The Media
in Your Life

FOURTH EDITION

The Media
in Your Life

An Introduction to Mass Communication

Jean Folkerts
The University of North Carolina at Chapel Hill

Stephen Lacy
Michigan State University

Ann Larabee
Michigan State University

PEARSON

Boston • New York • San Francisco
Mexico City • Montreal • Toronto • London • Madrid • Munich • Paris
Hong Kong • Singapore • Tokyo • Cape Town • Sydney

Acquisitions Editor: Jeanne Zalesky
Editorial Assistant: Brian Mickelson
Senior Development Editor: Carol Alper
Marketing Manager: Suzan Czajkowski
Senior Production Administrator: Donna Simons
Composition Buyer: Linda Cox
Manufacturing Buyer: JoAnne Sweeney
Cover Administrator and Designer: Joel Gendron
Associate Editor: Deb Hanlon
Editorial Production Service: Pine Tree Composition, Inc.
Electronic Composition: Pine Tree Composition, Inc.
Interior Designer: Roy Neuhaus
Photo Researcher: Laurie Frankenthaler

For related titles and support materials, visit our online catalog at www.ablongman.com.

Between the time website information is gathered and then published, it is not unusual for some sites to have closed. Also, the transcription of URLs can result in typographical errors. The publisher would appreciate notification where these errors occur so that they may be corrected in subsequent editions.

Library of Congress Cataloging-in-Publication Data
Folkerts, Jean.
    The media in your life: an introduction to mass communication / Jean Folkerts, Stephen
    Lacy, Ann Larabee. — 4th ed.
        p. cm.
    Includes bibliographical references and index.
    ISBN 0-205-52365-X
1. Mass media.   I. Lacy, Stephen.   II. Larabee, Ann.   III. Title.
    P90.F628 2007
    302.23—dc22

                                                                            2007007124

Printed in the United States of America

10   9   8   7   6   5   4   3   2   1   RRD-OH   11   10   09   08   07

For Leroy and Jenny Towns and Sean Lange

For Leslie, Katie, and Laurie Lacy

For Noah, Lissa, and Maksen

Brief Contents

Contents

CHAPTER 10
Journalism: Information and Society
250

CHAPTER 11
Public Relations
278

CHAPTER 12
Advertising
306

PART THREE
Media Issues
334

CHAPTER 13
Ethics
334

Features at a Glance

MEDIA IN YOUR LIFE

DATELINE

CULTURAL IMPACT

GLOBAL IMPACT

MEDIA CONVERGENCE

PROFILE

DISCUSSING TRENDS

NAVIGATING THE WEB

Preface

Since the laying of the first transatlantic cables, a communications system has developed that can instantaneously transmit information and entertainment around the world. At the beginning of the twenty-first century, global inhabitants are witnessing a major shift in the way they receive and interact with media forms. This change is driven by complicated economic, political, cultural, and technological forces that deeply affect mass media producers and consumers. With many of our colleagues, we believe that our societies benefit from citizens who participate in critical thinking about the media and who make conscious decisions about its development. Therefore, we have written this textbook as a contribution to a conversation about the meaning, evolution, and impact of mass media.

The Media in Your Life helps students understand what it means to live in a media-saturated environment. It serves as a basic introduction to mass media processes, functions, industries, and issues and provides different lenses for interpreting media, such as economics, history, cultural studies, and the social sciences. Therefore, readers will gain from several interrelated perspectives that together enrich their understanding of context. Students who are planning careers in the mass media will benefit from descriptions of the changing institutions in which they may work, but they will also gain ways to reflect on the meaning of economic convergence, technological change, and cultural impact. Generalist students will benefit from greater insight into their daily interactions with media technologies and content, as well the behind-the-scenes influences that shape that environment.

As teachers, we could not find a text that covered the multiple dimensions of economics, technological convergence, globalization, and cultural change as well as gave students an historical grounding in the development of mass media. Historical insight enables us to perceive changes in mass media over time, and sharpens skills of comparison and analysis. It keeps us from either overemphasizing or discounting developments such as the Internet. This textbook proceeds from the history of mass media industries in the United States, but avoids provincialism in its attention to global flows of media content and technology.

We have continued with the basic concepts introduced in the first three editions of this textbook that are still relevant today. However, the fourth edition is a very different book. We have included more extensive discussions of media convergence and consolidation, new and emerging technologies, and cultural and global impacts. The fourth edition is attuned to the ways in which digital media are transforming the relationships between media producers and audiences, acknowledging that audiences are gaining much more power to interact with content in increasingly mobile media systems. With many updated examples and other content, *The Media in Your Life* serves as an up-to-date guide to media studies.

MEDIA IN A STUDENT'S LIFE

Each chapter of *The Media in Your Life* begins with an exercise that asks students to examine dimensions of their personal use of media texts. This approach guides students from immediate experience towards deeper levels of knowledge and analysis, using appropriate critical tools. References to contemporary media forms and technologies that are familiar to students will help them enjoy the study of media and understand the day-to-day relevance of critical thinking about media.

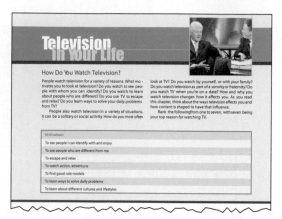

The book's scope is geared to a broader audience than many introductory texts for mass media courses. It is appropriate for majors in journalism and mass communications programs as well as for nonmajors who seek a general education course in media literacy. With this wide audience in mind, the book can best be characterized as having a liberal arts approach—an approach that is consistent with the needs of nonmajors, but an approach that, nevertheless, also meets accreditation standards of the Accrediting Council in Journalism and Mass Communication. Although a large amount of information as to how the media work is provided for those planning to become professional journalists, the book is relevant for general audiences and communicators as well.

GOALS FOR THIS BOOK

Our goals for this edition are to provide students with a broad knowledge of the media environment in which they live and work, as situated in a national and global scene. This emphasis and the examples we have chosen encourage students to seek explanations for the way the media functions in cultures and societies, rather than limiting students to a microscopic examination of the day-to-day operations of media organizations.

The text's three axes are economics, history, and culture, accompanied by continuing discussions of technology and globalization. Knowledge of the commercial aspects of media is fundamental to understanding how organizational decisions are made about technological development and the production and distribution of content. Furthermore, the convergence and consolidation of media are primarily driven by economics. Students must grasp these trends to think critically about the apparent power and influence of traditional media organizations, as well as the challenges of new media.

Historical context helps students see how current trends emerge from prior developments, including the introduction of new forms and technologies and social and political change. Each chapter tells a story of a media industry, process, function, or issue that gives students a sense of coherence over time. Because many schools no longer require a separate media history course, this picture may be unavailable, even to media majors. We believe that an understanding of media in contemporary society is based on an understanding of the history of media.

The fourth edition includes more extensive attention to cultural perspectives on media. One dimension of this approach is introducing students to the idea that they live in a media culture that shapes their values, beliefs, and perceptions of the world. Another is to provide greater discussion of diversity in media producers and audiences, including alternative and ethnic media, hiring practices in media organizations, and unequal access to media technologies. And finally, a comparative view shows how other cultures produce and respond to media flows. Cultural perspectives help students reach beyond the immediacy of their own experience to understand media as a variety of objects, meanings, and practices that may differ from group to group.

NEW TECHNOLOGIES, NEW FORMS, NEW PRACTICES

While giving students a coherent history of media industries, this textbook recognizes that digital technologies are transforming those industries and are changing the media landscape across the world. Since the original conceptualization of this book, the impact of digital technologies has been tremendous, leading to massive changes in media organizations, altering the way media content is produced and delivered, and ultimately changing the relationship between producers and audiences. Throughout the chapters, we have also provided readers with insight into economic and technological convergence, raising questions about the direction and consequences of these developments. *The Media in Your Life* traces the history of technological change in media systems, describes the current state of communications technologies, and discusses their foreseeable evolution without lapsing into utopian predictions or apocalyptic warnings.

Because of the spread of digital technologies around the world and the rise of multinational media conglomerates, the mass media has become a global system as never before. Nevertheless, beginning students often see media forms as being solely produced by the United States, and have limited understanding of cultural flows that carry media forms from one place to another, the global economics of mass media, and the presence of media in other countries. Although a complete coverage of the media's global scope is impossible in a single book, we have provided windows of insight through special boxes that highlight global impacts, as well as continuous discussion of global issues throughout the chapters. As media audiences or future media professionals, students can address the meaning of living in a networked, mediated world where inhabitants negotiate between the local and the global.

THE PLAN OF THIS BOOK

To reflect the way many instructors teach introductory mass communications courses, the book has been reorganized for the fourth edition. The first nine chapters deal with particular media and media industries. These include books, newspapers, magazines, movies, radio, television, music and recordings, and computers. Despite media convergence, the communication businesses continue to use these familiar categories of media. While many media professionals work in radically altered, converged environments, they often still see themselves as part of separate media industries with their own cultures and practices. In this time of transformation, we have maintained the discussion of these traditional industries as distinct entities. However, we have taken care to point out the limitations of this view by noting the ways in which technologies and industries are converging and subsequent changes in workplaces.

The next three chapters deal with the processes and functions of mediated communications that take students into reflection beyond specific industries. Media companies produce content to inform, to entertain, and to persuade. These three purposes are a useful way for students to think about the aims and intentions of media producers. When media inform, they provide content that helps people understand their lives and helps them make decisions about their world. That is why people read and watch news. When media entertain, the content brings enjoyment to people in a variety of ways. That explains why people go to movies and watch television. Organizations and people use media to try to convince someone to believe things or act in certain ways. Journalists, advertisers, and public relations professionals all aim to persuade.

The third section of the book takes students into a deeper examination of social and political issues that affect media producers and audiences. It includes chapters on ethics and regulation, including many controversies such as violence in media content and intellectual property rights. A final chapter on media research methods gives students a variety of tools for understanding media without limiting them to a single approach. Therefore, the text moves students toward more complex ways of thinking critically about media.

Starting with Chapter 2, each chapter has a similar organization. An introductory vignette and a "Media in Your Life" feature provide timely, relevant questions and introduce the exploration of a particular media industry, process, function, or issue. Each chapter proceeds to a narrative that discusses the media within the context of U.S. social and technological history. This narrative is followed by a description of the economic and institutional processes that affect each segment of the media, including production and distribution. The "Trends" section is divided into "Technology" and "Culture" subsections that discuss important developments, such as emerging technologies and changing audience demographics. This section also includes a set of questions that stimulate a further response to these developments.

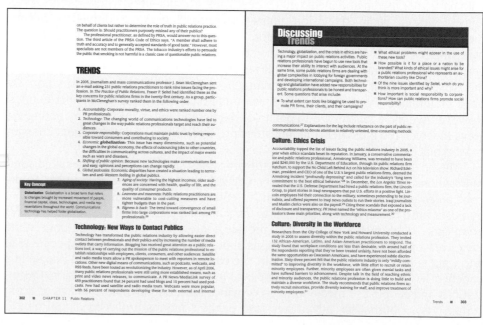

GUIDANCE FOR LEARNING IMPORTANT IDEAS, CONCEPTS, AND TERMS

The fourth edition of *The Media in Your Life* continues its unique learning system with the "Key Concepts" listed at the beginning of each chapter. These key concepts reappear along with definitions or explanations throughout the chapter in relevant sections. The ideas encapsulated under the key concepts are central to the media topic in each chapter and are highlighted as guideposts to students when reviewing main ideas. The key concepts, along with the issues posed in the chapter introduction, are designed to help students focus on main ideas and terms to make sense of the media story and to follow the thread of each chapter. In addition to these learning guides, distinctive **media terms** within the chapter text are boldfaced and featured with glossary definitions in the margin. Although these media terms function to ensure that students absorb the unique terminology of the media without confusing their grasp of larger concepts, they can also be used by individual instructors as the focus of learning goals for a more technical understanding of each of the media formats. Finally, after students have completed the chapter and are ready to review, they will find the issues listed in the introductory section reinforced at the end of the chapter with "Questions for Review" and "Issues to Think About."

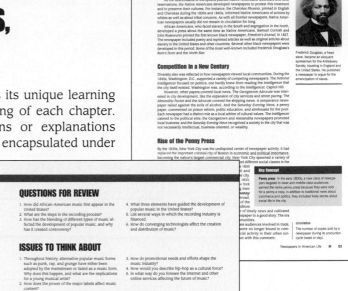

SPECIAL FEATURES TO FOCUS INTEREST AND LEARNING

A number of special features have been retained and updated in the text at appropriate intervals to highlight key ideas and to serve as the focus of special instructional units.

Chapter Opening Vignette   Each chapter begins with a vignette and accompanying photo to help the reader put the content of the chapter into a real-life context.

Media in Your Life   The introductory vignette of each chapter concludes with an interactive "Media in Your Life" feature, which alerts readers to how their everyday media behavior relates to forthcoming issues in the chapter. This feature is not a quiz or learning check; it is a chance for readers to take note of their own media awareness and to relate issues in the chapter to their own media attitudes and behavior.

Graphic Charts, Diagrams, and Photos   An array of illustrative material in each chapter provides supplementary data, useful charts illustrating key ideas, and historical and current photos that provide visual examples of concepts presented in the text.

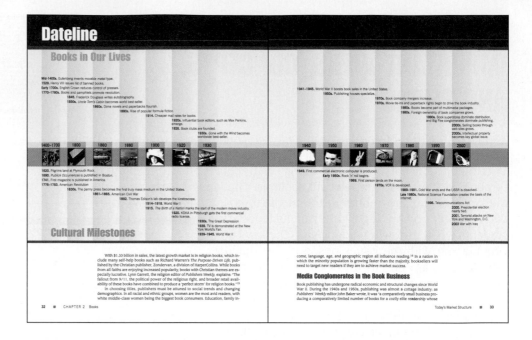

Datelines A graphic continuum, "Dateline," spreads out major media events across time, which helps students relate events and sequences in the media story with historic events that may be familiar to them.

Impact Features Three special-feature boxes throughout the chapters are presented to illustrate key social and technical influences that intersect with the media. To focus attention on key concepts and themes, the text includes the following boxed features: "Cultural Impact" (highlighting the ways the media influence and represent American culture), "Media Convergence" (stressing the continuing overlapping and blending of media functions as technologies develop), and "Global Impact" (calling attention to international influences in key areas).

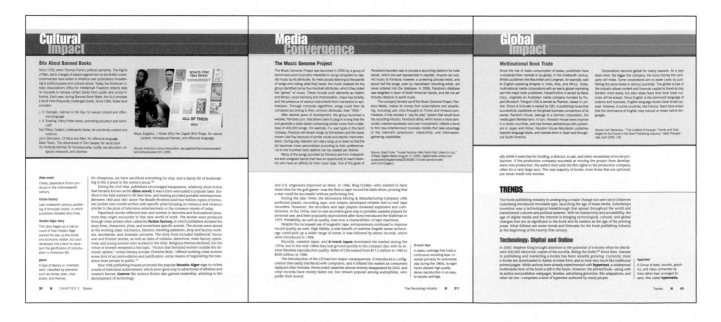

Profiles A prominent person in each medium is highlighted with a special portrait to focus attention on key roles of typical and influential players. This feature provides a miniature case study of a career that can be analyzed in assignments.

Navigating the Web Each chapter has a special section listing web sites that pertain to the material in the chapter. These sites provide information about the topic of the chapter and can be consulted for special projects, collaborative discussions, or term papers.

SUPPLEMENTS FOR THE INSTRUCTOR

Instructor's Manual/Test Bank The Instructor's Manual features a wide variety of student activities, Internet exercises, chapter summaries, chapter outlines, and questions to spark classroom discussions. The Test Bank includes 1,200 multiple choice, true/false, matching, fill-in-the-blank, short answer, and essay questions.

Computerized Test Bank The questions in the printed Test Bank are also available electronically through our computerized testing system, TestGen EQ. The fully networkable test-generating software is now available on a multiplatform CD-ROM. The user-friendly interface enables instructors to view, edit, and add questions, transfer questions to tests, and print tests in a variety of fonts. Search and sort features allow instructors to locate questions quickly and arrange them in a preferred order. The program is also available for download on our Instructor's Resource Center, at www.ablongman.com/irc.

PowerPoint™ Package Available at www.ablongman.com/irc, this presentation package provides slides combining graphic and text images in modular units to accompany each chapter. The package is compatible with Windows and Macintosh systems.

MyMassCommLab MyMassCommLab (www.mymasscommlab.com) is a state-of-the-art interactive and instructive solution for introductory Mass Communication courses, providing you and your students access to a wealth of resources geared to meet the individual teaching and learning needs of every instructor and every student. Designed to be used as a supplement to a traditional lecture course or to completely administer an online course, MyMassCommLab combines multimedia, video, activities, research support, tests, and quizzes to make teaching and learning more productive, efficient, and fun!

Allyn & Bacon's Mass Communication Interactive Video Specially selected news segments from ABC news programs include on-screen critical-thinking questions and deal with a variety of media issues and problems to help bring media issues to life in the classroom. An accompanying video user's guide can be found online at www.ablongman.com/irc.

Allyn & Bacon's Digital Media Archive for Communication, Version 3.0 The Digital Media Archive CD-ROM contains electronic images of charts, graphs, maps, tables, and figures, along with media elements such as video, audio clips, and related Web links. These media assets are fully customizable to use with our pre-formatted PowerPoint™ outlines or to import into instructor's own lectures (Windows and Mac).

Allyn & Bacon's VideoWorkshop for Introduction to Mass Communication: Instructor Teaching Guide with CD-ROM   Our complete VideoWorkshop program, by Elsa Peterson, includes quality video footage on an easy-to-use CD-ROM, plus a Student Learning Guide and an Instructor's Teaching Guide—both with textbook-specific correlation grids. The result? A program that brings textbook concepts to life with ease and that helps your students understand, analyze, and apply the objectives of the course.

The A&B Mass Communication Video Library   Adopters of this text have access to a rich library of videos about the media, created through Insight Media and Films for the Humanities. Some restrictions apply.

SUPPLEMENTS FOR THE STUDENT

MyMassCommLab   MyMassCommLab (www.mymasscommlab.com) is a state-of-the-art interactive and instructive solution for introductory Mass Communication courses, providing you with access to a wealth of resources geared to meet your learning needs. Designed to be used as a supplement to a traditional lecture course or to completely administer an online course, MyMassCommLab combines multimedia, video, activities, research support, tests, and quizzes to make teaching and learning more productive, efficient, and fun!

Allyn & Bacon's Introduction to Mass Communication Study Site   This website, accessed at www.abintromasscomm.com, features Introduction to Mass Communication study materials for students, including flashcards and a complete set of practice tests for all major topics. Students also will find Web links to sites with speeches in text, audio, and video formats, as well as links to other valuable sites.

ResearchNavigator.com Guide: Mass Communication, Theatre, and Film   This updated booklet, by Ronald C. Roat of the University of Southern Indiana, includes tips, resources, and URLs to aid students conducting research on Pearson Education's research website, www.researchnavigator.com. The guide contains a student access code for the Research Navigator database, offering students unlimited access to a collection of more than 25,000 discipline specific articles from top-tier academic publications and peer-reviewed journals, as well as the *New York Times* and popular news publications. The guide introduces students to the basics of the Internet and the World Wide Web, and includes tips for searching for articles on the site and a list of journals useful for research in the discipline. Also included are hundreds of Web resources for the discipline, as well as information on how to cite research correctly. The guide is available packaged with new copies of the text.

Allyn & Bacon's VideoWorkshop for Introduction to Mass Communication: Student Learning Guide with CD-ROM   Our complete VideoWorkshop program, by Elsa Peterson, includes quality video footage on an easy-to-use CD-ROM, plus a Student Learning Guide with textbook-specific correlation grids. The result? A program that brings textbook concepts to life with ease and helps you understand, analyze, and apply the objectives of the course.

Becoming Media Literate! Critical Consumer Projects & Worksheets   This exciting new print workbook, by Meredith Everson of the University of Pennsylvania, provides activities that will help students develop into critical consumers of media products. With more than 75 worksheets and projects included, this valuable workbook provides students with a way to activate their developing media literacy skill set.

Allyn & Bacon's Study Card for Introduction to Mass Communication   Colorful, affordable, and packed with useful information, Allyn & Bacon/Longman's Study Cards make studying easier, more efficient, and more enjoyable. Course information is distilled down to the basics, helping you quickly master the fundamentals, review a subject for understanding, or prepare for an exam. Because they're laminated for durability, you can keep these Study Cards for years to come and pull them out whenever you need a quick review.

Careers in Media This supplement by Frank Barnas and Michael P. Savoie, both of Valdosta State University, profiles employment opportunities in media and points out often overlooked options for students seeking jobs in the highly selective and competitive media world. Included is a discussion of portfolio development and valuable appendices with state and job web sites.

ACKNOWLEDGMENTS

This text has evolved over time and through experience in teaching at two major mass media programs at George Washington University and at Michigan State University. We offer a special thank-you to Lucinda Davenport of Michigan State University, who helped conceptualize and write the first edition. We also thank Pamela Laucella and Keith Kincaid for their contributions to the public relations and advertising chapters. We wish to thank our other colleagues at these schools who encouraged us to shape an introductory course in the direction that this book has taken. In particular, we thank Leslie Lacy and Leroy Towns of the Michigan State University staff, and Maria George, executive aide, and Tracy Cook Pannozzo, communications director, in the School of Media and Public Affairs at George Washington University. We would also like to thank Dwight Teeter, whose advice across the years has been thoughtful and sustaining and whose great joy in being an administrator has been invaluable in helping others along their way.

At Allyn & Bacon, many editors and marketing people have helped bring this book to a level that best expresses our approach to the course. In particular, Allen Workman, the development editor for the first edition, motivated us to complete the project and systematically helped conceptualize the pedagogical elements of the text. For the second, third, and fourth editions, Carol Alper, the development editor, kept us on course. We also thank Karen Berry of Pine Tree Composition, Inc., for her dedication to this project. Karon Bowers, our editor-in-chief, provided support and guidance. We thank Molly Taylor, series editor, for her commitment to and work on the third edition.

For all four editions, a number of our colleagues have provided helpful manuscript reviews at each stage of development. We hope they feel the book has benefited from their comments and advice. We wish to thank the following reviewers:

Linus Abraham, University of Minnesota, Minneapolis
Edward Adams, Angelo State University
Bryan Brown, Missouri State University
Tom Buckner, McClennan Community College
Larry Campbell, University of Alaska, Anchorage
Richard E. Caplan, University of Akron
David W. D'Alessio, University of Connecticut, Stamford
Bill Dean, Texas Tech University
Thomas Draper, University of Nebraska, Kearney
Anthony J. Ferri, University of Nevada, Las Vegas
Donald G. Godfrey, Arizona State University
Colin Gromatzky, New Mexico State University
James L. Hoyt, University of Wisconsin
Jack Keever, Seton Hall University
Joanne Kostides, Holyoke Community College
Kevin C. Lee, Western Carolina University

Kenneth J. Levine, Illinois State University
Carol M. Liebler, Syracuse University
Rebecca Ann Lind, University of Illinois, Chicago
William M. Lingle, Linfield College
Toni J. Morris, University of Indianapolis
Jack A. Nelson, Brigham Young University
Fred Owens, Youngstown State University
David J. Paterno, Delaware County Community College
Elizabeth M. Perse, University of Delaware
Evelyn Plummer, Seton Hall University
Randall K. Pugh, Montana State University at Billings
Ronald C. Roat, University of Southern Indiana
Jeanne Rollberg, University of Arkansas at Little Rock
Marshel Rossow, Mankato State University
Cara Schollenberger, Bucks County Community College
Kim A. Smith, Iowa State University
Roger Soenksen, James Madison University
Andris Straumanis, University of Wisconsin, Eau Claire
Hazel Warlaumont, California State University, Fullerton
Susan Weill, Texas State University
Sandra Wertz, The University of South Carolina

In addition to those who specifically read chapters and provided comments during the writing and revision of this text, we wish to thank all those who worked with us on research and teaching projects over the years, whose guidance led us to incorporate our knowledge—and much of theirs—into this text. These individuals include:

David Coulson, University of Nevada–Reno
Wayne Danielson, University of Texas at Austin
Carolyn Dyer, University of Iowa
Douglas Gomery, University of Maryland
Owen Johnson, Indiana University
Peter M. McGrath, The George Washington University
Robert Picard, Turku School of Economics
Shirley Quate
Stephen Reese, University of Texas at Austin
Dan Riffe, Ohio University
Mary Alice Shaver, Michigan State University
Pamela Shoemaker, Syracuse University
Todd Simon, Kansas State University
Jeffery Smith, University of Wisconsin–Milwaukee
Ardyth Sohn
Christopher Sterling, The George Washington University
Jim Tankard, University of Texas at Austin

The Media
in Your Life

We the People
Media and Communication

When Hurricane Katrina broke through the New Orleans levees and devastated the city in August 2005, it was the most destructive natural disaster ever covered by the U.S. media. Tens of thousands of mostly poor, African-American residents of the city lost their homes and were left without adequate food, water, shelter, or aid. Newspaper and television journalists often had difficulty interpreting what they saw, but their reports revealed difficult truths about race and poverty in the United States to its citizens and to the world. In the months following the disaster, debates about the nation's hidden social problems and inadequate government response filled news programs, magazines, daily papers, webpages, and blogs. The media, too, came under examination, both praised and criticized for its coverage.

For some, news journalists became the heroes of the disaster. Prestigious Peabody Awards were given to local television stations WWL-TV in New Orleans and WLOX-TV in Biloxi, Mississippi, which kept broadcasting throughout the storm. WLOX lost its roof and two transmitting towers, but, as the Peabody committee noted, "courageous employees of the station broadcast 12 consecutive days of life-saving news and information to its storm-shocked Gulf Coast viewers." CNN also received an award for its coverage. During the hurricane, it opened a Gulf Bureau and a web portal that fed more than a million video streams to visitors.

Newspapers came in for their share of praise. The *Times-Picayune* of New Orleans and the *Sun Herald* of Biloxi won Pultizers for public service. When the *Times-Picayune* lost its office, it began reporting from the journalism school at Louisiana State University and formed a partnership with a tourism Website to provide information on rescue work and missing persons. The staff of the *Sun Herald* handed out free copies of its newspapers in tents and shelters.

Other journalists praised their colleagues for bravery and humanity. Writing in the *American Journalism Review,* former network correspondent Deborah Potter said, "The storm seemed to free TV reporters from their customary role as detached observers, letting them show their feelings and act like human beings without fear of compromising their journalistic integrity."[1] The journalists who were there described their shock and horror at what they had witnessed. Local reporters explained their feelings of loss and compassion for their fellow citizens.

However, the media was also strongly criticized for its sometimes inaccurate portrayal of conditions in the city. Critics noted that violence and crime were inflated out of all proportion. CNN put the New Orleans police superintendent next to the host of *America's Most Wanted,* confusing serious news coverage and infotainment. The most noteworthy criticism came from rapper Kanye West. During a fundraising concert produced by NBC News, West diverted from his assigned script to lambaste the federal government and the media: "I hate the way they portray us in the media. You see a black family, it says, 'They're looting.' You see a white family, it says, 'They're looking for food.' And, you know, it's been five days [waiting for federal help] because most of the people are black."[2] West's statement resonated with many people who were angry about social causes and effects of the disaster.

Hurricane Katrina and the new stories that followed reinforce a long-held belief: The mass media help define community and nation through the events they cover, the voices they bring us, and the stories they tell. They are entwined with politics, economics, cultural identity, and freedom of expression. Sensitive to changes in technology, media industries are taking advantage of different outlets like webpages and cell phones to reach audiences even further in their daily lives.

Young adults consume media at high levels. In an average week, they spend approximately 50 hours using the Internet, watching television, listening to the radio, and reading.[3] They respond to what they experience. Inspired by stories about Hurricane Katrina, college students from all over the country volunteered in New Orleans to help clean up houses and streets.

This chapter provides a set of definitions and concepts to help you understand how media affect your life. These concepts have been developed from a few simple questions:

- What are mass communications? The mass media?
- How did the media system in the United States evolve and how is it structured today?
- What are the converging technological, regulatory, and content issues that affect our ability to communicate?
- What are the implications of changing media for a democratic society?
- How do media affect cultural and social change?
- What is meant by media culture?
- How does the globalization of media affect communication among citizens of the world?
- What are the specific functions of mass media?
- How do individuals and groups use media in their lives?

Communication in Your Life

Interacting with Others and Using Media

This chapter discusses the importance of the mass media in our lives. It also explains how mass media systems work. Think about the role of communication in your life. As you read this chapter, think about the following questions. Your answers will help you better understand how media affect your life.

- Can you describe a recent experience that involved both the use of media and interaction with another person?

- How was the interpersonal interaction different from your experience using a particular mediated communication?
- How was the media product (program, newscast, advertisement) designed to affect you and others?
- How did you use the media product, and how did you share your experience with others?

The role, structure, and economic nature of the system of mass communication in the United States are all concepts that affect our everyday lives. These elements characterize media as an institution, similar to the institutions of government, education, and religion.

In this book, we trace the history of the media because we believe the context in which different forms of mass media emerged significantly affected their role in modern life. Content is affected by economic structure as well as by the cultural values of consumerism. The key to understanding media is to understand such relationships. Thus we have chosen the following media markers—the context of history, economic structure, cultural change, globalization, and technological development/convergence—as the structural elements for this book.

MASS COMMUNICATION

People share their experiences and impressions through language, which is a collection of symbols. Communication requires the exchange of information with at least one other person. The exchange can be face to face with no intervening technology, or it can be mediated, which requires some mechanism, such as television or the Internet, to communicate these symbols. Mediated communication directed at a large audience is called ***mass communication,*** and usually involves a **professional communicator.** Most people agree that **mass media** include newspapers, magazines, books, films, television, radio, and recordings. In this book, the Internet is treated as a mass medium, although some scholars believe that its interactivity distinguishes it from traditional mass media. Direct mail, telemarketing, and outdoor advertising may also qualify as mass media even though the particular medium involved may not be considered "mass" by most people.

Most media companies employ professionals to construct, organize, and deliver messages, whether the messages be informative, entertaining, or persuasive. The communicator's role can be defined as that of a **gatekeeper of information,** a term defined by a communication theorist, David Manning White, in 1950.[4] He said that journalists tend the gates that control the flow of information; they select what others will receive as news. In the years since the original study, the term *gatekeeper* has come to mean anyone who controls information.

EVOLUTION OF MASS MEDIA IN THE UNITED STATES

Men and women have always sought ways to communicate with one another and with groups of people. As the groups grew larger, the necessity for technology increased. From listening to the lectures of Socrates in ancient Greece to hearing the beating of drums in Africa, individuals have recognized the importance of information to personal survival and to the development of civilization. As long ago as 2000 years before the birth of Christ, Mediterranean civilizations used technology to create a system of movable type by pressing signs into clay. Carvings in stone and hand printing on thin paper made from the papyrus plant are historical remnants of attempts to communicate. In about 1041, the Chinese printer Pi Sheng printed books using movable type made of hundreds of clay blocks bearing Chinese ideograms. That printing technique was introduced to Europe when Marco Polo returned from his travels in China in 1295. However, the development of movable metal type in the Western world by Johannes Gutenberg in the fifteenth century paved the way for the expansion of a

professional communicator

Person who selects information from sources and processes them for delivery to an audience.

mass media

A form of communication (radio, newspapers, television, etc.) used to reach a large number of people.

At his press conference, President George W. Bush serves as a source of information. The journalists at the event serve as communicators who gather, select, and interpret the information for a mass audience. When President Bush speaks directly to the nation via radio or television, he acts as both source and communicator.

Cultural Impact

Media Culture

Inhabitants of highly technological societies live in media-saturated environments. We are constantly surrounded by media messages from newspapers, televisions, radios, computers, cell phones, advertising circulars, billboards, logos, and a host of other images and texts. We not only perceive these media messages, but incorporate them into the patterns of our lives, into what we wear, what we do, and who we are. They shape our perceptions, our dreams and our identities as citizens of a community, a nation, and a world. Therefore, cultural critics say we live in a media culture.

The study of mass media can be approached from many directions, such as economics, politics, history, and the social sciences. Each lens gives us a different view. We can also look at culture: the way the mass media shapes our beliefs, values, perceptions, and behaviors and is shaped by them.

Because they are owned and managed by social elites, media systems often promote the political and social preferences of these more powerful groups. For example, as children, we may learn our social roles partly from television programs. However, media systems also reveal how groups compete for visibility and influence in a media culture.

Media culture is undergoing revolutionary change so that the old forms of power and influence that went along with traditional broadcasting are also changing. In the midst of such change, predictions are very difficult. However, many media critics believe that new digital technologies are allowing people to interact with the media as never before, creating new forms of expression that

may be radically altering our cultural landscapes on a global scale. Media scholar Henry Jenkins calls this convergence culture. He explains: "Entertainment content isn't the only thing that flows across multiple media platforms. Our lives, relationships, memories, fantasies, and desires also flow across media channels. Being a lover or a Mommy or a teacher occurs on multiple platforms. Sometimes we tuck our kids into bed at night and sometimes we IM them from the other side of the globe."

Source: Henry Jenkins, "Welcome to Convergence Culture," *Receiver #12*, Vodaphone, www.receiver.vodafone.com/12.

---

print culture. Gutenberg first carved wood so that letters stood in relief on tiny blocks that could be rearranged into different words; he then inked the blocks so multiple copies of documents could be made. The wood blocks made fuzzy letters, but Gutenberg's assistant, Peter Schöffer, soon realized that metal could be used instead of wood to produce a cleaner type. He used this method to print the English Bible in 1455.[5]

Technological development altered types of communication and social and business relationships; it affected the adoption of cultural norms. In medieval Europe before Gutenberg's invention, religious elites controlled information, and the Catholic Church acted as an early gatekeeper of information by dominating the dissemination of official notices. Books were copied laboriously by hand by monks secreted away from the world of trade; official notices also were hand copied and carried as letters or posted where those who could read could see them and pass on the information to those who could not.

Even then, informal networks spread alternative messages and challenged ideas, transmitting a social heritage with a greater dimension than that conveyed by official proclamations. After Gutenberg's invention, the economics of distribution affected the marketplace of ideas. This intellectual marketplace became a commodity market in which books containing a variety of ideas were bought and sold. The mass production of books not only loosened the church's grip on information. It created new

The First Printing Press.

The flatbed press from the Gutenberg era and the improvements that followed it brought books containing a variety of ideas to the eager public.

relationships between the church and the entrepreneur or merchant. Soon merchants began to produce and sell books, providing an outlet for ideas and values that had been kept out of print and confined to oral transmission. The public eagerly sought the histories, religious books, travelogues, and romances that were traded on the open market. Some books that offended the official gatekeepers were prohibited by the church, but they still were sold on the black market. Once printing was available, it was not easily controlled despite the best efforts of kings and church officials.[6]

Communication Networks in North America

The English model of printing was carried to North America, but the lack of a transportation system kept the colonies relatively isolated from one another. Ships from Europe brought letters, newspapers, and books for elite colonists about the government and church in their homelands. In the absence of widely distributed printed forms of information, ministers acted as a powerful elite, conveying official information and moral instruction from the pulpit. Such communication was supplemented, but not replaced, by the first printing press, which was established by Elizabeth Glover in 1638 in Cambridge, Massachusetts. Glover's press issued *The Freeman's Oath,* a formal contract of behavioral rules that citizens in the colony were required to sign, and the *Bay Psalm Book.* Those books and documents were intended not for casual reading but for creating standards for the public life of the community. Religious elites used information channels to promote prosocial values such as keeping one's word, maintaining faith in public worship, and advancing literacy.

Once postal routes were established, information became a commercial as well as a political and social commodity. Newspapers circulated first in local communities and then along some of the more popular trade routes, which also served as the delivery system for books.

From the 1830s through the end of the nineteenth century, communication industries expanded. Advanced technology in transportation systems and printing presses allowed for communication systems to serve new audiences and increased the number and type of products available. As railway lines spread throughout the massive geographic area that was to define the United States, products were marketed nationally. The new transportation lines provided new circulation routes for newspapers and fledgling magazines, and national marketing ensured a wide advertising base for at least the mainstream publications. Circulations expanded, and the distribution of newspapers, magazines, and books spread throughout the country. The introduction of rotary printing presses meant that a printer, with the same number of motions required to print a single page on a flatbed press, could feed a roll of paper through the press and produce enormous numbers of printed pages. Whereas in the late 1700s a circulation of 2,500 was considered excellent, by the 1890s newspapers such as the *New York World* reached 1,000,000 people.

Technology, Transportation, and Communication

In the beginning, communication was linked to transportation because information could travel only as fast as a horse and rider. Information traveled along trade routes along with other commodities.

The Telegraph   The link between communication and transportation was broken in 1844 when Samuel Morse opened the nation's first telegraph line with the question, "What hath God wrought?" No longer was the speed of communication dependent on how fast a horse could gallop; information could travel instantaneously by means of wires from its point of origin to a publisher's desk.

By 1846, newspapers in upstate New York were using the wires to transmit news between the state capital of Albany and other New York cities. In 1848, a group of New York newspapers, including the *Courier and Enquirer, Sun, Herald, Journal of Commerce, Tribune,* and *Express,* hired a steamer to retrieve news from the major port of Halifax, Nova Scotia. The group also negotiated a joint arrangement to use telegraph

Communication via telegraph depends on an infrastructure of telegraph poles and wires. During the Civil War, wires were often cut, and soldiers had to restring them to establish connections with the rest of the country.

lines to transmit news from Boston to New York. Those ventures resulted in the establishment of the Associated Press, a **wire service** that dominated delivery of national and international information until the early 1900s.[7]

Radio Revolution   By the early twentieth century, the advent of radio had broken a second link between transportation and communication: Not only could news travel from its source to an editor's desk as fast as the wires could carry it, but news also could travel from the editor or commentator to the public as fast as it could travel across the air waves.

Radio technology played an important role in World War I in ship-to-shore communications and was regulated by the U.S. Navy. Amateurs also enjoyed building and using radio sets, but few had conceived of it as a broadcasting—or mass communication—tool. At the end of the war, the U.S. Navy strongly opposed returning the rights to the British-owned Marconi Company, which had a monopoly on radio parts. With what historian Christopher Sterling labeled "tacit government approval," Owen D. Young, chairman of the board for General Electric Co., organized a new corporation to hold all U.S. patents. General Electric, together with American Telephone and Telegraph, United Fruit, and Westinghouse Electric, formed the Radio Corporation of America (RCA) and bought out American Marconi for $2.5 million.[8] The companies operated together until 1926. That arrangement set the stage for further radio development organized and controlled by big business and government.

As Westinghouse, General Electric, and RCA established stations in the early 1920s, radio became so popular that RCA sold $11 million worth of receivers in 1922 alone. By 1927, 700 U.S. stations were operating, and in 1929, $135 million worth of sets was sold. In 1923, only 7 percent of U.S. households owned a radio set; by 1930, almost 35 percent owned sets.

wire service
Organization that collects and distributes news and information to media outlets. Referred to as "wire" because before computer transmission, these services relied on use of the telegraph wires.

Motion Pictures and Television   The motion picture industry was well under way by the beginning of World War I, and experimentation with television began in the 1930s. The movies were a popular form of entertainment during the financial depression of the 1930s because people sought an escape from the harsh realities of daily life. Television arrived after World War II in the midst of an

Farm families heard news of the world, as well as classical music and comedy shows, over their radios. For the first time, the distribution of information was not tied to the speed of transportation.

expanding consumer society. The prosperity of the post–World War II era and the new technology together began to shape media as a basis for creating a consumer culture. The media attracted mass audiences, and the information provided by the media helped homogenize the audience, stripping it of regional characteristics, dialects, and mores.

Computers and Communication   Computers entered the mass media as typesetting machines during the late 1960s, but computer technology had a more powerful impact on mass media with the development of the home personal computer, or PC. Although traditional media such as newspapers benefit from computer-based technology, such new technologies also create forms of information exchange that were not possible with the old styles of production and distribution.

Communication by means of the computer began in the late 1960s, when the U.S. government connected four computers in Utah and California. The goal was to develop the framework for an emergency communication system by sending information across special high-speed telephone lines. After the mid-1970s, smaller networks such as that used by the National Science Foundation (NSF) decided to work together—to internetwork. Today, the Internet links millions of academic, governmental, and commercial sites. No one owns the Internet. Rather, it is a loose collection of computer networks whose users pass along information and share files.[9] Costs are shared rather informally by a variety of institutions.

It is the Internet that allows students to e-mail their professors and allows researchers to exchange ideas worldwide. Students regularly communicate through sophisticated software programs based on the Internet and designed specifically for the classroom. Programs such as educational software allow professors to create automatic e-mail lists, to construct electronic grade books, to give students assignments, to create interchanges among students, and to provide feedback. No longer is access to a professor limited to two class periods a week and a few office hours. Messages can be sent, received, and answered in a matter of minutes.

Key Concept

New media   Media forms and content that are created and shaped by changes in technology. The term most often refers to electronic communications like mobile computing, streaming video, and Internet messaging.

Key Concept

Media convergence   Digital transmission has made convergence possible. Technological convergence refers to the merging of different devices. Economic convergence refers to the relationships between different media outlets owned by a single company, especially the ability to distribute and promote content across different platforms.

Key Concept

Media consolidation   Media consolidation, also called concentration of media ownership, means that a single company possesses several media outlets, such as newspapers, Internet businesses, and radio stations. It is often used to describe the rise of large multinational media conglomerates that own many different types of media properties.

Media Convergence

In every generation, there are old media and new media. During the colonial period, books and newspapers were old media and magazines were new media. Today we use the term *new media* to refer to media forms and content that are created and shaped by technological changes, especially digital. In the twenty-first century, old media are still very much alive, but media industries and technologies have been marked by *convergence*, so that information is more able to flow easily across many devices and among many people across the world. Convergence has called into question whether we can still talk of separate media like print, radio, and television.

Technological convergence has been made possible by the digital revolution. The personal computer has been overtaking the television as the household media center. With the increasing capacity of PCs to provide audio and video, business analysts have predicted the convergence of the two devices into a single household screen, a system that will centrally manage many kinds of information. However, other devices like cell phones and video game systems are converging as well. The change has been driven by cheaper and faster bandwidth, larger memory storage, and the development of cross-platform formats that allow content to be delivered across different devices, such as computers, televisions, cell phones, video game players, and iPods.

Economic convergence is the delivery and promotion of content across several media channels owned by the same company. It is closely related to *media consolidation*,

Technological convergence has changed the way journalists receive information and transmit news content around the world.

which is the act of buying and owning different kinds of media properties, such as newspapers and television and radio stations that operate under a central management. In August 2006, the six largest of these corporations were CBS, Disney, General Electric, News Corp., Time Warner, and Viacom. Large media conglomerates own book publishers, radio stations, Internet services, phone services, television networks, newspapers, advertising companies, and other media properties. While media consolidation refers to the formation of these media **conglomerates,** economic convergence refers to the relationships formed between the media outlets they own. For example, a company's book imprint may produce a how-to book on home decoration while its television outlet runs a crafts show featuring the author of the book. Some advantages to these companies are that they require less labor and fewer resources, they can create content that can be used in several outlets, and they can promote their products and brands across these outlets. Economic convergence has been made possible by digital technologies and changing government regulations.

In the 1990s, many industry analysts viewed the struggle for the control of technology as a mere battle for profit, but the implications of that struggle are much broader. As the editors of the *Media Studies Journal* wrote, "The more enduring issues have to do with access to information, the quality of news and entertainment, the diversity of media in the marketplace and, most important, freedom of expression itself."[10]

Convergence has implications not only for content but also for *media regulation* and policy. By 1996 the evolution of technology had created conditions that required major policy changes for the first time in 60 years. The Telecommunications Act of 1996 changed existing media ownership rules, deregulated cable television, and required television makers to install a computer chip in new TV sets that allows people to block shows that are electronically labeled for violence and other objectionable content.[11]

Key Concept

Media regulation Governments enforce rules and regulations to promote social stability and mediate social conflicts. Because the media and the public "space" they occupy can affect many members of society, the government has always been particularly concerned with regulation of the media.

THE MEDIA SYSTEM IN THE UNITED STATES

The United States, like every country, has a communication system that coordinates its activities. Highly industrialized countries have complex systems and depend on computer technology. Oral tradition, print media, and radio dominate the communication

conglomerate

Large company formed by consolidating two or more small companies.

Media Convergence

The Cell Phone

A third of the world's 6.5 billion inhabitants have mobiles phones. In some parts of the world, the mobile phone and the radio are more important devices than the personal computer and the television. A generation of young consumers is driving the global cell phone market because of their affection for social networking. Text messaging is fast, inexpensive, and private, and has become the communications method of choice among the world's teens and young adults. Cell phones are also attractive because they are connected to fashion and image.

A growing number of phone users around the world, especially in wealthy places like Europe, South Korea, and Japan, use smartphones. Equipped with color screens, powerful processors, and richer broadband connections, smartphones can be used as multimedia devices, with an increasing capacity for networking, music, video, and gaming. Older users are more likely to rely on the phone's expanded capabilities to answer office e-mails, exchange data, and bank online. Younger users are more likely to take advantage of the social possibilities for dating and sharing thoughts, ideas, opinions, music, images and video that they create and record on their phones.

Devices like personal computers and cell phones challenge older ideas of what has traditionally constituted the mass media: fixed systems like the television and the radio tied to certain kinds of content. Now video and audio clips can be played on a variety of devices and with much greater interactivity from the user. Cell phone users can take short video clips of themselves and send them to friends along with text messages. They thus become their own media producers.

Sources: Pew Research Center, "The Cell Phone Challenge to Survey Research," May 15, 2006, people-press.org; ChildNet International, *Children, Mobile Phones and the Internet,* UNICEF, March 7, 2003, iajapan.org/hotline/mobilepdf/proceedings.pdf.

---

systems of less industrialized countries. Most media systems can be defined as **market** or **nonmarket systems.** In market systems, consumers demand information and media companies supply it. Media companies in market systems supply the types and amounts of information for which people will pay. Nonmarket systems supply information based on what some institution, usually a government, decides people should have.

In market systems, such as the one found in the United States, profit—the difference between revenue and costs—plays a motivating role. Media organizations consider many factors when they set **profit margins,** the amount of "extra" revenue they intend to seek. Profit does not play a role in nonmarket systems. The institution that controls information pursues other goals, which often include maintaining power. This basic difference in market and nonmarket systems has a profound impact on how the systems function within societies. However, as the world becomes a global village and as satellite delivery crosses national boundaries, the line between the two systems becomes less defined.

Figure 1.1, which we refer to throughout this chapter, explains how a market system works. The center of the diagram shows the individuals and groups who participate in the mass communication system. They include almost all people in the United States—anyone who sees a movie, reads a newspaper, listens to the radio, or watches a television show. People have different information needs and wants, which come from their psychological states and from their understanding of their identities in families, local communities, and nations. Those needs and wants translate into a demand for information and ideas.

> ### Key Concept
>
> **Market and nonmarket media systems** In a free-market society, mass communication can be described as a system that produces information on the basis of the interaction between two forces: audience demand and the ability of media companies to supply content. Media companies produce what someone will pay for. In a highly structured nonmarket or authoritarian society, mass communication may function as a system in which content is decided by an institution, usually a government. In such societies, the media produce not what the public will pay for, but what the authorities want the public to know.

profit margin

The difference between revenue and expenses.

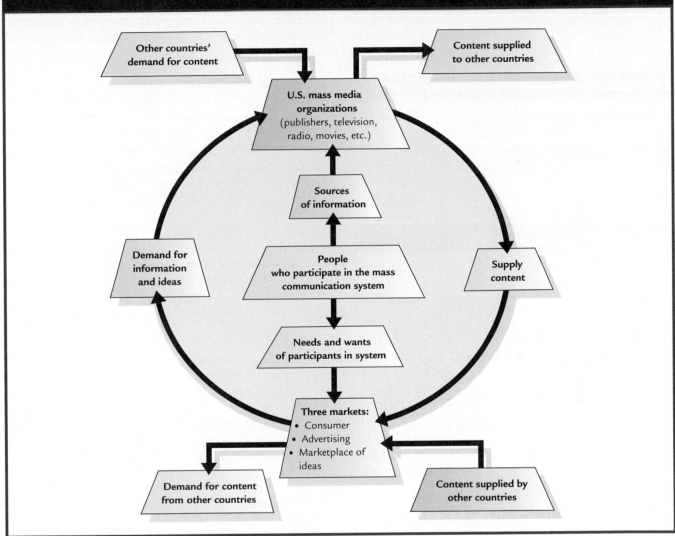

Figure 1.1

The Mass Media Market System

The U.S. mass media market system is cyclical, with people at the center. People have needs and wants, which they take to the three types of markets in the system (consumer, advertising, and the marketplace of ideas). These wants and needs become demand for information, advertising space and time, and ideas to help society function properly. The media companies observe the demand and supply content to the three markets to satisfy the wants and needs. At the same time people are exercising their demand, they also act as sources of information for the media organizations. This mass media system is not isolated from the rest of the world. It serves the demand from other countries by sending content to them. At the same time, other countries supply content to the U.S. system based on demand from that system.

Not only do individuals and groups fulfill wants and needs through the mass communication system, but they also act as sources for that system. When a newspaper runs a story about a fire, for example, sources of information may include a neighbor who called the fire department or firefighters who fought the blaze.

Three Communication Markets

When we look at mass communication as a market system, we see that people seek information, and businesses either sell or give information through communication markets. People can use the information for a variety of purposes, but as in all markets, exchange takes place. A consumer might buy a book or a recording, thus exchanging money for information or entertainment. In another instance, a business might buy an advertisement, thus exchanging money for access to public attention. Further, people might exchange ideas in a political debate—the marketplace of ideas. Three markets emerge in this view of the U.S. system: the consumer market, the advertising market, and the marketplace of ideas.

People use the two commercial markets—consumer and advertising—to satisfy their individual needs (e.g., surveillance, decision making, identity formation, self-understanding, diversion) that emerge from their cultural situations. Economic status, cultural identity, and educational attainment all have an important role to play. Communities use the marketplace of ideas to find ways to satisfy their information needs (e.g., coordinating group actions, transmitting heritage).

The users of mediated content by individuals and groups may not be consistent with the goals of the suppliers. Suppliers create content with three purposes in mind: to inform, entertain, and persuade.

Key Concept

The media as a consumer market The mass media can be described as operating in a market that sells useful information to readers, viewers, and listeners.

Key Concept

The media as an advertising market The mass media can be described as operating in a market that sells the attention of readers, viewers, and listeners to product advertisers.

Consumer and Advertising Markets   In the *consumer market,* the media deliver information to readers, viewers, and listeners. The purpose of the information varies from entertainment to persuasion to education. Those who acquire information pay either with money or the attention they give to advertisements. People buy newspapers, watch television, and listen to recordings in this market. The consumer, not the originator, of the information determines how a particular bit of information is used.

The *advertising market* involves selling the attention of readers, viewers, and listeners to advertisers. Businesses and other groups buy time or space in this market to influence what people buy or believe. An organization that advertises wants people to buy some good or service. Images of Tiger Woods wearing Nike apparel entice golfers to buy Nike products.

Assigning transactions to one of the two commercial markets is easier from the media company's perspective than from the consumer's perspective. Media organizations have different departments that serve the advertising and consumer markets. Often, media organizations label advertising to separate it from news and editorial content. However, readers, listeners, and viewers do not necessarily make the distinction between markets. When people want to buy a car, they may consult *Consumer Reports'* guide to cars on the Internet, check local prices in newspaper advertisements, and watch the Jeep Grand Cherokee climb an off-road hill in a television advertisement. Just how much each of these influences a particular buyer depends on the individual. Because people seek information from both advertising and news and often don't distinguish between the two, some advertisers deliberately create ads that masquerade as news.

The Marketplace of Ideas   The consumer and advertising markets are both commercial markets. An identifiable exchange of money takes place between supplier and user. The *marketplace of ideas* does not require money. In this market, ideas compete for social acceptance. People and groups seek to influence this exchange of ideas because the arguments made in the marketplace of ideas may help create laws and norms for behavior.

Key Concept

The media as a marketplace of ideas The mass media can be described as operating in a market in which ideas interact and compete for acceptance. A free exchange of ideas in the marketplace is considered necessary for a democracy.

Efforts to develop a national health-care policy is an example of how the marketplace of ideas works. Politicians make speeches, newspapers publish editorials, and radio stations accept listener call-ins with comments about health care. Eventually, Congress holds public hearings, drafts legislation, and votes on a health-care bill. The president signs or vetoes the bill. All the steps include communication, much of it through mass media. The ideas compete in the marketplace of ideas for final acceptance as official policy.

Although the three markets are distinct, information produced for one can be used in another. Political candidates try to influence the marketplace of ideas by purchasing advertisements. When Walt Disney portrayed Donald Duck rushing to the mailbox to pay his taxes on time during World War II, he used his Hollywood reputation to influence the marketplace of ideas by building patriotic spirit. In the same period, movies provided diversion in the consumer market by entertaining viewers with stories that emphasized cultural stereotypes of the enemy. Advertisers such as Benetton often use cultural ideas in the consumer market to promote their products in the advertising market.

Role of Media Organizations in the Marketplace

The needs and wants that people take to the three communication markets result in a demand for information and ideas. Media organizations in a market system supply that demand with media content, which flows into the three markets. Some needs and wants are fulfilled, and the cycle starts again. In that circular process, media organizations must (1) evaluate the demand for information and ideas in the three markets, (2) draw on people as sources in the system, and (3) supply content to fulfill the demand.

Media organizations take a variety of forms. Individual television stations, newspapers, or magazine and book publishers are media organizations. But the term also can be applied to corporations that own and/or manage several newspapers, television stations, or magazines. Most media organizations are part of larger conglomerates, or groups, that own varied types of media.

Table 1.1 shows some of these multimedia groups and their holdings. In 2007, Gannett owned 90 daily newspapers with a circulation of 7.3 million (up from 74 in 1999), including *USA Today*; 1,000 nondaily publications; and 23 television stations covering 18.05 percent of U.S. households. Gannett also has more than 130 websites in the United States and United Kingdom.

Gannett has a global reach, with operations in Canada, Belgium, Germany, Hong Kong, and Singapore. In the U.K., it owns the second largest regional newspaper publisher, Newsquest. Other operations include Gannett News service, a direct-mail

Table 1.1	Types of Media Outlets by Multimedia Groups		
Group	**Daily Newspapers**	**Television Stations**	**Radio Stations**
Freedom Communications	28	8	0
Gannett	90	23	0
Lee Enterprises	52	0	0
New York Times Co.	18	9	2
Media General	25	30	0
Scripps Howard	21	10	0

Sources: Company websites.

advertising company, an Internet advertising technology firm, a mobile phone search service, and a network that delivers programming to television screens in elevators.

Groups can be owned publicly or privately. Under public ownership, the corporation sells stock to the public. Anyone who has enough money to buy stock can become part owner of the public corporation. Under private ownership, a person or group of people owns all the company stock. Ownership type has a significant impact on organizations. For example, the higher the percentage of stock owned by the public, the less likely the company is to reinvest its profits in the company. This happens because the profit is returned to investors in order to keep the stock prices high.[12] The danger in this policy is the potential lowering of content quality.

Demand for Information and Ideas

Demand in the U.S. mass communication system reflects social and economic changes. Today, an increase in disposable income and leisure time provides many viewers with more time and money to buy new technology that can supply needs for entertainment and information. In addition, the population is nationally—even internationally—oriented as the role of the federal rather than state and local government dominates decision making that affects our lives. Events such as the September 11 attacks or the Indian Ocean tsunami focus audience attention on the international scene.

Demand for information and ideas comes from individual needs and wants. Media organizations cannot meet individual demands one person at a time because media can supply information and ideas only at the market level. Demand structure determines the nature of the aggregate demand and has three characteristics: audience similarity, the geographic nature of the market, and available technology.

Audience similarity can be charted on a continuum ranging from everyone being exactly alike to everyone being entirely different. Members of any audience share characteristics, but those members also are different in many ways. For example, readers of the *Tuscola County* (MI) *Advertiser* share more similarities than do readers of the *Washington Post.* Tuscola County is an agricultural area populated primarily by people who were born and raised there. Washington, D.C., is a giant metropolis populated by people from all over the world. Because the audience of the *Post* is more diverse, it costs more to provide the diversity of content needed to appeal to the broader group.

In addition to audience similarity, geography also defines demand structure. Information helps define communities, sometimes through audience similarity, as in the women's suffrage movement of the early twentieth century, and other times through geography. The success of *USA Today*'s page of short, informational blurbs about individual states capitalizes on people's identification with their home states. Geography also affects demand because geographic features such as lakes, rivers, and mountains determine the history, economy, and culture of people in a given market. Those factors in turn affect the type of information and advertising the audience demands. Whereas Kansas farmers might pay attention to fertilizer ads on television, such ads would be wasted on a Los Angeles, California, audience.

The final determinant of demand structure is technology, a factor that can make geography less important. Just as the telegraph expanded mass media audiences in the mid-nineteenth century, now cable and satellite technology have expanded the political, social, and economic range of those who have access to television. In addition, satellites transmit newspaper content to printing plants across the United States, making a local or regional daily newspaper available throughout the country. The expansion of national and international media distribution reduces the distinctions among separate cultures. In the process, some cultures may join to share common ideas, and some local or minority cultures may be left out. The convergence of technology will continue to give consumers more choice, opening up new avenues of distribution for print media and fostering interactive communication in television and other electronic media.

Demand in the Consumer Market Consumer demand for media content varies considerably depending partly on household decisions about **media mixes.** For example, one person might mix media by watching an hour of television a day and reading a couple of newspapers. Another person might watch television and not read newspapers or magazines. A person's mix represents his or her wants and needs. However, other factors such as price and accessibility also affect demand. Generally, as the price of a media commodity increases, some consumers will substitute different content or media. The ability to read or to use a computer also will affect media choices.

Demand in the Advertising Market Demand in the advertising market is straightforward compared to demand in the consumer market. Advertisers want to pay the lowest possible price to send their message to the highest possible percentage of potential customers. To do this, the advertiser must identify the location of potential customers and the best medium for reaching those customers. In most cases, advertisers use a combination of media to target the media mixes used by their audience.

Advertisers choose between mass and **targeted advertising,** depending on the size and type of audience they want to reach. A local department store uses mass advertising aimed at a diverse group because individuals with different levels of income or different interests will all buy products from its store. However, a Mercedes Benz dealership targets only those with a large enough income to buy its cars.

Demand in the Marketplace of Ideas Demand in the marketplace of ideas is more complex than transactions in the two commercial communication markets. Transactions in this market involve no money. The demand is for ideas, information, and reinforcement of cultural values that allow society to maintain and improve itself. The demand is diffuse and difficult to quantify because not all members of society agree on how to maintain and improve society.

In the United States, society uses the marketplace of ideas to form majority views about government and social norms. People and groups compete—often through media—to have their ideas accepted. Media coverage of an issue can help it gain political attention, but the U.S. system of government ensures, for better or worse, that political change is evolutionary rather than rapid. The right of a woman to choose whether to have an abortion has been a political and social issue for many decades. Abortion continues to gain media attention as a political and social issue because people are divided. *Roe v. Wade* established the right of women to choose and maintained that right for over 30 years, but subsequent legislation and court decisions have chipped away at that position. The marketplace of ideas continues to entertain varying points of view.

Access to the marketplace of ideas varies from country to country. A dictatorship allows very little influence from the outside world. Dictators want to retain power, which becomes difficult if people have open access to outside information and ideas. When a dictator is able to control the marketplace of ideas, the country may suffer economic and social harm. For example, in North Korea, Kim Jong II strictly controls government television and radio while many of his people live in dire poverty.

As national economies become more international through growing exports and imports, a global marketplace of ideas will increase in importance. Many media corporations have global reach. For example, the British Broadcast Corporation (BBC) transmits radio programming worldwide in 40 languages and owns 18 television channels with offices in France, Germany, Canada, the United States, Australia, Japan, and Hong Kong. To what extent are the politics, economics, and cultures of other nations influenced by their importation of news, entertainment, and advertising? What control should and can a government exercise over the international flow of information? These and other questions are debated in the global marketplace of ideas.

media mix

Consumers' use of a variety of media, such as newspapers, television, and the World Wide Web.

targeted advertising

Trying to sell a product or service to a particular group of people.

Supply of Content

As shown in Figure 1.1, mass media organizations supply content to the three communication markets to meet demand. In order to do this, every mass media organization must go through six processes:

1. Media organizations must *generate content.* Sometimes organizations create original content, and sometimes they buy content from other sources.
2. Once the organization generates content, it must *produce and reproduce content in quantity.* That is how media become mass media. Content must be replicated many times over to serve large audiences. The replication comes about because a printing press prints thousands of copies or because a million television sets change electronic pulses into pictures and sound.
3. Content must be *delivered to users.* Once it has been reproduced, the content must somehow reach users. A delivery person might throw a newspaper onto a porch, or a cable may carry electronic pulses into living rooms.
4. Mass media must *generate financial support.* Most mass media organizations either sell information to users or sell space and time to advertisers. However, other forms of financing are available. The selling of information and advertisements reflects the commercial nature of U.S. economic, social, and political systems. Some media organizations, such as public television and radio, are supported by grants, donations, and even the government.
5. The products of the organization must be *promoted.* Because so many media options are available today, an organization cannot assume that potential users will even know its product exists. Advertising and public-relations activities inform and persuade people to buy or use their products.
6. The first five processes must be *managed.* The generation, reproduction, delivery, financing, and promotion of mass media must be coordinated so that certain activities are accomplished in specific periods of time.

Effective strategies for carrying out these processes differ according to the size and complexity of each organization. At a weekly newspaper with a circulation of 5,000, the editor and one or two reporters write stories, take pictures, and compose headlines. A computer produces plates that go on a printing press. When the newspaper copies are printed, someone, often the editor, picks up the copies and returns to the newspaper office. After address labels are placed on subscribers' copies, most of the newspapers are delivered by mail. Promotion for the weekly paper might include annually delivering a paper containing a subscription flier to every household in town. Advertising salespeople collect money from advertisers; subscription fees are paid by mail. The editor and publisher manage the newspaper processes. A weekly paper can often be managed by only four to six full-time employees and three to six part-time employees.

In contrast, a metropolitan daily with a circulation of 350,000 has a department for each process. The newsroom and advertising department create the content. A metropolitan daily owns its own presses. The circulation department places copies in news racks and delivers newspapers to customers' doorsteps. The promotion department buys advertising on radio, television, and billboards, as well as running telemarketing campaigns. The accounting office bills advertisers and collects subscription money. The publisher, department heads, and dozens of assistant managers coordinate the activities, which might involve 500 or more people.

Key Concept

Interaction between supply and demand The interaction of media organizations' supply and consumers' and advertisers' demand determines the type of information and ideas available in a media market system. This interaction involves media organization managers researching what people demand and finding ways to supply it. The reaction of individuals to the supply determines the content that media companies produce in the future.

Interaction of Supply and Demand

Interaction between supply and demand in the consumer and advertising markets determines the amount and nature of media products and how financial resources are distributed among media companies. Consumers demand information to help them live. Mass media companies provide the content to make money. Ideally, consumers will get useful information, advertisers will get effective advertisements, and media companies will make a reasonable profit. However, market interactions often fail to achieve this ideal.

Three important factors create interaction problems: the level of competition for consumers, an organization's understanding of its customers, and the organization's goals. All three affect the responsiveness of media organizations to consumer and advertiser demand.

Competition moves power from producers to consumers. If some readers do not like *Time,* they can subscribe to *Newsweek.* Competition allows for choice, and choice forces companies to respond to consumer demand. Typically, media companies respond to competition for consumers by keeping the price of their product low, by increasing spending on content, and by trying to improve the usefulness of the information to the consumer. The goal of these responses is to provide a better product at a lower price than the competition.

A similar effect results from competition in the advertising market. If an advertiser does not like the price that one television station charges for advertising time, it can buy time from another. Competition holds down advertising prices and improves service to advertisers.

Although competition serves the consumer and the advertiser, it costs the media company. It is more expensive to produce and deliver information in competitive markets than in monopoly markets. The result of higher cost is lower profit. If media managers are given a choice, most will pick a less competitive market.

Even though competition forces media companies to respond to consumer demand, it does not guarantee that the company managers will accurately understand the customer's needs. The increased spending and lower price that results from competition will benefit the consumer only if companies produce more useful information or more attractive content. The managers of media organizations must predict, through intuition, experience, and research, what type of information would be useful to the consumer.

The final factor affecting the outcome of market interaction is organizational goals. Most mass media organizations seek profits, but some aspire to higher profits than others. To increase profits, media organizations must either lower their expenses or raise their revenues. Efforts to increase revenues are risky, but cutting costs is not, at least in the short term. As a result, the local daily newspaper, which is usually the only one in town and thus has little direct competition, may get by with fewer reporters than it might be expected to have in order to cover news well. Similarly, organizations with higher profit goals will keep a closer watch on advertising prices to make sure they are getting the best price possible. Over time, however, efforts to cut costs and hike prices often result in lower quality and fewer customers.

The profit goal is basic to the market system, but the impact of that goal differs depending on whether managers take a short-term or long-term approach. Profit goals motivate some media businesses to invest in long-term quality, which usually increases long-term profits because many consumers are attracted to quality information. Profit goals motivate others to cut costs to the bone for short-term profits. Over time new technology usually allows more companies to enter a market, and the effect of more companies is to reduce the ability of individual companies to squeeze profits from consumers and advertisers during the short term.

Media systems are cyclical. That is, each cycle allows media organizations to adjust to the changing demands of consumers, advertisers, and society itself. The nature of many of the cycles varies, but some are consistent. For instance, the broadcast television networks in the United States traditionally have a yearly cycle. Every fall networks drop some programs and add new ones designed to attract more viewers. The more successful a network was the previous year, the fewer changes it makes.

Often the interaction of supply and demand in a market system reflects a level of tension between societal values and pushing social boundaries. Although critical

Some researchers believe that tragic events, such as the school shooting in Littleton, Colorado, may be connected to repeated exposure of young people to violence in the media.

discussions of media have been ongoing since the mass production of books, modern media criticism and concerns about the impact of media on society began in the 1920s with the introduction of radio and intensified in the 1930s with the advent of feature-length sound films. Critics worried that radio would corrupt traditional values. They believed that adolescents, watching movies in a dark theater, would be influenced by sexual content, and that teenagers might adopt screen behaviors that did not conform to traditional standards. Critics also believed that media influences would make it more difficult for parents to maintain control over their children.

Through the years, social scientists have looked at the social effects of the media, particularly the effects of television, that ubiquitous screen that brightens nearly every living room or family room in the United States. Many studies have focused on the effects of television on individuals and on societal norms. In the aftermath of the rash of school shootings, particularly that in 1999 at Columbine High School in Littleton, Colorado, critics began to search for causes of the violent behavior of some students. Many political figures were quick to conclude that repeated exposure to violent TV programming might increase individual violence. We now know that media do have effects—both negative and positive—on individuals and that the effects are a complicated result not only of media influence but also family and societal behavior. With the advent of social networking and the Internet, critics and consumers once more are concerned about what kind of information their children are acquiring.

USE AND FUNCTIONS OF MEDIA IN THE MARKETPLACE

In 1948 Harold Lasswell, a political scientist who is considered one of the founders of communication research, formulated a statement of the "functions" of mass communication in society, with the idea of illustrating how media perform essential tasks for the maintenance of society. Lasswell argued that media performed three functions: (1) surveillance of the environment; (2) correlation of the parts of the society; and (3) transmission of culture. Looking at function in a slightly different way, some media scholars have identified the individual "uses" involved when people seek

Global Impact

Mass Media Worldwide

The June 2006 World Cup finale between Italy and France drew 1.1 billion in-home television viewers around the world. That's around 20 percent of the world's vast, diverse population. Media companies in most countries bought broadcasting rights. Even the reclusive North Korea, in which the government strictly controls the media, allowed its citizens to see pretaped World Cup broadcasts from South Korea. Coverage of the game also revealed the global spread of the Internet. At the height of the action, several million fans a day visited the Fédération Internationale de Football Association's official World Cup webpage to watch streaming video highlights and sign up for play-by-play text messages. Through the mass media, people around the world can share an experience of events such as sports matches. While retaining national loyalties, they become inhabitants of a much larger world.

The global media consists of a vast number of businesses and institutions in every country, though large multinational corporations based in the United States and Europe have a great deal of influence and control over what kinds of media products are exchanged in a global marketplace. In order to carry over into other markets, they create a readily identifiable consumer brand, like Disney or Microsoft, that either evokes an emotional response or is tied to product quality.

Many young people around the world are attracted to Western brands because they symbolize wealth, power, and cosmopolitanism. However, these brands also take on local meanings as young people fit them into their own social networks. Trends in media production are frequently influenced by ideas from other cultures that appeal to the youth market.

News, too, spreads around the world, and news organizations are concerned with their ability to broadcast and collect information across borders. Information about wars and disasters touches people's emotions, incites political debate, and can arouse awareness and action. But collecting news across borders is sometimes a hazardous occupation. From 2003 to 2005, 60 journalists were killed in Iraq. Other journalists have been attacked and kidnapped while covering the Israeli–Palestinian conflict.

Michael Parks, former editor of the *Los Angeles Times* and director of the School of Journalism at the University of Southern California, says that news executives must deal not only with the safety of their journalists but also with the "more fundamental question of when a story is too dangerous to cover."

---

information to fulfill their needs and wants. Those uses fall into five types: surveillance, decision making, social and cultural interaction, diversion, and self-understanding.[13]

Surveillance involves monitoring one's environment. It occurs in two types of situations: everyday surveillance, such as checking baseball scores or stock prices, and extraordinary surveillance, such as keeping up with events during a war or natural disaster. Surveillance keeps people in touch with environmental and other social and political changes that are crucial to their lives. When people watched CNN at the height of the U.S. military action in Iraq, they were surveilling, or monitoring, their environment. Surveillance also helps people decide how to use information for decision making, social and cultural interaction, and diversion.

Decision making involves collecting information in order to select among options. The decision may be as minor as which TV program to watch or as important as for which presidential candidate to vote. Use of information for decision making is purposeful and specific. Surveillance and decision making overlap because surveillance often determines what types of decisions need to be made.

Social and cultural interaction involves using information that defines, identifies, and maintains membership in a group. All groups define themselves with information, which allows individuals to hold and demonstrate membership in the group. The group may be as large as a country or as small as a household. Sometimes people get information formally, such as through classes for people who want to become U.S. citizens. Other times information passes informally through conversations among group members, such as in discussions during fraternity and sorority rushes.

Marshall McLuhan argued that the "medium is the message." McLuhan believed that the nature of technology was as important as its content.

His ideas were so controversial for the time and had so much influence on scholars of mass media that the term *McLuhanism* appears in the *Oxford English Dictionary*. The dictionary distills his entire work into a statement that the introduction of mass media deadens the critical faculties of individuals.

Herbert Marshall McLuhan was born in Edmonton, Alberta, Canada, on July 21, 1911, to a Protestant family of Scottish-Irish descent. His mother, Elsie, was an actress, and his father, Herbert, was a salesman.

Marshall McLuhan

He went to the University of Manitoba to become an engineer but switched his major to English literature. He graduated with a bachelor of arts degree in 1933 and earned a master's degree the following year. He then studied literature at Cambridge University in England, where he obtained a B.A. in 1936 and a doctorate in 1942. McLuhan married Corinne Keller, a Texan who studied drama at the Pasadena Playhouse in California.

McLuhan established his teaching and scholarly career at the University of Toronto, where he was influenced by Harold Innis, a pioneer in communication studies. In 1963, McLuhan was appointed director of the University of Toronto's Marshall McLuhan Center for Culture and Technology, where he worked for 14 years before retiring.

McLuhan wrote more than 15 books, including *The Mechanical Bride: Folklore of Industrial Man*, published in 1951.

That book was his first attempt to examine the effects of mass culture and "the pressures set up around us today by the mechanical agencies of the press, radio, movies, and advertising." He made a greater impact with his second book, *The Gutenberg Galaxy*, written in 1961, which discusses the effect of movable type on Western European culture in the fifteenth century.

In 1964, McLuhan earned popular acclaim with *Understanding Media: The Extensions of Man*, in which he contends that the introduction of electronic circuitry made behavior less isolated and more conformist than before. He expands on his concept of the "global village," arguing that media bring different cultures closer together. Another popular book, *The Medium Is the Message*, published in 1967, illustrated McLuhan's ideas of "hot" and "cold" media. His objective was to show that a medium is not neutral, but it transforms life.

McLuhan earned praise as the media guru of the 1960s, but he also was the target of criticism from scholars. He received many honors, awards, and medals, including citations from the British and Italian governments. McLuhan died on December 31, 1980, at the age of 69.

Sources: Alden Whitman, "Marshall McLuhan, Author, Dies," *The New York Times*, January 1, 1981: sec. 1, 1; Alan M. Kriegsman, "Marshall McLuhan Dies," *The Washington Post*, January 1, 1981: sec. C, 16.

Diversion involves using information for entertainment and enjoyment. Watching football on television or reading a short story may make a person feel sad, happy, or even horrified. Individuals seek different types of diversion, which is why some people prefer films by Spike Lee and others prefer films by Steven Spielberg.

Self-understanding requires that people use media to gain insight into their own behaviors and attitudes. A person feeling alone and isolated might gain solace from listening to a song about loneliness. A college student reading a news story about the consequences of binge drinking might seek to avoid excessive alcohol consumption.

The five distinct individual uses of information often are related. The seemingly simple process of selecting a movie to go to includes checking the newspaper to find out what is showing (surveillance), asking friends about the two or three films you are considering (social and cultural interaction), picking one (decision making), and going to see the movie (diversion).

The same information can be used in more than one way. For example, people may see a movie for entertainment. The next day they may discuss it with people at work (social and cultural interaction). The following year, they may remember how much they enjoyed a particular actor and decide to see a new movie starring the same person (decision making). The more different uses a person has for a given message, the more utility that message has.

Although individual members of a group may use mass communication to create social and cultural interaction, communication also may serve a group by correlating actions of its members and by transmitting its social and cultural heritage. Groups vary in size from a small group of friends to a tribe to an entire society, but they all involve member interactions and a common culture and heritage.

Large groups such as societies follow economic, political, and social agendas. *Economic actions* involve the exchange of goods, services, and money. News, as well as advertising, can affect economic actions. If Mary intends to buy an imported car, she might postpone her purchase if she reads a newspaper article that suggests Congress might cut import taxes, which could increase the cost of cars from other countries.

Media correlate *political actions* by providing information about politicians and the political process. John and Catherine might watch the television coverage of presidential debates either to make up their minds about a candidate or to reinforce their closely held beliefs. An irate property owner might write a letter to the newspaper editor complaining about the actions of a city council member. In countries where citizens have a great deal of political power, the media gain importance because of their role in the political process. The need to correlate political activities forms the basis for the First Amendment to the Constitution. Without a free flow of information, people in a democracy cannot decide who should run their country.

Media correlate social activities and actions. The correlation may be as simple as helping a community to coordinate and attend a Memorial Day parade, local club activities, or school events. Or media may help correlate a national march in support of integration—an act that is both political and social. The media's coverage of the 1963 March on Washington helped convince Congress and the population that civil rights legislation was needed to promote equality in the United States.

In addition to correlating a society's activities, fostering the transmission of social heritage is another important function of mass communication. Societies are defined by their common heritage. Although education plays the most important role in this transmission, media often contribute to the common understanding of social and cultural heritage. People who say they are Americans recognize a common history with others who claim the same label. History can be shared at the local, regional, national, or international level. The 1996 Olympic Games in Atlanta gave the South an opportunity to transmit its social heritage to the world. The closing ceremonies included a concert that featured jazz, blues, Latino music, and country music—all part of the southern and American heritage.

This book is organized to incorporate the role or functions of the media into descriptions of the various types of media and uses of communication. You will note that the book is organized into three parts: (1) Media Industries; (2) Media Processes and Functions; and (3) Media Research, Regulation, and Restrictions. In Part I, you will see how various media are organized and how they operate within market systems. In Part II, you will read about how the media functions of informing and persuading are incorporated into the basic activities of journalists and advertising and public relations professionals. And in Part III, you will see how regulation, ethics, and research shape the media landscape.

SUMMARY

■ Content and behavior of media are closely tied to the development of technology and the economics of big business. Media operate within a context of political behavior, social and cultural development, and globalization.

■ Typically, media include newspapers, magazines, television, radio, books, recordings, and movies. The authors here include the Internet, although some scholars argue that its interactivity makes it different.

- The convergence of technologies is ongoing. In the past, as new technologies developed, old ones adapted. New technologies, alone and in combination with older forms of media, have an impact on our daily lives, but no one can predict exactly the impact of each technology.
- Media companies are delivering content across multiplatforms because of converged technologies.
- The U.S. media system involves a circular process through which media providers and consumers meet desires and needs.
- Demand occurs in the consumer market, the advertising market, and the marketplace of ideas.
- As suppliers of content, all media organizations carry out six processes. Content must be generated, reproduced, and delivered; those three processes must be financed, promoted, and managed.
- Supplying the consumer market involves selling or giving information to people in exchange for their potential attention to advertising.
- Supplying the advertising market means selling space and time primarily to businesses and other organizations so they can transmit messages that influence the behavior of their audience.
- Supplying the marketplace of ideas involves contributing ideas and information to political leaders and other citizens.
- Individuals use mass communication for surveillance, decision making, social and cultural interaction, diversion, and self-understanding.
- Groups use mass communication to coordinate the political, economic, and social activities of their members and to transmit their social and cultural heritage.
- No media system can be isolated from other systems in the world. The U.S. system supplies and demands information and ideas from systems in other countries.

NAVIGATING THE WEB Communication

Media institutions and industries use World Wide Web sites to generate interest in their activities and to provide information about business ventures. At the other end of the spectrum are research sites that provide critical information about media as institutions.

Media Communications Studies
aber.ac.uk/media
The Media Communication Studies site was established by Daniel Chandler at the University of Wales, Aberystwyth. Included among its numerous pages is one about media institutions. It also provides other links and materials by Ben Bagdikian and Noam Chomsky about media institutions and society.

Media Education Foundation
mediaed.org
The Media Education Foundation encourages critical thinking about media and democracy, commercialization, and media ownership.

Media History Project
media.history.umn.edu
The Media History Project covers everything from oral and scribal culture to digital media.

QUESTIONS FOR REVIEW

1. Why was Gutenberg's invention of movable type important?
2. What does *technological convergence* mean?
3. What is *economic convergence*?
4. How do social groups use mass media?

5. What are the differences between market and non-market communication systems?
6. What are the three communication markets described in this chapter?
7. What is meant by demand for information and ideas?

ISSUES TO THINK ABOUT

1. How will media convergence affect your life?
2. What are some of the problems of applying advertising models to online and other computer information services?
3. How do images dominate our views of society at home and abroad?
4. What are the positive and negative impacts on society of market and nonmarket systems of communication?
5. How important is interactivity in a media system to the development of individuals and of society?
6. If you were the president of a developing country and you wanted to create a market system of communication, what modifications in the U.S. system would you seek to make?
7. What are the primary functions of media in a democratic society?

SUGGESTED READINGS

Altschull, J. Herbert. *Agents of Power: The Media and Public Policy,* 2nd ed. (White Plains, NY: Longman, 1995).

Bagdikian, Ben H. *The Information Machines: Their Impact on Men and Media* (New York: Harper & Row, 1971).

Bogart, Leo. *Commercial Culture: The Media System and the Public Interest* (New York: Oxford University Press, 1995).

Jenkins, Henry. *Convergence Culture* (New York: New York University Press, 2006).

Kovach, Bill, and Tom Rosenstiel. *Warp Speed: America in the Age of Mixed Media* (New York: The Century Foundation Press, 1999).

McChesney, Robert. *Corporate Media and the Threat to Democracy* (New York: Seven Stories Press, 1997).

Steven, Peter. *The No-Nonsense Guide to Global Media* (New York: Verso, 2004).

CHAPTER 2

Books

When Oprah Winfrey chose Jonathan Franzen's new novel, *The Corrections,* for her influential monthly book club, the author had mixed feelings. He compared himself to an indie rock star, telling an interviewer, "Now [that] I've signed a big label deal and I'm playing stadiums, how good can I be?"[1] On his book tour, Franzen expressed further concerns that Oprah's Book Club picks were corporate driven and often lightweight, sentimental, and targeted to women.

Offended, Winfrey cancelled Franzen's scheduled appearance on her show, and announced, "We're moving on to the next book." Nevertheless, *The Corrections* remained on the Book Club list. Media coverage of the event was extensive, and editors and publishers joined in attacking Franzen for ingratitude, egotism, and snobbery. The mainstream publishing industry had greatly benefited from Oprah's Book Club selections, which could increase sales of a book by hundreds of thousands of copies. Critics were divided into two camps. Some defended Oprah's Book Club for promoting public literacy. Others criticized it for a lack of judgment over whether a book selection had true literary quality or not. In the midst of the uproar, Franzen made a public apology, blaming his media inexperience. His book not only remained a bestseller, but won the 2001 National Book Award.

Since merchants first began to selling books to the general public, questions have arisen over who determines their purpose, meaning, and value. In our own time, these questions are set against the background

KEY CONCEPTS

- Scribal Culture
- Democratization of Knowledge
- Book Distribution
- Quality versus Quantity
- Youth Market
- Global Brands
- Intellectual Property
- Markets and Processes in the Book Industry

of a dramatic drop in reading in all segments of the population. The National Endowment for the Arts has reported that less than half of adult Americans read literature and that the decline in general reading is accelerating.[2] People are becoming more likely to browse the Internet, go to the movies, watch a television show, or read a magazine than read a novel. Everyone in the book trade has had to consider her response to these changes, whether she is an author promoting her book on television, a critic defending traditional literary values, a bookstore owner attracting customers by selling coffee, or a publisher negotiating the film rights for her latest bestseller. Technological developments such as web-based publishing and global marketing are further altering the production and sale of books. While predictions about the death of the book have proven to be greatly exaggerated, the future of the book remains to be seen.

The Oprah Book Club has promoted the value of books to a popular audience, creating greater profits for publishers. Debate over the club and its selections represents broader issues in book publishing, such as:

- What are the economics of publishing decisions? In a market system driven by consumerism, what relationship exists between literary quality and profit?

- Who determines quality? To what extent are literary elites such as acquisitions editors and critics in a better position than general readers to define quality?

- What kinds of audiences exist for what kinds of books? How are audiences created and identified?

- How has technological development affected books? What changes have taken place for publishers, writers, and readers?

- In what ways are books important to culture and citizenship? What impact do publishing decisions have on social values and vice versa?

GROWTH OF LITERARY CULTURE

In literate cultures, books transmit knowledge and are therefore associated with social, political, and economic power. During medieval times, the reproduction of books was restricted by the Catholic Church for the most part to monasteries, where scribes hand-copied treasured manuscript books that then made up the important libraries of Europe. In that **scribal culture**, copying books was an art, which we can appreciate when we look at rare books, such as the *Book of Kells,* on exhibit in museums. Scholars often traveled across Europe to the famous libraries to have access to knowledge. Such scarce books rarely, if ever, were owned by individuals, and students relied on teachers to read books to them, producing the "lecture" system of education that is still prevalent in U.S. and European colleges and universities. When your professor lectures to the class, he or she is reenacting an ancient tradition born of necessity.

Key Concept

Scribal culture In the Middle Ages, before the invention of the printing press, written material was reproduced almost exclusively by monks who served as scribes, or copyists. As the sole repository of books, the medieval church was able to control what information reached the population.

With the advent of the printing revolution in the mid-1400s as a result of Gutenberg's cast-metal movable type, books became objects to be printed and sold. They were no longer confined to libraries but become the domain of public culture. Soon books, printed in lots of 200 to 1,000 copies, circulated among the wealthy classes. The production of books opened the way for printer-merchants, who published books and searched for new markets for their products. The Bible, soon printed in English as well as in Latin, circulated freely. No longer did the educated classes depend on the authorities to interpret the word of God; they now could develop their own interpretations. The circulation of books threatened the power of church and state because knowledge, a powerful tool and weapon, was accessible to anyone who could read.

Books in Your Life

Judging Their Quality

You be the judge. If you're familiar with any of these books, give them a couple of letter grades: A, B, C, D, F. Judge their quality and their popularity according to how you think most of your friends would rate them. Think about whether quality and popularity can be combined in the same package.

As you read this chapter, you will find these books mentioned in connection with important issues for the book industry, including the apparent dilemma of quality versus popularity. Do you think quality and popularity are mutually exclusive?

Book Title	Quality Rating	Popularity Rating
Harry Potter and the Sorcerer's Stone (J. K. Rowling)		
The Da Vinci Code (Dan Brown)		
Little Women (Louisa May Alcott)		
Lord of the Rings (J. R. R. Tolkien)		
Paradise (Toni Morrison)		
For Whom the Bell Tolls (Ernest Hemingway)		
Hearts in Atlantis (Stephen King)		

In European towns, the printer's shop became a meeting place and educational center. As the British settled the North American colonies, bookshops there also became important cultural centers.

Because of the perceived power of books, nearly all governments and societies at one time or another have sought to restrict the printing or distribution of books. From the early 1500s until the end of the 1600s, printing in England was strictly controlled by the monarchy. In 1529, Henry VIII issued a list of prohibited books and imposed a system of **prior restraint** that required printers to have a license before printing. However, in spite of the severe punishments that were handed down to those who printed outside the system, by the mid-sixteenth century in England, nearly one-third of all books were printed outside the official channels. In 1695 the British Parliament allowed the licensing system to expire, and newspapers and books flourished throughout London and expanded into the provincial towns.[3]

BOOKS IN AMERICAN LIFE

As the printing business expanded into the provinces in Britain, it also expanded in the British colonies in America. Information was a highly prized commodity in British America, and colonists bought books to read for pleasure as well as to maintain their connections to the British homeland. Because books were expensive, the industry at first appealed to elite sensibilities and to those who had extra money and leisure time. However, throughout the nineteenth and twentieth centuries, the book industry was

prior restraint

Restricting publication before the fact rather than banning material or punishing an individual after the material is already printed.

democratized. Today, books are produced cheaply and quickly and appeal to all classes of people.

Throughout the seventeenth century, almost all books in the colonies were imported from Europe, although a few religious books and histories were published in Cambridge, Massachusetts. Later, as colonists sought more books, printers such as Benjamin Franklin imported books for sale and helped to establish public libraries. Franklin and a group of his Philadelphia friends contributed £40 in British sterling to start the Library Company in Philadelphia in 1731 to import books for reading and discussion. The colonists imported mostly religious books, but they also asked for professional books to expand their knowledge of law, medicine, and navigation. Popular literature also was imported and then published in the colonies. Such material included cheap forerunners to paperbacks, 16- to 30-two-page pamphlets known as **chapbooks,** which included tales of pirates and highway robbers. Cookbooks, household manuals, fortune-telling books, and even primitive weather forecasts also were published separately or were included in popular almanacs.

Books posed a problem when it came to circulation. They were bulky and expensive to distribute, and postage rates did not favor distribution through the mail. Before the Civil War, many books were circulated by book peddlers, who traveled from town to town with a horse and cart, selling books or exchanging stock with other dealers. Romantic novels, as well as the traditional religious, professional, and historical books, were sold throughout the rapidly expanding United States. The industry was well enough developed by the mid-1850s to play an important role in social movements and in creating a popular culture.

Books and Social Change

chapbooks

Cheaply printed paperback books produced during the 1700s.

serialized book

A book printed in parts in a magazine or newspaper over a certain period of time.

The first mass-market bestseller in the United States was Harriet Beecher Stowe's *Uncle Tom's Cabin,* published in 1852. Written for a popular audience, the novel was a powerful indictment of slavery that energized the abolition movement. Like many nineteenth-century novels, *Uncle Tom's Cabin* began in **serialized** form, appearing in the *National Era,* an abolitionist weekly. Stage plays and minstrel shows based on the story immediately began to appear and became popular entertainment. After publication in book form, the novel sold 20,000 copies within 3 weeks, and 300,000 within the first year. Stowe earned more than any other American or European author had on a single book. *Uncle Tom's Cabin* had its critics, who accused Stowe of exaggerating and writing with an overly emotional, sentimental woman's hand. In the South,

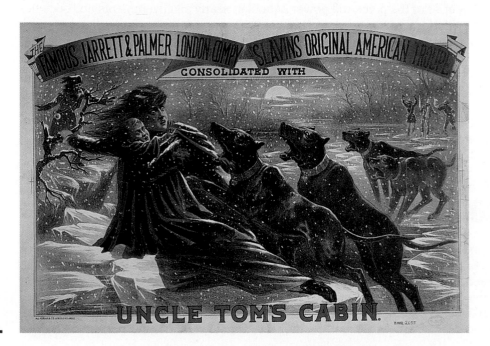

The first national best-seller, *Uncle Tom's Cabin*, depicted the evils of slavery and intensified the national discussion about slavery.

the book was received with denial and anger. Students at the University of Virginia publicly burned it, and peddlers were sometimes driven from Southern towns where they attempted to distribute it. Despite more recent criticisms of the book's racial stereotyping, *Uncle Tom's Cabin* has remained a classic because of its enormous popular influence on a vital national issue.[4]

The expansion of the book publishing industry provided opportunities for other writers dedicated to freedom and social justice for African Americans. Slave narratives—first-hand accounts of life under the slave system—were published and widely circulated by abolitionists. Some of these books and pamphlets reached sales of tens of thousands of copies and influenced works like *Uncle Tom's Cabin.* One of the most famous was the *Narrative of the Life of Frederick Douglass,* written by an escaped slave who became the country's most influential African-American voice, speaking for the Union cause and advising President Lincoln. After the Civil War, Douglass remained a tireless advocate of social justice, speaking and writing on black voting rights, urban development, economic opportunity, and women's rights. He reached his audience through his autobiographies, newspaper articles, and lectures, eventually taking his message abroad. Other former slaves continued to publish accounts of their experience, providing an important witness to history, ensuring that the nation would never forget the evils of slavery.[5]

Paperbacks and Popular Culture The development of the paperback book industry signaled to society that books were no longer for elites only and that the middle and lower classes would read popular fiction. For many years, books had belonged to the elites, and access to "refined" and "socially respectable" forms of reading reinforced elite values. The development of inexpensive paperbacks created the perception of pandering to popular taste and appealing to those who could be entertained by formulaic fiction. Accessibility to reading material helped to expand the middle class, but it also challenged elite social control. The result was a ***democratization of knowledge,*** or expansion of information to a wide group of individuals.

Economic and political conditions fueled the development of paperbacks. First distributed before the Civil War, paperbacks benefited from the less expensive printing technology associated with newspapers and from a lack of government regulation. Because the U.S. government refused to recognize foreign **copyrights,** books from other countries could be cheaply reproduced as paperbacks.

Further, newspapers printed cheap editions of French and English novels that masqueraded as newspapers so they could be distributed by newsboys and sold in the mail using inexpensive newspaper rates. Later in the nineteenth century, publishers printed books that resembled pamphlets and tried to distribute them as magazines. The practice ended in 1901 when the postmaster general declared that book publishers could not use second-class mailing rates under any conditions. Publishers took their case to court but ultimately lost. By 1914, ***book distribution*** finally gained a favorable mailing status. The move laid the groundwork for the development of book clubs in the 1920s, which promoted popular consumption of best-sellers as well as histories and biographies. Publishers sold hardback books through the clubs, successfully competing with the paperback industry.

Popular Paperback Formats The growth of the paperback industry stirred the debate over ***quality versus quantity,*** and in 1884 *Publishers Weekly* reported, "In the rage

---

Key Concept

Democratization of knowledge As books became more accessible in the 1800s, knowledge spread widely among the middle and lower classes, creating an increasingly democratic reading public. Wide distribution of books depended on cheap postal rates, inexpensive book production, and the portrayal of various classes of people in fictional works.

Key Concepts

Book distribution The ability to produce and distribute more books to more people depended on publishers' ability to make books known and physically available to potential readers. Wealthy social elites tended to favor limiting wide distribution and opposed low postal rates for books. However, cheap postage and improved marketing techniques eventually made books accessible to large numbers of readers.

Key Concepts

Quality versus quantity Book publishers traditionally have faced an apparent dilemma: Must they choose between publishing high-quality material or publishing to maximize their profitability? Different publishers have responded to this dilemma in different ways. Some have found that they can make a profit by producing work of high literary quality; others choose to produce work that appeals to more stereotyped and fleeting tastes.

copyright

A law that protects authors, playwrights, composers, and others who construct original works and keeps others from reproducing their work without permission.

Dateline

Books in Our Lives

Mid-1400s. Gutenberg invents movable metal type.

1529. Henry VIII issues list of banned books.

Early 1700s. English Crown reduces control of presses.

1770–1780s. Books and pamphlets promote revolution.

1845. Frederick Douglass writes autobiography.

1850s. *Uncle Tom's Cabin* becomes world best-seller.

1860s. Dime novels and paperbacks flourish.

1890s. Rise of popular formula fiction

1914. Cheaper mail rates for books

1920s. Influential book editors, such as Max Perkins, emerge.

1926. Book clubs are founded.

1930s. *Gone with the Wind* becomes worldwide best-seller.

1400–1700	1800	1860	1880	1900	1920	1930

1620. Pilgrims land at Plymouth Rock.

1690. *Publick Occurrences* is published in Boston.

1741. First magazine is published in America.

1776–1783. American Revolution

1830s. The penny press becomes the first truly mass medium in the United States.

1861–1865. American Civil War

1892. Thomas Edison's lab develops the kinetoscope.

1914–1918. World War I

1915. *The Birth of a Nation* marks the start of the modern movie industry.

1920. KDKA in Pittsburgh gets the first commercial radio license.

1930s. The Great Depression

1939. TV is demonstrated at the New York World's Fair.

1939–1945. World War II

Cultural Milestones

---

for cheapness, we have sacrificed everything for slop, and a dainty bit of bookmaking is like a jewel in the swine's snout."[6]

During the Civil War, publishers encouraged inexpensive, relatively short fiction that became known as the **dime novel;** it was a form well suited to popular taste. Soldiers in the field wanted to fill their time, and reading provided portable entertainment. Between 1860 and 1861 alone The Beadle Brothers sold four million copies of formulaic pocket-size novels written with specific plots focusing on romance and violence similar to the plots of television entertainment or the romance novels of today.

Paperback stories reflected men and women in factories and fictionalized situations they might encounter in that new world of work. The stories were produced through

dime novel

Cheap, paperback fiction produced in the midnineteenth century.

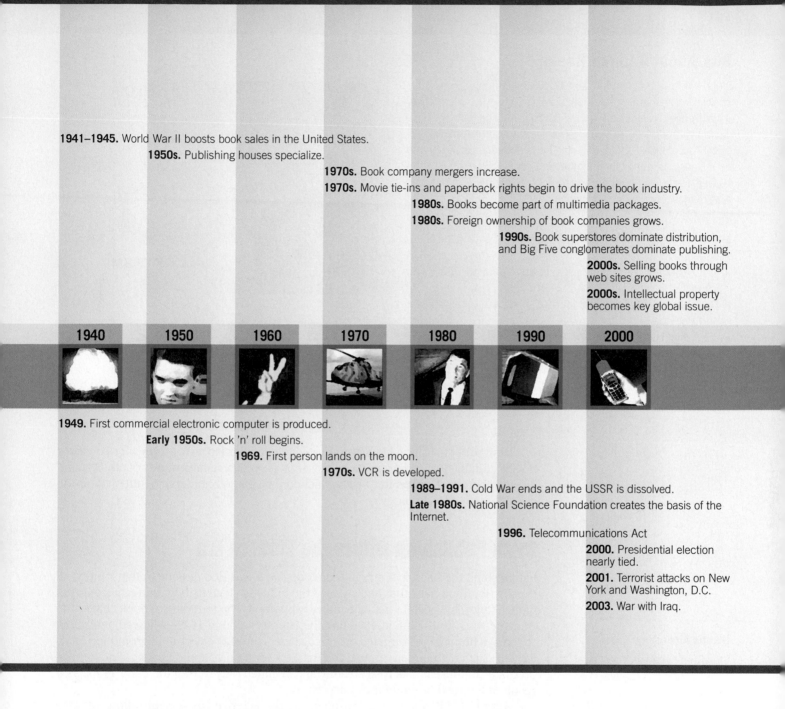

1941–1945. World War II boosts book sales in the United States.

1950s. Publishing houses specialize.

1970s. Book company mergers increase.

1970s. Movie tie-ins and paperback rights begin to drive the book industry.

1980s. Books become part of multimedia packages.

1980s. Foreign ownership of book companies grows.

1990s. Book superstores dominate distribution, and Big Five conglomerates dominate publishing.

2000s. Selling books through web sites grows.

2000s. Intellectual property becomes key global issue.

1940	1950	1960	1970	1980	1990	2000

1949. First commercial electronic computer is produced.

Early 1950s. Rock 'n' roll begins.

1969. First person lands on the moon.

1970s. VCR is developed.

1989–1991. Cold War ends and the USSR is dissolved.

Late 1980s. National Science Foundation creates the basis of the Internet.

1996. Telecommunications Act

2000. Presidential election nearly tied.

2001. Terrorist attacks on New York and Washington, D.C.

2003. War with Iraq.

what writers often called the **fiction factory,** in which publishers dictated the story lines, characters, plots, and sometimes specific scenes. The stories were aimed at the working class: mechanics, farmers, traveling salesmen, shop and factory workers, secretaries, and domestic servants. The story lines included traditional, heroic war and frontier stories, as well as tales of outlaws, detectives, male factory operatives, and young women who worked in the mills. Religious themes declined, but the virtue of women remained a hot topic. "Fiction that heroized women outside the domestic sphere," writes literary scholar Christine Bold, "offered working-class women some kind of accommodation and justification, some means of negotiating the transition from private to public."[7]

fiction factory

Late nineteenth-century publishing of formulaic books, in which publishers dictated story lines.

Cultural Impact

Bits About Banned Books

Since 1702, when Thomas Paine's political pamphlet, *The Rights of Man,* led to charges of treason against him by the British crown, controversies have arisen in America over publications threatening to political power and cultural values. Today, the American Library Association's Office for Intellectual Freedom collects data on requests to remove certain books from public and school libraries. Each year, during Banned Book Week, the ALA provides a list of most frequently challenged books. Since 1990, these have included:

- J. D. Salinger, *Catcher in the Rye,* for sexual content and offensive language
- J. K. Rowling, Harry Potter series, promoting occultism and witchcraft
- Dav Pilkey, Captain Underpants Series, for anti-family content and violence
- John Steinbeck, *Of Mice and Men,* for offensive language
- Mark Twain, *The Adventures of Tom Sawyer,* for racial slurs
- *It's Perfectly Normal,* for homosexuality, nudity, sex education, religious viewpoint, and abortion

- Maya Angelou, *I Know Why the Caged Bird Sings,* for sexual content, homosexual themes, and offensive language

Source: American Library Association, ala.org/ala/oif/bannedbooksweek/bannedbooksweek.htm, 2006.

New York publishing houses promoted the popular **Horatio Alger** rags-to-riches novels of individual achievement, which soon gave way to adventures of athletes and western heroes. **Genres** like science fiction also gained readership, attesting to the development of technology.

Book Publishing Enters the Modern Era

Establishing the book industry in the modern era was tied directly to the solution of the distribution issues that had stymied the industry since its beginning. Once books gained favorable postal rates, the industry boomed. The founding of book clubs—the Book-of-the-Month Club in 1926 and the Literary Guild in 1927—allowed publishers to reach a national but targeted group of readers through direct-mail promotion techniques. Such distribution opened the markets for an astounding array of new titles. Profits from these books rose steadily and declined only during the early 1930s as a result of the worldwide financial depression.

After World War II, book publishing was characterized by specialization. Publishers significantly increased the number of scientific and technical books they published and shifted emphasis to subjects that emerged from war-time trends. Themes reflected the struggle to maintain individualistic, small-town American values while taking advantage of new technology. Americans were ready to move forward technologically. Popular subjects included science fiction, aeronautics and aircraft manufacture, automotive construction and maintenance, radio, television, navigation, and radar. Books that probed the human personality, including those in the areas of psychology, psychiatry, and psychoanalysis, flourished. "How-to" books in home construction, furniture design, and interior decoration catered to those faced with

Horatio Alger story

Story that began as a real account of how Horatio Alger worked his way up the social and economic ladder, but soon developed into a term to represent the glorification of individualism in American life.

genre

A type of literary or cinematic work, classified by elements such as similar plots, characters, and themes.

housing shortages or lack of skilled labor, as well as to people interested in manual craftsmanship.

Expansion of secondary schools and the creation of the GI Bill, which financed higher education programs for returning soldiers, created a demand for educational texts. College enrollment increased from 1 million in 1940 to 12 million in 1960. A variety of federal legislation packages created programs that expanded libraries, in schools and communities, thereby creating an even larger demand for books. Most of the major book publishers developed extensive educational divisions.

TODAY'S MARKET STRUCTURE

The major issues in book publishing—quantity, profits, and quality—are debated today, even as the market structure changes. In 2005, the book publishing industry had net sales of $25.1 billion, up 9.9 percent over 2004.[8] However, the publication of new titles decreased by 18,000 in 2005. Small and medium-sized publishers suffered most, with only the largest publishers able to produce the same number of titles they did in 2004. The drop affected nearly all categories, especially adult fiction and children's books. The number of nonfiction histories and biographies experienced steep falls, with continuing declines in computer and technical books.[9] Fewer books with higher prices account for the larger profits, as publishers choose between quality and quantity. Two hundred bestsellers drive the market, making up about 10 percent of book sales. In 2005, J. K. Rowling's *Harry Potter and the Half-Blood Prince,* published by Scholastic, took 1 percent of the market, with sales of 13.5 million copies.[10] There are many social implications in these trends, including fewer publishing outlets for writers, less diversity of ideas to be found in serious books, and the rise of a global audience that shares the experience of reading a few bestsellers.

Children are of special interest to the publishing industry since they constitute a strong marketing demographic and will be the consumers of the future. Fueled by the Potter phenomenon, juvenile hardcover books are doing the best of any category, with a growth rate of 19.6 percent between 2000 and 2005.[11] The hope is that encouraging a new generation of readers will offset a 20-year trend that has seen the drastic decline of literary reading among young adults, 18–34.[12] With their hot visual elements, graphic novels, especially the Japanese comic, *manga,* tripled their sales between 2004 and 2005.[13] Also designed for a young readership, textbooks are a robust market, with 2005 sales at $10 billion.[14]

With $1.33 billion in sales, the latest growth market is in religion books, which include many self-help books such as Richard Warren's *The Purpose-Driven Life,* published by the Christian publisher, Zondervan, a division of HarperCollins. While books from all faiths are enjoying increased popularity, books with Christian themes are especially lucrative. Lynn Garrett, the religion editor of *Publishers Weekly,* explains: "The fallout from 9/11, the political power of the religious right, and broader retail availability of these books have combined to produce a 'perfect storm' for religion books."[15]

In choosing titles, publishers must be attuned to social trends and changing demographics. In all racial and ethnic groups, women are the most avid readers, with white middle-class women being the biggest book consumers. Education, family income, language, age, and geographic region all influence reading.[16] In a nation in which the minority population is growing faster than the majority, booksellers will need to target new readers if they are to achieve market success.

Media Conglomerates in the Book Business

Book publishing has undergone radical economic and structural changes since World War II. During the 1940s and 1950s, publishing was almost a cottage industry; as *Publishers' Weekly* editor John Baker wrote, it was "a comparatively small business producing a comparatively limited number of books for a cozily elite readership whose

The availability of dime novels expanded reading for middle- and working-class people. Heroic tales appealed to men and women.

access to bookstores was limited by geography."[17] Like many other companies, small, independent book publishers were swallowed up by conglomerates, although a variety of small, new firms still are being created today. The large inventories needed after World War II to supply increasing demand required large capital investments. Capital came from a variety of sources, including **public investment;** books, like newspapers, went public. Magazine publishers and motion picture magnates plowed some of their profits into the book industry; electronic companies, in anticipation of the computer revolution, also invested. Ownership went international. By 1992, five of America's largest book publishers were foreign owned.[18] Even more significant, a few publishing houses dominated the industry. In 2004, the five largest publishing houses in the United States took half the profits, with $4.80 billion in sales.[19] Table 2.1 indicates the global power of the big houses.

The Simon & Schuster story reveals what media consolidation has meant to the industry. Begun in the 1920s, Simon & Schuster developed a solid reputation as a publisher of scholarly, scientific, and artistic books that appealed to popular taste. In 1944, the Chicago department store magnate Marshall Field III bought a substantial interest in the company and simultaneously invested in Pocket Books, a paperback publisher. In 1966, Simon & Schuster acquired Pocket Books, and in 1976, both companies were brought under the Gulf + Western umbrella, which later became Paramount Communications. In 1983, Simon & Schuster acquired Allyn and Bacon; in 1984, it acquired the venerable publishing firm of Prentice Hall; and in 1991, it acquired Macmillan Computer Publishing. Then in 1993, Simon & Schuster, under the umbrella of Paramount, acquired Macmillan, a publishing firm with English origins dating to 1843.

In February and March of 1994, Viacom, Inc., and QVC Network, Inc., battled for control of Paramount. Viacom won by bidding more than $10 billion. The purchase affected all media industries, not just publishing. In addition to its massive publishing holdings, Paramount also owned Paramount Pictures and a vast movie library, television studios, a theme park division, the New York Knicks National Basketball Association team, and the New York Rangers of the National Hockey League. Viacom also has many other holdings, including MTV, VH-1, and the Nickelodeon networks. In 1994, as a unit, Viacom and Paramount owned 12 television stations, 14 radio stations, Showtime, the Movie Channel, syndicated reruns such as *Cheers,* and 3,790 films. They controlled 1,927 movie screens, 3,500 home video stores, and 507 music stores.[20] But the story doesn't end here.

public investment

The buying of stock in a company by the general public.

Table 2.1	Largest Trade Publishers, 2005	
	Owned by	**Worldwide Sales (in millions)**
Random House	Bertelsmann, AG	$2,393
Penguin Group	Pearson	$1,383
HarperCollins	News Corp.	$1,327
Simon & Schuster	CBS Corp.	$ 763
Time Warner Book Group	Hachette	$ 500
Total		$6,366

Source: Company annual reports; *Hoover's Company Records; Wall Street Journal,* February 7, 2006, B2.

Toni Morrison

Toni Morrison is one of the most outstanding writers of her generation, and is known for her depiction of African-American history and rich portrayal of the human condition. Long involved in the book industry as an editor and author, Morrison provides a model of excellence and dedication to literature.

Morrison was born Chloe Anthony Wofford in 1931 in Lorain, Ohio. She received a B.A. degree from Howard University in English, then her master's from Cornell. In the late 1950s Morrison taught at Texas Southern University in Houston before returning to teach at Howard. At Howard she became friends with a number of individuals active in civil rights. One of her students was Stokely Carmichael, who became a leader of the Student Nonviolent Coordinating Committee.

Morrison began writing after she moved to Syracuse, New York, as an associate editor in a textbook subsidiary of Random House. She moved in 1967 to New York and became a senior editor at Random House. In 1970 she published her first novel, *The Bluest Eye,* to great critical acclaim but with little financial success. In 1973 her second novel, *Sula,* was nominated for the 1975 National Book Award for fiction. A third novel, *Song of Solomon,* won the National Book Critic's Circle Award and the American Academy and Institute of Arts and Letters Award. In 1988 *Beloved* won the Pulitzer Prize for fiction. And in 1993, Morrison received the Nobel Prize in Literature.

Toni Morrison recently has won praise for *Paradise,* her seventh novel, which is a story about an Oklahoma convent that is assaulted by a group of men from a nearby Oklahoma town. She now teaches writing at Princeton, where she is known for encouraging young writers who come to work with her.

Sources: "Distinguished Women of Past and Present," www.distinguishedwomen.com; Zia Jaffrey, Interview with Morrison, *Salon,* salonmagazine.com/books/int/1998/02/cov_si_02int.html, January 27, 2000.

In late 2005, Viacom split into two companies, Viacom and CBS. Simon & Schuster became the publishing arm of CBS, and began producing books related to CBS's television networks. For example, Larry McMurtry's novel, *Comanche Moon,* is published by Simon & Schuster and was turned into a miniseries for CBS.

Conglomeration and Media Convergence

Concentration has advantages and disadvantages. Book publishing is a risky business; only 20 to 40 percent of books published make a profit. Therefore, concentration allows for greater profit by producing fewer books in large quantities. However, it also tends to contribute toward homogenization. If one type of book is successful, publishers look for a similar book to appeal to the same broad audience. This in turn can negatively affect the marketplace of ideas because fewer ideas will be available for discussion. The building of conglomerates has resulted in the production of media packages in which books, movies, television programs, and other products are combined.

AUDIENCE DEMAND IN BOOK PUBLISHING MARKETS

The book publishing market can be divided by types of publishing houses, as well as by types of books. Publishing houses can be further divided by size. Large publishers often have several divisions and publish different types of books within each division. A large house such as Pearson Education, for example, may have a **trade book** division as well as a **textbook** division. Trade publications, or books published for general distribution, include hardcover books, quality paperbacks, and mass market paperbacks. Textbook divisions include college textbooks, high school textbooks, and

trade book

mass marketed books sold at bookstores or through book clubs. Excludes textbooks.

textbook

Book used for elementary school, middle school, high school, or college classroom work.

elementary school textbooks. In addition, some **specialized publishers** may produce a particular type of book, such as children's books, religious books, and professional books. Scholarly books occasionally are published by large houses, but they are more commonly the province of university presses. **Niche publishers** target tiny specialized audiences, such as antique collectors. Publishers strive to supply the demand within a well defined market.

Financing and Convergence

Books traditionally have relied little on advertising for financial support; rather, they have been financed by individuals, such as by those of us who buy books. Increasingly, as the audience demands varied products in addition to a book, the industry is supplying the content for packages that include several media. Movie rights, television specials, and other related products often boost the proceeds for a publisher and an author while supplying audience demand.

When *Titanic* won eleven Oscars in 1998, at least 30 new and backlist titles related to the disaster hit the best-seller lists. Children's books such as *Voyage on the Great Titanic,* as well as older accounts of the disaster, became popular.[21] Such packaging represents one type of media convergence adding to the blurring of definitions between media—in this case, between books and films. Similarly, news events can lead to book sales. After the 9/11 attacks, books about Islam and the history of the World Trade Center had an unexpected rise in sales.

Word of mouth, called "buzz" in the book trade, is one of the best ways to ensure a book's success. To stimulate buzz, book marketers develop packages with reading guides for book clubs, like One Book community-wide reading programs initiated in 1998 by the Washington Center for the Book. One Book made a bestseller of Khaled Hosseini's first novel, *The Kite Runner,* about a boy in Afghanistan who immigrates to the United States.

During 1996, Oprah Winfrey became a new force in the book industry. Oprah began a reading club for her television program, and the selection of a book for Oprah's show pushed it to the top of the best-seller lists. The first book selected for the reading club was *The Deep End of the Ocean* by Jacquelyn Mitchard. It went from 100,000 copies in print to 640,000 within weeks. This example shows the power of celebrity, but it also illustrates a potential new source of demand for books. In an industry in which 30,000 copies represents a big success, an Oprah Book Club selection could bump up sales to 1,000,000 copies. This has become known as "the Oprah Effect." Oprah's early choices were mostly written by less-known **mid-list** women authors, and many of them have featured spiritual messages and individuals who overcome adversity. In April 2002, Oprah announced the end of the club, saying that she was finding it harder to choose a new book every week about which she could be passionate. This caused dismay among publishers. She resumed the club in 2003 to promote the classics. Her first pick, John Steinbeck's *East of Eden,* jumped from 80,000 copies in print to 1.8 million.[22] Two years later, when her audience's interests in the classics waned, Oprah again turned to promoting contemporary authors. Despite their importance in promoting literacy and shaping audiences for certain kinds of books, book club sales have declined since 2002.

Electronic Publishing

Because the book industry deals with nonstandard formats and sometimes small print runs, it was difficult for publishers to justify early investments in page-making software. Today, however, the use of computerized artwork, cover designs, and promotional pieces is standard. Skill, or at least familiarity, with computerized technology is rapidly becoming a requirement for entry-level professionals, who must use technology-related tools such as specialized graphics and database software. One result of the new technology has been more streamlined production, which results in the publication of "instant books" such as the *Starr Report,* a publication of Kenneth Starr's investigation into the relationship between former President Bill Clinton and Monica Lewinsky.

specialized publisher

Publishing house that produces a particular type of book, such as religious or children's books.

niche publisher

Small publishing house that serves very narrowly defined markets.

mid-list

Titles that sell less than the "frontlist" bestsellers or are on the "backlist" of older titles.

Howard Stringer, Chairman and CEO of Sony Corp., introduces Sony's Reader e-book device at a consumer electronics show.

Digital Books   Digital books take various forms, including reproduction of books in print as well as enhancements for print volumes. CD-ROM also is used for the production of customized textbooks, in which professors might choose particular passages and articles to be reproduced for their students in one newly created text.

One of the reasons that CD-ROMs and electronic books (e-books) are better marketed as enhancements is because print remains a relatively cheap, popular, portable, and accessible medium. It is hard to envision leisurely reading a popular novel on a computer screen while sitting in a lounge chair at the beach. However, some small e-book readers have made portability a positive factor for many people who travel, and increasingly books are available for downloading on small computer devices similar to palm pilots or other personal organizers.

Audio Books   The popularity of the iPod has revolutionized the audiobook market. Publishers have typically been wary of digital downloading because of rampant piracy, but must reach young consumers with technological savvy. Since fall 2003, Random House has experienced rapid growth in audio book sales through its children's website, Listening Library, which carries hundreds of titles with tens of thousands of downloads a year. In 2006, Apple's iTunes became the exclusive distributor of the audio versions of the Harry Potter series, despite author J. K. Rowling's initial fears of piracy. With the U.S. publication of *Harry Potter and the Half-Blood Prince* in paperback, Scholastic ran a sweepstakes in which Potter fans could win an iPod loaded with the first six Potter books and etched with Harry's school crest. In a further example of convergence, Apple offered a Harry Potter video game. Digitized audio books are easier and cheaper to make than CDs, since they don't have high production and distribution costs. However, authors and publishers will continue to struggle with the escalating problem of illegal copying and file sharing.

Market Dimensions of a Best Seller

J. K. Rowling's Harry Potter series has become a global commercial phenomenon created by good writing and market savvy. Children all over the world turned out to buy the sixth book in the series, *Harry Potter and the Half-Blood Prince,* which instantly reached best-seller status in several countries, including the United States, Germany,

Because of good writing and savvy marketing, J. K. Rowling's Harry Potter books have won readers around the world. In China, impatient fans produce and circulate illicit translations long before the official Mandarin versions appear.

France, and Sweden. In India, the book sold 139 copies a minute on the first day of release. Translations of *The Half-Blood Prince* were eagerly awaited and celebrated at publication parties, often with children dressed in costumes of Harry Potter characters. At the end of 2005, the Harry Potter series had been translated into 62 languages and had sold 270 million copies worldwide.[23]

The Harry Potter stories chronicle the life of a young wizard and his band of cohorts at the Hogwarts School of Witchcraft and Wizardry. They were written by J. K. (Joanne Kathleen) Rowling. Rowling graduated from Exeter University and moved to Portugal in 1990 to teach English. She married a Portuguese journalist. When their daughter was born in 1993, she had already begun the book, but after her marriage ended in divorce, she moved to Edinburgh to be near her sister. She was struggling to support herself and her daughter Jessica on welfare while she completed the first of the Harry Potter books, which she finally sold—after several rejections—for about $4,000.

Rowling's second Potter book, *Harry Potter and the Chamber of Secrets,* was published in 1998 and hit the adult hardback best-seller lists within a month of publication. It also won numerous prizes, and Rowling was voted BA (Bookseller Association) Author of the Year in 1999. In 1999, just as *Harry Potter and the Prisoner of Azkaban* was published with much press attention, the *Philosopher's Stone* was topping the paperback charts. (The book was titled the *Sorcerer's Stone* in the United States.) The fourth book in the series, *Harry Potter and the Goblet of Fire,* was published during the summer of 2000 with a record first printing of 5.3 million copies; it quickly broke all records for the greatest number of books sold on the first day of publication, as well as shooting to the top of the best-seller charts.

The U.S. corporation Warner Bros. owns the film rights for the Harry Potter books. *Harry Potter and the Sorcerer's Stone* was released in November, 2001. It debuted on a record 8,200 screens and smashed the previous box office record, earning an estimated $9.35 million ($20 million more than the previous recordholder, *The Lost World: Jurassic Park*). By the summer of 2002, it had grossed $966 million worldwide. The production of the films has a global dimension. They are shot with British casts and locations, and involve international special effects and distribution companies. As of 2006, three of the Potter films were among the top five international box office hits of all time.[24] The films and books support each other in their success through economic convergence.

The reason for the global appeal of Harry Potter is partly due to the rise of a world-wide middle-class **youth market**. These young consumers have extra spending cash and new tastes in popular culture and technological gadgets. Marketers banking on the Harry Potter phenomenon are able to advertise and create tie-ins through a range of media channels. Interactive contests, games, and discussions on publisher and author websites help shape and solidify audiences. Young people can experiment with identities and feel part of a global youth community. J. K. Rowling's website (www.jkrowling.com) is offered in several languages. Visitors can experience a connection to the celebrity author, navigating through what appears to be her mysterious house, and find links to other fan sites. In the United Kingdom, tours of Harry Potter book and film locations have become popular, and the U.K.'s premier news provider, the BBC, offers a website with Harry Potter games, quizzes and chat (news.bbc.co.uk/cbbcnews/hi/specials/harry_potter). This site is visited by children from all over the English-speaking world. Numerous product tie-ins, such as Hogwarts scarves and pens, further entice children into the Harry Potter fantasy. Harry Potter is much more than a book—he is a phenomenally successful **global brand**.

In the midst of Potter mania, Rowling has struggled to keep control over her **intellectual property**. Within hours of publication of *Harry Potter and the Half-Blood Prince,* digital and audio copies could be found online. Eager fans in non–English-speaking countries snap up bootleg translations, available both in print and on the Internet. Rowling has also sought to maintain control over her identity. The UN's World Intellectual Property Organization decided in Rowling's favor in her case against a Uruguayan who had registered the domain names kjkrowling.com and www-jkrowling.com. Fans who set up websites devoted to Potter characters may receive a letter from the Warner Bros. legal department warning them of copyright infringement. In the global exchange of texts, images, and consumer products, the question is, who owns Harry Potter?

Key Concept

Youth market In the 1950s, children, teenagers, and young adults with extra spending cash became an important consumer force in the United States and Europe. Today, in many other parts of the world, the same trend is occurring among middle-class youths who are becoming globally oriented and media savvy. They make up an important market for multinational corporations like media conglomerates.

Key Concept

Global brand A brand is a corporate identity, and is sometimes associated with a celebrity, like Michael Jordan, or a product, like Coke. Consumers often choose technical brands, like Microsoft and Apple, because of their perceived quality. But they choose other brands, like Disney or Nike, because of emotional connections. Global brands that appeal to consumers worldwide are increasingly important to multinational corporations' marketing strategies.

Key Concept

Intellectual property The protection of intellectual property through copyright law is important to ensure that authors and publishers receive compensation for their labors. However, strict copyright enforcement is controversial because it inevitably curtails freedom of use and access. Technology has made it much easier to violate copyright protections.

Key Concept

Markets and processes in the book industry The book industry serves the distinct market needs of general consumers, educators, and professionals. The processes of book production and distribution vary to fit these distinct markets.

SUPPLYING THE AUDIENCE'S DEMAND

Markets and processes in the book industry differ depending on the publisher; trade books and textbooks are published using different processes. Trade books gain greater publicity than do textbooks, but they constitute only 25 percent of the market. The bulk of the market is composed of textbooks, scientific books, reference and scholarly publications, Bibles, and other specialized books.[25]

Textbooks

Producing books for elementary and secondary schools is a process that is exceedingly **capital intensive** and politically and culturally sensitive. In school publishing, authors play the role of consultant-contributor more than that of writer. They contribute

capital intensive

A production process that requires a large investment of money.

The textbooks used in this middle-school Spanish class have undergone a rigorous production process resulting in a product that is politically and culturally acceptable to a wide range of school systems.

to the production of a book or educational package that is constantly shaped and reshaped in response to what market leaders want as analyzed by marketing professionals. The process is predominantly driven by the big state bureaucracies in California and Texas, which are large enough to have the power to determine content. Sample modules are tested on groups of students and teachers who record what works and what doesn't, providing feedback that might send a project back to the drawing board before a final huge investment is made. Sometimes special editions are printed to cater to local demands if printing cost can be justified. Often, videotapes or CD-ROMs are given away or sold at cost to encourage schools to adopt specific books. Because at the public elementary and secondary level taxpayers usually pay for the books, culturally sensitive issues often hit the media and become political footballs for citizens' pressure groups of all kinds. The danger, of course, is that catering to the educational demands of large states such as California and Texas also requires catering to the cultural needs and demands of powerful groups in those states.

Although the college book industry also is market driven, there are significant differences between it and the public school market. In the college market, authors are the writers; students, rather than taxpayers, usually pay for the books; the economic stakes are much lower; and books that grate on culturally sensitive nerves sometimes are used for a purpose. Although professors often generate ideas for college textbooks, sales representatives and editors evaluate whether those ideas will produce books that are competitive with other books in the field. The author's primary responsibility in the college textbook field is producing the manuscript. The contract between the publisher and the author determines who will locate photographs, provide rough sketches for charts and graphs, write photograph captions, and provide an index.

Once the book is finished, it is marketed by the publisher's marketing department. For public school adoptions, the marketing professionals contact curriculum committees in states and municipalities; for college adoptions, they contact professors at various colleges and universities who might adopt the book for their classrooms or departments.

Thus the publisher assumes almost all the financial responsibility for the book, as well as for production and promotion. The publisher selects what will be published, produces the book, advances the financing for production, promotes and distributes the book, and, if the book is successful, makes a profit. The authors produce the copy, examine the changes made by copyeditors, sometimes locate photographs, read page proofs, and sometimes provide an index.

The Trade Market: Fiction and Nonfiction

Trade books can be broadly classified as fiction and nonfiction. For both fiction and nonfiction, an author usually hires an agent to market a proposal. However, in an exceedingly small number of cases, authors send completed manuscripts to a publisher. A manuscript is read by a reader hired specifically to scan incoming manuscripts. The manuscript then is forwarded to an editor and accepted for publication (or rejected). Sometimes an author is successful first with a small publisher, and then a larger publishing house will entice the author away, as happened to best-selling author Tom Clancy, who struck it rich on the publication of his first novel, *The Hunt for Red October*. Clancy's book was first published by the obscure Naval Institute Press, but he soon joined with the Putnam-Berkley Group, Inc., and increased sales with each successive book he wrote. Altogether, Putnam-Berkley has shipped more than 31 million copies of Clancy's books.

Once a book is accepted, an editor is assigned to work with an author. In trade divisions, the editor has a great deal of power and often helps the author shape the book. Through the 1960s, editors helped develop great writers. Probably the best-known editor was Maxwell Perkins, who in the 1920s and 1930s worked with F. Scott Fitzgerald, Marjorie Kinnan Rawlings, Ernest Hemingway, and Thomas Wolfe. Editors such as Perkins regarded themselves as part of the literary class and were aware of their roles as developers of culture and literature and as contributors to the marketplace of ideas. During the past 20 years, power has shifted to some degree from those editors to people in subsidiary rights and marketing. Although editors are still influential in shaping a work, they tend to have less power in the organization and often remain anonymous to the general public. Nevertheless, many editors helped shape the best-sellers listed in Table 2.2.

Production Book publishing has long made use of the process of contracting out work. The typical production process involves a book being formatted into one of

Periodicals like the *New York Times* compile national best-seller lists by polling thousands of major bookstores.

Table 2.2	Top Ten Worldwide Bestsellers
In May 2004, these fiction titles topped the list at Amazon websites in the UK, France, Germany, and Japan:	
Dan Brown, *The Da Vinci Code*, Doubleday	
J. K. Rowling, *Harii Pottaa to Fushichoo no kishidan*, Say-zan-sha Publications	
Ian Caldwell and Dustin Thomason, *The Rule of Four*, Dial Press	
Mitch Albom, *The Five People You Meet in Heaven*, Hyperion	
Dan Brown, *Angels & Demons*, Pocket Star	
Stephen King, *The Song of Susannah* (*The Dark Tower*, Book 6). Donald M. Grant, Publisher.	

Source: The Economist, June 5, 2004, 84.

Media Convergence

Multimedia Packages

The impact of converging technologies on the creation of multimedia packages can be seen by viewing websites devoted to books and their spin-offs. For example, if you access www.lordoftherings.net, you will get to the homepage of the film; the page is produced by New Line Productions, Inc. The site shows the integrative possibilities of the Web, but the information found at the site reveals the increasing multimedia impact of a basic print. The site offers commercial products in various media forms. You can purchase the three films in the series on DVD and VHS after watching movie trailers and interviews with the director and cast. After listening to an audio clip and watching a video of the *Return of the King's* theme song, you can buy the soundtrack. A link will take you to Verizon Wireless where you can join communities and receive games, quizzes, and other messages related to *Lord of the Rings*. New Line Productions makes you part of their advertising campaign by offering e-cards, screensavers, and free downloadable posters.

several standard designs produced by in-house artists and designers or being designed by an independent firm under contract to the publisher. If a design contract is commissioned especially for a project, the author may work with the designers in all phases of the production process. Freelancers and other suppliers usually copyedit, typeset, and print a book. The freelancers may be individuals, or they may be production or printing firms outside the geographical confines of publishing centers. With the evolution of word-processing programs and desktop publishing, documents can be formatted directly on the computer. The publisher has access to people with specialized skills without hiring full-time employees for what may be seasonal work. The publisher does not have to pay for benefits associated with full-time employees and does not have to provide office space or other amenities such as child-care facilities.

Distribution   Chain bookstores are now the primary distribution network and account for almost half of bookstore sales. The top three chains are Barnes & Noble, with 800 stores; Borders, with about 1,250; and Books-a-Million, which has 200.[26] Other major distributors include Amazon and the superstores Walmart, Target, and Costco that sell large numbers of a few selections. The marketing of books through suburban bookstores affiliated with these chains actually has historical roots: Nineteenth-century novels were published in great numbers as the middle class, especially women, began to read for leisure. Waldenbooks specifically targets suburban, middle-class readers, many of them women. Furthermore, the chain stores provide statistics on sales that often are used by publishers to determine in advance the number of books to be printed. Surveys show that the average per-book press run is 10,000 copies. To appear on a best-seller fiction list, a book must sell about 100,000 copies. Unless the suburban book chains carry the book, it is unlikely to reach best-seller status.[27] However, there are major exceptions to this rule: *Snow Falling on Cedars, The Joy Luck Club, Cold Mountain,* and *Midnight in the Garden of Good and Evil* were all sold by devoted independent sellers before they became best-sellers.[28]

Because they are able to offer books at deep discounts, the large bookstore chains have driven out many independent booksellers. In turn, the superstores are threatened by online book sellers like Amazon that also carry used books, making almost-new books cheaply available.

option

A contractual agreement between an author and a producer, giving the producer temporary rights to a story.

Book to Movie   Many movies, such as *The Godfather* and *The English Patient,* are adapted from books. A writer's literary agent may try to sell film rights for a book, and a production company may **option** those rights. With an option, the author agrees to let the production company have control of the story for a limited period of time,

Multinational Book Trade

Since the rise of mass consumption of books, publishers have considered their markets to be global. In the nineteenth century, British publishers like Macmillan and Longman, for example, sold to English-speaking émigrés in India, Asia, and Africa. Today, multinational media corporations with an eye to global marketing own the major book publishers. HarperCollins is owned by News Corp., originally an Australian media company founded by Rupert Murdoch. Penguin USA is owned by Pearson, based in London. Simon & Schuster is owned by CBS. A publishing house that successfully capitalizes on the global business connections of its owner, Random House, belongs to a German corporation, the media giant Bertelsmann. In turn, Random House owns imprints in a dozen countries, and has formed partnerships with publishers in Japan and Korea. Random House Mondadori publishes Spanish-language books, and markets them in Spain and throughout South America.

Corporations become global for many reasons. At a very basic level, the bigger the company, the more money the company will make. Some corporations aim to lower costs by publishing the same books in various countries. The global scope of the industry allows content and financial capital to travel across borders more easily, but also raises fears that local book cultures will be erased. Since English is the dominant language of science and business, English-language books have broad appeal. However, in some countries, like France, fears have arisen that the dominance of English may corrupt or erase native languages.

Source: Iain Stevenson, "'The Liveliest of Corpses': Trends and Challenges for the Future in the Book Publishing Industry," *Aslib Proceedings,* April 2000, 135.

usually while it searches for funding, a director, a cast, and other necessities of movie production. If the production company succeeds at moving the project from development into production, the author then sells the film rights to the production company, often for a very large sum. The vast majority of books, even those that are optioned, are never made into movies.

TRENDS

The book publishing industry is undergoing a major change not seen since Johannes Gutenberg introduced moveable type, launching the age of mass media. Gutenberg's invention was a technological breakthrough that spread throughout the world and transformed cultures and political systems. With its interactivity and accessibility, the age of digital media and the Internet is bringing technological, cultural, and global changes that are as significant to the book and its readers as the age of the printing press. What follows are some trends and forecasts for the book publishing industry at the beginning of the twenty-first century.

Technology: Digital and Online

In 2000, Stephen King brought attention to the potential of e-books when he distributed 500,000 electronic copies of his novella, *Riding the Bullet.*[29] Since then, interest in publishing and marketing e-books has been steadily growing. Currently, most e-books are downloaded in Adobe Acrobat form, and so look very much like traditional printed pages. While authors have already experimented with **hypertext**, a widespread multimedia form of the book is still in the future. However, the printed book—along with

hypertext

A group of texts, sounds, graphics, and video connected by links rather than arranged linearly. Also called **hypermedia.**

its author and publisher webpages, fansites, advertising gimmicks, film adaptations, and other tie-ins—comprises a kind of hypertext authored by many people.

More books, both old and new, soon will be digitized and become available online. Books already old enough to be in the **public domain** will be available for free. The Library of Congress has already partnered with the University of Michigan Library and the Cornell University Library to digitize thousands of nineteenth-century books and antislavery pamphlets. In 2005, the Library of Congress announced plans for a World Digital Library, partnering with Google and other institutions to digitize and bring together multilingual texts from cultures around the world, especially Chinese, Indian, and Islamic. Google is engaged in its own Print Library Project, which has begun to scan and index millions of books, including newer books, with the help of Harvard, Stanford, University of Michigan, and University of Oxford. For a very new book with copyright-protected content, Google users can see only the index and a sentence or two, and can then decide whether to buy it. Google says it wants to make information widely available to a global public, but publishers object on the grounds of copyright violation. The battle over intellectual property is one of the key issues facing the publishing industry.

With a declining readership and increasing competition from online businesses, publishers are striving to reduce production costs, especially those involving a cumbersome distribution system and the rising price of paper. New inventory software is beginning to improve and streamline book distribution, so the publishers will have fewer unsold books returned to them. More publishers are also considering print on demand (POD) to reduce production costs. POD books are printed one at a time, on order from a customer, thus reducing the costs of printing too many copies for the demand. As PODs become more established, publishers will be able to keep lower inventory. Not all book technologies are inevitable. Various efforts to market handheld e-book devices have not met with much success. For now, at least, readers still seem to prefer experiencing books on paper.

public domain

The status of publications that are not under copyright. No one has exclusive rights to them, and the public owns them.

A digitized version of the 700-year-old Sultan Baybars' Qur'an in the British Museum allows visitors to turn its pages by moving their hands across a screen.

In discussing trends, the most elusive factor is content. Publishers would never worry if they could always predict the next hit. In the last decade, inspirational, religious-themed, and children's books have become big sellers, and the trends seem steady. But no one knows how long they will last. Some bets don't pay off; for example, publishers tried to bank on the popular young women's fiction "chick lit" by investing in "lad lit" about young urban slackers. "Lad lit" never took off.

"Content is king" is a concept that book publishers have not abandoned. Heads of publishing companies anxious to do multimedia deals and provide electronic products insist that "the book is the beginning in the content chain that leads to other products," "books are the seeds in the soil from which other projects spring," and "the core assets for many of these new delivery systems come from print." Time Warner's Trade Group Chair Larry Kirshbaum notes that "everything starts with a story and our role is to be the originator of those stories."[34] So the questions become related to content. For example,

- Do consumers who buy online want different books than consumers who visit traditional bookstores?
- In devising multimedia packages, what content is most appealing to various age, racial, ethnic, and gender groups?
- What content can be delivered most effectively as print on demand?

Culture: Finding Book Readers

Because of their rigorous editorial process, major publishing houses have traditionally emphasized the quality and authority of the books they produce. However, they are driven by the need for profit. Book publishers seriously promote only a limited number of new books, usually either by authors who have become celebrities or celebrities who have become authors. The aim is to discover and nurture authors who will become worldwide celebrities, like J. K. Rowling and Dan Brown, or to bank on already existing celebrities who can attract a ready audience. The biggest events at the U.S. book publishing industry's premiere annual event, BookExpo America, tell the tale. Many authors invited to BookExpo are well known religious, political, or business leaders and television and film celebrities. Billy Crystal spoke on the first night of the 2005 conference, promoting his book *700 Sundays.* Kim Cattrall, *Sex and the City's* Samantha Jones, was on hand to sign her *Sexual Intelligence,* published by Bullfinch Press, which is owned by Time Warner. Accompanying the release of the book was a documentary shown on the Time Warner network, HBO, which also produces *Sex and the City.* But the question remains whether popular books by celebrities have any art or substance. *Publishers Weekly* dismissed *Sexual Intelligence* as fluff.[30]

The publishing industry's efforts to attract readers through celebrity appeal are due, in part, to its real fears of a declining readership. Analyzing recent industry statistics, media consultant Paula Berinstein concluded that the reading population is "aging and shrinking."[31] The theme of the Association of American Publishers' 2006 annual meeting was "Where Have All the Readers Gone? And How Can We Find New Ones?" Publishers and government agencies, such as the Department of Education, are teaming for national reading initiatives to encourage literary reading. Other solutions have been proposed, such as marketing books in movie theaters, interesting readers through multimedia packages, making books simpler and more relevant, offering free books, and tapping African-American and Hispanic readers; according to the National Endowment for the Arts, the number of Hispanic adult readers in the United States rose from 3.4 million in 1982 to 6 million in 2002.[32] While the NEA and many others blame digital devices, video games, and the Internet for the decline in reading, others argue that reading has just taken a different form.[33] Whatever the case, publishers will need to find ways to adapt to these changes.

SUMMARY

- Books are the oldest commercial form of mass media. They have evolved from serving a highly elite audience to serving the masses of ordinary people. Books have become a form of popular culture that has spread throughout most literate societies.
- Publishing as an economic enterprise progressed from the control of the church, to small printers in European cities, to the provinces, including the American colonies.
- Publishers have traditionally emphasized the importance of their editorial process in maintaining the quality of their books. However, their need to make a profit raises questions about the importance of quality in the selection and marketing of new books.
- The advent of the paperback in the nineteenth century, the development of book clubs in the 1920s, and the current widespread publication of all types of books in paperback form helped to democratize the book industry.
- Book publishing has moved from business conducted in the atmosphere of a "gentlemen's club" to conglomerate ownership.
- Reading as a leisure activity is on the decline. Publishers must therefore find new ways to promote reading in order to sell books.
- Superstores have driven out many independent booksellers. In turn, they are threatened by the boom in online book sales, including an expanding market for used books.
- With the development of conglomerates, the book industry has become more multimedia oriented. Book success is often related to technological convergence. Successful films and audio or video products can hike book sales.
- Books often provide the stories, or content, for other media.

NAVIGATING THE WEB Books

Book-oriented websites are used to sell books and promote bookstores, provide reviews and introduce readers to authors, and deliver information about the industry. You can find information about the art and commerce of publishing on the following sites:

Bookwire
bookwire.com
Bookwire deals with a wide range of book issues and also has links to several good sites about books and the industry. It is a server for reviews, and it has a database of books, best-sellers, and publishing companies.

Book Industry Study Groups, Inc.
bisg.org
This industry association is concerned with a variety of publishing issues. The site carries news releases about the industry, including yearly data.

Publishers Weekly **Interactive**
publishersweekly.com
The online version of the leading trade publication for the industry, this site gives access to a wide range of

articles about authors, publishing companies, and the industry itself, although it does not provide the full content of the magazine.

The following site publishes reviews of books, author interviews, and advice for writers:

Book Page
bookpage.com

Order sites include:

Amazon.com
amazon.com
Amazon.com is one of the original high-volume book order sites on the Internet.

Barnes & Noble
barnesandnoble.com
Barnes & Noble is providing competition for Amazon.com.

QUESTIONS FOR REVIEW

1. What developments signified the emergence of mass market best-sellers in the United States?
2. What trends in book production were represented in the fiction factory?
3. Why is intellectual property an important issue for publishers today?
4. What is a media conglomerate?
5. What is the difference between a trade book and a textbook?
6. How does selling books online affect the industry as a whole?

ISSUES TO THINK ABOUT

1. During the American colonial period, information was a highly prized commodity. Do you think it is still so highly valued? How do converging technologies affect this concept?
2. Discuss the evolution of postal policy that affected the distribution of books in the United States. Why is postal policy an important factor in the development of print media?
3. Discuss the importance of the paperback industry to widening access to fiction and other printed works.
4. What does the trend toward multimedia packaging mean for the way books are sold and read?
5. What are the implications of producing schoolbooks for children and young adults that are targeted to the most populous states of the nation? Who makes the decisions about those books? Why are the decisions sometimes political?
6. How does consolidation of the book industry affect the circulation of ideas in an intellectual marketplace?
7. How might a decline in literary reading affect national culture?

SUGGESTED READINGS

Coser, Lewis A., Charles Kadushin, and Walter W. Powell. *Books: The Culture and Commerce of Publishing* (New York: Basic Books, 1982).

Davis, Kenneth. *Two-Bit Culture: The Paperbacking of America* (Boston: Houghton Mifflin, 1984).

Dessauer, John. *Book Publishing: What It Is, What It Does* (New York: R. R. Bowker, 1981).

Johns, Adrian. *The Nature of the Book: Print and Knowledge in the Making* (Chicago: University of Chicago Press, 2000).

Miller, Laura J. *Reluctant Capitalists: Bookselling and the Culture of Consumption* (Chicago: University of Chicago Press, 2006).

Stern, Madeleine B. *Publishing for Mass Entertainment in Nineteenth-Century America* (Boston: G. K. Hall, 1980).

Newspapers

When its stockholders decided to put the U.S.'s second-largest newspaper chain Knight Ridder up for auction in 2005, Wall Street financiers and journalists reacted with gloomy forecasts. The business press warned that too low a sales price would signal the death of the newspaper industry. *Fortune* declared, "The sale will tell us what newspapers are worth in the Digital Age."[1] Some editors and reporters at Knight Ridder's 32 newspapers feared not only for their jobs, but for the future of serious journalism.

Knight Ridder was proud of its eighty-five Pulitzer Prizes, including the *Biloxi Sun Herald*'s Gold Medal for Meritorious Public Service in its print and online coverage of Hurricane Katrina. But its newspapers had been experiencing falling circulations and ad revenues. Business analysts blamed competition from Internet sites, especially Craigslist, Monster, and eBay, which were replacing newspapers' all-important classified ads. Insiders blamed the company's cost-cutting measures for damaging journalistic excellence and driving away readers.

Fears were relieved when a family business, the McClatchy Co., acquired Knight Ridder for a decent price. Owner of twelve dailies, McClatchy also had a reputation for good journalism. But it almost immediately announced that it would be selling off twelve of its newly acquired newspapers, including the well respected *Philadelphia Inquirer.*

KEY CONCEPTS

- Nonmainstream Media
- Penny Press
- Yellow Journalism
- Market Structure for News
- Public versus Private Ownership of Newspapers
- Competition
- Credibility
- Ethnic and Minority Press
- Representation
- Market-Oriented Newspapers

Wall Street considered McClatchy's choice to buy Knight Ridder risky, but McClatchy CEO Craig Pruitt argued that "newspapers are strong and viable and have good futures." He laid out a plan to emphasize the local. McClatchy papers were not just newspapers, but "the leading local media company, the leading local Internet company."[2] On the Internet, newspapers could deliver their content, including traffic and entertainment reports, twenty-four hours a day. Executive editor of the *Miami Herald,* Tom Fiedler, approved of his new boss's approach and told his reporters that they would all have web responsibilities.

Since the early days of the Republic, newspapers have played an important civic role in providing information and a forum for opinion. Many would argue that newspapers are crucial to a robust democracy. However, like other print media, newspapers are changing in the digital age, redefining the way they reach audiences. The future of newspapers depends on how they will fit into the life of the reader and the lives of people in the nation and around the world.

Despite indications of prosperity, newspapers' role in society continues to change, bringing several challenges for the industry. Newspapers face the following issues:

- Changing reading patterns. Readers increasingly say they do not have time to read a daily newspaper.

- Changing community demographics. Most daily newspapers during the mid-twentieth century appealed to white male readers. This segment has been shrinking as a proportion of the total population. The percentage of Americans who are African American, Hispanic, Asian American, and Native American is growing.

- Aging readers. The baby boom generation, which grew up during television's infancy, is aging. These individuals form the bulk of the daily newspapers' readership. Younger readers do not read daily papers as often as their parents and grandparents.

- Changing content needs. The news and information that people want and need today differs from what newspapers provided even thirty years ago. Most parents work outside the home, which increases the demands on people's time. They need information to help them deal with these demands. Also, the growing diversity of the population requires a growing diversity of content.

- Changing technology. As digital media evolves, newspapers must find their place in people's lives. Newspaper managers must decide how and when to use developing technology to deliver the news, information, and advertising their organizations produce. They also must react to the growing competition for time and advertising that technology brings.

NEWSPAPERS IN AMERICAN LIFE

Throughout U. S. history, newspapers fulfilled two important roles: They served as a watchdog on the government and they provided perspective and information about the daily and weekly activities of their communities. Both roles were established from the beginning of the newspaper industry and continued to evolve as early editors fought for political independence and as politicians battled over postal laws that would determine where newspapers could circulate and at what price.

Local Newspapers and Challenges to Elite Authority

During the early colonial period, newspapers focused primarily on foreign events and covered local events to a lesser degree. Some newspapers challenged the British government while others cooperated.

Newspapers in Your Life

What Are Your Newspaper Reading Habits?

What you look for in the news and where you go to find it depends on who you are and what things are important in your life. News content can be found both in print and on-line, and has competition from other sources, such as television and blogs. Think about where you are most likely to look for news. Do you read a newspaper's print version? Do you browse newspapers online? Are there certain kinds of content that seem better in print? What could managers of your campus or local paper do to make it more interesting to you? In the table, note where you are most likely to find news on the listed topics.

	Network Television	Cable Television	National Newspaper	Local Newspaper	Online News Source	Blog	Radio
International affairs							
National affairs							
Campus news							
Sports							
Weather							
Business							

In 1690, Benjamin Harris published the first newspaper in America, but the royal government prohibited him from producing a second issue that critically analyzed local affairs. In 1701, postmaster John Campbell wrote the *News-Letter,* summarizing news from abroad and publishing colonial and business dispatches. The *News-Letter* was produced under prior restraint, which meant that the British government could exercise censorship.

Being a postmaster like Campbell gave a publisher several advantages, including free distribution and government allotments. In 1719, William Brooker succeeded Campbell as postmaster. Because Campbell refused to relinquish his editorship of the *News-Letter,* Brooker started a competing newspaper, the *Boston Gazette.* In 1721, James Franklin began the *New England Courant.*

Franklin is often credited with starting the first local newspaper and the first newspaper crusade because he confronted the local Puritan establishment and introduced items of wit and humor. The *New England Courant* covered local public controversies, which was a clear challenge to the elite authority. Thomas Leonard wrote, "Defiance was the soul of the *Courant,* the spirited cry of newcomers bumping against an old elite, of artisans mocking the more respectable classes, of provincials picking up the language of London coffee houses, and of eighteenth-century men recovering the nerve to mock and amuse in the face of the grave."[3] When Franklin turned his satirical pen toward the government, however, he landed in jail. While he was in jail, he continued to run the newspaper through his brother, Benjamin Franklin, a noted printer, philosopher, and inventor. James Franklin was released on the condition that he not publish his newspaper, and in 1726 he moved to Rhode Island and became a government printer.

Publick Occurrences, one of the earliest newspapers in America, was shut down by authorities because of its controversial content.

Governors in the colonies did not like criticism of themselves or the British government. The colonial editor had to walk the line between independence and political loyalty. As the country moved toward the War for Independence, patriot editors showed little tolerance for those who championed Britain.

Postal Rates and Serving the Community

From the time that the founders began to shape the laws of the United States, Congress and publishers have debated whether newspapers should be local entities or the fabric that binds the nation together. Should newspapers be the vehicles of communication that enable communities to identify themselves as part of a nation and a federal government? The establishment of postal rates for newspapers, books, and magazines was pivotal in the debate because out-of-town newspapers were distributed by mail.

Although magazines did not gain favorable postal rates until the mid-nineteenth century, Congress considered newspapers from the beginning to be important vehicles of public communication. The fight was not over whether to give newspapers favored status. It was over whether economic favoritism should be used to preserve local voices and traditional values or whether big-city newspapers and forces for modernization should be given the advantage. In an effort to give the advantage to urban newspapers, some members of Congress attempted several times during the early 1800s to abolish newspaper postage altogether. If postage did not exist, the urban newspapers could freely distribute their newspapers to wide geographic areas. But the U.S. Post Office Committee argued that such a move would allow city papers to displace local papers. The decline of the rural papers, they said, would mean that "freedom, that manliness of spirit, which has always characterized the great body of the common people of our country, and which constitutes the safeguard of our liberties, will gradually decline."[4]

Congress resolved the postal rate issue with a compromise that ensured the survival of the local paper. A new postal law in 1852 greatly simplified newspaper rates. In-county newspapers could be distributed free, but any newspaper could cross the continent for a penny.[5]

The early postal battle over newspapers established an important principle: Newspapers were significant factors in the building of a society across wide geographical territory and across the social boundaries of varying value systems.

Congress recognized the value newspapers had for the new nation and for serving local communities with news and information.

Key Concept

Nonmainstream media *Mainstream* describes the social groups with the political power to dominate a society. In the United States, the mainstream traditionally included descendants of white European Christians. Mainstream media cater to the interests of the mainstream groups. Nonmainstream media provide news and information to less powerful social groups, which are often defined by gender, race, ethnic, religious, or economic characteristics.

Benjamin Franklin—colonial printer, inventor, and diplomat—financed the beginning of several early American newspapers, extending his printing dynasty from Pennsylvania to South Carolina along the major trade routes of the colonies.

Serving a Diversified Society

U.S. newspapers always have reflected the diverse interest of our society despite historians' failure to chronicle adequately the history of **nonmainstream media.** When people moved west and trade routes developed across the Alleghenies, ethnic newspapers developed alongside English-language publications. Immigration patterns produced ethnic enclaves that naturally created concentrated market segments for ethnic newspapers. These nonmainstream publications were essential to ethnic and racial minorities. The mainstream publications either failed to serve the needs of these groups or worked to deny them equal rights.

From as early as 1739, foreign-language newspapers provided immigrants with news from home. German-language newspapers were among the first to appear.

They dominated the ethnic-press field until World War I, but newspapers written in French, Welsh, Italian, Norwegian, Swedish, Spanish, Danish, Dutch, Bohemian, Polish, Portuguese, and Chinese all appeared during the nineteenth century.

As the descendants of Europeans pushed Native Americans westward and onto reservations, the Native Americans developed newspapers to protest this treatment and to preserve their cultures. For instance, the *Cherokee Phoenix,* printed in English and Cherokee during the 1830s and 1840s, informed Native Americans of actions by whites as well as about tribal concerns. As with all frontier newspapers, Native American newspapers usually did not remain in circulation for long.

African Americans, who faced slavery in the South and segregation in the North, developed a press about the same time as Native Americans. Samuel Cornish and John Russwurm printed the first known black newspaper, *Freedom's Journal,* in 1827. The newspaper included poetry and reprinted articles as well as original articles about slavery in the United States and other countries. Several other black newspapers were developed in this period. Some of the most well-known included Frederick Douglass's *Ram's Horn* and the *North Star.*

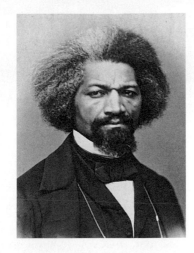

Frederick Douglass, a freed slave, became an eloquent spokesman for the Antislavery Society, traveling in England and the United States. He published a newspaper to argue for the emancipation of slaves.

Competition in a New Century

Diversity also was reflected in how newspapers viewed local communities. During the 1840s, Washington, D.C., supported a variety of competing newspapers. The *National Intelligencer* focused on politics; one hardly knew from reading the *Intelligencer* that the city itself existed. Washington was, according to the *Intelligencer,* Capitol Hill.

However, other papers covered local news. The *Georgetown Advocate* was interested in city development, like the expansion of city services and street paving. The *Alexandria Packet* and the *Advocate* covered the shipping news. A temperance newspaper railed against the evils of alcohol. And the *Saturday Evening News,* a penny paper, commented on prison reform, public education, and almhouses for the poor. Each newspaper had a distinct role as a local arbiter of cultural values. The *Intelligencer* catered to the political elite; the Georgetown and Alexandria newspapers promoted local business; and the *Saturday Evening News* recognized a society in the city that was not necessarily intellectual, business oriented, or wealthy.

Rise of the Penny Press

By the 1830s, New York City was the undisputed center of newspaper activity. It had replaced the important colonial city of Boston in economic and political importance, becoming the nation's largest commercial city. New York City spawned a variety of competing newspapers edited by men who championed different social classes in the city and by men who intended to make a profit. Before 1830 most newspapers had **circulations** between 2,000 and 3,000 and appealed to the commercial interests of the city. But Benjamin Day, who started the *New York Sun* in 1833, and James Gordon Bennett, who established the *New York Herald* in 1835, increased their circulations by selling their newspapers cheaply—for one cent a copy. These **penny press** publishers no longer relied on letters from abroad, political documents, or letters written by members of the elite for news. They hired reporters and managing editors and began to seek news. They recognized the power of timely news and cultivated reporters to get the scoop, to beat the competing newspaper to a good story. The era of the penny press intensified the focus on local communities.

The penny press newspapers targeted middle-class audiences involved in trade, transportation, and manufacturing. However, they were no longer bound to commerce and politics; they reflected the increasing social activity in their urban surroundings. Benjamin Day announced his *New York Sun* with this comment:

Key Concept

Penny press In the early 1830s, a new class of newspapers targeted to lower and middle-class audiences earned the name *penny press* because they were sold for a penny a copy. In addition to traditional news about commerce and politics, they included lively stories about social life in the city.

circulation

The number of copies sold by a newspaper during its production cycle (week or day).

Dateline

Newspapers in Our Lives

1690. *Publick Occurrences* is published in Boston.
1704. John Campbell publishes the Boston *News-Letter*.
1734–1735. John Peter Zenger is tried in New York for seditious libel.
Mid-1700s. Newspapers promote dissatisfaction with English rule.
1827. First African–American newspaper is started.
1830s. Penny press becomes the first truly mass medium in the United States.
1846. Newspapers begin to use telegraph to send news.
1847. Frederick Douglass starts the *North Star*.
1849. First newsgathering association is founded.
1861–1865. Press is censored during the Civil War.
1890s. Period of yellow journalism
1917–1918. Government imposes censorship during World War I.
1920s. Tabloid journalism flourishes in large cities.

1400–1700	1800	1860	1880	1900	1920	1930

1620. Pilgrims land at Plymouth Rock.
1690. *Publick Occurrences* is published in Boston.
1741. First magazine is published in America.
1776–1783. American Revolution
1830s. The penny press becomes the first truly mass medium in the United States.
1861–1865. American Civil War
1892. Thomas Edison's lab develops the kinetoscope.
1914–1918. World War I
1915. *The Birth of a Nation* marks the start of the modern movie industry.
1920. KDKA in Pittsburgh gets the first commercial radio license.
1930s. The Great Depression
1939. TV is demonstrated at the New York World's Fair.
1939–1945. World War II

Cultural Milestones

The object of this paper is to lay before the public, at a price within the means of every one, ALL THE NEWS OF THE DAY, and at the same time afford an advantageous medium for advertising. The sheet will be enlarged as soon as the increase of advertisements requires it—the price remaining the same.[6]

The National Stage

By the 1890s, newspapers in towns as small as Emporia, Kansas, where William Allen White edited the *Gazette,* accepted national advertising and carried national and international news provided by the Associated Press or other wire services, thus becoming

1941–1945. Government censors the press during World War II.

1950s. Television takes national advertising from newspapers.

1960s. Boom in newspaper public ownership begins.

1970s. Weekly newspaper circulation grows dramatically.

1970s. Newspaper groups go public to finance expansion.

1982. Gannett starts USA Today.

1990s. First newspapers go online.

1998. American Society of Newspaper Editors releases credibility study.

2000s. Newspapers push to eliminate regulation that prevents them from buying TV stations.

2000s. Newspapers begin to charge to download archived stories as Internet advertising stalls.

1940	1950	1960	1970	1980	1990	2000

1949. First commercial electronic computer is produced.

Early 1950s. Rock 'n' roll begins.

1969. First person lands on the moon.

1970s. VCR is developed.

1989–1991. Cold War ends and the USSR is dissolved.

Late 1980s. National Science Foundation creates the basis of the Internet.

1996. Telecommunications Act

2000. Presidential election nearly tied.

2001. Terrorist attacks on New York and Washington, D.C.

2003. War with Iraq.

national in scope. Nevertheless, White and like-minded editors still regarded the local community as the audience for their newspapers. In large cities such as New York, Boston, Philadelphia, and Chicago, newspapers played on a larger stage, but their audience remained primarily local. During the 1850s, Horace Greeley marketed his New York *Tribune* to Westerners as well as New Yorkers, and later in the century, William Randolph Hearst with the *New York Journal* and Joseph Pulitzer with his *New York World* commanded large national circulations and claimed influence with major political figures. Newspapers published in large eastern cities had an audience in Washington, D.C. Nevertheless, New Yorkers were their main subscribers, and New York advertisers paid most of their bills.

Advertising took on a national scope during the mid-1800s. Editors carried advertisements for nationally distributed brands as well as local products. For editors such as William Allen White, this posed a dilemma. To accept national advertising was to encourage readers to buy from the large surrounding cities and from mail-order houses rather than from merchants in their hometowns. White carried national advertising but constantly exhorted his readers to "buy at home."

Meanwhile, technology was changing, which facilitated large print runs and large circulations. The rotary press, which printed from rolls of paper rather than from sheets, new folding machines, and new techniques for making plates into paper mats that could be bent around a cylinder to accommodate rolls of paper all contributed to the expansion of the newspaper business.

In the expanding market, newspaper editors competed for circulation, using information, entertainment, and the sensational presentation of news as their tools. Henry Raymond, who started the *New York Times* before the Civil War, appealed to the business classes of New York and Washington, D.C., and established a reputation for solid information without entertainment. Charles Dana, who bought the *New York Sun* in 1868, advocated artisan republicanism, a philosophy maintaining that all people, including the working class, should have equal rights and full participation in the political system. Ultimately, however, Dana could not compete with Joseph Pulitzer's *New York World*. Pulitzer and William Randolph Hearst, with his *New York Journal,* played to the crowds. Catering to the working and middle classes, their newspapers hummed with the vitality of New York City life. They covered stories that had not been covered before, reporting New York gossip among the social set as well as political debates over the organization of labor and the rights of property owners.

The newspapers pursued what has become known as **yellow journalism,** which is the printing of stories that emphasize crime and personal tragedies presented with big headlines and illustrations. These newspapers were highly sensationalistic, although Pulitzer, except during the most highly competitive years, operated from a sense of journalistic integrity. Pulitzer introduced an editorial platform that called for taxing luxuries, inheritances, large incomes, monopolies, and privileged corporations, which he viewed as tools of the rich. He also called for reforming the civil service and punishing corruption in political office. The *New York Times* countered the sensationalists with a sober writing style and point of view.

The New York City papers were not the only ones to capitalize on new developments. E. W. Scripps offered a different kind of competition. Avoiding the urban cities of the Northeast, he established dailies in medium-size cities in the Midwest, supporting organized labor and advocating independence from powerful advertisers. After acquiring a number of newspapers in Ohio, Scripps expanded to the West Coast. With his Midwest papers and significant holdings in Oregon, Washington, and California, he shaped one of the first effective newspaper chains. Scripps required his editors to operate on a very small budget. His formula included heavy reliance on subscriptions and on revenues from multiple advertisers because he feared the power large advertisers might gain if a newspaper relied too heavily on them. Scripps, who disliked the sensationalism of Hearst and Pulitzer, sought to provide local information as the mainstay of his smaller newspapers.[7]

> ## Key Concept
>
> **Yellow journalism** In the late 1890s, in a battle for readership, William Randolph Hearst's *New York Journal* hired the artist who drew the popular cartoon "The Yellow Kid" away from Joseph Pulitzer's *New York World*. The *World* retaliated by hiring a new artist to draw the cartoon. Thus began the "Yellow War," in which the two papers published increasingly lurid stories with bold headlines and lots of graphics. The term *yellow journalism* is still used to denote content that is considered irresponsible, unethical, or lacking in professional standards of news judgment.

Maturation

Shortly after the beginning of the twentieth century, the number of daily newspapers began to decline as the industry grew more concentrated and profitable. Advertisers were looking for efficient advertising, and they placed their ads in the largest newspapers. Those newspapers that increased circulation experienced a growth in advertising and thus in profit. Those that did not eventually went out of business.

As daily newspapers began to consolidate and close, radio confronted the industry with a new form of competition. During World War II, both newspapers and radio faced some government censorship, but on the whole they cooperated with the government in reporting the war effort. Radio's role in news became increasingly important, particularly in reporting international events. President Franklin Delano Roosevelt's "fireside chats" and Edward R. Murrow's reports from London challenged newspaper superiority in reporting on the war. Nevertheless, it was not until the 1960s, when news of civil rights and subsequently of the Vietnam War exploded on television screens in American homes, that newspapers faced a major challenge from television news.

With some exceptions, the strength of newspapers is still the local audience. National newspapers have difficulty achieving financial stability, let alone high profit margins. During the 1960s, the *National Observer* acquired a national, politically sophisticated audience with its well written interpretive pieces, but it never obtained the advertising that would have enabled it to succeed in its appeal to a relatively elite national readership. The *Wall Street Journal* succeeds as a specialized national newspaper, appealing to the business community across geographical boundaries. *USA Today* targets a middle-class national audience. After two decades, it reached a 2.3 million daily circulation with a stable advertising market.

The *New York Times,* while definitely targeted toward New Yorkers, also maintains a loyal audience among intellectuals across the nation and at times has exerted major influence nationwide. For example, *New York Times v. Sullivan,* a landmark libel case in 1964, resulted when an Alabama police commissioner sued the newspaper because he resented the influence the *New York Times* had in the civil rights movement. The *Times* has begun a campaign to expand its national edition, including a readership program on many large college campuses.

TODAY'S MARKET STRUCTURE

Two major types of newspapers exist: daily and weekly. The daily newspaper is usually found in larger markets, has a large staff, and covers local, national, and international news from a variety of sources. Daily newspapers may or may not produce a longer Sunday edition, and some newspapers exist only as Sunday editions. Some daily metro newspapers, like the *New York Times* and the *Los Angeles Times,* reach a wide national or even international audience, while others are targeted locally. The weekly newspaper has a smaller staff and generally covers local news and often extensively features classified advertising.

Newspaper **markets** have been defined in a variety of ways. Newspapers are considered vehicles of mass communication that target generalized audiences within a local geographic area. However, exceptions are common. The *Wall Street Journal,* for example, targets a national market when defined by geography, but a specialized market when defined by editorial or advertising content. Furthermore, communities are being identified differently than they were in the past; suburban dailies not only compete with metropolitan newspapers but also supplement them with even more local news and information. Suburban newspapers also have the advantage of attracting local advertisers. Because of these strengths, investors have become very interested in suburban newspaper chains and have been buying and consolidating them. For example, the Clarity Media Group bought three newspapers in the Washington, D.C., metropolitan area and replaced them with its free tabloid, the *Examiner,* containing local news and advertising. Targeted to wealthy suburbanites, the *Examiner* has editions in other metropolitan areas across the country and has a national website. In Washington, it competes for readers with the renowned *Washington Post* and the *Washington Times.*

The **market structure for news** determines the degree of competition in a media market and, therefore, how responsive newspapers must be to readers. The market structure for newspapers has three components.

> ### Key Concept
>
> **Market structure for news** The market relationship between newspapers and their buyers is based on costs, competition, and availability of substitute products, such as other newspapers, television news programs, and websites.

market

A geographic area in which businesses and consumers exchange goods and services for money. *Major markets* include a metropolitan area and have many media choices; *outstate markets* are removed from metropolitan areas but are not rural and include some diversity in media choice; *isolated markets* include rural areas with limited media choices.

Media Convergence

Online Experiments

Many newspaper editors in larger markets are working to create a customized, interactive online version of their papers. Since the mid-1990s, newspapers have experimented with web delivery. At first, news stories were simply transferred to websites. More recently, many newspapers have added features that allow users to personalize the content. Rather than seeing general news, visitors can customize access so that they see news stories related to their interests, such as tracking stock performance. They may be able to post opinions, photographs, and other responses on the newspaper's website.

A notable early experiment with interactivity was the *Houston Chronicle*'s Virtual Voyager, which drew its audience into realtime, virtual experience of the news. Site visitors could follow the road trip of two journalists traveling for a month down Route 66 with a camera in the back seat. To increase interactivity, they could send the journalists public e-mail and e-cards.

In 1998, New Jersey Online, a joint website of three New Jersey newspapers and a television station, launched Community Connection. Using the web's capacity for allowing users to easily publish their own webpages, Communication Connection offered nonprofit organizations the opportunity to put their information online. The site eventually hosted 3,000 sites.

More recently, the *Lawrence Journal-World* (ljworld.com) won the Newspaper Association of America's 2006 Digital Edge Award for its interactive website, which includes podcasts, photos and commentaries posted by readers, and reader forums.

Source: Pablo J. Boczkowski, *Digitizing the News: Innovation in Online Newspapers* (Cambridge, Mass.: MIT Press, 2005).

The first component is how many choices are available within the market. Residents of Lawrence, Kansas, a town centered between Kansas City, thirty miles to the east, and Topeka, thirty miles to the west, have several choices. They can buy the *Kansas City Star,* the *Lawrence Journal-World,* or the *Topeka Capital-Journal.* Because Kansas City straddles the Missouri–Kansas state line and is a large city, the *Star* offers more cultural news for the area, Missouri state government news, national and international news, and advertisements for shopping in a larger city. The Topeka newspaper offers more Kansas state news. The Lawrence newspaper offers the best local news. Now the question becomes "How will residents deal with this choice?" Will they buy one newspaper? Several newspapers?

The second component is the probability that buyers will substitute products. For example, what is the probability that a person living in Lawrence will buy the *Kansas City Star* instead of the *Lawrence Journal-World?* The component of substitution becomes increasingly important when different types of media are available.[7] Then people have the ability to substitute television, for example, for newspapers. To head off the competition, newspapers have been developing online editions to capture web surfers and capitalize on the dramatic increase in Internet advertising revenues. Since newspapers make most of their profit from advertising, this is a critical issue. Since 2001, ads on newspaper websites have experienced a 30 percent to 60 percent growth, but online rates are lower than print rates.[8]

The third component is the number of barriers new firms face when trying to enter the market. In any major market area, new publishers find it exceedingly difficult to crack an already established newspaper market with a newspaper that competes for the same audience and the same advertisers as an existing newspaper. To challenge the *Washington Post,* for example, requires enormous resources. Although the *Washington Times* has spent huge sums of money, it has been unable to compete successfully with the *Post*'s broad advertising and subscription base. The *Post* serves its advertisers better than the *Times* does because the *Post* can reach more potential buyers at less cost. The overwhelming advantage held by most established newspapers in major markets remains the most important barrier to new competition.

AUDIENCE DEMAND IN NEWSPAPER MARKETS

Editors and owners are having increasing difficulty determining what content readers want, in part because they do not understand the three components of market structures discussed in the previous paragraphs. In the 1950s, white male editors of the mainstream newspapers concentrated on the city beat and basic suburban themes such as road development, schools, and protection from crime and catered to a middle-class white audience. Newspapers included a women's section that focused on fashion, food, and children. Ethnic and minority newspapers targeted other specific audiences. However, the composition of the United States has changed dramatically in ethnic diversity, the distribution of power, the number of women working, and the makeup of the typical family. The proportion of young people reading newspapers has declined since the 1950s as the use of other media has grown. Editors must serve a more diverse audience, and they face great difficulty in selecting the specific content that these segments of their market want to read. For example, professional women may want newspaper content that is more similar to the content that professional men read rather than to what women who work at home read. Although market research increasingly is used to explore readers' needs and preferences, this "fuzziness," or blurring of the boundaries of desired content, increases the difficulty of identifying the factors that would make an individual or family buy a particular newspaper rather than turn to another source of news.[9]

Newspaper editors no longer can assume that most middle-class households will subscribe to a newspaper. Even though the number of daily newspaper copies sold is greater now than it was in 1950, the **household penetration** (the percentage of households in a market subscribing to a newspaper) has steadily declined. Many reasons exist for this long-term decline, including changing work patterns and consumption patterns and competition from television, radio, and the Internet. Newspapers have traditionally had the advantage of thorough coverage and analysis, but television and radio have rich visual and auditory stimuli and allow for viewers to multitask, such as cooking dinner while listening to National Public Radio.

In 2004, the circulation decline accelerated dramatically. In a 6th-month period in 2005, circulation went down by 2.6 percent for dailies and 3.1 percent for Sunday papers.[10] As Table 3.1 shows, the decline in circulation has affected many daily newspapers. Circulation is only part of the story. Readership also is down in most demographic groups, even among highly educated people, raising fears that an informed citizenry is disappearing. Several factors have contributed to the loss, but the number one reason is that readers are now turning to websites for their news. A newspaper's own website can draw readers away from its print version. In September 2005, the public's need for information about Hurricanes Katrina and Rita helped increase online newspaper readership by 15.8 percent.[11] However, newspapers have not yet figured out how to capitalize on a highly competitive medium that also offers television network and other newspaper websites, as well as blogging, shopping and entertainment.

With increasingly diverse market structures, newspapers can no longer count on the generalized mass markets that supported their development throughout the nineteenth and early twentieth centuries. Faced with the difficulty of identifying content demanded by diverse readership and adapting to new technologies, newspaper managers have begun to think of newspapers as media aimed at the market's educated and high-income citizens. Some reporters for the *New York Times,* for example, say they write not for the general public, but for the political and intellectual elite as well

household penetration

The number of households subscribing to a newspaper compared to the number of potential households in an area.

Table 3.1   Change in Weekday Circulation at Ten Large Metropolitan Newspapers

Newspaper	March 31, 2006	March 31, 2002	Percentage Change
New York Times	1,131,170	1,194,491	–5.3
Los Angeles Times	905,107	1,001,610	–9.6
Washington Post	715,181	811,925	–11.9
New York Daily News	693,382	733,099	–5.4
Newsday (Long Island)	431,975	577,796	–25.23
Houston Chronicle	524,571	545,727	–3.9
Chicago Tribune	585,587	535,469	+9.4
Dallas Morning News	478,950	526,430	–9.0
Arizona Republic	435,338	496,373	–12.3
San Francisco Chronicle	429,721	525,369	–18.2

Source: Audit Bureau of Circulations, accessabc.com.

as for other newspaper reporters and editors.[12] Newspaper publishers have to decide whether to continue as mass media or to turn toward segmented audiences. If newspaper managers adhere to the basic concept of a newspaper as news for everyone, they need to identify themselves as suppliers of information, not just of news, because the demand for content will be wide ranging. If they turn instead to specialized audiences, their markets may be easier to define. They can choose, for example, to aim at the political elite; at business entrepreneurs; or at the under-30, entertainment-oriented upper middle class.

Newspapers have some advantages over other media. Their role in the community has a historical tradition as well as solid First Amendment protection. To maintain that traditional role, however, newspapers need to be seen by community members as essential reading. Newspapers need modernized forms of delivery, such as fiber optics, telephones, satellite transmission, and computers. Diversifying newsrooms in terms of the lifestyles, economic backgrounds, gender, education, and ethnic origins of reporters and editors can help newspaper managers respond to audience demand.

SUPPLYING THE AUDIENCE'S DEMAND

During the last four decades of the twentieth century, the newspaper industry experienced rapid change. Most newspapers came under group ownership, other forms of media expanded and developed, and competition among newspapers declined. During this same period, newspapers experienced a significant decline in their credibility among the general public. Many people no longer trust journalists and the content they create.

Ownership

Newspaper ownership may be **public,** meaning the public can buy shares of ownership in the form of stock traded through a public stock exchange, or it may be **private,** meaning the public cannot buy stock. In addition, newspapers may have *independent ownership* if a company owns only one newspaper, or it may have *group ownership* if the company owns more than one newspaper. About twenty newspaper companies own 39 percent of the nation's daily newspapers.[13] Most corporations that own newspaper groups, such as Gannett, also own several types of media. There is an increased probability that these media corporations will be bought by conglomerates, which own both media and nonmedia companies. For instance, General Electric now owns NBC television.

Corporations buy newspapers because, despite declining penetration, they generate profit rates two or three times greater than the rates of most businesses. This continuing profitability results from strict cost control and newspapers' domination of classified advertising. Factors contributing to increased corporate ownership include the fact that families who own newspapers sometimes have difficulty resolving tensions among their members about how the business should be run, and the tax structure encourages families to sell inherited property rather than keep it. Furthermore, it is much easier for a group to acquire a newspaper and manage it successfully than to start a new one. Starting a daily newspaper requires millions of dollars to buy printing presses and to run the newspaper for years while it builds name recognition. In Washington, D.C., the *Washington Times* was started to compete with the *Post,* but the *Times* has yet to earn a profit. It continues to exist because it is subsidized by a religious organization.

During the 1990s, the concentration of newspaper ownership continued in a new form. Companies began to "cluster" their newspapers by buying several newspapers in the same geographic region. In late 1998, for instance, the Liberty Group bought thirty-eight weekly and twice-weekly newspapers near Chicago. Clustering allows companies to provide better advertising coverage in an area by placing the same ad in all their newspapers. It also allows them to cut circulation expenses because their newspapers no longer compete with one another. This decline in competition has been criticized as leading to reduced newsroom budgets and lower quality.

Ownership concentration also continued in the 1990s as groups started to buy the alternative weekly papers found in most large cities. The weeklies were first published during the cultural movements of the 1960s and totaled more than 250 in 1999, with more than $400 million in yearly revenue. These newspapers typically emphasize politics and entertainment. Some of these alternative newspapers joined together to avoid being bought by daily chains. The fifty-year-old weekly, The *Village Voice,* is known for its investigative journalism and irreverent writing. Until October 2005, the *Voice* was owned by Village Voice Media, founded in 1969 by leftist university students. Village Voice Media merged with New Times, Inc., of Phoenix, creating a company that owned seventeen weeklies across the country. Some journalists warned that the new entity would impose a moderate, cookie-cutter editorial policy on all of its papers, robbing weeklies like the *Voice* of their critical perspective and distinctive character.[14]

Group ownership has been criticized since the first chains were formed during the nineteenth century. Some community leaders and journalists fear that group ownership will standardize newspapers at the expense of their local distinctiveness, that absentee owners are less likely to invest in the newsroom, and that ownership groups will impose their editorial will on a local newspaper. Supporters of group ownership argue that financial strength makes groups less vulnerable to manipulation by advertisers or political groups; that groups have more money to invest in staff and equipment; and that when managers are moved from one location to another, they are less likely to become part of the local power establishment with policies and interests

Doug Ray

Doug Ray is the award-winning publisher of the *Daily Herald,* a suburban newspaper with the slogan, "Big Picture, Local Focus." With readers from a wide demographic spectrum, including Mexicans, Poles, Vietnamese, Filipinos, and Indians, the *Daily Herald* emphasizes diversity in all of its activities. Since 2000, the newspaper has been sending journalists to the homelands of its immigrant readers to cover issues such as the imprisonment of children in Filipino jails. The combination of local sensitivity and good national and international journalism has spelled success for the *Daily Herald,* despite its competition with the *Chicago Tribune* and the *Chicago Sun-Times.* From 1995 to 2005, the paper increased its circulation by 19.9 percent, and from 2003 to 2005 increased its advertising revenue by 10 percent. In 2005, the paper boasted a circulation of 150,000.

Ray's first job was as an intern for a southern Illinois newspaper, where he worked as a reporter in the morning and sold advertising in the afternoons. Graduating from Southern Illinois University in 1969 where he worked on the student *Daily Egyptian,* Ray took a job as a beat reporter with the family-owned *Daily Herald,* then called the *Arlington Heights Herald,* a weekly which covered only local news. At the age of 28, Ray became managing editor, helping the *Daily Herald* make the transition from weekly to big city daily. Becoming the paper's CEO in 2002, Ray has made a strong commitment to journalism, creating an overstaff newsroom of 275 employees.

To attract more readers, Ray acquired the weekly Spanish-language *Reflejos,* and launched the website Beep, targeting 21- to 34-year-olds. In keeping with its own tradition of community involvement, the *Daily Herald's* Leadership Program honors young people who give public service as tutors, mentors, and coaches. In 2006, *Editor & Publisher* named Ray Publisher of the Year for growing a newspaper in time of downturn in the industry.

Source: Editor & Publisher, April 2006: 7.

to protect. Researchers have found that many of these problems have little to do with whether a newspaper is owned by a group or by an individual or family. The impact of ownership comes from local commitment and management goals—two elements that vary among newspapers regardless of whether owners are groups or individuals. For instance, research indicates that publicly held ownership can negatively affect local newspapers. The more stock is owned by the public, the higher the profit rate a newspaper company will pursue.[15] This reflects management goals. The high profit keeps stock prices up, but the result is reduced newsroom budgets that can lower the quality of the local coverage.

Competition

Direct **competition** among daily newspapers has all but disappeared. In 1920, 552 of 1,295 U.S. cities with daily newspapers had two or more dailies owned and operated by different companies. By 1960, only 61 of 1,461 cities had separately owned and operated dailies. Currently, about twenty cities have two or more daily newspapers that are separately owned and operated.

Why this downward trend? Newspapers serve more than one market. The diverse reading audience chooses from a variety of media outlets in the consumer market. Potential advertisers compose another market. These advertisers want to reach the most people possible for the least amount of money per individual. Accordingly, advertisers buy newspaper space according to the number of readers. This factor is referred to as cost-per-thousand, or the price an advertiser pays to reach 1,000 subscribers. In a two-newspaper town, the newspaper losing readers has a higher cost-per-thousand because newspapers rarely reduce their advertising prices. As a result, advertisers take advantage of the better buy at the other paper. Because

> **Key Concept**
>
> **Competition** Newspapers compete with other papers and media outlets for audiences, advertising revenues, and breaking stories. Competition ensures that communities hear more than one editorial point of view, pushes reporters to be more creative and aggressive, and forces newspapers to spend money on improvements to attract readers.

readers buy newspapers for ads as well as for news, readers of the trailing newspaper switch to the competing one. Once a newspaper begins to lose readers, it also loses advertisers, and as it loses advertisements, subsequently it loses readers. A downward spiral begins. One newspaper gains a disproportionate amount of advertising, and before long, a two-newspaper town becomes a one-newspaper town.

Competition is an important factor in newsroom quality. Research shows that competition gives the reader choice and, therefore, power. Usually, as the intensity of competition increases, publishers spend more money on the newsroom, resulting in better quality reporting. With more news and advertising space available in each market, advertisers get lower advertising rates, and reporters and editorial writers strive for new ideas for stories. The existence of two editorial sections also increases the possibility that the marketplace of ideas will become more lively and that readers will have access to varied points of view.

With these competition factors in mind, Congress in 1970 created the Newspaper Preservation Act, which allows two newspapers in the same town to combine all of their operations, such as business and circulation, with one exception: the newsroom. This legislation exempts newspapers from the antitrust laws that regulate competition. Congress felt that the political role played by newspapers in a democracy warranted efforts to maintain two daily newspapers in the same city. In 2007, twelve of the twenty-seven joint operating agreements (JOA) approved by the Justice Department since 1970 remained in operation. Research indicates that the quality of JOA newspapers is not as good as that in competitive markets but that it is much better than the quality in cities with one daily newspaper.[16] However, JOAs do not end the downward circulation spiral that forces newspapers out of business, and eventually at least one newspaper in all the JOAs is likely to close.

Even though daily newspapers have lost most of their local market newspaper competition, other forms of competition have taken its place. Since daily newspapers serve local communities, their competition for advertising revenues is local. Free newspapers, cable television, and direct mail all vie for local advertising dollars. Metro dailies have responded to surrounding regional and suburban newspapers by **zoning** their coverage. For example, in the late 1990s, the Pulitzer Prize–winning *San Francisco Chronicle* began five-day-a-week regional coverage to compete with the *San Jose Mercury News* and the *Contra Costa Times*. It cut back to one day a week because, as editor Phil Bronstein put it, zoning "was more fig-leaf coverage than real coverage."[17] The expansion of the Internet has posed new challenges for newspapers, especially in loss of classified advertising. In 2006, urban dailies were especially concerned about Craigslist, a site that offers free classified listings for cities across the world. Running eight million classifieds a month, it is popular with urban young adults looking for dates, apartments, pets, and jobs. The online trading site, eBay, and job search sites, such as Monster and Hotjobs, also siphon away ad listings. Rural newspapers have so far avoided this problem because their older, more settled readers have less access to the Internet.[18]

zoning

Printing an edition of a newspaper for a specific geographic area (or zone) that has content aimed at that area, usually in a specific section of the paper.

Declining Credibility

Newspapers cannot prosper as suppliers of news and information unless their readers trust what they read. The decline in newspaper *credibility* has become a primary issue facing newspapers at the beginning of the new century. A study conducted by *Time* magazine in 1998 found that newspaper credibility had sunk to a level at which only 21 percent of Americans believed all or most of the content in the local newspaper, representing a decline from 28 percent in 1985.[19] In response to the continuing decline, the American Society of Newspaper Editors (ASNE) began a $1 million project to improve credibility.

A 2006 Pew Research Center poll found that public opinion of news media continues to decline. For example, in 1998, 42 percent of television viewers familiar with CNN ranked it

Key Concept

Credibility Newspaper content has credibility with readers when readers believe what they read. If a newspaper reporter or company has no credibility with readers, the readers will not trust the facts and opinions about which the reporter writes or that the newspaper publishes.

Dan Rather's credibility suffered damage after he reported a story, using documents of questionable authenticity, about George W. Bush's service in the Texas Army National Guard. He retired from CBS News seven months later.

high in believability, while in 2006, that number had fallen to 28 percent. The poll also found that respondents considered television more reliable than print sources, and that they tended to be politically partisan in choosing news outlets, with Republicans favoring Fox News and Democrats favoring the *NewsHour with Jim Lehrer* and NPR.[20]

The decline in credibility in all news media does not make publishers and editors feel any better about their slipping public image. In 2001, the National Credibility Roundtables Project was formed to help newspapers build trust with their readers. By 2006, 195 newspapers had sponsored roundtables on issues such as bias, factual accuracy, and minority concerns. The interest in credibility is also important in the face of online competition. One of the ways newspapers set themselves apart from the web's bloggers and citizen journalists is to defend their experience and resources in providing accurate, credible content.

Key Concept

Ethnic and minority press Publications targeting minority and ethnic populations are a vibrant force in their communities; however, they have largely been ignored by the dominant culture. Recently, the attempt to provide a collective voice to ethnic media has brought it to the attention of investors, advertisers, and politicians.

Key Concept

Representation An image of an object, place, person, or event. Images often appear to mirror reality, but *re-present* it in a new form. Great social power lies in a dominant group's ability to represent other groups of people, through media, according to its own needs, ideas, and expectations.

Ethnic and Minority Press

As mainstream newspapers struggle to keep up circulation and ad revenues, *ethnic and minority newspapers* in many languages are surging in growth. A national poll by an organization of ethnic news organizations found that 20 million ethnic adults, who comprise 13 percent of the U.S. population, prefer ethnic radio, television, and newspapers.[21] Historically, immigrants and other minority groups have used their own publications to share news in their own language and keep in touch with their homelands. Often unfairly treated and stereotypically portrayed in the mainstream press, ethnic and racial minority groups have used their own press to organize politically and control their own *representation.*

Despite their expansion and cultural importance, ethnic and minority newspapers constantly struggle with adequate financing, especially in attracting advertising revenues. African-American newspaper executives report that their main threat of survival is lack of advertising dollars, even though they maintain steady circulations. The growth of metro dailies owned by media conglomerates threatens further strain on African-American newspapers.[22] However, conditions are improving for the Hispanic press.

Between 1990 and 2004, spending on Spanish-language print ads rose from $151 million to $1.25 billion.[23]

African-American Press

African-American newspapers have made important contributions to community building and the fight against racism and discrimination. The first African-American newspaper, the *Freedman's Journal,* was founded in 1827 to organize against slavery. After the Civil War, other newspapers, such as the *Chicago Defender* and the *Pittsburgh Courier,* developed to challenge segregation laws.

In 2006, 221 newspapers belonged to the National Newspaper Publishers Association, also known as the Black Press of America. This almost seventy-year-old federation of black community newspapers has also served as the industry's news service since World War II. It initially competed with the Associated Negro Press, but that organization dissolved in 1970.

Twenty-five percent of African Americans read African-American newspapers.[24] The African-American press brings attention to crucial issues affecting its readers, such as racial profiling, affirmative action, and inequalities in education. It provides a refuge from the mainstream media with its stereotypical portrayals of African Americans as criminals and drug addicts. African Americans turn to their own newspapers for news they can trust. Robert Bogle, the CEO of the *Philadelphia Tribune,* the oldest black newspaper in the country, doubts that coverage in the mainstream press can ever replace African-American newspapers. He says, "Our nation is still divided by race. No one can tell our story better than we can. You have to live it. You have to be part of it to understand it."[25]

Native-American Press

Like the African-American press, the Native-American press covers issues of a people mostly ignored or stereotyped by the mainstream media. The first Native-American newspaper, the *Cherokee Phoenix,* was first published in 1828. The first bilingual newspaper in the Western hemisphere, it defended American Indians against relocation and the encroachment of settlers on the frontier. Before the Civil War, Native publications flourished, including the first paper by Cherokee women, who were residing in a boarding school. One scholar estimates that 250 papers were published in the Indian Territory before 1900.[26] Today about 280 reservation newspapers and 320 other publications serve Native Americans.[27] Most Native-American publications take the form of newsletters for their small, local audiences. In 2002, graduates of the Freedom Forum's American Indian Journalism Institute started Reznet, the first online Native-American student newspaper.

Twenty-three percent of Native Americans turn to their diverse tribal newspapers as their primary source of news.[28] Native-American newspapers cover tribal business, tribal sovereignty, community safety, and national issues such as the long-standing battle against native mascots for sports teams. Because reservation newspapers are controlled by tribal governments, a hot issue in recent years has been their censorship. In answer, the National Congress of American Indians passed a resolution in 2003 calling for tribes to ensure a free, independent, and objective Native press.[29]

Hispanic Press

In 2006, Hispanics and Latinos made up the fastest growing segment of the U.S. population. However, Hispanics constitute diverse groups, having come from a variety of Spanish-speaking countries at different times in U.S. history. Because the United States seized large amounts of land from Mexico, the largest group of Hispanics are of Mexican descent. Newspapers serving these descendants are called the Chicano press and are printed in Spanish, English, or sometimes both languages.

The Chicano press can trace its roots to the area that is now Texas. Newspapers such as *La Gaceta* and *El Mexicano* were printed in the 1810s as Mexico sought independence from Spain.[30] The 1960s saw growth in the Chicano press as Hispanics battled for political power and civil rights. From 1990 to 2006, Hispanic dailies and weeklies grew from 355 to 700, with circulation well over twelve million.[31]

The strength of Hispanic media has attracted larger conglomerates, such as Impre-Media, that have been buying Spanish-language newspapers. One-fifth of Hispanic

Cultural Sensitivity

In 1994, the *Minneapolis Star Tribune* instated a new policy for its journalists. They would no longer use the terms "Redskins," "Skins," "Braves," "Indians," "Tribe," and "Chiefs" in referring to sports teams. The paper's executive sports editor explained that after conversations with Native Americans about team mascots: "We have come to believe that discontinuing the use of these offensive nicknames is the right thing to do. And we believe newspapers make decisions about language all the time. Many racist and sexist terms have been eliminated over the years."

The *Star* joined five other daily newspapers that had policies related to mascot team names and logos depicting Native Americans, such as the Cleveland Indian's Chief Wahoo. The *Oregonian*, the *Portland Press Herald*, the *St. Cloud Times*, the *Kansas City Star* and the *Lincoln Journal Star* have maintained these policies for over ten years. Photographs of fans doing the "tomahawk chop" are also discouraged.

In 2003, arguing on the principle of reality and accuracy in reporting, the *Minneapolis Star Tribune* changed its policy, allowing its reporters again to use the official team names. However, it encouraged sensitivity and alternate references, such as using the Cleveland Indians "I" rather than its Chief Wahoo logo.

The Native American Journalists Association reacted by releasing a report on the mascot issue, a followup to its 2002 study of stereotypes, inaccuracies, and false perceptions of Native Americans in the mainstream press. The Association argued that newspapers that continue to use sports team names deemed offensive "erode what credibility they have among Native Americans and others, including communities of color and religious communities." Further, the use of such names and logos helps creates a climate for Native American youth that leads to low self-esteem and self-destructive behavior. In 2006, six Native Americans filed a petition with the U.S. Patent and Trademark Office to cancel the trademark of the Washington Redskins. The petitioners are between eighteen and twenty-four years old. The mascot issue

remains a heated one, at a time when Native Americans have very little representation on mainstream newsroom staffs.

Sources: Indian Country Today, Feb. 2, 1994: A1; Native American Journalists Association, Reading Red Report 2003, naja.com.

adults turn to Spanish-language newspapers rather than the mainstream press.[32] Hispanic newspapers play a variety of roles in their communities, from providing the national and international news in Spanish to promoting community activism on issues such as immigration and legal discrimination. Gerardo Lopez, editor of *La Opinion*, has explained, "We gather facts with the same rigor and discipline as *Los Angeles Times* reporters do, but we also must do public service journalism by informing our readers how to become citizens, acquire health care and participate in the political process."[33]

Asian-American Press   The Asian-American press covers a wide variety of publications catering to many different language groups, including Indians, Vietnamese, Koreans, Filipinos, Chinese, Hmong, Japanese, and Thais. Immigrants who came to

Ethnic communities in the United States often turn to ethnic newspapers in their own languages for news that is relevant to their cultures.

the United States in the nineteenth century founded their own newspapers to communicate in their own languages and keep abreast of news from their homelands. The first Chinese-language papers in the United States were intended for railroad workers and written mostly by missionaries. Nineteenth-century Indian newspapers promoted radical action against British imperialism in their native land. Before World War II, 17 Japanese-language newspapers in the United States had a circulation of 60,000. They disappeared during World War II, as their publishers and editors were rounded up and interned in camps with other Japanese Americans.[34] Today, about 500 Asian-American print media organizations strive to reach a population of 13.5 million Asian-Americans.[35]

Until New America Media, a collaboration of 700 ethnic news organizations, conducted a poll on the reach of the ethnic press, Asian-American newspapers received little attention outside of their communities. Its survey of Asian-American readers found that half or more of Chinese, Vietnamese, and Korean adults regularly read ethnic newspapers, sparking the interest of advertisers and investors. Publications targeting first-generation immigrants are more focused on maintaining community and homeland ties. Publications for second-generation ethnic populations have a different focus. These immigrants, especially English-speaking young people, are seeking news about cultural survival and identity as they struggle with assimilation, racism, and the stereotype of the "model minority" who is peaceful, hard working, and successful.

NEWSPAPERS AS ORGANIZATIONS

By the mid-nineteenth century, newspapers had begun to expand their staffs. The small papers of the colonial and early republic years generally were four pages long and were published by a printer–editor or by a printer who compiled writings by anonymous behind-the-scenes editors. As newspapers expanded in size and circulation, editors began to hire reporters. Throughout the nineteenth century, the reporter was a hired hand, paid space rates by the column inch, and not given job security or benefits. The few women who were hired as reporters had the same lack of security. During the late nineteenth and early twentieth centuries, reporters joined together in press clubs to establish themselves as professionals. Their desire for professional status reflected a growing movement in many of the occupations of the day.

Newspaper Departments

To most people, the term *newspaper staff* brings images of reporters and photographers chasing a story. Although these jobs are crucial to a newspaper, getting the news and advertising to readers also requires other activities. Newspaper organizations typically divide their staffs into newsroom, production, advertising, and circulation departments. The content starts in the newsroom and the advertising department. The newsroom staff produces the stories and photographs and graphics (drawings, cartoons, tables, and charts) that make up the news and information in the newspaper. The newsroom staff organizes the elements of each page on a computer screen in a page layout. At the same time, the advertising department sells ad space and creates the advertisements for the space not given to news and information. The production department runs the newspaper copies on the presses after receiving the laid-out pages from the newsroom and ad department by means of computers. As the newspaper copies come off the press, the circulation department puts them in trucks to be delivered to carriers, news racks, and newsstands.

These four departments have been a part of newspapers for more than 150 years. More recently, newspapers and newspaper groups have added marketing departments. The marketing department conducts research, develops promotional activities, and creates advertising to sell the newspapers to readers and advertising space to businesses and individuals. Newspapers that emphasize the role of the marketing department in creating news and information are called **market-oriented newspapers.** These newspaper organizations typically require communication among the various departments in order to increase sales to readers and advertisers.

Critics of market-oriented newspapers fear that the advertising department will influence content to the detriment of readers and that newspapers will produce only news that entertains readers. As a result, independent public affairs reporting will be reduced. Advertisers can influence coverage at some newspapers, and examples of newspapers pandering to potential advertisers are not difficult to find. For example, the *Waco Tribune-Herald,* hoping to attract advertising from a new supermarket, ran a front-page story and two pages inside the paper about the opening of a new store.[36] A 1998 study conducted by Randal Beam, a professor at Indiana University, found that seeking reader input and serving readers' needs and wants through marketing does not necessarily mean pandering by producing only entertainment-oriented news.[37] However, the study also found that at market-oriented newspapers, editors interacted more with managers from other departments, creating the potential for influence across departments.

> ### Key Concept
>
> **Market-oriented newspapers** Market-oriented newspapers emphasize using research to determine what readers and advertisers want in the newspaper in order to increase circulation and ad sales. The debate about market-oriented newspapers centers on the relative influence managers give to the marketing department and journalists over news content.

Newsroom Staffing

Newsrooms typically include reporters, photographers, designers, copyeditors, desk editors, a managing editor, and an editor. Reporters interview sources, conduct research, and write articles. Photographers provide the photographs that illustrate articles. Sometimes several photographs printed together create a picture story that emphasizes images more than words. Copyeditors edit stories written by reporters and write headlines for them. Designers produce graphics for the newspaper and organize the graphics, text, and photographs into the layout that becomes the printed pages. Desk editors supervise other staff members who are assigned to specific areas of news coverage. The city editor supervises the staff that covers the city in which the newspaper is located, and the sports editor supervises reporters and editors who put the sports section together. The managing editor supervises the daily operations of the newsroom, which includes coordinating the activities of the various desk editors. The editor is the top manager in the newsroom with responsibility for all activities and staff in the newsroom.

As the size of the paper increases, so do the degree of editorial specialization and the staff. For example, the advertising departments of large newspapers employ several people who specialize in classified advertising, including salespeople and designers as well as people who specialize in demographics and client relations. On the editorial side, the number of editors increases. Large metropolitan dailies tend to be organized by **desks,** or departments, which may be classified as national, business, news, city, education, health and science, and real estate. Reporters are assigned to each desk, and the editor in charge of that department ensures that reporters cover regular **beats,** such as the police department, county courthouse, city hall, or statehouse. General assignment reporters pick up developing stories, **spot news,** and **features.**

The traditional bureaucratic structure of newspapers has been highly criticized in recent years; some critics believe that the traditional structure creates barriers to innovative stories and coverage. In reaction to the criticism, some newspapers have created different ways of structuring the newsroom. In addition to the traditional beats organized around government organizations such as the police and city hall, newspapers have created topical beats such as science, the environment, and minority issues. These beats allow reporters to consider a broad range of topics and issues in depth.

Topic beats are only one of the developments identified with the modern newsroom. Some newsrooms now pursue a team approach. The teams include reporters, photographers, and designers who have a team leader, not an editor. The team leaders help team members develop stories rather than telling them how to cover the stories, as traditional editors might. As part of a marketing approach, newspapers such as the *Orange County Register* and the *Minneapolis Star Tribune* created teams to cover certain topics in order to better serve readers. Debate continues over the impact of teams on the quality of news coverage, but a study of the health and science team at the *Portland Oregonian* concluded that it produced better coverage than the traditional approach.[38]

An important member of the news teams is the designer. At some newspapers, the way the news and information is packaged is as important as the news and information itself. A newspaper's **design** must attract and retain readers; it has become a key part of the marketing approach practiced by some newspapers.

Newspaper Design

The trend toward more readable news and graphic displays began with the introduction of Gannett's *USA Today* in 1982. The newspaper distributes over 2 million copies a day. It provided a wake-up call to the nation's newspaper editors, serving notice that readers would respond to "news you can use" and to graphic displays that made information more accessible. *USA Today* also has pioneered technological developments by using new digital photographic techniques and satellite distribution to regional printing plants. The *New York Times* and the *Wall Street Journal* use similar techniques to produce and distribute those newspapers nationally.

Much of the attractive design that now appears in newspapers came from research conducted during the late 1980s by several newspaper chains. Publishers wanted to find out, in a scientific fashion, what readers would read and what attracted them to newspapers. Thus began the new period of market-oriented newspapers, which emphasized design.

Knight Ridder launched a project at the *Boca Raton News* in southern Florida that led to major changes in newspaper design, although Knight Ridder papers enjoy local autonomy in applying the design lessons learned through market research. Another major effort by a group to get its newspapers in touch with their readers and look to the future was Gannett's News 2000 project. In June 1991, Gannett introduced the program to 230 Gannett executives, instructing each publisher to address the issues that were in

desk

A newspaper department with an editor in charge. Most newspapers, for example, have a city desk and a sports desk.

beat

A regularly covered topic of news such as police and science. Reporters contact sources on a beat regularly to check for events that might be newsworthy. Desks have one or more beats connected with them.

spot news

News based on one-time events such as accidents or crimes.

feature story

Story that emphasizes activities of people instead of "hard news events" such as crime and disasters.

design

Visual elements, including headlines, photographs, and graphics, organized to make the newspaper interesting and easy to read.

Newspaper design has increasingly turned to the tabloid format to save on printing costs.

the minds of the community. Using surveys, **focus groups,** and readership studies, Gannett staff developed comprehensive designs for each paper. Many of the changes involve presentation, including dramatic designs, **breakout boxes,** and fewer stories that jump from page to page.

Reflecting the importance of design in the industry is the formation of the Society for News Design, an international professional organization with more than 2,600 members in the United States, Canada, and fifty other countries. Members include editors, designers, graphic artists, publishers, illustrators, art directors, photographers, advertising artists, website designers, students, and faculty.

Newspaper Content

Newspapers contain a variety of information, most of which is not news. The information falls into five broad categories: advertising, opinion material, news, graphics, and photojournalism. Each category has several subcategories.

Advertising   Advertising in print newspapers includes three major types: classified ads, display ads, and inserts. Classified advertisements are the lists of ads set in small type that advertise jobs, items for sale, and garage sales. Display advertisements, found throughout the paper, incorporate photographs, drawings, and large type. Inserts, which are similar to small catalogs, most often advertise merchandise for sale at department stores and supermarkets.

Opinion   Opinion appears on the editorial and op-ed (short for "opposite the editorial") pages. On these pages, editorial writers, political **pundits,** and local citizens express their opinions about current political and social issues. These pages make up the heart of the marketplace of ideas. For example, the opinion pages of the *Lansing State Journal* carry letters, columns, and editorials about conflicts between Michigan State University students and permanent residents in East Lansing. Permanent residents want limits on late-night parties, whereas students want lower priced housing. Ideas exchanged through editorial material allow the community to explore better ways for these two groups to live together.

News   The bulk of nonadvertising information is news. News includes features, current events, and investigative series. Because newspapers tend to emphasize local news, proximity is important for most staff-prepared stories.

Graphics   The term *graphics* covers a range of newspaper content, from the information graphics that present data in tables and graphs to comics and political cartoons. Newspapers have included graphics for more than two centuries, starting with political cartoons before the American Revolution. Currently, newspapers use graphics extensively to create visual interest and to communicate complex ideas and data.

The comics and political cartoons remain the mainstay of newspaper graphics. According to the Newspaper Association of America, more than 70 million people in the United States read newspaper comics and look at political cartoons every day. Comics provide entertainment and a lighter look at some of people's problems. Political cartoons comment on political, social, and cultural events and the people who influence those events. Comics appeal to the consumer market; political cartoons contribute to the marketplace of ideas. The difference between the two is not always obvious because some comics aimed at entertaining, such as "Dilbert," also provide commentary on social and cultural issues.

focus group

Group of individuals representing different interests who are assembled to discuss a topic. A form of research used to get in-depth information, but not information that is representative of an entire audience.

breakout box

Shorter pieces of information, often direct quotes, that are connected to the larger story being covered. They are used to emphasize specific points and for design relief.

pundit

An expert on a particular topic; a person consulted because of his or her knowledge.

Reaching an International Audience

With their predominantly local, community focus, most U.S. newspapers do not worry about attracting a global readership. Two notable exceptions are the *International Herald Tribune,* owned by the New York Times Co., and the *Wall Street Journal*'s international edition. Both target wealthy, highly educated, middle-aged, European and Asian senior managers who often travel. These business people help shape the global economy and speak the international language of business: English. They also want news they can download into their PDAs and mobile phones, a service both papers provide.

Launched in 1887, the *International Herald Tribune* was the first newspaper to be distributed by airplane, taking the morning paper from London to Paris. In its early days, it was read mostly by Americans living abroad. Distributed in 180 countries, the *Herald* publishes the work of its own correspondents, and reprints stories from the *New York Times.* 60 percent of the *Herald Tribune*'s readers are in Europe and 35 percent in Asia. About a third of those are Americans residing overseas. The paper's business coverage provides a global perspective on technology, European politics, mergers and acquisitions, media, and communications. The *Herald Tribune* also has partnerships with newspapers in other countries to provide editions with local sections. For example, in Russia it is published with the *Moscow Times,* in Korea with *JoongAng Daily,* and in Japan with *Asahi Shimbun.*

Owned by Dow Jones & Co, the *Wall Street Journal* has a total circulation of 2.6 million. That figure includes its Asian edition, launched in 1976, and its European edition, launched in 1983. Like the *Herald Tribune,* it has partnerships with papers in other countries, especially in Central and South America. Global advertisers can also take advantage of deals involving Dow Jones' financial news channel, CNBC. In 2005, the *Journal* announced that it would begin publishing its foreign editions in a smaller tabloid form. Like many other newspapers, the *Journal* was hit with declining ad revenues and made the move to save on printing costs.

Of other newspapers, *USA Today* lacks an international perspective but is published in sixty countries. Japan's *Yomiori Shimbun* is the most read paper in the world, demonstrating that an international readership is not necessarily focused on the United States.

Source: Susan Paterno, "International Intrigue," *American Journalism Review,* February/March 2006, ajr.org.

Any newspaper editor can explain the importance of a comics section to readers. About 95 percent of all daily newspapers carry a separate and identifiable comics section on Sunday,[39] and more people read comics regularly than read sports, editorials, letters to the editor, food pages, and in-depth investigative reports.[40]

The use of information graphics boomed in the late 1980s and became a newspaper mainstay because of offset printing, the use of computers, and the development of *USA Today.* Information graphics such as tables, maps, and graphs have become so important that the number of newspaper graphic artists and designers has grown significantly. Most important news stories have a designer who packages the story, and the nature and extent of graphics and photographs available to tell the story can affect the location of the story. At many papers, a story without good art (graphics and photography) will not make the front page.

Photojournalism   Photojournalism, which integrates words and photographs, attempts to explain people's behavior and the nature of the world. Effective photojournalism involves skilled editing and assumes that informing the public is essential.

Photojournalism is capable of powerfully affecting an audience's interpretation of an event and often defines public memory. Many people's memories of September 11, 2001, are defined by the photograph of firefighters raising the flag at the site of the World Trade Center.

Photojournalism may be more critical to society than other forms of photography because its goal is to alter our vision of the world and it is mass distributed. Photojournalism opens up arenas of action and images that people would otherwise never see.

TRENDS

The greatest challenge facing the newspaper industry today is the same one facing book publishers: the transition from print to digital media that has changed readers and the ways they read. Many newspapers cling to old ways, not only in a reluctance to embrace technological innovation, but also in a lack of diversity in the newsroom. At a time when media conglomerates drive for more profits, journalists emphasize the importance of maintaining depth of coverage, good writing, and the importance of the news itself to democracy and citizenship. They also see value in the fast delivery of content that the Internet makes available. The troubles in the industry with falling circulations and ad revenues are intensifying a perceived need for newspapers to change rapidly to accommodate the technological and cultural developments around them.

Technology: News Online

Since the mid-1990s, some 1,500 newspapers have acquired an online presence, but their ability to produce any significant profit from the venture remains unclear. Online ad revenues are growing, but still account for only 3 percent to 5 percent of total revenues.[41] Readers access the news for free on many sites, including Google, which provides an extensive, timely news service. An exception is the *Wall Street Journal*, which successfully charges for an online subscription for access to its full online content. In 2005, banking on its excellence and reputation, the *New York Times* announced that it would charge a paid subscription for opeds on NYT.com, which would also allow readers to chat with columnists and access video and audio of them. Another scheme, used by many papers, is to provide the week's news for free, but charge for older stories in an electronic archive. Most newspapers still struggle with a way to turn online news into a product.

Another issue with online delivery is staffing. The *New York Times* was the first major national paper to merge its online and print staffs, shortly before the paper announced substantial layoffs.[42] It was following the pattern of many other newspapers that had already made a similar move. With serious cutbacks in staffing at many metropolitan newspapers, harried journalists in newsrooms are now expected to publish online content 24/7. News organizations are experimenting with further convergences of newspapers and online sites with television stations. As newspapers invest in technology but reduce staff, observers wonder about the fate of ambitious, cutting-edge journalism.

Major newspaper organizations are setting their sights well beyond their traditional mission to provide the news. In 2005, the New York Times Co. bought About.com, an online encyclopedia of topics with "human guides" that create its content. Industry analysts expected that links from About.com to the *New York Times* and other company-owned websites would triple. In similar moves, the *Wall Street Journal* bought Monster.com, the Washington Post Company bought *Slate,* and Rupert Murdoch's News Corp. bought MySpace, drawing complaints that the popular site would soon be conformist and mainstream.

Technology: ePaper

Another effort to win readers was the *New York Times*'s partnership with Microsoft to promote ePaper, a portable advice that allows readers to turn pages of the downloaded newspaper electronically.

Culture: Young Readers

As in the book industry, newspapers must begin to attract young readers to ensure their future. Before television gained popularity, young people learned the newspaper-reading habit from their parents. With television's arrival, families began to move away from newspapers as their source of entertainment. A 1999 study found that only 3 percent of the 1,200 teenage participants thought that reading was "enjoyable" or "entertaining."[43] Various strategies have been tried to lure young readers back to newspapers, including specially targeted websites, niche tabloids, front page redesign, and reading programs in schools.

Content is the key to attracting young readers, or any readers for that matter, and newspapers use market research to help them identify the content that readers want. In 2005, the Readership Institute, with the *Minneapolis Star Tribune,* conducted a study of under-30s to see what attracted them. They developed an experimental "experience paper" with the following hot buttons: It gave its target audience something to talk about, stimulated their sense of surprise and humor, and looked out for their interests. From this experiment, the Institute suggested that young adults prefer papers that are designed sensitively for them.[44]

Culture: Diversity

Larger newspaper organizations have become much more interested in attracting growing ethnic and minority populations by offering special language editions and other features. But newspaper staffs are predominantly white, and partly for this reason, these populations mostly find their own press more credible. A serious question exists as to whether a white, mainstream press can speak for racial and ethnic groups.

In 1978 the American Society of Newspaper Editors (ASNE) realized that journalists who make decisions about what and how to cover news should be representative of groups who might read the newspaper. However, racial minorities made up only 3.95 percent of newsroom employees. As a result, the ASNE announced its goal of having the percentage of journalists who are minorities equal the percentage of minorities in the general population by 2000. By 2001, 12.07 percent of daily newspaper journalists were minorities, but minorities represent more than a quarter of the general population. The ASNE revised its goal and set the year of reaching equivalence at 2025. In 2005, the percentage had increased only slightly, to 13.87 percent.

The progress of newspapers in increasing diversity continues to be dismal. In 2004, a Knight Foundation study found that 73 percent of the 200 largest newspapers in the country employed fewer minorities than they did in 1990.[45] At the campus newspapers of 19 of the nation's highest ranked universities, only 2.6 percent of editors were African American. At 17 other universities with undergraduate programs in journalism, the percentage was 4.4 percent.[46] Native Americans make up only one half of 1 percent of all newsroom employees. Only 309 Native Americans work on mainstream daily newspapers.[47]

Not only have changes been slow, but newsroom managers and minorities often have different perceptions of newsroom reality. A survey conducted by the National Association of Black Journalists (NABJ) indicates that African-American journalists feel that they work in an unfriendly, unsupportive environment. Although 94 percent of newsroom managers said that their organization showed a serious commitment to retaining and promoting black journalists, 67 percent of the black journalists disagreed. NABJ's investigation of the coverage of the 1992 Los Angeles riots found that the lack of African-American decision makers in determining story coverage was a critical problem according to black reporters who were assigned to cover the riots. Many black reporters indicate that they are afraid to bring up racial issues because they believe it will hurt their careers. Although many newsroom executives seemed surprised

In the early twentieth century, newsrooms were all-male bastions. Although efforts to integrate them have been slow and less successful than desired, today's newsrooms include minority and female journalists as well as white males.

Discussing Trends

Communities have ties to their newspapers. Newspaper associations have repeatedly discovered this when trying to analyze credibility and other factors. The challenge for newspaper owners is how to capture a younger audience, how to use technology in productive ways, and how to diversify to attract wider populations. Otherwise, as the now over-fifty age group becomes the over-seventy group, newspaper audiences could dwindle even further. Some of the questions that need to be answered include:

■ If you were a newspaper publisher, how would you attract young readers?

■ What would cause you to read a newspaper?
■ Do you think newspaper publishers could use the Internet more effectively to build audience loyalty?
■ If so, how would you do that?
■ Are newspapers worth preserving, or are they a dying medium?
■ If you were analyzing these trends as a newspaper editor, how would you address the issues?

at this claim, Geneva Overholser, former editor of the *Des Moines Register,* said that it is not just blacks who are afraid to speak up in newsrooms, but "[w]omen are afraid to speak out, young people are afraid to speak out. I certainly know that people of color are afraid to speak out."[48]

SUMMARY

■ Newspapers historically focused on their local communities and provided information about local events. However, they also carried national and international news, and Congress debated early the relative merits of local versus national circulation of newspapers.

■ During the revolutionary period, newspapers helped to develop political rhetoric that supported independence. In doing so, they were seldom tolerant of competing voices.

■ With developments in manufacturing during the nineteenth century, newspapers began to carry national advertising and expand their markets.

■ Newspaper markets today are determined by several components, including the number of choices available within a geographic area, the probability of product substitution, and barriers to entering the market.

■ Changing demographics make it difficult for newspaper editors to understand the components of the market. Publishers can no longer assume that middle-class readers will subscribe to the newspaper.

■ Newspaper readers now have many choices. They can choose to read a newspaper, subscribe to cable television, listen to the radio, watch network television, or subscribe to a computer online database service.

■ Newspaper content includes advertising, opinion material, and news. It comes from newspaper staff reports, wire and news services, and feature syndicates.

■ To combat changes in the markets, newspaper executives are trying new approaches. Some newspapers use survey research and focus groups to determine the needs of their particular communities and then target their reporting and writing to those needs. Others have reorganized their newsgathering operations, relying less on institutional news and more on topically defined news.

■ Newspapers will remain an important component of the media mix, as long as their staffs take advantage of new technologies and ensure that their content serves their audiences.

■ Newspaper publishers recognize the opportunities of online delivery of information, but they have not yet determined how to be profitable using this new technology.

■ Newspaper owners must learn to attract younger and more diverse audiences if they are to maintain a steady audience base.

■ Many ethnic and minority readers turn first to the ethnic fairness press for news. They distrust the credibility and fairness of white, mainstream newspapers.

NAVIGATING THE WEB Newspapers

Websites about newspapers contain information about the industry and online versions of newspapers. With the Internet, a person can access newspapers from all over the world and find articles and data about the industry.

Associated Press Managing Editors
apme.com
The APME is maintained by newspaper managing editors who are members of the Associated Press, which is a news service that serves news media around the world. The site carries information about a variety of news media on the "Industry News" page, and it has links to several other newspaper industry pages, including the Associated Press web site.

Editor & Publisher
editorandpublisher.com
Editor & Publisher is the oldest journal in the United States devoted to the newspaper industry. On its web-site, a user can find articles and statistics related to newspapers, including trends, circulation, and advertising. Some content on the site is available only to subscribers.

New America Media
news.newamericamedia.org
A collaboration of 700 ethnic news organizations, the New American Media provides news stories, polls, and a directory of ethnic media.

Newspaper Association of America
naa.org
The NAA represents more than 1,500 newspapers in the United States and Canada. Its site provides a variety of information about marketing, public policy, diversity, and operations in the newspaper industry. The NAA "Facts about Newspapers" page carries detailed data about the industry in the United States and Canada.

QUESTIONS FOR REVIEW

1. Discuss the significance of colonial newspaper editors in the debate over independence and revolution.
2. List the characteristics of the penny press.
3. What is a newspaper market?
4. If most newspapers are making a substantial profit, why are publishers worried?
5. Why are newspapers facing problems with credibility?

ISSUES TO THINK ABOUT

1. If newspapers have traditionally appealed to local readers, what should they do to attract young readers who will make up the buying public during the next 10 to 20 years?
2. Why should newspaper newsrooms reflect the demographic makeup of society? How can newspapers reach the goal of having newsroom demographics reflect those in society?
3. If you, as an editor, were to redefine how your newspaper was organized, what ideas might you have for change?
4. Suggest some innovative ways to integrate newspapers with the Internet.

SUGGESTED READINGS

Bagdikian, Ben. *The Media Monopoly,* 4th ed. (Boston: Beacon Press, 1997).

Bogart, Leo. *The Press and the Public: Who Reads What, When, Where and Why in American Newspapers,* 2nd ed. (Hillsdale, NJ: Lawrence Erlbaum Associates, 1989).

Martin, Shannon E., and David A. Copeland, eds. *The Function of Newspapers in Society: A Global Perspective.* (Westport, Conn.: Praeger, 2003).

Underwood, Doug. *When MBAs Rule the Newsroom: How Marketers and Managers Are Reshaping Today's Media* (New York: Columbia University Press, 1993).

Wallace, Aurora. *Newspapers and the Making of Modern America: A History* (Westport, Conn.: Greenwood, 2005).

Woods, Keith, ed. *2001 Best Newspaper Writing Winners* (St. Petersburg, FL: Poynter Institute, 2001).

CHAPTER 4

Magazines

Weddings are big business for Martha Stewart and Condé Nast. Over 2 million couples walk down the aisle every year after spending an average of $27,000 per wedding, for a total of $50 billion.[1] To get ideas for the most extravagant day of their lives, many of them read magazines like *Martha Stewart Weddings* or Condé Nast's *Brides, Modern Bride,* or *Elegant Bride.*

There, brides find pleasurable dream worlds of picture perfect days and couples dressed in haute couture.

But wedding magazines are more than pictures and stories. They are advertising engines that market fashions, invitations, flowers, decorations, and honeymoon packages. As a product of Martha Stewart Living Omnimedia, *Martha Stewart Weddings* can advertise across media platforms, including the company's radio station, television shows, and e-commerce websites that sell greeting cards, flowers, and CDs of wedding music. Similarly, Condé Nast operates brides.com, where visitors can feel part of a community on forums about tuxedos and wedding cakes. The company also sponsors bridal fairs with marketers, party planners, and etiquette experts. Couples will only read wedding magazines during a year of planning, but advertisers expect them to develop brand loyalties that will last into the future.

In magazines, more than any other medium, advertisements and editorial content flow together to create an experience. Usually featuring white, middle- to upper-class heterosexual couples, wedding magazines present audiences with conventions of what a wedding should

KEY CONCEPTS

- Magazines as a Unifying Force in American Life
- The Industrial Revolution and Magazine Technology
- Era of Democratic Reading
- Specialization in Publishing
- Muckrakers
- Consumer and Business Magazines
- Market Segments for Magazine Advertisers
- Magazine Start-Up and Financing
- Magazine Publishing Process

be like. They therefore reinforce social codes as they attract readers to buy a vision, convincing them of the right way to look, act, and think. Audiences develop a shared knowledge and worldview; that, in turn, informs magazine contents in a two-way flow. Therefore, magazines and other media forms don't just appeal to already existing audiences, but create new ones.

Magazines have social power, but their readers do, too. Readers from minority and ethnic groups may not see themselves represented in the experience of magazines that feature only Euro-American models and put the magazine aside. Readers may misunderstand, reject or refine ideas to suit their own tastes. Therefore, publishers work to identify the desires of audiences and involve them in the magazine experience as best they can. Today, the trend is toward specialized magazines targeted to highly specific audiences, such as aging baby boomers, gay parents, or "tweenies" (eight- to twelve-year-old girls).

Throughout our nation's history, magazines have been collectors, producers, and distributors of social knowledge. They have also been aids to economic expansion. These activities still continue, but magazines must adapt to changing demographics and rapidly evolving technologies in a global scene.

In a world in which individuals have unprecedented choice regarding which media to buy and use, magazine industry personnel have to consider the following issues:

- How are converging technologies affecting magazine content, advertising, audience, design, and distribution?

- What is the balance between editorial content and advertising in magazines? To what extent are they converging?

- What are the changing demographics that may affect the magazine industry? What specialized magazines might emerge in response?

- As magazines expand into international markets, what issues do they face? What kind of magazines appeal most to global audiences?

MAGAZINES IN AMERICAN LIFE

The magazine business, like all business ventures, has been dependent on supply and demand. Once magazines became established in the British colonies in America, they successfully occupied a niche within the world of print and publishing as the nation's conscience, the conveyors of social knowledge. Although newspapers supplied quick information and books offered professional materials and fiction, magazines provided the long, thoughtful essays that encouraged people to think about politics, to plan their travels, and to engage in debates about social policies. At first magazines catered to the elite, but they soon began to reach a broader class and became a *unifying force in American life.*

Key Concept

Magazines as a unifying force in American life
Magazines have allowed people across class, social, and racial divisions to read common material, thus providing the basis for mutual understanding.

Magazines Experience Slow Growth

The colonists were eager for information from their home countries and from adjacent colonies where they had family and friends. They imported books from England and read the fledgling newspapers in the colonies. Magazines developed more slowly because they were expensive, postal regulations did not favor their distribution until the mid-1800s, and early America lacked a professional class of writers to supply articles.

In fact, it was a full fifty years after the first newspaper was published in the colonies that Andrew Bradford sold the first magazine: *American Magazine, or A*

Magazines in Your Life

Do Magazines Bring People Together?

As you read this chapter, consider how magazines shape audiences. Think about the types of magazines you, your friends, and your family read. Are your family's magazines so specialized that you don't enjoy them? What about your magazines? Would your parents or your children read them? What kinds of magazines bring people together? What perspectives and tastes do your favorite magazines convey?

Types of Magazines	Titles You Read	Titles Your Family Reads	Other People Who Read Your Magazines
News			
General interest			
Specialized			
Men's			
Women's			

Monthly View of the Political State of the British Colonies. It first appeared on February 13, 1741. Although Benjamin Franklin had intended for his *General Magazine, and Historical Chronicle, for All the British Plantations in America* to be the first magazine in the colonies, Bradford's was published three days earlier. Bradford's magazine lasted three issues; Franklin's survived six. The first American magazines boldly published articles that appeared in British magazines and rarely used local material.

Reading magazines was a pastime of the colonial elite, who not only had the education to read but also the time. Because most colonists were engaged either in subsistence agriculture or the trades, they had little leisure time for reading. Inadequate distribution and printing methods contributed to the slow growth of magazines. Magazines never enjoyed the favored postal rates to which newspapers quickly grew accustomed. To reach audiences outside the growing towns of Boston, Philadelphia, and New York, magazines traveled by stagecoach, which had to contend with rough and sometimes washed-out roads. Most publishing operations were family owned, sometimes with husband and wife sharing equal responsibilities, and profits could be earned more easily from printing, stationery sales, or newspaper publishing than by publishing magazines.

Magazines in the Nineteenth Century

Although only twelve magazines existed at the beginning of the nineteenth century, by 1850 that number had grown to about 685. Despite a severe setback during the Civil War, the industry experienced a sharp turnaround, with 3,300 magazines in circulation by 1885. The **Industrial Revolution** that began in England in the late eighteenth century had a major impact on **magazine technology.**

Key Concept

The Industrial Revolution and magazine technology In the mid- to late nineteenth century, developed societies were completing a transition from an economy based on handwork and agriculture to one based on mechanized industry. The shift from handwork to mechanized production increased efficiency and radically lowered the cost of printing, which made magazines and newspapers affordable for a large population.

Mathew Brady and his photographers chronicled the Civil War. Magazines such as *Frank Leslie's Illustrated Weekly* carried engravings of the photographs to inform the nation of the carnage of the war.

The change from an agricultural to an industrial society after the Civil War made magazines cheaper, more attractive, and more efficient to produce. New printing technologies, including the steam press, **stereotyping,** and **electrotyping,** sped up production. These innovations also reduced the amount of heavy labor needed, often allowing young women, who could be paid less, to handle many aspects of publishing, thus reducing labor costs. Papermaking machines allowed paper to be produced in continuous rolls. Photographic and engraving developments also were important to magazines because they allowed publishers to use engravings and drawings more frequently at less cost.

Technology improved transportation and contributed to an advanced postal system that facilitated faster and less expensive distribution of magazines across wider geographical areas. Newspapers could rely on local forms of distribution, but magazines were expensive and needed a wider geographical base from which to attract readers.

In 1845, a five-ounce magazine cost six and one-half cents to mail; by 1852, the same magazine could be mailed for five cents. If postage was paid in advance, charges were reduced by half. Postal laws were even more favorable by 1863, setting the rate at one cent for four-ounce magazines published less than weekly, with rates rising proportionally for each additional four ounces.[2]

stereotyping

The use of a paper mat to make cylindrical molds for printing.

electrotyping

A metal plate used in letterpress printing by coating a lead or plastic mold of the page to be printed.

Social Impact A rapidly growing population, a steady migration to cities, and national distribution of products helped consolidate the magazine audience and create an *era of democratic reading.* As manufacturing made the transition from locally produced products to nationally distributed brand names, magazines became the perfect national advertising vehicle. They circulated to all regions and appealed to national businesses and national audiences. Magazines gave meaning to situations and helped readers understand significant social, economic, geographic, industrial, and educational events. Children were expected to read in order to become good citizens, and young adults strived to expand their knowledge in order to advance their careers. The search for social knowledge was important to those seeking upward mobility.

A new generation of educated, middle-class women looked to magazines for advice on fashion and home economics. Magazines began blending content with advertising and product endorsement for this audience. They were becoming the most important group of consumers.

With this historical context in mind, think about the magazines you listed in Magazines in Your Life at the beginning of this chapter. Can you think of magazines you read today that help you understand significant social and political events?

Quality Monthlies The showcase magazines of the mid-nineteenth century were the quality monthlies, known for their travelogues, light fiction, and political commentary, as well as for their elegant covers and finely drawn illustrations. Among these were *Century Magazine, Scribner's, Atlantic Monthly,* and *Harper's.* Those magazines helped to develop a class of American writers and created a forum for criticism of American art and literature. By 1870, *Harper's,* which relied heavily on British authors, had a circulation of 150,000. This magazine, owned by The Harper Brothers, Inc., provided an excellent advertising vehicle for books produced by the company. The *Atlantic Monthly* was one of its chief competitors, building its reputation on American authors such as Ralph Waldo Emerson.

Financing a New Industry

Advertising not only provided the funds for magazine growth but also provoked social and cultural controversy. Some magazine publishers shunned advertising, believing that ads for such items as **patent medicines** cheapened their product. However, some publications sold space publicizing contraceptives and abortion-inducing drugs, forcing readers to confront the issue of unwanted pregnancies. Magazines such as *Ladies' Home Journal* eventually abandoned patent medicine advertising and published articles to educate middle-class women about the alcohol content of drugs they routinely took.

General-interest and women's magazines dominated the nineteenth-century market; however, publishers began to recognize the value of **market segments,** or specific categories of readers. By midcentury, publishers began to develop specialized magazines, targeting particular social and economic interests. Early *specialization in publishing* focused on subjects such as southern living, public affairs, agriculture, antislavery, medicine, law, education, banking, and the insurance industry. By the end of the nineteenth century, specialized audiences included druggists, hardware dealers, railroad enthusiasts, telegraphers, coach makers, children, and literary types. In the twentieth century, targeting specific market segments enabled magazines to survive economic hard times and competition with new media such as radio and television.

The best example of large-scale specialization and technological innovation appeared in the specialized market of philosophy and religion. The American Bible Society and antislavery societies circulated publications as an integral part of a widespread religious revival that preceded the Civil War. These societies were the first to use technological innovations. They used newly developed, inexpensive methods of printing and expanded the distribution of their messages to create the illusion that their movements were larger than they really were.

> **Key Concept**
>
> **Specialization in publishing** As early as the mid-nineteenth century, magazines adopted the practice of targeting specific segments of an audience rather than appealing to the general public. Magazines continue this trend in the twenty-first century.

Mass Production and Assembly-Line Magazines

The magazine industry mushroomed, fueled by technological change and a rising middle class. The technological improvements allowed magazines to increase their circulations. By 1890, 4,400 magazines were being published and circulated to eighteen million readers. Circulation reached sixty-four million fifteen years later. In 1915, advertising revenues for general-interest and farm publications combined topped $28 million. The elite magazines of the nineteenth century, such as *Harper's* and *Godey's Lady's Book,* gave way to mass-produced, assembly-line products.

Magazines exploited the social trends and changing values that emerged with the rising middle class. Public education, opportunities for college education, and business expanded. In this new world of rapidly developing products and new

patent medicines

Packaged drugs that can be obtained without a prescription. Before the Food and Drug Administration was created, these drugs often contained large amounts of alcohol and sometimes opium.

market segments

The target audience. The group of individuals a magazine selects to target for its readership.

technology, national advertisers bought magazine space to appeal to the middle-class potential consumers of new products.

Publishers strove to achieve large circulations, realizing that advertisers would tolerate higher advertising rates if they could gain wide exposure for their products. Increased advertising rates enabled publishers to reduce subscription prices, which made magazines available to a larger audience.

Magazines began to define their audiences broadly, but they remained an expensive medium. The quality monthlies sold for a quarter, whereas a newspaper sold for two or three cents. However, in the late 1890s, the muckraking magazines dropped their prices to ten cents in order to broaden their targeted audience. The *Ladies' Home Journal* had more than a million circulation in 1904, but until World War I few magazines fared as well.[3] Among those that did were *Collier's, Cosmopolitan, McCall's,* and the *Saturday Evening Post.* Most of the successful magazines of the first two decades of the twentieth century were general-interest magazines such as *McClure's, American Magazine, Independent, Literary Digest, Leslie's Weekly, Scribner's Magazine, Century Magazine,* and the *Saturday Evening Post.*

Before television became a nationwide visual medium for mass audiences, general-interest family magazines, such as the *Saturday Evening Post* and *Collier's,* were dominant and accessible forms of visual information.

The Muckrakers

The dramatic social force on the magazine front was the inexpensive muckraking magazines. Despite massive economic growth and an improved standard of living during the late nineteenth and early twentieth centuries, a growing recognition of corporate greed and political corruption provided opportunity for criticism. The magazine industry began to attack corporate giants and their struggle for political power. Theodore Roosevelt, despite his own inclinations toward reform, called these writers **muckrakers.** Roosevelt likened the writers to the man with the muckrake in John Bunyan's seventeenth-century *Pilgrim's Progress:* "A man who could look no way but downward with the muckrake in his hands; who was offered the celestial crown for his muckrake, but would neither look up nor regard the crown he was offered, but continued to rake the filth of the floor." Through the **dime magazine,** crusading journalists reached almost three million readers. They used the magazines as responsible tools for public education, describing the close relationship of politics and government and pointing out the advantages of the wealthy and privileged classes. *McClure's,* for example, published articles on the consolidation of the oil industry, corruption in state government, and right-to-work laws. Such magazines, including *McClure's,* the *Munsey,* and the *American Magazine,* thrived until the start of World War I.[4] Although exceedingly popular, the scandal magazines were relatively short lived. It is possible that by 1915 when the magazines lost popularity the public was tired of reform or believed that corruption had subsided. Perhaps the public had shifted its attention to the looming war in Europe. Nevertheless, the muckraking magazines were a social force that informed readers about corporate and political behavior inappropriate for a democratic society.

dime magazine

Magazine that cost ten cents and appealed to a broad class of readers. These magazines were less expensive than the quality monthlies that preceded them.

35 millimeter

Photographic film that has a frame for exposure 35 millimeters in length. It is used for both still and moving pictures.

fast film

Generic term for the film that photographers use to stop fast action. Does not need long exposure to light to capture the photographic image.

News and Pictures Revolutionize Magazines

Issues of social reform did not belong to the muckrakers alone. As the Kodak box camera began to revolutionize public photography after 1900, the development of the **35-millimeter** camera and **fast film** created new opportunities for photojournalism, which was an extension of the type of photography social reformers had used between 1880 and 1915 to document the negative social effects of the Industrial Revolution.

Some journalists tried to expose these problems through articles and illustrations. Muckrakers, who often were magazine journalists, and their newspaper counterparts attacked corporations and fought for changes in labor, agricultural, and business laws. Jacob A. Riis and Lewis W. Hine photographed the plight of the poor

The photojournalism magazines captured emotion as no medium had before. Here on the pages of *Life*, C. P. O. Graham Jackson plays "Goin' Home," expressing his own and the nation's sorrow at the death in 1945 of Franklin Delano Roosevelt.

and homeless to show what can happen to unskilled workers in an unregulated capitalist economic system.

In the 1920s, social documentary photography was greatly enhanced with the introduction of the small Leica camera, made by E. Leitz of Germany. With the Leica, a photographer could work unnoticed while recording a scene. In addition, film became "faster," needing less light and less time to record an image. These technological changes led to flourishing picture magazines, first in Germany, then England, and then the United States. Magazines that used high-quality paper and printing processes benefited more than newspapers from the new technology.

Henry Luce, who later developed the Time, Inc., publishing empire, capitalized on the need for news, the development of the 35-millimeter camera, and the public's desire for interpretation of social and political events. He and Briton Hadden started *Time* magazine in 1923, at first clipping and rewriting items from daily newspapers and later adding their own staff and building the weekly into one of the most renowned news vehicles in the nation. In 1930, when the Great Depression was already under way, Luce successfully founded the business magazine *Fortune.* Although some thought he was foolhardy to initiate such a venture at that time, he recognized that businesspeople and the public needed to understand the consequences of business decisions.

Then, in 1936, he created *Life. Life* and Gardner Cowles's *Look* became showcases for photojournalists who chronicled the later years of the Depression and set the standard for war photography during World War II. Unlike photographers in previous wars, *Life* and *Look* photographers, with their small cameras and fast film, could photograph action. They conveyed the horrors and glory of war, including the blood, effort, and grief, transporting readers to the battlefields.

Roy Stryker of the Farm Security Administration employed talented photographers in this New Deal program, designed to put artists to work and to photograph the Great Depression. Many of the photographers later became famous.

Perhaps the most notable group of photographers during the depression years worked for photographer Roy Stryker and a government agency, the Farm Security Administration (FSA). Photographers such as Arthur Rothstein, Walker Evans, Dorothea Lange, and Gordon Parks photographed migrant farmers in California, African-American sharecroppers in the South, drought-stricken farmers in Oklahoma and Texas, and federal work projects throughout the country. The FSA photographers' records of that period demonstrate how effectively a camera can function as a sociological commentator and historical recorder.

Magazines in Our Lives

1741. First magazine is published in America.

1800s. Increasing literacy and technology enhance magazine growth.

1850. Number of magazines published in the United States reaches 685.

1863. Price to ship magazines by mail declines.

1890. 4,400 magazines reach 18 million circulation.

1893. *McClure's* starts mass circulation of muckraking magazines.

1904. *Ladies' Home Journal* passes 1 million circulation.

1915. Magazine muckraking dies out.

1922. *Time* becomes first news-weekly.

1936. *Life* becomes first U.S. picture magazine.

1400–1700	1800	1860	1880	1900	1920	1930

1620. Pilgrims land at Plymouth Rock.

1690. *Publick Occurrences* is published in Boston.

1741. First magazine is published in America.

1776–1783. American Revolution

1830s. The penny press becomes the first truly mass medium in the United States.

1861–1865. American Civil War

1892. Thomas Edison's lab develops the kinetoscope.

1914–1918. World War I

1915. *The Birth of a Nation* marks the start of the modern movie industry.

1920. KDKA in Pittsburgh gets the first commercial radio license.

1930s. The Great Depression

1939. TV is demonstrated at the New York World's Fair.

1939–1945. World War II

Cultural Milestones

Maturation and Competition

Despite improved printing technology and the audience appeal of photojournalism, magazines struggled through the 1930s. A massive economic depression, in which one-third of U.S. workers were unemployed, resulted in lower advertising and subscription revenues. Although the end of the war in 1945 generated prosperity and record amounts of buying, it also resulted in rising costs, including an 89 percent increase in postal rates.

Advertising—the golden financier of magazines—became a commodity for which to fight. It had fueled the magazine industry, but as radio and television entered the

1941–1945. *Life* plays important role in reporting World War II.

1950s. TV takes national ads from magazines.

1969. *Saturday Evening Post* closes.

1970s. Niche magazines begin boom that continues into 1990s.

1972. *Life* closes as a monthly. *Ms.* magazine starts publication.

1990s. Magazines begin publishing on the Internet.

1990s. Magazines use customized printing to target audiences for advertisers.

2000s. Magazine consolidation continues but at slower pace.

2000s. Magazine companies look for international growth.

1940	1950	1960	1970	1980	1990	2000

1949. First commercial electronic computer is produced.

Early 1950s. Rock 'n' roll begins.

1969. First person lands on the moon.

1970s. VCR is developed.

1989–1991. Cold War ends and the USSR is dissolved.

Late 1980s. National Science Foundation creates the basis of the Internet.

1996. Telecommunications Act

2000. Presidential election nearly tied.

2001. Terrorist attacks on New York and Washington, D.C.

2003. War with Iraq.

media picture, magazines began to lose their competitive edge. Now they had to share advertising resources not only with newspapers but also with new and dynamic media that captured people's ears as well as eyes. Ads with sound and motion made stronger impressions on consumers than print ads. And the cost for television ads was cheaper: In 1971 the expense per thousand persons reached through *Life* was $7.71; by means of television, it was about $3.60.

Three historic general-interest magazines ceased publication with the growing popularity of television. The magazines failed not because of loss of circulation but because of loss of advertising. Although the *Saturday Evening Post* had a paid circulation of 6 million and a **pass-along rate** of 14 million readers, it ceased publication

pass-along rate

The total number of readers who read a magazine regularly, including those who read copies that were given, or passed along, to them by other readers.

in 1969. *Look*'s paid circulation was 8 million with an estimated 18 million readers when it folded in 1971. *Life,* which boasted a circulation of 7 million and was read by 21 million people, folded in 1972. (*Life* was later revived as a feature magazine published monthly.) These giants had retained huge circulation lists, but they lacked the advertising money needed to keep them afloat financially. Whereas television's share of national advertising more than doubled in the 1960s, from $1.5 billion to $3.5 billion, magazines' share went from less than $1.0 billion to only $1.2 billion.

Specialization, however, kept the magazine industry in business by targeting specific audiences and addressing changing **demographics.** Specialized magazines thrived because, rather than competing for the same audiences as broadcast television, they delivered to advertisers audiences with particular interests and consumer habits. For example, advertisers can count on subscribers to *Skiing* to buy advertised skiing products. Particularly successful niche magazines have addressed changing demographics, trends, and technologies. For example, they have targeted increasing numbers of working and single women, emphasized fitness and health, and exploited the popularity of computers.

Key Concept

Consumer and business magazines The two main types of magazines are magazines for general audiences of consumers and magazines for specialized audiences of professionals and businesspeople. Consumer magazines are distributed to the public through either subscriptions or retail sales, carry advertisements for consumer products, and may cover any general or specialized topic. Business magazines, sometimes called trade journals, are distributed through controlled free subscriptions or paid subscriptions and contain articles and advertisements that are of interest to small target audiences.

TODAY'S MARKET STRUCTURE

The magazine industry, like other media industries, is big business, producing both *consumer and business magazines.* Ownership is highly concentrated, with Time Warner far ahead of other publishers. After strong growth in the 1990s, the number of consumer and business titles began to fall. In 2005, 9,336 fewer titles were produced than in 2001, making a total of 22,054 titles.[5] The industry was in a slump, with big layoffs at major publishers and advertising revenues up only 0.5 percent.[6] Eighty-nine magazines had circulations of over a million in 2005. Targeted to a growing population of retirees, the *AARP Magazine* topped the list at 22,675,655. *The AARP Bulletin* was next, followed by *Reader's Digest* at 10,111,773. Five of the magazines in the top ten, including *Better Homes and Gardens* and *Good Housekeeping,* were targeted to women.

Consumer Magazines

Consumer magazines are those directed to the consumer. They may be of general interest or specialized, and they often follow trends. Though the overall number of titles has fallen, 2005 saw the launch of 257 new magazines, including 31 targeted to women and 26 to African Americans and Hispanics. Between 1996 and 2006, the number of regional and national Hispanic magazines grew from 124 to 329, proving the importance of this growing audience.[7] In 2005, a spinoff of *Sports Illustrated* for Latinos appeared, the new *Boom Hispanic* provided stories on Latino hip hop, and *Siempre Mujer* covered home décor, health, and relationships for Hispanic women. Other significant trends in consumer magazines include an increase in lifestyle, celebrity, and sports magazines. Listed in Table 4.1 are the top paid-circulation consumer magazines.

Business-to-Business Magazines

Business-to-business magazines occupy a large segment of the magazine business. Traditionally, the top ten categories of business magazines have been computers, health care, engineering and construction, media, automotive, banking and finance, business, building, advertising and marketing, and industrial manufacturing. In 2005, publications pertaining to conventions, meetings, insurance, travel, architecture, design, lighting, and automotives saw increases in advertising revenues.[8]

demographics

Characteristics of an audience for mass media based on age, gender, ethnic background, education, and income.

Table 4.1 Top Paid-Circulation U.S. Consumer Magazines, 2002	
1. *AARP Modern Maturity*	22,675,655
2. *NRTA/AARP Bulletin*	22,075,011
3. *Reader's Digest*	10,111,773
4. *TV Guide*	8,211,581
5. *Better Homes and Gardens*	7,620,932
6. *National Geographic*	5,403,934
7. *Good Housekeeping*	4,634,763
8. *Family Circle*	4,296,370
9. *Ladies Home Journal*	4,122,460
10. *Woman's Day*	4,048,799

Source: Magazine Publishers of America, www.magazine.org. Reprinted by permission.

controlled circulation

Technique of sending magazines free to individuals within an industry to increase identification with an organization.

association magazines

Magazines published by various associations to publicize their activities and communicate with their members.

In **controlled circulation,** magazines are sent free to individuals within an industry. This method was developed as a distribution technique in the specialized business-press arena and, unlike consumer magazines, more than half of the specialized business publications use this method of circulation. For example, *Offshore Engineer* is mailed only to named individuals who prove they are involved in specifying and buying equipment and services for the offshore industry.

However, controlled-circulation magazines are recognizing that they need to try different approaches to support growth. **Association magazines** in particular can no longer afford to exist on dues alone. "They have to generate revenues from selling ads and doing all the things that consumer publications do," says Elissa Myers, vice president and publisher of *Association Management,* the 21,400-circulation magazine published by the American Society of Association Executives. Myers points out that the average association now draws only 40 percent of its revenues from dues, compared to the 95 percent drawn in the 1960s. As a result, more and more association magazines are beginning to consider nonmembers as subscribers.[9] Association magazines are a traditional and solid approach to conveying information. Nearly every organization, from county medical societies to the Home Builders' Association, publishes a magazine for its members.

Magazines on the Web

Like newspapers, magazines have a growing interest in developing a strong, innovative web presence. Magazines exist on the web independently or as a supplement to print magazines. In 2005, the five consumer print magazines with the top distribution of digital

Many of the top-circulation magazines, such as *TV Guide* or *Reader's Digest,* appeal to the general population. Others, such as *Essence,* focus on a narrower audience segment.

Many magazines appear in both online and print versions. Others, like *Slate*, appear only online and are sustained by advertising revenues rather than subscriptions.

editions were *PC Magazine, Seventeen, U.S. News and World Report, Cosmo Girl,* and *Computer Shopper.*[10] The top five most-visited websites associated with print magazines were *Sports Illustrated, Entrepreneur, People, TV Guide* and *Slate.*[11] Digital magazines and magazine websites are usually in a supporting role, used for marketing the print edition and its products. For example, in 2005, *Self* sponsored a fitness challenge online, and received over 100,000 new subscriptions.[12]

Some profitable online businesses have launched successful print magazines for their audiences. Online entrepreneurs see print as making their businesses more credible and bringing in more advertising revenues and customers. Examples include *WebMD the Magazine; Beverage Spectrum* for retailers; *BabyCenter;* and *EnergyBiz,* a spin off from the Internet publication Energy Central. The wedding site, Knot, spawned a national magazine, regional publications, and an Oxygen network TV show entitled *Real Weddings from the Knot.*

Magazine Ownership

Despite the growth in small-circulation magazines, magazine publishing is big business, and a handful of conglomerates dominate as they do in other industries. Some owners publish in a variety of subject categories, and others specialize. Market analysts predict that the pace of consolidation will slow, but magazine publishers will continue to realize benefits by being big. Size brings decided advantages in marketing and distribution. However, companies are more concerned about whether a particular magazine fits the company's business profile. Those that don't fit into an apparent long-term strategy may be sold off.

Conglomerates also have the advantage of staff pools. When one of the conglomerate's magazines is successful, its editor may be moved to another of the conglomerate's magazines. Nevertheless, critics continue to worry about the standardization that comes with conglomerate ownership. If conglomerates prevail, how will the independent magazines survive? Industry analysts and some critics answer that there will always be room for a good editorial product.

AUDIENCE DEMAND IN MAGAZINE MARKETS

A magazine has to be in demand to succeed. People can be looking for news on a general topic, advertising about companies or products, or information about new ideas. In response to demand, magazine publishers produce certain kinds of content. The two major markets are consumer, with magazines selling editorial content to readers, and advertising, with magazines selling readers to advertisers.

Consumer Market

All publications need to find a **market niche.** Magazine publishers have done so by providing information in greater depth than newspapers and by being more disposable than books. In addition, they carefully target their audiences. Audiences may be defined through various categories. Some are listed below.

- Geography—worldwide (*National Geographic*); regional (*Southern Living*); state (*Texas Monthly*); city (*Atlanta*)
- Gender—female (*Working Mother, Cosmopolitan*); male (*Esquire*)
- Ethnic background—African American (*Ebony*); Hispanic (*Hispanic Times*)
- Age—children (*Sesame Street Magazine*); teenagers (*Seventeen*); seniors (*Modern Maturity*)

market niche

Portion of the audience a particular magazine gains as subscribers or buyers.

Global Impact

Adapting to Other Cultures

Many popular consumer magazines are expanding into world markets. Because of global communications, affluent people in many cultures seek Western images of bodies, celebrities, brands, and luxury goods that they associate with freedom, wealth, and status. Advertisements are part of magazines' visual appeal that carries across languages and cultures. A variety of magazines is available in international editions. Examples include *Business Week, Elle, Prevention, Men's Health, Shape, Car Magazine, National Geographic,* and *Sports Illustrated.*

Typically, when magazine executives decide to expand into another country, they find a publishing partner there. International Federation of the Periodical Press in London helps match publishers with foreign partners. The foreign edition of a magazine may have different artwork and editorial content, but is expected to preserve brand recognition. The design of the cover is especially important. For example, *Rolling Stone* is published in Turkey, and looks very much like the U.S. edition. It has the same distinctive logo and art photography of band members. However, the Turkish edition includes stories about the Turkish music industry and its celebrities.

As of June 2006, *Cosmopolitan,* published by the Hearst Corporation, boasted 55 foreign editions. It also has its own TV channel for young women in Latin America, bringing them *Sex and the City.* The *Cosmopolitan* global brand includes watches, handbags, and jewelry sold worldwide. *Cosmopolitan's* cover of an inviting, scantily clad model is recognizable around the world. Since Helen Gurley Brown became its editor in 1965, *Cosmopolitan* has promoted sexual freedom and confidence for women, a brand identity that has encountered trouble in some countries with authoritarian governments and laws against sexually explicit material.

Cosmopolitan is not available in North Korea, which has the strictest government censorship of popular culture in the world. A 20-year ban against *Cosmopolitan* in Singapore was finally lifted in 2005. In South Africa, the magazine frequently has had to defend itself against pornography complaints that are heard by the government's Film and Publication Control Board. In May 2006, an objection was made to the magazine's inclusion of a "sealed sex section." The board ruled in the magazine's favor. Editor Vanessa Raphaely said in the magazine's defense, "Our editorial follows a policy of empowerment and education which is very important to us in a country where a lot of the sex is non-consensual and violent."

Magazine executives hope that their brand will carry easily into a foreign market if they just find the right universal hot buttons. A former executive at Hearst, Gil Maurer, listed these buttons as "how," "why," "secrets," "doctors," "fat," "sex," "now," "easy," "thin," and "win." But as they expand into the global marketplace, magazines like *Cosmopolitan* sometimes find that their brand identity does not always play well in other cultures with different morals and values.

Sources: Gil Maurer, "What Makes a Great Magazine," speech, Los Angeles, CA, April 12, 2005, magazine.org; "Cosmo Cleared of the 'Pornographic' Charge in South Africa," International Federation of the Periodical Press, April 21, 2006, fipp.com.

- Lifestyle—raising children (*Parents Magazine*); owning a home (*Coastal Living*)
- Occupation—*Farm Journal, Nursing, Chemical Engineering News, Editor & Publisher*
- Hobby or sport—*Art & Antiques, Game & Fish Magazine*
- Socioeconomic background—wealth (*Fortune*); education (*Harper's*)
- Application—entertainment (*TV Guide*); decision making (*Consumer Reports*)
- Ideology—liberal (*Mother Jones*); conservative (*National Review*)

Almost every literate person in the country is a potential magazine consumer. Many **market segments for magazine advertisers** overlap, bur rarely do two magazines target the identical audience. For example, *Parents Magazine* and *Working Mother* overlap, but fathers may also read *Parents.* Similarly, readers of *Parents* may also read *American Baby* because their child is an infant, but they may eventually graduate to *College Parent Magazine. Gay Parent, Jewish Family & Life, Twins Magazine,* and *Sports Parent* all identify different kinds of parenting readers.

Changes in audiences force magazines to change their content. Therefore, as social change enabled more African Americans to earn higher incomes, advertisers began to recognize that African Americans had increased purchasing power. Publishers then began to target magazine

Key Concept

Market segments for magazine advertisers Each magazine strives to sell content and advertising to a specific segment of the total population that the publisher has selected as its target readership. The tastes of the target audience determine the nature of the magazine's offerings.

content to specific African-American interests, convinced that they could attract advertisers for the new market. Thus economic and cultural forces intertwine—as do consumer and advertising markets.

Advertising Market

Initially, magazine publishers relied primarily on subscriptions for revenues. However, they soon recognized that they could broaden their audience by allowing advertisers to pay part of the costs. Today, advertisers search for media that are most appropriate for their product and message. Magazines compete with all media for consumers and for advertising. However, a few magazines, such as *Ms.* and *Consumer Reports,* publish without advertising because their publishers wish to avoid advertiser control and also have found that some subscribers support content that does not appeal to advertisers.

Magazines allow companies to match their messages with specific audiences. For example, suppose that a national software company that publishes an interactive database for evaluating entry-level jobs wants to reach people in their late teens and early twenties. Radio and newspapers tend to be too local, and national television advertising costs too much. That leaves national magazines that appeal to young people. *Jane* would allow the software company to reach young women, and *Details* would allow it to reach young men.

SUPPLYING THE AUDIENCE'S DEMAND

To continue making money and survive as a business, magazine organizations have to stay in touch with their readers. As society changes, so do readers' wants. For example, *Seventeen* magazine caters to teenage females. Every few years, the magazine's audience "ages out," and *Seventeen* has to recruit new readers. The magazine targets not a set of particular women, but a particular age group whose demographics, backgrounds, wants, and needs are always changing.

The readers change, and so do the topics that interest them. Today's *Seventeen* includes stories and information that were not considered necessary or even proper ten or twenty years ago. *Seventeen*'s October 2007 web survey, "Does IM Rule Your Relationships?" would probably never have appeared in the 1970s. Chances are that in 1970 gun violence in the schools and beepers for staying in touch would not have occurred to an editor of a teen magazine as possible topics.

Seventeen readers see a much different magazine than their mothers read, yet in many ways, the topics remain the same: dating, school, and beauty. Enough historical and cultural continuity encourages mothers to buy *Seventeen* for their daughters because they remember their own fondness for the magazine.

Creating and Financing Magazines

Ideas for new magazines start with a concept that gets refined through the reactions and suggestions of others.[13] This process is referred to as **magazine start-up and financing.** Only one in every ten ideas presented to publishers makes it to the start-up stage, and even then, market success is not guaranteed. An idea must be original, but not so far outside the mainstream that it will not attract an audience. Furthermore, a magazine must have staying power: If it addresses a trend, the trend must be here to stay. For example, computer magazines have proliferated, addressing a permanent new development in our society. In 1988, as the computer trend gained strength, about 180 ideas for computer magazines were presented to major magazine publishers. Eighteen were seriously pursued, but only three were still in existence three years later. Of course, many specialized computer magazines now are available on newsstands.

Cultural Impact

Teen Magazines

Teenage girls look to magazines to help shape their identities and relate to their peers. In the voice of a helpful friend, teen magazines provide advice and guidance. Like women's magazines, they also present powerful, often sexualized visual images and consumer products that seem to offer teens the chance to buy an identity. They socialize girls to take on accepted gender roles by associating beauty and sex with personal power. Teenagers have some influence on magazine content. As they choose to either consume or reject the magazine and its advertised products, they confirm or challenge the identity offered to them.

In 2006, the largest selling teen magazines were *Seventeen, Teen People,* and *CosmoGirl!.* Launched in 1944 to give adult advice to white, middle-class high school girls, *Seventeen* is the oldest, with a 2006 circulation of 2 million. The little sister of *People, Teen People* was launched in 1998, with a 2006 circulation of 1.5 million. An offshoot of *Cosmopolitan, CosmoGirl!* had a 2006 circulation of 1.37 million. Since girls often share their magazines with friends, the readership of these magazines is much larger than the circulation figures.

The magazines promise teens that they will achieve greater social status through association with celebrities or luxury goods. The top three teen magazines cater to an audience of mostly middle-class girls. They advertise products that such teenagers can afford, offering a way to imitate the stars with clothes from Target and American Eagle Outfitters. Another magazine, *Teen Vogue,* appeared in 2003 as the offshoot of *Vogue,* a women's fashion magazine. Like its big sister, *Teen Vogue* targets a more affluent audience with designer products such as Louis Vuitton and Christian Dior. A similar magazine, *Elle Girl,* lasted only a few years. In general, commercial teen magazines struggle to keep reader interest. Their main competitor for girls' time is the Internet and text messaging.

Another kind of publication aimed at teens is the expanded shopping catalogue, which offers magazine features as well as products. Known for its sexualized images of teens, Abercrombie & Fitch ran into trouble in 2003 when its Christmas Field Guide included a section called "Group Sex." Upset at the marketing of sex to teens and preteens, feminist and family groups called for a boycott, the company's profits fell, and it withdrew the catalogue.

Some girls have rejected the identity offered in commercial teen magazines by starting their own print and online grrrl zines, self-published magazines often produced on a copy machine. In 2004, the Grrrl Zine Network listed 377 zines in print, 176 with print and online versions, and 86 appearing only online. Emerging from the punk underground, grrrl zines offer friendship, creative expression, and support for alternative lifestyles in a free, public media space.

Sources: Frances E. Gorman, "Advertising Images of Females in *Seventeen:* Positions of Power or Powerless Positions?" *Media Report on Women* (Winter 2005): 13–20; Jon Fine, "Teen Titles Hit Awkward Phase," *Crain's New York Business,* October 4, 2004: 22.

More important than a great idea is its execution; an idea must be packaged as a marketable product. Table 4.2 shows some start-ups and what happened after their first five years.

An entrepreneur must be both an editor and a marketer.[14] As marketer, the entrepreneur must secure financial backing. Initial financial support for starting commercial magazines comes from three sources. First, entrepreneurs can seek support from companies already established in the industry—for example, major publishers—to launch a new idea. Second, they can look for **venture funding** from small investors who are willing to endure higher risk for bigger payoffs than traditional capital investors. For that, a strong business plan is crucial. Third, start-ups can be funded by private investors who know the publisher and believe in that person's ability to make the magazine work.

Not all magazines are commercial ventures. However, they usually are financed by governments, special interest groups, or commercial companies.

venture funding

Funding of an enterprise with cash from several investors who are interested in innovative enterprises that carry both risk and the potential for large profits.

Table
4.2   The Fate of Magazines Launched in 2004

Title/Publisher	Targets	Fate
Cargo, Condé Nast	Bimonthly magazine, with an advertising rate base of 300,000, for urban men who like shopping	Folded 2006
Suede, Time, Inc.	With nine issues a year and an initial rate base of 250,000, the magazine targeted fashion-conscious women of color.	Folded 2005
Vitals, Fairchild Publications	Quarterly publication with an initial advertising rate base of 150,000, for fashion-oriented men with household incomes of $100,000 or more	Still quarterly, with a rate base of 200,000
Cottage Living, Time, Inc.	Home magazine, with an initial rate base of 500,000, featuring decorating, gardening, food, and travel	Still publishing with a rate base of 650,000

Sources: *Media Week*, June 27, 2005: 52–53; *Folio*, April 2004: 24–25; *Advertising Age*, October 25, 2004: S12; *Mediaweek*, August 23–30, 2004: 25.

Government   Although some government agencies publish magazines, they tend to be geared to government employees. Usually government publications are newsletters or pamphlets.

Special Interest Groups   Some organizations, such as a city chamber of commerce or a nonprofit organization, publish magazines. Some associations, such as the National Association of Home Builders, publish magazines that rival commercial publications in quality and cost. Others publish smaller, less professional magazines.

Commercial Companies   The vast majority of magazines are commercial, and their financial support comes from readers, advertisers, or a combination of the two.

Advertising

Advertising is the primary source of revenue for most magazines. However, as previously discussed, some are financed through other means. Nevertheless, magazine publishers always must make a decision about advertising. The decision often reflects the philosophy of the magazine's owners.

Advertising-Free Magazines   Some magazines survive without advertising; they are supported solely by readers who pay for subscriptions or for issues on the newsstand. These magazines are published by individuals who believe that advertising would compromise the integrity and principles of the magazine. For instance, *Ms.* magazine, after initial disputes with advertisers, reinvented itself as a nonadvertising publication. Because the magazine's editorial stance is that a woman looks and feels best without excessive use of cosmetic products, *Ms.* wanted to avoid the hypocrisy of printing advertising that contradicted the editorial position. However, *Ms.* magazine has had a difficult time sustaining its readership. Beginning in 1965, Reiman Publications has catered to a rural audience with ad-free magazines like *Crafting Traditions, Birds & Blooms,* and *Country Woman.* Reiman's fourteen publications have a combined circulation of 13 million.

Free Magazines with Advertising-Only Financing   Although some magazines are supported by readers only, others are financed by advertising only. Consumers read or receive the magazines at no charge. Membership in the American Association of Retired Persons, for example, guarantees a subscription to its flagship publication, *Modern Maturity.*

Combination Financing   A third type of financing is a combination of advertising and circulation. Most commercial magazines fall into this group, and advertising rather than circulation provides most of the revenue stream. Magazines that rely on a combination of advertising and reader support traditionally competed for readers, but now they more often compete for advertising dollars. Advertising rates are closely tied to circulation figures, so publishers must be careful not to price their magazines out of the market. If they do, the decrease in circulation will result in a subsequent decrease in advertising revenue. Therefore increased costs often must be absorbed by increased advertising revenue.[15]

Advertising Tie-Ins   Although prestigious newspapers have established their independence from advertising pressures, magazines have allowed, and sometimes even courted, editorial/advertising **tie-ins**. **Package deals** are commonplace for many magazine editors who guarantee preferential editorial treatment to advertisers. Take, for example, one issue of *Where to Retire,* a magazine aimed at baby boomers considering retirement in the next ten years. An article featuring Georgetown, Texas, as an award-winning hill country town, is surrounded by advertisements for Georgetown Village, a retirement community, and Texas travel guides from the Texas Department of Economic Development.

Advertisers and Editorial Content   Advertisers also specify placement of some ads and react negatively when editorial content does not support their products. Many advertisers even hire resident censors who sit in the ad departments of major magazines. Dow specified that ads for its Spray 'n Wash products had to be adjacent to pictures of children or editorials about fashion, and ads for its bathroom cleaner next to home-furnishing and family features. Revlon refused to advertise in a magazine because the Soviet women on the cover were not wearing makeup. (The story later won a prestigious Front Page Award.) And during the Gulf War, Procter & Gamble successfully stopped *Sassy* from running a page covered with the word *peace.*

However, if a magazine too often crosses the fine line that separates credibility and promotion, the industry and the magazine's readers may lose faith in it. If circulation drops as a result, advertisers lose interest as well, and the magazine is left to wither from lack of reader or advertiser support.

> **Key Concept**
>
> **Magazine publishing process**   To publish, magazines need the combined efforts of publishers, editors, writers, graphic artists, production staff, printers, ad managers, subscription managers, and distributors. These staff members provide content, physical print production, ad or subscription support, and distribution to the magazine's reading public.

PUBLISHING A SUCCESSFUL MAGAZINE

The masthead, or list of owner, publisher, and staff of a magazine, usually appears near the table of contents in the first few pages of a magazine. The list emphasizes that *publishing is a process.* The number and size of departments and types of positions vary with each publication; large consumer magazine staffs may employ several hundred people, whereas small specialized business publications might have fewer than ten people. The positions and departments in the following sections are common for all sizes of magazine staffs.

Publisher   The publisher, to whom all staff members are ultimately responsible, may also be the magazine owner or editor. The publisher defines the personality of the

tie-in

The connection made when a magazine runs a story about a product advertised in the magazine.

package deals

A series of media tie-ins.

publication and works to ensure its financial success. Some publishers with particularly forceful personalities and deep pocketbooks can breathe life into a publication or kill it with an easy blow. When *Lear's* ceased publication in March 1994, the *New York Times* reported that the magazine had died as it had lived. "It was created by Frances Lear, who, after a bitter divorce from television producer Norman Lear, was at a crossroads. She invented the magazine for a particular reader: herself. She gave the magazine her vision, her energy, her money and her name. She sustained it with her enthusiasm, and when she lost interest, she pulled the plug."[16]

Editor   Once the publisher has defined the magazine's personality, the editor develops and shapes its identity. To successfully complete an editor's mission, the managing editor, the articles editor, and department editors work together to give readers the information they want. Editors edit and proofread stories, approve design and graphics, accept freelance submissions, and contract with designers.

Large-circulation magazines pay from $1.00 to $2.00 a word. For example, if you write a 5,000-word article, you could expect to earn about $10,000. However, this is true only if you have already established a reputation and have created a relationship with an editor. Now, to have a gross income of $50,000 (before taxes and expenses), you would have to write five such articles each year—and be successful at placing all of them. *Salon Magazine* reports that many freelancers are willing to accept $1.00 a word for the visibility they get at a publication such as the *New York Times Magazine,* which a *Times* editor says now pays star writers $80,000 for four pieces. Only a few writers, such as Norman Mailer, achieve real fame and real money. Mailer reportedly was paid $140,000 for two pieces for the now defunct *George.*

Advertising   Advertising is often a magazine's lifeblood. According to Magazine Publishers of America figures, advertising revenue increased steadily but slowly from $6.7 billion in 1990 to $17.7 billion in 2000.[17] In 2005, ad pages in magazines gained only 0.5 percent, with industry analysts speculating that the decline might be from online competition.[18]

Advertising staffs may include only an advertising director and several salespeople. At larger magazines, divisional managers contribute specialized knowledge about readers and advertisers in specific geographic areas or about specific types of products.

Design and Production   Convergence of technology is readily apparent in the design and production departments of large and small magazines. The design department designs the actual paper product that readers hold. The production staff includes artistic experts, technological wizards, and people who buy supplies for production, such as ink and paper. **Desktop publishing**—the integration of design and production—has saved magazines millions of dollars and cut production time. For example, when the National Geographic Society converted to desktop publishing for *National Geographic Traveler and World,* it saved $200,000 annually.[19] Technology also has allowed publishers to print split runs and use selective binding, in which pages are changed according to geographic locale. Advertising copy may be based on zip codes. Geographically divided runs allow publishers better to target their markets.

Circulation   The circulation staff gets the magazine to the reader through either subscriptions or newsstand sales. Each method has different costs. A new subscription costs publishers about $15 in promotion expenses; each renewal costs about $3. For single-copy sales, every stage of transport between publisher and newsstand takes a percentage of the copy price.

Soliciting subscriptions is one facet of circulation, and experts have become adept at using demographic background information about individuals in personalized, target-market selling. Publishers also design websites aimed at attracting subscribers.

Newsstand, or single-copy, sales go through a variety of stages before hitting the display racks. Each publisher works with one of about ten national **distributors.** The

desktop publishing

Writing, illustrating, and designing publications with a personal computer.

distributor

Company that helps get magazines from the printer to the wholesalers.

In September of 2002, *Mother Jones* magazine published this intro to an article about Gloria Steinem:

> More than two decades after founding *Ms.* magazine, Gloria Steinem remains America's most influential, eloquent, and revered feminist. Her 1992 book, *Revolution from Within: A Book of Self-Esteem,* was a number one bestseller and has been translated into 11 languages. Last winter, shortly after publishing a book of six essays titled *Moving Beyond Words,* she canceled a national speaking tour because of a rare nerve disorder that left her bedridden. Now rejuvenated, the 61-year-old Steinem spoke with us about politics, aging, and why her best activist days are still to come.

Gloria Steinem

danced in chorus lines. She graduated from Smith College and then spent a year in India with the followers of the spiritual leader Mahatma Gandhi before starting her professional career. She advises women to use their backgrounds to learn and to grow.

When she returned to the United States from India, she wrote for *New York Magazine* and *Esquire,* building a reputation as a reporter and establishing a network. Her political involvement in women's causes began in 1969 at an abortion-law reform rally, where she heard women talk about being offended by sexist jokes and about having abortions and other experiences, some of them similar to hers. Inspired, Steinem cofounded the national feminist publication *Ms.* Although the magazine went through several changes of ownership, in December 1998, Gloria Steinem and a group of investors bought the publication from MacDonald Communications Corp. The investors, a group of women who call themselves Liberty Media for Women, paid between $3 million and $4 million for the magazine.

Since the founding of *Ms.* magazine in 1971, Gloria Steinem has been a feminist ideal for young women and men. She has devoted her life to persuading all kinds of women to believe in themselves, has lent an influential voice to the cause of immigrant farmworkers in California, and has helped to persuade Democratic political leaders to include women's issues in their platforms.

As a feminist, Steinem has had a major impact on the magazine industry. She developed a solid reputation as a reporter and magazine writer, founded *Ms.* in 1972, and later helped convert it to a no-advertising publication to avoid the impact of sexist advertising on its content.

Steinem grew up in a tenement in Toledo, Ohio. Her emotionally ill mother, Ruth, had been a newspaper journalist who wrote under a male pseudonym. Steinem's parents were divorced when she was ten.

When Steinem was old enough, she worked evenings and weekends as a waitress and shop assistant. She also tap

Today, Steinem is president of Choice U.S.A., which sponsors the Gloria Steinem Leadership Institute to mentor promising young people in the pro-choice movement, helping them hone their communication skills.

Sources: Sarah Lyons, "Daughter of the Revolution," *South China Morning Post,* July 6, 1996: Books sec., 8; Joan Smith, "The Unexplained Feminist," *Financial Times,* May 4, 1996: Books sec., 11; Rosie Boycott, "Sex and Feminism," *Daily Mail,* April 20, 1996: 36; Maureen Freely, "Gloria and Me," *The Guardian,* April 18, 1996: Features sec., 6; Katie Donovan, "Feminist Enigma," *The Irish Times,* April 9, 1996: News Features sec., 9; and "New Group Buys *Ms.* Magazine," abcnews.com; Cynthia Gorney, "Gloria," September 2002, motherjones.com/mother_jones/ND95/gorney.html.

distributor supplies the printer with the mailing labels of some of the four hundred regional **wholesalers.** The printer mails bundles of issues to the wholesalers, which deliver the copies to dealers. Popular newsstand dealers include owners of grocery stores, convenience stores, pharmacies, and bookstores. At the same time that magazines are delivered, the wholesaler picks up and discards the previous week's or month's unsold ones.

Magazine Employees

Salaries for the entry-level position of associate editor and editorial assistant are between $25,000 and $30,000. Some companies pay overtime, which can double that income, but to do so means working sixty hours a week. Copy editors and researchers make between $35,000 and $45,000 and reporters, $40,000 to $60,000. Managing editors and senior editors earn $55,000 to $70,000 while the editor-in-chief averages

wholesaler

Company that delivers magazines from a warehouse to dealers, such as bookstores.

$93,561.[20] On the production side, art directors make between $52,000 and $63,000; production managers between $47,000 and $52,000, and production directors between $65,000 and $83,000.[21] The gender gap in these jobs is closing, but still significant, with women production directors making on average $13,000 less than their male counterparts.[22] Sales directors, managers, and executives make between $80,000 and $113,000, with women once again lagging behind by approximately $30,000.

TRENDS

As with other forms of print media, today's magazines are operating in a climate of massive change wrought by digital technology and changing demographics. Some print publications, like *Newsweek* and *Cosmopolitan,* have established readerships and advertising bases for their continued economic health. Other start-ups, like the men's magazine *Cargo,* quickly come and go. In a heavily competitive environment, magazine publishers must decide to what extent they will put advertising and editorial content on the web, depending on what readers they hope to attract. In 2006, experiencing a decline in readership, *Time* was revamped, boosting its web presence so that it could provide news twenty-four hours a day and switching its publication dates from Mondays to Fridays so that its advertisers could hook weekend shoppers.[23] In making these decisions, magazine publishers who rely on advertising must consider how best to attract advertising revenues in order to survive.

Technology: Driven by Economic Need

Technology is driven, at least in part, by economic need. As publishers see the need for innovation in order increase profits, they finance the development of technology. At other times, technological developments in fields other than publishing can be adapted for innovation.

In July 2005, *Folio,* a publication for magazine managers, outlined the six most significant trends in technology affecting the industry:

1. *The Internet:* The importance of the Internet to the magazine industry lies especially in the opportunities it provides for marketing the magazine and its vendors' products. It also helps save money, since subscriptions can be done online and content can be circulated in digital form, both in the production and distribution process, rather than through mailing. However, this feature also poses a threat to the magazine industry, since news and entertainment content is readily available for free on the web.
2. *Digitization of content:* The digitization of content within the production and printing process has also reduced costs and provided greater opportunities for creativity. For example, digital photographs can be easily manipulated.
3. *Desktop software:* Programs such as Adobe InDesign and Adobe Photoshop have made publishing easy on the Internet; proofing for design elements like color and size can be carried out more quickly and efficiently.
4. *Print manufacturing:* Greater efficiency and automation in the printing process has made it faster, cheaper, and easier to produce a magazine. Different versions of a magazine can be printed for different audiences. For example, *AARP* has three regional editions.
5. *Database publishing:* Database management software allows magazine publishers selectively to target audiences through personalized advertising.
6. *Wireless, mobile publishing:* Magazine staff can communicate with each other more easily, sending sales orders, artwork, and stories to each other in real time.[24]

Men's magazines, especially, are pushing into mobile platforms like cell phones and PDAs to deliver content and advertising. *GQ* ran a promotion in which a reader could text message the magazine, mention an ad, and receive prizes. In 2006, *Maxim* was working on a service by which a user could order products through a cell phone. Readership of *T.V. Guide* was declining when its publishers turned to high tech to energize sales. Users of the *Guide's* cell phone technology can selectively download its content and, if predictions are right, will be able to program their DVRs remotely with this information. However, such measures did not save Condé Nast's magazine, *Cargo,* which folded despite offering downloadable purchasing guides that readers could take with them on their PDAs and cell phones. The magazine attempted to target men who liked to shop.

Culture: Diverse Readership

Magazine publishers are targeting new audiences for the twenty-first century. In the United States, slower population growth, an aging society, changing lifestyles, and an increasingly diversified population are making new demands on magazines. And these changes are not strictly American characteristics, but are occurring throughout the world. If magazines are to survive, magazine publishers must learn how to satisfy the new demands.

In 2004, the Magazine Publishers of America began an initiative to encourage diversity in all aspects of the industry. It argues that the representation of many groups adds a range or ideas, fosters innovation, helps salespeople to understand and reach niche audiences, increases the customer base, and ensures that the editorial staff represents multicultural groups appropriately. The association also features market profiles of African Americans, Hispanics, and Asian Americans.

Between 1990 and 2000, the African-American/black market grew 22 percent. That market has unique features. African Americans are heavier magazine readers than other adults and they are, on average, younger consumers with more children at home. African-American teens spend more than the average U.S. teen on clothing, jewelry, computer software, and athletic footwear. Music magazines are more popular among African Americans, ranking fifth in favorite magazine categories.

The fastest growing ethnic group in the United States, Asian-American consumers, are younger, better educated, and have higher household incomes than the average adult. This population also represents many language groups, though most speak English very well. About 75 percent of Asian Americans read magazines, especially preferring the business/finance publications like *Fortune* and *Business Week.*

Hispanic magazine readers are younger and more urban, and though they come from different cultures, are bound by their shared language. The purchasing power of this group is growing at a phenomenal rate, and by 2007 is expected to top $926 billion. Hispanic youths are trendsetters, and are an important influence on music and fashion.

Culture: Women and Minorities in the Workforce

The magazine publishing industry is becoming more aware of the potential of diverse readerships. But diversity among its executives and employees must also follow. From the late nineteenth century, women have been the biggest readers of magazines. They are also the top consumers of household products, and their business drives much of the consumer magazine industry. Yet, with a few notable exceptions like Helen Gurley Brown, women have not fared well as employees in publishing. They make significantly less than their male counterparts, and in 2002, headed only 28 percent of over 550 magazines.[25] Despite the growth of ethnic and minority populations in the United States and their importance as media consumers, they are even less well represented in publishing. When one of the most respected African-American women's magazines, *Essence,* was bought by the media conglomerate Time Warner in 2005, readers reacted with sadness that a black-owned business was being taken over by a white company. *Black Enterprise* noted that *Essence's* readers were "crushed" and

Discussing Trends

The traditional function of the magazine has been to correlate the various parts of American society and to provide a forum for political and social discussion. Because magazines were less immediate and less disposable than newspapers, it was assumed they would provide more thoughtful commentary on events and trends.

However, the magazines that have survived economically in recent decades have been those that specialized, targeted niche markets, promoted shopping, and experimented successfully with enhanced features online. Some of the questions that need to be answered include:

■ To what extent have magazines become mere catalogs for advertisers?

■ What new forms might magazines take as they expand into multimedia platforms?

■ How do magazines shape audiences and identities?

wondered whether African-American women would "lose a strong voice that spoke to their aspirations and has served as the bully pulpit in the fight against racism, sexism, and other barriers to their ascension."[26]

SUMMARY

■ Magazines helped develop the nation's social conscience.

■ Limited technology and lack of an economic base, together with a primitive postal system, hampered the development of the U.S. magazine industry.

■ Rapidly advancing technology and mass marketing of goods reduced production costs and created an advertising base that fostered magazine development.

■ A rising middle class, increased public education, and the opportunity for social advancement encouraged a reading audience. By 1900 that educated middle class used magazines as the medium for social protest.

■ Magazines survived competition from radio and television by targeting groups of readers. This specialization was attractive to both the audience and the advertiser.

■ In today's market, specialization is key. Consumer magazines and literary journals make up the bulk of magazine publishing.

■ Huge business conglomerates are the primary owners of magazines. However, in response to the recession of the early 1990s, magazine publishers downsized and decentralized.

■ During the economic downturn of the early 2000s, magazine advertising revenue declined.

■ Magazines not only meet the needs of existing audiences, but create audiences. These audiences buy into the experience and models of identity.

■ Combined—or converging—technologies foster new methods of production and distribution. Magazine publishers increasingly are enhancing their products with websites and online magazines.

■ Editors argue about whether magazines will continue to function as important generators of a national conversation about political and social issues, or whether they will emerge as "super catalogs" and other forms of media.

NAVIGATING THE WEB Magazines

Magazine websites include sites for the magazines, sites for companies that publish magazines, and sites for information about the industry. Although industry information and company sites are usually free, some magazine sites require users to purchase a subscription.

American Society of Business Publication Editors
asbpe.org
The goal of this association is to enhance knowledge and practices of editors and writers employed in the business, trade, and specialty press. The ASBPE has local chapters in fourteen national regions.

Folio
foliomag.com
Folio Magazine provides articles, event notices, and trade information related to the magazine industry, business-to-business, consumer, association, and city and regional publications.

Magazine Publishers of America (MPA)
magazine.org
The MPA site provides research material about magazines and news about the industry.

The Write News
writenews.com
Writers who are targeting magazines use the Write News site, which contains writing tips, job information, and other helpful ideas.

Ziff-Davis Magazines
Ziffdavis.com
Ziff-Davis is one of the largest publishers of computer and electronic media magazines. This site connects to the texts of magazines published by Ziff-Davis, including *PC Magazine* and *Games for Windows.*

Some magazines online include the following:

People
people.com

Business Week
businessweek.com

PC Magazine
pcmag.com

QUESTIONS FOR REVIEW

1. Why were magazines slow to develop in the early United States?
2. How did mass production affect magazines?
3. How are magazines financed?
4. How is technology used for distribution?
5. How are magazines adapting to online possibilities?

ISSUES TO THINK ABOUT

1. What cultural roles have magazines occupied?
2. What experiences do readers find in magazines?
3. How are economics and cultural issues intertwined in magazine development?
4. Should magazine editors and consumers be concerned about influence on content by advertisers? If so, why?
5. What are the advantages and disadvantages of conglomerate ownership?
6. Will magazines use online technologies to enhance the print product or to replace it?
7. How are magazines expanding beyond their print form?

SUGGESTED READINGS

John, Arthur. *The Best Years of the Century* (Urbana: University of Illinois Press, 1981).

Vincent, Theodore G., ed. *Voices of a Black Nation: Political Journalism in the Harlem Renaissance* (San Francisco: Ramparts Press, 1973).

Wilson, Christopher. "The Rhetoric of Consumption: Mass-Market Magazines and the Demise of the Gentle Reader, 1880–1920," in *The Culture of Consumption,* Richard Wightman Fox, and T. J. Jackson Lears, eds. (New York: Pantheon, 1983), pp. 39–64.

Wilson, Harold S. McClure's *Magazine and the Muckrakers* (Princeton, NJ: Princeton University Press, 1970).

Yagoda, Ben. *About Town: The* New Yorker *and the World It Made* (New York: Scribner's, 2002).

The Movies

Socially conscious, reality-inspired, low-budget motion pictures swept the 2005 Oscars. Putting aside the standard blockbusters like *King Kong* and *Batman Begins,* the Academy of Motion Pictures honored movies about love between gay cowboys, the evils of pharmaceutical companies in Africa, the ethics of true crime writing, urban racial tensions, and the conflict between civil liberties and the state.

Accepting his award for best supporting actor in the political drama, *Syriana,* George Clooney praised Hollywood for tackling sensitive subjects in the past, such as AIDS, civil rights, and racism. In particular he mentioned Hattie McDaniel's 1939 Oscar for her portrayal of a slave in *Gone with the Wind.* But director Spike Lee was not impressed with Clooney's sense of history. He pointed out that McDaniel's win reinforced the stereotype of black women as "Mammies" and that a black female actor would not win again for another sixty years. Thus, the Academy Awards ceremony dramatized the country's difficulties with race, even as it celebrated the film industry's efforts to tackle racism.

Hollywood films are the United States' most recognizable cultural form, and the Academy Awards is an experience shared by millions of movie lovers every year. Movies appeal to psychic and social needs: to have a fantasy life, to be loved, to be wealthy and beautiful, to create possible identities, to understand one's role in the world. Films both create culture and reflect upon culture. Hollywood is not only a dream factory but a stage on which social harmonies and differences are played out.

Hollywood is associated with the wealth, glamour and power of the United States, but most of its films have international dimensions in their financing, production, and distribution. The 2005 winner of best picture, *Crash,* was an independent production distributed by a Canadian company, Lions Gate Films, which acquired the film at the Toronto International Film Festival. *King Kong,* which won Oscars for sound and visual effects, was directed by a New Zealander, made in New Zealand, and distributed worldwide by the U.S.-based Universal Studios, which is partly owned by the French company, Vivendi. Even the gorilla was an international construction. The English actor behind the beast, Andy Serkis, learned gorilla mannerisms during a visit to a primatology research center in Africa.

Dominating the world market for motion pictures, Hollywood is many things: a specific place, a state of mind, a creative synergy of artists, and a global network of investors, production companies, and distributors. The industry is facing significant changes because of digital technologies, which makes it much cheaper and easier to make and distribute movies. Some movie makers see the digital revolution as opening up greater possibilities for people worldwide to create their own cinema. Spike Lee explains, "I think that what this technology is going to do is make this whole media thing more democratic. That anybody could buy a digital camera now, buy some tape, and make a film." Others, like Hollywood director Steven Spielberg, still use traditional film, resisting technological change. Spielberg says, "Audiences will not be drawn to the technology; they'll be drawn to the story."[1]

As you read this chapter, consider the following issues facing filmmakers and those who are interested in the impact of moviemaking and moviegoing:

■ What are the economic and cultural impacts of film viewing? Are films significant in shaping the culture of our future?

■ Economic interests are an important component of filmmaking. How do you think corporate interests and the studio system have contributed to (or limited) the subject matter and impact of film?

■ Increasingly, film production houses are internationally owned. How will this increased international economic concentration affect film as a "culture machine"?

■ How do you think new technologies will affect the production and delivery of film and its convergence with other media?

■ Film viewers can choose different settings in which to see films in a variety of technological formats. "Movies in Your Life" outlines some of the choices available and points out that different types of viewing may serve different functions.

FILM IN AMERICAN LIFE

Film historians Louis Giannetti and Scott Eyman write that moving pictures are, for some, "art, science and schooling all in one."[2] They also are—and have been since 1920—big business. The emergence of moving pictures was part of the experimentation with entertainment in the United States during the 1880s and 1890s that included concert saloons, peep shows, and vaudeville variety acts.

The Movies in Your Life

How Do You Watch Movies?

College students are major consumers of movies. How important are they in your life? As you read this chapter, think about the different ways in which you view movies. Do you think your viewing habits and those of your friends influence the movie industry? What do your friends think?

Take a moment to think about how the form, type, and function of movies you view are intertwined. Do you view movies on DVD for relaxation and in a theater for social reasons? Do your goals differ when you view movies in different places? Are the results different? For example, do large-screen films viewed in a theater have a greater impact on you than a film viewed on a television does? Is form—or the convergence of technology—affecting the impact, the content, or the use of film? As you read this chapter, you will see that the movie industry is concerned about some of the very same considerations that influenced you in responding to these issues.

Form of Viewing	Type of Film	Time/Day	Purpose of Viewing
Movie theater			
Broadcast TV			
Cable TV or direct broadcast satellite			
VHS/DVD (rental)			
VHS/DVD (own film)			
Computer			
Other (please specify)			

Technological and Economic Development

The fascination with pictures in motion goes back to ancient Greek and Arab civilizations, but not until the mid-1800s did technology make such pictures available to broad audiences. Motion pictures evolved from two sets of developing technologies: experimentation with photographic processes and the development of moving picture devices. Photographic processes that evolved in the mid-nineteenth century paved the way for moving pictures. By the late nineteenth century, a French scientist had developed a camera that produced twelve pictures on a single plate. The development of gelatin emulsions and the production of celluloid during the 1880s furthered photographic technology. In 1878, Eadweard Muybridge achieved a sense of motion by positioning cameras at different intervals along a race track and arranging for the shutters to click in sequence. In the early 1890s, several scientists were experimenting with viewing devices in the United States, Thomas Edison's labs produced the **kinetoscope,** a device that allowed for viewing a film by moving loops of film over a series of spools.

A contemporary observer wrote,

> The ends of the film are joined, forming an endless band passing over two guide drums near the top of the case. One of these drums is driven by a motor and feeds the film along by means of sprocket teeth which engage with perforations along the edges of the film. Just above the

kinetoscope

A boxlike mechanism used to view short films during the late 1800s. The viewer looked into an opening and watched film move past a lightbulb.

Short action films were among the first popular films to appear in theaters of the early 1900s. One of these, Edwin Porter's *The Great Train Robbery*, helped launch the popularity of the cowboy movie.

film is a shutter wheel having five spokes and a very small rectangular opening in the rim directly over the film. An incandescent lamp . . . is placed below the film between the two guide drums, and the light passes up through the film, shutter opening, and magnifying lens . . . to the eye of the observer placed at the opening in the top of the case.[3]

The new motion picture technology set the stage for the peep show, which featured short films that could be viewed by looking through a viewfinder on a machine about the size of an upright piano. Kinetoscopes became popular in hotel lobbies and other public places, but they never produced the great profits Edison had anticipated.

Vaudeville provided the entertainment milieu in which technical projection developed as a form of theater. Vaudeville acts were popular from the beginning of the nineteenth century, though their form and acceptance varied with specific historical periods. Until the 1880s, vaudeville was considered legitimate theater and appealed to all classes. During industrialization in the late 1800s, audiences developed a greater sense of class consciousness, and upper-class theatergoers began to object to the "lower class" that cheered and booed from the galleries. The upper class then excluded the working class from theater, and variety acts became more important as entertainment in working-class neighborhoods, often in saloons. However, entertainment entrepreneurs, not content to appeal only to a drinking crowd, sought to establish the **vaudeville show in a theater** environment that would attract working-class and middle-class audiences. Once variety moved back to the stage—this time as its own genre rather than as an extension of theater—it was established as vaudeville with high appeal to the middle class. In this environment, entrepreneurs marketing new technologies made inroads.

In the late nineteenth century, agents who booked acts for vaudeville, looking for new acts for their demanding audiences, often sought visual presentations to enhance their shows. "Magic lantern" slide shows had been popular during the 1880s, but the invention of projection machines posed interesting possibilities for new types of entertainment. Several competing machines entered the market at about the same time. Auguste and Louis Lumière introduced the Cinématrographe, Francis Jenkins and Thomas Armat the Vitascope, and Edison the kinetoscope.

Initially, films were short exhibitions of moving images. They were popular in Asia, Europe, and the United States. Between 1896 and 1903, travelogues, local features, comedy, and news often were the subjects of short films. Depictions of movement also were used to create a physiological thrill. In 1902 and 1903, Edwin Porter produced several American films, including *Life of an American Fireman* and *The Great Train Robbery.* These 12-minute productions pioneered storytelling techniques in film and led the way to the development of feature films.

Films were shown in the vaudeville theaters and by traveling showmen, who projected them at tent shows or fairs. By 1906, storefronts known as **nickelodeons** exhibited films that attracted working-class audiences. To broaden their audience, nickelodeon operators began moving their operations into theaters and adding one or two vaudeville acts to the attraction. This small-time vaudeville relied more heavily on motion picture entertainment and less on live acts than did the traditional variety show. By 1910, nickelodeons attracted an audience of 26 million each week, a little less than 20 percent of the national population. By 1914, the weekly audience had increased to 49 million.[4] The moving picture was now considered respectable middle-class entertainment, and theaters began popping up in middle-class neighborhoods and small towns.

In 1908 a variety of companies were competing in the movie industry. Industry leaders were spending so much energy defending their patents and jockeying for position that, in an effort to increase profits and to standardize the industry, they decided to form a monopoly. Led by the Edison Manufacturing Company and the American Mutoscope and Biograph Company, they formed a trust called the Motion Picture

Key Concept

Vaudeville show as early movie theater In the early 1900s, popular comedy, dramatic skits, or song-and-dance entertainment was presented in local vaudeville theaters. Early silent films, usually with piano accompaniment, also were shown in these theaters.

nickelodeon

Small storefront functioning as a theater; popular about 1910. These preceded the grand movie palaces.

Patents Company (MPPC). Creating trusts was a common business strategy in the late nineteenth century to acquire and pool patents. For a short time, the MPPC controlled production of raw film, manufacture of motion picture and projection equipment, distribution, and exhibition. All members were required to purchase film from the Eastman Kodak Company, and the company refused to sell to outsiders.

The trust was dissolved in 1915 because of the government's success in *United States v. Motion Picture Patents Co.,* an antitrust case against the MPPC. The MPPC certainly had increased its own profits and was known for its strong-arm tactics, which included raiding independent studios and smashing equipment. However, it also had ended squabbles among different segments of the U.S. film industry and had improved film quality. Through competition and standardized distribution and exhibition practices, the MPPC helped create an internationally competitive motion picture industry.[5]

Although members of the MPPC had tried to eliminate independent movie production, its standardization of production and distribution became too rigid. The MPPC clung to the concept of short films and at first rejected the multiple-reel feature films that became successful during the teens. Independents saw big feature films as a way to gain a market niche and sought financing on Wall Street. By 1915 the MPPC was gone and independents were producing feature films. Film exhibition moved from the storefront nickelodeon and the small vaudeville houses to theaters that were designed exclusively for the showing of movies. The movies had become big business.

The Audience and New Expectations

When D. W. Griffith's long, controversial, and popular feature film *The Birth of a Nation* opened in New York's Liberty Theater on March 3, 1915, it established the importance of feature films. The three-hour film was based on a popular novel published in 1905 that had become a successful play. This story of the aftermath of the Civil War roused enormous controversy because of its underlying racist message. The film depicted a northern family and a southern family adapting to the postwar period, but the point of view was decidedly southern. African Americans who were not loyal to their southern masters were depicted as subhuman. The last half of the film was dominated by Ku Klux Klan activity that would never be condoned today. Nevertheless, the film opened to a packed audience. Each audience member paid two dollars for a reserved seat, an orchestra accompanied the performance, and costumed ushers handed out souvenir programs. The exhibition format resembled that of an upper-class theater. The film played for forty-four consecutive weeks at the Liberty and showed in leading theaters across the United States, breaking records and generating controversy because of its racist tones. The production yielded $5 million on an investment of less than $100,000.

Griffith's follow-up picture, *Intolerance,* ran 3½ hours, and although the film is regarded as an artistic classic, it failed miserably to reward its financial backers. Griffith, who personally stood behind the losses, never recovered financially.

Why did *Intolerance* fail? Critics debate the issue. Griffith's message of love, tolerance, and the uselessness of war might have been popular before 1916, when Americans were resisting involvement in what many considered a European war. However, by 1916, when the film was released, the message alienated many viewers as the United States prepared to go to war.

Pioneer filmmaker D. W. Griffith perfected the art of cinematic continuity and storytelling necessary for the modern feature film. His film *The Birth of a Nation*, a controversial story dependent on racial stereotypes, was a box-office hit, but his subsequent film *Intolerance*, loaded with pacifist scenes, failed to gain an audience on the eve of World War I.

Griffith made other successful films, but he was a poor businessman and always struggled with finances. By 1920, his films were no longer regarded as groundbreaking. Nevertheless, Griffith's innovative film techniques redefined the expectations of film audiences. He created grand epics with spectacular scenery and introduced lighting and **editing** techniques that established film as a medium for exploring social and cultural themes.

Sound and Money

Companies that experimented early with adding sound to motion pictures were the first to realize vast profits from introducing the technology, but this introduction changed the industry economically. Once big money was needed for big technology, few companies could make the switch without help from bankers. The adoption of sound also signaled a solidifying of big business interests.

As audience reaction to feature films and the appearance of stars ensured that movies would indeed continue to be an important entertainment medium, companies such as Western Electric, Warner Bros., and Fox experimented to develop technology for sound, hoping that it would accelerate profits. Although some critics thought such investments were a waste of money, sound soon became accepted through an economic process of invention, innovation, and diffusion.[8] In 1926, Warner formed the Vitaphone Corporation in association with Western Electric, a subsidiary of American Telephone & Telegraph Co., to make sound pictures and to market sound production equipment. Although Warner lost $1 million in 1926, the loss was anticipated and was necessary to finance the expansion. Vitaphone initiated a sales campaign to encourage exhibitors to introduce sound equipment. Such planning paved the way for the success of The Jazz Singer, which premiered in October 1927. Because Warner was first to market sound, it earned extraordinary profits. During the last half of the 1920s, Warner was able to solidify its position by acquiring other companies with production and exhibition facilities.

After the success of The Jazz Singer, most of the major companies rushed to switch to sound. RCA developed a competing sound system called Photophone. The company became a massive firm by merging with a motion picture giant, the Radio-Keith-Orpheum Corporation, and with the Keith-Albee-Orpheum circuit of vaudeville houses. Major companies had signed long-term, exclusive contracts with AT&T, but RCA challenged the giant with unlawful restraint of trade and reached an out-of-court settlement in 1935. By 1943, RCA supplied about 60 percent of all sound equipment. Production costs rose as a result of the new technology. The major companies and studios were able to make the capital investment needed to switch to sound, but smaller independent companies did not have enough financial backing or capital to make the transition. Many of the independents simply closed their doors or sold out to the bigger companies. By 1930 the industry was an **oligopoly.**

The Studio System

By the 1920s, the movie industry had moved to California, where the studios could use nearby locations to depict desert, mountain, or ocean scenes and the weather permitted year-round filming. However, many decisions affecting the industry were made in New York offices by film company executives. The corporate chief executives (such as Harry Warner, Nicholas Schenck of Loew's/MGM, and Joseph M. Schenck of Fox) made the most important decisions, such as the titles and number of films to be produced in any given season, total production budgets, and the number of **A and B pictures.** Once the New York executives had prepared a release schedule, the head of the studio took control. But the chief executives who controlled the business aspects of the industry made the most important creative and business decisions. Because they valued stability, they used popular stars in familiar roles. In this way, economic structures affected film style and content.

editing

The technique of joining pieces of film or of digitally manipulating images in a creative process.

oligopoly

A business situation in which a few dominant companies control enough of the business that each one's actions will have a significant impact on the actions of the others.

A and B pictures

A films are usually high-budget films that studios expect to be box-office hits. B films are low-budget films designed to make money.

Unlike the chief executive officers (CEOs), the heads of the studios were familiar to the public: Louis B. Mayer at MGM, Darryl Zanuck at Twentieth Century Fox, and Jack Warner at Warner Bros. The heads promoted and negotiated contracts with the stars, ensured that production schedules were met, and assigned material to producers.

The glamourous stars were encased in a **star system** created by studio heads and had little control over their own lives; the studios controlled many of their personal and private actions. Their contracts usually ran for seven years, and the studios could drop or renew the contracts yearly. A star who rebelled could be loaned out to work for other studios on pictures that had little chance of succeeding. Furthermore, stars were cast repetitively in similar roles. Once the studio discovered someone with star potential and groomed the actor, it tried to stay with the winning formula. Such formulaic casting made it difficult for stars to get more demanding roles. Publicity departments at the big studios promoted the stars and worked hard to ensure the public would view each star in a particular wholesome but glamorous light. Moviegoers contributed to the development of the star system as they began to select movies on the basis of particular stars who were cast in them. Thus the studio heads, combined with audience responses, contributed to the star system.

The star system could punish or reward actors. It made a superstar of Clark Gable, shown here with David O. Selznick and Louis B. Mayer of MGM signing for the part of Rhett Butler in the 1939 film *Gone with the Wind*.

Domination by the Big Five

By 1930, five companies dominated United States movie screens: Warner Bros.; Loew's, Inc., the theater chain that owned Metro-Goldwyn-Mayer; Paramount; RKO; and Twentieth Century Fox. Each company was vertically integrated; each produced motion pictures, operated worldwide distribution outlets, and had a theater chain. Three other companies—Universal, Columbia, and United Artists—had significant holdings but no chain of theaters. Universal and Columbia supplied pictures to the majors, and United Artists was a distribution company for a small group of independents. Theaters owned by the big five companies formed an oligopoly and took in more than 75 percent of the nation's box-office receipts. Through the 1930s and 1940s, these eight companies defined Hollywood.

The depression of the 1930s caused movie revenues to plummet. The major studio companies had difficulty meeting their financial obligations. They had overextended themselves in a market that was declining rather than expanding.

When President Franklin D. Roosevelt introduced the National Recovery Act (NRA), with provisions for cutting competition among industries, the federal government allowed the big five to continue practices they had already established to limit competition. These included **block booking** (requiring all theaters to buy a season's package of films rather than individual productions) and **blind booking** (forcing a theater owner to buy a season's package of films sight unseen). The NRA also allowed the companies to continue the **vertical integration** they had established, which brought them great profits. In return, the studios were supposed to make certain concessions. Although the studios had vociferously opposed unionization, now they readily recognized trade unions of production personnel, which formed some of the least expensive parts of the business, as a way of complying with the act. However, they continued to fight to keep stars outside the collective bargaining system.

Key Concept

Star system By the 1930s, the New York–financed Hollywood studios had developed a system for ensuring financial stability based on movies featuring popular stars in familiar roles. Ironclad contracts forced actors to accept scripts that enhanced the particular image the studio wanted the star to project. Stars also were required to behave as their fans expected them to, both inside and outside the studio.

block booking

The practice of forcing a theater to book movies as a package, rather than individually. Declared illegal in the 1940s.

blind booking

Marketing strategy common in the 1930s and 1940s that required theaters to book movies before they were produced.

vertical integration

A system in which a single corporation controls production (including obtaining the raw materials), distribution, and exhibition of movies. Declared illegal in the 1940s.

Dateline

The Movies in Our Lives

1878. Eadweard Muybridge uses stop-action photography.

1892. Thomas Edison's lab develops the kinetoscope.

1895. Vaudeville theaters begin to show magic-lantern shows.

1903. *The Great Train Robbery,* the forerunner of feature films, is shown.

1900s. Nickelodeons become popular.

1915. *The Birth of a Nation* marks the start of the modern movie industry.

1927. *The Jazz Singer* popularizes sound in feature-length films.

1930. Five large movie companies dominate the industry.

1934. Studios establish decency code for films.

1939–1945. Movie industry helps government promote war effort.

1400–1700	1800	1860	1880	1900	1920	1930

1620. Pilgrims land at Plymouth Rock.

1690. *Publick Occurrences* is published in Boston.

1741. First magazine is published in America.

1776–1783. American Revolution

1830s. The penny press becomes the first truly mass medium in the United States.

1861–1865. American Civil War

1892. Thomas Edison's lab develops the kinetoscope.

1914–1918. World War I

1915. *The Birth of a Nation* marks the start of the modern movie industry.

1920. KDKA in Pittsburgh gets the first commercial radio license.

1930s. The Great Depression

1939. TV is demonstrated at the New York World's Fair.

1939–1945. World War II

Cultural Milestones

Key Concept

Domination of the domestic film market By 1930, five giant Hollywood studios dominated world filmmaking. World War II cut Hollywood off from film markets abroad, but demand for movies intensified in the domestic market.

Growth in the Domestic Market

When World War II began, the film industry lost most of its worldwide business that had been established during the late 1930s. But the **domestic market** improved dramatically because U.S. citizens were earning relatively high

1948. Supreme Court breaks up the industry's vertical integration.

1950s. Television begins to affect movie attendance.

1952. Supreme Court extends First Amendment rights to film.

1960s. Networks begin showing movies during prime time.

1968. Film industry begins using a ratings system.

Late 1960s. Graphic violence and sex become prominent in independent films.

1972. HBO starts satellite distribution to cable systems.

1980s. Video recorder technology is sold to consumers.

Late 1980s. Cable channels increase their financing of feature films.

1990s. Movies are promoted on the World Wide Web.

1990s. Cable systems experiment with movies on demand.

1999. *Star Wars: Episode I-Phantom Menace* Shot with digital system.

2000s. DVD replaces VHS for viewing movies at home.

2006. Warner Bros. offers films online through BitTorrent.

1940	1950	1960	1970	1980	1990	2000

1949. First commercial electronic computer is produced.

Early 1950s. Rock 'n' roll begins.

1969. First person lands on the moon.

1970s. VCR is developed.

1989–1991. Cold War ends and the USSR is dissolved.

Late 1980s. National Science Foundation creates the basis of the Internet.

1996. Telecommunications Act

2000. Presidential election nearly tied.

2001. Terrorist attacks on New York and Washington, D.C.

2003. War with Iraq.

wages and had few commodities on which to spend them. Movies were affordable and available. Domestic **studio film rentals** for the top eight studios increased from $193 million in 1939 to $332 million in 1946. In this peak year, an average of 90 million Americans, or 75 percent of the U.S. population, went to the movies each week.

studio film rental

Movie produced by studios to rent to distributors and/or theaters.

Post–World War II Decline

The movie business declined at the end of the war—even before the rise of television. Returning soldiers bought houses in the suburbs, went back to college on the GI bill, and started families. The decline in movie attendance paralleled a restructuring of the industry after the Supreme Court in 1948, in *United States v. Paramount Pictures, Inc., et al.,* forced the companies to divest themselves of their theater chains and thus limited the vertical integration that had been the norm for thirty years. The Supreme Court's *Paramount* decision ended block booking, fixing of admission prices, and other discriminatory practices, which were declared to be in restraint of trade.

With the *Paramount* decision came increased freedom for producers and stars. Although the major companies continued to dominate the industry, the number of independent producers more than doubled from 1946 to 1956. In response, the major studios competed to provide space and facilities for such producers. Foreign films had more access to the U.S. market, and small **art theaters** sprang up, particularly in university towns and large urban areas. Stars were more reluctant to sign long-term, exclusive contracts, so their talent became more widely available.

Nevertheless, the big companies continued to dominate the production business, both at home and abroad. Because access to movies made in the United States had been limited during the war and many European production facilities were shut down, studios made huge profits from European rentals. Foreign operations, both rentals and production, continued to gain importance; by the 1960s, more than half the revenue of the major studios came from operations overseas.

art theater

Outlet for films designed for their artistic quality rather than for their blockbuster audience appeal that usually are produced by independent companies rather than by the big studios.

Cinerama

Trade name for process that produces wide-screen images.

3-D

Film technique designed to create a sense of depth. Viewers wore special glasses for viewing.

Key Concept

Response to television In the 1950s, the movie industry, desperate to recapture audiences lost to television, competed by offering technical novelties, including 3-D Panavision. Soon Hollywood also collaborated with television, providing studio facilities for making innovative TV series.

Response to Television

By the early 1950s, the movies had a major contender for audiences' time: television. For young families with children, television was simpler and less expensive than going to the movies. For older people, television did not require as much effort. The motion picture industry formulated its ***response to television,*** using the natural advantages of the theater format. Studios began to produce more films in color, to experiment with screen size, and to introduce **Cinerama** and **3-D.** The most lasting innovation was

The post–World War II decline in major movies opened the market for independent producers such as Ingmar Bergman, who experimented with new film techniques. Bergman's *The Seventh Seal* is still shown regularly at university film series.

Panavision, which was introduced by Fox in 1962 and gave the illusion of depth without seeming contrived.

Before long the film industry began to collaborate with television. In 1949, Columbia converted a subsidiary into a television department that produced programs for *Ford Theater* and the comedy series *Father Knows Best.* In 1953, when television made the transition from live to filmed production, Hollywood became the center for television production.

By 1955, Hollywood was also releasing many of its older pictures for television broadcasting. For example, RKO sold its film library to a television programming syndicate for $15 million. During the 1960s, however, the studios realized that they had undervalued their old films. ABC paid Columbia $2 million for the 1957 film *The Bridge on the River Kwai,* and when the film was shown on television on September 12, 1966, sixty million people watched it. Television became a regular market for films, and competitive bidding continued to rise.

In the late 1960s, studios began producing made-for-television movies. In television movies, production costs were kept low, and these movies soon glutted the market, diminishing the demand for older movies. Between television movies and acquired film libraries, the networks discovered that they had enough films stocked for several years and stopped bidding for studio productions. The studios retrenched, but by 1972 they were again selling to the networks. ABC, the youngest network, increased its ratings and forced CBS and NBC to be more competitive. The three networks bid the prices of movies such as *Alien* as high as $15 million in the early '80s. When cable television became widespread in the 1980s, movies became an even hotter commodity. Film ultimately benefited from *converging technologies.* The coming of television and cable increased film viewing.

The development of cable television and direct satellite broadcasting has altered the use of movies on television. Home Box Office (HBO), a cable television channel that began operation in 1972, allowed its subscribers to see movies after their theatrical release, but before the major broadcast networks could acquire them. HBO's success led to the establishment of other premium channels such as Showtime and Cinemax.

In the 1990s, the expansion of channels made possible by fiber-optic cable allowed cable companies to offer pay-per-view movies. These differ from premium channels in that the viewer pays for each viewing rather than a flat monthly fee. Pay-per-view makes films available to the cable and broadcast satellite subscriber at the same time that the movie appears in video stores, before it appears on a channel such as HBO. Some hotels even offer pay-per-view showings of movies that are currently in first-run movie theaters.

Increasingly, movies, whether made for theaters or directly for television, have become a basic building block of television content. The strong film libraries held by Disney, Turner Broadcasting System, and Time Warner were important factors in the mergers between Disney and Capitol Cities/ABC and between Turner Broadcasting System and Time Warner. Television and theaters are no longer competitors. Instead, they are different distribution systems for reaching viewers.

CULTURAL AND POLITICAL DEVELOPMENTS

Before 1952, when the Supreme Court handed down a decision that granted First Amendment protection to film, movies were considered a simple amusement, like a circus. The courts had previously ruled that movies were not a "significant medium for the communication of ideas."

Movies as Art and Social Commentary

The studio, the star system, and a system of repeating popular **film genres,** such as Westerns and science fiction movies, enabled the Hollywood studios to maximize profits. They also guaranteed that a certain type of movie would emanate from Hollywood. U.S. filmmakers left intellectual movies to foreign producers. During the

Panavision

System of lenses used in filming that enabled a film shot in one wide-screen version (Cinemascope, for example) to be shown in theaters without the lenses for that type of projection.

film genre

A kind or style of movie.

silent era, slapstick comedies, Westerns, and melodramas were the most popular genres. However, D. W. Griffith and his contemporaries in the teens and early twenties introduced more sophisticated narratives dominated by characters who were not only goal oriented but also in a hurry to succeed. These narrative structures were linear and came almost directly from the stage. Griffith's *The Birth of a Nation,* for example, was a stage play before he adapted it to film.

Popular culture films such as gangster pictures, musicals, and screwball comedies became popular during the talkie era, and the studio and star systems propelled Hollywood to produce big-budget spectaculars. Yet despite the emphasis on popular culture films and the box office, Hollywood managed to produce, sometimes by accident, lasting classics. Certain artistic directors earned international recognition. For example, Orson Welles wrote, directed, and starred in *Citizen Kane* in 1941, when he was twenty-six years old, and became known throughout the world for his contribution to cinematic technique. *Citizen Kane* was based loosely on the life of newspaper tycoon William Randolph Hearst. Welles included unusual camera angles, backlighting, and condensed time sequences and introduced other film techniques that continue to influence moviemakers today. Many film critics consider *Citizen Kane* to be the greatest American film ever made. However, it was a box-office failure when it was released because Hearst used his immense power in the newspaper and entertainment industries to encourage negative reviews and to force theater owners to boycott the film.

From the 1940s to the early 1960s, films used a narrative structure that featured wholesome heroes and heroines. Although there were attempts at **social realism**, such as Tennessee Williams's *A Streetcar Named Desire,* positive tones and outcomes dominated the big screens. In *Streetcar,* Marlon Brando played Stanley Kowalski, a brooding, unkempt antihero who brutalizes both his wife and her sister. In the 1960s, film content and character changed in dramatic ways. Some critics date the shift to the 1967 production of *Bonnie and Clyde,* a movie about two 1930s gangsters, which critic Pauline Kael described as a film of violence that "puts the sting back into death."[7] The strident films of the 1960s reflected the nation's conflicts over the Vietnam War, youthful rebellion, the civil rights movement, and militant black power efforts. Social conflict and social statement films dominated the decade and the early 1970s.

Since the 1960s, some filmmakers, especially independent **auteurs**, have moved away from highly structured, linear plots to more episodic narratives with finely drawn characters. Their films seek to expose social problems and contradictions. Films include Robert Altman's *Nashville* and *Gosford Park,* John Sayles' *Matewan* and *Lone Star,* and Paul Haggis's *Crash.* In 1994, director Quentin Tarantino ushered in a new kind of **postmodern film** with *Pulp Fiction.* An independent film with a fragmented storyline and dialogue full of popular culture references, *Pulp Fiction* drew from many forms and genres, such as comic books, gangster and Blaxploitation films, and 1950s nostalgia. The film's unexpected financial success ushered in independent film as a significant force in the box office.

After the release of the *Star Wars* science fiction epic in 1977, many films turned to escapism. The early 2000s saw the culmination of fantasy and science fiction in film series such as Harry Potter, Spiderman, and Lord of the Rings. Action pictures with cartoon violence and larger than life male heroes have become the staple of summer blockbusters. Disney has continued its imagineering with *The Little Mermaid, Aladdin, The Lion King, Toy Story,* and *Monsters, Inc.* **Historical epics**, such as *Braveheart,* and **melodramas**, such as *Titanic,* remain favorite traditional genres. These blockbusters are often extremely popular worldwide (see Table 5.1), but have been criticized for their generic storylines and often one-dimensional or stereotypical characters.

Movies and the Marketplace of Ideas

Until recently, Hollywood had rarely produced explicitly political films. Despite the cultural and social impact of movies, the motion picture was not considered "speech" until 1952 and therefore was not protected by the First Amendment to the U.S. Con-

auteur

A director with a highly personal cinematic style who maintains creative control over his or her film.

postmodern film

Using various techniques such as a collision of styles and a suspension of historical time, a postmodern film emphasizes artificiality and creates emotional detachment in its audience.

historical epic

Film genre focusing on heroic myths, legends, and historical incidents and requiring an expensive, large-scale production.

melodrama

Film genre characterized by exaggerated emotions, stereotypical characters and overblown storylines having to do with fate.

Table 5.1	All-Time Box Office Outside the United States and Canada	
1.	*Titanic* (1997)	$1,234,600,000
2.	*The Lord of the Rings: The Return of the King* (2003)	$752,200,000
3.	*Harry Potter and the Sorcerer's Stone* (2001)	$651,100,000
4.	*Harry Potter and the Chamber of Secrets* (2002)	$604,400,000
5.	*Harry Potter and the Goblet of Fire* (2005)	$602,200,000
6.	*The Lord of the Rings: The Two Towers* (2002)	$581,200,000
7.	*Jurassic Park* (1993)	$563,000,000
8.	*The Lord of the Rings: The Fellowship of the Ring* (2001)	$546,900,000
9.	*Harry Potter and the Prisoner of Azkaban* (2004)	$540,100,000

Source: Internet Movie Database, www.imdb.com. Used with permission.

stitution. In 1915 in *Mutual Film Corp. v. Industrial Commission of Ohio,* the U.S. Supreme Court declared that exhibiting films was a business pure and simple, a decision that allowed for the control of film content. To avoid including film under the protection of the First Amendment, for nearly forty years courts adhered to the "simple business" standard and did not recognize movies as "a significant medium for the communication of ideas." However, in 1952 in *Burstyn v. Wilson,* the Supreme Court declared that film content entertained and informed and therefore was subject to First Amendment protection.

In 1922, the motion picture industry voluntarily organized the Motion Picture Producers and Distributors of America (MPPDA) and named Will H. Hays as its president. The move was designed to avoid government regulation and to combat negative publicity about stars, divorce, and the prevalence of drugs in the industry. Twelve years later, a group of Catholic bishops organized the National Legion of Decency to develop lists of films that were acceptable and not acceptable for Catholic viewers. Hollywood responded by establishing a production *code of film content* that forbade sex, excessive violence, and vulgar language. Violators of the code were to pay a $25,000 fine to the MPPDA, although the fine was never publicly invoked. The code, although often skirted or challenged, remained on the books until 1968, when the industry adopted a ratings system. The ratings system shifted responsibility to the movie viewer by specifying the type of audience the movie had been designed to attract. In 1984 and again in 1992, the industry revised specific ratings, but the principle of alerting the audience rather than controlling content remained as the guide.

> ### Key Concept
>
> **Code of film content** Various regulations have been in place, particularly at the local level, to control the content of films shown in communities. The film industry, constantly facing pressure to produce exciting films yet avoid moral injury to young audiences, developed a production code to comply with various local government restrictions. In 1968, the industry altered its position from controlling content to developing a system of ratings to identify levels of sexual and violent content and adult language.

Government opinions of the motion picture industry's activity during World War II were mixed. Major producers cooperated to produce war films on what they termed a nonprofit basis. Nevertheless, during 1941 and 1942, the Army Pictorial Division alone spent more than $1 million in Hollywood. Critics claimed the producers filmed for the government during slack times, or when the studios otherwise would have stood idle, and that by cooperating, the industry managed to remain relatively untouched by the war. Therefore, despite Walt Disney's portrayal of Donald Duck's willingness to pay taxes with patriotic enthusiasm and Frank Capra's direction of the Why We Fight series designed to train new soldiers, the motion picture industry still had a variety of enemies in Congress.

The Motion Picture Bureau, a division of the Office of War Information (OWI), attempted to influence Hollywood producers to support the war effort. One of its tasks was to try to motivate producers to incorporate more realistic pictures of African-American life into films. A 1942 survey conducted by the Office of Facts and Figures revealed that 49 percent of the African Americans in Harlem thought they would be no worse off if Japan won the war. In response to this evidence, OWI wanted Hollywood to tone down its racist images of African Americans to foster a sense of unity in the country.[8]

Although the industry had catered to the Legion of Decency and various economic groups, when OWI attempted to promote more positive images of African Americans, the industry cried censorship. For example, MGM in 1938 had hand carried its script of Robert Sherwood's antifascist play, *Idiot's Delight,* to Italy for approval after drastically altering it to avoid offending Benito Mussolini. Warner Bros.' coal mining saga, *Black Fury,* was altered to blame labor unrest on union radicals rather than on mine operators after the National Coal Association protested.

OWI efforts to promote positive African-American images had little effect. A 1945 Columbia University study found that of one hundred African-American appearances in wartime films, seventy-five perpetuated stereotypes, thirteen were neutral, and only twelve were positive. OWI hesitated to push very far, claiming the war came first.[9]

Congressional frustration with the film industry was not limited to its concern about treatment of minorities in wartime. In the late 1940s and 1950s, conservative members of Congress attacked the industry in hearings before the House Committee on Un-American Activities. This committee and Senator Joseph McCarthy's parallel committee in the Senate pummeled the media industries, taking special delight in attacking the motion picture and broadcast industries. Congressman and committee chairman Thomas Parnell intended to prove that the film industry had been infiltrated by Communists who introduced subversive propaganda into the movies.

At the 1947 hearings, ten screenwriters, later dubbed the Hollywood Ten, refused to say whether they had been members of the Communist Party, invoking the First Amendment guarantee of freedom of the press and freedom of association. The Hollywood Ten all went to jail for contempt of Congress. Although recent research shows that these writers had in no way tried to formally propagandize or commit any type of subversion, Hollywood did not stand behind them. Rather, it panicked. Many Hollywood liberals such as Humphrey Bogart and John Huston supported the writers initially, but most support disappeared when the heads of the large studios threatened the supporters' careers. The Hollywood Ten were suspended from work, and executives invited Hollywood's talent guilds to help them eliminate any subversives from their ranks.

From 1951 to 1954, a second round of hearings investigated Hollywood further. Director Elia Kazan, who would later win an Academy Award for *On the Waterfront,* eagerly testified and lost many friends. The result of the hearings was an informal blacklist of actors, directors, writers, and producers whom the major studios would not hire. A few found work with independent production companies, often using false names. Once the national scare ended and Senator McCarthy was exposed as an irrational manipulator of fear, the film industry enjoyed relative freedom from government interference and regulation. In 2005, George Clooney's *Good Night, and Good Luck* explored the history of McCarthyism while giving a timely warning against governmental control over the press.

An anticommunist witch-hunt fueled attacks on Hollywood stars during the late 1940s and early 1950s. Ten film writers were jailed for refusal to answer trumped-up charges of communist affiliation. A chill effect followed, with panicky Hollywood executives refusing to employ many actors and producers.

The story of Edward R. Murrow's work to expose Senator McCarthy's tactics was depicted in the 2005 movie *Good Night and Good Luck.*

After the 9/11 attacks, political documentaries gained an unprecedented international popularity and financial viability. For example, Michael Moore's *Fahrenheit 9/11* won an Oscar for best documentary in 2003. Other films of social criticism followed, including *Super Size Me,* which exposed the medical impacts of fast food; *The Corporation,* which described multinational corporations as psychotic; and *Uncovered: The War on Iraq,* which critiqued the government's reasons for going to war. Former Vice President Al Gore's *An Inconvenient Truth,* on global warming, received two standing ovations at the Cannes Film Festival. Critics have put forward various reasons for the success of such films, including the urge to rebel against what some see as conservative mainstream media, a taste for realism and fact-based film after 9/11, and a new personable style in such films which often feature an ordinary person trying to make sense of a social problem.

The Role of Women in Movie History   Since the beginning of feature films, most women in the movie business played second billing to men, just as minorities played minor roles. ***Stereotypes of women and minorities*** abounded. A female actor could not open a movie, which means "attract a large audience," by herself. Even acclaimed actresses such as Katharine Hepburn and Bette Davis were defined in most films as much by their leading men as by their own star power. Few women were movie executives, and even fewer directed films.

Today, women have a greater impact in the movie business. Actors such as Sandra Bullock and Julia Roberts open films and attract large audiences. Women sit on executive boards of major studios, and female directors produce quality, money-making movies. Penny Marshall directed *Big* and was executive producer of *A League of Their Own.* Oprah Winfrey also won kudos for her production of Toni Morrison's best-selling novel-turned-screenplay, *Beloved.* In 2004, director Sofia Coppola was nominated for an Academy Award for *Lost in Translation.*

Despite their advances, women still face problems in Hollywood. Young actors often feel typecast in roles that depend on looks more than talent, and these roles often stereotype women. In 2002, Halle Berry won the Oscar for best actress in *Monster's Ball* after Angela Bassett, who was nominated for best actress in the 1993 movie

Halle Berry, seen here with her costar Billy Bob Thornton, won the 2002 Best Actress Academy Award for her performance in *Monster's Ball.* Berry was the first African American to win the best actress award.

What's Love Got to Do with It, turned down the role because she said the role was a stereotype of black women's sexuality.[10] Interestingly, the controversy involving this stereotypical treatment of women received far less media attention than the treatment of women in the 1991 movie *Thelma and Louise.* This film was labeled as male bashing, mostly by male columnists, because it showed two strong women refusing to be intimidated by men.

People of Color in Film

An analysis of movies and race begins with the history of stereotypical treatment of people of color by white filmmakers. From the early presentation of people of color in film during the 1890s, the images have been inaccurate and limited. During the 1930s, 1940s, and 1950s, movies presented African Americans as lazy and slow thinking. This stereotype has been called the "Step 'n Fetchit" role—a term that came from the stage name of Lincoln Perry, who made a career of playing this type of character. Native Americans have been presented either as the "noble savage" or the "blood-thirsty savage."[11]

The stereotypes associated with Hispanics and Latino movie characters have varied from the Latin lovers of the 1920s to the bandidos of the 1930s and 1940s to the gang members and drug dealers of the 1960s. Early portrayals of Asian Americans often showed them as scheming and untrustworthy. However, more often than not, Asian Americans were just missing from films or had minor roles.[12]

Often ignored in history are the films made by filmmakers of color. The first black film company, for example, was the Lincoln Motion Picture Company, formed in 1915 in Los Angeles to showcase black talent. In 1916 the Frederick Douglass Film Company formed on the East Coast to counteract antiblack images in the movie *The Birth of a Nation.*[13] Hampered by financing and distribution problems, both companies closed during the early 1920s. They were replaced by other African-American film companies. Oscar Micheaux became the best-known black filmmaker of this period, producing dozens of silent and talking films. Many of these films dealt with racial issues and presented African-American life in greater variety than was found in major studio films.

From the late 1930s to the 1950s, a variety of companies produced movies with all-African-American casts for the segregated theaters of the black community. These films tended to imitate films produced by whites and were made cheaply. As film historian Daniel J. Leab said, "The leads remained very Caucasian-looking and spoke good English; the villains and comic figures, who were more Negroid in features and darker skinned, tended to speak in dialect."[14] The failure to present African Americans in a more realistic fashion in these films can be largely attributed to the financial and distribution control that whites continued to hold over the black film industry. In order to be seen, films about African Americans had to fit white stereotypes.

Movies by Chicano and Hispanic filmmakers in the United States came much later than those by African Americans. Although a few films were produced by Chicano filmmakers during the early and mid-1960s, the early 1970s saw the blossoming of Chicano-made movies. Mostly documentaries, such as *Requiem-29: Racism and Police Repression against Chicanos* by David García, these films dealt with the problems confronting Chicanos and were part of the overall social unrest of the late 1960s and early 1970s.[15] However, fictional films by Chicanos and Hispanics developed even later.

In the 1960s, major studios discovered that African-American actors could make money at the box office. Sidney Poitier became an acclaimed actor and bankable star. The change in Hollywood reflected the changing mood of a nation whose consciousness was being raised by the civil rights movement. The late 1960s and early 1970s saw the arrival of the black action film. *Shaft,* directed by famous black photographer Gordon Parks, came out in 1971 and made $6.1 million.[16] Hollywood liked these profits, and similar films followed, including two *Shaft* sequels. Although these films starred African Americans, they were produced by major film studios, and some critics said they exploited the anger that black audiences felt about the lack of changes in society. In fact, they are now referred to as **"Blaxploitation" films**.

For many years, independent black filmmakers struggled for financing and recognition. Then, in the 1980s and 1990s, the New Black Cinema emerged, led by directors Spike Lee and John Singleton. Lee's *Do the Right Thing* and Singleton's *Boyz N the Hood* receive critical acclaim and made a profit, prompting further investment in African-American cinema. Some critics worried that films like *Boyz N the Hood* and *Menace II Society* were creating new stereotypes of young, criminalized black men in urban ghettoes. Others thought the films revealed a realistic world not normally seen in Hollywood cinema. African Americans still struggle for representation in mainstream cinema, but have been able to direct and star in a variety of films that resist any single definition.

Although the number of titles remains small, Latino and Native American filmmakers began to produce movies during the 1980s. *Zoot Suit* (1981) and *La Bamba* (1987) by Luis Valdez, *Born in East L.A.* (1987) by Cheech Marin, and *American Me* (1992) by Edward James Olmos were early Latino films. More recently, Robert Rodríguez, whose first film *El Mariachi* in 1992 was made with $7,000 and earned more than $1.8 million, has moved into the movie mainstream with the critical and box-office successes *Spy Kids* and *Spy Kids 2.* Independent Latino/Hispanic cinema has had a number of art house successes, including *The Motorcycle Diaries, Maria Full of Grace, Real Women Have Curves,* and *Amores Perros.* But the market for Spanish-language commercial films is not yet successful.

Films made by Native American filmmakers are even more of a rarity. In 1998, *Smoke Signals,* a film advertised as the first feature film written, acted, directed, and produced by Native Americans, was shown to rave reviews at the Sundance Film Festival in Utah. The movie was directed by Chris Eyre from a book by Sherman Alexie titled *The Lone Ranger and Tonto Fistfight in Heaven.* Despite this film's critical success, it continues to stand alone as an example of how Native Americans can find their own voice to speak about themselves. Few movies feature Native American actors or are made for Native American audiences.

Asian-American filmmakers have yet to emerge as a force in Hollywood. This may reflect the strength of the Asian film industries in Japan, China, and Taiwan. For example, *Crouching Tiger, Hidden Dragon,* directed by Ang Lee, was nominated for the Academy Award as best picture in 2001, and Jackie Chan, who was born in Hong Kong, has had several American hits, such as *Rush Hour* and *Rush Hour 2.*

South Asian director Mira Nair has made a number of successful, award-winning films, such as *Monsoon Wedding* and *Mississippi Masala.* N. Night Shyamalan, whose parents are Indian, has been called the next Steven Spielberg. His 1999 film *The Sixth Sense,* with Bruce Willis, grossed almost $300 million in the United States.

Although people of color continue to be stereotyped in films and struggle for roles in Hollywood, events in 2002 raised hopes that improvement is underway. For the first time ever, a woman of color, Halle Berry, won the Oscar for best actress, and

Blaxploitation films

A film genre that arose in the 1970s featuring black actors, urban scenes, and funk and soul music.

Mira Nair

Known for her lush, sensitive portrayals of immigrant communities, director Mira Nair has made a number of award-winning movies with a distinctive personal vision. Born in India in 1957 to a civil servant, Nair has also lived in the United States, Uganda, and South Africa, giving her a unique, global perspective on the experience of people moving from place to place.

As a university student, Nair became involved in political theater in New Delhi, and her concern with social activism continues to shape her films. In 1976, she came to the United States to study at Harvard where she learned photography and film. Nair began as a documentary filmmaker, returning to Delhi to record the lives of people on the street.

Nair's first big fiction film was *Salaam Bombay!,* which chronicles the life of Krishna, a street boy navigating the dangers of the city. She recruited twenty-four Bombay street children to act in the film. After the *Salaam Bombay!* world premier at Cannes, the crowd applauded for fifteen minutes, and it won the 1988 Caméra d'Or for best first feature film.

Nair then gained studio backing for *Mississippi Masala,* starring Denzel Washington and Sarita Choudhury. Exploring the complexities of global identities, the interracial love story focuses on Meena, a young woman born in India and raised in Uganda before her family immigrates to the United States. The Hindu word "masala," means a spice mixture, and characterizes Nair's cinematic vision. *Mississippi Masala* was an artistic success, winning three awards at the Venice Film Festival. Nair has continued to make feature films about the immigrant experience, including *The Perez Family* about a Cuban family in Miami and *My Own Country* about an East Indian doctor treating AIDS in Tennessee.

Nair's *Monsoon Wedding* was released in 2001 to great popular and critical acclaim and grossed $14 million at the U.S. box office. Shot in thirty-days with a handheld camera, the film is a lavish spectacle set in India and inspired by the traditions of Bollywood, the Indian film industry. Nair's success led to further opportunities to direct an adaptation of *Vanity Fair* and the HBO original film *Hysterical Blindness.*

Nair splits her time between New York and Kampala, Uganda, where she has founded the Maisha film lab to encourage East African and South Asian filmmakers. Nair explains, "Maisha is built on the premise that if we don't tell our stories, no one else will. It was always time for our stories, but now is the time we will make them our way."

Sources: India Abroad, September 2, 2005: A5; John Lahr, "Whirlwind," *New Yorker,* December 9, 2002: 100.

Denzel Washington won the Oscar for best actor. This occurred on the night Sidney Poitier was recognized for his lifetime achievements as an actor and director by the Academy of Motion Picture Arts and Sciences.

TODAY'S MARKET STRUCTURE

The film industry is still dominated by a group of major studios. It has survived repeated challenges, including the breakup of theater networks; the rise of television, cable, and pay-per-view; and the popularity of the videocassette recorder (VCR) and the DVD player. The studios have not only survived, they have adapted, prospered, and grown. For example, Rupert Murdoch, the Australian press lord, merged Twentieth Century Fox with his chain of metropolitan television stations acquired from Metromedia Television. The Fox television stations give the corporate family instant access to wide distribution of a film after it appears in the nation's theaters.[17] In 1985, Ted Turner bought MGM and acquired its film library for his superstation before reselling the movie company. The major studios still control about 80 percent of the business in the United States and much of the market in countries like Australia, Italy, France, Germany, and Mexico. Although the number of independent producers has increased during the past twenty years, all of them contract with the studios to distribute their films.

In 2005, a film about a Memphis pimp, *Hustle and Flow*, was nominated for two Oscars and won for Best Original Song, by Three 6 Mafia. Three 6 Mafia was the first hip-hop group to perform at the Academy Awards, making movie history.

The key to the studios' success continues to be their domination of movie **distribution.** The studios see all the forms of distribution—theaters, DVD/VHS, pay-per-view, television networks, cable channels, satellites, and premium networks—as windows of opportunity for distributing their films. In each of the windows, consumers pay a different price for the same material. Watching a movie in a theater costs more than buying it through pay-per-view on cable or renting a DVD. Renting a DVD costs more than getting a movie as part of HBO, and HBO costs more than watching a movie on the TNT cable network. In each window, consumers pay less, but they have to wait longer after the initial distribution to see the film.[18] Movies hit the video stores and pay-per-view about six months after they leave theaters. After another six months or so, the film will be on HBO. This "windows" process allows studios to reach people who will not pay $7 to $10 to see a film in the theater. It also explains why studios have become part of multimedia corporations. By controlling the windows, the corporations squeeze more profit out of each viewing opportunity. This is why Viacom, for example, owns the CBS Network, Paramount Pictures, Showtime, and Blockbuster video stores.

distributors

The people of the movie industry who arrange to engage movies in theaters, then on television.

The Hollywood movie industry often relies on remakes of previously successful films. Peter Jackson's *King Kong* uses award-winning special effects to create an even more realistic version of the famous ape.

AUDIENCE DEMAND IN MOVIE MARKETS

In 2004, Hollywood's major studies reported a drop of 9 percent in theatrical admissions, to 1.4 billion moviegoers. The next year, the decline continued with a 6 percent drop in box office sales. International receipts also dropped, from 2004's record high of $25.23 billion to $23.24 billion.[19] Industry analysts blamed piracy, competition with DVDs and video games, and a lack of quality films. In 2006, Hollywood studies banked on tried-and-true formulas with sequels of *Pirates of the Caribbean, X-Men,* and *Mission Impossible.* Because religious controversy can bring in box office receipts, *The Da Vinci Code* was expected to be a success, and despite bad reviews, sold $224 million in tickets worldwide, just behind *Star Wars: Episode III, Revenge of the Sith.*

In the early days, movies catered to the family audience. From the era of the nickelodeon to the age of Panavision, mothers, fathers, and children flocked to neighborhood movie houses and to the theater palaces in the cities. After the advent of television, as couples settled down to raise children in the suburbs, the movies became less attractive. For parents, going to a movie meant paying for a babysitter, tickets, and transportation, so many chose to stay home and watch television. Slowly, the audience changed, and from the late 1960s until the late 1980s, the seventeen-year-old was the most reliable moviegoer. Demographics have changed, however, and aging baby boomers now far outnumber teenagers in the United States and present a viable group for studios to target.

The movie viewing audience became older during the 1980s and early 1990s, according to data published by the Motion Picture Association of America. In 1981, 24 percent of moviegoers were between the ages of sixteen and twenty, but by 1992, that percentage dropped to 15 percent. Admissions for people between forty and forty-nine rose from 6 percent to 16 percent during that period. However, since 1992 the age distribution of moviegoers has remained relatively stable.

Younger viewers retain great influence over which films are made. People between ages twelve and twenty-four made up 19 percent of the U.S. population but 28 percent of total theater admissions in 2005 according to the Motion Picture Association. Nearly half of all teenagers go to the movies at least once a month, compared to just one in four adults. Young people rarely wait for recommendations and reviews; they go to movies as soon as they open. They attend movies as part of their social activity with friends, choose movies on impulse, and are heavily influenced by television advertising. By contrast, older adults attend movies selectively, preferring films that represent more sophisticated fare than they can find on television. They choose movies after reading reviews and listening to their friends' recommendations.

Adults accompany young children to family movies and appreciate the music, acting, story lines, and animation. Adults, as well as the children they accompany, are partly responsible for the success of films such as the Harry Potter movies, along with classics such as *Beauty and the Beast, Aladdin,* and *Home Alone.* The movie industry's ratings system has emerged as a **labeling system targeted to specific demographics.** In general, films rated G and PG earn more money than films rated R or NC-17. None of the top ten all-time grossing films has an R rating.

A movie with an R rating can't be advertised on television and isn't allowed in some theaters. A producer wishing to make an R-rated film must negotiate with major studios, which have a policy against releasing NC-17 films. The meaning of an NC-17 rating is frequently under challenge, with some family groups, pediatricians, and educators arguing that the ratings system doesn't adequately protect children.

Increasingly, the U.S. audience in all its various segments is only a portion of the audience to which U.S. movies are directed. Profits can be doubled by showings in the international market. Furthermore, studios are measuring the popularity of particular stars and genres in the international markets before film scripts are even developed.

Key Concept

Labeling for audience demographics Movie ratings systems have been developed to target the various demographics that constitute the filmgoing public. As family audiences gave way first to the teenage audience, then to the baby boomers, the ratings system adapted. The current ratings system is as follows: G: general audiences; PG: parental guidance suggested; PG-13: special guidance for children under thirteen; R: people under seventeen must be accompanied by an adult; NC-17: no one under seventeen admitted.

Violence in Film

Speaking at an Amnesty International meeting in 2004, actor Patrick Stewart lambasted the movie industry for its depictions of violence against women. In particular, he took on Quentin Tarantino's *Kill Bill*, calling it "a deeply offensive film." Tarantino has often been criticized for the ultraviolence his movies, such as *Reservoir Dogs* and *Pulp Fiction*.

While pediatricians, social scientists, and politicians have been concerned about the effects of media violence on children, cultural critics have explored film violence as a question of history, meaning, and ethics. Cinematic violence is as old as the medium, with plenty of blood and gore in early shoot-em-up Westerns, war epics, slasher films like *Psycho,* and gangster movies like *The Godfather.*

Cultural critic Henry Giroux has given us three useful categories for thinking about film violence: ritualistic, hyperreal, and symbolic. In action films, the violence is ritualistic: formulaic and repetitious. The very definition of an action film lies in the mounting body count, as in *Die Hard's* 264 killings. The audience is not expected to think about the violence, or about who is being killed, but rather to experience the film as entertainment even thought it might contain racist and sexist messages.

Hyperreal violence is connected to a genre of film that features realistic, ultra-violent scenes combined with gritty dialogue, irony, and humor. Tarantino's films, like *Reservoir Dogs* and *Pulp Fiction,* aim to distance the audience emotionally from hyperreal violence, so that they can watch without feeling guilt at their pleasure in it. The characters in the films, and subsequently the audience, are neither good nor evil, but exist in a moral limbo.

Finally, symbolic violence provokes us to think about human actions and conditions. Clint Eastwood's *Unforgiven* critiqued the

ritualistic violence of the Western and the image of the hero that Eastwood himself had often played. The violence in *Schindler's List* provokes us to think of a society's capacity for terror and genocide. Symbolic violence engages our emotions and asks us to reflect morally on the social conditions that lead to violence.

Giroux suggests that thinking through the kinds of violence connects to questions about the ethical responsibilities of filmmakers and the social causes and cultural effects of violence.

Sources: Henry A. Giroux, "Pulp Fiction and the Culture of Violence," *Harvard Educational Review* 65 (Summer 1995): 299–315; BBC News, March 4, 2004, news.bbc.co.uk/1/hi/entertainment/film/3537707.stm, accessed June 13, 2006.

SUPPLYING THE AUDIENCE'S DEMAND

Movies meet the demands of the audience and make profits not only through traditional showings at theaters but also through release to the international market, pay-per-view television channels, home videos, premium channels, and television networks. Movie theaters usually split box-office receipts with distributors, who also charge booking fees to moviemakers. Exhibitors make a good deal of their money, however, on refreshments, which often are marked up by 60 percent over their wholesale cost.

In the 1990s, U.S. theater operators expanded to accommodate strong movie attendance. They built new, improved theaters with state-of-the-art sound systems and stadium-style seating. A blockbuster film could open on five thousand to six thousand screens and make its cost back in two weeks. But the rush to build backfired during 2000 and 2001. Six of the nation's largest theater chains filed for bankruptcy, and after a spate of consolidations, only a few companies such as AMC and Cinemark had control over domestic moviegoing. The Motion Picture Association reported a net loss of

Movies and Video Games

The relationship between the movie industry and the video game industry flows both ways. Movies are made into video games, and video games are made into movies. In the domain of media convergence, content such as narratives and characters can ideally be adapted to any platform. Industry resources, such as advertising, creative development, and digital technologies can be shared. However, video games and movies are significantly different. Players spend many hours emotionally involved in the levels of the video game, while moviegoers expect more complex characters and a linear storyline that resolves itself in two hours.

Much of the profit made from a Hollywood movie no longer comes from its box-office release. Instead, money comes from licensing of the content to be used for TV programs, cartoons, official toys, DVDs, Pay-TV, and video games. The latest video game release is greeted by gamers at least as avidly as the latest blockbuster film is greeted by moviegoers. The combination of the two can mean big profits.

Movie producers often begin early to develop a video game tie-in. For example, when director Peter Jackson began filming *King Kong*, he approached famed game designer Michel Ancel of Ubisoft Entertainment, located in France, to make a video game adaptation. A gamer himself, Jackson had a vision for the game, such as providing an alternative ending in which the ape is saved from death and returned safely home to Skull Island. After agreeing to the project, the Ubisoft team met with *King Kong's* writers to make sure the game script followed the tone of the film. The team also worked with Jackson's studio to incorporate visual elements, creatures, and the voices of the film's cast. *King Kong: The Official Game of the Movie* was released a month before the film, sharing its holiday promotional push. The collaboration was successful. The game was widely praised and won Spike TV's award for best game based on a movie.

After dismal failures, such as the 1993 attempt to turn *Super Mario Bros.* into a movie, collaborators on films and video games are learning how to bring the forms together for profitable entertainment for both mass audiences and serious gamers.

Sources: Edward Jay Epstein, "Hollywood, the Remake," *Wall Street Journal*, December 29, 2005: A10; Xavier Poix, "Ubisoft's Peter Jackson's *King Kong*," *Game Developer*, April 2006: 28–36.

401 screens from 1999 to 2001.[20] With the growth of DVD, pay-per-view, flat-TV home studios, and the potential of Internet-delivered films, the number of screens will likely decline even more in the coming decades. Distributing movies will take on a new meaning as movie studios search for outlets other than the movie theater.

Product Placement: Supplying the Advertising Market

For the first one hundred years of the U.S. movie industry, advertising played a small part in the financing of movies. However, that is changing. Movie companies face blockbuster budgets in excess of $100 million, and companies concerned about people's increasingly cynical response to television commercials constantly search for ways to sell their products more effectively. These two needs have seen an increase in an advertising strategy called ***product placement***. This involves displaying a clearly identifiable product in a film, such as having a popular star in a film drinking not just any soft drink, but specifically a can of Pepsi. Critics argue that product placement is deceptive because the viewer does not recognize the ad for what it is. Industry spokespeople have another point of view: Director John Badham notes that film budgets have become so large that producers need to look for new types of revenue. "From a producer's or a director's view, product placement is a great way to reduce the budget and keep the studio quiet."[21]

The technique is not new. In 1945, film star Joan Crawford downed Jack Daniels bourbon whiskey in the Warner Bros. production *Mildred Pierce*. However, in 1982

Key Concept

Product placement Movie production has been financed primarily by admission revenues rather than sponsored ads. However, since the 1980s, significant indirect advertising income has come from the product placement system, whereby a product, such as a Coca-Cola can, is clearly discernible in the movie.

product placement hit the big time when sales of Reese's Pieces soared 66 percent in three months after the candy was showcased in Steven Spielberg's *E. T. the Extra-Terrestrial.* Hollywood-featured releases became an important element of every consumer marketing program.[22] Spielberg struck again in 2002 with the release of *Minority Report.* Product placement of brands such as Burger King, Century 21, and Guinness brought in $25 million to cover almost a quarter of the film's $102 million budget.[23]

Minority Report was not alone in the increasing use of product placement. The Austin Powers franchise has been aggressive in product placement. Who doesn't know that Dr. Evil stocks Starbucks coffee in his lair? In 2002, Coors Brewing Co. signed a deal with Miramax Films to be the official sponsor of theatrical premieres of Miramax films in the United States. However, controversy arose over the Coors product placement in *Scary Movie 3* because the film was directed at a teenage audience and rated PG-13. Since then, Coors products have not appeared in any Miramax movies. With the need to reduce risk for blockbuster movies, studios will continue to sell placement aggressively in their movies. At issue is the influence this may have over viewers.

The Home-Viewing Revolution

Television brought movies into the home, but viewers had no choice but to watch what was available or to turn off the TV set. When Sony introduced the Betamax home videocassette recorder in 1976, people could select what they wanted to watch at home and when they wanted to watch it. With the advent of video rental stores, people no longer had to go to theaters to see the films they wanted to see. However, the high cost kept many people from purchasing VCRs. JVC introduced VHS technology a few months later and provided the competition that drove down the cost and led to the eventual demise of the Beta format.

When the VCR first appeared, it was not a popular piece of equipment among movie moguls. Jack Valenti, president of the Motion Picture Association of America, called the VCR a "parasitical instrument."[24] Valenti was about to witness a **home-viewing revolution**. At first the studios attempted to sell movies on videocassettes directly to the public, but high costs made that impractical. Sensing a business opportunity, some entrepreneurs bought the expensive videocassettes and rented them out at affordable rates. As rental stores began to spring up in neighborhoods, film studios capitalized on the new market by releasing more and more films on video. As more videos became available, more people bought VCRs, and the purchase price of popular videos decreased. Today, popular family movies such as *Harry Potter and the Sorcerer's Stone* first make money at the box office. Then the theater popularity prompts buyers to pay $15 to $20 for a videocassette or DVD that they can watch again and again.

> **Key Concept**
>
> **Home-viewing revolution** At the time of its appearance in the mid-1970s, the videocassette recorder (VCR) was perceived as a threat to the traditional film industry. Movie producers feared consumers' ability to record movies from television to watch at their leisure. However, the industry quickly learned to join the revolution, to profit by spinoff sales of tapes of popular films, and to create products directly for the home-viewing market.

The home-viewing revolution took a new twist with the introduction of digital videocassette players in 1997. DVDs have sharper images and carry far more material than do tapes and have moved quickly to supplant the VCR as the technology of choice for home viewing. Movie studios continue to increase the number of their older titles available on DVD, which allows them to sell more copies of older titles.

Many DVDs now provide extra content, such as director interviews and added scenes. When moviegoers leave the theater, about 42 percent of them plan to buy the DVD.[25] More women than men prefer seeing movies at home. Children's films are especially popular, with some, like Disney's *The Return of Jafar* and *Tarzan and Jane,* released directly to DVD and VHS.

Although the home-viewing revolution is more than a quarter-century old, it remains far from over. The delivery of movies over the Internet and video-on-demand over cable broadband will give viewers even more control and choice, which is something viewers enjoy and will pay for. Home theaters with flat screen TVs and rich audio sound combined with digital delivery of movies will make staying at home even more appealing.

SUPPLYING THE INTERNATIONAL MARKET

Film has always been an international medium. In 1895 the first public screening of short films occurred in France, the United States, Germany, and Belgium.[26] Today, despite the dominance of U.S.-made films in most markets, movies remain essentially international. Three trends demonstrate the global nature of films: strong domestic film industries in many countries, growing exportation of films from many countries, and increasing coproduction of films across national boundaries. ***Competition in the international market,*** therefore, takes a variety of forms.

Key Concept

Competition in the international market The international sale of films has been an important source of profit for the U.S. movie industry, which sometimes earns more on violent or sensational U.S. movies abroad than at home. Some countries see U.S. films as a threat to their domestic film industries. However, several nations have vigorous movie traditions of their own, and British, French, and Chinese film styles have influenced U.S. filmmaking.

Film Around the World

European countries have had strong film industries for more than one hundred years. British, French, and Swedish films have had a small market in the United States, although Hollywood would often remake the European films with American actors. The Indian film industry, often called Bollywood, out-produces all other countries with over 800 films per year. However, it makes much less profit than Hollywood, which produces fewer films. In the twenty-first century, Bollywood has begun to compete more strongly against Hollywood in the world market, catering to millions of South Asians who have immigrated to other countries. With a new wave of globally minded directors and higher budgets and technological investments, Bollywood is following Hollywood's lead in its marketing campaigns, tying local products to native and imported films.

Nigeria's film industry, known as Nollywood, has become the third largest in the world. Nollywood produces about 2,000 films a year, usually in English, shot with handheld cameras, and distributed all over Africa on compact discs. Supplanting U.S. imports, Nollywood films feature voodoo horror, epics from African history, and African stories about love and family.

China has had a strong cinematic tradition, beginning in the early twentieth century with films depicting legendary scenes of ancient swordfighters. In the 1940s, Hong Kong became the center of the Chinese film industry, and, in the 1960s, its kung fu films, like Bruce Lee's *Fists of Fury,* attracted ethnic and working class audiences in the United States. Lee is so well known worldwide that a statue was erected to

Film industries outside the United States, such as India's Bollywood, present serious international competition for Hollywood. Bollywood films like *Devdas* (2002) feature a distinctive film-making style with colorful costumes and sets, melodramatic plots, and song and dance numbers.

Global Impact

Conflicts in Power and Values

The popularity of Hollywood exports has sometimes been met with criticism that U.S. cultural values and economic power are being imposed upon the world's people. When Jackie Chan visited India's film capital, Mumbai, in 2005, he told an audience that young people try too hard to imitate Western film stars and that film industries outside of the United States should fight to preserve their own cultures. While many film scholars dismiss the notion that Hollywood movies threaten local cultures and their filmmaking enterprises, the debate continues on the negative influences of the world's most successful film business.

The influence of Western sexual mores on India's Bollywood film is one example of conflict. Before the 1990s, Bollywood films were family centered and even a kiss on the lips was considered taboo. However, when Bollywood films began to languish at the box office, filmmakers began to produce steamy love stories with provocative scenes. Social critics have attributed the success of these new films as coming from a middle-class Indian audience's exposure to Western media, broadcast on satellite TV. Not everyone has been happy with the change. Some Indian traditionalists would prefer a return to what they see as an uncontaminated culture with strong Hindu family values.

Another problem is that Hollywood films sometimes misrepresent the cultures to which they market. When it was released in Japan, *Memoirs of a Geisha* caused an uproar because of its historical inaccuracies, stereotypical portrayal of an exotic East, and the use of Chinese actors.

Some countries control and censor Hollywood imports to help promote their own domestic films and preserve their cultural distinctiveness. China allows only 20 imported movies per year and blocks them out completely during the summer months. Although *Mission Impossible III* was filmed partially in China with the help of the country's film industry, the government censored it for violence and what it perceived as a negative portrayal of Shanghai. Venezuela's President Hugo Chavez began the Film Villa Foundation to produce Latin American film with its own superheroes for children, offsetting the U.S. media portrayals of Latinos as criminals and drug traffickers. In 2005, members of the United Nation's cultural agency, UNESCO, approved a convention stating that countries should have the sovereign right to promote and protect their distinctive cultural expressions. The United States refused to sign because of fears that the treaty would interfere with free trade.

Hollywood's expansion into world markets has been commercially successful, but it has not been without question, conflict, or resistance.

Sources: Herald Sun, December 13, 2005: 63; *Global Information Network*, October 20, 2005: 1; *Financial Times*, December 13, 2005: 15.

him in Bosnia to stand as a symbol of ethnic harmony. Jackie Chan, from Hong Kong, is also beloved of global audiences for his comic action films that stand up for the little guy. In 2001, the respected Taiwanese director Ang Lee transformed the martial arts film into a high art spectacle with *Crouching Tiger, Hidden Dragon,* a worldwide box office hit that was nominated for a Best Picture Oscar.

In addition to growing domestic markets, several countries have seen growth in the exportation of their films. Australian and New Zealand movie companies have found both financial success and critical acclaim in the United States. The string of successes include Australia's *My Brilliant Career* (1979), the Mad Max movies, and *Crocodile Dundee* (1986). Following the success of these films, several members of the Australian movie industry, including actor Mel Gibson and director Peter Weir, moved to Hollywood. The Australian film industry continues to enjoy its renaissance, however, with successes in the United States in the late 1990s with films such as *Muriel's Wedding* and *Me, Myself, I.* Foreign films have succeeded not only in the marketplace but in U.S. award competitions. In 1993, *The Piano,* a New Zealand film starring a New Zealander and two Americans, was nominated for an Academy Award for best picture. In 2001, the Australian film *Moulin Rouge* achieved both financial and critical success in the United States.

An important element of the growing exportation of films from a variety of countries is the number of serious filmmakers throughout the world. Beginning in the 1980s, Satyajit Ray of India, Aki Kaurismaki of Finland, Luis Puenzo of Argentina, and

Pedro Almodovar of Spain have represented a new wave of serious directors. These filmmakers and others use film to explore personal problems and social relations in a way that transcends geographic boundaries.[27] Even smaller film industries abroad are beginning to compete successfully with Hollywood. Russia ranks tenth of Hollywood's foreign markets, but is reviving its national film industry. In 2004, its fantasy thriller *Night Watch* beat out *Spider-Man 2* at the domestic box office and made more than *Lord of the Rings: Return of the King.*

Hollywood International

Hollywood studios, as well as other international film industries, now depend on international talent, international audiences, and international financing and distribution to make profitable pictures. A Hollywood blockbuster can be sold to dozens of markets worldwide, especially as countries build U.S.-style multiplexes. Even in its creative ideas, Hollywood often remakes foreign movies, such as *Vanilla Sky,* based on *Abre Los Ojos* from Spain, and *The Ring,* based on *Ringu* from Japan. Actors are selected to appeal to foreign audiences. Liv Tyler was chosen for *Lord of the Rings* because she was popular in Japan, where the series was expected to do well. Foreign backers are tapped for money. *Terminator 3* and *K-19* were made possible by German investors. Film crews in many parts of the world cooperate on a project like *Lord of the Rings.* International trade agreements protect Hollywood's intellectual property against rampant piracy. Through overseas divisions, Hollywood studios have expanded beyond exporting English-language films to coproducing films with foreign film industries and making more movies in other languages, such as Spanish, Chinese, and Japanese.[28] In all dimensions of filmmaking, Hollywood is becoming less tied to its national origins.

TRENDS

As it has in the past, the movie industry will continue to take advantage of new technologies and respond not only to changes in demographics of the U.S. population but also to the demands of international markets.

Technology: Digital Moviemaking

Digital movie cameras and other technologies are significantly altering the way movies are made. The movie crew no longer has to wait overnight for film to be developed. Instead they can shoot a scene, load it onto a computer, and immediately see the results. Digital moviemaking has other benefits: better special effects, crisper images, and less spending on lab costs. A proponent of digital moviemaking, George Lucas shot *Star Wars: Episode 1—The Phantom Menace* in high definition with Sony's 24p CineAlta system, and other directors have followed suit. Lucas argues that digital technologies allow for greater creativity and that epic movies can be made for much less.[29] Many independent filmmakers have turned to digital technologies because they are so much cheaper to produce. Despite fears of piracy, Hollywood studios have also begun to favor digital movies, including a switch from reels to high definition digital projection and satellite distribution.

Technology: Digital Delivery

The move to digital distribution of content affects the movie industry as it does every other medium. The conglomerates that own numerous media companies are experimenting with new digital distribution of movies to homes and to movie theaters. Digital home delivery already includes DVDs, pay-per-view, and movies on demand. The next generation of digital technologies allows downloading feature-length films into TVs, computers, iPods, and cell phones. The success of this distribution method depends on the saturation of broadband connections. In 2005, the number of broadband connections worldwide rose by 37 percent to 221 million, making for a large potential market for digital downloads.[30] In 2006, Warner Bros. Home Entertainment Group began licensing movies to BitTorrent, which offers file swapping. Movielink and CinemaNow were the first services to offer movie downloads such as *Poseidon* and *V for Vendetta* for sale.

Technology: Piracy

The increasing ease of video downloading has created many new opportunities for piracy. Typically, pirates use digital camcorders to record new releases off the movie screen and then sell them on the street or upload them to the Internet. Along with China, Russia, Mexico, India, and Malaysia, Canada has become one of the most notorious countries for video piracy with camcorders. When *Harry Potter and the Goblet of Fire* was released in Montreal, police frisked moviegoers and showed them an antipiracy video. Many pirated movies also come from workers at film studios or in DVD stamping plants. The Motion Picture Association of America estimated that $6.1 billion was lost to illegal copying in 2005, with half of that figure attributed to digital downloading.[31] To beat the pirates, newly designed DVDs have copy protections that are difficult to crack. But if many movies become available online, protecting them from file sharing and the ingenuity of hackers will be difficult.

Media conglomerates are increasingly interested in releasing content across a variety of platforms at the same time. This strategy is partly intended to reduce piracy. Timing is important. If a movie is released in one place, pirates may acquire it, copy it, and distribute it in another place before the movie is released there. To cut pirates off at the start, studios are releasing blockbusters in major cities worldwide at the same time. At the risk of losing moviegoers, Hollywood studios may release films in theaters, on DVD, and through digital stream on the same day.

Culture: Demographics Issues

Demographics have always been an integral part of the movie business. Film producers and distributors aimed primarily at the family audience during the first sixty years of the industry. This changed when baby boomers became teenagers and dominated the moviegoing market. The aging of the baby boomer generation has seen a growth in moviegoing among those older than fifty. However, the younger market still has an edge on influencing filmmakers.

Family-oriented pictures still dominate the box office. Of 20 blockbusters released in 2005, 17 had a G or PG-13 rating. Nevertheless, film habits have changed, with fewer people going out to movie theaters and many staying home instead to watch cable television or a DVD. In 1948, two-thirds of the U.S. population went out to the movies every week. Now, it is only one-tenth.[32] However, the attention to the movie box office is misleading, since ticket sales account for only 15 percent of the movie industry's revenues.[33] Movie studies make their money on licensing rights to home entertainment and other tie-ins.

While the youth market still has an edge on influencing filmmakers, many young men in their teens and twenties are less interested in traditional media, including films.[34] The loss of this important demographic of moviegoers is leading Hollywood studies to rethink their focus on action films. They also are searching for other niche markets both domestically and abroad. Overseas, largely untapped markets, such as Vietnam, are of increasing interest to studios.

Much studio attention has also turned to Christian audiences and faith-based movies. In the 1950s, Hollywood studios turned out a slew of faith-based films, including *The Robe, The Ten Commandments,* and *Ben-Hur.* In 2005, Hollywood recognized the marketability of films with religious themes when *The Passion of the Christ* and *The Chronicles of Narnia: The Lion, The Witch and the Wardrobe* proved popular. *The Da Vinci Code* sparked a controversy among Christians that added to its publicity. With two-thirds of Americans declaring themselves Christians, the market for faith-based music, film, and books is growing. Ten thousand Christian retail stores supply the niche.[35] At

The movie industry has always been a fluid industry. As demand for certain types of movies came and went, the studios reacted to that demand. This reflects the commercial nature of movies and the desire of studios to make a healthy profit. Because the cost of production is directly reflected in profit, the desire for profit affects how films are made and distributed. New technology, audience demographics, and the international market also will affect how movies are made. Some of the questions that need to be answered include:

- How will increasing digital moviemaking and distribution affect the types of movies you see and the form in which you see them?

- What might digital technologies mean for the Hollywood film industry?
- In order to appeal to a wide audience, is it possible to make films that cross age and gender barriers?
- Will the baby boomer generation become more influential in Hollywood than teenagers?
- Do common concerns exist across cultures that would lead to similar films based on age or gender rather than on nationality?
- Why do fantasy films attract audiences so well across national boundaries?

the same time, movies like *Brokeback Mountain,* with its sensitive portrayal of a gay relationship, show that Hollywood may not always please this demographic.

Like other traditional media industries, the film business is undergoing change as it faces the challenges and opportunities of technology, shifting demographics, and social and economic globalization. The creation and experience of film is becoming much less bound to the local theater.

SUMMARY

- U.S. filmmaking has been dominated by large studios since the early years of the industry.
- Films first targeted family audiences, then, with the advent of television, switched to the teenage audiences that spent their money indiscriminately on movies.
- Film represented two lines of development: the perfection of the photographic process and the fascination with moving pictures.
- Vaudeville influenced the content and style of the first projected shorts.
- Edwin Porter's 1903 short films *Life of an American Fireman* and *The Great Train Robbery* pioneered storytelling techniques that led toward feature-length films.
- The Motion Picture Patents Company controlled early film production. Although it edged out independents, it also stabilized a fledgling industry.
- During the teens and early twenties, film became middle-class entertainment, and studios introduced the star system to attract large audiences.
- By 1930 five movie companies dominated the U.S. film industry.

- The peak year of movie attendance in the United States was 1946.
- After World War II, the domestic audience dwindled because of the population shift to the suburbs, the baby boom, and ultimately more attention to television.
- However, the foreign audience grew and by 1960 provided nearly half of the U.S. film industry's revenues.
- Movies constitute art, social commentary, and entertainment.
- Movies were not given free-speech protection until 1952.
- Movies usually target a young audience, although aging baby boomers constitute a dynamic secondary market.
- Product placement is a form of advertising in which identifiable brand-name products are consumed or used by characters in movies.
- The advent of the VCR created a new challenge for the film industry. The industry responded by supplying videos through rental stores and directly to the consumer, increasing revenues by $15 billion.
- Merchandising products is a successful profit-making venture of movie studios.

NAVIGATING THE WEB The Movies

Movies and films are at the top of the popular culture list of websites. Sites cover the history, business, and criticism of film. Many are created by interested individuals; others are produced by the large movie corporations. Some experimentation inevitably will be done with showing movies directly on websites, but as yet movies are still more suited to the television set or the big screen for general viewing. The following sites contain research material about movies and their history.

MovieWeb
movieweb.com
MovieWeb has information about current movies and those screening within the past five years. It also contains useful statistical information about movies.

BitTorrent
bittorrent.com
The BitTorrent site provides a software interface that allows users to download digital content, including movie files.

The Academy Awards
oscar.com
The Academy Awards site, maintained by the Academy of Motion Picture Arts and Sciences, lists all Academy Awards and includes a summary of the films that have been screened over the years.

Internet Movie Database
imdb.com
An index and directory of motion pictures.

The following two sites contain information about the entertainment industry. They have current information about the film industry, including upcoming films and box-office receipts.

The Hollywood Reporter
hollywoodreporter.com

Premiere
premieremag.com

QUESTIONS FOR REVIEW

1. What type of technology did magic-lantern shows use?
2. Which studios have retained dominance over time?
3. Why was the First Amendment not applied to film until 1952?
4. What is the star system and why is it important?
5. Why is *Bonnie and Clyde* sometimes considered a turning point in the development of modern film?
6. What is the home-viewing revolution?

ISSUES TO THINK ABOUT

1. Some people argue that movies have been the U.S. dream machine. As more films are made with an international audience in mind and more international films are imported into the United States, how will the dream machine transmit social and cultural heritage?
2. How do new movie technologies affect the content and reaction? Do you react differently if you watch a film on a DVD at home or in a dark theater? With friends or parents?
3. How has the Hollywood system affected the development of U.S. film?
4. What do you think the technology of the future will be? How will it affect the production, distribution, and marketing of movies?
5. What are the implications of product placement?

SUGGESTED READINGS

Adair, Gilbert. *Flickers: An Illustrated Celebration of 100 Years of Cinema* (Boston: Faber & Faber, 1995).

Alexander, George. *Why We Make Movies: Black Filmmakers Talk About the Magic of Cinema* (New York: Harlem Moon, 2003).

Decherney, Peter. *Hollywood and the Culture Elite: How the Movies Became American* (New York: Columbia University Press, 2005).

Ellis, Jack C. *A History of Film*, 2nd ed. (Englewood Cliffs, NJ: Prentice Hall, 1985).

Giannetti, Louis D. *Flashback: A Brief History of Film*, 3rd ed. (Englewood Cliffs, NJ: Prentice Hall, 1996).

6

Radio

Radio free speech advocates seemed to win a victory in 2003 when the FCC reversed its 2001 decision against KBOO-FM for playing Sarah Jones' "Your Revolution," a song with sexually explicit lyrics. After a complaint from a listener, the FCC ruled that the lyrics were intended to "pander and shock" and fined the station $7,000. Sarah Jones, KBOO, and the American Civil Liberties Union objected to the censorship on First Amendment grounds, and Jones defended her music, saying that it was a feminist response to music on the radio "which often treats women as sex objects and playthings." The FCC reversed its decision after further deliberation, swayed in part by Jones' and KBOO's argument that Jones had been frequently asked to sing the song at high school assemblies.[1]

Despite the FCC's admission of error in this case, its censorship of radio and television intensified after Janet Jackson flashed her breast during the 2004 Super Bowl. Howard Stern's employer, Viacom, was fined $3.5 million for complaints against the shock jock, who moved to satellite radio to be free of regulators. Smaller radio stations have worried about the hefty fines the FCC now imposes, and many broadcasters have complained that the FCC's standards are unclear.

The Sarah Jones and Janet Jackson incidents are part of a growing controversy surrounding radio and television content. Broadcasters are prohibited from playing indecent material between 6 A.M. and 10 P.M., but both music and talk programming increasingly include material that some listeners find offensive. In 2002, FCC Commissioner Michael

KEY CONCEPTS

- Broadcast Radio
- Network Broadcasting
- Airwave Scarcity
- Federal Communications Act of 1934
- Commercial and Noncommercial Broadcasting
- Drive-Time Broadcast
- Radio Markets for Consumers and Advertising
- Radio Station Types
- Internet Radio and Satellite Radio

opps said, "It's become a rare morning when I don't walk into my office and find 30 [complaints] in one day."[2]

The conflict over the nature of radio content represents two of radio's many faces. Radio influences individuals and groups within society through ideas and information. Government regulators often see their goal as making sure the impact is not negative. At the same time, radio is a commercial medium that attracts listeners through entertainment. Listeners' attention is sold to businesses in the advertising market. Some stations care little how they attract that attention and purposely play controversial material. Radio has had other faces as well. The powerful medium once was an innovative journalistic tool that brought a war home to listeners around the world. In countries where television is not widely available, radio is still a primary source of news and entertainment. It remains one of the most portable media available, as well as one of the most influential information and propaganda tools. Perhaps the most notable characteristic of radio is its availability. According to UNESCO, households in developing countries are ten times more likely to have radio sets than TV sets.

The most consistent characteristic of radio has been its ability to survive in emerging competitive markets. Radio began as a medium for live entertainment and short news broadcasts. It developed situation comedy programs and dramatic fare that eventually transferred to television. After television sapped the best performers and programs from radio, radio altered its format, turning primarily to music, news, and talk. In the 2000s, especially in developed countries, radio faces increased competition from computer-based interactive technologies. Listeners can create their own playlists from online databases. Software allows online listeners to hear live music broadcasts from rock and blues clubs. Users of the Internet and online services can access the latest news on demand. Even radio's grip on talk could be loosened as individuals communicate with one another over the Internet. As radio continues to compete with other media and enters the world of converging technologies, the major issues will be the following:

- Will interactive programming delivered by satellite and Internet force broadcast radio to shift content, or will radio's music, talk, and news formats still appeal to tomorrow's population?

- How will radio reflect or contribute to cultural life?

- What effect has consolidation had on radio and its listeners?

- Will the growing use of sexually explicit material lead to increased government content regulation?

- Will radio continue to be significant as a carrier of international news and information, crossing boundaries of countries that try to block external influence?

RADIO IN AMERICAN LIFE

Radio was the first national electronic mass medium, and politicians, corporate managers, and advertisers were quick to recognize its potential power. Radio allowed millions of people throughout the country to listen simultaneously to the same carefully tailored message. Despite the introduction of newer technologies, people throughout the world still use radio more than any other mass medium for information and entertainment. Even in the United States, where television seems to dominate the mass media, radio retains a significant audience—and significant political and social influence. By the beginning of 2007, the United States had more than 13,700 licensed radio stations.

Delivery of news is a critical radio function; more than 2,000 stations listed themselves as either news/talk or news stations in 2007.[3] These news and talk stations provide information and often try to persuade though opinion. Radio's ability to entertain with music is also important; in fact, music, especially music heard on the radio, has

Radio in Your Life

How Many Roles Does Radio Play?

Think about your own use of radio: What purposes does it serve for you, your family, and your friends? Do you use it for news? For entertainment? For background study music? Do you listen to the talk shows? Do you find yourself using the computer to listen to radio?

As you read this chapter, think about how you use radio and how many minutes a day you spend listening to rock, alternative rock, top 40, country, rap, classical music, jazz, talk, and news.

Type of Station	Use	Hours Per Day	Other Media Used for Same Purpose
Rock			
Alternative rock			
Top 40			
Country			
Rap			
Classical			
Jazz			
Talk			
News			
Public radio			
Other			

defined several generations of youth. This music often shapes norms and beliefs while entertaining.

The Magic Starting Point

As with most technology, finding an exact starting point in **broadcast radio** history is not easy. Radio was not invented by one person. Rather, a variety of inventors contributed to specific aspects of radio development. The scientific understanding gained by James Clerk Maxwell and Heinrich Hertz during the 1870s and 1880s furthered radio's development. Nathan Stubblefield experimented with transmitting voice and foresaw radio not merely as a point-to-point communication form, but as a method of transmitting news.[4] In 1895, Italian inventor Guglielmo Marconi produced a device that sent a message without wires. The message, however, was in code, like that of the telegraph. For radio to be a significant force, voice and wireless transmission had to merge.

Others contributed as well. John Ambrose Fleming developed a type of vacuum tube, Lee de Forest made amplification possible, and Reginald A. Fessenden experimented with

Key Concept

Broadcast radio The technology of radio airwaves, which was originally conceived as a wireless telephone system or a narrowcast system, reaching a limited number of listeners, became predominantly a medium for sending out signals for wide-area reception by many radio receivers—a mass media system.

David Sarnoff, airwave pioneer and radio czar, began his career in radio's infancy. His role in forming RCA and the NBC network dramatically shaped the broadcast industry as a commercial medium.

the technology and began broadcasting. Edwin Howard Armstrong and de Forest fought bitterly in court over the patents to the regenerative circuit—a circuit that used the **audion** as a transmitter, amplifier, and detector in a radio receiver. Although engineers familiar with the technology believed that Armstrong understood the process far better than de Forest did, the court awarded de Forest the patent. Armstrong later invented frequency modulation (FM), but its development was hampered by the Radio Corporation of America (RCA). Armstrong committed suicide after losing his legal battles and watching FM languish in the shadow of television development.

By 1915, the technology to send and receive music and voice was well established. On September 30, 1915, David Sarnoff, then a lowly employee of American Marconi Company but later president of RCA, wrote a memo to his boss. He predicted that the "Radio Music Box" would become as common in households as the piano or phonograph. But it took more than five years for radio to become a commercial enterprise because the demand had not yet developed and because of patent infringement disputes.[5]

The development of the radio station ensured that radio would be a mass medium that sent content to a large number of radio receivers, rather than remaining a wireless telephone. Several stations claimed to be "first." The first experimental license after the federal government began regulating radio was given to St. Joseph's College in Pennsylvania. The University of Wisconsin was granted an experimental license in 1919, two years after it first broadcast music; this license became a regular license in 1922.[6] KDKA in Pittsburgh was the first radio station to schedule programming and to offer continuous voice service. It received a commercial license on October 27, 1920, to experiment with voice transmission for a year.

KDKA's first broadcast was election returns from the Harding–Cox presidential race. The station also broadcast church services, sports, and market reports. Less than a year after KDKA started broadcasting regularly and shortly before its experimental license was converted to regular status, WBZ in Springfield, Massachusetts, received the first regular broadcasting license.

Radio as a Mass Medium

Radio became a mass medium during the 1920s. This decade saw rapid growth and change in the number of stations, the percentage of U.S. households with radio receivers, the forms of financing radio, and the nature of programming.

The United States went from 30 licensed commercial AM stations in 1922 to 618 by 1930. Despite radio's development as a broadcast medium, the influence of the telephone company persisted. American Telephone and Telegraph (AT&T) invented the broadcast network, simultaneously broadcasting on January 4, 1923, over its stations in New York and Boston. Two years later, AT&T had regular **network broadcasting** over 26 stations from New York to Kansas City.[7]

In 1926, AT&T withdrew from the radio industry and sold its radio subsidiary to RCA. RCA soon acquired all stock in the National Broadcasting Corporation (NBC) and began to build a dominant network. Starting with 19 stations in 1926, NBC had 56 stations two years later. The network grew to 154 stations in 1938 and 214 by 1940. There were actually two NBC networks: the Red and Blue networks. The Blue network's flagship station was WJZ, NBC's first station in New York. The Red flagship station was WEAF in New York, which NBC acquired from AT&T. Each network offered its own programming.

NBC soon had competition when the Columbia Broadcasting System (CBS) emerged as the second network. CBS had 16 stations in 1929 and had expanded to 113

audion

A three-electrode vacuum tube amplifier, which was the basis of the electronic revolution that permitted the development of radio.

by 1938. In 1934, Mutual Broadcasting Network entered the field with 4 stations; by 1940, it had 160 outlets. Mutual differed from the other networks in that it did not own any stations but shared programs among independent member stations. In 1943, when the Federal Communications Commission (FCC), in an effort to reduce the power of the networks, forced NBC to sell one of its networks, the American Broadcasting Company joined the competitive field. FM stations continue to proliferate, although growth has slowed.

Networks provided programs at lower cost than it would have cost individual stations to produce them, which meant higher profits. From an advertiser's perspective, networks simultaneously connected homes throughout the United States. A company could reach millions of people with the same message at the same time. A modern mass medium had arrived.

Although networks could connect the people in the United States, people had to want to be connected—and they did. Demand for radio receivers expanded as fast as radio stations did in the 1920s. With radios selling for as low as $9, the percentage of households with radios rose from about 7 percent in 1923 to 20 percent in 1926 and 35 percent in 1930.[8]

These broadcasts often used wire service material that was available from newspaper sources. During the 1920s, the news services—the Associated Press (AP), United Press (UP), and International News Service (INS)—waffled in their stance toward this potential competitor. They were unsure whether allowing wire service reporters to supply news to radio should be part of their service or whether radio would threaten their newspaper clients.

Cecil Brown reported on World War II on the radio for CBS. By the beginning of the war, the network had established itself as a highly credible news source.

However, when radio networks used wire service material to beat newspapers in delivering election results of the 1932 Roosevelt–Hoover presidential race, the radio–newspaper war was officially declared. Journalists became embroiled in an industry battle. After the 1932 election, the AP, a newspaper-based and -funded service, refused to sell news to radio networks, ordered newspapers with radio stations to limit broadcasting of AP news to brief bulletins of thirty words, and charged additional fees for the use of its material on radio. UP and INS created similar constraints on radio.

The news service actions led to the growth of separate radio newsgathering organizations. CBS started the fledgling Columbia News service soon after the AP decision, though it was discontinued when NBC and CBS signed an agreement to end the radio–newspaper war. This agreement, which limited the networks' ability to gather their own news, lasted less than a year. The wire services provided only limited copy to the networks and maintained a structure that favored newspapers. The radio industry was not strong enough to consider staffing its own worldwide bureaus.

Competition emerged from a news service that was not tied to the newspaper industry. Transradio Press Service, begun in 1934, acquired 150 clients during its first year and provided news from other wire services such as Havas in France and Reuters in England as well as domestic news. The service sent an average of 10,000 words a day. Fearful of the competition, the wire services declared independence from newspaper dominance and began to sell news to radio stations. The networks also returned to gathering their own news.

As you read in Chapter 1, Edward R. Murrow made radio news a household term during World War II with his remarkable coverage of the European front. Murrow's broadcasts were expanded as CBS expanded its activities abroad.

The Advent of Advertising

As late as 1922, the primary purpose of radio programming was to sell radio sets. Without programs, no one would buy radio receivers. That year, AT&T started *toll broadcasting,* or the selling of time, at WEAF in New York. Secretary of Commerce

Radio was initially conceived as a technological device to be experimented with in garages and workshops, but as programming developed, the device was encased and moved into the living room as a piece of furniture. Radio was advertised as a cultural device that could bring the best symphonies into every middle-class home.

Herbert Hoover feared that a speech by the president would "be used as the meat in a sandwich of two patent medicine advertisements." Nevertheless, station owners quickly envisioned a future of broadcasting financed by advertising. By 1929, advertising had been included in the first National Association of Broadcasters code of standards. NBC made more than $15 million in advertising that year.[9]

Because radio was new, the audience responded even to relatively simple and inexpensive programs. On 1920s radio, dance music reigned supreme. Many stations broadcast bands and orchestras live. Religious programming was also popular. University stations and, to some degree, networks broadcast educational material. Educational programming declined during the 1920s as university stations closed from lack of funding, and commercial stations, whose owners actively opposed licenses for educational institutions, got control of more radio frequencies.

Early Regulation

Technological chaos ruled in the early days of radio. Stations attempted to broadcast over the same **radio frequencies,** resulting in noise rather than useful programming. The problem of allocating stations to the limited number of air waves led to several regulation efforts. The Radio Act of 1912 gave the Secretary of Commerce and Labor the right to license radio stations and assign frequencies. However, failing to anticipate that demand would far exceed availability, the act created no criteria for licensing.

Finally, Congress passed the Radio Act of 1927 and established the Federal Radio Commission (FRC) to regulate broadcasting. Such legislation represented a major departure from the government's stance toward the press. Regulation of radio was justified on the basis of *airwave scarcity,* and the commission was instructed to act in the "public interest, convenience and necessity." However, this departure was acceptable to industry representatives. The Radio Act ensured that commercial interests would dominate the medium, networks would retain power, and government would not interfere too directly. The number of educational licenses fell from 129 in 1925 to 52 in 1931.[10]

Even though the FRC reduced the chaos in the radio industry, several agencies still shared regulation of radio, telephone, telegraph, and cable; this overlap created confusion as to which regulations applied. Congress passed the *Federal Communications Act of 1934,* establishing the Federal Communications Commission (FCC) as the regulator of wired and wireless communication. Congress also charged the FCC with recommending action on the long-standing debate between *commercial and noncommercial broadcasting,* but the pattern set by the 1927 act persisted. The commercial forces, well financed and well organized, dominated the debate. Noncommercial interests were unable to create a unified front that would present a cohesive message to Congress. It would be decades before frequencies would be set aside specifically for educational purposes.

Radio's Golden Age

radio frequency

An electromagnetic wave frequency used in radio transmission.

During the 1930s, radio matured as a mass medium. Through the 1940s, radio was the electronic bridge to world affairs, quality entertainment, national sports events, and urban progress. The 1930s and 1940s were the Golden Age for radio. The number of homes with receivers, the interest of advertisers, and the types of programming expanded rapidly. News, comedy, drama, mysteries, and "entertainment news" emerged in radio programming. As the medium matured, audiences began to regard radio as a reliable source of news and information. The World Series was carried by some stations as early as 1922, and sports became a mainstay by the end of the decade.

Drama was a favorite, and in 1934 the *Lux Radio Theater* began presenting radio adaptations of films, using movie stars to provide the voices. Soon, more than 30 million people listened weekly. Because of radio's credibility, influence, and popularity, when Orson Welles and his *Mercury Theater* players broadcast an updated version of H. G. Wells's *War of the Worlds* on Halloween night in 1938, some listeners did not realize that it was meant to be entertainment. The program started with dance music, which was interrupted by a realistic-sounding news flash announcing that Martians had landed in New Jersey. Although the program contained periodic statements identifying it as a dramatization, tens of thousands of listeners reacted as if it were real.

The mix of drama and news entertained and informed, and some early radio programming foreshadowed the television docudrama. *The March of Time,* which began in 1931, dramatized news, using actors to recreate (sometimes in altered form) actual news events. *The March of Time* was broadcast on and off for the next fourteen years, reaching as many as 9 million homes at one point, and it spawned several imitators.

During the day, soap operas such as *Guiding Light* and *Backstage Wife* attracted a primarily female audience. At night, game shows such as *Twenty Questions* and *Truth or Consequences* were family listening fare. Mysteries, crime shows, Westerns, and comedy series added diversity. Comedy shows ranged from *Amos 'n' Andy,* which used racist stereotypes of African Americans, to *Blondie,* which featured a bumbling, unlucky husband named Dagwood Bumstead. The king of the radio comedians was Jack Benny. By 1938, Benny had an audience of 7 million families and was making $25,000 a week.

The growth of radio listening during the 1930s reflected an increase in radio ownership and a hunger for news and entertainment spawned by the Great Depression. Between 1930 and 1940, the number of radio sets in the United States increased from 13 million to 51 million.[11] During the depression, people bought the relatively cheap radio receivers and sought escape from their everyday difficulties.

As radio matured as an advertising medium, companies bought time to sponsor particular shows rather than simply airing commercials. For example, General Foods' Jell-O sponsored Jack Benny. Networks rented time to companies, which were responsible for the content of the entire program. This enabled advertisers to dictate the type of programming that aired. A similar pattern dominated the early years of television.

Competition from TV

At the end of World War II, radio was at the height of its dominance as a mass medium. By this time, 14.6 percent of advertising expenditures went to radio, up from 6.5 percent only ten years before. But ten years later, the percentage had dropped to 6.1 as television moved into households across the nation.[12]

The advent of television caused a rapid decline in the comedy and drama shows on radio. As radio stars such as Jack Benny, George Burns, and Gracie Allen moved to television, many critics predicted an end to radio as a mass medium. But radio reshaped itself and survived, becoming the music box of a new generation. Radio created a forum for ethnic music. And furthermore, millions of young baby boomers found rock 'n' roll, which distinguished them from their parents' generation.

New Technology and the "Music Box"

The development of **FM** radio and the creation of the transistor, which made portability possible, combined to recast radio as the music box it had once been. FM had three major advantages: (1) It had better sound quality than **AM;** (2) smaller communities that were bypassed by other media forms would have access to frequencies; and (3) with its wider **wave band,** FM could carry the new **high-fidelity** and stereo recordings

FM

Frequency modulation that attaches sound to a carrier wave, varying the frequency of the carrier wave.

AM

Amplitude modulation that attaches sound to a carrier wave by varying the intensity, or amplitude, of the carrier wave.

wave band

An electromagnetic wave within the range of radio frequencies.

high fidelity

Reproduction of sound with minimal distortion.

Dateline

Radio in Our Lives

1895. Guglielmo Marconi sends a message without wires.

1912. Radio Act of 1912

1920. KDKA in Pittsburgh gets the first commercial radio license.

1922. First advertising is sold for radio.

1926. NBC becomes the first radio network.

1927. Radio Act of 1927

1932. Radio networks begin their own newsgathering.

1934. Federal Communications Act of 1934; the FCC is established.

1938. Orson Welles's *Mercury Theater* broadcasts "War of the Worlds."

1938. Edward R. Murrow begins broadcasting reports of war in Europe.

1400–1700	1800	1860	1880	1900	1920	1930

1620. Pilgrims land at Plymouth Rock.

1690. *Publick Occurrences* is published in Boston.

1741. First magazine is published in America.

1776–1783. American Revolution

1830s. The penny press becomes the first truly mass medium in the United States.

1861–1865. American Civil War

1892. Thomas Edison's lab develops the kinetoscope.

1914–1918. World War I

1915. *The Birth of a Nation* marks the start of the modern movie industry.

1920. KDKA in Pittsburgh gets the first commercial radio license.

1930s. The Great Depression

1939. TV is demonstrated at the New York World's Fair.

1939–1945. World War II

Cultural Milestones

---

transistor

A small electronic device containing a semiconductor. A key component of an integrated circuit that paved the way for portability.

that were enhancing the quality of recorded music. The **transistor,** invented in 1948, made possible portability and better car radios. By the late 1950s, teenagers could listen to rock 'n' roll anywhere and just about any time they wanted.

AM radio stations send long wavelength, low-frequency radio signals, and FM stations send short wavelength, high-frequency signals. The longer the wavelength, the greater the distance the signal will travel because it is not easily absorbed by the

1942. Voice of America begins broadcasting in several languages.

1948. Transistor radio is invented.

1950s. TV's development forces radio to use music format.

1971. National Public Radio begins operation.

1990s–2000s. Radio industry concentrates as a result of the Telecommunications Act.

1995. Radio begins transmitting over the Internet.

1996. Telecommunications Act

2000. Radio changes to digital broadcasting.

2002. FCC expresses stronger concern over indecency on radio.

1940	1950	1960	1970	1980	1990	2000

1949. First commercial electronic computer is produced.

Early 1950s. Rock 'n' roll begins.

1969. First person lands on the moon.

1970s. VCR is developed.

1989–1991. Cold War ends and the USSR is dissolved.

Late 1980s. National Science Foundation creates the basis of the Internet.

1996. Telecommunications Act

2000. Presidential election nearly tied.

2001. Terrorist attacks on New York and Washington, D.C.

2003. War with Iraq.

ground and other solid objects. This explains why a person in Montana can pick up an AM station in Forth Worth, Texas, late at night when atmospheric interference is low. High-frequency signals, however, produce higher quality sound.

FM stations dominate radio ratings today because of the higher sound quality. Music is the primary format on radio, and FM provides higher fidelity for stereo radio. Nevertheless, AM radio staged a comeback in the 1990s, as talk radio boomed. Talk

High Definition Digital Radio

Once confined to broadcast AM and FM, radio listeners now have a range of choices, from streaming audio on computers to satellite radio. Radio has become available for cell phones, and audio programs can be downloaded as podcasts. Peer-to-peer file sharing on the Internet allows users to create and download playlists, much like listening to traditional radio without commercial interruption. In this scheme, everyone can become a radio broadcaster. Because of these new outlets, traditional FM and AM radio stations are facing competition, especially from satellite radio systems that provide nearly 200 channels mostly without commercials.

AM and FM stations are turning to high-definition digital radio as a way of attracting and keeping listeners. As of June 2006, 800 radio stations were broadcasting in high definition, with hundreds more expected to follow. The cost for the station upgrade is about $80,000.

For high-definition digital channels, a station's digital transmitter sends signals to the listener's digital receiver. The station can broadcast both analog and digital signals which share the same radio spectrum. Thus, the station is able to simulcast music and news programs on the same frequency. Digital technology offers more choice of channels, crisper sound, and other on-demand data services such as programming guides, sports scores and traffic warnings. Unlike pay satellite radio, the service is free, though listeners must pay an average of $300 for a receiver. These radios also provide information such as song titles, artists' names, weather forecasts, and translations in Spanish. Eventually, technology forecasters say, high-definition receivers will allow storage and replay.

However, the adoption of high definition radio faces challenges. While most American homes have cheap, standard radios, listeners must be convinced to buy a new, expensive high-definition radio, mostly on the basis of sound quality. Rich Russo, director of broadcast services at JL Media, believes that most consumers don't care that much about high quality sound since popular devices like iPods have less fidelity than CDs. Further, a survey by Bridge Ratings of 500 HD listeners who had owned their HD radio for less than six months found that 23 percent were unsatisfied. They mostly complained of bad reception and lack of technical clarity. Because of these problems, some business analysts have suggested that HD radio will have difficulty attracting more listeners.

Critics of HD radio say that media conglomerates like Clear Channel may force out more independent channels in the switch to digital. Further, because both satellite and HD digital radio allow greater opportunities for piracy, the FCC may implement technologies that control radio use. For example, HD radio owners may not be able to save songs or skip commercials. Digital rights advocates argue that these measures are excessive, limiting innovation and preventing consumers from using content as they traditionally have.

The case of HD digital radio reveals typical responses to new technologies, which are often accompanied by both hype and criticism. However, the case is not yet closed, and whether U.S. consumers will end up with HD rather than analog radio remains to be seen.

Sources: Rich Russo, "It Stands for Huge Debacle," *Mediaweek,* July 24, 2006: 11; Bridge Ratings, *HD Radio Study: Consumer Satisfaction,* 2006, bridgeratings.com; Michael Kanellos, "High Definition Radio Gears Up for Reality," CNET News, May 26, 2005, news.com.com.

and information do not require high-quality transmission, and the long reach of AM opens up a big market for the talk shows.

TODAY'S MARKET STRUCTURE

By the end of the 1960s, as television became the favorite mass medium for national advertising, radio lost its mass appeal. Local stations began to tailor their formats to attract local, specialized audiences. The shift has been a lucrative one. Between 1996 and 2003, radio's advertising revenues grew from $9.6 billion to $14.7 billion, and have held steady. Most of these revenues come from local advertisers. Most communities have the choice of a number of free stations in several formats. Rural areas have access to fewer free stations and formats.

These formats, which are described in Table 6.1, deliver a particular type of audience to advertisers, who buy time to present their goods and services. The audience for each format is carefully defined by music or content taste, age, lifestyle, and buying habits. Stations use a variety of strategies to build a loyal audience, often creating programming around distinctive **on-air personalities.** Stations with similar formats compete for advertisers, particularly during the *highly lucrative drive times*—6:00 to 10:00 A.M. and 3:00 to 7:00 P.M.

In 2006, 93 percent of people over age twelve listened to the radio in an average week. Senior citizens are more likely to listen to radio in the afternoon, while working-age people tune in during their morning commute. Teens listen to radio after school and on weekends. The lowest rate of listening occurs between 7:00 P.M. and midnight, when young people are more likely to tune in.[13]

Syndicated programming increasingly dominates radio, especially in non–drive-time periods. A disc jockey (DJ) at a central location plays songs and supplies chatter

Key Concept

Drive-time broadcast Significant audiences are available to broadcasters during the morning and afternoon periods when people are driving to and from school and work. These drive times represent prime markets for radio—and for radio advertisers.

on-air personality

A personality listeners identify with and tune in to regularly on the radio. Whether the radio host reads the news or announces music, the on-air personality gives a station a singular identity.

syndicated programming

Nationally produced programming that is supplied to stations through telephone lines and by satellite.

Table 6.1 Commercial Radio Formats—by Frequency of Use

Country: Country music in a variety of forms: traditional, contemporary, and country-rock. Appeals to ages 25 to 64 with a variety of socioeconomic backgrounds.

Alternative Rock: Plays rock music from lesser known groups and singers who would not appeal to top 40 listeners. Aimed at people in the 18 to 30 age group.

News-Talk: Twenty- to thirty-minute cycles of local, state, national, and international news and a variety of talk and call-in shows. Targets listeners between 25 and 65 and can narrow the group according to content.

Spanish: Variety of music, news, and talk in Spanish. Aimed at Spanish-speaking people in a particular market.

Religion: Music, information, and talk designed to appeal to people who support the religious beliefs of the organization that runs the station. Aimed mostly at adults.

Urban/African American: African American–oriented music, ranging from soul, gospel, and rhythm and blues to jazz and rap. Aimed at African Americans between 18 and 49. Also attracts many white listeners.

Adult Contemporary: Current and former popular music. Attracts wide range of adults between 18 and 35.

Classic Rock: Music mostly from the 1960s, 1970s, and 1980s, with an emphasis on particular artists. Aimed at those over 35, especially men.

Oldies: Mostly rock 'n' roll hits from the 1950s and 1960s. Targets people over 35.

Easy Listening: Slow, instrumental versions of current and older hits. Aimed at older listeners.

Top 40: Current 40 top-selling rock and pop songs. Targets ages 18 to 24 but has many younger listeners.

Jazz: Jazz music, from big band to fusion. Appeals to a limited number of upper income listeners.

Middle of the Road: Variety of music and information. Music list includes contemporary popular music. News, sports, weather, traffic, and talk are included in the mix. Attracts 25- to 45-year-olds.

Classical: Recorded and live opera, symphony, and chamber music. Aimed at educated groups.

Album-Oriented Rock: Emphasizes current and old hits of particular artists. Album cuts and entire sides are played. Particularly attractive to people 18 to 35, especially men.

to stations around the country through telephone lines and by satellites. Standardized programming, which sometimes eliminates the DJ, is often less expensive than local programming. Syndication has become particularly prevalent in the talk format, in which hosts such as Rush Limbaugh, Dr. Laura, Don Imus, Tom Joyner, and Howard Stern draw millions of listeners from across the United States. However, this type of programming lacks local flavor and reduces diversity. Even though syndicated radio does not have local flavor, some supporters argue that there simply is not enough talent to provide high-quality DJs, news, and talk for the more than 13,000 radio stations throughout the United States.

Radio Station Organization

Organizational patterns are similar for AM and FM stations. A general manager supervises the entire operation; makes business decisions with the assistance of other department heads; and runs the business department, which handles payroll, hiring, billing of advertisers, and buying of supplies.

At least three departments—programming, sales, and engineering—report to the general manager. The programming department and its manager select and produce all of the station's programming. If a station has a news format or substantial news programming, it may have a separate news department and news director.

The sales department sells radio time—and, implicitly, the attention of its listeners—to advertisers. A sales manager runs the department, and account executives sell time and serve the advertisers. This service includes helping advertisers pick the best time for their ads to air and helping them develop the advertisements.

The engineering department, headed by the chief engineer, is responsible for the technology at the station. This includes a variety of equipment, from CD players to **modulators** and antennas. Members of this department make sure the station's broadcasting meets the requirements of the FCC.

The **traffic** manager works with the sales and programming departments. She or he prepares a log of what is supposed to play every day and keeps a record of what actually goes on the air. The traffic manager supplies the information that is used to bill advertisers for time on the radio.

Large stations may have additional departments, such as a promotions department, which is in charge of advertising and public relations for the station. At small stations, the general manager usually handles these responsibilities.

Radio Ownership

Congress drastically changed ownership rules for radio stations with the 1996 Telecommunications Act. Before the act, companies could own no more than thirty stations, and those stations could have no more than 25 percent of the national audience. The 1996 law removed all national limits on audience and stations. It also expanded the number of stations a company could own within a market, which varies by market size.

As a result of the changes in ownership limits, large radio corporations grew rapidly, buying independent stations and other groups. By 2006, 21 radio companies owned more than 40 stations. The largest was Clear Channel, with more than 1,200 stations in 190 markets. The company received about 27 percent of listeners.

The expansion of these large companies has generated a range of concerns from many quarters. Some critics say this concentration has reduced minority and women ownership. Others say it has reduced the number of independent voices in local markets, which limits those who have access to the airwaves. The American Federation of Television and Radio Artists claims that the large corporations use cookie-cutter playlists that keep independent artists off the radio. The companies have denied they require such playlists.[14]

modulator

Device that processes the carrier wave so that its amplitude or frequency varies. Amplitude modulation (AM) is constant in frequency and varies the intensity, or amplitude, of the carrier wave. Frequency modulation (FM) is constant in amplitude and varies the frequency of the carrier wave.

traffic

Department that controls movement of programming through the day, logs what goes on the air, and supplies information for billing advertisers.

AUDIENCE DEMAND IN RADIO MARKETS

Radio does not aim for the mass; it aims for targeted audiences. Station managers strive to identify content that will appeal to dedicated listeners with particular demographic characteristics. Gaining a loyal and identifiable segment of the audience, rather than trying to attract a large percentage of the total available audience within a given geographic area, has enabled radio to survive in a competitive media environment. The attention of the targeted audience is sold to advertisers, which connects the **markets for consumers and advertising.**

Key Concept

Radio markets for consumers and advertising The structure of radio markets requires that stations deliver content that listeners want, such as music, news, and talk, in order to gain an audience for advertisers' sales messages.

Consumer Market

Radio listeners demand music, news, and talk. A few nostalgia stations continue to carry radio drama and comedy, and some stations broadcast sports, but music makes up the bulk of programming.

Demand for Music   Music programming provides background for people's daily lives. Students study, mechanics repair cars, and commuters drive, all to the sound of radio music. Music helps us to endure exercise and to transcend boring tasks, and it bonds us with people who share common interests. It is the shared interest that makes the format approach work. In general, people who want to listen to country music tend to have some common characteristics—characteristics that can be associated with certain buying habits that attract advertisers. Without correlations between demographics and music and demographics and buying habits, radio advertising would lose its effectiveness.

Demographics that lead to demand for a particular type of music might involve educational level, race, or gender, but they most often reflect age. Music has been the language of adolescence, and the various demographic groups have been given names that reflect their music tastes in adolescence. The members of the so-called Generation X tend to share musical tastes, as did the bobby-soxers and baby boomers before them. The Xers have rap and grunge, the boomers had folk rock and acid rock, and the soxers had Frank Sinatra and swing. The radio and recording industries have addressed the music of each generation, capitalizing on the ability of radio to create and spread popular music to those who want to listen.

The connection between age and radio format can be seen in the numbers of stations within format types. The formats reflect consumer demand. For example, in 2003, 807 stations carried the oldies format, which aims at most baby boomers, while 491 stations carried the top 40 format aimed at younger listeners. Another 692 carried the adult contemporary format, which fits in between the oldies and top 40. With 2,088 stations, country music is the most popular in the United States, especially for people thirty-five to sixty-four years old.[15]

Format is not just a function of age, however. Men listen to radio slightly more than women, with men more likely to listen to sports stations and women more likely to listen to country music.[16] Hispanic stations have been booming, with 750 stations in 2006. Some stations have been switching formats to capture Hispanic listeners.

Demand for News and Talk   Radio news ranges from the in-depth reporting of national and international news found on National Public Radio to a quick survey of the city's most important stories. In between falls extensive coverage of local news. Large markets have enough demand for these types of news to support either an all-news

Radio provides musicians with airplay to generate bigger audiences for their music. U2 owns its own private radio station, Zoo Radio, broadcast from Dublin and available over the web.

or a news/talk station. Smaller markets must often rely on public radio stations to meet the demand for news.

In 2005, Arbitron reported that 16 percent of listeners tuned into the news/talk stations. The news/talk format has held steady, and is second only to country music in attracting listeners. However, the category is broad enough to include sports and talk/personality stations, so listeners are not necessarily drawn by serious news.[17] Twenty-nine percent of the audience for news/talk is sixty-five and older; 19 percent falls within the fifty-five to sixty-four-year-old range. Only 1–3 percent of teenagers are news/talk listeners. National Public Radio has an especially loyal following of more highly educated, wealthy patrons. The audience for news/talk on commercial stations is predominantly male and less well educated.

Advertising Market

Advertising demand is expressed by the potential advertiser, not by the audience. Because each radio station targets a demographically defined group of people who listen to a specific format, no station can deliver an audience that would include all the people a business might want to reach. Therefore, businesses often buy radio advertisements as a part of a total media package. A pizza parlor might run a coupon in the local newspaper and buy radio ads on one, two, or several stations to tell people about the special price. One study of two medium-size cities found that the average company bought ads from about five different types of media outlets.[18]

Advertising rates reflect an independent assessment of audience size. Advertisers learned early not to rely on media companies to estimate audience size and supported the rise of ratings companies, whose sole job is to measure audiences. Arbitron, the primary radio ratings service, assigns counties to 250 geographic regions, labeled **areas of dominant influence (ADI),** and reports listener data for these areas and smaller geographic components on either an annual or a quarterly basis.

The numbers of listeners are reported in two forms: rating and share. A *rating* is the percentage of *all people in a market* who are listening to a particular station during a 15-minute segment. A *share* is the percentage of *people with their radios on* who are listening to a particular station during a 15-minute segment. The data come from

area of dominant influence (ADI)

Area defined by the ratings company Arbitron for purposes of reporting listener data.

Catherine Hughes

In 1980, Catherine Hughes purchased WOL-AM in Washington, D.C., launching a brilliant enterprise that would become Radio One, a large company with 70 stations. Hughes has had a number of firsts. She was the first woman to head a radio station that was number one in its market, and she was the first African-American woman to head a publicly traded company.

Born in Omaha, Nebraska to a nurse and an accountant, Hughes became interested in radio as a child when she received a transistor radio as a gift. After attending Creighton University and the University of Nebraska–Omaha, she became a lecturer at Howard University, where she also served as general sales manager of the campus radio station.

After her success in building the Howard University station's revenue, she took advantage of an FCC rule that allowed women and minorities to purchase failing radio stations for a discount. After many attempts to get a loan to buy WOL-AM, she was finally granted one by a female Puerto Rican loan officer. After losing nearly everything in this venture, Hughes transformed herself into a radio talk show host, a move that brought attention to her radio station and gave her confidence. WOL-AM finally began to make a profit in 1986. Hughes used this money to begin buying other stations in Washington, D.C. and Baltimore, eventually expanding her empire to include 70 stations. After building Radio One into a publicly trade company, she made her son CEO, and is now the company's chairman and secretary.

One out of five stations in the United States with a black-oriented format belongs to Radio One. Reaching 18 million listeners, the company has been a force in promoting hip hop, gospel, and R&B. A pioneer of "24-Hour Talk from a Black Perspective," Radio One syndicates talk shows focusing on African-American issues with hosts like Rev. Al Sharpton and author Michael Eric Dyson. Hughes's company mission is to empower the black community not only through programming but through hiring with 1,500 of Radio One's employees being African American. Catherine Hughes and Radio One have been a significant social and economic force for African-American communities and for the radio industry in general.

Sources: The Museum of Television and Radio, shemadeit.org; *Miami Times,* May 18–May 24, 2005: 2A.

---

surveys in which randomly selected listeners fill out a week's worth of daily logs detailing their radio listening.

To understand ratings and shares, look at the Pit Viper's hard rock drive-time program on station JIMI. The ratings service estimated that 10,000 people listened to the Viper's show from 8:15 to 8:30 A.M. on May 15. Of the 1 million listeners in the ADI, 100,000 were listening to the radio at that time. Table 6.2 shows how the rating and share for the show are computed.

Table 6.2 — Ratings and Shares for the Pit Viper

	Total Market (Basis for Rating)	Total Listeners with Radio on During Segment
May 15 Segment: 8:15 A.M. to 8:30 P.M.	1,000,000	100,000
Pit Viper's hard rock listeners	10,000	10,000
	Rating: $\dfrac{10,000}{1,000,000} = 0.01 \ (1\%)$	Share: $\dfrac{10,000}{100,000} = 0.10 \ (10\%)$

Arbitron also keeps track of demographic information, such as the age and sex of listeners who listen to various radio formats and at what time of day. For example, from 6 to 10 A.M. on weekdays, 78 percent of Urban Adult Contemporary listeners are twenty-five to fifty-four years old. From 7 to midnight on weekdays, 32 percent of Spanish regional listeners in the South Central United States are women.

In 2005, radio rating systems were under challenge. The leader in radio audience measurement, Arbitron changed its method, and found that the figures for listeners during morning commutes dropped dramatically. Since this was the hottest advertising window, the new figures caused Clear Channel to look elsewhere for ratings services. The competition among ratings companies is changing the way listeners are counted.

SUPPLYING THE AUDIENCE'S DEMAND

Key Concept

Radio station types The demand for information from various audiences is met by eight types of radio stations in the United States. In addition to the dominant commercially financed stations, there are stations run by governments, public consortiums, community groups, special interests, and educational institutions as well as shortwave operators and unregulated pirate broadcasters.

The type of content broadcast by a radio station depends on its purpose and who owns it. As shown in Table 6.3, there are eight *radio station types,* which can be classified on the basis of ownership and type of financing: commercial, state-run, public, shortwave, educational institution, community, special-interest, and pirate stations. The types of stations available vary by country, depending on the nature of government and regulation. In the United States, about 85 percent of all stations are commercial, although all eight types can be found. In Asia and Africa, state-run and commercial stations have been the most common.[19] U.S. commercial stations program primarily music, and public radio remains the prime source of news and information. Talk radio has

Table 6.3 Types of Radio Stations

Commercial: These stations seek to make a profit. Programming is mostly music, interview and call-in shows, and news.

Educational: Educational radio stations are owned and operated by universities, colleges, and even high schools. More than 800 U.S. educational institutions have broadcast licenses.

State-Run: Owned and operated by governments with direct control of content on a day-to-day basis.

Community: Low-power stations that promote community participation in solving local problems. In the United States, many serve ethnic communities.

Public: Noncommercial stations that receive money from the general public, private foundations, and governments. Receive government grants but are shielded from day-to-day government intervention.

Special Interest: Financed by noncommercial groups that advocate particular political or religious beliefs.

Shortwave: Shortwave radio is used to beam international programming. During 1995 it gained new attention in the United States because of its use by the militia movement.

Pirate: Unlicensed stations. For example, WTRA/Zoom Black Magic Liberation Radio in Springfield, Illinois, battled the FCC over the right to broadcast without FCC approval. The low-power station promoted communication among people who lived in a low-income housing project.

Sources: Carolyn Weaver, "When the Voice of America Ignores Its Charter," *Columbia Journalism Review* (November–December 1988), 36–43; Michael C. Keith, *Radio Production: Art and Sciences* (Boston: Focal Press, 1990), 228; Robert Chapman, *Selling the Sixties: The Pirates and Pop Music Radio* (London: Routledge, 1992); and Ron Sakolsky, "Zoom Black Magic Liberation Radio: The Birth of Micro-Radio Movement in the U.S.," in *A Passion for Radio,* Bruce Girard, ed. (Montreal: Black Rose Books, 1992), 106–113.

emerged as a cultural force, and it has emerged on commercial and public radio, special-interest stations, and shortwave.

The Public Radio System

In 1967, after a period of concern that television was becoming a "vast wasteland," Congress responded to the recommendations of a prestigious study group, the Carnegie Commission, and created the Corporation for Public Broadcasting (CPB). In 1969–1970, CPB joined with public television and radio stations to form the Public Broadcasting Service (PBS), which serves television, National Public Radio (NPR), and Public Radio International. These organizations provide programming for noncommercial stations.

NPR started in 1971 in one room with part-time journalists. Early programming was offbeat, and the small budget encouraged an emphasis on feature stories. One reporter writing in a closet commented on whether Wint-o-Green Life Savers spark in the dark when someone bites them.[20] By 2005, NPR had 25.3 million listeners, up from 22 million in 2004. Besides its on-air programming, NPR was an early pioneer in podcasting, putting many of its shows on the web.

NPR makes up an important part of public radio, but the over 800 public radio stations produce the bulk of programming. Classical music and jazz make up a significant portion of program time on many stations. Public radio stations tend to reflect the needs and wants of those in the community who supply the money that allows the station to operate, a practice that has opened the system to charges of elitism. Each public station operates independently as a public corporation. Each station originates its own programming but also carries NPR programs about national and international issues. Funding for public radio stations comes from about 13 percent in allocations from the Corporation for Public Broadcasting, 24 percent in corporate underwriting, and 34 percent in listener support.[21]

Corporate sponsorship of public radio has increased since the 1980s, when the FCC allowed corporations to mention more than their name and location in on-air spots. In 2002, NPR had sold underwriting to 161 corporate sponsors, and by 2005, that number had climbed to 236. Some listeners complain about the new commercialism of public radio, which they see as pandering to McDonald's and Starbucks.[22]

NPR's commitment to providing in-depth news in longer segments attracts talented broadcasters like Ted Koppel and an increase in listeners. News programs like *All Things Considered* and *Morning Edition* are popular. From 2001 to 2005, NPR's audience grew by 50 percent.[23] That audience is an interesting political mix, with 30 percent identifying themselves as liberal, 33 percent as moderate, and 31 percent as conservative. In contrast, commercial call-in radio attracts 45 percent conservative listeners, with only 18 percent identifying themselves as liberal.[24]

NPR's major competitor is Public Radio International (PRI), originally called American Public Radio, which also receives funding from the Corporation for Public Broadcasting. Public radio stations can select programming from both NPR and PRI. PRI serves 730 affiliate stations; its programs are distributed internationally by the World Radio Network. The Corporation for Public Broadcasting also supports Satélite Radio Bilingüe which provides programming to stations on Hispanic issues, and AIROS Native Radio Network, which serves 33 stations controlled by Native Americans.

Commercial Radio News

The growth and development of NPR coincided with a decline in the amount of commercial radio news, especially in smaller markets. The growth of television, the development of FM radio, and deregulation all combined to restructure radio news after 1960. However, commercial radio news continues to survive and even shows signs of resurgence.

Commercial radio stations that carry news generally list themselves as news or news-talk. Both types of format have content other than straight news. All-news formats have interview programming and even call-in shows. The difference between the two is primarily one of degree and emphasis. All-news stations emphasize the information elements, whereas talk programming includes a greater element of persuasion as guests and listeners express their opinions.

All-news stations typically have ongoing news packages, similar to *CNN Headline News* on television, that summarize important happenings around the world, nation, state, and local community. A second form of commercial news can be found on music format stations. However, this news is usually limited to short news summaries that run for a minute or two on the half-hour. The thirty-one radio networks often syndicate these reports, with stations adding local news from the newspaper.

Deregulation and increasing competition for radio advertising have hurt smaller news operations. Before the deregulation of the 1980s, most radio stations provided news every thirty minutes as part of their public service requirement for a license. When the public service requirement was dropped, about 8 percent of the stations dropped news. The increasing number of stations chasing dwindling advertising funds in the early 1990s contributed as well. Many stations simply cannot afford news. In a 2005 study of news reporting on commercial radio, the Project for Excellence in Journalism found that the news was "thin," focusing mostly on headlines.

Talk Radio

Between 1990 and 1995, the number of stations that devote the bulk of their programming to talk almost tripled, from 405 to 1,130. Since 1995 the number increased slightly to about 1,200 at the beginning of 2006. With talk, radio stations have discovered a way to boost their ratings among higher income older audiences and to attract advertisers who want to reach this group. A more recently developed format is talk personality, which appeals to younger people in the twenty-five to thirty-four age bracket. Those stations have edgier programming and less sports and news.

Talk radio as a format was developed in the 1960s by conservatives Joe Pyne and William Buckley. Murray Levin, a Harvard professor who wrote *Talk Radio and the American Dream* in 1980, told a *Los Angeles Times* reporter in 1995 that talk shows

Controversial radio "shock jocks," such as Howard Stern, challenge the limits of acceptable speech on the radio. Stern moved his show to Sirius satellite radio in 2006 to avoid censorship by the FCC.

Commerce and Culture: Who Decides What We Hear?

The U.S. Congress and the Federal Communications Commission have long wrestled with the issue of how big a broadcast company can become before it has too much power to influence what people see and hear. The issue resurfaced with a vengeance in 2002 as a result of Clear Channel's aggressive acquisition of radio stations, with more than 1,200 stations and efforts underway to acquire another 186. The federal government reacted by postponing and investigating these acquisition plans and by introducing legislation that would control potential abuses from economic concentration.

At the forefront of the complaints was a wide range of organizations that represent artists, including the Recording Association of America, American Federation of Musicians, American Federation of Television and Radio Artists, and the Recording Academy. Their complaints centered on the practices of using a national playlist that limits the variety of music heard locally, of artists and recording companies financing station promotions and receiving airtime for particular artists, of stations not playing artists who do not use Clear Channel's concert-promotion service, and of using other companies to buy radio stations and hold them for Clear Channel in anticipation of policy changes at the FCC.

Critics argued that all of these practices, if true, limit consumer access to a wider range of content and stop smaller companies from buying stations. Hillary Rosen, president of the Recording Industry Association of America, says, "There is no question that radio consolidation and radio promotion have raised questions about access to the airwaves."

Executives at Clear Channel denied the charges. Randy Michaels, chief executive officer for Clear Channel Radio, said no national playlist exists.

While Clear Channel became known as the "King of Vanilla" for its cookie-cutter programming, its strategies began to change in 2005 with the advent of satellite and high-definition radio. Competing with XM Satellite and Sirrus Satellite, Clear Channel has chosen to target niche audiences through its HD channels. Early efforts have included a southern rock station, Mother Trucker; a new-age Relaxation Channel; and a Spanish-music station, La Bomba.

Clear Channel has also earned praise for its coverage of Hurricane Katrina. In 2002, a Clear Channel station in North Dakota had come under fire for not reporting a toxic spill because it was running automated programming. However, during the 2005 hurricane as many smaller stations ceased operating, the Clear Channel stations were able to keep transmitting emergency information

and invited emergency call-ins from people who could not reach 911.

In late 2006, as part of a merger, Clear Channel announced that it would sell 448 of its smaller market radio stations. The move opened the door for new and smaller owners to acquire radio stations.

Sources: Paige Albiniak, "Clear Channel Challenged," *Broadcasting & Cable,* January 28, 2002, broadcastingcable.com; Bill McConnell, "Clear Channel Fights Back," *Broadcasting & Cable,* May 13, 2002, broadcastingcable.com; Paige Albiniak, "Music Biz Asks for Radio Probe," *Broadcasting & Cable,* May 27, 2002, broadcastingcable.com; Daisy Whitney, "Outlets Kept News Flowing After Storm," *TelevisionWeek,* February 27, 2006: 24.

capitalize on emotional subjects. "When I studied talk radio," Levin said, "there was no issue that aroused as much anger and emotion as homosexuality. The talk-show hosts, they knew this. They would talk more about it than the subject warranted. They'd get heated debates and would push people to further extremes. That boosted ratings."[25]

The popularity of talk radio has created a wide diversity of hosts. They range from conservative Rush Limbaugh to outrageous Howard Stern and include a range of political figures including perennial presidential candidate Pat Buchanan, who was among the first to realize the potential of talk radio as political communication.

In 1993, political scientist Richard Hofstetter surveyed San Diego County and found that about one-third of adults had listened to political talk shows at one time or another. Those who were more interested in political issues and well informed about candidates were more likely to listen. Most were mainstream in their views, Hofstetter said. Eighty percent said that they disagreed with the talk show host at least occasionally, but 30 to 40 percent said that they disagreed often. "That was surprising," Hofstetter told the *Los Angeles Times.* "That suggests this is a sort of titillating, cheap thrill for these listeners. I think what's happened is people stuck in automobiles want to listen to something besides music."[26]

The popularity of talk radio has caused critics and scholars to speculate about why it has been so successful. One argument holds that talk radio is the new town meeting of a fragmented society whose members never meet in person but use electronic media such as radio and the Internet to connect. In this town meeting, the populace speaks rather than relying on official voices. In fact, in *Talk Radio,* Levin attributes the public fascination with talk radio to an increasing distrust of official institutions.

Critics often attack talk radio as a negative force. Peter Laufer, in *Inside Talk Radio,* concludes that many hosts put forth "fallacy" as "fact," "uninformed opinion" as "thoughtful commentary," and "groundless innuendo" as "investigative journalism."[27] Critics suggest that talk radio exploits and fans groundless fears and feeds paranoia.

INTERNATIONAL RADIO

Radio is a powerful medium in many countries. Even with new technologies, radio continues to be significant because programming is inexpensive to produce, can be transmitted across borders, and does not rely on expensive receiving equipment. These features, combined with portability, make radio a tool both for governments and for those who seek to challenge governments. In countries where print media are not widely distributed or where governments deny access to news, portable radios often are the only connection to factual information.

Broadcasting Across Borders

Broadcasting across borders dates to 1926, when the Soviet Union ran a brief radio propaganda effort against the government of Romania. The first ongoing broadcast for people outside a country occurred in 1927, when Holland directed domestic programming to Dutch citizens living abroad. During the next seven years, Germany, France, Great Britain, the Soviet Union, and Japan created their own "colonial" broadcasts.[28]

During World War II, several combatant countries broadcast programs aimed at the enemy's population in an effort to undermine opposition, lower morale, and create confusion. Germany, for example, broadcast anti-British messages into India in eight Indian languages.

Known personalities tended to attract listening audiences. One of the most famous of the radio personalities, "Tokyo Rose," broadcast to the Allied troops in the Pacific in an effort to lower their morale. After the war, an American typist, Iva Togura, was convicted of treason and spent ten years in prison for being the infamous Tokyo Rose.

Border Radio

On the tense U.S.–Mexico border, government patrols attempt to keep illegal immigrants from crossing, but the radio waves do not honor such barriers. Music, news, advice, and politics in a variety of languages, including English, Spanish, and Mixteco (the language of Mesoamerican Indian people of southern Mexico) pass from the United States to Mexico and back, catering to the multicultural border populations.

Radio stations began to proliferate on the border in the 1930s, as media entrepreneurs traveled away from the increasing commercialism and government regulation of the airwaves. They crossed into Mexico and worked out special licensing agreements for stations built with special transmitters that could send a signal that could reach as far as Japan. These stations were known as "border blasters." In World War II, the United States signed a broadcasting treaty with Mexico that threatened to shut down border stations, but they continued to thrive, attracting audiences with country and Western music, evangelical programs, and advertisements that promised oil bonanzas and amazing cures. The most famous personality to broadcast from a border blaster was the mysterious Wolfman, whose voice was used as the soundtrack to the 1973 George Lucas film, *American Graffiti.* In 1972, the United States and Mexico agreed to regulate the FM band to control border blasters and protect radio stations from interference. But the problem continues with stations in Tijuana, including one owned by Clear Channel, broadcasting at 150,000 watts.

Radio stations of all kinds dot the border. Many Mexicans rely on radio as their primary medium. People living near the border in Tijuana hear mostly radio from big U.S. cities like San Diego and Los Angeles. Smaller stations on the U.S. side broadcast to Tijuana with hip hop, country and Western, talk shows, and sports news about the San Diego Padres. Even though they broadcast in Spanish, they tend to imitate U.S. formats for commercial radio, but some preserve a more Mexican-style programming with ranchero music. In Tijuana, Radio Latina broadcasts top 40 hits. In both radio and television, broadcasters on the border try to ignore it by providing similar programming to its audiences on both sides, and selling advertising that will appeal to all markets. But some public stations have different roles. Radio Bilingüe serves Mixteco farm workers with special programming, including a message service to help reunite families and friends divided by immigration.

The population in border cities is expected to double in the next thirty years, and border radio will grow with it. The radio represents the permeability of national borders, especially in terms of language and culture.

Sources: Gene Fowler and Bill Crawford, *Border Radio: Quacks, Yodelers, Pitchmen, Psychics, and Other Amazing Broadcasters of the American Airwaves* (University of Texas Press, 2002); Monica Campbell, "Good Morning, Mexico," *San Francisco Chronicle,* February 16, 2006: sfgate.com.

Togura, who was trapped in Japan during the war, admitted to working for Japanese radio. In reality, Tokyo Rose did not exist. The name had been applied to every woman announcer on Japanese radio.

From the end of World War II until the late 1980s, the Cold War, a war of ideology, relied heavily on the dissemination of information and propaganda. The Western and Eastern bloc countries fought for domination through propaganda extolling the virtues of one political system over the other.

The two dominant broadcast units for the West were the British Broadcasting Corporation (BBC) and the Voice of America (VOA). The BBC began broadcasting to the Soviet Union in 1946, and the VOA followed a year later. The VOA reached its zenith under then-President John Kennedy in the early 1960s, when it also received its greatest support from Congress.

It is difficult to say how much international broadcasting contributed to the changes that swept the world during the past decade. However, Western radio broadcasts to other countries claimed audiences in the tens of millions throughout the Cold War period. Chinese immigrants talk about listening to the broadcasts while they were banished to the villages during the Cultural Revolution, and others profess to have learned English by listening to the broadcasts.

Europe Most European countries have mixed systems with both public and commercial stations. Public stations are financed by license fees, which theoretically represent licenses to obtain radio content but in practice are fees for using a radio receiver. Commercial stations raise revenue from advertisers, and during the 1980s they increasingly took advertising revenues from other media. In Austria, Ireland, Portugal, France, and Greece, a higher percentage of advertising dollars is spent on commercial radio than in the United States.[29]

Programming on European public networks includes classical and popular music, sports, news and current affairs, and educational material. As in the United States, commercial stations in Europe target segmented audiences. In Britain, the keen interest in radio, largely because of the success of the BBC stations, has driven technological innovation. The number of digital radios owned by Brits increased from 60,000 in 2002 to 3.12 million in April 2006.[30]

Africa With little Internet penetration on the continent, radio is the most popular, accessible, and affordable medium for many Africans, especially in poor, rural areas where literacy rates are low. Since radios can run on batteries, solar power, or hand crank, users do not need electricity. Setting up a radio station involves relatively low start-up costs. Until economic and political liberalization in many African countries, the radio was often government controlled. Since the easing of such controls in the 1990s, independent and community radio stations have proliferated in many parts of Africa. Radio is used for political organizing, health and safety education, local music promotion, investigative reporting, and community events.

Foreign investors and governments see the potential of radio in Africa. African countries are served by multinational satellite companies like WorldSpace, which delivers programming through digital receivers. As a major player in African radio, the BBC partners with African stations to serve Britain's own African immigrant communities. Nongovernmental agencies use local radio to educate Africans on HIV and other health and safety issues. Missionary organizations provide religious programs and radio services. And the U.S. government provides the Voice of America throughout Africa and Radio Sawa in the Middle East to promote U.S. interests.

Radio is the most important medium in many parts of the world because it is portable and inexpensive to own and operate.

Latin America Commercial programming in Latin America is similar to that found in North America, with an emphasis on music and entertainment. Global satellite networks, such as SES Americom, provide commercial services. Religious stations are also prevalent in some areas. For example, HCJB's Voice of the Andes began in Ecuador in 1931 and has its own six-million-watt hydroelectric plant to help power its station, which provides evangelical programming.[31] As in Africa, many people in Latin America have little access to electricity that powers phones and televisions, and community stations provide most of their news. Some countries, such as Bolivia, El Salvador, and Argentina, experienced a growth in community and private radio stations during political unrest in the 1980s. During this period, hundreds of illegal FM stations sprang up in Argentina, which had no federal licensing agency. They served people in small communities by running local information and educational programs and by offering advertising to small businesses. When politicians discovered in 1991 that these stations provided an effective way to reach voters, the central government tried to close them down. However, many pirate stations continue to operate today.

Recently, NPR has teamed with local stations, including college stations, to encourage public radio programming in Central and South America.

Asia Radio in Asia has similarities with radio in both Latin America and Africa. Because of European colonial influence, countries such as India have adopted systems modeled after the BBC. Some Asian nations such as Singapore have highly developed commercial systems. Some, such as South Korea, have radio systems with extensive religious programming.

In China the government has traditionally maintained tight control of radio at both national and local levels. Lately, the control has loosened, but control remains stronger than in most other populous countries.

The variety of systems reflects variations in economic and political development. People in the rural areas of some countries, such as Bhutan and Bangladesh, have limited access to radio sets, whereas people in countries such as Japan and Korea have nearly as many radios per inhabitant as in Australia or the United States. The importance of radio as a mass medium varies as well. In some isolated parts of China, radio is the primary source of national news. In Japan a highly developed television system has replaced radio as the primary source of information.

Australia Australia, with its vast geography and scattered population, has a natural demand for radio. The distances between population centers far exceed the broadcast capabilities of nonsatellite television. Australia has 38 million radios, second in the world only to the United States.

The Australian radio system is overseen by the Australian Broadcasting Commission (ABC), which also provides programming through a network of stations. The programming is similar to that of public stations in the United States, with music and news making up most of the content. During the 1980s, ownership rules were changed to allow more stations per company, and commercial radio grew in popularity.[32] The Australian government has set 2009 as the start-up year for digital radio.

TRENDS

Radio is not struggling as much as traditional print media to retain its audience, though that audience is changing. Still, radio's advertising growth from 2003 to 2005 was unimpressive, leading industry analysts to worry about the medium's investment future. Other major challenges to the industry include changing technologies, such as high-definition radio and podcasting, increased competition, and changing demographics. For audiences, access to the most innovative technologies with the greatest choice will be limited to wealthier consumers. The trends will determine both how we receive radio and the nature of radio content.

Technology: Internet Radio

In 2006, satellite radio had 9 million subscribers, the Internet had 30 million weekly listeners, and terrestrial radio had 230 million subscribers.[33] Traditional radio was still far in the lead, but the new media were already influencing the market. Internet streaming has been gaining popularity, with the number of weekly listeners jumping by 50 percent in 2005 and weekly on-demand streams increasing by 1,000 percent from January to June 2006. The most popular destinations were Yahoo.com, with 2.6 million listeners, and America Online, with 1.9 million.[34] To grab a share of this audience, terrestrial radio stations, such as NPR and Clear Channel, have been simulcasting their programs, taking them to a worldwide audience over the web. However, in 2006 only 19 percent of online users had listened to the simulcast of the radio station they listened to over the air.[35]

Technology: Satellite Radio

Even newer than **Internet radio** is **satellite radio.** XM began broadcasting in late 2000, and Sirius came on board the next year. Both charge about $13 per month for a subscription. Satellite service accommodates radio listening on long trips because signals are not lost as a car moves from one signal area to another.

A central feature of the competition between terrestrial and satellite radio is to what extent listeners will be willing to pay for radio service and to what extent advertisers will provide revenues. Satellite radio banks on big stars like Bob Dylan, who hosts *Theme Time Radio Hour* on XM, to attract subscribers. Many listeners followed Howard Stern to Sirius. But celebrities are expensive, and the listeners who can afford satellite radio are wealthy, with one in four living in households that earn $100,000 per year.[36] For upscale audiences, the opportunities presented by new media have meant expanding choices and greater control over what they consume. The greater ability to select content may mean that listeners will soon be able easily to tune out advertising, and that will seriously impact the medium.[37]

> **Key Concept**
>
> **Internet radio and satellite radio** These two distribution systems resulted from the development of computer technology during the 1990s. The two forms of converging technology free radio stations from the geographic limits of terrestrial broadcasting and open up new audiences and markets.

Technology: Portable Digital Devices

While the technology was still in its infancy in 2007, the latest cell phones were being equipped with the ability to play radio broadcasts from the Internet and satellite stations. iPod users can download Internet radio listings, sort through them, capture songs as MP3 files, and transfer them to their devices. Satellite companies have devices to create playlists and download selected music. These digital recording capabilities concern some artists, who worry about the pirating of their music and lack of any royalty compensation, while other musicians argue against further regulation of such technologies, which they feel gives an advantage to big recording studios.[38]

Culture: Changing Demographics

As in other mass media, radio must adapt to changing demographics and attract diverse audiences. Of increasing interest has been the growing Hispanic population. Hispanic radio is growing faster than mainstream radio stations, and attracts more Hispanic ad spending.[39] Thirty-seven percent of Hispanics turn first to ethnic radio stations over mainstream ones.[40] In 2005, over 750 Spanish-language stations were operating, targeting mostly forty to forty-nine-year-old men and teenage girls. Unlike the mainstream population, Hispanics over sixty-five years old are least likely to listen to radio. The most preferred Spanish-language format is Mexican regional, which features mainstream hits by Mexican and Latin-American performers. Spanish news/talk ranks fourth after other music formats. An up-and-coming format in 2006 was the Latin hip hop, reggaeton, popular with urban Latino youth. In 2004, Clear

Changes in trends occur for a variety of reasons, and these often are related to technology and regulation. A new president, for example, appoints new members to regulatory boards such as the FCC, and these new members bring new interests. Currently, the FCC is concerned about the sexual content on radio. This concern is far from new. However, with each generation the material seems to become more explicit. The reemergence of this issue raises the following questions:

- Why do sexually explicit lyrics offend some people?
- What sort of negative impact can these lyrics have?
- Should FCC fines for such lyrics be removed?
- Should the context of playing these lyrics—information versus entertainment—be considered when the FCC investigates a complaint?

Regulatory boards are not the only groups in Washington, D.C., that react to trends. Congress has become concerned about the concentration of ownership and has introduced legislation to control potential abuses. At the heart of this issue is whether abuses have occurred or whether there is the potential for such abuses. Think about these questions concerning the negative impact of ownership concentration:

- Has the concentration of ownership limited the number of different formats available in your radio market?

- Does concentration make it more difficult for independent artists to have their music played on the radio?
- Is it wrong for recording companies to pay for radio promotional events and then to receive play time for their music in return?

The final trend is connected by the move to digital radio. By digitizing the content signal sent by radio stations, it has become very easy to distribute the material in ways other than broadcast waves. Today, digital radio can be sent by satellite and Internet, but both of these distribution systems face difficulties. The Internet has a new fee structure for using recordings that many think will cripple the Internet as a stand-alone distribution system. Questions to be answered include:

- Should satellite, cable, and Internet radio broadcasters continue to pay higher fees than regular broadcasters?
- What kinds of content protection technology, if any, should be implemented for digital radio?
- High definition will require new receivers that will cost more than analog sets. Do you think many people will purchase high-definition radios?
- Will satellite and Internet radio run local broadcast radio stations out of business?

Channel began changing its rock stations over to Spanish-language to attract the Latino youth market.[41] Some Hispanic listeners complain that such commercial radio stations produce too narrow a list, ignoring the many varieties of Latino music in a diverse population from many parts of the world. Listeners of the old rock stations feel upset by the switch, reflecting unsettling changes they feel in the wider culture.[42]

Nearly 95 percent of African Americans listen to the radio in an average week, and are equal to Hispanics in their primary consumption of ethnic radio.[43] African-American men aged fifty to fifty-four have the highest consumption, listening to radio an average of twenty-six hours, thirty minutes per week, well over the average. African-American listeners are more likely than the general population to tune in at night. Formats that appeal equally to general listeners and African Americans include top 40, adult contemporary, and news/talk, while other formats such as gospel, smooth jazz, and rhythmic contemporary hit radio attract more African-American listeners. An African-American owned company, Radio One, is one of the largest broadcasting companies in the United States, with seventy stations. Predicting the influence of new technologies on the radio business, Radio One's CEO Catherine Hughes says, "I think the last community to be impacted will be the African-American community. Radio is so much a part of our culture. Black radio is to the African-American community what black newspapers were to our ancestors."[44]

Hispanic and African-American populations are considered of special interest to a radio industry expanding into niche markets. However, minorities make up only 7.9 percent of the radio workforce.[45] There are no African Americans employed as radio news directors, and only 8.8 percent of directors are Hispanic. On a more positive note, Arbitron set up a special website in 2007 to help minority investors acquire radio stations being sold by Clear Channel.

Culture: Content Regulation

Because the airwaves belong to the people, radio and television have never been given complete First Amendment rights. As a result, the FCC has a right to regulate material that it considers indecent. This is "programming that describes or depicts sexual or excretory organs in a patently offensive way."[46] The degree of regulation has varied over the years, but recent events suggest that we may be in for a period of growing regulation. The FCC has been imposing heftier fines for indecency after a wave of complaints. In February 2006, complaints to the FCC increased to 141,868, over the 44,109 received at the end of 2005. Christian and profamily groups such as the Parents' Television Council have organized e-mail campaigns to protest what they perceive as unacceptable radio and television content.[47]

The heart of this conflict is the issue of just how much regulation government should exercise over broadcast content. A more conservative FCC, which reflects appointments by President George W. Bush, suggests that regulation may grow. Yet the popularity of mainstream rap with explicit lyrics indicates that commercial music interests and many listeners may not want increased regulation.

SUMMARY

- Radio began as a point-to-point communication form before becoming a mass medium during the 1920s.
- Radio became the center of home entertainment during the 1930s, much as television is today.
- During World War II, radio news gave war coverage a speed and intimacy that never existed before.
- A central debate throughout the history of radio is whether it should be a commercial medium serving owners or a noncommercial medium serving society.
- In the United States, radio has become a medium that attracts demographically defined audiences and sells the attention of those audiences to advertisers.
- Music for entertainment makes up most of radio's programming, but news and talk radio remain important sources of information, especially in larger markets.
- More than two dozen music formats are available to radio stations.

- There are eight types of radio stations: commercial, state-run, public, educational institution, community, special interest, shortwave, and pirate.
- Radio remains the most used medium throughout the world.
- International broadcasts grew during the 1980s as more countries used improved technology to communicate their ideologies.
- Radio stations face increased competition during the twenty-first century from Internet and satellite distribution of radio.
- Radio ownership concentration has increased greatly as a result of the 1996 Telecommunications Act, and some critics have feared this will reduce the diversity of news and information.
- Driven by talk radio and the explicit lyrics of rap music, the debate over regulation of radio content has reemerged during the past few years.

NAVIGATING THE WEB Radio

Radio on the web is growing as stations set up websites. Software allows users to easily set up their own Internet radio servers and to stream radio play.

Inside Radio
mstreet.net
Inside Radio provides insider radio news on the web or by means of fax.

Sites also include information about the history and current state of the radio business. The following sites contain historical and industry information.

Old-Time Radio
old-time.com
Programming logs, pictures, and catalogs of tapes from the Golden Age of radio are available at this site. It contains historical material about the 1930s and 1940s.

The Museum of Television and Radio
mtr.org
The MTR site is an introduction to the two museums about radio and television. One is located in New York and the other in southern California. The site contains information on the museums, which have scholarly material about the history of radio and TV.

Radio-Locator
radio-locator.com
Maintained by Theodric Technologies LCC, Radio-Locator allows users to link to over 10,000 Internet radio stations, classified by geographic location and format. It also provides a search for unused FM frequencies for use with satellite radio and MP3 players.

The following sites have information about radio news and radio companies.

Westwood One Radio Networks
westwoodone.com
The Westwood site is maintained by the Westwood radio networks. It contains information about the company, its programming, and its affiliate stations.

National Public Radio
npr.org
The home site for the National Public Radio network contains audio and text versions of news events and information about NPR, its programs, and its affiliates.

QUESTIONS FOR REVIEW

1. Was radio first conceived of as a broadcasting system?
2. What is a network?
3. When did radio journalism become significant?
4. What is significant about radio formats?
5. How might the development of Internet and satellite distribution of radio affect local radio stations?
6. Describe the types of radio stations.
7. How did the Telecommunications Act of 1996 affect ownership?
8. Why is the FCC considering increased regulation of radio content?

ISSUES TO THINK ABOUT

1. Describe radio's flexibility across the years. How has this contributed to its staying power as a mass medium?
2. Does specialization strengthen or trivialize radio as a news and information medium?
3. Does public radio make a unique contribution to society? How might the reduction of federal support for public radio affect content?
4. Why is radio a significant international medium? How does it differ from other media in this respect?

SUGGESTED READINGS

Balk, Alfred. *The Rise of Radio, from Marconi through the Golden Age* (Jefferson, NC: McFarland, 2006).

Chantler, Paul. *Local Radio Journalism* (Oxford, England: Focal Press, 1992).

Land, Jeff. *Active Radio: Pacifica's Brash Experiment* (Minneapolis: University of Minnesota Press, 1999).

Murray, Michael D. *The Political Performers: CBS Broadcasts in the Public Interest* (Westport, CT: Praeger, 1994).

Regal, Brian. *Radio: The Story of a Technology* (Westport, Conn.: Greenwood, 2005).

Seib, Philip M. *Going Live: Getting the News Right in a Real-Time, Online World* (Lanham, MD: Rowman & Littlefield, 2000).

CHAPTER 7

Television

During the 2004 U.S. Presidential election, many young voters regularly learned campaign news from *Saturday Night Live* and *The Daily Show with Jon Stewart.* Politicians hit the late-night comedy shows to drum up support. When John Edwards announced his candidacy on *The Daily Show,* Stewart quipped, "I guess I should probably tell you now, we're a fake show. So this may not count."

But while Stewart downplayed the importance of his show, its influence was undeniable. During the Democratic and Republican conventions, more eighteen to thirty-four-year-olds watched coverage on *The Daily Show* than on CNN, MSNBC, or Fox. For the first time, late-night comedy shows rivaled mainstream news programs as information sources for this audience demographic.

Political and media analysts wondered what the phenomenon might mean for the future of democracy. Some worried that by combining news with entertainment, comedy shows gave young people only a shallow view of the issues. Bill O'Reilly, of Fox News, called viewers of *The Daily Show* "dopey college kids," but a survey by the Annenberg Public Policy Center found that these viewers were better informed and had deeper campaign knowledge than nonviewers.[1] Other analysts theorized that even if young people were informed, they were in danger of becoming cynical and apathetic about citizenship because of their exposure to satire of the political process.

KEY CONCEPTS

- Community Antenna Television (CATV)
- Network Affiliate
- Broadcasters as "Trustees" of the Airwaves
- Single-Sponsor System
- Network-Owned and -Operated ("O and O") Groups
- Demographic and Psychographic Approaches to Broadcast Marketing
- Digital Television (DTV)
- TV News and Information Formats
- Entertainment Formulas
- Cost per Consumer in the TV Advertising Market
- Market Factors in International Television
- Cultural Imperialism
- Interactive Television

On the other hand, supporters of *The Daily Show* argued that it attracted young viewers because it criticized mainstream journalism that under the guise of objectivity served only the interests of social elites. *The Daily Show* served an important role of challenging mainstream television news to do better. Young people responded to this message, which engaged them with its humor and heart.[2]

Arguments about television shows do not surprise media historians. Television has often been a controversial medium. In the 1960s, the chair of the Federal Communications Commission (FCC), Newton Minow, called television "a vast wasteland." Critics argue that television robs us of cultural sophistication and distorts reality. Others believe that in the service of social elites, television creates a homogenous consumer culture without viable alternatives and alters our feelings, perceptions, thoughts, and behaviors without our control. A more optimistic view of television sees it as fostering opportunities for us to participate in accepting or rejecting cultural ideas and identities. It expands the worlds of us who have limited experience with faraway places and events. Television is a powerful institution that has changed the social and political landscape and, in turn, has undergone many changes in its technology, ownership, and influence.

As you read this chapter, you will see that changing technologies affect how people watch television as well as what they watch. Television content and the amount of television being watched remain concerns for people who are interested in cultural identity, social change, political life, and the evolution of a democratic society. Consider the following issues:

- How has the commercial nature of television shaped its content? Is content shaped by advertisers? By public need and desire? By the overwhelmingly commercial structure of the medium?

- Until recently, the broadcast television industry was dominated by three networks. Now many viewers have access to more than one hundred channels. What effect has this change had on the public?

- How do you think the content of television has shaped or changed U.S. culture and society? Has television fostered democracy? Has it turned politics into entertainment? Has it made people more accepting of violence? Has it encouraged tolerance of diversity?

TELEVISION IN AMERICAN LIFE

The history of television is a history of technology and policy, economics and sociology, and entertainment and news. Television has never been a static medium. Rather, it evolved through changing technologies, including changes in presentation (such as color programming) and distribution (by cable, satellite, and fiber optics). These changes have been affected by government regulation. But television was not merely a technical invention. It changed people's lives, even down to the arrangement of their homes. As Lynn Spigel has demonstrated, for example, women's magazines of the 1950s discussed how to rearrange household furniture to accommodate the television as a replacement for the fireplace and the once traditional piano. The magazines also noted that television could provide a unifying influence in family life.[3] In later decades, televisions were often placed where they could be watched during meals. Today, many households have more than one television, and family members may watch individually rather than together. Television revolutionized not only the home, but also news, politics, and information. Some say that it revolutionized an entire society.

Television in Your Life

How Do You Watch Television?

People watch television for a variety of reasons. What motivates you to look at television? Do you watch to see people with whom you can identify? Do you watch to learn about people who are different? Do you use TV to escape and relax? Do you learn ways to solve your daily problems from TV?

People also watch television in a variety of situations. It can be a solitary or social activity. How do you most often look at TV? Do you watch by yourself, or with your family? Do you watch television as part of a sorority or fraternity? Do you watch TV when you're on a date? How and why you watch television changes how it affects you. As you read this chapter, think about the ways television affects you and how content is shaped to have that influence.

Rank the following from one to seven, with seven being your top reason for watching TV.

Motivations
To see people I can identify with and enjoy
To see people who are different from me
To escape and relax
To watch action, adventure
To find good role models
To learn ways to solve daily problems
To learn about different cultures and lifestyles

Development of Television

Television resulted from a long line of early experiments by many inventors, including Vladimir Zworykin, Philo T. Farnsworth, Edwin Armstrong, and Lee de Forest. The finished product represents the efforts of combined technologies and vicious patent disputes. Although experimentation began a century ago, the first test broadcasts did not begin until the mid-1920s. Development of television was not an exclusive American phenomenon; television was on the air in England in the mid-1930s.

Battles between the radio networks such as Columbia Broadcasting System (CBS) and electrical giants such as Radio Corporation of America (RCA) determined the course of television in the United States. David Sarnoff of RCA became the dominating force in both radio and **television network** development. In 1933, Sarnoff opened the RCA Building in midtown Manhattan, which included a studio designed to provide live TV programs. RCA first demonstrated its all-electronic television system to the **trade press** in 1935, and television sets went on sale in a Bronx furniture store in 1938. In 1939 many people in the United States saw their first television on five- and seven-inch screens at the New York World's Fair.

During 1939, several radio networks and radio manufacturing companies, including General Electric, RCA, CBS, and DuMont, began transmitting from experimental television stations in New York. RCA and DuMont, which manufactured early

television network

A system of linked communication technologies that transmits video, audio, and text to many stations. Network-affiliated stations rebroadcast programs and advertising to viewers in a geographic area, and may also provide locally produced content.

trade press

Periodicals that target a specific industry. *Broadcasting & Cable* magazine, for example, targets the broadcast and cable industry and is an example of a trade magazine.

Television arrived in the home and changed not only people's vision of the world but also the spatial arrangements of their homes. Household furniture was shifted to accommodate the television as a replacement for the fireplace and the once traditional piano.

receivers, slowly increased the size of the viewing screen to twelve inches. After several years of debating technical standards, the FCC authorized a standardized system for resolution quality and transmission.[4] By the end of 1941, which was television's initial year of commercial operation in the United States, CBS and NBC had converted their New York stations from experimental to commercial status, and about ten thousand sets were sold.

Television's progress came to a halt in 1942 as manufacturers devoted themselves to war production. New television sets could not be made, and old ones could not be repaired. Only six experimental stations stayed on the air, and these for only an hour or so a week.

Although the technology was in place and regulation allowed for expansion, commercial television faced major challenges at the end of the war. First, TV station start-ups were expensive, requiring $1.5 million (about $7 million in today's dollars) or more. Second, the nation still suffered a shortage of critical materials. Third, advertisers were wary of television's high costs. Owners correctly expected their stations to operate at a loss for several years before a large enough viewing audience began to attract advertisers.

Each segment of the industry was reluctant to commit resources because of uncertainty in other segments. Station owners were concerned about whether consumers could afford sets to receive their broadcasts; set manufacturers needed on-air programming to entice set buyers; programmers needed advertisers' financial support; and advertisers needed viewers. One entity had to create the impetus for the other players to take the plunge, so development was slow. Nevertheless, the potential market encouraged risk-taking, and each segment stumbled its way to success.

Postwar Challenges

After World War II, television began to emerge as a mass medium, and networks rapidly became the dominant force in shaping station ownership and programming. By 1934, the regulation of broadcasting had been assigned to the Federal Communication Commission (FCC), which was created by the Communications Act. In 1948, because of signal interference and because the number of channels assigned for television proved inadequate to meet the demand, the FCC froze the granting of television station licenses. Until it ended in 1952, the freeze limited stations to the 108 that were already in operation. During the freeze, a few big cities had several stations, and many had none. In areas that had no television, people used ingenious methods to get signals. In some communities, companies built tall antennas on hilltops to receive station signals and then transmitted those signals through **coaxial cable** to subscribing homes, thus initiating *community antenna television (CATV).* By 1952, about 15 million homes (10 percent of the U.S. population) had TV sets, and advertising revenues were about $324 million. Total advertising revenues for radio in the same year were about $445 million.

By late 1948, four television networks broadcast from New York with limited links west to Chicago. Three of the networks—ABC, CBS, and NBC—were based on radio networks; the fourth, which was television only, was run by DuMont with help from its partner, United Paramount Theaters of Hollywood. In addition, National Education Television (NET) was founded in 1952 by the Ford Foundation and became a network in 1954. It ceased operation in 1970.

Good programming and solid *network affiliate* stations developed because they allowed the local broadcast stations to share the expense of producing quality programming. Local stations could not afford individually to pay national radio stars such as Jack Benny, but by forming networks, better programs could be produced and broadcast locally. CBS and NBC offered the strongest programming and so gained the most affiliates. ABC and DuMont competed for the rest. DuMont was the only network that had no radio connections; its financial support came from a successful television manufacturing business. DuMont hoped to pick up stations along the Atlantic seaboard and then move inland as the number of receivers increased and as the AT&T coaxial cables necessary for carrying television signals moved west. But the new stations tended to affiliate with one of the major networks. Unable to compete financially, DuMont closed its doors in 1955.[5] ABC, CBS, and NBC continued to dominate television until the coming of the Fox network in the late 1980s.

During the 1950s, CBS and NBC competed for the top spot. One of their early battles involved the development of color television. CBS, RCA (which owned NBC), and other companies had experimented with color systems beginning in 1940. As often happens with innovative technologies, technical standards clashed. In 1948, CBS claimed it could implement its system, but RCA argued that further experimentation was necessary before standards could be set. In 1950, after considerable political pressure from Congress and from CBS, the FCC first chose CBS's partly mechanical color system. However, in 1953 the FCC reversed its decision and authorized the all-electronic RCA system, which was compatible with black-and-white sets. David Sarnoff, chairperson of the board of RCA, announced on television that color had arrived. "This day will be remembered in the annals of communications," he said, "along with the historic date of April 30, 1939, when RCA-NBC introduced all-electronic black-and-white television as a new broadcast service to the public at the opening of the World's Fair in New York. At that time we added sight to sound. Today, we add color to sight."[6] However, Sarnoff's claim was mostly public relations hype, and it was not until the mid-1960s that color receivers became widely available.

Policy and Politics

Industry players cooperated with the government to ensure a profitable commercial broadcast system. Broadcast regulation is treated thoroughly in Chapter 14, but it is important to note here that the basic outlines of radio regulation were applied to television, guaranteeing that it too would be primarily a commercial medium. The act extended principles of the 1927 Radio Act that assigned licenses to *broadcasters as "trustees" of the airwaves* and charged broadcasters with operating in the public interest.

> ### Key Concept
>
> **Community antenna television (CATV)** The first form of cable system, CATV was created in 1948. It used signals that were beamed to widespread communities via hilltop antennas; coaxial cable then carried the signals to households. The CATV system brought television signals to many rural areas that previously were unable to get them or received only poor-quality signals.

> ### Key Concept
>
> **Network affiliate** A television station typically contracts to carry one network's programming and commercials; the station thus becomes an affiliate of that network. In return, the network pays the station for use of its time. The three major networks—CBS, ABC, and NBC—historically gained much of their strength through powerful affiliation agreements.

coaxial cable
Cable that contains two conductors: a solid central core surrounded by a tubelike hollow one. Air or solid insulation separates the two. Electromagnetic energy, such as television transmission signals, travels between the two conductors.

> ### Key Concept
>
> **Broadcasters as "trustees" of the airwaves** Basing its regulations on the concept that airwave scarcity produces a common space that is subject to public laws, the U.S. government has long required that broadcasters function as trustees of the airwaves, operating by license in the public interest.

The FCC had difficulty addressing the issue of radio and television political content, particularly when it involved opinion, from the early days forward. The FCC argued that broadcasters' editorializing might not serve the public interest because broadcasters might propagate their own opinions without providing airtime for opposing points of view. Therefore, in a 1941 broadcast licensing hearing, the FCC ruled in the *Mayflower* decision that a broadcaster could not advocate a specific point of view. In 1946 the FCC codified much of its previous thinking into a document titled "Public Service Responsibility of Broadcast Licensees," generally referred to as the "Blue Book." This document outlined the rationale for FCC programming regulation and set standards for public service. It also argued that some profits should be reserved for public service programming. The TV industry attacked the Blue Book, arguing that the FCC was moving too close to censorship, which is prohibited by the U.S. Constitution. In 1948–1949 the FCC reconsidered its position on editorializing and encouraged reasonably balanced presentation of responsible viewpoints.[7]

This FCC policy statement became the basis of the *fairness doctrine.* Under the fairness doctrine, a station broadcasting one side of a controversy had to offer time to someone representing the other side of the controversy. The doctrine was eliminated in 1987, when the FCC concluded that the growing number of media outlets provided for enough diversity of opinion about public controversies.

In the aftermath of World War II, fear of Communism infected U.S. society. Legislators, business groups, and others attacked the film and television industries, labeling performers, producers, actors, and writers **fellow travelers,** or sympathizers with those who advocated bringing Communism to the United States. In the atmosphere of anti-Communist hysteria fostered by Wisconsin Senator Joseph McCarthy, the entertainment industry faced sharp challenges from the House Un-American Activities Committee.

In 1950, Counterattack, a right-wing political group, published *Red Channels: The Report of Communist Infiltration in Radio and Television,* which named many writers, performers, and other broadcast employees as Communist Party members or sympathizers. This and other **blacklists,** many of which went unpublished, destroyed the careers of many aspiring broadcasters because those named on the blacklist were denied employment in the industry.

fellow travelers

During the period of intense fear of Communism in the 1950s, people in the broadcast and entertainment industry who were unfairly accused of sympathizing with the beliefs of the Communist Party.

blacklist

A list of individuals compiled with the express purpose of forcing them out of their jobs. Blacklisting was used during the 1950s to label certain individuals as Communists and to force them out of the information and entertainment industries.

anthology

A favorite television format of the 1950s that consisted of stage plays produced for TV.

Entertainment Programming

Television programming successfully adapted radio's best offerings by the early 1950s. This movement from radio to TV served the networks because their programs had recognized stars, and it served the stars because it gave them access to a new, growing audience. **Anthologies** quickly became standard fare. *Kraft Television Theater, Studio One,* and *Fireside Arena Theatre,* produced live from New York, mimicked live stage performances. With live television, "every night was opening night," recalled costume designer Bill Jobe, "with fluffed lines, ties askew, flies open, and overstuffed merry widows."[8] Critics acclaimed the tasteful performances, and sponsors seeking sophisticated audiences raced to finance independently produced high-quality programming.

Comedy–variety shows hosted by successful radio comedians, quiz shows, dramas, and Westerns were standard prime-time television fare. Local programming also increased as stations began to broadcast during the day. "Every station had its cooking expert; a late afternoon children's program host, usually a cowboy or a clown; a general interview host for daytime shows; and a small local news staff."[9]

By the late 1940s, the networks had added situation comedies (sitcoms), which were mostly borrowed from radio. One of radio's most popular comedies was *Amos 'n Andy,* which debuted under the name of *Sam 'n Henry* in 1926. In 1931, the two white radio actors who spoke as *Amos 'n Andy* on radio starred at the *Chicago Defender*'s second annual picnic. The *Defender* was Chicago's nationally known black weekly newspaper. But even as actors Charles Correll and Freeman Gosden appeared at the *Defender*'s picnic, another prominent black newspaper, the *Pittsburgh Courier,* attacked *Amos 'n Andy* for being demeaning to African Americans.

Amos 'n Andy became a television hit in 1951, with black actors replacing the white radio voices. It was the first television show to have an all-black cast. The black community was split in its response. The NAACP denounced *Amos 'n Andy* for depicting "the Negro and other minority groups in a stereotyped and derogatory manner" that strengthened "the conclusion among uninformed or prejudiced people that Negroes and other minorities are inferior, lazy, dumb, and dishonest." But the *Pittsburgh Courier,* which had panned the radio show, found the television version to be "well-paced, funny more often than not, directed and produced with taste." *Amos 'n Andy,* the television show, won an Emmy nomination in 1952, but CBS did not renew the program for a third season. CBS syndicated the show, however, selling it to local stations and foreign countries until 1966. Correll and Gosden continued to act in a radio version of the program until 1960.[10]

Other popular sitcoms soon became part of television fare. *I Love Lucy, Father Knows Best, Our Miss Brooks,* and *Burns and Allen* enjoyed long runs. However, many programs lasted only a few months.

Live performances continued to dominate television programming through the mid-1950s, but broadcasters soon realized that television lent itself to recorded programs. Filming programs for later broadcast was efficient and economical. By the late 1950s, the national programming from New York and much of the creative local programming that had originated in Chicago had moved to Hollywood. There, television producers had access to the technology and talents of the film studios, and the climate allowed outdoor filming all year. Film was the primary recording method; videotape was not in widespread use until the early 1960s.

Television comedy borrowed from its predecessor, radio. *The Red Skelton Show* specialized in slapstick that contained vestiges of vaudeville.

The Influence of Advertising on Programming

From the beginning of television, advertising and programming were intertwined through network personnel and through sponsorship. For example, Harry Ackerman, appointed vice president to head network programs for CBS in Hollywood in 1951, had worked at CBS radio and then for the prestigious Young & Rubicam Advertising Agency. At first, television programs were owned by advertisers, which based the content of the shows on the interests of the audiences they wished to reach. The names of the anthology dramas reflected their sponsors: *Kraft Television Theater* and *Goodyear TV Playhouse,* for example. The sponsor's advertising agency bought time from a network, and the agency produced and controlled the program and supporting ads. Sometimes the line between advertising and entertainment blurred. "A girl breaks into song," the *New Yorker* reported, "and for a moment you can't quite pin down the source of her lyrical passion. It could be love, it could be something that comes in a jar."[11]

Through the 1950s, networks and advertisers struggled over who would control content. NBC introduced the concept of *magazine programming,* which meant selling time to several advertisers to share the support of a single show. The networks improved their production facilities and brought more production in house. As the expense of programming and advertising rates increased, TV networks and stations increasingly sold time, not shows. At first only one product or service appeared in each commercial break, but later each break contained multiple ads.

The downfall of the **single-sponsor system** came with the 1950s **quiz show** scandals. These popular shows were cheap to produce because they required little in

Key Concept

Single-sponsor system In the early days of television, a single advertiser often sponsored an entire show. This system declined as television time became more expensive and the reputation of sponsors suffered from the quiz show scandals of the late 1950s.

quiz show

Show on which contestants answer questions that show their knowledge of selected material.

Television in Our Lives

1927. First experimental broadcast

1934. Federal Communications Commission is established.

1948. FCC freezes television station licenses to examine allocation policies.

1948. Cable television systems begin.

1400–1700	1800	1860	1900	1920	1930	1940

1620. Pilgrims land at Plymouth Rock.

1690. *Publick Occurrences* is published in Boston.

1741. First magazine is published in America.

1776–1783. American Revolution

1830s. The penny press becomes the first truly mass medium in the United States.

1861–1865. American Civil War

1892. Thomas Edison's lab develops the kinetoscope.

1914–1918. World War I

1915. *The Birth of a Nation* marks the start of the modern movie industry.

1920. KDKA in Pittsburgh gets the first commercial radio license.

1930s. The Great Depression

1939. TV is demonstrated at the New York World's Fair.

1939–1945. World War II

1949. First commercial electronic computer is produced.

Cultural Milestones

the way of sets or staging. Individuals appeared onstage and answered questions, much like *Jeopardy* contestants do today. The shows appealed to large audiences. The famous *$64,000 Question,* developed by an advertising agency and sold to Revlon, achieved one of the highest ratings of the decade. But the *$64,000 Question* and other highly rated quiz shows, including *Twenty-One,* were rigged to make them more exciting. The scandal broke during the summer of 1957. In the fall of 1958, Charles Van Doren, star contestant on *Twenty-One,* confessed that the producers (and by implication the sponsors) had given him advance answers to the questions he would be asked.[12] (Van Doren's story was the basis for the 1994 film *Quiz Show.*) Although the

Early 1950s. 15-minute network news broadcasts

1952. FCC unfreezes station licensing.

1952. Networks cover presidential campaign.

1955. DuMont network closes, leaving three broadcast networks.

1960. First televised presidential debates between Kennedy and Nixon

1963. NBC starts 30-minute network newscasts.

1960s. Color television becomes popular.

1972. HBO becomes first premium cable channel.

1979–1980. *60 Minutes* becomes first news program to top the ratings.

1980. CNN begins operation.

1980s. Large-market local television expands newscasts from 30 minutes.

1987. Fox network begins broadcasting.

Early 1990s. Direct satellite broadcast starts using 18-inch dishes.

1996. Telecommunications Act

2000. Direct satellite broadcast increases its share of pay television.

2009. All broadcast TV stations must change to digital broadcasting.

1950   1960   1970   1980   1990   2000

Early 1950s. Rock 'n' roll begins.

1969. First person lands on the moon.

1970s. VCR is developed.

1989–1991. Cold War ends and the USSR is dissolved.

Late 1980s. National Science Foundation creates the basis of the Internet.

1996. Telecommunications Act

2000. Presidential election nearly tied.

2001. Terrorist attacks on New York and Washington, D.C.

2003. War with Iraq.

networks were in some cases reluctant to take over the management of advertising and programming, they used the scandal to claim that because sponsors were too greedy for high ratings, the networks themselves should control programming.[13]

Polls and Television

Television is the dominant medium when it comes to national election coverage. In 1960, John F. Kennedy defeated Richard Nixon, largely because he looked young and handsome on camera. Each presidential election year, the television networks race

Charles Van Doren was first a celebrity, then an outcast, on the TV quiz show *Twenty-One.* Quiz shows, many of which were proved to be fraudulent, attracted wide audiences.

to see who can predict the election outcome first. The predictions are based on exit polls, which involves asking people about their votes as they leave the polls. In 2000 the networks created confusion because early in the evening their exit polls predicted Democratic candidate Al Gore would win the popular vote in Florida. They later reversed this prediction and said George W. Bush would win Florida. The voting was so close that the final winner of Florida and the presidential election were not declared for six weeks. In the 2004 election, problems with exit polls surfaced again, when they were skewed in favor of the Democrats, causing television commentators to suggest a John Kerry win. Furthermore, exit poll data was leaked prematurely and could be found on Internet blogs. The networks may continue to use exit polls for predictions, but may be more careful in the process of collecting and analyzing data, as well as timing the release of exit poll information.

TODAY'S MARKET STRUCTURE

Until the mid-1980s, television was dominated by three major broadcast networks: CBS, NBC, and ABC. PBS, which began broadcasting in 1970, also drew a share of viewers. Cable was targeted at a small, largely rural audience. However, in the 1980s, cable companies took advantage of satellite technology to expand their distribution. They found that even urban viewers, with a range of network affiliates and small local stations from which to choose, would pay to receive the additional channels that cable offers. In addition, some new networks arose to challenge the dominance of the big three.

Major New Networks

Although networks had long dominated television, by the early 1990s forecasters were predicting their deaths. The share of prime-time audiences held by ABC, CBS, and NBC eroded from a high of 91 percent in 1978–1979 to 33.7 percent in 2003.

The lost audience moved to other networks and to cable. However, predictions of the networks' deaths were premature. The companies that own the networks remain financially strong as a result of deregulation in the 1990s that allowed them to expand their holdings. These companies provide original content and continue to attract viewers to their stations in the face of stiff competition.

Fox Rupert Murdoch, who started his career managing a family-owned newspaper in Adelaide, Australia, managed to do in ten years what no one in the United States had been able to do in the past—pose a serious competitive challenge to CBS, NBC, and ABC. Targeting a young audience, with shows like *The Simpsons,* Murdoch took advantage of the FCC's desire to foster competition against the networks and used his own resources and nerve to battle the dominant business structure of U.S. television.

Murdoch built a single paper into a chain of tabloid newspapers, then moved to London in 1969 to buy a tabloid weekly, *News of the World.* By 1985, Murdoch and his News Corporation had collected a group of powerful media companies in Britain, including the *Sun,* the nation's largest-circulation daily, and the prestigious *Times,* and had begun laying the groundwork for a satellite television service called Sky

Channel, which beams programs to cable systems throughout Europe. In 1985, Murdoch's News Corporation moved into electronic media with the purchase of Twentieth Century Fox Film Corp., with its rich film library. In the same year, Murdoch bought six big-city television stations from Metromedia in New York, Los Angeles, Chicago, Dallas, Houston, and Washington, D.C.[14]

Murdoch's deal needed approval by the FCC, but he was not a U.S. citizen, and the Communications Act prohibits ownership of broadcast stations in the United States by foreigners. Murdoch changed his citizenship as soon as legally possible, and the FCC seemed to ignore the fact that his News Corporation was made up primarily of foreign investors.

Ten years after Murdoch started the network, which he named the Fox Network, the foreign ownership issue resurfaced. After an eighteen month investigation, the FCC reversed its 1985 decision, declaring that Murdoch's company, despite his U.S. citizenship, was indeed a foreign company. However, the FCC simultaneously granted Murdoch a waiver from the foreign-ownership rule, allowing him to continue business.[15] In 2004, Murdoch moved his company's base of operations from Australia to the United States.

Despite confrontations with the FCC, Murdoch has continued to expand and diversify his empire, acquiring DirecTV; a direct broadcast satellite service; IGN Entertainment, which holds video-game websites like GameSpy and TeamXBox; and Intermix Media Inc., which owns MySpace.com.

CW/UPN and WB As Fox illustrated that a new network could achieve success, two others joined the competition. United Paramount Network (UPN) and Warner Bros. Network (WB) joined the field during 1994 and 1995 respectively. In their first season, UPN reached an average of about 4 percent of households, and the WB reached about 2 percent. By 1999 the new networks reversed these positions, as the WB became the fifth-ranked network.

Faced with declining ratings and rising costs, UPN and WB closed down in 2006. Their programming, including *America's Next Top Model* and *7th Heaven,* migrated to a new combined network, CW. The National Association of Black Owned Broadcasters expressed concern that the merger disproportionately affected African-American television station owners who were affiliates of the two networks.

The UPN show, *Everybody Hates Chris*, survived the merger of UPN and WB into the new CW network. However, five out of eight other shows with African-American casts were cancelled.

PAX TV/ i: Independent Television The number of networks grew to seven in August 1998. A born-again Christian and founder of the Home Shopping Network, Lowell "Bud" Paxson started a broadcast station network that featured family-friendly programs, like *Touched By an Angel,* that avoided sex, violence, or strong language. After PAX's prime-time programming reached an all-time high of one million households in 2001, it lost 55 percent of its viewers by 2005. The network's name was changed to i, and it began featuring content by independent producers and softening its line against sex and violence. Shortly after, Paxson resigned from the company, now ION Media Networks.

Univisión In 1955, Raúl Cortés, who founded the first U.S. Spanish-language radio station, launched a companion television station in San Antonio, Texas. KCOR-TV, now KWEX-TV, produced its own soap operas, news, and game shows. Cortés sold his station in 1961 to the Spanish International Network (SIN), owned by the Mexican company, Televisa. In 1986, Televisa was forced to sell SIN to Hallmark Cards because of FCC rules against foreign ownership, yet much of the programming on the renamed network, Univisión, still came from Televisa. Univisión became the fifth largest television network in the United States, featuring news, sports, variety, and talk shows and very popular **telenovelas**. While its audience is largely Spanish speaking, many non-Hispanics tuned in for Univisión's coverage of the 2006 World Cup, more than any other network.

Television Delivery Systems

About 111 million households in the United States have one or more television sets, and the average home has access to nearly one hundred channels. In 2005, 68 percent of households received a cable signal and 22 percent a direct satellite broadcast (DBS) signal.[16] The rest did not subscribe to a cable or satellite service and received only an analog signal.

Broadcast Stations The United States has about 1,700 **full-power television stations.** More than 1,300 are *commercial,* in business primarily to make a profit. They are licensed by the FCC, transmit programs over the air, and carry commercial messages to pay costs and make a profit. *Noncommercial* stations, often referred to as educational or public television, are not operated for profit. These 381 stations are financed primarily by grants from foundations, viewers' donations, and government funds, and carry no traditional advertising. *Low-power broadcast* stations serve limited areas because the stations' signals cannot reach long distances. There are about 2,200 low-power broadcast stations. Broadcast operations can be further classified according to their spectrum location in the very high frequency (VHF) or ultrahigh frequency (UHF) band. The 589 commercial VHF broadcasting stations use larger radio waves to carry their television signals than do the 782 UHF broadcasting stations. The VHF signals travel farther and provide a clearer picture than UHF TV signals.

Cable Distribution Cable television systems distribute television channels through optical fibers, coaxial cables, and broadband amplifiers. Signals are collected at a central point and then sent through cables to subscribers. A cable company usually negotiates with local authorities for a franchise in a region.

By the mid-1960s, broadcasters began to fear the power of cable competition and asked the FCC to design protective regulation that would keep cable operators from competing with traditional broadcast stations. From 1966 until the late 1970s, the FCC imposed heavy restrictions on cable development. However, such regulations did not hold up under Supreme Court scrutiny, and during the late 1970s the FCC reversed its position on cable regulation. In 1984, Congress passed a strongly deregulatory Cable Communications Policy Act, which limited interference in cable operations by local communities, state governments, and the FCC. Recent disputes over cable have centered primarily on subscriber rates, with a fair amount of government and

telenovela

A soap opera with a finite number of episodes.

full-power television station

A station that reaches a large percentage of households in its market and that must broadcast a schedule of programs.

The Telenovela

The telenovela has been a staple of Spanish-speaking television for over fifty years. Originating in Central and South American countries, telenovelas helped launch the career of stars like Salma Hayek and cement the positions of the Univisión and Telemundo networks, among the largest in the United States. Relatively cheap to produce, telenovelas have a finite number of episodes, and are usually shown daily for four months to a year. They share characteristics of English-speaking melodramas, involving difficult romances, characters that can be easily identified as good or evil, a dramatic conflict usually involving social class, strong emotional displays, and a happy ending. A chief writer at the Telemundo network describes the formula: "A telenovela is the story of an impossible love."

Telenovelas often reflect their time and place, and over the years have taken on themes such as urbanization, police corruption, immigration, assimilation, racism, the environment, and changing family life. They have also adapted to appeal to young people. For example, the Mexican-produced *Rebelde* is set in the private "Elite Way School" where some of the students form a rock band. These students are played by the members of an actual rock band, RBD, who drew 65,000 fans at the Los Angeles coliseum in 2006 and won Best Pop Album in *Billboard*'s Latin music category. The show also heavily features product placements and has its own product spinoffs such as ringtones and candy. The telenovela format has been adapted to other languages. In 2006, Fox's new My Network TV included two telenovela-inspired programs in its lineup—*Desires* and *Secrets*.

The telenovela is a global popular culture phenomenon. Originally, telenovelas were made and shown in Mexico, Cuba, Venezuela, Colombia, and Brazil. Televisa, a Mexican company, exported these shows to the United States, where they were sponsored by soap companies and had strong, loyal followings. Telenovelas are now produced in every Spanish-speaking country, and studios can be found in Miami and Los Angeles. Depending on the production company, some of the telenovelas made in the United States have a national slant with references to the country's immigration policy. Others remain generic enough to appeal to a worldwide audience; for example, actors may avoid regional accents.

Telenovelas, including old reruns, are shown in over one hundred countries, such as China, Poland, Bosnia, Indonesia, Japan, Bulgaria, and Russia, where they have avid followings. Many reasons have been proposed for this popularity. Some cultural observers suggest that while offering escape for the working class, more traditional telenovelas avoid the display of luxury in U.S. television shows or the intellectualism of European ones. Others say that the storytelling carries universal themes that allow emotional identification and provide a sense of justice. Even if they respond to common themes, viewers must make sense of these programs out of their own experiences and cultural background. For Spanish-speaking immigrants, telenovelas offer a connection to cultural tradition and ways of thinking about identity. Dulce Terán, Venezuelan producer of the popular *Olvidarte Jamás,* explains, "In the U.S., telenovelas are the way to keep yourself welded to your traditions. It's the way you remember your country, and your language."

Sources: Emily Witt, "Never Forget You," *Miami New Times,* March 2, 2006, Proquest; Araceli Oriz de Urbina and Abel Lópes, "Soaps with a Latin Scent," Unesco, 1999, www.unesco.org/courier/1999_05/uk/connex/txt1.htm; Josh Kun, "We Are a Band," *New York Times,* July 9, 2005: late ed., 2.

---

private concern directed toward the rapidly increasing costs of cable television to the consumer.

Deregulation paved the way for cable **superstations.** In 1976, Ted Turner turned the lowest rated Atlanta TV station, UHF Channel 17, into superstation WTBS. He contracted with a satellite company to **uplink** his signal to RCA's SATCOM I for distribution to cable systems. At first, only twenty systems **downlinked** WTBS, but within two years more than two hundred systems downlinked programs from the station, and by 1979 more than two thousand systems were participating.[17] Using WTBS, Turner made the Atlanta Braves, which he also owned, one of the most popular baseball teams in the United States.

The 1984 Cable Communications Act and the 1996 Telecommunications Act continued the creation of a deregulatory environment for the cable industry, spurring its expansion. Even though the United States has more than 11,000 cable systems, a few

superstation
A station that reaches hundreds of markets throughout the country by means of satellite distribution of a signal to cable systems.

uplink
Transmitting an electronic signal to a satellite for storage or further distribution.

downlink
Transmitting an electronic signal from a satellite to a ground facility.

companies own most of them. These companies are called multiple system operators (MSO). Comcast is the largest of these, with 23.3 million subscribers in 2006. Time Warner Cable is in second place with 14.4 million. In 2006, both companies benefited from splitting the acquisition of the fifth largest cable company, Adelphia, which had declared bankruptcy in 2002 after its founder was accused of fraud.

Satellite Distribution   Satellite distribution is the fast growing segment for delivering TV content. This growth resulted from the conversion of satellite systems from analog to digital, and federal legislation in 1999 that allowed satellite systems to distribute local station broadcasts into those stations' home markets. This had been illegal and the largest stumbling block for Direct Broadcast Satellite (DBS). Mergers in the industry in the late 1990s reduced the number of major satellite providers to EchoStar and DirecTV, which uses a transmission format called Direct Satellite Service (DSS). In 2003, DirecTV was purchased by Rupert Murdoch.

Television on the Internet   In 2005, a video boom began on the Internet. By July 2006, YouTube was receiving 16 million visitors, MySpace Videos 20 million, and Yahoo! Video 21.1 million to view videos, including clips from television shows.[18] Seeing a new market ahead, television networks began making their programs available online. ABC cut a deal with Apple in October 2005 to sell episodes of *Lost* and *Desperate Housewives* through iTunes. With that success, the networks began offering episodes of these programs for free as streaming video. CBS provided video streams from the NCAA men's college basketball team, while MTV already had 8,000 music videos available online.[19] In January 2006, Sky Television launched a subscription service in the U.K. and Ireland, allowing their viewers to download video to their PCs. While TV on the web receives far fewer viewers than on regular TV, the Internet is becoming an important delivery system.

Television Station Ownership Patterns

When buyers consider purchasing a television station, they must first examine the other media they own within that market. FCC regulations limit multiple ownership of the same medium and cross-ownership of other media (radio and newspaper) within the same market. The intent is to prevent a controlling media monopoly and to encourage a variety of voices within the marketplace.

Network Owned and Operated Groups   Of all ownership types, **network-owned and -operated ("O and O") groups** receive the most attention. The stations in these groups tend to be in larger markets such as Chicago, New York, and Los Angeles because they attract larger audiences and profits than they would in smaller markets. The major networks generate or acquire programming that runs on their own stations and on affiliated stations. The networks make money not only by carrying network advertising, but by selling advertising time on single stations. Because of declining network ratings and increasing production costs, networks make more profit from their stations than from network advertising.

Other companies besides the networks own groups of stations. Some of these companies are major players in the media industry. For example, Gannett, which is known more for its newspapers than for television stations, owned twenty-two stations in 2006, and Media General owned thirty stations. Stations that are owned by groups may or may not be affiliated with networks. Affiliates make money from networks, which pay them to run programming, and by selling advertising at their stations. Affiliated stations use network shows and also buy syndicated programs.

Independently Owned Stations   Independently owned stations are owned by individuals or families. They are not part of groups and may or may not be affiliated with networks. Programming can be expensive for independently owned stations that do not have a network on which to rely. However, independent stations have total freedom in deciding content, and much creative programming has originated at these stations.

Public Television Stations   Public broadcast stations are supported mostly by private donations, tax revenues, grants, and corporate underwriting. They do not carry direct advertising. Public television is known for its long-running popular educational programs such as *Sesame Street* and *Masterpiece Theatre* and explorations of nature and science. It is also known for carrying important congressional proceedings such as the Senate Judiciary Committee's confirmation hearings when Clarence Thomas was nominated to the Supreme Court. However, C-SPAN and CNN now generally provide more thorough coverage in this area.[20]

The public service channel C-Span provides citizen access to the U.S. political process.

C-SPAN is a private, nonprofit company created in 1979 by the cable television industry as a public service. Their mission is to provide public access to the political process. C-SPAN receives no government funding; operations are funded by fees paid by cable and satellite affiliates who carry C-SPAN programming.

The federal government supports public television by giving money to the Corporation for Public Broadcasting (CPB), a private, nonprofit corporation created by Congress in 1967, which in turn partially funds one thousand public radio and television stations. With some of this money, public stations produce or buy programming. Television stations buy shows such as *The News Hour with Jim Lehrer* from the Public Broadcasting Service (PBS), a network created by CPB.

The federal government's portion of the $2.3 billion spent on public television continues to decline; it was only 19.5 percent in 2006. Congressional critics of PBS argue that its programming has a liberal bias, pointing to shows like *NOW with Bill Moyers.* When it planned to carry an animated cartoon about a lesbian couple, the network received sharp criticism from the Bush administration. The politics of PBS have created an uncertain climate for its continued funding. Table 7.1 illustrates where public television gets its money.

As the result of declining federal funds, PBS stations carry underwriter spots that look like commercials. PBS also licenses books, toys, and other merchandise, especially based on characters such as Elmo, Bob the Builder, and Barney. In 2005, PBS teamed with Comcast, Sesame Workshop, and HIT Entertainment to launch a new twenty-four-hour cable channel for preschoolers, PBS KIDS Sprout, that includes advertisements. Some critics have questioned whether PBS still provides an alternative to commercial television.

AUDIENCE DEMAND IN TELEVISION MARKETS

Television caters to the advertising market and the consumer market with news and entertainment. Networks, cable systems, direct broadcasters, and syndicates provide programming that supplies the demand. The chief goal, except in public television, is to make profits, which is usually done by achieving high ratings. However, high profits are increasingly associated with targeted audiences rather than mass audiences. In such cases, lower ratings can still attract advertisers. For example, golf events on television earn low ratings but are still attractive to advertisers because people who watch golf on television are high earners with disposable income to spend.

Table 7.1 Who Funds Public Radio and Television?

Total Revenue: $2,395,228

Subscribers	26.5%
Corporation for Public Broadcasting	16.3%
Business	15.3%
State governments	12.5%
Colleges and universities	10.3%
Foundations	6.8%
Local governments	3.4%
Federal grants and contracts	2.8%
Auctions	0.5%
Other	5.7%

Source: Corporation for Public Broadcasting

Consumer Market

TV shows have traditionally been divided into two types: entertainment and news. In the 1950s, the major networks relocated their entertainment divisions to be near Hollywood studios, while their news divisions remained in New York. Most television stations and networks have separate departments for providing these types of programs. However, the line between entertainment and news has not always been easy to distinguish, and the rise of infotainment and reality TV shows like *Cops* has made that line even fuzzier.

Delivering the news has been an important mission of television, and has met the people's interest in international, national, and local affairs. In the 1970s, the news became profitable when many viewers turned on their sets to follow the Watergate scandal. Furthermore, with new technologies and newly hired consultants, local news channels began running sensational crime stories combined with light banter from attractive anchors. Television had an advantage over print in that it provided powerful images that seemed more immediate and real than text, and the news could be appealingly dramatized in shows like the long-running *60 Minutes.*[21] Television has shaped cultural perceptions of many important events, from the civil rights movement to the September 11 attacks. However, in recent years, network news has been losing its audience, which declined from 52 million in 1980 to 28.8 million in 2004. The audience is also graying, with the median age of viewers at 60.[22] In recent years, many critics have expressed concern that the large media conglomerates who own most television stations are more concerned with ratings and profits than with hard-hitting journalism, and that entertainment has become more important than news.

Entertainment programming has also been undergoing change. In the early days of television, families spent an evening together tuned to a single station to watch sitcoms like *Leave It to Beaver* and variety shows like the *Ed Sullivan Show.* Now, the

Social satires like the controversial *Family Guy* are popular with young adult viewers.

members of households may be viewing different shows on different TVs, and are less likely to sit through an entire show, much less an evening of a single station's programming. The audience share for programs has dropped. In 1978, the most popular show on TV, *Laverne and Shirley,* reached 31.6 million households, while in 2006, the top show, *American Idol,* reached 14.9 million households.[23] The kinds of programs have changed, so that reality TV and crime dramas have ascended over sitcoms, and the types of shows have become much more diverse across many channels. The traditional types of programs, such as sitcoms, talk shows, and news, overlap to create new **hybrid** forms, often using irony, parody, and satire. For example, *The Daily Show* combines the news and comedy formats, *Family Guy* combines the children's cartoon and the sitcom, and *Reno 911!* combines the cop show with comedy.

The changes in the number of channels and their lineups have resulted in what media analysts call **fragmentation,** the process that divides audiences into small groups consuming specialized offerings. Cable channels, especially, engage in **narrowcasting,** broadcasting programs that appeal only to a specific demographic. For example, ESPN draws sports fans, BET caters to an African-American audience, and MTV targets young people with music videos and shows like *Pimp My Ride.* Some channels carry **syndicated material,** like *Golden Girls,* that appeal to senior citizens. Some critics have argued that fragmentation has eliminated the potential of a common, national culture in which everyone is watching the same programs and sharing the same experience of television viewing. They fear that audiences will exist in separate niches without exposure to any content that falls outside their narrow tastes and social and political interests.[24] Others argue that even when only three channels existed, their programming catered to a white, middle-class audience and did not reflect the diversity of American life, which is more evident in fragmentation.[25]

The centralized control over programming is in further transition with the advent of TV on Demand, recording devices that can be programmed according to users' interests, and the ability of users to access video content anywhere, anytime, through devices like computers, cell phones, and iPods. Tech-savvy users have more ability to inexpensively create, circulate, and market their own video programming, as can be seen on the popular webpage YouTube.

hybrid

A new form created from the combination of two or more different elements.

audience fragmentation

The division of audiences into small groups consuming more specialized offerings of diverse media outlets.

narrowcasting

Transmission of data, like a television program, to a specific demographic of viewers, listeners, or subscribers.

syndicated material

Programs made available for sale directly to stations or cable channels rather than distributed by networks to affiliates. Examples are *Xena: Warrior Princess* and *The Oprah Winfrey Show.* Discontinued network shows that have had long successful runs, such as *Cheers,* are also candidates for syndication.

It appears one career is not enough for Bill Cosby. In his forty years as an entertainer, he has been a standup comedian; broken racial barriers as a costar of the 1960s television series *I Spy;* changed the face of television situations comedies with *The Cosby Show;* sold four million copies of his first book, *Fatherhood,* and two million of his second book, *Time Flies;* had two comedy albums in *Billboard*'s Top 10; and been awarded eight gold records and five Grammy Awards as well as Emmy Awards for *I Spy* and *The Cosby Show.*

Much of Cosby's work is based on his family life and his experience as a father—areas he says he knows best. Cosby believes in keeping comedy and situation comedies clean, and he has been successful doing so.

Cosby was born in Philadelphia on July 11, 1937, and was the first of three boys. The family lived in a housing project, where, he says, their needs were met and there was no place for prejudice. His mother, Anna Pearl Cosby, was his role model; she raised the boys while working sixteen hours a day as a domestic. His father served in the navy.

Cosby was the captain of his high school track and football teams, but he dropped out of school in his sophomore year. He joined the navy, finished high school through a correspondence course, and received his GED. He went to Temple University on a track scholarship but quit three years later to concentrate on his comedy career. He later obtained his degree from Temple and went on to obtain master's and doctorate degrees in education from the University of Massachusetts. His wife, the former Camille Hanks, also has a doctorate in education. The Cosbys have four daughters; their son Ennis was murdered in 1997.

Bill Cosby

Cosby played the first minority lead role in television when he starred with Robert Culp in *I Spy* from 1965 to 1968. Before the series was over, he had won three Emmy Awards. Cosby went on to perform in other TV shows, several specials, and many successful concert performances. He also has recorded more than twenty comedy albums and has written four books during his career.

His most famous accomplishment was *The Cosby Show,* a family show in which the parents were strict but loving and children and parents learned from each other. Cosby took his idea to all three networks, but only NBC accepted it. By its second season, *The Cosby Show* was the highest-rated weekly television series, attracting sixty million viewers. The show ran for eight years, from 1984 to 1992.

Today, Cosby is one of the richest people in the entertainment business, and he has been number one on *Forbes*'s list of top-earning entertainers several times.

In 2004, Cosby garnered both praise and criticism for his remarks at an NAACP event marking the anniversary of the landmark Supreme Court decision, *Brown v. the Board of Education.* In that speech, he urged African Americans to fix their own communities, including their speech and spending habits, to help young people overcome poverty.

Sources: Don Heckman, "Common Cos," *The Los Angeles Times.* June 11, 1995: sec., 8; Bob Thomas, "Cosby Talks," *Good Housekeeping,* February 1991: 167; and Todd Klein, "Bill Cosby," *Saturday Evening Post,* April 1986: 42.

Advertising Market

Advertisers use media to persuade potential buyers. Television advertisers have traditionally addressed a mass market, and products that are advertised on television reflect such an audience. A popular actress, Betty Furness, opened refrigerator doors on television repeatedly during the 1950s to advertise Westinghouse refrigerators to homemakers; Procter & Gamble advertised its cleaning products on Ed Sullivan's Sunday night variety program in the 1950s and 1960s; and a new line of automobiles rolled across the screen each year on Dinah Shore's variety show sponsored by Chevrolet.

With the development of multiple cable channels and narrowcasting, advertisers use **demographics and psychographics** to target audiences. Although traditional demographics give advertisers some guidance in targeting audiences, some larger audiences are bound together more

Key Concept

Demographic and psychographic approaches to broadcast marketing Research analysts looking for TV advertising markets identify program preferences using two common approaches: Demographic approaches stress statistical links between program features and factors such as age, education, income, and gender. Psychographic approaches stress links between programs and potentially measurable factors in audience lifestyles or in categories of personal likes and dislikes.

by attitude than by demographics. The Discovery Channel, for example, divides its audience not merely into people over and under fifty years of age, but into categories that include "scholars," "practicals," and "boy's toys."[26] In 2006, IBM released a report on the future of television that divided viewers into two main categories that would continue to influence the medium. The "lean back" segment, or "massive passives," have lifestyles that do not make them likely to change their television viewing habits. The "lean forward" segment consists of the "gadgetiers," affluent working parents with a fondness for TiVotoGo and iTunes, and the "koolkids," tech savvy-teenagers whose interactive media activities revolve around the mobile phone.[27] These categories are shaped by both age and lifestyle behaviors.

Advertising and Television Content

Networks and stations sell time for ads, known as *spots,* during a television show, and product placement strategies are often used to reinforce their message. Attracting 41.6 percent of all households, the 2006 Super Bowl was accompanied by ads from Coca-Cola, Anheuser-Busch, McDonald's, and others, who paid an average of $2.4 million for a thirty-second spot.[28] Advertisers are attracted to the Super Bowl because it can target a large, diverse audience. During the game, advertisers included Dove's Self-Esteem Fund, thus acknowledging the large female audience. Super Bowl advertising also reveals the way a large media conglomerate markets across its many businesses. Owned by the Disney Corp., ABC ran spots for its other business properties, like Buena Vista films and Mobile ESPN. One of its commercials used Steelers and Seahawks players saying "I'm going to Disney World."

With new technologies and delivery systems that allow viewers to flip past or block advertising, many advertisers are moving beyond the traditional thirty-second spot to experiment with different marketing strategies. Greater effort is made to integrate advertising into television shows, so that the products are visibly featured and actors promote them. For example, in 2006, Hewlett Packard signed on as sponsor of the MTV game show, *Meet or Delete,* in which participants selected dates, roommates, or band members based on what information people had stored in their computer files, such as links to websites and music lists. Hewlett Packard products were featured in each episode, which ran on three MTV networks as well as on its wireless platforms and mtvU.com. ABC's *Extreme Home Makeover* featured products from its sponsor, Sears. For these kinds of shows, companies may pay all or part of the production costs.

Advertisements are also made to look like televisions shows, featuring characters and a plot that evolves in a series of spots. The hope is that such advertainments will involve viewers so much that they won't switch the channel. A question for the television industry is whether viewers would rather pay for programs without advertisements or receive programs with advertisements for free. However, the line between television program and advertisement is not as clear as it once was.

Audience Measurement and Station Survival: The Ratings Game

Measuring audience demand for particular programs is important because prices charged for advertising are based on the number of households and people watching. The measurement also helps programmers evaluate the demand for various types of shows. If crime dramas get high ratings one season, more such programs will surely appear the next season.

A. C. Nielsen Media Research dominates the audience measurement business. Nielsen measures viewing of programs and breaks down the number of viewers into a variety of demographic and psychographic categories.

Using statistical techniques, the Nielsen reports can tell an advertiser that in October 2005, *Invasion* was the most popular new show among 25–54-year-olds in Boston, while *My Name is Earl* was the most popular show among the same demographic group in New York.[29]

Nielsen uses a variety of techniques to measure audiences. These include diaries, people meters, and set-tuning meters.

- *Diaries.* Viewers keep pen-and-pencil journals detailing what they are watching. In 2006, Nielsen announced that it was phasing out pen-and-pencil diaries in the 154 smaller markets where it still used them.
- *People meters.* People meters measure what is being watched and who is watching. A box is placed in five thousand randomly selected households in the United States. Each person presses a button to record when he or she is watching.
- *Set-tuning meters.* Nielsen places these meters on the back of TV sets in randomly selected households in the forty-nine largest TV markets. They record what is watched on a daily basis.[30]

Nielsen Media Research measures audiences for television much the way Auditron measures audiences for radio, except that the unit measured for television is sometimes the household as well as individual people. In addition to the number of viewers watching a program, Nielsen reports findings in the form of ratings (the percentage of TV households in a market watching a program). In the week of July 31, 2006, Nielsen reported that among African Americans, the most popular show was the NBC *NFL Pre-Season,* attracting 9.2 percent of 13,280,000 African-American television households. That rating included DVR playback up to 3 a.m. on the next day.

Nielsen also reports its findings in the form of shares, the percentage of households watching television that are tuned to a particular channel. Shares are significant figures because they show how viewing is distributed across channels, and they can be compared across markets. For example, in May 2006 in Toledo, Ohio, WTVG-TV beat out its rival, WTOL-TV for the first time since 2003. Among twenty-five to fifty-four-year-old viewers, WTVG's audience share for its newscasts was 28 percent compared to 19 percent for WTOL.[31] This was good news for WTVG, since the twenty-five to fifty-four-year-old demographic is the biggest target for advertisers.

Nielsen's rating system is undergoing change because of convergence technologies like streaming video on the Internet, video-enabled portable devices, video-on-demand, and DVRs. In 2006, the company began combining data measurements from Internet and television usage, and testing software and wireless meters. This data could be used, for example, to monitor the way viewers access both a television channel and its webpage or playback programs on their iPods. The company also began to monitor the television habits of college students, who watch television away from home.

The accuracy of audience measurements can be a controversial issue. Different methods and meter placement can produce different ratings and shares. Advertisers require that ratings be measured by an independent company because stations might inflate their own audience measures to increase ad rates. At times, Nielsen Media Research has come under fire for monopolizing the ratings industry and for an alleged bias and inaccuracy in its sampling.

SUPPLYING THE AUDIENCE'S DEMAND

Supplying the demands of the consumer market and supplying the demands of the advertising market are intertwined. Sometimes, while trying to target (attract) a certain segment of the audience, television executives manage to deter other segments, causing lower ratings and decreased advertising support. This happens when networks provide programs to attract specific age groups, but it also can occur with other types of demographic groups.

In 1999, the National Association for the Advancement of Colored People (NAACP) began monitoring the participation and representation of African Americans in television. In 2006, the organization noted that the fall lineup of ABC, NBC, CBS, and Fox had no sitcoms starring African-American actors. Furthermore, the merger of UPN and WB programming into the new CW network eliminated several of the African-American comedies that UPN had featured.[32] Unlike UPN, which targeted African Americans, the CW targeted eighteen to thirty-four-year-old baby boomers. Broadcast stations are supposed to serve the general public, but because of discriminatory hiring practices and content that reflects the interests of targeted advertising groups, the issue of minority representation on television may continue to cause controversy.

Station Organization

Most television stations contain six core departments. The size of each department depends on how big the station is. The engineering department manages the technical equipment used by all departments, especially the news and programming ones; the news department produces newscasts and public affairs reporting; the programming department buys and produces content to attract viewers for advertisers; the advertising or sales department solicits advertisers; the business office maintains financial records; and the promotions department uses advertising, special events, and public service to attract viewers and develop a positive image of the station.

Television Transmission Technologies

Television, just like newspapers and magazines, has to be distributed to the audience. Television transmission technologies can be either wireless, such as broadcast, microwave, and satellite, or wire based, such as coaxial or fiber-optic cable. Many of these technologies are used in combination with each other.

Over-the-air Broadcast   Over-the-air broadcast television, including both ground-based and satellite television, is similar to broadcast radio in that the information is transmitted from a station antenna on a specific radio frequency, or channel, to an antenna on a television or a satellite. The FCC assigns a portion of the spectrum to each television channel: 54–88 MHz for channels 2–6, 174–216 MHz for channels 7–13, 470–890 MHz for UHF channels 14–83. Broadcast television stations share the airwaves with other users such as radio stations, mobile communication companies, wireless computer networks, garage door openers, and heart rate monitors. With the advent of many new wireless technologies, these airwaves have become an important issue.

Before 1998, all broadcast television stations used analog technology to transmit their signals. By 2009, all television stations in the United States will have moved from **analog technology** to **digital technology,** as mandated by the U.S. Congress. *Digital television (DTV)* improves the quality of the picture by increasing the number of lines on the screen and facilitates the convergence of television, personal computers, and portable devices. The switch affects the spectrum because digital signals, using the MPEG-2 compression system, free up air space for other uses such as advanced wireless and public safety services. Providers can use a DTV channel either as a single **high definition television (HDTV)** channel or as a carrier for several subchannels. Changing to DTV disproportionately affects lower income senior citizens, African Americans, and Latinos who have analog televisions without converter boxes for digital signals. In 2006, the FCC had begun work on a program to provide coupons for converter boxes to eligible households; however, analog televisions will eventually be phased out and replaced by digital televisions.

Another type of broadcast television is low-power television (LPTV), operating on conventional frequencies but covering distances less than fifteen miles. LPTV stations are comparatively inexpensive for both producer and viewer, and have fewer FCC regulations on content. Confined to a local area, they are often operated by schools, local governments, businesses, religious groups, and individual citizens. In 2006, Telemundo, the second largest Spanish-language network, owned nine LPTV stations.

Cable Transmission   Cable television transmits its programming through coaxial or fiber-optic cables instead of broadcasting it over the air. Cable transmission has several

Key Concept

Digital television (DTV) Digital television converts TV programming into a digital format rather than the analog format used since television was invented. By sending the programs as a series of ones and zeros, the picture is sharper than it would be with analog distribution. All TV programming must be digital by 2009.

analog technology

Transforms one form of energy into another to transport content, as when a telephone converts sound vibrations into electrical vibrations.

digital technology

Transforms information into binary form, as when computers convert sound vibrations to 1s and 0s.

high-definition television (HDTV)

Digital transmission that produces the highest level of TV reproduction quality.

advantages: Cables, strung on utility poles or laid underground, are not subject to line-of-sight obstruction or most other electronic interference; two-way interaction back and forth along the same cable is possible; and a subscriber can receive many channels, typically sixty-five but sometimes as many as two hundred, from one cable system instead of one channel from one broadcast station.

Digital cable technologies have created the possibility for transmission of 1,000 channels in a system and fostered convergence of radio, phone, computer, and television. Because of the capacities of fiber-optic cable, cable companies provide **broadband** Internet access and voice-over-Internet-protocol (VoIP) phone service. Analog-to-digital conversion has also facilitated video on demand (VOD) that allows viewers to watch programs when they choose.

In the late 1990s, cable companies upgraded their cable equipment to broadband networks that could carry high-speed Internet, two-way voice, multichannel and advanced video services. At the beginning of the new century, the companies continued to expand into VOD, interactive and high definition TV, and VoIP telephone.

Direct Broadcast Satellite (DBS)

Like broadcast television stations, DBS systems are wireless, using a radio signal to transmit programming, in this case from a large antenna on a satellite to a smaller antenna. Satellites provide a relatively inexpensive way of transmitting information nationally or globally and have made instantaneous global communication possible. Most communications satellites orbit 22,300 miles above the equator. At this distance, they seem to remain stationary over one point on Earth. As a result, these satellites can continuously receive uplink signals from Earth dishes and send downlink signals to Earth dishes within their footprint. The *footprint* is the geographic area that can be covered by a satellite.

The number of DBS subscribers grew from 5.3 million in 1997 to 24.95 million in 2005. Prediction is that this total will reach 39.8 million by 2010.[33] The accuracy of this prediction will depend on competition from cable and telephone firms.

Multichannel Multipoint Distribution Service (MMDS)

MMDS, also called wireless cable, uses microwave frequencies that are picked up by a special antenna and a set-top box on a television set. Initially designed for cities that did not receive cable, MMDS had less expensive installation and start-up costs. In 2006, the FCC began reallocating MMDS frequencies to Advanced Wireless Services (AWS-1), a wireless technology that facilitates convergence of mobile data services, video, and messaging for portable devices like cell phones. Sprint Nextel owns most of the spectrum allotted for MMDS.

Internet Protocol Television (IPTV)

With IPTV, high quality video is delivered through an Internet protocol (IP) broadband network. Telecommunications companies are upgrading their equipment to deliver IPTV, competing with cable and satellite distribution companies for a share of the market. In 2006, the technology was still developing in the United States, but China, Hong Kong, Taiwan, and Italy had functioning IPTV networks.

broadband

Fiber-optic cable with the capacity to carry large amounts of information.

Supplying News and Information: The World in Our Living Rooms

Local stations, national networks, cable and satellite networks, and news syndicates generate programming in a variety of *TV news and information formats.* Local stations usually produce their own community news, and satellite technology allows them also to carry national and international news. CNN, Fox News Network, and MSNBC use cable and satellite technology that provides twenty-four-hour access to news. TV news syndicates take the form of either a video exchange by local stations joined in a cooperative or a pay service.

Television networks supplement their programming with round-the-clock news through their webpages, e-mail and text alerts, and RSS feeds.

Evening Newscast   The evening news format, as exemplified by the network shows featuring anchors like Katie Couric, is the most basic news presentation model. Chet Huntley and David Brinkley popularized the anchor format, in which one or two anchors present the news, usually with video or other visual accompaniment.

Local stations have their own news teams. Teams include the anchors and supporting team members who report on local weather, sports, and other topics, such as health and consumer information. Station reporters videotape reports or report live from story sites. There also may be remote feeds, usually from stations affiliated with the same network, for stories of special interest.

News magazines   Magazine programs contain several stories in each segment. Newsmagazines reached the level of prominence they enjoy today in the late 1990s. Magazine programs such as *Dateline NBC* air more than once a week, and they often receive high ratings, especially during summer when most entertainment programs are reruns.

The shows vary in the degree of hard and soft news they carry and in the degree of sensational treatment. However, they are profitable because they cost less money to produce than a prime-time drama, and they allow the networks to share the high salaries of news personalities among several programs.

Interview Shows   *Meet the Press* and *Face the Nation,* in which journalists interview one or more prominent people in the news, are some of the longest running programs. They provide the public with the opinions of prominent politicians, military leaders, and other important public figures. In doing so, these programs serve the marketplace of ideas.

Morning Shows   Since 1952 when the *Today Show* first aired, television viewers have been waking up to morning news shows. While the evening news has experienced declining viewership, the morning new shows, like *The Today Show* and *Good Morning America,* provide most of the ad revenue for the networks' news divisions. They appeal to more affluent women, and are more likely to carry news about runaway brides than a hard-hitting expose of war causalities.

Tabloid Television   Tabloid television includes confrontational talk shows such as *Jerry Springer,* Hollywood gossip shows such as *Entertainment Tonight,* and so-called reality-based shows such as *Cops* and *America's Most Wanted.* These are inexpensive to make, easy to syndicate, and wildly profitable.

Supplying Entertainment

Entertainment Formulas   Television programming goes through stages of development, including funding and contract negotiations, casting, and scripting, usually by staff writers. It then moves into production, including taping and editing. The process can generate creative ideas, but they tend to become **entertainment formulas,** repeated until the audience grows tired of them. Costs are high and risks are great. When a network's new show pulls good ratings, other networks quickly produce shows with similar plots or casts of characters.

> **Key Concept**
>
> **Entertainment formulas** Because of financial risks, producers of television entertainment tend to rely on standard entertainment patterns or formulas that have been successful in the past. They often extend adult formulas into entertainment for children; if violent programs attract young adult audiences, a similar violent format may be used in children's programs.

With the large number of broadcast and cable channels available, viewers see several different types of formulas generating copycat programming during the same season. For instance, the fall primetime lineup in 2006 was full of formulaic spinoffs. The reality-TV genre remained strong, with *America's Next Top Model, Survivor, Dancing with the Stars, Trading Spouses, Wife Swap, Extreme Makeover: Home Edition,* and *Nanny 911.* Comedies retained much of their favorite 8–9 P.M. slot with *The Class, How I Met*

How Real Is Reality TV?

Reality TV is rooted in a television past that included PBS's *An American Family,* which taped the daily upheavals of the Loud family, and *Candid Camera,* which secretly recorded people making fools of themselves in rigged situations. The more contemporary form of reality TV took off in the 1990s, with shows like *Real World, Big Brother,* and *Survivor* that threw strangers together in an environment, sometimes as part of a contest. The promise of reality TV is that it truthfully shows ordinary people and reveals just how contrived other television programs are in contrast. But just how real is reality TV?

A critical look at a show like *Survivor* suggests: Not much. Though the show asks viewers to forget the contrivances like cameras, editing, and lighting, they are important in shaping the viewer's experience. Seventy-two hours of footage are taped for every *Survivor* episode, and in the editing process, shots are chosen and altered to enhance the drama of the plot and make the characters look good. *Survivor's* executive producer, Mark Burnett, has admitted that some scenes are reenacted with hired actors. The "Tribal Council" at the end of each episode uses props and a highly dramatic set-up. During the first season of the show, footage was rearranged to build suspense. Burnett himself uses the word "dramality" rather than "reality" to describe his show.

In 2004, the Writers Guild of America, a union that represents Hollywood screenwriters, began efforts to organize staff members who worked for reality TV shows. These staff members, the Guild argued, worked longer hours with less pay than other writers in the industry. But were the "story editors" for reality TV shows really "writers"? Over time, more details of how reality TV shows are made began to emerge from the clash.

When the staff producers of *America's Next Top Model* went on strike in July 2006, they argued that they actively script the show, line by line, from the available footage, adding drama, deciding how characters should be portrayed, and inventing "red

herrings." Therefore, they deserved the same working conditions as any other scriptwriter.

While the unreality of reality shows is obvious to many savvy viewers, most are not aware of the extent of the manipulation, which brings into question the difference between a contrivance and a transparent reality. Yet many viewers still search for social truths in *Survivor,* even when the contrivance is obvious. When the show presented teams divided by race, critics acknowledged that it was a gimmick to obtain more viewers and others were appalled at the calculated divisiveness. Yet some argued that the show was acknowledging the truth of a segregated society. Lewis W. Diuguid, of the *Kansas City Star's* editorial board, wrote that *Survivor* was an "honest view" that revealed how the set-up destroyed black unity and "enabled whites to maintain dominance and control over blacks, causing blacks to forever fall behind."

Sources: Lewis W. Diuguid, Editorial, *Knight Ridder Tribunes Business News,* September 20, 2006: 1; Christopher J. Wright, "Welcome to the Real: Simulation, Commodization, and Survivor," *Journal of American Culture* 29 (2006): 170–183; Gloria Hillard, "America's Next Top Strike: Reality Show Writers," NPR, August 15, 2006, npr.org.

Your Mother, Ugly Betty, 'Til Death, Happy Hour, America's Funniest Home Videos, Everybody Hates Chris, and *All of Us.* Crime investigation dramas remained popular. CBS featured *CSI: Crime Scene Investigation,* along with its spinoffs, *CSI: Miami* and *CSI: New York.* ABC had the now venerable *Law & Order* spinoffs, *Criminal Intent* and *Special Victims Unit. Bones* melded together forensic shows, like *CSI,* with hospital dramas like *Grey's Anatomy.*

Entertainment Programming
Entertainment programming includes prime-time network shows, which run between 8:00 and 11:00 P.M. EST. Syndicates' prime-time shows are first-run shows that are sold through syndicates and not by networks. Other programming is composed of syndicated reruns, which are former or current successful prime-time shows that produced enough episodes to run five days a week. Still other programming includes movies, sports programming, and public broadcasting.

Who produces entertainment programming? Overwhelmingly, television shows have been produced by Hollywood studios. However, freed from regulation during the early 1990s, networks began producing more of their own television programs. This allowed them greater control of the program content, but it also raised concerns among independent producers. With network-produced shows taking up more time slots, networks will buy fewer independent programs. As media companies have merged, corporations increasingly look to own a production company and a television company to distribute the film and video. For instance, Disney owns ABC, News Corp. owns both the Fox Network and Twentieth Century Fox.

Social Issues and Entertainment Content Although First Amendment considerations prevent government action in most content areas, Congress and public interest critics have repeatedly raised concerns about the impact of sexual and violent content on television, particularly its effects on children.

Programs aimed at young people typically emphasize relationships between boys and girls, which translates on television into sex. MTV has been successful in attracting young viewers with relational programming such as *Real World*. This age group is attractive to advertisers because teenagers spend much of their money on consumer goods and services. These programs also attract teenagers who see themselves as young adults. Proponents argue that these programs introduce social issues and teach teenagers how to deal with them. Critics are quick to point out that choices made by the characters seldom have lasting consequences and are unrealistic.

The public and Congress express even greater concern about the impact of programming on young children, particularly in regard to violence. Some people argue that parents should monitor what their children watch, others support installing V-Chips that can block specified programming, and still others advocate outright control of content production.

Extreme Makeover: Home Edition features products from its sponsor, Sears.

The high ratings of a show like *CSI* may encourage television networks to create spinoffs, like *CSI: Miami* and *CSI: New York*.

Increased concern about the influence of television content on children and the impact of violent programming on society led to a television program ratings system in 1997. The television industry developed the system not out of altruism but because the 1996 Telecommunications Act mandates a system that can be used with the V-Chip, which allows television broadcasts to be filtered according to a ratings system. For example, use of the chip would block children under fourteen from viewing shows like *The Simpsons* and *Family Guy.*

The Motion Picture Association of America helped to develop the ratings system, which is similar to the one used for movies. The system has been adopted by the networks and most basic cable channels. The system has six levels that are indicated by icons in the upper left corner of the TV screen during the first fifteen seconds of the program. The levels are based on age and run from TV-Y, which means that the program is suitable for all children, to TV-M, which means that it is not suitable for children under age seventeen. Table 7.2 lists all of the new ratings.

The ratings system has not received unanimous support. Critics argue that the ratings should address content more specifically and that separate ratings should be available for sex and violence. Others argue that determining the suitability of TV content should be left to parents, not a ratings system.

In 2006, as the television industry faced sharp pressure from the FCC to protect children from indecent programming, it began public service announcements to promote use of the V-Chip, which few people used. With the suggestion of the FCC, some cable operators also began putting together packages of family-friendly programming.

Supplying the Advertising Market

Several different entities—networks, groups, individual stations, and cable systems—sell advertising time. The price of the time varies with the geographic location and type of audience, which also varies in kind and number with the time of day. For example, advertising time within a network show is much more expensive than time within a local show because of the larger, national audience that the network can reach. The price for an ad within a Chicago local program would depend on the size and demographics of the audience.

Table 7.2 Television Ratings
TV-Y—All Children: The program is suitable for all children. It should not frighten young children.
TV-Y7—Older Children: Designed for children age 7 and older; may contain mild physical or comedic violence that may frighten children under 7.
TV-G—General Audiences: Program is appropriate for all ages. It contains little or no violence, no strong language, and little or no sexual dialogue or situations.
TV-PG—Parental Guidance Suggested: Program may contain limited sexual or violent material that may be unsuitable for young children.
TV-14—Parents Strongly Cautioned: Program may contain some material that many parents would find unsuitable for children under 14 years old.
TV-M—Mature Audiences Only: Program is specifically designed to be viewed by adults and therefore, may be unsuitable for children under 17.

The number of viewers a particular program attracts determines the fee that the network or station charges advertisers. The formula for determining the **cost per consumer** is called the cost per thousand (CPM), which is the dollar amount it costs to reach a thousand viewers with an ad. Take, for example, a thirty-second advertisement on *CSI: Miami*. The charge for such a spot in 2006 was about $465,000.[34] On a good night, the program might reach 14 million viewers. The cost per thousand viewers would be $14.66. Here is the formula broken into two parts:

$$\frac{\text{Total number of viewers}}{1,000} \quad \text{Example:} \frac{14,000,000}{1,000} = 14,000$$

$$\frac{\text{Cost of ad}}{\text{Result of first equation}} \quad \text{Example:} \frac{465,000}{14,000} = \$33.21 \text{ per thousand}$$

The same formula can be used for radio, magazines, and newspapers. Thus the cost of reaching a thousand people with a TV program can be compared to the cost of reaching the same number of people in other media. The higher a show's rating, the more a station can charge for a minute of advertising, as long as the CPM does not become too much higher than that of other media.

Television regulation also affects how stations and networks supply the advertising market. For example, cigarette advertising is prohibited. Cigarette manufacturers got around the ban on television advertising by putting cigarette ads in football stadiums, baseball parks, and basketball arenas, which appeared on TV. The Justice Department said that Philip Morris had ads placed near the field or scoreboards in fourteen football stadiums, fourteen baseball parks, and five basketball arenas. In 1995, Philip Morris agreed to remove such advertisements.[35]

The latest move toward regulating advertising concerns liquor advertisements. From 1948 until 1996, the companies that produce distilled spirits voluntarily refrained from advertising on television. But in fall 1996, Seagrams ran advertisements for Chivas Regal Scotch in Texas and Massachusetts, sparking the FCC commissioners and members of Congress to consider regulating liquor advertising. The FCC deferred to the Federal Trade Commission (FTC), which urged the alcohol industry to regulate its own marketing practices to protect young people from exposure. However, in 2004, young people viewed 196.6 alcohol ads on average, a steep increase from 2001.[36]

TELEVISION AND THE INTERNATIONAL MARKET

The worldwide spread of television is due to many reasons, including national and local politics, technological inventions and infrastructures, and cultural traditions and expectations. **Market factors** such as the rise of media conglomerates and the greater availability of content have helped shape the globalization of television. Wealthier countries like South Africa have complex, multifaceted broadcasting, cable, satellite, and multimedia systems. Poor countries like Namibia do not have a heavy investment in television, and their citizens rely more on radio. Some countries have television stations owned by the government, which controls information. In others, a single media corporation dominates the television market.

Media Convergence

The Broadcast Flag

The FCC approved a regulation in 2003 that would require all digital TV devices to recognize "broadcast flags." Broadcast flags are codes in the video data stream that tell a device, like a digital video recorder, that the content is protected. Depending on the broadcast flag, a user might not be able to play back or record a broadcast. If the flag allows the user to record the broadcast, she might not be able to transfer it to other devices, even in the same household network. The FCC's decision was fueled by the motion picture industry's concerns that digital TV and downloading would make it easier for pirates to copy and sell movies.

In 2005, the Supreme Court ruled that the FCC did not have the power to impose broadcast flags on consumer devices, but the U.S. Congress took up the issue again in 2006. The specific target was unauthorized recording and distribution of high definition radio and satellite radio broadcasts, but a favorable ruling would give the FCC power to impose broadcast flags.

The motion picture industry and television and radio providers argue that such protections are necessary to protect their intellectual property rights and that illegal copying damages them financially. But critics claim that such measures impinge on "fair use," which allows limited use of copyrighted materials for certain purposes like parody, education, and research. The broadcast flag would impose more restrictions than currently exist for older video recording devices. For example, users could be forbidden from excerpting clips and using them in their own creative videos. Amateur engineers would not be allowed to build their own devices and networks without implementing broadcast flag technologies.

The controversy highlights competing views of copyright as users become more involved in selecting, saving, and altering audio and video. Whether broadcast flags are finally implemented or not, the debate over fair use will continue, as new digital technologies threaten control over content ownership.

Source: Wendy Seltzer, "The Broadcast Flag: It's Not Just TV," *Federal Communications Law Journal* 57 (2005): 209–214.

Availability of Distribution Systems

At the center of global television proliferation are companies such as News Corp., which provides service in North America, Latin America, Asia, Australia, and Europe. About half of its business comes from the United States. News Corp. and other satellite companies use eighteen-inch satellite dishes to provide packages of channels to viewers in a variety of countries and are able to reach audiences without the expensive task of laying cable. Such corporations wield enormous power. Although NBC challenged News Corp.'s right to own U.S. TV stations, arguing that it violated FCC

The spread of global communications systems has allowed viewers to share the experience of television events like the World Cup.

regulations because it was foreign owned, NBC dropped its complaint after News Corp. agreed that NBC could use Star Television's satellite to reach Asian markets.

Availability of Programming

Satellite broadcasting has made it possible to send and receive news from around the world. In 1980, CNN, based in Atlanta, Georgia, introduced the then-revolutionary concept of worldwide twenty-four-hour news, and now has twenty-six foreign bureaus and reaches about two hundred countries.[37] Other networks have followed suit. For example, Al Jazeera, known as the Arabic CNN, broadcasts its uncensored and often controversial news to thirty-five million viewers from its home in Qatar.[38] Global twenty-four-hour news has made it possible for millions of fans all over the world to share the experience of the World Cup, watching the game in airport kiosks and bus stations.

Programming in various nations is as diverse as their citizens, though increasingly, television content flows across cultures and some formulas are copied from country to country. Endemol, a company in the Netherlands, introduced the reality show *Big Brother* along with *Fear Factor, Deal or No Deal,* and *Extreme Makeover: Home Edition.* Seven years after its debut in 1999, *Big Brother* had ten versions worldwide and reached viewers in dozens of countries.

Cultural Resistance

Many of the cultural debates around worldwide television explore how local cultures make sense of global television programming, including brand-driven advertising. An argument that often surfaces, especially among traditionalists, is that a glut of messages from wealthy countries like the United States is damaging the morals of the young and erasing languages, national identities, and cultural modes of expression. In this way, wealthy countries use **softpower,** or media persuasion, to influence cultures, or even engage in *cultural imperialism* as an act of domination. Religious and political leaders may use this argument to prevent the influx of foreign television programming, but opinion is often divided. In the Middle East, some opinion leaders argue that Western media is a cultural invasion which must be prevented, while others want to embrace it or adapt it to suit the interests of the people.[39] Studies of media reception in many countries, like India and China, have suggested that people are active in choosing, creating, adopting, and moderating media messages to suit their own cultural differences as well as create new global identities.

> ### Key Concept
>
> **Cultural imperialism** Cultural imperialism is the forcing of one country's cultural values on another country through dominance of media content. For example, many young people around the world imitate U.S. culture because of what they see on U.S. television programs and movies.

softpower

The use of media persuasion, rather than violence, to promote a nation's interests.

TRENDS

The television industry is in a state of flux, facing new technologies that are transforming the way video can be sent, new government regulations on ownership and content, and the demands of an increasingly diverse nation.

Technology: Broadband

The greatest change to television will come from faster broadband connections, which have made streaming video possible. Broadband reached 2.6 million households in 1999, but by 2005 had reached 31 million. In 2010, that number will have more than doubled.[40] This has raised the question of whether the Internet will become television's key delivery system. Because of these changes, over-the-air broadcast, cable, and satellite companies are competing with phone companies to reach households with combined voice, Internet, and television services. Regulatory and licensing decisions by the FCC will affect who gets to own what and who has what access to households. Some citizens who can't afford or interact with new technologies may be left behind, and others will not adapt. Older forms of content, such as the thirty-second advertising spot, may fade away. By 2010, many forms of video will be widely available, revising the way we think of television.

Technology: Interactivity

Digital technologies are providing more opportunities for interactivity. Advertisers, business managers, and media analysts often call this a transformation from "push" to "pull." Since *Wired* and *Business Week* introduce the terms in 1997, they have proven useful metaphors. The old broadcast medium was more "push." Couch potatoes sat back and passively received the programming from their television sets without much effort. The delivery of content was pushed on them. In some ways, push is seen as desirable because many people may want just to relax or don't want to waste a lot of time fiddling around with difficult media delivery systems. In the new digital media, the emphasis is on pull. Active users like to manipulate gadgets and selectively interact with content. This means big changes in the way content such as advertising is shaped and delivered. Push vs. pull is often connected to a divide in generation and lifestyle. The new digital mediascape is a combination of push and pull, so that a viewer may be passively watching a video on YouTube, but be inspired to respond to an advertising message by clicking on a link.

> ### Key Concept
>
> **Interactive television** The ability of computers and TV sets jointly to send messages to and receive messages from the company that provides the television signals. Typically, viewers can access video on demand and interact with program hosts and audiences in studios.

Interactive television can be as simple as switching channels with the remote, ordering a movie, blocking programming, or selectively recording and editing programs. However, services are expanding to include other possibilities, such as providing a portal for video game play or an advertising link on a television screen that can be clicked with the remote. Advertisers envision an interactivity that will allow them to customize these messages for targeted viewers, keeping track of their habits over time. Because these innovations may include advertising aimed at children, regulators are concerned. FCC head Michael Copps described the future at the Children Now forum in 2006: "Picture this: A child turns on a TV show, an icon pops up, the young viewer pushes a button on the remote and is immediately transported from the television show to a lavish Internet emporium where jingles, games, and commercial products are available to tease, manipulate, sell, and satisfy every desire."[41] However, full interactivity will require television companies to invest in upgrades. Marketers have not yet determined how much interactivity audiences want, what types of interactive programs they will watch, and how willing they will be to use and pay for complex technologies.

In the "pull" environment, viewers interact with television shows using other devices as well. For example, viewers can vote on *American Idol* contestants using text messaging from their cell phones, play online against game show TV contestants, or post online chat messages that then appear on shows such as *Star Trek 2.0*. They may also visit the websites of their favorite shows to chat and blog, and may set up their own websites to gossip about celebrities, post clips, and discuss plots. With digital camcorders, they can produce their own videos inexpensively and easily upload them onto video sites. With the popularity of sites like YouTube and Google Video, this user-generated content is gaining importance. In 2005, Al Gore founded Current TV, a cable and satellite aimed at providing a forum for young people and inviting them to submit short video "pods." A third of the programming comes from viewers, who can upload video onto Current TV's website. Community members vote on which new pods will be shown. Other networks are featuring viewer-generated content in their regular news and entertainment programming. While the idea has been around since *America's Funniest Home Videos* and *MTV News Unfiltered,* the advent of digital technology, combined with the popularity of social networking, has greatly increased the interest in user-generated content and interactive television.

Culture: Media Ownership

Media ownership is a contentious political issue. Some argue that regulations against ownership suppress competition and are outdated in an environment of sweeping change as old media converge into new media. Others hold that the increasing consolidation of media ownership puts too much political, economic, and cultural power into the hands of a few.

The passage of the Telecommunications Act of 1996 guaranteed massive changes in television station ownership and the mix of delivery services. The act changed regulations governing broadcast television and cable ownership, programming, and cable rates. The far-reaching law affects all areas of the television industry and will alter the nature of the industry well into the twenty-first century.

Old rules limited companies to ownership of twelve TV stations reaching up to 25 percent of the national audience. The 1996 act eliminated the limit on the number of stations one entity could own and increased to 35 percent the national audience a company's stations could reach. Companies quickly grew in size, and the broadcast lobby continues to push for a higher national audience percentage, which will make the media corporations even bigger.

As a result of the act, networks and TV stations now can own cable systems, and cable systems can own TV stations. A network can own a second network, provided it starts the second one rather than buying an existing network. The law also requires the FCC to consider whether it should relax the rule against a broadcaster owning only one TV station in a market. The FCC has taken a liberal stance toward ownership of a TV and radio station in the same market.

The conglomeration of media described in earlier chapters also affects television as a result of the Telecommunications Act. Perhaps the most drastic changes are in the cable industry. With the ending of rate regulation in 1996, cable rates outpaced the inflation rate by 200 to 300 percent. The success of cable-rate deregulation hinges on telephone companies' ability to provide programming. Regional operating companies can deliver programs as a cable system, which will require a franchise agreement from local government, or as an **open video system.** Open video systems do not have to get local franchise agreements and are subject to limited federal cable regulations. In return for more freedom, the open systems make cable channels available to unaffiliated programmers without discrimination in one of two ways: The system operators can rent entire channels to programmers without control of the content, or the systems can make a channel available that will vary in its content. A person or group could buy an hour of time on a given day to broadcast any message that falls within the limits of the law.

Open video systems allow greater access to people and organizations that are not affiliated with an existing network or television station. Economists would say that this lowers barriers to entry for nonestablished businesses and will make content more diversified.

Just as telephone companies can enter the cable business, cable companies can provide telephone service. Existing telephone companies must negotiate with new service providers about interconnections and a variety of other issues required to keep telephone use simple.

Almost as soon as the 1996 act was signed, corporations began to lobby the FCC to deregulate even further. In June 2006, the FCC revisited its ownership rules, calling for public comment on proposed changes. These include removing the 35 percent cap on households a company could reach with "O and O" TV stations, removing the radio–television cross-ownership limit, allowing a company to own more than one network, removing the limits on the number of radio stations a company could own in a market, and removing the ban on local newspapers owning broadcast stations.

A similar effort to make these changes in 2003 was overturned in court and led to a grassroots movement against the deregulation of media ownership.

As part of its review of media ownership, the FCC began conducting research projects that highlight the potential cultural impacts of its decisions. For example, the

open video system

A system that rents entire channels or time on channels to unaffiliated programmers without discrimination.

Discussing Trends

As with most media, technological, economic, and content trends will dominate discussion of television's future. Of course, the three trends are intertwined. Ownership determines financial goals and corporation content strategies. Technology determines how those strategies can be pursued and who will have access to the content. Content affects who watches and whether the financial goals can be met. Here are some of the many questions confronting the television industry in the next decade:

- How has the transition to digital technology affected the nature of television?
- Has the public benefited from or been harmed by ownership concentration that has resulted from the FCC changing ownership rules?
- Are the changes consistent with the idea that television owes a service to the public?

- The 1996 Telecommunications Act was supposed to promote competition in the television distribution industry, but has that happened?
- What can the viewing public do to affect diversity in television content?
- To what extent has television made the transition to a push-pull model for users?
- What influence will portable devices like iPods and cell phones have on the delivery of television programming?
- How much interactivity do television viewers want? What kinds of interaction are most successful?
- What is the impact of social networking on television channels, including their shows and websites?
- What new strategies are advertsers using to reach television audiences?

FCC is studying the impact of changes in ownership on people's newsgathering habits, local communities, diversity in programming, independent programming, children's and family-friendly programming, and minority participation in the media.

SUMMARY

- Television, as a medium and as content, has always been controversial in U.S. society.
- Television station licensees are charged with operating in the public interest.
- Getting the television industry on its feet after World War II was difficult because each important element (station owners, set manufacturers, programmers, consumers, and advertisers) was waiting for someone else to begin the process.
- Although blacklisting did not alter the structure of the television industry, it reminded television executives of their vulnerability and underscored the necessity for free expression.
- Three networks, CBS, NBC, and ABC, dominated television during the first forty years. This dominance declined during the 1980s and 1990s because of cable television and the advent of additional broadcast television networks.
- Early television programming borrowed from radio and was broadcast live.

- Early advertising took the form of sponsorship, and advertisers controlled the content of specific programs.
- Profitable entertainment formulas are often repeated, so that many television shows resemble each other.
- The traditional mode of television broadcasting is shifting to a multiplatform model with more user choice and interaction.
- Audiences are measured by demographic and psychographic approaches.
- The FCC has promoted technologies like the V-Chip and the broadcast flag in its efforts to regulate television programming.
- Television penetration is global, and news and entertainment are transmitted across borders.
- Young people are using video in new ways and are attracted to new kinds of programming.
- Audience measurement, such as ratings and shares, affects programming because it affects an advertiser's willingness to buy time in connection with specific programs.

NAVIGATING THE WEB Television

You can find sites related to your favorite television programs, or you can use television websites to find information about the industry. There also are sites that lead you to current news and information and station promotion.

Broadcasting & Cable
broadcastingcable.com
Broadcasting & Cable is the television trade magazine. The online version contains information about the print version as well as some content from the print edition.

The Museum of Broadcast Communications
museum.tv
A site that includes an encyclopedia of television history and an archive of programming.

***TV Guide* Online**
tvguide.com
This site provides information about current and historical television content. It is the online version of *TV Guide* magazine, which has a circulation of nine million.

TV Radio World
radiostationworld.com
This site is a directory for television and radio stations and networks around the world. It also provides information about technical information and regulations applicable to particular countries throughout the world.

QUESTIONS FOR REVIEW

1. What is the difference between cable systems and broadcast stations?
2. What was the *Mayflower* decision and why was it important?
3. How do public and commercial television differ?
4. How does television measure its audiences?
5. What are the consequences of the federally mandated move to digital television?
6. What is a V-Chip?

ISSUES TO THINK ABOUT

1. How has the primarily commercial ownership of television in the United States affected its development?
2. What changes do you see in politics since the advent of television? Do these changes foster democracy?
3. Has television news deteriorated, or is lower viewership merely reflection of changes in society?
4. How do varying distribution technologies affect the development of television content?
5. As television moves to the Internet, what changes do you see?
6. What will be the impact of interactive television?
7. What has been the impact of the Telecommunications Act of 1996?

SUGGESTED READINGS

Barnouw, Erik. *The Golden Web: A History of Broadcasting in the United States, 1933–1953* (New York: Oxford University Press, 1968).

Carter, Bill. *Desperate Networks* (New York: Doubleday, 2006).

Douglas, Susan. *Inventing American Broadcasting, 1899–1922* (Baltimore: Johns Hopkins University Press, 1987).

Garner, Joe. *Stay Tuned: Television's Unforgettable Moments* (Kansas City, MO: Andrews McMeel Publishing, 2002).

Gitlin, Todd. *Inside Prime Time* (New York: Pantheon, 1985).

Kumar, Shanti. *Gandhi Meets Primetime: Globalization and Nationalism in Indian Television* (Urbana, IL: University of Illinois Press, 2005).

Lasswell, Mark, ed. *TV Guide: 50 Years of Television* (New York: Crown Publishing, 2002).

Music and the Recording Industry

When the northern English post-punk band, Arctic Monkeys, released *Whatever People Say I Am, That's What I'm Not,* it became the fastest selling debut album ever to hit the U.K. charts. The band's success had not come from the usual route of finding a record label to promote it. Instead, the Arctic Monkeys had attracted a huge fan base by word of mouth over the Internet. Their fans had circulated music from the Monkeys' demos, given away for free at the band's gigs, and had set up a massively popular MySpace page. After the Monkeys finally agreed to sign to an indie label, music critics praised the band as "the new Beatles," while marketers wondered about the implications of a new model that circumvents the recording industry's traditional role as patron, gatekeeper, and promoter.

In the twenty-first century, because of digital technologies, recording artists are able to create, distribute, and promote their music in unprecedented ways, making it possible for musicians to gain a significant number of fans without a record label. Young musicians find that social networking on the web allows them to establish personalized relationships with fans, especially since music is an important cultural means to establish identity and group belonging. Even well established musicians are challenging established ways. The Barenaked Ladies abandoned their old label to successfully promote their 2006 album *Barenaked Ladies Are Me* through a variety of digital forms, such as ringtones, digital downloads through iTunes, a multimedia presentation on USB flash drive, and rough album tracks that allowed fans to remix them.

While the recording industry is scrambling to keep up with the new media, many digital utopianists see opportunities for democratizing the process by which artists find and reach audiences, promoting diversity and innovation. Others are more guarded. Co-author of *The Future of Music,* David Kusek, writes:

> The new artist model says anybody can make and distribute a recording. It is much less expensive to make a record today and recorded music is only going to become less valuable to everyone over time. The real hard part is promotion. The true nemesis of the artist is obscurity. There is a glut of music out there and the situation is only going to get worse. This is the reality of the future of music, abundance and saturation.[1]

Everyone involved in recording music is affected by these changes: musicians, songwriters, publishers, event coordinators, promoters, producers, and engineers.

Since the early twentieth century, a blend of technological change and youth culture has driven the rise of recorded music, especially popular forms like jazz, rock, and hip-hop. The evolution of this music is not a linear flow, but a series of disruptions brought by technological and cultural change, including rebellion against older social forms, mainstream popular taste, and the commercialization of art. The introduction of new forms, like bebop and punk, has challenged social and aesthetic boundaries around the world.

The digital revolution in music is not the first revolution in music, though it has unique characteristics that reflect dramatic changes to all media industries. The growth of user-generated content, the ease with which digital files can be manipulated and exchanged, and the ability conveniently to deliver content across media platforms are also affecting the recording industry. The most important question is who owns the music—listeners, musicians, or record company executives.

The social and economic implications of changes in the music scene pose significant issues such as the following:

- Recording companies have traditionally provided musicians with patronage, a system of approval and support. To what extent should the recording industry continue to serve as a gatekeeper of music? What effects, either good or bad, does patronage have on artists and their music?

- Digital technologies like peer-to-peer file sharing have made it easy for musicians and fans to share music. However, the recording industry exists to make a profit through music sales. What legal and social measures, if any, should be taken to ensure that the industry maintains control over content? To what extent should peer-to-peer file sharing of copyrighted material be allowed?

- What varied forms of music are achieving popularity as more musicians are able to produce, distribute, and promote their music online? In what ways will music change as computer users are able to manipulate and arrange digital tracks for themselves? Will traditional forms, like the album, become defunct?

Music in Your Life

Music as Rhythms and Ideas

Music can be listened to merely for entertainment, but it also may educate. Think about how music has affected your life. Why do you listen to it? What does it do for you?

As you read this chapter, think about the many ways in which music pervades life in the United States. Think about how you use music—to tell stories; to relax; to worship. Also try to relate some issues to the commercialization of music and the impact of corporate music makers on popular content.

What You Learn	Technologies You Use	People You Listen With	Purposes of Music
New ideas	Radio	Friends offline	Religion
About people who are different from you	Television	Friends online	Excitement
About people who are like you	Compact discs	Date	Making friends
About the world around you	iPod	Family	Relaxing
About emotions	Cell phone	People in restaurants/bars/stores	Other

PRINTED AND RECORDED MUSIC IN AMERICAN LIFE

American music is the result of cross-cultural exchanges as inhabitants listened to and adapted the new musical forms they encountered. The roots of Native American music lie in sacred songs accompanied by percussion instruments, flutes, and whistles. When Europeans arrived they brought with them sacred and secular musical forms, such as hymns, dances, and folk songs. African slaves brought their various musical traditions, and used them as the basis for spirituals and work songs. Of these early three strains, the African-American and European came to dominate U.S. popular music. African-American music forms transformed into blues and jazz; and European music forms transformed into bluegrass and country music.

African-American Music

African music arrived in Virginia with the slave ships even before the *Mayflower* landed in New England, and it appeared in printed form during the Civil War. It evolved into black spirituals, work songs, blues, and jazz. Although the Africans sang tribal songs with a **syncopated beat** that was foreign to most European songs, during the 1700s and 1800s the early African Americans blended these songs with European religious music to create spirituals. The first black spiritual appeared in print in 1862, and the first collection of black spiritual sheet music was published five years later.[2] African Americans sang work songs on the docks and in the cotton fields of the South. These songs had no instrumental accompaniment, and workers used them both to help them

syncopated beat

The regular metrical accent that shifts temporarily to stress a beat that is normally weak. Syncopation is important in African and African-American musical traditions and is considered the root of most modern popular music.

Early jazz music developed from the ragtime and blues played in New Orleans and was spread northward by musicians such as Louis Armstrong, whose career paralleled the growing popularity of jazz. Elements of jazz and blues ultimately became a critical element in rock 'n' roll.

bear harsh working conditions and as clandestine protest songs, which created the base of the blues tradition.

Blues songs were personal music about an individual's troubles. After the Civil War, wandering musicians helped to spread the spontaneous music with impromptu lyrics, and at the turn of the twentieth century, W. C. Handy immortalized the genre with his song "The St. Louis Blues." The song was so popular that it earned Handy $25,000 a year in royalties forty years after it was written.[3]

African Americans also composed music for entertainment and dancing. These fast-paced banjo songs were adopted by white performers in the traveling **minstrel** shows that were popular among white audiences from the 1840s to the early twentieth century. In these shows, white men blackened their faces with burnt cork and sang black songs. Successful songwriters such as Stephen Foster gained fame by imitating the songs of black Americans, who were not allowed to perform their own music. Such music eventually made a successful transition from performance to motion picture. Al Jolson, famous for his blackface movie roles, carried the minstrel tradition into the twentieth century. Despite its appeal to some white audiences, African Americans felt minstrel shows mocked their tradition.

In the late 1800s, the minstrel shows also gave rise to ragtime, which originated in the African-American dance music called the cakewalk. Ragtime emphasized intricate syncopated rhythms in march tempos. Ragtime composer Scott Joplin, who first studied classical European music, stunned his audiences with songs such as the "Maple Leaf Rag." Ragtime developed as commercial music, particularly in urban areas with large concentrations of African Americans.

At the turn of the twentieth century, African-American musicians performed in the bars and brothels of the Storyville section of New Orleans. They combined ragtime and blues forms, creating jazz in the relatively tolerant environment of the southern port city.[4] City authorities closed down Storyville in 1917 under pressure from the U.S. Navy, which had a large military base in New Orleans. New Orleans' loss was the United States' gain as jazz spread through the nightclubs of Chicago, St. Louis, New York, Kansas City, Memphis, and San Francisco. In the 1920s, the economy boomed, young people looked for excitement, and jazz thrived.

A decade later jazz became the basis for the big band, or swing, sounds of the 1930s and 1940s played by black, white, and mixed bands. Many jazz musicians criticized swing because it sanitized jazz to make it more commercial. Nevertheless, jazz flourished and grew in complexity. It underwent a revitalization in the 1950s and is found in a variety of forms today.

minstrel

An entertainer, with blackened face, performing songs and music of African-American origin.

European-American Music

Europeans brought both religious and *folk ballad traditions* with them to America. The religious songs came with the settlers, many of whom were escaping religious persecution in Europe. The folk songs came with the sailors and adventurers who saw the New World as a way to make money and with the peasants and farmers who settled on the expanding frontiers. Serious music did not gain a foothold until the first half of the nineteenth century, when an elite class began to look toward European forms of entertainment.

Because of the efforts to break away from Europe, patriotic songs were popular in this early period. British soldiers used "Yankee Doodle" to taunt colonists, but during the American Revolution it became a standard on the battlefield. Patriotic songs remained popular throughout the 1800s and reached their peak with the marches of John Philip Sousa in the latter part of the nineteenth century.

Origins of Western, Bluegrass, and Country Music   European folk music blended with other traditions. In some urban areas, folk ballads were integrated into African-American minstrel music, and in the West they formed the basis of western songs, expressing the tales of the lonesome cowboy. Hill music—bluegrass, hillbilly, and country—had its roots in European folk music. In the mountains of Tennessee, Kentucky, Virginia, and North Carolina, people used folk tunes and religious songs, played on traditional instruments such as the fiddle and banjo, to ease the burdens of life.

Urban Popular and Tin Pan Alley   The popularity of music culminated in the late 1800s in *Tin Pan Alley*, which was both a place and an approach to commercial music. The popular music industry was centered in New York City around Union Square. Here, the music houses employed people to write songs for sheet music, vaudeville, and theater. Writers incorporated classical and folk melodies and wrote their own tunes to please the taste of the average person. In 1893 the music producers moved to West 28th Street. Monroe H. Rosenfeld, a press agent and journalist, named the street Tin Pan Alley after the sound made by a piano that had been modified with newspaper strips woven through its strings to muffle the noise.

> **Key Concept**
>
> **Tin Pan Alley** The sound of pianos in the commercial music district of New York City gave the name "Tin Pan Alley" to the industry that produced popular songs for sheet music, vaudeville and minstrel performances, and early recording in the United States. Today, popular music writing is concentrated in New York and California.

Tin Pan Alley dominated popular music for almost twenty-five years, producing thousands of mostly forgettable songs for sheet music sales. It ended in the 1920s as radio, phonographs, and movies began to distribute not only notes and lyrics, but sounds as well. Today the term describes formula commercial music aimed at pleasing large numbers of people.

Elite Music   Although music aimed at the educated and wealthy elite did not develop as quickly as popular and religious music in the United States, it made giant strides from 1865 to 1920 and even today is significant as a form of music available on radio, tape, compact disc, and even television.[5] The increased availability of higher education, the expansion of the middle class during the Industrial Revolution, and the invention of the phonograph created large audiences for serious music. Private citizens funded conservatories and concert halls, and by 1920 symphony orchestras had been established in New York, Philadelphia, Chicago, Cincinnati, Minneapolis, Pittsburgh, San Francisco, Cleveland, Detroit, and Los Angeles. Opera did not fare as well, with only two permanent opera companies performing in 1920.[6]

> **Key Concept**
>
> **Rock 'n' Roll** The increased demand for varied radio and recorded music in the post–World War II era encouraged a blend of styles that eventually merged the African-American, urban popular, and country traditions to form rock 'n' roll in the 1950s.

From the 1930s to Rock 'n' Roll

By the middle of the 1920s, African and European music had become interwoven to form specific strains of popular music, and radio facilitated the wide distribution of popular forms of music. The United States had jazz, blues, country, western, theatrical and movie songs, Tin Pan Alley tunes, and dance music. Jazz entered the mainstream musical arena and paved the way for *rock 'n' roll*.

The hot jazz of the 1920s, born in the brothels of New Orleans, gave way to **swing** during the late 1920s. Gone were the small improvisational groups, replaced by bands of more than a dozen musicians. Some African-American swing musicians, such as Duke Ellington, garnered an audience and a reputation during this period, but swing

swing

Big band music played with a jazz rhythm that was popular during the 1930s and early 1940s. Swing enjoyed a revival during the 1990s.

Dateline

Music in Our Lives

1600s. African and European folk and religious music arrive in America.

1800s. Blues develops from African roots, and country music develops from European roots.

Late 1800s. Sheet music sales boom.

1887. Edison invents the recording machine.

Early 1900s. Records are mass produced.

1930s. Swing grows from jazz.

1940s. Les Paul invents the electric guitar.

1940s. Tape recording develops.

1947. Columbia develops 33⅓ rpm long-play records.

1948. RCA develops 45 rpm records.

1400–1700	1800	1860	1900	1920	1930	1940

1620. Pilgrims land at Plymouth Rock.

1690. *Publick Occurrences* is published in Boston.

1741. First magazine is published in America.

1776–1783. American Revolution

1830s. The penny press becomes the first truly mass medium in the United States.

1861–1865. American Civil War

1892. Thomas Edison's lab develops the kinetoscope.

1914–1918. World War I

1915. *The Birth of a Nation* marks the start of the modern movie industry.

1920. KDKA in Pittsburgh gets the first commercial radio license.

1930s. The Great Depression

1939. TV is demonstrated at the New York World's Fair.

1939–1945. World War II

1949. First commercial electronic computer is produced.

Cultural Milestones

bop

Jazz that developed during the 1940s as a reaction to big band swing music. Usually performed by small groups with fast tempos and conflicting rhythms. Also called be-bop.

was dominated by predominantly white bands headed by Benny Goodman, Glenn Miller, and Artie Shaw.

Even as mainstream singers such as Frank Sinatra, Bing Crosby, and the Lennon Sisters sold millions of records during and after World War II, some areas of music were changing. In jazz, African-American artists such as Charlie Parker and Dizzy Gillespie reacted against swing and the white commercial exploitation it represented. They developed **bop,** which returned jazz to its improvisation roots and boosted its ability to compete in the recording industry.

Early 1950s. Rock 'n' roll begins.

1950s. High-fidelity and stereo technology is introduced.

Early 1960s. Beatles become the most popular rock group ever.

Late 1960s. Rock 'n' roll fragments into various strains of rock.

Mid-1970s. Punk and new wave music develop.

Late 1970s. Hip-hop develops in South Bronx.

1979. Sony Walkman is invented.

1980s. Compact disc is invented.

1981. MTV begins broadcasting.

1985. Digital audiotape is introduced.

1990s. Music begins broadcasting over the Internet.

1990s. MP3 technology is developed for the Web.

2000s. Rap becomes international and more mainstream.

2001. The iPod is introduced.

2005. Cell phones that play MP3s are widely introduced.

1950	1960	1970	1980	1990	2000

Early 1950s. Rock 'n' roll begins.

1969. First person lands on the moon.

1970s. VCR is developed.

1989–1991. Cold War ends and the USSR is dissolved.

Late 1980s. National Science Foundation creates the basis of the Internet.

1996. Telecommunications Act

2000s. Presidential election nearly tied.

2001. Terrorist attacks on New York and Washington, D.C.

2003. War with Iraq.

The bop movement represented only one genre of African-American music that flourished. Count Basie gained white fans with his **jump music,** and blues singers such as Blind Lemon Jefferson and Big Mama Thornton recorded hits. The term *rhythm and blues (R&B)* was applied to all kinds of black music, replacing the term *race music.*[7]

Country music flourished along with rhythm and blues. The lonesome songs of Hank Williams, the western songs of Gene Autry, and the foot-tapping bluegrass of Bill Monroe made country music commercially attractive for the recording industry. The

jump music

Small band music that merged swing and electric blues during the late 1940s. Jump developed into rhythm and blues music.

Grand Ole Opry in Nashville broadcast weekly over radio, and performing there became the goal of every country-and-western singer.

Blending Music to Make Rock 'n' Roll

People disagree about who invented rock 'n' roll, but everyone agrees that it vitalized the recording industry. Many say that Louis Jordan's rhythm and blues music of the 1940s was rock 'n' roll. Others argue that Bob Wills and his Texas Playboys' western swing of the 1930s was the root of rock 'n' roll. Other influences include urban blues singers such as T-Bone Walker, who adopted Les Paul's solid-body electric guitar during the late 1940s.[8] Elements of gospel music can also be heard in early rock 'n' roll.

Without question, however, rock 'n' roll was born in the deep South, and it emerged from rhythm and blues. By living in the South, young musicians were able to hear the black R&B and white hillbilly music that formed the core of rock 'n' roll. Two streams emerged. One involved identifiable rock 'n' roll music from rhythm and blues, by musicians such as Little Richard, Bo Diddley, and Chuck Berry. The other stream was the rockabilly music, which dated to Bob Wills but incorporated more rhythm and blues. Early rockabilly musicians, such as Johnny Cash, Carl Perkins, Buddy Holly, and Elvis Presley, folded gospel and rhythm and blues into their music. Often they covered R&B artists' music, as Elvis did with Big Mama Thornton's "Hound Dog." At the same time, some African-American artists, such as Chuck Berry, found influence in the country music they heard growing up in the South.

Elvis Presley incorporated rhythm and blues with rockabilly roots to establish himself as a rock 'n' roll star.

Alan Freed, a Cleveland disc jockey, helped to popularize the music in the North. His show boomed in popularity after June 1951, when he began playing the R&B records he had heard on African-American radio stations. Freed called the music "rock 'n' roll."

Though early rock 'n' roll made African-American rhythms more acceptable to white audiences, the major recording companies resisted. Company executives saw no future in music that adults considered too loud, and the sexual energy demonstrated in rock 'n' roll dancing alarmed adults. This was "trash" music to most white people older than age eighteen. Early production and distribution of rock 'n' roll were left to small record companies such as Sun Records of Memphis and Chess Records of Chicago. Figure 8.1 illustrates the evolution of rock 'n' roll and other strains of music in the United States.

CREATIVE, ECONOMIC, AND CULTURAL IMPACTS

The evolution of music is guided by artistic, economic, and social forces. Musicians share ideas, techniques, and forms with other musicians, often including those outside of their own musical circles. Therefore, music is in a constant state of creative flux as new forms rise, blend with other forms, and fade. Many musicians aspire to reach large audiences and make money from their music, and so economic influences become important in what types of music are created and sold. Finally, musicians create their pieces for audiences, and therefore have a cultural impact. Audiences may shape identities and communities around particular genres of music, like crunk or reggaeton. Music may confirm the elite status of certain groups, like opera lovers, or rally audiences to social or political action or to rebel against the status quo. These

Figure 8.1 The Evolution of Rock 'n' Roll

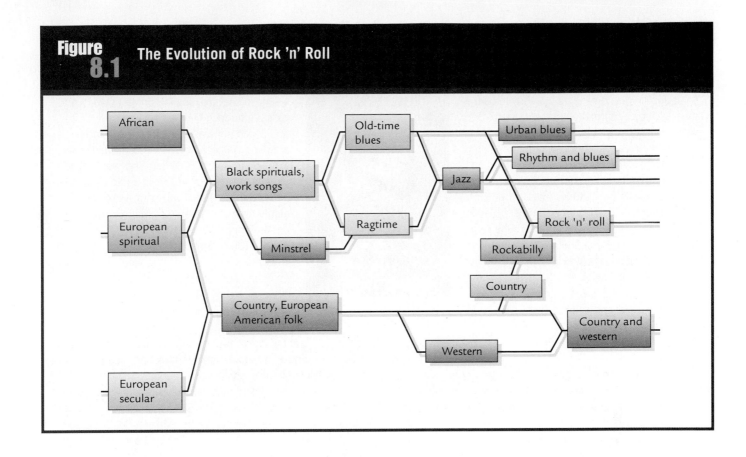

dimensions of music—creativity, economics, and social meaning—have been influenced in recent years by new technologies, the rise of the recording industry, and changes in identities and communities.

Creativity: Blending Musical Forms

Of the many creative aspects of music, one is the ***blending of forms***. Often this has happened casually as musicians have adopted features of music they have heard. Sometimes, artists have deliberately sought out music from other places to invigorate their own styles. In the late nineteenth century, classical musicians incorporated popular and folk music, as in Rimsky-Korsakov's *Capriccio Espagnol* and Verdi's *Aida*. Jazz blended African musical forms with those from the United States and Europe, and has continued to incorporate other world sounds, such as Japanese native instrumentation. Emerging in the 1980s, world music commercialized the blending of ethnic, folk, pop and dance music, especially from third world countries. Most recently, digital music files and other technologies have created many opportunities for **sampling**—the electronic borrowing and incorporation of sounds and rhythms from prior recordings.

The borrowing of musical styles has, in the past, been partly driven by colonization, as dominant powers appropriated elements of cultures they conquered and considered inferior, but also interesting and exotic. The cultural flow went both ways, as conquered and enslaved peoples adapted the musical forms of the colonizer. Because of these political and cultural histories, musical borrowings have sometimes been controversial. Social critics have leveled charges of **cultural appropriation** especially at White twentieth-century musicians, from Benny Goodman to Elvis to Paul Simon. These musicians were seen as stealing and capitalizing on musical forms that belonged to disempowered social groups who did not have the same access to

Key Concept

Blending of musical forms Popular music evolves as musicians blend different strains of music. Rock 'n' roll was born and developed this way. Sometimes social controversy emerges as critics and scholars debate whether culturally based music should be blended and who should be credited with changes in popular music.

sampling

The electronic borrowing and incorporation of sounds and rhythms from prior recordings.

cultural appropriation

Capitalizing on musical forms that belong to disempowered social groups.

During a period of male-dominated rock 'n' roll, Janis Joplin was considered by many to be the most exciting performer of her generation. "She was not just a singer, but a symbol of the liberation and excess of hippy San Francisco in the late '60s," reminisced Harper Barnes, who had reviewed Joplin's performance in front of 11,000 fans at the outdoor Mississippi River Festival in Edwardsville in the summer of 1969. "Joplin simply tore the place up. . . . She flings herself into every song, her voice scooping up notes and slamming them down, her body moving like a bawdy majorette. At one point, she looked out at the audience with the grin of a naughty child and said, 'Now do you know what rock 'n' roll is all about?'"

Janis Joplin

Janis Joplin was born into a middle-class family on January 19, 1943, in Port Arthur, Texas, an oil town on the Gulf of Mexico. It seemed that the plain, chubby girl and then teenager was often unhappy and had trouble fitting in with others her age. After graduating from high school, she attended the local college briefly, then set out to San Francisco. In North Beach, where the beat writers such as Jack Kerouac had gathered, Joplin sang in bars and coffeehouses, experimenting with folk and blues songs before settling into rock 'n' roll.

For a while, Joplin gave up music. She returned home and started school again in Austin, Texas. But she left after a short stay. Friends in the fading band Big Brother and the Holding Company convinced her to join them in San Francisco

in 1966. The band's new sound combined an energetic beat with Joplin's powerful blues- and gospel-influenced voice.

Joplin pursued pleasure with the same energy, and life became an incessant whirl of sex, alcohol, and drugs. When she was not too strung out to sing, she "drove audiences into a frenzy with her harsh yet soaring voice and the highly charged, openly sexual energy of her performances," wrote Barnes.

By 1967, Janis Joplin was a star. She, Jimi Hendrix, and Otis Redding were the hottest American performers in rock 'n' roll. When the album *Cheap Thrills* came out in 1968, she became world famous. Over time, however, the alcohol and $200-a-day drug habit took their toll. In 1970, at the age of twenty-seven, Joplin died of an accidental overdose of heroin. Jimi Hendrix had died from suffocation related to drug use a month earlier.

Some of Janis Joplin's most famous songs included "Summertime," "Ball and Chain," "Piece of My Heart," and "Turtle Blues." Three months after her death, "Me and Bobby McGee" was released and became Janis Joplin's first song to be number one on the pop charts.

Sources: Harper Barnes, "Full-Tilt Boogie Janis Joplin Came and Went Like a Texas Tornado," *St. Louis Post Dispatch* October 14, 1992, Everyday Magazine sec., 1F; Susan Whitall, "Polishing the Tarnished Janis Joplin," Gannett News Service, October 14, 1992.

---

audiences, distribution systems, and commercial success. Sampling of indigenous music in Western pop, especially when the true source has been unacknowledged, has raised similar ethical questions about piracy and plagiarism. For example, Eric Mouquet's and Michel Sanchez's sampling of a Baegu song on their album *Deep Forest* resulted in legal wrangling over the song's ownership and charges that the Baegu community had never been compensated.[9] The issue often involves not only lack of financial compensation, but lack of cultural respect.

Made possible by recording technologies like tapes, vinyl records, synthesizers, and digital samplers, sampling has become increasingly common in many forms of music. It first gained hold as a musical practice called *dub,* created by Jamaican musicians in the 1970s. By switching vinyl records and using mix boards, dub musicians manipulated recorded songs to create new versions, usually by adding percussion, heavy base, echo, and reverb. Introduced in the 1980s, low-cost musical instrument digital interface (MIDI) devices allowed many musicians to work with sampling, which became an integral part of rap and hip-hop music. Hip-hop producers combed through earlier music by artists such as James Brown and Isaac Hayes for vocals, drum sounds, and other elements that could then be manipulated and repeated through looping. In the twenty-first century, the formation of vast, online music resources has made it easier for musicians to find and incorporate samples into their own creations, which can be easily distributed. However, tension exists between record companies, who see

Cultural Impact

Rise of the Ringtone

Made possible by digital technologies, ringtones have become so prevalent that they have become an important part of the music industry. Recording companies receive increasing revenues from them. In 2006, ringtone sales were expected to reach $600 million in the United States, up from $68 million in 2003. Accomplished musicians are hired by entertainment companies to create new ringtones, and major artists like Madonna and 50 Cent produce voice tones, voice ringbacks, and ringtones as part of their recording process. *Billboard Magazine* charts the Top 20 ringtones sales each week, demonstrating their importance as a pop music form. Causing irritation to some people who consider ringtones mere noise, their sound has become ubiquitous in many urban parts of the world, much more prevalent than radio.

After the Finnish company Nokia introduced text messaging in the late 1990s, a Finnish computer programmer, Vesa-Matti Paananen, realized that cell phones could be programmed to play simple, monophonic melodies. He made his software freely available to anyone who wanted to create these melodies. The earliest monophonic ringtones were mostly extracted from classical composers like Beethoven, Bach, and Mozart, and other works in the public domain.

In Europe and Asia, entrepreneurs began making and selling ringtones, sometimes composing them, sometimes arranging them from popular music for which they paid license fees to music publishers who owned the copyrights. Ringtones became more complex, and therefore more desirable, as programmers invented ways to turn phones into music synthesizers and MP3 players. Some musicians, such as English pop musician Boy George and Deep Purple's Steve Morse, began writing for cell phones, creating a unique form of twenty-second musical composition.

The new global business in ringtones expanded rapidly as phone users—predominantly, but not exclusively, teenagers—customized their phones to make personal statements about fashion and identity. Major music companies partnered with wireless telephone companies to provide mobile content, a move that the

music industry hoped would help save it from declining sales and competition from peer-to-peer file sharing.

An important component of commercial music, ringtones now officially fall under the U.S. Copyright Act. Under pressure from the Recording Industry Association of America, the Register of Copyrights ruled in 2006 that like other forms of music, ringtones are subject to compulsory licensing with mandatory royalty rates. Several organizations of songwriters and music publishers objected to the ruling, arguing that it did not protect the interests of content creators.

Sources: BMI, press release, April 3, 2006, www.bmi.com/news/entry/334746; Sumanth Gopinath, "Ringtones, or the Auditory Logic of Globalization," *First Monday* 10 (December 2005), firstmonday.org/issues/issue10_12.

sampling as copyright violation, and many artists, who view sampling as essential to creation and invention.

Economics: Commercialization

Another aspect of popular music is *commercialization*, which is a process that tends to move power from the artists to the recording executives and audiences. Popular music has two purposes. It can be an expression of an individual artist's vision, as in the rap of Tupac Shakur, or a highly

Key Concept

Commercialization Music that has the potential to attract a wide audience undergoes a process in which individual expression is converted into a form that is designed to appeal to a specific demographic group. The commercialization process tends to move power from the artists to the recording executives and audiences.

Global Hip-Hop

With elements of art, dance, music, fashion, knowledge, and often politics, the hip-hop movement has spread to nearly all corners of the globe through migration and communications technologies. While commercial rap in the U.S. stresses commercialism, violence, sex, and hustler authenticity, hip-hop has taken many forms as other people have adapted it according to their own aesthetics and cultural values. However, hip-hop around the world has a common thread, for it often speaks to the experiences of socially and economically disadvantaged urban youth.

As with many forms of music, hip-hop is a rebellion against social conditions, and some societies consider it a threat to order. For example, in the 1990s, Tanzanian youths began to hear rap music on new, independent radio stations. Prior to this time, the socialist government had exercised censorship over media, but had begun to liberalize its economic and social policies, allowing greater access to foreign influences. Tanzanian youths, especially in the city of Dar es Salaam, saw rap as a means for expressing dissatisfaction with severe unemployment, governmental corruption, and poor education. However, many older people saw the emergence of hip-hop culture as a dangerous force that would turn young people into dropouts and criminals. Rappers were labeled *wahuni*, meaning hooligans, while their defenders argued that hip-hop is socially empowering.

Other societies have embraced and supported hip-hop as an important means of cultural expression. In Cuba, rap first gained hold in black, working class urban areas in the 1980s. At parties, Afro-Cuban youths listened to Miami radio and circulated cassettes from the United States. An annual rap festival, started in 1995, brought U.S. rappers like Common Sense and Mos Def, to Cuba, and Afro-Cubans began to produce their own music to protest racism. With increased popularity, Cuban rap attracted funding from the U.S. recording industry and split into a more commercial form that incorporated popular Latin sounds like salsa, and an "underground" form that saw itself as maintaining the original influence. Interested in gaining popular support, the Cuban government began finding and promoting rap through its Ministry of Culture, and praised its message of social justice. However, some critics feel that the government's appropriation of rap has damaged the creative and political autonomy of artists.

From Vietnamese rappers in Toronto to Maori rappers in New Zealand, hip-hop has provided a means to speak about racism, poverty, and alienation, to assert cultural identity, and to connect with others around the world. However, in each community, hip-hop has intersected with particular social circumstances that have given it new ideas, new purposes, and new languages.

Sources: Alex Perullo, "Hooligans and Heroes: Youth Identity and Hip-Hop in Dar es Salaam, Tanzania," *Africa Today* 51 (2005): 74–102; Sujatha Fernandes, "Fear of a Black Nation: Local Rappers, Transnational Crossings, and State Power in Contemporary Cuba," *Anthropological Quarterly* 76 (2003): 575–608.

---

processed product as in the music of the Backstreet Boys. Although many people regard pop music that incorporates an individual's vision as more sincere than processed music, for recording companies, the music of individuals is risky. It is difficult to predict just whose music will have immediate popularity and whose will gain stature over the long term. To reduce risk and retain power, recording companies often look for the short-term profits of processed music. This was the approach of Tin Pan Alley, and it has been the approach of many recording companies since then.

> **Key Concept**
>
> **Music as a forum for rebellion** Popular music has often served younger generations as a way to express and encourage rebellion against existing social rules and norms. Music helps express the emotions people feel about their lives.

Social Meaning: Music and Rebellion

Music—particularly music as a form for mass media—has served each generation as a *forum for rebellion* against the status quo. As rock spread into a variety of subgroups defined by varying ethnic backgrounds, cultures, and classes, its breakthroughs and barriers in the recording industry represented cultural tension, not merely a change in musical form.

As each generation matures, its members see the world with a new perspective and with new values. The lyrics and music written by artists who are members of the new generation often express these values, which inevitably conflict with values held by their parents. When Bob Dylan wrote "The Times They Are A-Changin'" in 1963, he told parents to either help change society or get out of the way of young people who wanted to make the changes. Dylan's words were adopted by many baby boomers as an expression of their discontent with what they saw as an unjust and valueless society. Three decades later feelings of alienation among the children of baby boomers found expression in the rebellious lyrics of grunge and rap.

Sometimes the rebellion in music expresses itself through lyrics; other times the music itself is rebellious, as in the syncopated beat that made early rock 'n' roll different. Often the music represents the results of social change. The same generation that embraced the rebellion in folk music associated with Dylan accepted the blues of Ray Charles, which led to soul music and to the Motown sound from Detroit. The Supremes, Aretha Franklin, Four Tops, Temptations, Stevie Wonder, and Smokey Robinson and the Miracles sold millions of records to young white people whose parents would have condemned the music as "race music" just a generation before. The times did change.

The rock 'n' roll musical rebellion of the 1950s affected Europe as well as the United States. Young British rock 'n' rollers listened to American music on Radio Luxembourg and cheered when Buddy Holly and the Everly Brothers toured Britain during the late 1950s. The Beatles brought British rock to the United States and became the best-selling musical group in history. Hard rock, pop, and psychedelic rock boomed during the 1960s. Bands such as the Grateful Dead and Jefferson Airplane carried the rebellious hippie culture of the San Francisco Bay area to the rest of the United States.

Rock splintered during the 1970s and 1980s as major recording companies increasingly commercialized popular music and artists reacted to that commercialization. Taking its name from the discotheque (dance club), disco music had a relatively short life but made a big splash on television and in the movies. Disco, sung by groups such as the Bee Gees, was based on a heavy beat that was easy to dance to. It lacked the soul of other types of rock and, like Tin Pan Alley music, became crassly commercial.

As a reaction to this commercialization, rock returned to its rhythm and blues and country roots during the mid-1970s led by Bruce Springsteen and the E Street Band. Springsteen initially set his socially critical lyrics to a hard-driving beat that was reinforced by the saxophone of Clarence Clemons. A VH-1 television documentary about him proclaimed that Springsteen killed disco. By the 1990s, Springsteen was singing personal songs that resembled the sounds found in the Great Depression music of Woody Guthrie.

Rap is a popular creative form for artists around the world. Israeli rapper Subliminal has incited international controversy over his Zionist lyrics.

The Supremes attracted black and white audiences who rebelled against the previous generation by listening to "crossover" Motown soul music.

During the late 1970s, punk rock also emerged as a reaction to the commercial success of rock. Groups such as the Sex Pistols and the Ramones played angry, nihilistic music that projected little hope for the future. A somewhat milder form of rebellion against traditional rock came in the form of new wave groups such as the Talking Heads.

A second form, heavy metal, evolved from the acid and hard rock of the late 1960s. Led Zeppelin and Queen began the movement, and other groups such as Van Halen, Judas Priest, and Def Leppard carried it through the 1980s. Heavy metal underwent a resurgence in 1994 with Megadeth, Pantera, and several other groups, but it never regained the popularity of the earlier period.

Grunge and hip-hop carried the punk tradition into the 1990s. Grunge, led by groups such as Nirvana, originated in the northwest United States and projects images of a painful, materialistic, and uncaring world created by the earlier rock generations. The success of grunge is a contradiction because of grunge musicians' disdain for materialism. One of grunge's leaders, Kurt Cobain of Nirvana, killed himself in April 1994, becoming, at least for some, a cult figure and martyr.

Although grunge appealed primarily to white, young people, hip-hop music emerged from the African-American tradition. Hip-hop developed in the South Bronx in New York City during the late 1970s and formed the backdrop for 1980s rap music. DJs such as South Bronx's Lovebug Starski and Grandmaster Flash experimented with turntables as musical instruments, deftly stitching together pieces of different songs, which tended to have a heavy beat. Some DJs would rap while the music played. The first rap single, "Rapper's Delight," was released in 1979 by Sugarhill Gang. Rap and hip-hop have their roots in African call-and-response music and, more recently, the Watts poets in 1960s Los Angeles, Bo Diddley, and Cab Calloway.[10]

As rap moved into the 1990s, it diversified and attracted political attention. Some rappers, such as M.C. Hammer, had a softer sound, whereas gangsta' rap, with its emphasis on harsh ghetto conditions, had a violent edge. Gangsta' rap came under fire from Congress because of its emphasis on violence and its demeaning attitude toward women. Today, the beat and lyrical patterns of rap have become a strong element of the music industry. White young people listen to rap, and some, such as Eminem, perform it.

Other Forms of Popular Music

Rock and rap have come to dominate the popular music scene in the United States, but that domination is far from complete. Country in its many forms is next in popularity to rock. Traditional country music, such as that played at the Grand Ole Opry during the 1940s and 1950s, flourished until the mid-1970s, when Willie Nelson, a songwriter who had enjoyed limited success as a singer in Nashville, led a revisionist movement. His simple-sounding lyrics in songs such as "Crazy" evoked powerful emotions and memories of Hank Williams's songs of the 1940s and 1950s. Nelson, Waylon Jennings, Jerry Jeff Walker, and Kris Kristofferson incorporated rock, western swing, and blues in their songs and helped to reshape country music.

Traditional country music experienced a revival during the 1990s with artists such as Garth Brooks, Reba McEntire, and LeAnn Rimes. Brooks ranks second only to the Beatles in career record sales. In 1999, Shania Twain and the Dixie Chicks emerged as successful country artists and **crossover artists.** More recently, artists such as Toby Keith, Faith Hill, Deana Carter, and Lucinda Williams demonstrate the wide range of music that falls under the umbrella of country.

Jazz, too, continues to change. The bop of the 1940s and 1950s gave way to three types of jazz in the 1950s and 1960s: cool, hard bop, and free jazz. Cool jazz had an

crossover artist

A top-selling musical artist in more than one music segment. Country and rhythm and blues often cross over with Top 40 music.

intellectual quality, with sophisticated arrangements. Hard bop combined bop jazz with old jazz forms from New Orleans. Free jazz dropped the rhythm and tune of jazz and explored personal, impromptu music.[11] Since the 1960s, jazz also has incorporated rock elements. This fusion music continues today as jazz begins to merge with hip-hop and rap music.

A fusion of African, European, and indigenous musical forms, Latin music arrived with Puerto Rican and Cuban immigrants to New York in the 1930s. In contact with jazz and other musical styles, it became the mambo, the salsa, and the cha cha. The modern salsa, which combined the mambo with a funky backbeat, emerged in New York in the early 1960s, and became enormously popular. By the 1990s, Latin music had become an important segment of the market, reaching 5 percent of sales by 1999, fueled by stars like Ricky Martin, Christina Aguilera, and Enrique Iglesias.[12]

Latin beats further merged with rap and techno to create new fusions like salsa rap and techno merengue. Reggaetón combines reggae with Caribbean dancehall music and has been popularized by major stars like Daddy Yankee and Luny Tunes. The genre has become so popular that it inspired Universal Music to form a record label devoted to Hurban (Hispanic-urban) music.[13] With the growth of the Latino market for all media forms, many companies, from Apple to Wal-Mart, have begun to cash in on Latin music.

Colombian singer Shakira has won two Grammies and represents the ability of Latin American artists to crossover into a North American market for popular music.

Elite Music

Music for elite audiences, often referred to as classical music, has always had difficulty acquiring popular support and financing in the United States. This held true in the 1990s, but classical music still survives as a segment of the music and recording industry. In the 1990s, the sales of classical music recordings and the number of classical music radio stations continued to decline. The percentage of all recording sales for classical music dropped from 3.5 in 1999 to 2.4 in 2005.[14]

Declining support from the National Endowment for the Arts, labor disputes among orchestras, an aging of the audiences, and the closing of some prominent civic orchestras in cities such as Sacramento and San Diego indicate difficult times ahead for elite music.[15] The major record labels carry few classical selections, and most classical music releases are on independent labels like Naxos.

However, the Internet may be creating a more robust market for classical music, with classical downloads from Apple's iTunes accounting for 12 percent of its total sales in 2006. Orchestras have started posting their concerts for sale on iTunes and their own websites. In 2006, New York's Metropolitan Opera began streaming live productions over the web, and Opera America now delivers music appreciation courses online. Efforts to reach younger audiences also include more concert offerings of early baroque and Renaissance compositions, and music by innovative composers such as Gyorgy Ligeti, who wrote the score for the film, *2001: A Space Odyssey.*[16]

THE RECORDING INDUSTRY

The recording industry provides artists with the means to achieve mass distribution. It acts as a gatekeeper, searching for talent that it finds worthy of financing and promotion. Record companies handle the recording, mass production, and packaging of recordings and their distribution to retailers. They also manage publicity, from cover art for albums to tours for their performers, and legal aspects, such as contracts, licensing, and copyrights. However, the recording industry faces serious challenges from digital forms of creation and distribution that are now available to musicians at low cost. Once again, the industry must adapt to new technologies.

The precursor to recording technology was the printing press. During the 1880s, entrepreneurs cranked out sheet music to sell to budding pianists and singers. Some songs sold more than a million copies, and in 1910 two billion copies of sheet music were sold.

The phonograph hit the sheet music industry hard. By 1877, Edison had developed a machine that could record on a tinfoil cylinder, but it was not until the 1890s that Emile Berliner developed a way to engrave a zinc disk and mass produce copies of records. He joined forces with Columbia Phonograph, a company that developed a method of creating disks with wax in the early 1900s. The modern recording industry was born.

The famous opera singer Enrico Caruso became the first recording star to earn big royalties in the industry. He began recording records in 1901 and accumulated more than $2 million in royalties between 1904 and his death in 1921.

The recording industry boomed between 1910 and 1920. Industry sales reached $158 million in 1919, but the banking depression killed the boom. The Great Depression of the 1930s also caused low record sales. After World War I, radio promised to revive the industry, but the worldwide depression of the 1930s stunted its growth. In 1927, 104 million records were sold; in 1932 the figure dropped to 6 million. The economic recovery and improving technology during the 1930s and 1940s brought the recording industry back to prosperity.

Phonographs and Records

After World War II, the recording industry experienced a period of rapidly improving technology. Within a thirty-year period, companies moved from the 78 rpm record to 33⅓ rpm LPs (long-playing records) and 45s—the inexpensive "singles" that music-loving young people collected. Like many industries, the recording industry encountered **competing technologies.** The first records played at 78 revolutions per minute (rpm), and we get the term *album* from those days, when a long work or collection of songs consisted of several 78 rpm records packaged in a cardboard case that resembled a photo album. In 1947, Columbia developed the long-playing record that, at 33⅓ rpm, could play for longer than an hour. The next year RCA introduced the 45 rpm record, which played for only a few minutes, about as long as the old 78 rpm records. The 45 had one song per side and required an adapter to play on most record players, but RCA wanted to recoup its investment. The company pushed ahead in the battle of the speeds.

> ### Key Concept
>
> **Competing technologies** The 1950s saw an interruption in the steady advance (from zinc to wax to shellac to plastic disks) that major recording companies had developed in marketable audio technology. When an explosion of new technology confused buyers with three competing turntable speeds and two record disk sizes, the major recording companies decided on a standard (33⅓ rpm) disk to regain the market. The smaller (45 rpm) record remained as a secondary format until the 1980s.

With so many types of records, the public was confused, and sales dropped dramatically until 1950. Columbia and RCA called a truce, and machines were manufactured that could play both 45s and LPs. The 78s disappeared almost immediately, and the 45s slowly gave way to the LPs, which could hold many more songs, as the most popular record format.

Audiotape and Digital Technology

Early radio popularized listening to performed music, and inventors searched for better ways to preserve musical performances. Initial efforts to record on wire were scratchy and unreliable. During World War II, the Germans developed magnetic tape-recording technology. Some Americans smuggled those machines to the United States,

The Music Genome Project

The Music Genome Project was launched in 2000 by a group of technicians and musicians interested in using computers to classify music by its attributes. By meticulously listening to thousands of songs and noting what they heard, the music analysts for the group identified some four-hundred attributes, which they called the "genes" of music. These include such elements as rhythm and tempo, vocal harmony and improvisation, major key tonality, and the presence of various instruments from mandolins to synthesizers. Through computer algorithms, songs could then be compared according to their common attributes, their "DNA."

After several years of development, the group launched a website, Pandora.com, that allows users to plug in a song they like and generate a radio station comprising similar music from a database of 400,000 songs. For example, if a user types in the band Coldplay, Pandora will stream songs by Shinedown and the lesser known Lola Ray because of similar vocals and electric instrumentation. During play, listeners can vote a song up or down so that the list becomes more personalized according to their preferences. Up to one hundred radio stations can be created per listener.

Many of the songs provided by Pandora are from independent and unsigned bands that have an opportunity to reach listeners who have an affinity for their music type. One of the goals of Pandora's founders was to provide a launching platform for indie bands, which are well represented in playlists. Anyone can submit music to Pandora; however, a screening process exists, and about half the songs, even by mainstream recording artists, are never entered into the database. In 2006, Pandora's database was weighted in favor of North American bands, and did not yet include classical or world music.

The company formed out of the Music Genome Project, Pandora Media, makes its money from subscriptions and advertising, including user click-throughs to iTunes and Amazon.com. However, it has resisted a "pay for play" system that would favor the recording industry. Pandora's ethos, which favors a more democratic creative expression and user involvement, reflects a trend to find new entertainment business models that take advantage of the Internet's eclecticism, interactivity, and information-gathering capabilities.

Source: Brad Fuller, "Inside Pandora: Web Radio that Listens to You," *O'Reilly Digital Media,* August 17, 2006, digitalmedia.oreilly.com/pub/a/oreilly/digitalmedia/2006/08/17/inside-pandora-web-radio.html?page=1.

---

and U.S. engineers improved on them. In 1946, Bing Crosby—who wanted to have more time for his golf game—was the first to tape-record his radio show, proving that a star could be successful without performing live.

During the late 1940s, the Minnesota Mining & Manufacturing Company (3M) perfected plastic recording tape, and Ampex developed reliable reel-to-reel tape recorders. However, the recorders and tape players remained expensive and cumbersome. In the 1970s, reel-to-reel recorders gave way to portable cassette players for personal use, and their popularity skyrocketed after Sony introduced the Walkman in 1979. Portability, as well as quality, was now a characteristic of tape machines.

Despite the increased use of magnetic tape, entrepreneurs continued to improve record quality as well. High fidelity, a side benefit of wartime English sonar technology, could pick up a wider range of tones; it was followed by stereo records, which were introduced in 1958.

Records, cassette tapes, and **8-track tapes** dominated the market during the 1970s, but in the mid-1980s they lost ground quickly to the compact disc, with its almost flawless reproduction quality. Sales of CDs soared from $17.2 million in 1983 to $930 million in 1986.

The introduction of the CD had two major consequences. It introduced a configuration that easily interfaced with computers, and it inflated the market as consumers replaced older formats. Prerecorded cassettes almost entirely disappeared by 2003, and vinyl records have mostly faded out, but remain popular among audiophiles, who prefer their sound.

8-track tape

A plastic cartridge that holds a continuous recording tape. Invented primarily for automobile play during the 1960s, its eight tracks allowed high-quality stereo reproduction in an easy-to-handle cartridge.

Table 8.1	How Music Fans Are Buying Music (Units sold in millions, United States)	
Configuration	**1999**	**2005**
Vinyl album	2.0	1.0
Cassette	123.6	2.5
CD	938.9	705.4
Music video	19.8	33.8
Download album	0	13.6
Download single	0	366.9
Mobile	0	170.0

Source: Recording Industry Association of America, *2005 Year End Statistics*, riaa.com/news/newsletter/pdf/2005yrEndStats.pdf.

The CD, in turn, has begun dying out with the development and spread of MP3 (MPEG-1 Audio Layer 3) technology. In October 2006, Alain Levy, the chairman of EMI's record division, responded to rapidly declining CD sales, declaring, "The CD, as it is right now, is dead."[17] The MP3 made it nearly effortless to upload and download music from a computer or other portable digital device. With the introduction of MP3 players, especially the iPod, and the expanded music capacity of the cell phone, MP3 downloads grew rapidly, with global digital music revenues for record companies reaching $1.1 billion in 2005 (see Table 8.1). Forty percent of those were from downloads to mobiles.[18] Overall, however, the recording industry was in dramatic decline, and in the same year, music fans downloaded 20 billion songs illegally through peer-to-peer file sharing, far outpacing legal downloads. Therefore, with little control over the technology, the record industry is struggling to find ways to transform music-loving file sharers into paying customers. Digital technologies, like social networking sites, are also making it possible for artists to connect with their fan bases without an intermediary, and offer their songs for direct sale. The consequences of these developments on the music industry are still unfolding.

The iPod and other portable MP3 players have revolutionized the way people buy and listen to music.

TODAY'S MARKET STRUCTURE

After a period of expansion with the introduction of the CD, the recording industry revenues began to decline in the early twenty-first century, facing competition from new technologies that allowed listeners to share music easily. Worth $14.5 billion in 1999, revenues had dropped to $12.2 billion in 2005.[19] However, music sales statistics do not account for the importance of music in cultural life or in relation to other media, such as television, radio, and film. U.S. sales of musical instruments, especially recording software, portable and digital keyboards, drums, and fretted instruments like guitars, have been growing, demonstrating the interest people have in creating music.[20]

Of the three media goals of entertainment, information, and persuasion, the primary one in the recording industry is entertainment. Although music often can aim to inform and persuade, as occurred with the folk songs of the Great Depression, the protest music of the 1960s, and rap of the 1980s, the recording industry's commercial nature causes most recorded music to aim at entertaining listeners.

The Record Labels

In 2006, the world recording industry was dominated by five **major** recording companies: Universal Music Group, Warner Music Group, Sony Music, BMG, and EMI. These companies are multinational companies, and reveal the global nature of the industry. Universal is based in France, Warner in Canada, Sony in Japan, BMG in Germany, and EMI in the United Kingdom. A merger between Sony Music and BMG had been initially approved by the European Union in 2004, but that decision was overturned in court in 2006, forcing the two companies to resubmit their request.[21] The merger would give the new music company 71 percent of the world market. In 2006, EMI and Warner Music were also discussing a merger that would further reduce the number of majors. Critics argue that this consolidation will give companies too much control over pricing and drive out independent labels with cheaper offerings.

Independents, often called "indies," account for about 25 percent of the world market.[22] These production companies have often taken risks on new talent when the majors behaved much more conservatively. For example, grunge might have remained a local fad in Seattle if Subpop Records had not offered recording contracts to Soundgarden and Nirvana. Some independents have a relationship with the major labels and sell music through them. Some hope to become important enough to be bought by the majors.

Artists may want to gain the attention of the majors by using independents as a stepping stone to bigger contracts. However, when artists move from the independent labels that have nurtured them, their music may change. For example, rap music was transformed when it was picked up by major labels. While rap artists on independent labels made statements against the mainstream music industry and emphasized local surroundings, commercial rap emphasized the artist's quest for material success, creating the image of the hustler.[23]

Historically, the independents have provided a chance for innovative music to reach listeners, but an even greater opportunity lies in digital offerings which can be provided directly by the artists. A majority of musicians in the United States use the Internet to find ideas and collaborate, and to promote and sell their music.[24] On sites like PureVolume .com and MySpace, bands can attract millions of listeners, who then may turn out for posted concert dates. In 2006, MySpace had user profiles for about three million unsigned bands and musicians, as well as commercial recording artists like Madonna, Gnarls Barkley, and John Mayer. With the expansion of services on social networking sites that allow musicians to sell their music directly to fans, the market has become further democratized. Many more kinds of music—from gothic ambient to Indian ragas—are available to niche audiences, often for free.

Key Concept

Majors versus independents With their deep pockets and their ability to mass-produce copies of recordings at low average costs, the five largest recording companies have the economic advantage over independent companies. The independents try to counter this by promoting relatively unknown musicians who are creating new and exciting kinds of music.

Combining rap with an interest in martial arts, Wu-Tang Clan developed a fan base with the release of their independent single, "Protect Ya Neck" before signing with a major label.

Because of the explosive growth of online music, the major recording companies are searching for new business models to take advantage of the profit potential in online sales. However, digital music has also meant that new major players like technology companies have entered the scene. In 2006, *Billboard* listed among the most influential entertainment companies to drive the music industry: Apple, Microsoft, Yahoo Music, MySpace, KDDI (a Japanese mobile operator), T-Mobile, Verizon Wireless, Real Networks, and YouTube.

Control of Content

In order to make profits, recording companies must maintain some control over the content they produce. Therefore, they uphold the principle of copyright. In copyright law, the production of music is divided into two separate streams. Composers and songwriters produce compositions that, when put in some concrete form such as musical notation, fall under one form of copyright protection. Artists often assign their copyrights to a music publisher that handles the licensing to recording companies and other entities, usually for a negotiated fee. Recording companies produce the mechanical sound recordings, called **phonorecords,** that fall under a second form of copyright protection. Phonorecords can be on any recording medium, from phonograph to MP3. A recording, like a CD, holds a copyright for the musical composition and a copyright for the sound recording. A musician that wants to use another musician's recorded composition for some purpose has to ask both the artist and the record company for permission, unless both copyrights are owned by the same entity.

Copyright protection of music has been debated since 1899, when commercial music began to be recorded on cylinders and platters. Since then, each successive introduction of recording technology, which has made copying easier, has led to further discussions of copyright law and, often, new legislation. In the United States, the trend has been to impose ever stricter copyright restrictions, including extension of the term of copyright and greater restrictions on use of content. Often, these laws are refined in court cases involving alleged copyright infringement.

The advent of digital recording on compact discs and subsequent computer file sharing raised alarms in the recording industry. The struggle between the record labels and digital audio tape (DAT) recorder manufacturers in the late 1980s led to the Audio Home Recording Act of 1992. In some ways, the act preserved prior rulings that allowed copies to be made for consumers' private use. But it also imposed a requirement that DAT recorders contain an anticopying system and that consumers be charged extra to include a royalty fee to the owners of sound recording copyrights.

The situation became more complicated with digital file sharing, since it involved service providers and other entities worldwide. The first case involving file sharing on the Internet arose in 1993, when 141 music publishers sued service provider CompuServe for allowing users to create MIDI versions of "Unchained Melody," used in the soundtrack for the movie, *Ghost.*[25] CompuServe agreed to pay licensing fees. However, the problem grew large enough to provoke the U.S. Congress into passing the controversial **Digital Millennium Copyright Act** in 1998. This act protected service providers from liability for copyright infringement as long as they took down any user-generated illegal material posted to their sites as soon as they were notified of its existence. The act also prohibits the disabling of copyright protection devices and requires that webcasters pay a flat licensing fee determined by the U.S. Copyright Office.

The case of Napster in 1999 challenged the ability of users to connect to each other's computers and share music through peer-to-peer file sharing. Napster allowed people to exchange copyrighted and noncopyrighted music through the Internet. The five majors responded to Napster with lawsuits for copyright violations. In 2001, a federal judge ruled that Napster had to filter music that was not in the public domain. As a result, Napster shut down in summer 2001 in hopes of returning as a company that sold music online. However, Napster declared bankruptcy when it was unable to

phonorecord

Mechanical sound recording that falls under copyright protection.

Digital Millennium Copyright Act

Act that protects service providers from liability for copyright infringement.

find financial backing for the change. Roxio Inc. bought the Napster name, web domain, and technology in November 2002 for $5.3 million.

Similar cases were brought against services like Kazaa, MusicCity, and Grokster, and in 2005, the U.S. Supreme Court ruled that peer-to-peer file sharing services could be held liable for copyright infringement. In the meantime, the record companies had begun suing individual file sharers, many of them college students. By November 2005, that number had reached over 15,000.[26] Critics argue that the recording industry exaggerates the impact of illegal file sharing on revenues, and that file sharers often buy the CDs of music they download, much as they would if they heard it on the radio.

Digital technologies also brought a greater capacity for sampling and remixing recorded music that has led to copyright issues. While for years the recording companies and music publishers made only sporadic attempts to curtail sampling, they eventually formed departments to hunt down copyright violators, even retroactively. In April 2006, Notorious B.I.G.'s 1994 album, *Ready to Die,* was pulled from the shelves for including a six-second sample from the Ohio Players' "Singing in the Morning." Critics of the crackdown on music sampling argue that these measures have stifled creative expression, especially in hip-hop music. A sampling license is expensive, averaging between $1,000 and $5,000, but sometimes reaching $25,000.[27]

AUDIENCE DEMAND IN RECORDING MARKETS

People demand music for entertainment and for affirmation of cultural values. Music can distract people from boring or difficult tasks. It also plays important **social roles,** fostering rebellion, blending forms to make new cultural statements, and promoting certain cultural norms through commercialization. It contributes to ceremonies and rituals that define social groups. National anthems praise and affirm the glory of a country. Weddings, funerals, graduations, and other life passages incorporate music as a basic element. Music gives generations of people an identity because the shared values expressed in music create feelings of commitment and membership and help to pass on the social heritage.

> **Key Concept**
>
> **Social roles of music** Music serves as an important part of cultural rituals, helps promote rebellion among youth, provides an identity for generations, and promotes cultural norms through commercialization.

Audiences exist for a variety of recorded musical forms, though public taste has often been shaped by offerings from the mainstream music industry. Dominant types of music are, in order of popularity: rock, rap/hip-hop, R&B/urban, country, pop, religious, classical, and jazz.[28] Small, but notable, audiences exist for oldies, new age, gothic, ethnic, big band, movie soundtracks, and Broadway show tunes.

Changes in music popularity can be sudden and dramatic. The rapid growth in the demand for rock 'n' roll during the 1950s caught many music companies off guard. In the mid-1980s, sales of rock music took 50 percent of the market, but had declined to 23.9 percent in 2004. On the other hand, rap grew from 6.7 percent in 1995 to 13.8 percent in 2002, dropping off slightly by 2004. Religious music followed a similar pattern, growing from 3.1 percent to 6.7 percent in 2001, and then falling off to 6.0 percent in 2004. These market ups and downs reflect a complicated mix of creative, economic, and social changes.

SUPPLYING THE AUDIENCE'S DEMAND

The recording industry meets audience demand by discovering artists, financing their creative output, and distributing and promoting their music. Through its relationship with other industries, the recording industry distributes its products in a variety of ways. Audiences hear live music in small venues and large concert halls, and recorded music through the Internet and the radio and while watching movies and television shows. Each of these venues is a different system with its own audiences, personnel,

A new era in the recording process began when the popular group the Beatles produced the breakthrough album *Sgt. Pepper's Lonely Hearts Club Band*. It featured layered sounds using high-tech blending techniques.

and ways of using music. For recording artists, the first stage of reaching an audience is the recording process.

The Recording Process

As an essential part of the production process, recording studios supply the demand for music by transferring an artist's musical creation to a fixed medium, such as an MP3 or CD, that can be mass produced and distributed. Once the music is in any fixed medium, it falls under copyright law.

Recording studios range from small private studios owned by individual artists to large profitmaking studios that provide either analog or digital recording. In the 1990s, the declining cost of recording technologies made it easier for musicians to set up their own home studios, causing some competition for commercial studies. Sometimes, in order to save money, musicians work out some elements of the recording process at home before going to a commercial studio, where hourly rates are steep. Rates at commercial studies range from $25–$300 per hour, and the time per song is usually 10–20 hours.

While the commercial process varies according to the type of music and the number of musicians involved, it follows these basic steps:

1. *Preproduction:* This stage involves budget planning, locating musicians, booking studio time, selecting and arranging songs, taking care of any copyright issues, and rehearsing.
2. *Tracking:* In the studio, after equipment is arranged, the backing tracks are recorded. These may include drum, bass, and rhythm guitar. Musicians may play to a scratch vocal that is later discarded.
3. *Overdubbing:* Vocals are recorded, corrections are made to the first tracks, and sweetener tracks, such as subtle keyboard effects, are added.
4. *Mixing:* The tracks are tuned for levels, balance, and equalization, and then added together and sequenced for the final mixdown on tape, CD, or hard disk.
5. *Mastering:* At a mastering studio, the recording is prepared for mass production. This may include sequencing songs, adding pauses, and making further corrections and adjustments to the sound before making the final master.

The amount of time involved in the **recording process** varies greatly with the type of recording and the artist involved. The Beatles' *Sgt. Pepper's Lonely Hearts Club Band* album required more than seven hundred hours in the recording studio because of the amount of overdubbing and multitrack recording used.[29] The result was an album that changed rock 'n' roll.

Financing

Financing in the recording industry takes many forms. People buy CDs and tapes, which is a direct source of income. Because recording production, distribution, and promotion are expensive, most recording titles that are released do not make a profit. So profit potential of blockbuster recordings is important.

A secondary source of **revenue comes from licensing** existing music. Someone who uses a copyrighted piece of music must pay the copyright holder. Copyright owners

Key Concept

Recording process The recording of music involves several steps of planning and assembling sections of taped sessions. They may be recorded directly all at one time, or multiple tracks may be recorded. In the editing and mixing process, complex studio equipment is used to merge the sections or the multiple tracks to make a single tape, which is then edited to produce the best possible mix of vocals and instrumentals that has the sound qualities the producer desires.

Key Concept

Revenue from licensing For recording companies and artists, the licensing of performing and recording rights is an important way to increase revenue beyond the uncertain profits from direct record sales. The copyright owner (usually a record company) collects revenue whenever a piece is performed or rerecorded or whenever a recording is played in a public setting.

receive revenue, known as royalties, under three conditions. Under *performing rights,* the copyright holder is paid every time a song is performed. *Mechanical rights* ensure that the copyright holder is paid when the song is recorded. *Public performance rights* require that the copyright holder be paid when an actual recording is played commercially.[30]

Rights are overseen by music licensing organizations such as the American Society of Composers, Authors, and Publishers (ASCAP) and Broadcast Music Incorporated (BMI) in the United States, the Performing Rights Society (PRS) in England, Gesellschaft für Musikalische Aufführungs (GEMA) in Germany, and the Société des Auteurs, Compositeurs et Éditeurs de Musique (SACEM) in France. The organizations act as agents for the publishers and composers of music whom they represent. The organizations collect fees and distribute money on the basis of formulas that incorporate several factors, such as the number of performances of a particular song and the writer's prestige and seniority.

Distribution

The two keys to a hit recording are ***recording promotion and distribution***—getting airplay on radio and television and obtaining adequate distribution of copies. Play time involves promotion, which is the attention-grabbing side of the industry. Distribution tends to be rather mundane in comparison, but it is no less important.

Distribution can take several forms. Recordings are sold in record stores such as CD Warehouse; in department and discount stores such as Wal-Mart; by mail clubs such as Columbia House; and over television, as in the ads for a singer's greatest hits or songs of a certain era. The last two forms often involve direct selling, which means that the production company handles the distribution without another company between it and the buyers. The last two forms involve at least one intermediate company.

Since the early 1970s, the five major recording companies have expanded their distribution branches. The branches sell directly to record stores and to rack jobbers. *Rack jobbers* handle sales of recordings in department and discount stores. They stock the CD and tape racks and split the sales money with the store. Other independent distributors also serve the industry by distributing independently produced recordings and even some recordings from major companies.

> **Key Concept**
>
> **Recording promotion and distribution** Companies traditionally promote a recording by making people aware of it through performances on radio and television. They distribute a recording by selling it directly to record stores or indirectly to discount and department stores. The latest electronic technology offers new opportunities for promotion and distribution. Many record stores provide listening stations that allow customers to sample records before buying them. The Internet offers sampling and downloading of music.

In the competition for distribution, the majors have three advantages. They can provide many copies of hit recordings; they can afford expensive national promotions; and they have strong financial backing.

Throughout the twentieth century, music was delivered to people either by radio or through some recording technology that uses a physical object. The move to digital technology at the end of the century is reshaping how people receive music. Satellite radio makes music available on dozens of channels no matter where the radio receiver is located. Fiber-optic cable provides dozens and potentially hundreds of music channels. But the most influential form of distribution has become the personal computer.

The rise of MP3 technology as a system for trading and selling music continues to reshape the industry.

Three basic models exist for making revenues from music downloads. The music can be offered for free, but accompanied by advertisements, such as banner ads or product placements. The music can be offered as part of a subscription service, where users pay a monthly or annual fee for unlimited downloads. Finally, the music can be offered as single tracks or albums, with users paying per download. Through software blocks, content providers usually limit the number of copies a user can download and share. However, because many music fans resent the limitations, providers also offer unprotected downloads for a higher fee.

Promotion

Sales of records or sheet music have always depended on making the largest number of people aware of the music's existence. When sheet music dominated the industry, vaudeville performers increased sales of a particular song by performing it. As radio attracted more listeners, radio airplay became essential to a record's reaching the charts. Today, performance tours supporting a new album and exposure on television, such as on a music video channel, are crucial in promoting recordings. Reaching and staying at the top of the national pop charts requires play time on MTV's *Total Request Live* and dozens of live performances throughout the United States and abroad. Despite the importance of video music promotion, the number of TV video music channels is limited and the time they spend showing music videos declined during the 1990s. So radio remains the most frequently used promotion tool. If a recording can get extensive airplay on radio stations, it has a chance of making the top-selling recordings list. The station format and the location are crucial considerations in promoting recordings on radio. Contemporary hit radio formats that run recordings from the Top 40 chart provide the best exposure. However, recording companies sometimes select stations with other formats for promotions because those stations better fit the recording. Stations in markets with a **cumulative weekly audience** of more than one million are vital for promotion. These markets, such as New York, Los Angeles, and Chicago, generate a high percentage of recording sales. Exposure in these markets can make or break a recording.

Promotion involves sending traditional **press releases** and **media kits** to reviewers and radio stations. However, the key link in recording promotions is the independent promoter, sometimes called a "plugger." Independent promoters are hired by recording companies to help increase record sales. They use a variety of techniques to promote recordings, including providing information to media about the artists and the recording, arranging personal appearances by artists, and helping with tours that promote new recordings. The crucial role of the independent promoter is getting a recording played on the radio. During the late 1980s, promoters became very powerful in either getting or stopping airplay. Without independent promoters, it is difficult for a recording to become a hit.

Key Concept

Payola in music promotion When record promoters pay DJs or program producers to play specific songs on a radio station or video channel to enhance the song's popularity they are engaging in payola. Investigated by Congress since the 1950s, the conspiracy between the recording and broadcasting industries is probably impossible to uproot, especially as combined ownership affects more sectors of the media and recording industries.

cumulative weekly audience

The total number of people who listen to radio during a given week in a given market.

press release

An announcement of some event, such as a recording release, sent to various news media outlets.

media kit

A collection of information about a particular event or person, such as a recording release. The kit can include text, photographs, recordings and videos.

Promotion's Influence on Music Because promotion significantly affects the sales of music, it also is a prime source of corruption. A recurring problem in the record industry has been the phenomenon of *payola*, or paying a programmer or disc jockey to play a specific song. In the 1950s, the situation became so critical that Congress held hearings that revealed an industry in which payola ruled. For example, 335 disc jockeys reportedly received $263,245 in "consultant" fees.[31] Stations offered deals that were thinly disguised payola plans. One station in Los Angeles offered a "test record plan," which cost $225 a week for eight plays a day, and a New York station had a deal of six plays a day for six weeks for $600.[32] As a result of the congressional hearings, the Federal Communications Act of 1934 was amended in 1960 to outlaw payola. Punishment is one year in jail with a maximum $10,000 fine. However, these hearings concentrated only on rock 'n' roll music—a controversial genre in the 1950s—and ignored payola in other areas of popular music. Furthermore, payola is difficult to monitor. Although it has been outlawed, independent promoters are still known to deliver money, gifts, or more tangible services to those in positions to get music on the radio.[33]

Video: A Powerful Promotional Tool In 1981, MTV began featuring short music videos on its twenty-four-hour channel, making them an important aesthetic form that appealed to youth culture in the United States. Before the 1980s, musicians had made films as creative expressions, such as the Beatles' *Yellow Submarine* and Frank Zappa's *200 Motels*. Television programs, such as Dick Clark's *American Bandstand*

and the *Ed Sullivan Show* offered musicians the opportunity to promote themselves. However, MTV changed the music industry by distributing videos widely through satellite and cable transmission. Record company executives were willing to invest substantially in videos such as Michael Jackson's *Thriller,* and licensed them to MTV for free.[34] Through MTV's reach into global markets, many people around the world were exposed to promotional music videos for artists like Madonna and Britney Spears. In the late 1980s, because of declining ratings, MTV shifted its programming to feature reality TV shows.

The music video was in a lull until the advent of other cable channels like Fuse and streaming video websites, which once again made music videos popular and gained the interest of record companies. On YouTube, user-generated videos like OK Go's *Treadmill Dance,* filmed and choreographed by the sister of one of the band members, gained wide viewership. In 2006, record companies like Universal and web companies like Google began working out business deals that would allow profits to be made from streaming music videos, either through advertising revenues or licensing fees. Major record labels also hoped that adding video content to CDs would help boost sales of what seems to be a fading technology.

TRENDS

The late 1990s and early 2000s have not been kind to the recording industry, which has begun to see a slump in sales. Various reasons have been given for the decline, including the industry's aging business models, the decline of traditional radio, the lack of diverse and interesting music, the high cost of the CD, and competition from other media. The record industry also blames piracy, both from bootlegged CDs and P2P file sharing, for cutting into its profits. In regard to file sharing, the claim has been disputed by many digital freedom advocates, and a few academic studies have shown mixed results. Some have found that digital file sharers are more likely to buy music, while others show a correlation between file sharing and a decline in music purchases, especially among college students and in households with children.[35]

Having for some time looked with distrust upon the digital world, the recording industry is in the process of shifting its energies to it. Chairman of EMI, Alain Levy, has called digital technologies "the bright future of our industry," explaining that customers will still want compelling, recognizable content that is screened by music companies.[36] That is a similar argument made by other media companies, who defend their roles as gatekeepers who can recognize quality. Nevertheless, the recording industry faces considerable challenges in shifting its business culture to accommodate changes in technology and culture.

Technology: The Celestial Jukebox

Record companies make very little money from direct sales of the recordings they produce unless they are very big hits like Justin Timberlake's "My Love" or Akon's and Eminem's "Smack That." Therefore, record companies search for other ways to make profits, such as the licensing and reissuing of older recordings. They are also seeking to make money from a single recording by presenting it across as many revenue-generating platforms as possible, such as videos and ringtones. Deals with technology companies like Google and phone companies like Skype are

Madonna's music is available in many media forms, from music videos to ring tones.

increasingly important. For example, in a deal between France Telecom and Warner Music, Madonna's single, "Hung Up," was released as a ringtone and an MP3 file in France weeks before the album came out.[37]

Writing about recent changes in the music industry, communications theorists Patrick Burkart and Tom McCourt have called this trend "the **Celestial Jukebox**," by which they mean "the various systems whereby any text, recording, or audiovisual artifact can be made available instantaneously via wired or wireless broadband channels to the Internet or home computers."[38] Others have linked the concept of a Celestial Jukebox to a specific device: an all-in-one portable, wired music and video player like the Apple iPhone. Such a device allows users to access their music of choice anytime, anywhere. However, Burkart and McCourt argue that corporate interests, such as technology companies and the major record labels, are creating and controlling the Jukebox in a way that is detrimental to users, blocking access and exploiting user information. For example, recording companies are looking to **customer-relationship management (CRM)** that involves digitally collecting information about users to make music recommendations. Such recommendations and customized playlists may create "a niche market of one" that robs music of its traditional social role of bringing fans together to share meaning and taste.

Technology: Digital Rights Management

Digital rights management (DRM) refers to technologies that control the use of digital files and force users to adhere to licensing agreements. For example, using a protective software code called FairPlay, iTunes allows only five computers to be authorized to play downloaded music and makes it difficult for songs purchased from other sites to play on the iPod.

Many users resent the problems posed by such incompatible systems, and they have been easily hacked. Within eight hours of the release of iTunes 7, hackers had learned how to remove its protective code.[39] Some consumer advocates object to DRM because it curtails the ability of consumers to make multiple copies, as they would from a CD or cassette tape. Others say that only the technology companies benefit from DRM, rather than record labels, musicians, or consumers. The recording industry argues that an effective DRM is an essential way to protect copyrighted content.

Culture: Remix and the Struggle over Ownership

The **mashup** is a musical form that stitches two or more recordings together to create a new one. Usually, vocals from one source are combined with music from another, often in parody. Examples include Lazy Tramp's "Let's Pole Dance," remixing David Bowie and the Beastie Boys, and Freelance Hellraiser's "Stroke of Genius," remixing Christine Aguilera and the Strokes. As music critic Sasha Frere-Jones writes, "One of the thrills of the mashup is identifying two well-known artists unwittingly complementing each other's strengths and limitations: bacchanalian rapper Missy Elliott combined with morose English rock band Joy Division, ecstatic Madonna working with furious Sex Pistols."[40] Digital technologies such as software programs and file sharing have made it easy to remix recording and make mashups, and many such offerings have been created on home computers. The mashup gained commercial legitimacy with the release of Jay-Z's and Linkin Park's *Collision Course,* which combined the music of the two artists and made number one on the *Billboard* 200 in early 2005.

California DJ Brian Burton, aka Danger Mouse, is often credited with propelling the mashup into public consciousness, not only because of his artistic innovation,

customer-relationship management

A system that allows consumers to customize musical offerings.

mashup

A remix of two or more recordings that creates a new one.

As new technologies develop, the music industry will continue to be threatened. However, so far, it has survived and adapted to changes in both content and packaging. Some of the questions to be answered include:

■ How will the trends mentioned in this chapter affect the recording industry during the next ten years?

■ What effect will struggles over copyright issues have on musicians?

■ To what extent is it possible for music companies to control music file sharing?

but because he spurred a massive protest against recording labels who censored his work. In late 2003, Danger Mouse created a skillful remix of the Beatles' *White Album* and Jay-Z's *Black Album,* called *The Grey Album,* and released it online and in a few local record stores. He received a cease and desist order from EMI, which owned the rights to the *White Album* sound recording. In response, a grassroots campaign began among activists who organized a day of protest, Grey Tuesday, when 170 websites offered the album online.[41] These activists and their service providers received cease-and-desist orders from EMI and SONY/ATV, which owns the rights to the Beatles' musical compositions. In the end, the companies backed down, and EMI gave Danger Mouse a record contract for a mashup. The *Grey Album* remains freely available online.

These struggles over creativity and ownership have continued in other instances. In late 2005, a noncommercial mashup tribute to Green Day, created by Party Ben and team9, was suppressed after the hosting website received a cease and desist order from Warner Records. The incident launched another Grey Tuesday–style protest. After recording a parody of James Blunt called "You're Pitiful," "Weird Al" Yankovic had to pull the song from his album, *Straight Outta Lynwood,* after receiving a complaint from Blunt's label, Atlantic Records. Blunt had already given Yankovic permission. Parody is problematic for copyright law since it significantly alters the original work enough to be considered a form in its own right and is considered fair use. The problem for courts lies in the difficulty of defining a true parody, and so parodists like Yankovic usually protect themselves by obtaining permission from the original creator.

As recording companies attempt to define the terms by which music is used and distributed, these cases have instigated political activism to defend what copyright expert Lawrence Lessig has described as **remix culture**: "the creativity of mixing other creativity."[42] While this debate extends to many creative forms, from video to software, music has been at the heart of the issue as various stakeholders negotiate the roles of profit and ownership in cultural expression.

remix culture

A global movement to promote the creation of new forms remixed from former creative recordings and other products.

SUMMARY

■ Music's primary purpose is to entertain people, but it also serves important social and personal functions.
■ Music binds social groups together by creating shared experiences and by serving as part of ceremonies and rituals.

■ American popular music evolved by blending music from African and European cultures.
■ Popular music depends heavily on the connection between music and young people's rebellion against existing social norms.

- As music has become commercialized, control of the music has moved from the artists to the recording companies.
- The first technology used by the music industry was the printing press to print sheet music during the 1800s.
- During the 1950s, two record formats battled for supremacy. The 33⅓ rpm long-playing format won over the smaller 45 rpm format, only to lose out to tapes and compact discs during the 1970s and 1980s.
- Today's recording industry remains highly concentrated in the United States and the world; only a few companies produce 70 to 80 percent of all recordings.
- Digital technologies have made it easier for musicians to record, distribute, and promote their own music.
- Copyrights allow the holder of the copyright to be paid for reproduction and performance of music.
- Distribution of recordings occurs through record stores, discount and department stores, television, the Internet, and mail-order clubs.

- Because of their size, the major recording companies have economic advantages in distributing and promoting recordings.
- Promotion plays a key role in selling recordings, making people aware of the music, and encouraging demand. It also creates conditions for corruption.
- Music video emerged during the 1980s as an important promotion tool. Recent developments in streaming video have made this promotional tool even more important.
- The recording industry is global in reach, but most of the recording production and sales organizations are located in Britain, France, Germany, Japan, and the United States.
- Music copyright protection falls into two categories: copyright of the musical composition and copyright of the sound recording.
- Efforts to impose strict copyright protections have led to protests from musicians and consumers.

NAVIGATING THE WEB Music

Music is a growing presence on the World Wide Web because of improved sound quality. Sites take a variety of forms, from those owned by recording companies to sites on which the music of independent artists can be sampled and their recordings bought. The following sites are information sites for music and the recording industries and sites where music can be downloaded.

Downhill Battle
downhillbattle.org
Downhill Battle is a nonprofit organization that supports creative expression, collective licensing, and free culture, and seeks to overturn what it considers the monopoly of the major recording companies.

MP3
mp3.com
The MP3 homepage for leading technology for downloading music on the web also contains music for downloading and news about the music industry.

MTV
mtv.com
The oldest and largest music network provides access to commercial music videos. It has a number of companion sites for its worldwide networks, including MTV-Asia (mtvasia.com) and MTV Networks Europe (mtvne.com).

Pandora
pandora.com
Home of the Music Genome Project, Pandora is an innovative webcasting site that creates customized radio stations.

Rock and Roll Hall of Fame
rockhall.com
This is the official web site of the Rock and Roll Hall of Fame located in Cleveland, Ohio. It includes information about important musicians in the development of rock 'n' roll, as well as information about events occurring at the Hall of Fame.

VH-1
vh1.com
This is the official web site for the VH-1 music channel. It includes music news, tour information, links, the channel schedule, and biographical information about popular musicians.

QUESTIONS FOR REVIEW

1. How did African-American music first appear in the United States?
2. What are the steps in the recording process?
3. How has the blending of different types of music affected the development of popular music, and why has it created controversy?
4. What three elements have guided the development of popular music in the United States?
5. List several ways in which the recording industry is financed.
6. How do converging technologies affect the creation and distribution of music?

ISSUES TO THINK ABOUT

1. Throughout history, alternative popular music forms such as punk, rap, and grunge have either been adopted by the mainstream or faded as a music form. Why does this happen, and what are the implications for a young musical artist?
2. How does the power of the major labels affect music content?
3. How do promotional needs and efforts shape the music industry?
4. How would you describe hip-hop as a cultural force?
5. In what way do you foresee the Internet and other online services affecting the future of music?

SUGGESTED READINGS

Baskerville, David. *Music Business Handbook and Career Guide* (Thousand Oaks, CA: Sage, 2006).

Burkart, Patrick, and Tom McCourt. *Digital Music Wars: Ownership and Control of the Celestial Jukebox* (Oxford: Rowman & Littlefield, 2006).

Campbell, Michael. *And the Beat Goes On: An Introduction to Popular Music in America, 1840 to Today* (New York: Schirmer Books, 1996).

Chanan, Michael. *Repeated Takes: A Short History of Recording and Its Effect on Music* (New York: Verso, 1995).

Hamm, Charles. *Putting Popular Music in Its Place* (Cambridge, England: Cambridge University Press, 1995).

Hull, Geoffrey P. *The Recording Industry* (New York: Routledge, 2004).

Unterberger, Richie. *Unknown Legends of Rock 'n' Roll* (San Francisco: Miller Freeman Books, 1998).

9

Computers and the Internet

The popular social network Facebook was founded in 2004 by Mark Zuckerberg, a student at Harvard. Originally a local campus network, its founders perceived it as a physical place, like "the mall or lounging on the quad," where people could hang out. As it added more associated schools and workplaces, Facebook grew within two years to 9.5 million users in the United States, mostly college students. In December 2005, based on its own survey, Facebook estimated that 85 percent of students at supported schools had accounts. Most of them logged in at least once a day to communicate with friends in their network and organize campaigns and events.[1]

As Facebook grew and changed, it met with controversies about privacy, safety, and authenticity that are familiar to observers of cyberlife. The biggest controversy involved the introduction of "news feeds," which sent notice of any changes in a user's profile—including information about romantic relationships and uploaded files—to all the friends on the user's list. Hundreds of thousands of Facebook users protested the feeds because too much of their information was exposed, and some users felt more vulnerable to stalking. Facebook responded by adding more privacy features. However, Facebook users were also finding that their information was under surveillance from college administrators and law enforcement, including the U.S. Secret Service. Some students were expelled, questioned, and prosecuted for photos, remarks, and other damaging information on their sites.

KEY CONCEPTS

- Information Society
- Information-Based Economies
- Digital Divide
- Privacy and Anonymity
- Regulation in the Information Age
- e-Commerce
- Web 2.0
- Nomadic Computing
- Pervasive Computing

Social networking sites like Facebook have become important communities in which young people have emotional investments and feel a personal claim to virtual spaces. These sites have grown rapidly as young people seek entertainment, knowledge, meaning, identity, and friendship online. Digital media researcher Danah Boyd explains that social networks give young people a sense of community and access: "Youth are trying to map out a public youth territory for themselves, removed from adult culture. They are doing so online because their mobility and control over physical space is heavily curtailed and monitored."[2] Marketers, teachers, social scientists, parents, and politicians have weighed in on the impacts of social software, sometimes warning of the dire consequences of cyberstalkers and Internet addictions, sometimes extolling the potential shifts of political and economic power in a fading of old media. The rules of these social environments are still being debated, and reflect ongoing concerns about democratic community, freedom of access, privacy, safety, and control over technology. These concerns are common to most conversations about the role of networked computers in society.

As digital technologies evolve, they offer new possibilities and problems that affect economic, social, and political life.

■ How many people in the world will have computers in the future? To what extent will socioeconomic levels and governmental control influence who has access and who does not? What will this mean for global cultures, economics, and politics?

■ The Internet has become increasingly commercialized and politicized. Who should have control over the World Wide Web? To what extent should the web be a creative, intellectual commons? What aspects of the web should not be open to commercialization?

■ How are other media forms like radio and television changing as they go online? What new forms of mass media and journalism are emerging?

■ As we express ourselves online, will we be able to preserve privacy, maintain security, and preserve the tenets of free speech? What other social and psychological affects will online life have, especially on children?

Many media critics and historians say that networked computers are as important as the printing press in revolutionizing human communications. In homes and workplaces across the world, networked computers are social technologies that people use to converse, provide feedback, and form and modify their relationships with others. From e-mail to social networking sites like Facebook to digital devices like cell phones, digital communications are shifting the media landscape so that many more people are more actively involved in its creation. All other media, including movies, newspapers, books, radio, and television, are being profoundly affected by this change, so that thinking of these as separate media is more and more difficult. In countries where digital technology is prevalent, a networked generation has grown up with a very different experience of mass media than most of their elders.

Software developer Ray Ozzie writes that while digital technologies will not replace physical human contact, they "have the potential to have significant, fundamental impact on the types of relationships we maintain, on where we live and work, on when and how we are educated, on how we entertain ourselves and spend our leisure time, on our politics, and on how we conceive of time."[3] In their report, "We Media," Shayne Bowman and Chris Willis explain that a new media ecosystem is evolving. Its central component

Computers in Your Life

Tools and Toys

Computers and their linked devices, such as MP3 players and digital cameras, have become indispensable for many students. How do you use computers in your life? What kind of work do you do on computers? In what ways do you use them for entertainment and social contact? How much of your life is spent online? As you read through this chapter, think of ways in which societies have become dependent on computers and what our networked world might look like in the future.

How Do You Use Computers?	How Many Hours Per Week?
Doing school assignments	
Sharing music, photos, and videos	
Playing video games	
Watching online television	
Listening to online radio	
e-mailing teachers, family, and friends	
Making friends or dating	
Blogging	

is the web, the "greatest publishing system ever known," formed "without central planning and without government regulation, censor or sanction—an emergent, bottom-up process."[4] Generated by many participants worldwide, this process has shifted power away from traditional media, with its gate-keeping and agenda-setting functions and its emphasis on profitability. The digital revolution, including media convergence, has affected almost every process of mass communication—gathering, organizing, presenting, and disseminating information.

Whereas people once logged onto computers in offices and homes, they are now carrying digital technologies everywhere, making them an important part of their everyday lives. While many people may continue to buy a daily newspaper and watch primetime television in their living rooms, they have other options available to them. A vast library of information, including text, audio, and video, is available twenty-four hours a day, seven days a week to continually connected users, who contribute to the mix by uploading their own text, audio, and video.

As early as 1964, Marshall McLuhan described the spread of electronic technologies, with their power to transmit information instantaneously, as creating a "global village" where people were bound together and experienced the world in a new way. The proliferation of computers, broadband, and wireless connections has continued the trend, allowing greater global connectivity and transmission of content like brand advertising, music, and movies. However, diffusion and access are uneven, with some parts of the world lagging far behind. The consequences of the digital revolution for governments, media corporations, social institutions, and citizens and consumers are diverse and uneven, as they were at the introduction of the printing press. But indisputably, the global spread of networked computers is fundamentally changing the landscape of mass communications.

COMPUTERS IN AMERICAN LIFE

Computers have profoundly influenced our society by simplifying complex tasks and by informing and entertaining us in new ways. However, the computer has also complicated simple tasks—have you tried typing a form on a computer? Every day we encounter computing technology, just as we encounter other forms of mass media. A computer assists us each time we make a phone call, read a newspaper, watch television, listen to the radio, program our DVD players, get cash from a bank's automated teller, have our purchases scanned at the checkout counter, reserve an airplane seat, or pay with a credit card. In the coming decades, we will use computers even more for information and entertainment. The computer is the heart of interactive television, movies on demand, and individualized news delivery. An information or media center in a custom-built home today may well control not only temperature, lights, and appliances, but also the information that household receives and sends. These are representative of our *information society.*

Some historians date the computer to the ancient abacus, a handheld counting device, and mechanical devices that were in use by 1900 for tabulating large amounts of data. However, the military demands of World War II produced the first electronic computers. The breakthrough can be attributed to a variety of people. John Vincent Atanasoff, an Iowa State University professor, and an electrical engineering student, Clifford E. Berry, were in the process of constructing a computer when the war began. A huge computer, the Colossus, helped the British break German military codes, and Harvard mathematician Howard Aiken developed a computer to calculate artillery ballistics. When U.S. leaders saw the possibilities for defense and space applications of computer technology, they channeled government money to finance computer research and development.

In the landmark 1945 article "As We May Think" in the *Atlantic Monthly,* MIT researcher Vannevar Bush suggested that a machine, a "memex," could extend the powers of human memory and association and solve the problem of organizing and accessing information. "A memex," Bush wrote, "is a device in which an individual stores all his books, records, and communications, and which is mechanized so that

The enormous 1955 Remington Rand Univac computer had less processing power than a Pentium desktop computer used today.

it may be consulted with exceeding speed and flexibility. It is an enlarged intimate supplement to his memory."[5] Bush envisioned the machine as a desktop device with a keyboard; storage would be on microfilm, and dry photography would be used for input.

Doug Engelbart read Bush's article and recognized the problem he described but realized that the computer, not a microfilm machine, was the answer. The computer could manipulate symbols and allow individuals to compare data.[6] Engelbart went on to direct laboratory research at the Stanford Research Institute and was active through the 1970s in developing computer applications. Engelbart's group at Stanford initiated the field of computer-supported cooperative work and invented **WYSIWYG** word processing, the mouse, multiwindow displays, and electronic meeting rooms.[7]

Although Bush envisioned a mechanical device to sort information, electronic computers were the key to Engelbart's concept of being able to manipulate information. In 1946, the first electronic, general-purpose computer, Electronic Numerical Integrator and Computer (ENIAC), was developed at the University of Pennsylvania. The construction of the computer reflected the earlier work of Atanasoff and others.[8] ENIAC was eighteen feet high and eighty feet long and weighed thirty tons. It used 17,468 vacuum tubes connected by 500 miles of wire to perform 10,000 operations a second. To change its instructions, engineers had to rewire it. The research effort that produced it had been financed by the U.S. government in hopes that a computer would contribute to the war effort, and ENIAC was used to make some of the calculations in the building of the hydrogen bomb in the 1950s.

Engineers recognized at the beginning that computers had many possible applications. Not only could they manipulate numbers and sort information by topic, but they offered a platform for developing graphics programs that could serve as architectural and design tools. Already in the early 1950s, MIT laboratories were experimenting with **interactive** computing and computer graphics. Ivan Sutherland created Sketchpad, a graphics program in which the user drew directly on the screen using a light pen. Sketchpad introduced software inventions such as the cursor, the window, and clipping. In 1955, IBM released the **computer language** FORTRAN, which was designed to aid scientists in solving engineering problems.

Mildred Koss, one of Univac I's initial programmers, commented, "There were no limitations to what you could accomplish. There was lots of vision and new ideas as to where the computer might be used. We looked at the computer as a universal problem-solving machine. It had some rules and an operating system, but it was up to you to program it to do whatever you wanted it to do."[9]

But computers could be problematic as well. Grace Hopper, a mathematician who worked in computer research at Harvard and developed the first commercial,

WYSIWYG

Text on a computer screen that corresponds exactly to the printout: What you see is what you get.

interactive

Systems that involve two-way communication. The information receivers act as senders and vice versa.

computer language

An intermediate programming language designed for programmers' convenience that is converted into machine language.

high-level computer language, gave a name to those problems. While trying to determine what had caused a computer malfunction, Hopper found the culprit—a dead moth on a vacuum tube. From then on, "bug" became a common computer term.[10]

The Move to Micro

With the development of the silicon chip in 1959, the computer industry expanded to become a microelectronics industry. The silicon chip and programming languages enabled the electronics industry to develop **microcomputers** for general use. Software, rather than hardware, determined the application. By the early 1960s, this infant industry was garnering annual revenues of more than $1 billion. As computers were used for processing different applications, hardware and software manufacturers rapidly began to develop new products.

In 1974, Intel marketed its first computer chip, the Intel 4004. This chip, which combined memory and logic functions on the microchip to produce a microprocessor, launched the individual computer market. First, workstation terminals that were attached to a large mainframe began to proliferate in the workplace, and then stand-alone desktop computers appeared. However, the personal computer (PC) was designed primarily for ham radio operators and other electronics hobbyists.

In 1975, Paul Allen, the friend of a Harvard student named Bill Gates, was attracted to the cover of the January 1975 issue of *Popular Electronics.* The cover featured a photo of the very first personal computer, the MITS Altair 8800. After reading that article, Gates and Allen started Microsoft Corporation.

The Altair 8800 was the first practical mass market machine, produced by a hobby company called Micro Instrumentation Telemetry Systems (MITS), and it sold for $397, about the price of the Intel chip that made its production possible. But there was a catch. To be useful, an Altair required a video display terminal, storage disks, and a printer, which brought the price into the $5,000 range. For that price, the buyer had a computer that did real work, such as word processing, file management, and running BASIC, FORTRAN, COBOL, and PL/I programs. Programmers entered data with switches instead of a keyboard. Hobbyists and entrepreneurs[11] loved the Altair. Personal computing had arrived.

In 1977, Steve Wozniak and Steve Jobs, two college dropouts, perfected the Apple II, which sold for about $1,300, contained four **kilobytes** of memory, and came with a jack that converted a television set into a monitor. About the same time, the Tandy/Radio Shack TRS-80s—the first truly portable computer—became available. In 1981, Osborne introduced a machine with a built-in twenty-four-line monitor, and in 1981, IBM entered the market with the first IBM PC. "Totables" or "luggables" included the Kaypro, which sold for about $1,800, and Compaq's suitcase-style machine, which was about the size and weight of a portable sewing machine.

Software Revolution

By the mid-1980s, the personal computer had been revolutionized with the advent of **user-friendly operating systems.** The most widely used of these was DOS. DOS-based personal computers and the Apple Macintosh became affordable, revolutionizing not only the workplace, but the home. These machines enabled people to use a desktop computer for sophisticated engineering problems and at the same time for other applications such as word processing, graphics, design, **spreadsheets,** and **database** management. Personal computers became even more user-friendly in 1984 with the introduction of the small, light computer named the Apple Macintosh. The Macintosh provided an easy-to-use format characterized by the term **graphical user interface (GUI).** This arrangement used the metaphor of a desktop to display the range of tasks the Mac makes possible. In 1990, Bill Gates introduced Microsoft's Windows 3.0, and two years later followed with 3.1. This software replaced DOS's text-based interface with a GUI clearly modeled on the Macintosh. But the lower price of Windows machines, whose manufacturers had to compete with each other, attracted

---

microcomputer

A small computer using a microprocessor as its central processor.

kilobyte

A measure of memory size equal to 1,024 bytes.

user-friendly

Software that is designed for use by individuals who are not familiar with complex computer languages.

operating system

A program that tells the computer how to behave. DOS and Windows, produced by Microsoft, dominate the world market for operating systems. The Macintosh operating system is second, used by about one-tenth as many machines as the Microsoft systems.

spreadsheet

Software that allows for organization and tabulation of financial data; commonly used in planning budgets.

database

Software for recording data. Data can be sorted into categories and reports printed in various forms. Used by businesses that need to sort customers by zip code, for example.

graphical user interface (GUI)

Arrangement on the screen that imitates a desktop.

Until the mid-1970s, computers took up entire rooms. But in 1975, the first microcomputer kit—the Altair 8800—was developed, making computers affordable and usable in the home. Unfortunately, the operating system language for the microcomputer was the same as that for large mainframe computers, filling up most of the Altair's small memory capacity and leaving little room for data.

When Paul Allen read about the Altair 8800, he convinced his friend Bill Gates to work with him on developing a condensed operating system language, which the teenage math geniuses licensed to the makers of the Altair 8800.

One year later Allen and Gates established Microsoft Corporation. The young founders were convinced that they were in the forefront of a computer revolution. Software, said Gates, was where the money would be.

Microsoft's big break came in 1980 when the industry's leader, IBM, asked Gates to develop an operating system for its new personal computer. Gates declined at first, then bought a system from another small company for $50,000, reworked it, and licensed it to IBM for $125,000. He named the operating system MS-DOS, for "Microsoft disk operating system." Gates retained ownership and thus was ready to confront the microcomputer revolution. IBM introduced its PC in 1981, and clones (practically identical machines) using MS-DOS soon followed.

Today, Microsoft's operating systems—MS-DOS and Windows—run more than 90 percent of the world's personal computers.

On July 15, 1996, Microsoft and NBC each invested $220 million to launch MSNBC, the Microsoft–NBC news service that is available on cable and online. The companies claim they are preparing for the time when computers and television

Bill Gates

merge. Gates became a billionaire, and in 2006, was the richest person in the world.

In the early 1990s, the U.S. government became concerned that Microsoft was violating antitrust laws because of a monopoly on its operating system and, later, its web browser Explorer. In April 2000, after almost two years of legal maneuvers that threatened the existence of the company, a court settlement required Microsoft to disclose technical information and barred agreements on Microsoft products that were designed to exclude competitors. Microsoft's legal woes continued in Europe, where the European Commission imposed a 2004 antitrust ruling which ordered the company to release a version of Windows without its media player.

While Microsoft's legal problems had begun during Gates's tenure, he began to step away from the company, leaving his position as Microsoft chief executive officer in January 2000, and allowing his friend, Steve Ballmer, to become head of the corporation. Gates served for a time as chief software architect before announcing that he was quitting to devote his time to his charity organization, the Bill and Melinda Gates Foundation, which is devoted to ending poverty, improving health, and increasing computer access around the world. Since December 1994, the foundation has committed $11 billion in grants to organizations in more than one hundred countries.

Sources: Peter H. Lewis, "A Glimpse into the Future as Seen by Chairman Gates," *The New York Times,* December 12, 1993: sec. 3, p. 7; "Bill Gates," *Newsmakers,* Gale Research Inc., August 1993; Joel Achenbach, "The Computer King's Hard Drive; Billionaire Bill Gates, Cult Hero, Cracks Open a Window on the Secret of His Success," *Washington Post,* April 14, 1993: B1; Cynthia Flash "Microsoft, NBC Launch News Venture," *News Tribune,* July 14, 1996: 1; Fact Sheet, Bill and Melinda Gates Foundation, 2006, gatesfoundation.org.

---

cost-conscious buyers. And as Windows' share of the market grew, software companies had less and less incentive to write for the Macintosh. This was especially true of the burgeoning video-game sector. The result: Macintosh was relegated to specialized markets such as graphic designers, whereas Windows became the effective industry standard for desktop and laptop machines. Windows had sold 60 million copies by 1995, and Microsoft was supplying 80 percent of the operating systems worldwide. The company launched Windows 95 in August 1995. Subsequent versions of Windows, including Windows 98, Windows 2000, Windows NT, Windows XP, and Windows Vista, have since been introduced and dominate the market.

The introduction of user-friendly software, along with the trend toward microcomputers, has made computers a common household item. Within twenty-four years from the introduction of the personal computer, its household penetration had reached 50 percent. For comparison, Table 9.1 shows the number of years it took for some popular media technologies to reach 50 percent penetration.

Dateline

Computers in Our Lives

1943. Early electromechanical digital computer is developed by IBM.
1946. First electronic, general-use computer is developed.
1949. First commercial electronic computer is produced.
   1954. Computer graphics are introduced by MIT.
   1955. IBM invents the computer language FORTRAN.
   1959. Silicon chip is developed.

| 1400–1700 | 1800 | 1900 | 1930 | 1940 | 1950 |

1620. Pilgrims land at Plymouth Rock.
1690. *Publick Occurrences* is published in Boston.
1741. First magazine is published in America.
1776–1783. American Revolution
   1830s. The penny press becomes the first truly mass medium in the United States.
   1861–1865. American Civil War
   1892. Thomas Edison's lab develops the kinetoscope.
      1914–1918. World War I
      1915. *The Birth of a Nation* marks the start of the modern movie industry.
      1920. KDKA in Pittsburgh gets the first commercial radio license.
         1930s. The Great Depression
         1939. TV is demonstrated at the New York World's Fair.
         1939–1945. World War II
            1949. First commercial electronic computer is produced.
            Early 1950s. Rock 'n' roll begins.

Cultural Milestones

1974. Intel markets its first computer chip.

Mid-1970s. MITS develops the first personal computer, the Altair 8800.

1975. Bill Gates and Paul Allen start Microsoft Corporation.

1976. Steve Jobs and Steve Wozniak perfect the Apple II.

1980. Microsoft introduces MS-DOS.

1981. IBM manufactures its first PC.

1984. Apple introduces the Macintosh.

Late 1980s. National Science Foundation creates the basis of the Internet.

1995. Microsoft introduces Windows 95.

1996. Telecommunications Act.

2001. Total advertising revenue online declines.

2002. Microsoft antitrust case is settled.

2002. The dot.com bubble bursts.

2004. Web 2.0 companies grow.

1960	1970	1980	1990	2000

1969. First person lands on the moon.

1970s. VCR is developed.

1989–1991. Cold War ends and the USSR is dissolved.

Late 1980s. National Science Foundation creates the basis of the Internet.

1996. Telecommunications Act

2000. Presidential election nearly tied.

2001. Terrorist attacks on New York and Washington, D.C.

2003. War with Iraq.

Table 9.1	Number of Years to Reach 50 Percent of U.S. Households for Selected Technologies	
Technology/Medium	**Number of Years to Reach 50% Penetration**
Newspapers	100+
Telephone	70
Cable TV	39
Personal computers	24
Color TV	15
Cell phones	12
Radio	9
Black-and-white TV	8
DVD	6

Sources: Electronic Industries Alliance, U.S. Department of Commerce, 1996. Courtesy of John Carey; Adam D. Thierer, "Overcoming Mythology in the Debate over Media Ownership," *Cato Congressional Testimony,* September 28, 2004, www.cato.org.

COMPUTERS AND COMMUNICATION

Key Concept

Information-based economy The computer has paved the way for the development of the information-based economy in which a large portion of the national product is accounted for through production of information for entertainment, investing, and economic decision making.

Once computers became small and inexpensive enough for consumers to buy them as individual PCs, and software opened the door to a variety of uses, the next step was to connect computers in such a way that people could videoconference, send messages, and access information from other computer sources. This was achieved through the Internet, its graphical interface (the World Wide Web), and online services, and has led to the formation of *information-based economies.*

The Internet

network

Computers that are connected by communications lines. The computers may be connected within a restricted geographic area, such as a laboratory in a mass communication program. This network is a local area network (LAN). The Internet networks millions of computers worldwide through telephone and fiber-optic lines.

The Internet is a **network** of computer networks. These networks include computers found in businesses, universities, libraries, government, media companies, and homes. The Internet is available today because the federal government wanted to link computers in such a way that in times of disaster—either human or natural—defense and communications systems could still operate. In the 1960s, the U.S. Defense Department designed an experimental network called ARPAnet. As the type and number of network systems increased, it became apparent that allowing computers to "talk" to one another regardless of their operating systems would be beneficial to all. In the late 1980s, the National Science Foundation (NSF) created five supercomputer centers. At first the NSF tried to use ARPAnet to connect them, but bureaucracy and staffing problems got in the way. NSF, therefore, created its own network by connecting the centers with telephone lines. Then, through a chain system, the network linked universities and other commercial and noncommercial computer groups. In each area of the country, a group is linked to its neighbor group or institution rather than every one being fed to a central location. This saves primarily in the cost of telephone lines.

The success of the system came close to being its downfall as users multiplied rapidly and the telephone lines could not sustain the use. In 1987, the old network was replaced with higher capacity telephone lines.

The most important feature of the NSF network has been its commitment to universal access, opening up enormous sources of data and conversations for people using computers.[12] What is amazing is that connections occur within seconds, despite being linked from one institution to another across hundreds of miles or around the world.

The Internet is the carrier of a variety of services, including newspapers online, original Internet content, electronic shopping, music that can be downloaded and played through stereo and television equipment, and streaming video that offers real-time news feeds. The Internet distributes almost any content that can be imagined.

Commercialization of the Internet

In its early days, the Internet was used and managed by academic and military interests, who saw it as a research and defense tool. However, in the mid-1980s, private vendors and service providers became involved in setting up networks and expanding the Internet's user base. With the introduction of the Internet's graphical interface, the World Wide Web, the commercialization of the Internet began in earnest, as companies promoted their products, provided secure online shopping, and engaged in other commercial ventures. Previous forms of commercial-free electronic exchange, like e-mail and online gaming, became vehicles for advertising.

The historical vision of the Internet as a noncommercial space where knowledge and information could be freely exchanged persists in discussions of unlimited file sharing, digital copyright, and **open source code** in which programmers can view, change, and distribute code as long as they allow others to do the same in turn. The term "open source" has been broadened to apply to freely shared information and content that can be publicly viewed and altered. Yet much of the Internet has been given over to commercial interests that wish to control content, infrastructure, and access through encryption, copyright, and other restrictions. Many critics see this as a threat to the Internet, which they believe should be as open as possible to encourage creativity and information sharing. Others see the commercial aspects of the Internet as facilitating a global economy.

Social and Cultural Effects

Economists and social theorists claim that the United States and other developed countries have moved from industrial-based to information-based economies. Creating and distributing information for entertainment, investing, and economic decision making account for a large portion of the U.S. national product. Relying on information creates concern in three areas: (1) Who has access to the information? (2) What are the social, cultural, and political implications? (3) Is regulation necessary to protect individual privacy and commercial interests?

Access Information is a commodity that represents knowledge and the potential ability to transcend socioeconomic class.

Research reveals that because individuals with higher levels of education generally have more access to mass communication, they gather ideas and new information more quickly than those with less education. One of the concerns about the Internet has been whether the entire population will have access or whether only a select few will. As the Internet developed, scholars referred to this concept as the *digital divide*; there was major concern that those who were poor and less educated would be divided from those who had access to information. Within the United States, the overall number of Internet users also reveals inequities. In 2000, 92 percent of adults in households with annual income over $75,000 accessed the Internet, but only 53 percent of

> ### Key Concept
>
> **Digital divide** Only some people—for example, those with higher incomes, education levels, or connections to institutions—will have access to digitized information as is found through computer networking.

open source code

Programming code that is freely available to anyone to use and manipulate.

Identity in Cyberspace

Since the Internet became an active meeting place, social and cultural theorists have pondered the question of what becomes of our identities, relationships, and communities online. What happens when our self-presentations and our interactions with others take place mostly in cyberspace?

A prominent writer on cyberspace, Sherry Turkle, has observed that when we interact with computers through task windows, we take on different roles. For example, while on a computer, a student may be messaging family, writing a story for a creative writing professor, manipulating data for an economics class, and playing with online gamers. In each of these windows, the student takes on a different social role. Turkle has argued that this multitasking may be changing our idea of a unitary self: "The life practice of windows is that of a decentered self that exists in many worlds, that plays many roles at the same time." With the prevalence of digital devices like cell phones, virtual windows are folded into the physical spaces and routines of everyday life.

We can also represent ourselves in a multitude of ways on the Internet, which offers much opportunity for disguise and anonymity. Users of online games, chat rooms, social network sites, and other virtual spaces often take advantage of the Internet to affirm and enhance identities or experiment with new ones. They can create representations of self through the voices they use on their blogs, the names they choose, the photos and videos they post, and the friends they list. They can have different versions of their personalities and behaviors on different sites.

From the earliest days of the Internet, users have engaged in games that allow more extravagant experiments with identity. On massive multiplayer online role-playing games (MMORPGs) like EverQuest, users can create characters called "avatars," usually fantasy figures like Tolkienesque elves or wizards. In virtual communities like Second Life, avatars can be altered for gender, skin color, body size, eye color and size, clothing, accessories, and even skin wrinkles.

While virtual worlds may offer creativity and freedom in expressing identities, there are potential problems. The one most often discussed in the news media is the presence of stalkers and sexual predators who may disguise themselves to harass others and lure children and other vulnerable persons into dangerous situations. Virtual communities may also feel betrayed when a member turns out to have created an elaborate lie, as was the case with 19-year-old blogger Kaycee Nicole Swenson. Swenson wrote about her struggle with leukemia, gaining many readers who offered their support through comments and even talked to her on the phone. After Kaycee died, her "mother," Debbie Swenson, confessed that the girl had been a made-up persona who had never existed at all. Communications scholar John Jordan writes, "Only if everyone agrees that online interactions are just 'play' can the consequences of hoaxes and pranks be considered harmless fun. If others take these interactions seriously, however, and invest their real emotions in the community, then a hoax can have devastating effects, even in those situations where the perpetrator claims his or her actions were mere jest."

Virtual worlds provoke a host of questions as the Internet becomes ever more embedded in our lives. Do we behave differently online, and how might our personalities and psychologies be affected? Do we become more isolated from each other when we share only virtual space, or does the Internet expand our social interactions and make them more meaningful? What kinds of community are we creating online? Are there social costs, such as increased fragmentation and a lack of authenticity? Sherry Turkle writes, "Information technology is identity technology. Embedding it in a culture that supports democracy, freedom of expression, tolerance, diversity, and complexity of opinion is one of the next decade's greatest challenges. We cannot afford to fail."

Sources: John W. Jordan, "A Virtual Death and a Real Dilemma: Identity, Trust, and Community in Cyberspace," *The Southern Communication Journal* 70.3 (2005): 200–218; Sherry Turkle, "How Computers Change the Way We Think," *Chronicle of Higher Education*, January 30, 2004: B26; Sherry Turkle, *Life on the Screen: Identity in the Age of the Internet* (New York: Simon & Schuster, 1995).

Because of social factors like age and income, many people have been left out of the digital revolution. However, the gap is narrowing as computers become widespread among all social groups, including senior citizens.

adults in households with less than $30,000.[13] Race and ethnicity is also a factor in participation. Lacking even a telecommunication infrastructure, many Native American communities face difficulties in obtaining any Internet access. Nevertheless, because of lower cost, the national digital divide appears to be narrowing, with more growth in broadband lines among people with less income.

The digital divide is even more of a global concern, since many regions of the world lack access to computers and the Internet, especially in the Middle East, Africa, Latin America, Southeast Asia, and Eastern Europe. In September 2006, members of the United Nation's Global Alliance for Information and Communication Technologies and Development met for the first time to strategize how to connect the world's poor with information technologies in order to build stronger economies. The co-founder of MIT's Media Laboratory, Nicholas Negroponte, introduced a durable $100 laptop in 2005 that can be operated by hand crank, intended for distribution to needy children worldwide. In turn, Microsoft announced plans to produce its own low-cost option: a cell phone that would become a computer when plugged into a keyboard and TV. These initiatives attempt to close the digital divide in a world where wealth is increasingly attached to the power of information.

Social Interaction and Political Participation   As more people get online and become familiar with the information available to them, they are turning to the Internet for information about major life decisions. A 2005 Pew Internet & American Life survey found that many people go online to make decisions about major illnesses, financial investments, job training, home buying, and choosing schools and colleges.[14] Further, many of the 73 percent of Americans who use the Internet say it has improved the way they work, shop, and pursue leisure time activities.[15] While the Internet began as a social medium, bringing together people who shared research interests, many more have joined to share stories, photos, artwork, videos, songs, messages, sometimes just with friends and family, at other times with large networks of participants in sites like MySpace. Logging onto the Internet has become an important part of daily life for a growing number of Americans.

As information becomes more specialized, more technology based, and more expensive, sociologists and political critics worry that the participation of an informed public, necessary to support the foundations of a democracy, may erode even further than it already has. Sociologists are concerned that we will become a fragmented

Because of the Web's interactive capacity for streaming audio and video, many people are able to make and share their own digital creations.

society in which there is no longer such a thing as "common knowledge." We might have nothing to say to our neighbors because we choose the content and the information sources we want, which might be different from those our neighbors want.

Freedom of Expression   There are many issues having to do with privacy and security and the Internet. As you will read later in this chapter, many individuals are concerned about security of bank accounts and of shopping online. They also are concerned about hackers, and the ability of outsiders to break into their flow of information.

Another aspect of privacy that affects our social and cultural structure is the ability to express ourselves freely without undue interference by the federal government or other entities. With the passing of the 2001 Patriot Act in reaction to the attacks on September 11, 2001, the federal government has increased its ability to "look into" people's correspondence.

Another area that affects freedom of expression has to do with efforts by the government to regulate pornography on the Internet. Here, one must balance the needs of society, the rights of people not to receive information they don't want, and the rights of others to exchange ideas freely.

TODAY'S MARKET STRUCTURE

The computer industry and related services are highly diversified and competitive. The market consists of access providers such as Comcast, hardware manufacturers such as Intel, software manufacturers such as Microsoft, and online services such as Google, which provide e-commerce, information, and entertainment.

Beginning in 2000, a major upheaval occurred in the computer industry when many new Internet companies, called the dot.coms were formed, new business models were introduced, and investors threw money into risky ventures that ended in failure. When the **dot.com bubble** burst, it had wide repercussions in Western economies, leading to mild recession. Over the next few years, thousands of workers were laid off in all sectors of the computer industry, and companies restructured, selling off some of their divisions. For example, according to the U.S. Bureau of Labor, the number of software employees peaked at 274,100 in January 2001, but had fallen

dot.com bubble

A period of inflated expansion of new Internet business in the late 1990s.

to 233,500 by February 2005. The hardware company 3COM laid off 8,500 workers and sold off U.S. Robotics and Palm.[16] Companies like AOL, which had merged with the entertainment giant Time Warner in January 2000, began a downhill slide, ending in massive reinvention. Instead of having its users pay for broadband access, AOL began offering free e-mail and software to increase its website traffic, hoping to make its money from advertising revenues. The computer industry appeared to be recovering in 2005, but some analysts warned that a new dot.com bubble might be forming with investor enthusiasm in new online service companies.

The Technology of Access

With the advent of streaming audio and video, many people in the United States and in many parts of the world have acquired high-speed Internet. Slow telephone modems have been rapidly replaced by much faster **cable modems** and telephone-based **DSL** (digital subscriber line) hookups. Cable modem speeds, however, are somewhat mercurial, given that the speed can vary depending on the number of individuals using the cable service at the same time. DSL speed may also vary according to type and the customer's distance from the telephone facility. Customers may also opt for satellite broadband, which requires more equipment, or mobile wireless broadband for cell phones and PDAs. Interest is growing in broadband over power lines (BPL), which allows consumers in remote areas to have high-speed broadband access by plugging a BPL modem into an electric socket.

Competition has caused the price of broadband access to drop considerably, so that in 2006 DSL subscribers paid as little as $13 a month. Companies make more money by bundling Internet access, phone, and video services together, so that consumers may be charged a higher rate for buying only a cable modem service without an accompanying cable television service. The chief competitors are the cable and phone companies that now offer similar services. They have waged advertising and price wars and engaged in legal battles over who has what kinds of access to customers. As more technologies like BPL gain a footing in the market, providing even more competition, consumers may enjoy cheap or even free broadband.

Using a radio link, free wireless broadband is becoming increasingly available in public locations like libraries, community centers, coffee shops and parks. About 120,000 such "hot spots" existed by September 2006.[17] Many towns are interested in building their own downtown wireless networks to attract businesses and customers and bridge the digital divide, but cable and telephone companies consider these efforts direct competition, and have tried to block municipal networks through government regulation. Free wireless has downsides, since the connections are unsecured and users have no guarantee of privacy and data security.

Hardware

Computers, along with their parts and peripherals, constitute the hardware industry. It is a global industry, so that parts may be designed, tested, manufactured, and assembled in several different countries. Competition in this sector is intense, and companies compete by lowering prices or creating innovative products like tablet PCs and smaller, faster computer chips. As computers have become more embedded in the everyday lives of people in information societies, demand has greatly increased, with U.S. sales of 6.7 million personal computers in 1994 growing to 70 million in 2005. Most of those sales are desktops, at 58.4 percent, followed by laptops at 27.5 percent, and palmtops at 14.1 percent. The market is expected to reach 105.97 million PC sales by 2010.[18] Along with the rest of the computer industry, hardware companies faced tough times during the dot.com bust, and IBM transferred its PC business to Lenovo in order to focus instead on selling software and services. However, because speed, storage, portability, and capability to manage new applications continues to improve, a demand exists for new computer purchases. In 2006, the leading PC companies were Dell, Hewlett Packard, and Gateway.

cable modem

Device used to connect computers to the Internet and other online services that operate through cable, rather than telephone, lines.

DSL

Telephone lines that foster extremely fast connection to the Internet and other online services.

Software

Software is a term for programs, or the instructions that tell the computer's processor what to do. The software industry provides many different types of programs, including business software for managing production, sales, customer records, and inventory; operating systems for networks and mainframe computers; and packaged software, such as video games, PC operating systems, backup and virus programs, and office applications like word processing and e-mail programs. In 2005, the packaged software industry in the United States was worth approximately $90 billion, with business software accounting for $82 billion. Household consumption of packaged software comprised $5.5 billion, with the rest going to schools.[19]

Businesses are increasingly turning to **Software as a Service (SaaS):** on-demand programs delivered over the Internet through browsers and mobile devices. SaaS saves companies money because it helps them avoid upfront software licenses and they don't have to maintain, service, and upgrade applications across all their computers. Such services are also available to individual consumers. For example, Google has a free service that offers users the ability to create and save simple word processing documents and spreadsheets online. Microsoft has also begun to launch services that work along with its packaged software. However, SaaS causes some worry because of data privacy and vulnerability to system crashes.

Online Service Providers

Online service providers include companies like Comcast that sell network access, often with services like e-mail and web hosting, and companies like Google that allow users to access and exchange information online. In order to enjoy certain legal protections, a service provider must meet the definition as set out by the U.S. Digital Millennium Copyright Act. A service provider is "an entity offering the transmission, routing, or providing of connections for digital online communications, between or among points specified by a user, of material of the user's choosing, without modification to the content of the material as sent or received." According to the act, if a service provider meets this definition, it is not liable for illegal materials that users exchange through its service as long as it removes such materials when it learns of them.

Of all sectors in the computer industry, online service providers with free, innovative offerings experienced the greatest growth after the dot.com bust. Business models based on advertising revenues or offers of both free and purchasable premium content surpassed other pay services. Started by two Stanford graduate students in computer science, Google grew to the most highly valued media company in the summer of 2005, with its worth at $80 billion. Services based on user-generated content, like YouTube, FlickR, and MySpace, began attracting the attention of entrepreneurs. In October 2006, Google announced that it was buying YouTube for $1.65 billion, demonstrating the importance of these services.

AUDIENCE DEMAND IN COMPUTER MARKETS

The demand for computers in business is enormous. Nearly every professional office—whether it be a law office, a public relations agency, or a government agency—relies on computers. Educational institutions constantly struggle to fund up-to-date computer facilities in a rapidly changing technological environment. Stockbrokers and financial analysts use computers to keep up with constantly changing market conditions. In doctors' offices, appointments and medical and billing records are kept on computers. Reporters, advertising personnel, and public relations professionals seek information via the computer and then use the computer as a tool for the production of ads, news stories, public relations releases, and illustrations. Convergence is further evident as the advertisements are broadcast electronically for companies sponsoring World Wide Web sites.

Software as a Service

Software programs accessed over the Internet. SaaS providers make money either through usage fees or advertising.

Media Convergence

YouTube and User-Generated Video

By autumn 2006, users were uploading 65,000 short videos and streaming 100 million a day on the popular website YouTube. Most of these videos were amateur creations, such as altered commercials, music performances, mockumentaries and documentaries, comedy routines, and tapes of cute babies, pet antics, vacations, and local high school bands. Also in the mix were regular television shows, such as *The Daily Show* and *The Colbert Report*. YouTube had become the leader in user-generated content and "clip culture," a convergence of interactive web technologies and television that has transformed the way media producers and many media consumers think about video.

YouTube was founded in early 2005 by Chad Hurley, Jawed Karim, and Steve Chen. Having worked out how to post videos on the web without having to download special software, the team uploaded its first video of Karim standing in front of an elephant at the zoo. Internet users were attracted to other videos of the founders' everyday lives, and word of mouth spread quickly.

As it gained popularity, YouTube received the blessing of mainstream media critics. lonelygirl15's video diary attracted 10,000 subscribers and caught the attention of *New York Magazine* and NPR's *On the Media*, where critics debated issues of art and authenticity in user-generated video. (lonelygirl15 turned out to be a fake, created by a screenwriter and filmmaker.) Discussing lonelygirl15 and other YouTube contributors, former *Spin* editor Michael Hirschorn wrote, "Digital video is doing more than just providing infinite alternatives; it's making network product seem visually slow and outdated." Many media commentators noted the significance of user-generated video as overturning an old broadcast model of delivering content to a relatively passive audience. In the *Los Angeles Times*, media management consultant Randall Rothenberg wrote that YouTube represented "a remarkable, even revolutionary, democratizing of the means of production."

Utopian predictions about the new media were dampened by various issues related to authenticity, proper social conduct, and stealing. Criticisms arose over revelations that advertisers were slipping in fake videos purportedly from YouTube amateurs. During election season, concerns were expressed that negative campaign videos were harming the political process. Always a lurking issue, copyright infringement came to the fore. The Japanese Society for Rights of Authors, Composers and Publishers asked YouTube to remove 30,000 pirated clips, and after Google purchased the site for $1.65 billion, Comedy Central demanded that all clips of its shows be removed. Only a year before, the *Daily Show's* executive producer had encouraged viewers to share clips online, and in an agreement between Google and Comedy Central's parent, Viacom, the clips were restored.

YouTube had provoked the television networks, including Fox and ABC, into putting their shows online, using their own websites and iTunes. In that way, the networks had a hope of making money through advertising revenues and cross-promotion. However, YouTube had already irrevocably changed the mediascape, technologically, economically, aesthetically, and culturally.

Sources: Verne Kopytoff, "Copyright Troubles Surface vs. YouTube," *San Francisco Chronicle,* October 28, 2006; Thomas Goetz, "Reinventing Television," *Wired,* September 2005, wired.com/wired/archive/13.09/stewart.html; David Greising, "YouTube Founder Rides Video Clips to Dot-Com Riches," *Chicago Tribune,* October 15, 2006; Michael Hirschorn, "Thank You, YouTube," *Atlantic Monthly,* November 2006, theatlantic.com/doc/200611/youtube; Randall Rothenberg, "Tune In, Turn On, Click YouTube," *Los Angeles Times,* October 28, 2006.

Demand for Hardware

The decreasing cost of personal computers has helped foster their adoption in households. In 2006, a fast, well equipped desktop or laptop computer could be obtained for less than $1,000. A family could subscribe to an Internet provider for less than $20 a month. Some computers now cost about the same as a thirty-inch television set. The computer is still an expensive device for some families, but the decline in price makes it more accessible than in previous years. According to the U.S. Census Bureau, in 2003, 62 percent of American households owned a computer.

Low-cost computers provide the basic functions that most people use, such as e-mail, word processing, and social networking. Thus, computer manufacturers compete by introducing new products, such as tablet PCs with handwriting recognition, to attract high-end buyers. Gamers, for example, are willing to pay more money for faster processors and other multimedia features.

Demand for Software

Most home computers are sold with a solid complement of software, including the operating system such as Windows or MacOS. Consumers take for granted that basic software will be provided, and companies like Microsoft have gained market advantage over their competitors by providing this software. Proprietary software also comes with peripherals and devices such as digital cameras. Some computer users buy specialized software for activities such as manipulating photographs, building webpages, and gaming. However, similar programs may be available in freeware or low-cost shareware, or in open source code that can be manipulated by the user.

Demand for Privacy and Regulation in Networked Services

As computer networking becomes more a part of people's lives, including their banking and shopping habits, online security has become an important social and political issue. Fears concerning ***privacy and anonymity*** exist on many levels, from protecting credit card numbers to preventing Internet stalking. These issues fall into two general categories: the security of user information in increasingly vast electronic databases, and the protection of vulnerable persons from exploitation by criminals who may steal identities and disguise themselves in other ways. Concerns over censorship and access to information affect governmental attempts at ***regulation in the information age.***

As people navigate the Internet, they leave digital trails that represent a great deal of personal information, such as credit card and social security numbers, phone numbers, credit reports, home addresses, shopping records, information about household members, magazine subscriptions, and medical information. Small programs called cookies record website visitors' IP addresses, login times, and user identity and preferences. Almost every move a person makes on a computer can be traced. Internet users must weigh whether the benefits, such as convenience and ease of communications, outweigh the risks of losing privacy.

> ### Key Concepts
>
> **Privacy and anonymity** Courts have ruled people have a right to privacy, but sometimes that right conflicts with the need to find those who abuse access to free communication over the Internet.

> ### Key Concepts
>
> **Regulation in the information age** In the early days of the Internet, regulation was compared to law in the Wild West—there wasn't much. As more people use the Internet, pressures to make money increase, issues of security evolve, and regulation has grown. However, the extent and nature of Internet regulation continues to be an issue in courts and legislatures and will be for years to come.

When AOL released the search engines histories of 650,000 clients, Internet users were astonished to find out how much could be learned about them from these histories. Although AOL had stripped the search engines of any identifying information other than a number, two reporters for *The New York Times* were almost instantly able to track down user # 4417749, who turned out to be a widow living in Georgia. #4417749 had searched for other members of her family with the name "Arnold," "landscapers in Lilburn, Ga" and "homes sold in shadow lake subdivision gwinnett county georgia." She had also revealed very personal information in searches such as "numb fingers" and "60 single men."[20] AOL apologized and took the search histories offline, but the data had already migrated to other websites. It gave a fascinating glimpse into the kinds of people who use the Internet, but a reminder of how much potentially damaging information search engine companies are collecting. For example, included in the search histories were credit card and social security numbers. Search engines like AOL and Google not only collect this information, but can tie it to other identifiers such as user name and computer network address. They use the data to improve their applications and marketing. However, since the Electronic Communications Privacy Act of 1986 does not cover more recent network technologies, few protections exist to shield search engine users from government surveillance and other uses of personal information.

The federal government has compiled hundreds of millions of entries in its "Investigative Data Warehouse," and has developed software to monitor and intercept electronic communications through the Internet and digital devices like cell phones. However, the FBI has been unresponsive to requests to provide a description of what is in its databases or what kind of information is collected. Privacy advocates argue that such activities undermine democracy and should be made transparent, while legal scholars debate the limits of the Fourth Amendment guarantee against unreasonable searches and citizens' reasonable expectations of privacy. One of the cases made against the FBI's collection of such data is that citizens aren't protected against data leaks and have no ability to challenge false data.[21] In a time of war and rapid technological change, these issues are more complex.

Some cybercriminals target user data like credit card and bank account numbers through interception and theft. For example, in phishing scams, criminals create phony e-mails, represented as being from legitimate banks, in order to gather account information from victims. Programs called password sniffers can surreptitiously allow criminals to access computers where they can steal or maliciously alter data or store illegal data such as child pornography. Internet users must possess knowledge and exercise caution to avoid these kinds of scams and intrusions. They also expect their financial, educational, medical, and governmental institutions to protect them against cybercrime.

Though anyone who puts sensitive personal information online is at some risk, children and the elderly are most vulnerable to cybercrime. The Children's Online Privacy Protection Act (COPPA), which took effect in April 2000, forbids online service and website operators from collecting, using, or disclosing information about persons under the age of thirteen without parental consent. Such operators must guard the "confidentiality, security, and integrity" of children, mostly to protect them against predators. Several companies have been fined under COPPA, including Mrs. Field's Cookies, Hershey Foods, and the social networking site Xanga. In August 2005, the U.S. Justice Department requested billions of user search records from AOL, Yahoo, Microsoft, and Google in order to investigate the protection of children from adult content. Only Google did not comply, arguing that the request violated the company's proprietary data and its users' privacy.[22]

Adult Internet users are largely responsible for protecting their own data from intrusion and unwanted surveillance. Many organizations, including some universities, try to educate people in strategies to enhance online security. Technical measures include anonymous login services, firewalls, and antivirus, antispam, and encryption programs. Users are also urged to exercise caution in their web searches and when they fill out forms. As social media encourage users to become more comfortable with sharing very personal information, the risk of unwanted exposure has increased. For example, students' online stories and photos about drinking binges can come to the attention of school officials and, years later, future employers. Most legal and business experts agree that neither society nor the law has caught up with the privacy issues posed by evolving digital technologies.

SUPPLYING AUDIENCE DEMAND

The audience for the content available through computer networks is growing, and covers a wide demographic spectrum with many information needs. This audience turns to computers for financial information, medical and legal advice, internal corporate data, business contacts, religious inspiration, creative outlet, romance and friendship, formal education, and job opportunities and training. As discussed throughout this text, mass media industries are increasingly involved in managing their businesses through networked computers and delivering advertising, news, and entertainment content over the Internet. The growing engagement of consumers in online activities is creating wide social, political, and economic impacts as business and organizations meet the demand for convenience, information, and social contact.

Health and Medicine

The Internet is transforming the way medicine is practiced and delivered, giving patients more control over their care. A 2005 Pew Internet survey found that 12 percent of Internet users had turned to the web to help another person with a major illness. Patients and caregivers can find online support groups and information from health providers about physicians, hospital facilities and equipment, prescription medicines and their side effects, cutting-edge research, and clinical trials.[23] Many professional medical journals allow free access online.

In hospitals and other medical facilities, networked computers are used to manage patient records and accounts, access medical databases, and communicate between healthcare workers and between doctor and patient. In some hospitals, patients may have computer chips implanted under their skin to help medical staff track them through the system. Surgeons can use imaging software in preoperative planning. When surgical patients arrive home, they can be monitored through wireless devices. Networked computers have also transformed medical education. Medical students can receive training through online courses and perform diagnoses and simulated operations on virtual patients. As in many other fields, networked computers have begun to significantly alter the activities and relationships among healthcare providers and their patients.

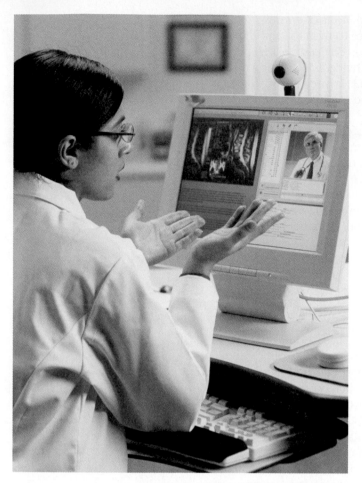

Computers have revolutionized the health care field. Patients turn to them for information and advice, and medical professionals use them for communication, training, record-keeping, and performing medical procedures.

Politics

The Internet is increasingly being used to conduct political campaigns and to gather campaign news. Candidates have webpages, campaign blogs, profiles on social networking sites like MySpace, and campaign videos on YouTube. In the 2006 election, Facebook had special election pages that provided profiles of 1,400 candidates and ranked them according to member support. Candidates have begun using the social nature of the web to reach potential voters, especially young voters, on a personal level. To create a better informed citizenry, voter organizations offer information on candidates and issues. In Michigan, for example, voters can visit the Publius website, where they can find out where to vote and view a sample ballot with links to candidates' webpages and campaign finance records. The number of citizens who have searched for political and campaign news online more than doubled between August 2002 and August 2006.[24] Such news may come from mainstream news media, political organizations, and individual bloggers.

While citizens can find voter registration forms at websites like rockthevote.com, online voting is controversial. During the 2004 election, after receiving criticism from computer scientists, the Pentagon canceled plans to allow military and civilian overseas personnel to cast votes online, using a pilot system. However, since 2000 some states, such as Arizona, Florida, Texas, and Utah, have allowed limited online voting, and many states have introduced computerized touch-screen voting machines. Computer experts feel that computerized voting is too vulnerable to fraud, viruses, and other security problems that could compromise ballots. However, proponents argue that online voting increases participation.[25]

Shopping and Finance

With customers buying a host of products from automobiles to flower arrangements, online retail shopping, also called *e-commerce* or e-tail, was worth an annual $211.4 billion in the United States in 2006, a small, but growing fraction of total retail sales.[26] Travel and hospitality services make up the bulk of sales, with consumers taking advantage of the convenience of reserving airline tickets and hotel rooms online. Online sales peak during the holiday season, when last-minute shoppers buy gifts and take advantage of expedited shipping. Some retailers, like Amazon, may conduct their operations solely online, while others, like Barnes & Noble, have both websites and brick and mortar stores. Wired shoppers now expect businesses to have some presence on the web, and many retailers take advantage of e-mail and online advertising to promote their products. Because of faster connections and more user-friendly websites, Internet users are increasingly happy with the convenience of online shopping, but become irritated with bad customer service and websites that respond slowly and crash.[27]

More Internet users now trust computer systems to handle their financial transactions. In December 2006, 35 percent of bills were paid online, up from 25 percent the year before.[28] Consumers also use the Internet to make deposits, check their credit histories, submit their tax forms, and play the stock market. Some large banks, such as ING Direct, have only an online presence and no brick and mortar sites. The rise of online banking and other financial activities is having an effect on labor, since fewer employees are needed to handle routine transactions. However, knowledgeable employees are still in demand for customer service.[29] The shift in investment strategies to online trading may also have global impacts. *The New York Times* columnist Thomas Friedman has argued that online trading allows individuals to participate in the global economy as never before, and that, taken collectively, the "electronic herd" can have a powerful effect on global markets.[30]

Education

In 2004, a Pew Internet survey of digital technology experts expressed surprise that educational institutions had changed so little with the introduction of computers and the Internet into classrooms. Nearly all schools had computers and Internet access by

Computers have become an integral component of the educational experience for both teachers and students.

Global Impact

Broadband in South Korea

South Korea is only slightly larger than Indiana and has a population of about 49 million, yet it has the highest household broadband penetration in the world, with a quarter of the population accessing the Internet at extremely high speed. Overall, it has the fourth largest Internet penetration of any country, with 65 percent of its citizens online.

Because of its high-tech infrastructure, South Koreans are at the forefront of digital convergence technologies. By 2006, they were able to receive multichannel satellite television through their cell phones and DMB (digital mobile broadcasting), and commuters watch flat screen television in their cars on the morning drive. South Koreans are avid online gamers, with 3,000 video games companies and a substantial portion of the population participating in a social networking site called CyWorld. Therefore, South Korea is an interesting case for thinking about the future of the global Internet.

The growth of South Korea's high-tech culture is largely a result of government initiatives to revive its weak economy with technological investments. After the Asian financial crash in 1997, South Korea's economy was devastated. The government embarked on an ambitious plan to give everyone high-speed Internet through a national broadband infrastructure, and gave further incentives for research and development in its high-tech industry, which includes multinational companies like Samsung and LG Electronics. The resulting transformation of South Korean society has been called a techno-revolution.

The social consequences of a wired society have been featured in some sensational cases from South Korea that made global news. A young South Korean man collapsed and died after playing fifty hours of the video game, Starcraft, in an Internet café.

Commenting on the case, psychologists weighed in on the compulsion players may feel when they are immersed in online worlds, and advised them to seek help if they suffered from Internet "addiction."

In another case, a South Korean man found himself the target of vicious attacks, including harassing phone calls to his employer and death threats on his cell phone, after his former girlfriend committed suicide. Allegations of abuse had been posted on the dead woman's webpage and quickly spread throughout the South Korean Internet community, along with the man's phone number and other personal information. A similar case was the harassment of the "dog-poop girl," who had been recorded in a cell phone photograph when she did not clean up her dog's mess on the subway. She ended up dropping out of school after the photograph circulated on the Internet. The Korea Internet Safety Commission said that such incidents of cyberviolence and harassment have skyrocketed, and the government was taking measures to make Internet users more accountable by making anonymity more difficult. A majority of South Koreans support curtailing free speech on the Internet.

The dramatic changes in South Korean society, including problems associated with online life, may speak of the future for other global citizens as fast broadband connections spread even to remote parts of the world.

Sources: John Borland and Michael Kanellos, "South Korea Leads the Way," CNET, July 28, 2004, news.com.com; Michael Kanellos, "Nation: Techno-Revolution in the Making," CNET, June 23, 2004, news .com.com; "S. Korean Man Dies After Games Session," *BBC News,* August 10, 2005, news.bbc.co.uk/1/hi/technology/4137782.stm.

2003, and the number of teenagers who say they use the Internet at school grew 45 percent from 2000 to 2004. However, 32 percent of teenagers do not use the Internet at school, and integration and development of these resources have been uneven.[31] A common complaint among educators is that technology is introduced without adequate teacher training and technical support. Another concern is that the digital divide has affected whether economically disadvantaged students have access to computer-assisted instruction.

The use of digital technologies in college classrooms has increased since the early 1990s, with many institutions requiring students to own computers. In college education, computers are used for multimedia presentations in the classroom, mostly through PowerPoint; simulations and modeling; educational games; research databases; and online course materials using programs like Blackboard and Angel. Some professors have begun delivering lectures and sharing other course materials through podcasts, and many colleges and universities provide distance education and online courses to make education more convenient and cost-effective. However, the increase in computer-assisted instruction is not without social controversy. For example, some question whether such instruction is more effective than traditional teaching, whether technologies like PowerPoint impose too much control over the classroom environment, and whether technologies like distance education are simply a way for universities to make profits at the expense of education.[32] Computer technologies also pose many issues for higher education, such as budget allocations, privacy and security of student records, intellectual property, and teacher training and support.

TRENDS

One trend, more than any other, is driving the changes in people's use of computers: high-speed Internet connections. In February 2005, 56 percent of U.S. households and 82 percent of businesses had broadband. Worldwide, the household penetration rate was 4.5 percent in 2006, with the most subscribers in the United States, China, Japan, South Korea, and France. Many regions of the world lag far behind, with Africa, the Middle East, Eastern Europe, and Latin America caught on the other side of the digital divide.[33] A more diverse population in the United States is gaining high-speed access, with increased subscriptions among African Americans, senior citizens, inhabitants of rural areas, and those with less than a high school education.[34] Broadband over power lines (BPL) may bring more access to remote populations.

Broadband connections are central to the growth of rich multimedia, the use of portable digital devices, and the convergence of radio, television, movies, and other media. They promote increased user-generated content and interactivity, such as multiplayer online gaming and music and video sharing. They have reshaped workplaces, and have begun to alter educational and health care institutions. And they have created an environment in which users can be connected to their computers twenty-four hours a day. As more people around the world gain access, while others either refuse or have no opportunity for it, the cultural, social, economic, and political implications are vast.

Technology: Web 2.0

Web 2.0 has become a popular term among many Internet software and content developers, and broadly refers to new companies and applications, like Google, Napster, and Wikipedia, that arose after the dot.com bust of 2001. Knowledge consultant Tim O'Reilly, who helped introduce the concept, has defined its features:

1. Instead of software, Web 2.0 companies provide services. For example, Google operates as a facilitator, bringing together content from many sources, like websites, newspapers, and digitally scanned books.
2. Web 2.0 companies own important, unique databases. For example, through peer-to-peer file sharing, services like Napster have formed a vast, global musical resource.
3. Web 2.0 companies trust users as participants in development of resources. Individual clients provide music, videos, news stories, and other content for the database. The service acts as an intermediary in a decentralized system of content providers.
4. Therefore, these Web 2.0 services represent a collective intelligence. The more users who participate in adding links and content, the smarter the service becomes.

5. Web 2.0 companies allow users to select among many kinds of content or products, each with low demand, but that add up collectively to a large demand. For example, unlike a mainstream bookstore, which must carry mostly bestsellers to make a profit, Amazon may sell an obscure book with a limited readership because all of these small sales generate large profits. Amazon allows users to serve themselves according to their unique interests.
6. Users can access Web 2.0 services from a variety of devices, such as cell phones and PDAs.
7. Web 2.0 software development, user interfaces, and business models operate on principles of providing rich content, user-friendliness, and usability.

An overriding principle of Web 2.0 is that the services provide an "architecture of participation," inviting users to add to software projects and databases.[35] It is also facilitated by recent development like peer-to-peer (P2P) file sharing, **RSS** feeds that allow users to subscribe to content notices from webpages, and **folksonomies** that allow users to label and more easily share content through tagging.

RSS

A data file that notifies users of updates to webpage contents.

folksonomy

A method for users to label the content they create with identifying words and phrases.

Technology: Nomadic and Pervasive Computing

Key Concept:

Nomadic computing Portable digital devices have freed users from fixed computers. With nomadic computing they can use mobile devices to access computer networks from almost anywhere.

Key Concept:

Pervasive computing Some computer scientists envision a world in which the environment is saturated with computer chips. Pervasive computing, also called ubiquitous computing, refers to the integration of chips and other digital technologies into ordinary objects.

The portability of computer devices is transforming the landscape of how, why, and where people use them.

Wireless technologies like WiFi and 3G and portable digital devices like cell phones and PDAs have freed Internet users from their fixed home and office computers. This phenomenon has been called *nomadic computing*, in which users have "independence of location, motion, and platform and widespread access to remote files, systems, and services."[36] An increasing number of global businesspeople and telecommuters can access their email, contact lists, and corporate and government networks anytime, anywhere. Many organizations are encouraging the trend. For example, the U.S. government requires agencies to promote telework so that agencies can continue to function in the event of a disaster like a flood or flu epidemic.[37]

Nomadic computing is connected to *pervasive, or ubiquitous computing*, which is the increasing presence of computer chips, not only in portable devices, but in ordinary objects in everyday environments. An inhabitant of an information society may carry some combination of laptop, pager, mobile phone, GPS, and personal digital assistant, and own a pair of Nike shoes that communicates data to an iPod. But advocates of pervasive computing would like to have environments saturated with computer chips embedded in objects like credit cards, clothes, vending machines, cars, appliances, and even the human body. For example, the VeriChip, approved by the FDA for use in 2004, is a tiny chip implanted in hospital patients so that personal and medical information can be easily scanned. Radio frequency identification (RFID) chips are embedded in products in large stores like Wal-Mart for inventory purposes. But some computer scientists have a larger goal in mind, hoping to create smart environments in which every artifact has a chip that communicates with a user according to that person's profile. However, embedded chips are highly controversial, with critics of pervasive computing expressing concern about security and privacy.

In the twenty-first century, the spread of broadband access and the increased possibilities for convergence have had dramatic impact on almost all aspects of economic, political, and social life. Portable digital devices have freed users from fixed computers, and changed the way they receive media content. Digital media bring hopes and fears about the future of individuals, families, communities, nations, and the world. As the technologies evolve, many questions remain. These include:

- What new business models and audience behaviors may arise from the delivery of media content across digital media platforms? What will increased possibilities for interactivity mean for the future of media?

- How will cultures throughout the world change as broadband access becomes widespread? Will this change the way cultures relate to one another?

- To what extent will content be delivered through portable devices? How popular will that content be? How will portable digital devices change the way we work and play?

- How will governments and Internet users negotiate issues of privacy in the future?

Culture: Hopes and Fears

In 2004, the Pew Internet & American Life Project began surveying computer pioneers, social analysts, and other technology experts about the future of the Internet, proposing various scenarios to which they responded.[38] The project directors hoped that by gathering predictions, they could contribute to sounder planning and policy decisions. The answers provide a glimpse into prevalent fears and hopes about a technology that is still emerging.

Of the more fearful scenarios, many experts agreed that a terrorist attack on the information infrastructure is likely by 2014, either through a computer bug or a physical attack on a facility such as a power grid. As of February 2007, terrorist organizations had used cybercrime like credit card fraud to raise money, rather than attempting to attack computer systems; however, such an attack could cause a large power blackout, economic disruption, and loss of key data. Some experts hypothesize that an attack might come from a growing number of people who are opposed to accelerating technology and its negative social impacts. Other fears expressed in the report include an over-dependency on automated systems, an expansion of government and business surveillance with the increase of pervasive computing, and an increase in Internet addiction, as more people become involved in alternative virtual realities.

On a more positive note, the experts predicted that by 2020, a low-cost global network will exist that will be accessible to most of the world's peoples. However, ethnographer Tony Salvador and anthropologist John Sherry have outlined some of the challenges to a worldwide Internet. Places that have unreliable electricity, wet or dirty conditions, small living spaces, and unreliable roads for transport will have a tough time gaining access to PCs. Further, potential users must have either enough money to buy them or have public computers available. Governments do not always support computer use, either by imposing high tariffs on their importation or forbidding ownership of PCs and access to computer networks.[39] Therefore, a network that reaches all people faces considerable challenges.

A global network will have implications for cultures and languages. English has become the most common language used in cross-cultural transactions, especially in scientific research and business. Many of the Pew experts, however, predict that other languages, especially Mandarin, will gain in importance and that the Internet will help preserve languages and cultures threatened with extinction.

SUMMARY

- Computers are used in every application by traditional mass media organizations. They are also a medium in their own right and are used directly by consumers.
- The computer began as an attempt to create calculating machines, then evolved as scientists sought efficient means to organize, retrieve, and process information.
- Although the computer industry is highly diversified and competitive, giants such as IBM and Microsoft have held leading roles and dominated different portions of the industry at different times.
- Computer research and networking have been heavily funded by the U.S. government because of the implications for defense and strategic applications.
- The development of the silicon chip in 1959 made it possible for the computer to shrink in size.
- The modem is the connection to the computerized world, the device that makes possible the concept of an information highway. A major issue is whether the cable industry or telephone companies will win dominance to provide access to computer users.
- The Internet is a series of computers networked to other computers that provide the fundamental basis of an information highway.
- Convergence—the delivery of content across multiple digital platforms—is increasingly rapidly.
- Because of fast broadband connections, the Internet is increasingly becoming the key delivery system for text, audio, and video.
- People increasingly go online for information about health, politics, shopping, and education.
- Computing is becoming a nomadic activity, as people access the Internet through portable devices.

NAVIGATING THE WEB The Internet

Many people who use the web are interested in computers, technology, and the potential of the information highway. On websites, you can find information on the history of computers, new technologies, and the business of technology.

TechWeb
techweb.com

This publication provides news and analysis of development in the information technology business, including coverage of Internet media companies.

Digg
digg.com

On this Web 2.0 site, users submit content and vote on it. Many of the featured stories are related to new developments in computer technology.

Electronic Privacy Information Center
epic.org

EPIC is a public interest research center in Washington, D.C. It was established in 1994 to focus public attention on emerging civil liberties issues and to protect privacy, the First Amendment, and constitutional values. EPIC is a project of the Fund for Constitutional Government. It works in association with Privacy International, an international human rights group based in London, and is also a member of the Global Internet Liberty Campaign, the Internet Free Expression Alliance, the Internet Privacy Coalition, and the Trans Atlantic Consumer Dialogue (TACD).

Wired
wired.com

Launch in 1993 and inspired by the ideas of Marshall McLuhan, *Wired Magazine* and its website provide news about the political, economic, and cultural effects of cutting-edge technology.

ZDNet
zdnet.com

The ZDNet Webzine comes from Ziff-Davis, the largest publisher of computer magazines. It covers news about computers and the world of online businesses.

QUESTIONS FOR REVIEW

1. What was IBM's role in the development of computer technology?
2. Why is Microsoft a significant player in computer delivery of mass media?
3. What is an operating system?
4. What is the digital divide?
5. What is Software as a Service?
6. What is Web 2.0?

ISSUES TO THINK ABOUT

1. To what extent is a global computer network desirable? What are some of the obstacles to developing such a network?
2. What aspects of social life can't be transferred into online environments and exchanges? Why?
3. What will happen to traditional media forms, such as television shows and movies, as they become increasingly delivered through the web?
4. Develop your idea for a website that would meet the needs of a professional today. How would you structure the content of such a site and what links would you include?
5. If you were designing a newspaper for the future, how would you incorporate new technology?

SUGGESTED READINGS

Bakardjieva, Maria. *Internet Society: The Internet in Everyday Life* (London: SAGE, 2005).

Goldsmith, Jack, and Tim Wu. *Who Controls the Internet?: Illusions of a Borderless World* (New York: Oxford University Press, 2006).

Grier, David Alan. *When Computers Were Human* (Princeton, NJ: Princeton University Press, 2005).

Negroponte, Nicholas. *Being Digital* (New York: Alfred A. Knopf, 1995).

Taylor, Robert W. et al. *Digital Crime and Digital Terrorism* (Upper Saddle River, NJ: Pearson/Prentice Hall, 2006).

Vise, David A., and Mark Malseed. *The Google Story* (New York: Delacorte, 2005).

Journalism:
Information and Society

The year 2006 was a tense one in the relationship between journalists and the U.S. federal government. Pulitzer Prizes in national reporting were awarded to two stories the White House would have preferred not to see in print. Dana Priest, of the *Washington Post,* won for her article describing the detainment of al Qaeda prisoners in secret CIA prisons, called "black sites," in places like Eastern Europe, Thailand, and Afghanistan. James Risen and Eric Lichtblau, of the *New York Times,* won for their series on the government's use of wiretaps, without court-approved warrants, to eavesdrop on thousands of U.S. citizens.

In both cases, the White House had pressured the papers not to print the stories, which used unnamed government sources. Of the wiretapping story, President Bush said, "It was a shameful act for someone to disclose this very important program in a time of war. The fact that we're discussing this program is helping the enemy."[1] The Pulitzer Prizes were thus contentious, with proponents arguing that the committee had stood up for freedom of the press and the public's right to know, and critics arguing that the papers had been wrong, even treasonous, to reveal vital government secrets in the war on terrorism.

In U.S. history, tensions have often surfaced between the government and the press, which has traditionally had a watchdog role in providing information and holding public figures and institutions accountable for their actions. The press also must be accountable for its own actions, upholding journalistic standards and ethics. Sometimes,

KEY CONCEPTS

- Journalism
- Political Journalism
- Enlightenment Philosophy
- Journalism of Exposure
- Televised Presidential Debates
- Objectivity
- Narrative Tradition
- Agenda-Setting
- News Values
- Computer-Assisted Reporting
- Public Journalism
- Participatory Journalism

as in the case of the mentioned prize-winning stories, editors face difficult decisions in deciding whether to publish. In times of war, the stakes may be especially high.

Journalism—reporting on government, politics, policies, economics, and other news and issues—has become a cornerstonc of American life. The United States was founded on the assumption that a populace could govern if it was well informed. President James Madison wrote that "knowledge will forever govern ignorance, and a people who mean to be their own governors, must arm themselves with the power knowledge gives. A **popular government** without popular information or the means of acquiring it is but a prologue to a farce or a tragedy or perhaps both."[2]

In 1945, Supreme Court Justice Hugo Black reaffirmed the importance of information in American society, noting that the First Amendment guarantee of a free press "rests upon the assumption that the widest possible dissemination of information from diverse and antagonistic sources is essential to the well-being of the public."[3]

Although the history of journalism is often confused with the history of the newspaper because newspapers were one of the earliest and most common methods of distribution of information about public life, the two are separate and distinct. Newspapers are a delivery system. Today the delivery systems for journalism include radio, television, magazines, books, and websites. Some people define journalism as an act—a method and art of collecting and presenting information that ultimately is distributed through various channels; others describe it as a ritual—a way of sustaining, enriching, and challenging societal norms; still others see it as a form of public storytelling that helps define cultural identities, beliefs, and values.

Journalism has a changing face. As news professionals continue into the twenty-first century, these issues will need to be addressed:

- How will journalists maintain their credibility in the face of infotainment—a combination of news and entertainment designed to win profits for media companies?

- Who gets to tell the news? With many news outlets available, what is the role of the professional journalist?

- How does journalism foster the values of a society?

- What has been the impact of the twenty-four-hour news cycle on the thoughtful delivery of news?

- How does the role of the journalist change as she or he adapts to a variety of delivery systems including print, radio, television, cable, and online?

Key Concept

Journalism Journalism is the way news is disseminated through reporting on government, politics, policies, economics, and other news and issues.

Key Concept

Political Journalism This special type of journalism focuses on reporting on the political process, including campaigns and elections, Congress, the presidency, and other government and political entities.

JOURNALISM IN AMERICAN LIFE

Throughout U.S. history, *journalism* has helped make the government a government "of" and "by" the people. *Political journalism* has helped guard against secrecy and governmental power. Thus journalism's primary purpose has been to inform. But in different periods, it also has been a powerful persuasive tool. And from the earliest times, it has sought to entertain by providing information about unusual happenings and humorous incidents. In recent years, a move by

Journalism in Your Life

Information and Credibility

Most of us trust that journalists' goal is to provide news and information that helps us to adapt to our society and to make informed judgments about political and economic choices. What journalistic venues do you trust?

Journalistic Venues	TRUSTWORTHINESS (Rate from One to Five, with Five Being the Most Trustworthy)	REGULARITY OF USE (Rate as Daily, Several Times a Week, or Weekly)	TYPE OF INFORMATION (Rate as Breaking News, Analysis, or Entertaining News)
Network television news			
Cable television news			
Local television news			
Online news from newspapers			
Online news from national websites (CNN, MSNBC, etc.)			
Online news from Google or Yahoo			
Newspapers			
Magazines of information and opinion			
Radio news			

many media industries toward **infotainment,** a blur of information and entertainment, has caused many journalists to worry about redefining the essence of journalism.

Challenges to Elite Authority

During the early colonial period, journalists were not a separate occupational group; they were editors, postmasters, and elite businessmen who sought to earn a living by printing information and who wanted to play a role in the founding of a new country. These writers were citizens first and intellectuals or commentators second. This point is important because freedom of expression is not granted to an elite cadre of journalists—it is granted to citizens of the United States. Thus journalists do not have rights that ordinary citizens do not have.

Scholars debate how courageous journalists were during the colonial period. Some argue that journalists were quite cautious, rarely challenging the status quo. Others point out that despite the fact that governors in the colonies did not like criticism of themselves or the British government, journalists still spoke out.[4]

For example, in 1733, John Peter Zenger, printing the *New York Weekly Journal* for a radical attorney named James Alexander, was charged with **seditious libel** for openly criticizing the royal governor of New York. At that time, the law allowed a jury

popular government

Government that is controlled by the citizenry rather than an elite cadre of officials.

infotainment

A blend of information and entertainment. Critics believe such treatments masquerade as journalism and deceive the public.

seditious libel

Criticism of the government. In colonial times, such criticism was considered libelous even if it was true.

The acquittal of printer John Peter Zenger on charges of seditious libel made media history because it set a precedent for truth (as a defense for libel) in journalism.

to determine only whether a printer had actually published specific material, not whether the material was true or was, indeed, seditious. After a highly publicized trial and an eloquent defense by Andrew Hamilton, the jury acquitted Zenger, thereby establishing a political, although not a legal, **precedent** for the right to criticize government. Hamilton argued that truth should be a defense in any seditious libel trial and that a jury should be able to judge not only whether an accused printer actually printed the material, but also whether it was libelous. He appealed to the colonists' dislike of arbitrary power, an aversion that would become even stronger as colonists began to consider independence.[5]

Independence and the Marketplace of Ideas

Journalists played an important role during the late-eighteenth-century struggle for independence. They not only recounted events but also presented competing ideologies for discussion in the marketplace of ideas. During the mid-eighteenth century—especially after the French and Indian War, which required colonists to contribute to what they considered a British cause—colonists began to entertain the idea of increased independence from Britain. Many of the imported books, local newspapers, and pamphlets read by the colonists spread the ideas of the Enlightenment, a philosophical movement during the seventeenth and eighteenth centuries that generated new ideas about scientific reasoning, democracy, rule by consent of the governed, and free criticism of government. These ideas challenged authoritarian control and championed individual rights and democratic participation.

Chief among intellectuals and editors who challenged British authority was Benjamin Franklin. He established a prominent newspaper in Philadelphia, ran a bookshop, printed a newspaper and various pamphlets, attempted publication of a magazine, and helped found a public library system. He extended his printing network to the southern colonies by financing printers so they could start bookshops and printing establishments in growing cities. He gained fame for both the lightning rod experiments that later earned him a place in elementary school science books and the "Join or Die" snake, a graphic representation of the need for the colonies to stick together in their fight against England or else undergo separate deaths.

When the British Parliament passed the Stamp Act, which assessed a tax on paper, newspaper publishers rebelled. The tax was designed to help pay for the French and Indian War, which started in 1756. The colonists argued that they had no say in whether or how the war should be fought and therefore should not have to pay the tax. In protest some of the newspaper publishers printed woodcuts with skull-and-crossbones emblems; others ceased publishing and refused to pay the tax. By the

precedent

A legal decision that sets a standard for how subsequent cases are decided.

time of the Revolution, most printers were notoriously patriotic. A lack of tolerance for diversity of political opinion characterized most communities, and printers who remained loyal to the British Crown were quickly exiled. Despite protests against British control of the press, colonists readily exercised their own control of public opinion by suppressing unpopular opinions. The resistance to free expression for everyone during times of stress became a characteristic of American media during the next two centuries, and the media often felt free to demonize and stereotype America's perceived enemies in times of social strife or war.

Newspaper editors and pamphleteers such as Thomas Paine cheered the colonists onward. During the struggle for independence, when George Washington's troops were mired in winter snows in Trenton, New Jersey, Paine offered eloquent pleas for steadfastness, such as, "These are the times that try men's souls."

The Fight for Political Dominance

Although the states ratified the Constitution with no provision for a free press, within three years (in 1791) a Bill of Rights was added to ensure civil liberties: among others, the right to assemble, to choose a religion, to speak and write freely, and to be tried fairly. Chief among the Bill of Rights was the First Amendment:

> Congress shall make no law respecting an establishment of religion, or prohibiting the free exercise thereof; or abridging the freedom of speech, or of the press; or the right of the public peaceably to assemble, and to petition the government for a redress of grievances.

From 1790 to 1830, during the constitutional debates and the establishment of political parties, most editors and commentators argued vociferously on one side. Eighteenth-century political writers did not value objectivity as an ideal. Journalists, often members of the social elite and appointed by a politician, helped establish the function of the press in a newly created democratic society.[6] They sometimes overstepped the boundaries of good taste, but they established the right of journalists to comment on political competition, a right that has fueled the political process ever since. These commentators sided with either the Federalists, who wanted a strong central government, or the Anti-Federalists, who argued to preserve the powers of the states.

The period of rabid political rhetoric has been labeled the **Dark Ages** of American journalism by many historians. Anti-Federalist Benjamin Franklin Bache, the grandson of Benjamin Franklin, accused the revered George Washington of having "debauched" the nation and argued that "the masque of patriotism may be worn to conceal the foulest designs against the liberties of a people." Bache was so outrageous that even his friends at times turned against him. But he stuck to his political principles, "in which he said that government officers were fallible, the Constitution good but not obviously 'stampt with the seal of perfection,' and that a free press was 'one of the first safeguards of Liberty.'"[7] A vituperative editor on the Federalist side, William Cobbett, called Bache black-hearted, seditious, sleepy-eyed, vile, and perverted.

Despite the First Amendment, a Federalist Congress in 1798 passed the restrictive Naturalization, Enemy Alien, and Sedition Acts. These laws, commonly called the **Alien and Sedition Acts,** made it possible to indict those who "shall write, print, utter, or publish . . . false, scandalous and malicious writing or writings against the Government of the United States, or the President of the United States, or either house of the Congress . . . with intent to defame . . . or to bring them into contempt or disrepute." Those who were convicted could be punished by a fine of not more than $2,000 and could be imprisoned for two years. Anti-Federalist editors across the land were indicted and jailed, and only when Thomas Jefferson took office as president of the United States in 1801 were those editors released. The Alien and Sedition Acts indeed marked a low point, with their restrictions against the criticism of government in a time of peace. Because those acts were passed but not renewed, such restrictions generally have been reserved for times of war.

Dark Ages of journalism

Period when the republic was formed and reporters and editors were highly partisan in their efforts to build a new political system.

Alien and Sedition Acts

Federalist laws passed in 1798 to restrict freedom of information. They were used to quell political dissent.

History of Press Responsibility

When the First Amendment was written, idealists adhered to the ***Enlightenment philosophy*** that all individuals are born equal to learn, improve, and make proper decisions from which to lead productive lives. The government was thought to exist only as an extension of the people. It was the responsibility of the press to provide information to individuals, who were considered rational beings who could discern truth from falsehood. The founders of the United States believed that if a variety of people contributed ideas to the discussion, a free marketplace of ideas would be created and the truth would emerge. For the marketplace of ideas to succeed, the market needs to provide free access for those who would contribute.

By the twentieth century, the Industrial Revolution had changed society and the press. Individuals became more interdependent, and national media developed as radio and television expanded. During the Great Depression, Franklin Delano Roosevelt introduced federal programs based on the concept that government has the responsibility to make sure people live in acceptable conditions. In addition, with the implementation of compulsory education, people gave government the responsibility of educating the children. To some degree, U.S. society had exchanged individualism for protectionism and collectivism. With that change came renewed calls for offering individuals information that would allow them to put events and issues into context.

In 1947 a commission chaired by Robert Hutchins expressed the change in society's expectations of the press system. The **Hutchins Commission,** funded primarily by Henry Luce, founder of *Time* and *Life,* said that the great influence of media and the concentration of ownership required that media be socially responsible. The commission, after reviewing press behavior, decried the state of American journalism.

The commission listed five "ideal demands of society for the communication of news and ideas":

1. A truthful, comprehensive, and intelligent account of the day's events in a context that gives them meaning
2. A forum for the exchange of comment and criticism
3. The projection of a representative picture of the constituent groups in society
4. The presentation and clarification of the goals and values of society
5. Full access to the day's intelligence

After evaluating the press in light of its ideal demands, the commission found freedom of the press in the United States to be in danger because of the monopolistic nature of the press. Concentration meant, the commission noted, that fewer people had access to communication channels and that those in charge had not provided a service adequate to society's needs.

Concerned with the potential of new technology to be developed for either good or evil, the commission discussed guidelines for regulation of new technology and international communications systems.[8] The commission chose, however, to assign the press the responsibility of "accountability," rather than recommending increased government regulation. The commission suggested that retraction or restatement might better serve victims of libel rather than suits for damages, and it recommended repeal of state syndicalism acts and the Alien Registration Act of 1940, saying they were of "dubious constitutionality." The commission also suggested that the government assume responsibility for disseminating its own news, through either private channels or channels of its own.

Hutchins Commission

Commission established in the 1940s to review press conduct. The commission argued that the press should provide intelligence that would enable the public to understand the issues of the day.

The commission suggested that the press should accept the responsibility of being a "common carrier" of information and discussion rather than assuming that ownership meant dissemination of a personal viewpoint. It encouraged owners to experiment with new activities, especially in areas in which profits were not necessarily

Cultural Impact

Data Mining and Student Privacy

A graduate student from the Medill School of Journalism at Northwestern University, Laura McGann, broke the story. The U.S. Department of Education had provided information from hundreds of student financial aid applications to the FBI, including Social Security and driver's license numbers. The data-mining operation, called "Project Strike Back," had begun just after the September 11 attacks as part of antiterror investigations. McGann had discovered her story in a reference to Project Strike Back in a document from the Government Accountability Office. She then filed a Freedom of Information Act request, and received heavily censored documents that allowed her to complete the research.

The story was distributed widely through the Associated Press and made the *New York Times* and the *Chronicle of Higher Education,* causing concern among privacy experts and students across the country. Educators worried that secret data-mining efforts could be extended to other student records, especially a new proposed system to track a student's progress that would include attendance, courses, fields of study, and financial information. Thus, McGann's story contributed to a national policy debate over maintaining the privacy of student information.

McGann had been working with a team of students on a News21 project, funded by the Carnegie Corporation and the John S. and James L. Knight Foundation. The project focused on privacy, civil liberties, and homeland security, and the students talked to government officials and privacy experts, used computers to analyze government databases, and researched publicly available documents to investigate how citizens' personal information is collected and used. The work led to McGann's piece, another national story on finger scanning at Walt Disney World, and a multimedia web presentation, *Digital Dilemma: Privacy in an Age of Security* (newsinitiative.org/project/data_dilemma).

In the opening to *Digital Dilemma,* News21 producers describe what they call the "digital trails" that we leave everywhere in an information-rich society: "We log onto computers at school and work, use our debit cards to buy lunch, scan our membership cards at the gym; the list goes on and on. With each of these everyday acts we leave a digital bread crumb that enables others to track our movements. But how often do we stop and wonder, who is following these virtual trails?"

Sources: Jeffrey Selingo, "Education Department Mined Hundreds of Students' Records as Part of FBI Antiterrorist Operation," *Chronicle of Higher Education,* August 31, 2006; Laura McGann, "Student-Loan Forms Combed for Names of Terror Suspects," *Fort Worth Star-Telegram,* September 1, 2006; Robert Mentzer, "Medill Students Break National News with News21 Project 'Liberty vs. Security,'" *Inside Medill News,* August 21, 2006, medill.northwestern.edu/medill/archives.html.

---

assured. The commission also encouraged vigorous mutual criticism by members of the press and increased competence of news staffs. It also chided the radio industry for giving away control to soap sponsors and recommended the industry take control of its programs by treating advertisers the way the "best" newspapers treated them.

Focusing on freedom as "bound up intrinsically in the collective good of life in society," the commission further suggested that the public had a social responsibility to ensure continued freedom of the press, requesting that nonprofit institutions help supply variety and quality to press service. It requested that educational centers be created for advanced research about communications and emphasized the importance of the liberal arts in journalistic training.[9]

Renewing the discussion of the importance of a free and accessible press to a democratic society, the Hutchins Commission finally recommended that an independent agency be established to appraise and report annually on the performance of

Dateline

Journalism in Our Lives

1600s. Journalists double as printers and editors.

1700s. Journalists covering Congress act as recorders of debate.

1733. Zenger attacks establishment.

1794. Senate opens press gallery.

1790–1830. Journalists debate values of competing parties.

1820s. Journalistic reports extend recording debate to reporting.

1830s. Occupational role of journalist develops.

1861–1865. Young reporters come to Washington, D.C., to cover war.

1890s. Journalists cover sports, social events, theater. Development of muckraking.

1920. Photojournalists take advantage of new technology.

1922. First noontime news broadcast

1932. Radio reporters cover Hoover–Roosevelt presidential race.

1400–1700	1800	1860	1880	1900	1920	1930

1620. Pilgrims land at Plymouth Rock.

1690. *Publick Occurrences* is published in Boston.

1741. First magazine is published in America.

1776–1783. American Revolution

1830s. The penny press becomes the first truly mass medium in the United States.

1861–1865. American Civil War

1892. Thomas Edison's lab develops the kinetoscope.

1914–1918. World War I

1915. *The Birth of a Nation* marks the start of the modern movie industry.

1920. KDKA in Pittsburgh gets the first commercial radio license.

1930s. The Great Depression

1939. TV is demonstrated at the New York World's Fair.

1939–1945. World War II

Cultural Milestones

the press. The commission worried, however, that too much emphasis was being placed on that recommendation. Nevertheless, it seemed to be the only solution commissioners could agree on, after acknowledging that the concept of laissez-faire, not government control, would eliminate the effects of monopoly.[10]

Needless to say, the owners of the agencies of mass communication reacted negatively. Many members of the press were critical because no one from its ranks was included on the commission. Responding to the criticism, the American Society of Newspaper Editors (ASNE) in 1950 appointed ten newspapermen and educators to investigate self-improvement possibilities. The editors' findings reaffirmed the concept

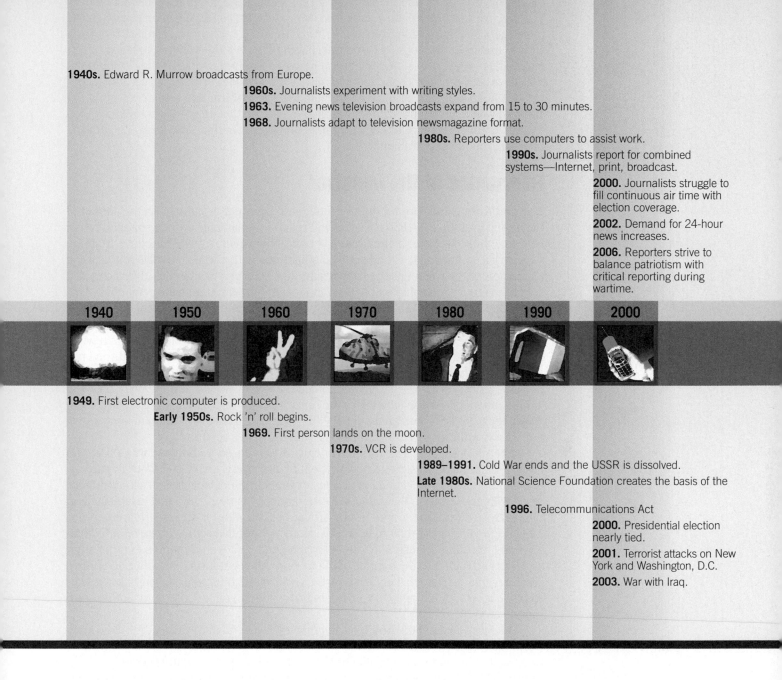

1940s. Edward R. Murrow broadcasts from Europe.

1960s. Journalists experiment with writing styles.

1963. Evening news television broadcasts expand from 15 to 30 minutes.

1968. Journalists adapt to television newsmagazine format.

1980s. Reporters use computers to assist work.

1990s. Journalists report for combined systems—Internet, print, broadcast.

2000. Journalists struggle to fill continuous air time with election coverage.

2002. Demand for 24-hour news increases.

2006. Reporters strive to balance patriotism with critical reporting during wartime.

1940	1950	1960	1970	1980	1990	2000

1949. First electronic computer is produced.

Early 1950s. Rock 'n' roll begins.

1969. First person lands on the moon.

1970s. VCR is developed.

1989–1991. Cold War ends and the USSR is dissolved.

Late 1980s. National Science Foundation creates the basis of the Internet.

1996. Telecommunications Act

2000. Presidential election nearly tied.

2001. Terrorist attacks on New York and Washington, D.C.

2003. War with Iraq.

of laissez-faire and rejected the commission's recommendations, claiming that improvement of U.S. newspapers depended on "the character of American newspaper-men" and their "acceptance of the great responsibilities imposed by freedom of the press." The ASNE study suggested that reporters and editors might be more willing to profit by the "intelligent criticism of the newspaper-reading public" than they would by suggestions made by a commission over which they had no control.[11]

For much of the twentieth century, **social responsibility theory** became the dominant theoretical model for media and still has influence. As coauthor of *Four Theories of the Press,* Theodore Peterson wrote, "freedom carries concomitant obligations;

social responsibility theory

As applied to freedom of the press, a philosophy that states that with freedom comes responsibility to the social good.

and the press, which enjoys a privileged position under our government, is obliged to be responsible to society for carrying out certain essential functions of mass communications in contemporary society." In this view, media should continue to be free from government in order to watch over government and should act as a gatekeeper representing the public's interest.

Many journalists and media analysts still accept the social responsibility theory in some form, but others have criticized its limitations, especially in an era when the public gets its information from many sources such as cable news, satellite radio talk shows, and political blogs. For example, people are no longer limited to a few newsmagazines, newspapers, and television news on three networks as they were in the mid-twentieth century. The traditional news media no longer have as powerful a central gatekeeping role that once offered limited ways of framing and interpreting social and political events. With its interactive capabilities, new media have allowed the public emergence of many viewpoints and interests that now compete with the mainstream news for influence.[12]

Emergence of the Reporter

The shift from editor/printer/intellectual to reporter/editor came with the advent of the penny press in the 1830s. As you will read in the chapter on newspapers, urban editors wanted to expand circulations, hoping that revenues would follow. In doing so, they recognized that strong political affiliations with parties would jeopardize the expansion of their readership. They began to rely more strongly on advertising and sought to report news that would be of interest to all. With this strategy in mind, Benjamin Day of the *New York Sun* hired a reporter—a person who collects information and presents it in a readable fashion to a wide range of readers.

Day hired George W. Wisner, a young reporter, and paid him four dollars a week to rise at four in the morning to cover daily police court sessions. Wisner turned police court charges of spousal assault and petty debt into action and drama for the *Sun's* news pages. Crime stories reinforced the social values of the day by showing what happened to those who broke the rules, but they also appealed to an interest in "bad people." Wisner was an ardent abolitionist, so he used his position to try to sneak antislavery editorials into the *Sun* along with his police reports.

When Wisner left New York for Michigan, Day hired Richard Adams Locke, an educated man who was interested in scientific discovery. Locke is famous in journalism history for his 1835 series of articles exploiting the discoveries of Sir John Frederick William Herschel, the greatest astronomer of his time, who had established an observatory near Cape Town, South Africa. Locke's story illustrates that entertainment, along with information, was considered a journalistic goal. Locke reported that Herschel, through the use of a new telescope, had discovered planets in other solar systems and had seen the surface of the moon with vegetation, animals, and winged creatures that resembled men and women. Locke cited the *Edinburgh Journal of Science* as his source and managed to fool not only the general public but the scientific community as well.

The *Sun* defended the **hoax,** saying that it was useful in diverting the public mind from such worrisome issues as the abolition of slavery. The Moon Hoax, as it came to be called, is often used to illustrate the claim that penny editors were less concerned with fact and objectivity than with entertaining their public. Sometimes a little fiction was useful in building circulation. Some critics speculate that Locke was trying to upstage the staid, political papers of New York City, which had rejected the penny press as sensationalistic. These papers could not ignore Locke's story, and most of them printed it. When the hoax was revealed, the papers had little argument with which to defend themselves against the penny press upstarts.

hoax

An act or story intended to deceive; a tall tale; a practical joke or serious fraud.

The reporter thus became established as a fixture in American journalism. Fictional accounts of reporters in the late nineteenth and early twentieth centuries depict them as semieducated "tough guys" who were out to expose corrupt businessmen and government officials. Women, though they began to enter the ranks, are relatively invisible in the fictional accounts. The intellectual role of the newspaper was relegated to the editorial page, and editors who often were heavily involved in politics made editorial decisions. The editors continued to separate themselves financially from political parties, but most editors strongly supported a particular party.

The Reporter and Social Conscience   During the mid-1800s, newspaper journalists began to expose the wrongdoings of city officials and to focus on city services and politics. During the late 1800s, reporters established the form of reporting called **muckraking,** unearthing corporate greed and exposing it to the masses. The food and drug industry had expanded quickly without regulation, and reporters found that many commercial food-handling situations were dangerous to the consumer. Although the articles were often labeled sensational, they were boring by today's standards. Filled with detail, they dutifully chronicled industry violations of safety and health standards. But they were sensational at the time because to that date no one had written publicly about the issues being discussed. People were shocked to see the material. Much of the material was in the same vein as the social documentary, which found a place in books and, after the turn of the century, to some degree in newsreels. Muckrakers established the *journalism of exposure* as a basic tenet of American journalism.

Photojournalism   As the Kodak box camera began to revolutionize public photography after 1900, the development of the 35-millimeter camera and fast film created new opportunities for photojournalism, which was an extension of the type of photography social reformers had used between 1880 and 1915 to document the negative social effects of the Industrial Revolution.

The *New York Sun* fascinated its readers in the 1830s with stories of observations of winged creatures on the moon. The stories and the illustrations turned out to be fakes.

muckraking

Using the journalism of exposure. The term was given to the press by Theodore Roosevelt, who claimed the press "raked the muck" but refused to regard the "celestial crown." Often used as a term for reporting on business.

This heart-wrenching example of photojournalist Jacob A. Riis's work as a social reformer shows street children in New York City in 1889.

Some journalists tried to expose these problems through heavy use of illustration. Jacob A. Riis and Lewis W. Hine photographed the plight of the poor and homeless to show what can happen to unskilled workers in an unregulated capitalist economic system. In the 1920s, social documentary photography was greatly enhanced with the introduction of the small Leica camera, made by E. Leitz of Germany. With the Leica, a photographer could work unnoticed while recording a scene. Film that could be quickly exposed and new printing techniques contributed to the development of picture magazines in Germany, England, and the United States. By the 1960s, *Life* and *Look* became showcase magazines for the work of photographers. However, television quickly eclipsed the magazines, and current visual images that moved captivated the public.

JOURNALISM ON RADIO AND TELEVISION

Print journalism—and print and wire reporters—dominated journalism through the first third of the twentieth century. At first radio was merely a voice for the newspaper; newspaper copy fashioned by print journalists was read across the air. Later, reporters developed specific styles oriented toward listeners and viewers. In July 1922, the *Norfolk* [Nebraska] *Daily News* started the first regularly broadcast noon news program. In 1932, radio reporters covered the Roosevelt–Hoover presidential race and launched radio news. They also started a major industry battle between newspapers and radio, and publishers sought to keep radio from competing with them by limiting radio access to news from the major wire services. Newspapers could not stop radio, however, and by the late 1930s radio news was becoming a standard feature.

Radio and World War II

Radio journalists became popular sources of news with their dramatic and complete coverage of World War II. Before radio, war news took hours, days, or even weeks to reach the general public. Radio was instantaneous. Furthermore, print could never match the immediacy of Edward R. Murrow broadcasting from London as German bombs ripped through the city. Murrow developed a radio style, an intimate conversation with his listeners.

During the 1938 coverage of Germany's invasion of Austria, Murrow set up the first simultaneous broadcast with reporters in Vienna, London, Paris, Berlin, and Rome. By the time Hitler invaded Poland in 1939, CBS and NBC had placed experienced reporters throughout Europe. By 1943, the amount of radio news in the networks' evening programming had tripled, and a majority of people in the United States rated radio as more accurate than newspapers in war coverage.

Television Journalism

Newsreels, shown in movie houses, and television offered the first electronic visual journalism. Although some experimentation with television news occurred as early as 1940, development of news programming was delayed until after World War II; the half-hour television network news shows did not appear until the 1960s.

In 1945, NBC set up an organization for production of news film. In 1948, the network presented *NBC Newsroom,* a program produced by radio journalists and broadcast from the NBC radio newsroom. Critics argued that pictures of a man reading the news did not add much to an understanding of world affairs, but ratings were sufficient to keep the program on the air and attract competitors. The current evening newscast format dates to NBC's *Camel News Caravan,* a fifteen-minute nightly program starring John Cameron Swayze. CBS inaugurated a similar program, *Douglas Edwards with the News. Camel News Caravan* solidified NBC's news operation for the short term. By May 1951, forty stations carried the program, which mixed newsreel footage with visual reading of the news. NBC Television News established bureaus in New York,

Long before the publicity machine peppered U.S. society with one-name idols such as Madonna and Eminem, people earned that sort of recognition through a lifetime of accomplishments. Of these career icons, perhaps the most influential journalist was Edward R. Murrow, who shaped journalism in radio and television. Although it seems that much of broadcast news has fallen into sensationalism and pandering, current standards for good public service journalism can be traced directly to Murrow.

Murrow was born in North Carolina in 1908 and moved to Washington State at age six. During his youth, he worked as a farmhand, a bus driver, and a logger. While attending Washington State College, where he changed his first name from Egbert to Edward, Murrow participated in campus politics; he graduated in 1930.

During the five years between graduation and the beginning of his twenty-six-year career with the Columbia Broadcasting System (CBS), Murrow worked with educational organizations and traveled throughout Europe. He started work for CBS in 1935 and was promoted to CBS representative in Europe two years later. It was in Europe that he shaped the values of radio news and trained a group of broadcast journalists who would guide both radio and TV news for a generation.

From Europe, Murrow covered the steady expansion of Hitler's power. His broadcasts from London during World War II, which started with the statement "This is London," allowed Americans to experience war as they had never before experienced it. Murrow said that during the war Winston Churchill "mobilized the English language and sent it into battle." This could be applied accurately to Murrow's reporting efforts.

Murrow did more than simply report. He trained other journalists such as Howard K. Smith, Charles C. Collingwood, Eric Sevareid, and Richard Hottelet. These colleagues would help define radio news and establish television news a decade later.

Edward R. Murrow

Following the war, Murrow became an executive with CBS before returning to journalism on television. Two of his programs, *See It Now* and *Person to Person,* helped shape the public's expectations of TV journalists. The high point of his TV journalism career came in 1954 when he attacked Senator Joseph R. McCarthy on *See It Now* for creating a witch hunt in the name of anticommunism. McCarthy attacked people from the floor of the Senate and caused many to lose their jobs; some even committed suicide. Few people had been willing to do battle with such a powerful senator. But Murrow used his thirty-minute program to criticize McCarthy with McCarthy's own words and images. He said of McCarthy's attacks, "We must not confuse dissent with disloyalty," and added, "We will not be driven by fear into an age of unreason if we remember that we are not descended from fearful men, men who fear to write, to speak, to associate and to defend causes, which were, for the moment, unpopular."

Murrow continued at CBS until 1961, when President John F. Kennedy appointed him director of the United States Information Agency (USIA). The USIA's mission was to spread information about the U.S. government and culture around the world. He served as director until 1963 and died in 1965.

During his career, Murrow grew to understand the power and potential of broadcasting. On October 15, 1965, he spoke at the convention of the Radio–Television News Directors Association and said of television: "This instrument can teach, it can illuminate, and yes it can inspire. But it can do so only to the extent that humans are determined to use it to those ends. Otherwise, it is nothing but wires and lights in a box."

Sources: "Edward R. Murrow," *Compton's Encyclopedia Online,* www.optonline.com/compton/ceo/03310-A.html, accessed in October 1999; "Edward R. Murrow: A WWW Information Source," Washington State University, www.wsu.edu/Communications/_ERM/index.html, accessed in October 1999; Jean Folkerts and Dwight L. Teeter Jr., *Voices of a Nation: A History of Media in the United States* (New York: Macmillan, 1989).

Chicago, Washington, D.C., Cleveland, Los Angeles, Dallas, and San Francisco. It recruited **stringers** from abroad, hired camera crews and photographers, and signed exchange agreements with affiliate stations for news film. Initially, this meant additional jobs for journalists, but in 1952/1953, as production costs increased and NBC's news programs encountered financial difficulty, the network dramatically reduced its news division.

Meanwhile, CBS also expanded its news operations. William Paley, along with his second-in-command, Frank Stanton, shaped CBS into a leader in entertainment and news programming. Paley solidified CBS's financing, then demonstrated an uncanny skill for negotiating with affiliates and with celebrities. He was willing to allocate resources to programming, and it didn't take Paley long to ensure that CBS would surpass NBC as a leader in news and information programming.

stringer

A reporter, often at a location remote from the newspaper, who sells occasional pieces at "space rates," or by the column inch.

Veteran news reporters remember the Edward R. Murrow days as the Golden Age of Television News, when money flowed through CBS newsrooms and news shaped the reputation of the individual network. Murrow, famous for his radio news broadcasts during World War II, debuted in television in 1951 with the first network public affairs series, *See It Now.* In later years, Murrow made CBS famous for its **documentaries,** such as *Harvest of Shame,* which depicted the plight of migrant farmworkers.

Political Reporting on Television

Just as television restructured U.S. entertainment patterns and the process through which people got their news, so it also reshaped the process of reporting on government officials. Television combined with expanding education, increasing mobility, participatory democratic legislation, and sophisticated research methods during the 1950s and 1960s to weaken political parties in the United States and increase the role of the media in selecting leaders.

Network journalists covered the presidential campaign of 1952, a race between the popular General Dwight D. Eisenhower, a hero of World War II, and Illinois Governor Adlai Stevenson, one of the nation's foremost intellectuals. During this race, politics began to conform to the requirements of television. Stevenson's long commentaries bored too many of his listeners; Eisenhower, although anything but a polished television star, at least learned the value of short spots.

Soon after being named Eisenhower's running mate, Richard Nixon was accused of being the beneficiary of a secret trust fund set up by wealthy businessmen. The public was scandalized. Fearing that Eisenhower would drop him from the Republican ticket, Nixon chose television as the medium for his defense. It was through television that Richard Nixon was able to bypass journalists. Television provided this politician the opportunity to present himself in public without editing by journalists. In what became known as "the Checkers speech," Nixon detailed his financial condition and vowed that, though his children's dog Checkers had been donated by an admirer, the family loved the dog and "regardless of what they say, we're going to keep it." This personalized use of television built on what Franklin Delano Roosevelt had accomplished with his "Fireside Chats" over radio before and during World War II. Politicians began to go directly to the public, rather than having information first sifted through reporters and editors for newspapers and magazines.

The Image

Image has always played a role in U.S. politics. Image helps to define candidates for voters. Television, with its strong visual impact, enhanced the ability of media and politicians to manipulate political images.

John Kennedy used presidential debates and press conferences to shape his image. His ready wit and handsome smile made him a natural for the cameras. In the first *televised presidential debate* between Kennedy and Richard Nixon in 1960, Kennedy established himself as a man with a vision for leadership and placed Nixon in the position of defending the status quo. The role of image was demonstrated further by the reaction of people who listened to the debate on the radio: The majority of radio listeners believed Nixon won the debate.

The Kennedy–Nixon debates set a precedent for future presidential campaigns. Debates are now an expected part of the campaign process, and their effectiveness or lack of it is controversial and thus interesting to voters. In the 1992 elections, the questioning of candidates in a town hall format, with citizens rather than journalists asking questions, gained more attention than did the formal debates. However, as the 2004 election debates showed, formal encounters continue to be a significant part of presidential campaigning.

In 1968 Richard Nixon hired people who understood the art of television advertising, and paid media became a significant force in political campaigning. Nixon's people knew how to research public taste and to create advertising. Although disarray in the Democratic Party in 1968 aided Nixon's victory, some critics charge that without

documentary

Film or video investigation. Based on the term documents—such accounts document the details of a historical or current event. Often used as a term that implies investigative reporting.

The precedent for televised presidential campaigns was set in 1960 as Americans sat riveted around their television sets for the Kennedy and Nixon presidential debates.

the mastery of the television image devised by his advisors, Nixon might never have become president.

Today, political candidates work hard to control their images through advertising and by making arranged appearances. Many candidates limit their exposure to journalists, preferring to display a crafted image rather than respond to impromptu questions. Whenever candidates do respond to the press, their spin doctors work to get the candidate's interpretation of an event or issue into journalists' stories. The promotion of image rather than issues and substance is also fostered by some of the current production values of television. News values that promote higher ratings through ever shorter **sound bites** allow candidates to shape a planned, desirable television image, no matter what their actual political history.

Expanded Television News
In 1963, only a few weeks before the assassination of President John F. Kennedy, whose funeral made television history, NBC expanded its evening news coverage from a mere fifteen minutes to a thirty-minute newscast featuring the anchor team of Chet Huntley and David Brinkley. CBS followed suit with a news program anchored by Walter Cronkite. ABC, whose newscasts were at best a fledgling operation, didn't expand to a half hour until 1967. Since the 1960s, the networks have often explored expanding their evening newscasts to an hour. However, the affiliated stations continue to run their own profitable local newscasts in the lead-in time slot (usually 5:00 to 6:30 or 7:00 P.M. EST) and retain the time slot following the network news for profit-making syndicated shows such as *Wheel of Fortune* and *Jeopardy.*

Expansion of network news came not in the prestigious and expensive evening hours but in morning news, in which a softer format appealed to audiences with shows such as *Good Morning America.* The definition of news also expanded to include **newsmagazines** such as *60 Minutes,* which began in 1968 but did not achieve a permanent slot on the weekly schedule until the late 1970s. The expansion also includes late-night news programs such as Ted Koppel's *Nightline,* which ABC introduced in 1979 during the height of the crisis arising from Iranian militants' seizure of hostages in the U.S. embassy in Tehran. In the late 1980s, the number of newsmagazines in prime time grew. In the late 1990s, because of competition with entertainment shows for ad revenues and ratings, television newsmagazines drifted away from in-depth investigative stories and began featuring more lifestyle and celebrity news.[13]

sound bite

A short quotation used on radio or television to express an idea.

newsmagazine

Fifteen- to twenty-minute news segments put together to form an hourlong electronic magazine such as *60 Minutes* or *Dateline.* Such programs combine soft features with hard-hitting investigative reporting.

OBJECTIVITY AND STORYTELLING

American journalism has emerged from two separate traditions, that of **objectivity** and that of storytelling, or the **narrative tradition.** Modern journalism exhibits a tension between these traditions, with many editors and station managers arguing that objectivity is the golden norm of journalism, while others struggle to retain and understand the narrative tradition and its importance.

We know that impartiality or objectivity was a criterion used as early as the colonial days. Benjamin Franklin speaks of being an "impartial printer." During the Civil War, J. Thrasher, head of the Press Association in the Confederate states, tells editors to be "objective." When Adolph Ochs strives to make the *New York Times* a newspaper of record in the mid-1800s, he speaks of "objectivity."

Traditionally, objectivity has included five components: detachment from the object of the story, nonpartisanship, a reliance on facts, a sense of balance, and use of the inverted pyramid style of writing.[14] However, many journalists believe it is impossible to be totally objective. In fact, journalists have dropped the word *objectivity* from such documents as the Society for Professional Journalists' code. The strive for objectivity has been replaced by use of the words *truthfulness, accuracy,* and *comprehensiveness.* However, journalists often endorse objectivity as a principal tenet. Leonard Downie, executive editor of the *Washington Post,* reveres the concept to the degree that he claims he does not vote because doing so would force him to take sides and make him less objective. Some media critics and journalists argue that objectivity has too often made news organizations passive recipients of information from powerful institutions, rather than active seekers of the truth.

The tradition of narrative journalism has remained strong. Telling stories was a component of colonial and frontier newspapers. Sometimes they were totally factual; at other times, they were representations of reality. Narrative journalism, or "literary journalism," was controversial as early as the 1880s, when it threatened literature, whose predominant form during the period was realism. The controversies centered on some themes that are still heard today: the conflict between "high" and "low" culture and the blending of fiction and fact. Many narrative journalists actually aspired to be novelists.[15]

During the late 1960s, when a young generation of journalists evaluated the role of journalism in the social change brought about by civil rights and Vietnam activities and debates, they turned to what they labeled "new journalism" as a way of expressing the social context of political arguments. Some of these young reporters abandoned the objective, straightforward approach of "Who? What? When? Where? and Why?" The demands of interpretation and the political and cultural context of the decade demanded new techniques, new language, and incorporation of styles that had distinguished alternative media for many years. Everette Dennis, in the *Magic Writing Machine,* divided **new journalism** into five types: (1) the new nonfiction, also called "reportage" and "parajournalism"; (2) alternative journalism, also called "modern muckraking"; (3) advocacy journalism; (4) underground journalism; and (5) precision journalism. David Halberstam wrote a journalistic account of Vietnam (new nonfiction); the *Village Voice* advocated political positions on issues such as free love (alternative and advocacy, which sometimes blend); underground newspapers were printed and distributed without acknowledgment of authorship; and precision journalists used new statistical methods to prove points.

Today, narrative journalism appears in works such as *Black Hawk Down* by journalist Mark Bowden. An account of the disastrous U.S. intervention in Somalia, *Black Hawk Down* began as a series in the *Philadelphia Inquirer.* The use of fictional techniques helps make such works adaptable across a range of media platforms, so that

Key Concept

Objectivity The journalism tradition of objectivity involves looking at a story as though through a perfect lens uncolored by a reporter's thoughts about a subject; trying to view a story from a neutral perspective. Some critics believe pure objectivity is impossible and that fairness and balance are more important.

Key Concept

Narrative tradition The narrative tradition of journalism looks at journalism as story. Many writers employ fictional techniques in writing nonfiction material.

new journalism

Journalism that expresses the social context. Used at different times in the history of journalism, in the 1890s, it defined sensationalism. In the 1960s, the term was used to describe experimentation in reporting strategies and writing styles.

Bowden's series became a book, a film directed by Ridley Scott, and a webpage with audio and video clips on the *Inquirer* website (inquirer.philly.com/packages/somalia). However, controversy about the method still abounds, especially as the news media faces broad questions of credibility in the wake of scandals like the revelation that *New York Times* reporter Jayson Blair had concocted his stories and presented them as fact.

TODAY'S MARKET STRUCTURE

Today's journalists operate in a highly competitive marketplace. Both objective and narrative traditions are used in reporting news for newspapers, radio, television, and the Internet. However, the marketplace has become increasingly competitive, and media companies have "gone public," or begun to sell stock on the markets, thereby creating a need to pay dividends to those individuals who buy the stocks. This has increased the attention paid to ratings of television and radio news, as well as to the circulation numbers of newspapers and to the numbers of hits on Internet sites. Entertainment has assumed more importance.

Although journalism has always been a business, during the last thirty-five years it has evolved into big business. Whether television, radio, newspapers, or online, the corporations that increasingly own large news outlets require ever-higher profit margins to please the stock analysts and mutual fund managers. The results have varied. In some cases, publicly owned companies such as the *New York Times* produce award-winning journalism. In other cases, such as that of Thomson newspapers, the journalism got so bad that companies lost large numbers of readers. Thomson eventually sold its newspaper holdings.[16] When newspapers seek profit levels that exceed those of most other industries, the result is often a reduction in the number of journalists and a corresponding decline in local, quality coverage.[17]

Despite these problems, journalism today is supported by thousands of devoted journalists in all media who aim to serve the public and society. The quality of journalism often rests on the initiative of the individuals who put in extra time just to get the story right. However, the tension between profit and quality journalism will continue as long as journalism is a commercial enterprise.

AUDIENCE DEMAND IN JOURNALISM MARKETS

An often debated question in newsrooms is whether the journalist should give the people what they "need" or whether the journalist should provide the material that audiences "want." Such an argument assumes that the journalist and editor know what people need to read. The public certainly does not agree and through its purchasing power does make its own decisions about what kinds of information it needs and wants.

The audience demands information that it can discuss; thus journalism provides the discussion points that help to create the marketplace of ideas. Through the marketplace, the public—individually and in groups—makes political, social, and economic decisions.

SUPPLYING THE AUDIENCE'S DEMAND

The supply for the marketplace of ideas comes from all sources of information, including social networking, newspapers, movies, television, recordings, computers, and radio. Consumers, journalists, lobbyists, public-relations personnel, and government officials determine, both as individuals and as groups, what content has use in the marketplace of ideas. Because people are both information sources and information consumers, they make the mass communication system an important part of the political and social process. Media serve as **agenda setters:** the content of media helps determine which topics and issues society considers important. Who gets to comment affects the information we all receive, so if only one political party were permitted to comment, content presented by the media would not reflect the social and political world we all must deal with. Likewise, if social issues were presented from only one point of view, such as that of the businessperson, the social context of those on welfare, of working single parents, or of educators would be excluded from the picture. When the agenda setters fairly present all points of view, society is best served.

Consumers want varying kinds of news. The bulk of nonadvertising information is news. News can be soft, hard, or deep. Soft news includes a variety of feature stories, such as the story of the first woman to serve as drum major of a university band or the story of the birth of a Siberian tiger at the local zoo. Soft news also includes advice columns, such as *Dear Abby*. Hard news focuses on current events that have serious effects on people, such as crime, politics, and disasters. If a child dies in a house fire, the story is hard news. In-depth news requires the story to go beyond breaking stories to incorporate background details and trends. Investigative articles often fall into this category. A series of stories about the impact of changing federal regulations on student loans is an example.

News in newspapers comes from primarily three sources: the newspaper staff, wire and news services, and feature syndicates. Staff and news service reporters share similar standards for selecting which events and issues become news. These standards are called **news values,** and their application to particular stories is called "news judgment." Over time, several news values have evolved. The following values are usually cited as the reasons behind news selection and are even taught in reporting courses in journalism school:

- Impact applies when a large number of people are affected by an event or issue or when a small number of individuals are intensely affected. A car accident that kills three people has a greater impact than one that causes a small cut on one person's forehead.
- Proximity deals with the geographic location of an event. The more local the event, the more news value it has. A story that shuts off electricity for eight hours in Lansing, Michigan, will be reported in the *Lansing State Journal* but not in the *Detroit Free Press* because the *Journal* is proximate to Lansing readers.
- Prominence concerns how notable or famous a person is. Politicians, sports figures, and entertainment stars are prominent figures. An illicit affair by a shoe store clerk would not be news, but President Clinton's affair was because of his prominence.
- Timeliness deals with recency of an event or issue. A bank robbery that happened yesterday has more news value than one twenty years ago. The focus is on breaking stories.
- Conflict relates to disagreement among people. The conflict can be physical, as in crime and war, but it need not be. Much political news involves conflict in the marketplace of ideas.
- Disaster includes both natural calamities such as earthquakes and human-caused catastrophes such as an oil spill in the ocean.
- Human interest relates to personal details that intrigue readers. The story of an eighty-year-old woman who drives a school bus and is called "Grandma" by elementary students has human interest.

Two news photographs from Hurricane Katrina, taken and captioned by different photographers, created racial controversy because they referred to white victims as "finders" and African-American victims as "looters."

News values may change as society changes. The penny press, for example, emphasized crime news, which contained conflict and impact. A more recent type of news is called "coping information." Life in the United States has grown more complicated. More readers want information that will help them live more efficiently. Articles about how to stay healthy through better eating and exercise help people cope with daily stress.

A story can have more than one news value. The more of these values in a story, the more likely it is that people will read it. In addition, some values are more important than others. Because newspapers tend to emphasize local news, proximity is important for most staff-prepared stories.

Journalists don't sit with a checklist of news values when picking events to be covered. Rather, they internalize these values and judge whether stories will be of interest to their readers. As the audience changes, however, the match between the journalists' and the audience's news values can change. Coping information emerged because readers wanted it.

Specialized Supply in the Marketplace

Information can be supplied in many forms through many different media. Listed in the following sections are some of the ways that information has been gathered and delivered in recent decades.

Computer-Assisted Reporting *Computer-assisted reporting (CAR)* is an umbrella term for several uses of computers in reporting. CAR activities range from finding addresses and phone numbers online, to accessing government databases, to using spreadsheets that manipulate data to create new interpretations of old data.

News reporters rely on government and industry databases and other electronic sources to create information-rich stories.

Initially, only investigative reporters at large newspaper organizations practiced CAR because it involved more computer and database skills than most journalists possessed. As journalists gained better computer skills and governments put databases online, CAR use increased. It plays a significant role in helping reporters understand everything from economic reports to census numbers. For example, Knight Ridder's Chris Adams and Alison Young constructed an award-winning series, *Discharged and Dishonored,* on veterans' issues using data from surveys and the claims database of the U.S. Department of Veterans Affairs. They found that 13,700 veterans had died while their claims were still being resolved.[18]

The Public Journalism Controversy Beginning in the late 1980s, the development of ***public journalism,*** also called civic journalism, as a theoretical and practical approach created a great deal of controversy. Newspapers and local broadcast news reports have always served communities. But during the mid-twentieth century, many reporters strived not to enter community journalism, because they viewed working for big papers such as the *New York Times, Chicago Tribune,* and *Washington Post,* or for network news, as the road to professional advancement and career success. On a smaller scale, journalists left the small towns for papers in the state capitals. Urban journalists could adopt the professional values of being detached, objective, tough, and critical. They stood apart from the communities they served.

> **Key Concept**
>
> **Public journalism** By creating a public conversation through journalism, modern news media hoped to inspire consumers of news to become more involved in their own communities. The media encouraged citizens, officials, reporters, and editors to identify and respond to the issues that confronted their neighborhoods and their cities.

As their audience and their competition changed, newspaper organizations found themselves with diminishing circulations and a lack of connection with their communities. Seeking to reestablish their identities, some newspaper editors, as well as academicians, began to explore a philosophy of public journalism. Many local newspapers partnered with broadcast stations in public journalism efforts. Many of these efforts also included online components of newsgathering and dissemination. The *American Journalism Review* listed five components of public journalism:

> asking readers to help decide what the paper covers and how it covers it; becoming a more active player and less an observer; lobbying for change on the news pages; finding sources whose voices are often unheard; and, above all, dramatically strengthening the bonds between news-

Media Convergence

Citizen Journalism and the London Bombings

In London on July 7, 2005, terrorists launched a coordinated attack on the public transport system during rush hour. Bombs went off on three subway trains and a bus, killing fifty-two people. The director of the BBC World Service and Global News division, Richard Sambrook, explains that "it was a day of intense pressure for our news teams to get things first, but more importantly to get things right."

Within hours of the attacks, citizens began sending in images and information, including twenty amateur videos, more than one thousand photographs, twenty thousand e-mails, and four thousand text messages. Cameraphones and videophones played an important role, with survivors recording the scene from inside the damaged subway. Sambrook says, "People were participating in our coverage in a way we had never seen before." Because of the immediacy and quality of the videos, the BBC newscast that night began with a series of amateur clips so that ordinary citizens became a collaborative part of the storytelling.

As a publicly funded broadcaster, the BBC understood that the relationship between journalists and the public had changed. New portable technologies, like camera cell phones, had given eyewitnesses a greater capability to record events as they happened, before journalists could arrive at the scene. The newsroom staff had to trust the information they were receiving. Previously, the BBC, as with many news organizations, had received videos, e-mails, phone calls and other amateur materials to report their stories. However, there had never been collaboration on this scale.

Not everyone thought that the role of the citizen journalist had been entirely positive. Some, like Xeni Jardin, coeditor of the group blog, BoingBoing, expressed concern that the images came from gawkers with a voyeuristic, morbid fascination. Such images were more likely to appear on unmediated sites like Flickr, an image service where users can post photographs and browse them according to subject of interest.

Mainstream news organizations argue that they serve as gatekeepers to filter out potentially offensive or manipulated images and provide direction for citizen journalists who are untrained in reportorial skills, standards, and ethics. For example, the BBC website's "Have Your Say" page (news.bbc.co.uk/2/hi/talking_point/2780295.stm) includes guidance in how to construct a photo essay and write captions, as well as the advice not to endanger anyone, "take any unnecessary risks or infringe any laws." However, the relationship between citizen journalists and mainstream media is still uneasy in the tension between professionalism and fully open, unmediated reporting.

Sources: Mark Glaser, "Did London Bombings Turn Citizen Journalists into Citizen Paparazzi?" *Online Journalism Review,* July 12, 2005, ojr.org/ojr/stories/050712glaser/; Richard Sambrook, "Citizen Journalism and the BBC," *Nieman Reports* (Winter 2005): 13–16.

---

paper and community. At its heart is the assumption that a newspaper should act as a catalyst for change.[19]

Words such as *involvement* invoked specters of political corruption from the past, and editors feared that trying to influence the outcome of public action would affect newspapers' credibility. In addition, some editors saw the new approach as a loss of control of their own product. Marvin Kalb, director of the Washington Office of the Joan Shorenstein Center on the Press, Politics and Public Policy at Harvard University, urged caution: "A journalist who becomes an actor, in my view, is overstepping the bounds of . . . traditional responsibility."[20]

From 1993 to 2002, the Pew Center for Civic Journalism funded many journalism projects involving newspapers, television, and radio stations. The *Portland Press Herald* and the *Maine Sunday Telegram* in Portland, Maine, used the money to allow teenagers to work with the news staff to publish news and features online. The *Savannah Morning News* in Georgia studied and wrote about the effects of an aging population on taxes, lifestyles, and services in the region. However, the Pew Center for Civic Journalism closed its doors in 2003, and the public journalism movement began to reinvent itself to take into account electronic communications that had provided new channels for citizen voices. As Leonard Witt wrote in the newsletter of the Civic

Journalism Interest Group, "Citizens, who are so much a part of public journalism philosophy, no longer have to be invited into the mix. They are part of the mix."[21]

GLOBAL JOURNALISM

There are 193 nations in the world with a range of relationships between the government and the press. In the worst countries, the press is completely controlled by the government, and journalists who stray out of line are treated with harassment, intimidation, imprisonment, torture, and even death. In the best, journalists enjoy the liberty to "hold opinions without interference and to seek, receive and impart information and ideas through any media and regardless of frontiers."[22] Reporters without Borders indexes 167 countries by press freedoms, and in 2005, placed Denmark, Finland, and Iceland at the top and Turkmenistan, Eritrea, and North Korea at the bottom.[23] The United States and other Western democracies like Canada and France did not do well in the index, largely because of interrogation and imprisonment of journalists who would not reveal their anonymous sources.

The differences in the ways journalists and press function in various countries makes it difficult to speak of a global journalism. Yet in recent years, three trends have stimulated more discussion of a need for journalists to have a global conversation. These are: the spread of communications technologies that allow for unprecedented flows of information; the rise of multinational multimedia conglomerates; and the movement of migrants and refugee populations who maintain their own cultures and connections to homelands. Serious news audiences are aware, as never before, of events on the far side of the world and of the interconnectedness of governments, cultures, and economies.

Some press organizations, government agencies, and academic researchers have attempted to address global issues through research agendas and training initiatives. For example, the Journalism Ethics for the Global Citizen project at the University of British Columbia promotes the formation of a global code of ethics in a world where "news reports, via satellite or the Internet, reach people around the world and influence the actions of governments, militaries, humanitarian agencies and warring ethnic groups."[24] Other organizations, like the Committee to Protect Journalists and Amnesty International, advocate for journalists who are kidnapped or imprisoned. Funded in part by the U.S. State Department, the Edward R. Murrow Journalism Program funds journalists to study in the United States, hone their skills, and acquire knowledge of democratic institutions. All of these programs recognize a commonality among journalists worldwide, but articulating a shared set of principles and concerns remains difficult.

In the United States, many U.S. journalists see their work as directed primarily at local audiences, and many people aren't interested in international news except when dramatic events are occurring. The Pew Foundation found that after a surge of interest in the war with Iraq, the number of Americans who said they followed international news closely had fallen from 52 percent in 2004 to 39 percent in 2006.[25] In an earlier report, the respondents attributed this lack of interest to inadequate background information and the negativity, remoteness, and repetitiveness of international news.[26] Since such news is expensive to cover and audiences seem indifferent to it, profit-driven media organizations are less likely to cover it. Nevertheless, many more international news sources are available than ever before through the Internet, increasing the possibility of globally informed publics.

Journalist Daniel Pearl was kidnapped and killed in Pakistan following his investigations of links between Al Qaeda and the 9/11 attacks.

Journalists at Risk

Journalism in many parts of the world can be a deadly activity. The Committee to Protect Journalists (CPJ) reports that during 1996–2005, 338 journalists were killed while carrying out their work. The vast majority do not die in the crossfire, but rather are hunted down and killed, often in direct reprisal for their reporting. According to CPJ statistics, only 67 journalists died in crossfire, while 298 were murdered. Others died while covering violent events such as disasters and street demonstrations. Photographers, camera operators, and radio journalists are more likely to lose their lives.

The most dangerous country, by far, is Iraq, which claimed the lives of sixty-four journalists between March 2003 and February 2006. Most were Iraqis who were purposely murdered. *Al-Arabiya* correspondent Atwar Bahjat was gunned down while covering the bombing of a Shiite shrine, and freelance photographer Safa Isma'il Enad was shot while visiting a photo print shop. CBS cameraman Paul Douglas and soundman James Brolan were embedded with the U.S. Army's 4th Infantry Division when they were killed by a car bomb.

In 2006, journalists were killed for many reasons. In Afghanistan, Abdul Qodus died while covering a suicide bombing that was followed by another attack. In China, Wu Xianghu was beaten to death by traffic police angry at an embarrassing story about high bicycle license fees. In India, Prahlad Goala was murdered for exposing corruption in the local forestry service. In Sudan, editor Mohammed Taha Mohammed Ahmed was decapitated for printing a story about the Prophet Muhammad. And in Mexico, Enrique Pérez Qintanilla, a freelance reporter who covered drug trafficking, was shot, probably by an organized crime group.

Like other organizations of its kind, the Committee to Protect Journalists maintains these stories and statistics to defend press freedoms and to reveal abuses around the world as a warning to journalists and news organizations. By publicizing abuses, the Committee hopes to create change in areas where press freedoms are endangered.

Source: The Committee to Protect Journalists, cpj.org.

TRENDS

Under the pressure of economic, cultural, and technological change, journalism is also changing. Audiences have become participants in the news with greater opportunities to do their own critiquing and reporting. The news media no longer have the same gatekeeping and agenda-setting roles, and must adapt to these changes while maintaining influence, credibility, and integrity.

Technology: Participatory Journalism

Digital technologies allow much greater access to the news, and some media critics speculate that a fundamental shift is taking place that will change the definition of journalism and journalists. Interactive abilities through the web have made it much more possible for citizens to participate in journalistic endeavors. For example, a survey by the Pew Internet & American Life Project found that 34 percent of bloggers consider their online writing journalism. In 2006, about twelve million people in the United States kept a blog, so the number of bloggers who considered themselves journalists was substantial.[27] J. D. Lasica, senior editor of the *Online Journalism Review,* has proposed some categories for describing the many activities of *participatory journalism:*

Key Concept

Participatory journalism Digital technologies have enabled participatory journalism, which empowers ordinary citizens to take part in journalism. While critics question its importance, others find that the trend is gaining legitimacy.

1. Audience participation at mainstream news outlets. This participation includes readers commenting on news stories and staff blogs; submitting photos, videos, and other information relevant to breaking stories; and writing their own stories and reviews that are published on news sites.
2. Independent news and information websites. These include community information sites like Backfence (backfence.com); political blogs like the Drudge Report (drudgereport.com); consumer sites like Consumer World (consumerworld .org), and specialized sites like Gizmodo (gizmodo.com).
3. Full-fledged participatory news sites. These sites, like South Korea's OhMyNews and Citizen Joe (citizenjoe.org), are organized by professional journalists, but contain substantial material from citizen journalists.
4. Collaborative and contributory news sites: These self-organizing, self-publishing sites, like Wikipedia (wikipedia.org) and Universal Hub (universalhub.com), are comprised of user-generated editorial content.
5. E-mail newsletters and mailing lists.
6. Personal broadcasting sites. On sites like YouTube (YouTube.com) and CurrentTV, users can post their own video and audio.[28]

These categories are not exhaustive. New, experimental projects are continually put online as the Citizen Media Initiatives List on CyberJournalist.net attests.

The view of online citizen media among professional journalists is mixed. Strong advocates, like syndicated technology columnist Dan Gillmor, argue that a grass-roots democratic movement is changing the face of journalism. Journalism, Gillmor says, is becoming a conversation rather than a lecture from media elites and changing the power relationship between media producers and audiences.[29] New York University journalism professor Jay Rosen, on his influential PressThink blog, writes that with the ascendancy of blogging, the mainstream press is losing its sovereignty over the news: "*Not sovereign* doesn't mean you go away. It means your influence isn't singular anymore."[30] One of the cases often featured is Dan Rather's fall from the anchor chair on *CBS Evening News,* attributed in part to bloggers who questioned the truth of a story about President Bush's special treatment in the Texas Air National Guard. Rather had reported the story on *60 Minutes Wednesday,* and after CBS put the evidence online, bloggers raised suspicion that the document was forged. Thus, bloggers seemed to gain some legitimacy as fact-checkers and watchdogs over the watchdogs.

However, other journalists question the importance of citizen journalism, citing a lack of professionalism, training, and dedication. Nicholas Lemann, professor of journalism at Columbia University, writes that the best citizen journalism has come mostly from witnesses of unexpected events, such as the Hurricane Katrina disaster. However, he writes, "the content of most citizen journalism will be familiar to anybody who has ever read a church or community newsletter—it's heartwarming and it probably adds to the store of good things in the world, but it does not mount the collective challenge to power which the traditional media are supposedly too timid to take up."[31] John Burke, of the Editors Weblog, has dismissed claims that a plethora of citizen journalists are producing quality news. He argues that blogs, by their nature, don't uphold standards of objectivity, accuracy, collaboration, and transparency. Further, blogs are "one-man shows" without editorial oversight.[32] Other critics fear that bloggers, because their journalism is unregulated under election laws, may increasingly be paid to swing political elections through mudslinging and rumor.[33] They point to the case of presidential candidate John Kerry, who was the subject of rumors spread by blogs that he misrepresented his military record.

Whether the role of the citizen journalist shifts the balance of power or not, elements of participatory journalism are increasingly part of the mainstream news scene, from readers posting comments on news sites to serving as invited reporters. The scale and worth of that participation has not yet been fully assessed, but it is undoubtedly changing the way news is produced and read. The form is still evolving, and many questions remain as to participatory journalism's defining principles, ethics, business models, and adherence to copyright and other regulations.

Technology: Online News Aggregators

Google News, Yahoo News, and other news aggregators collect headlines from a variety of sources such as mainstream news outlets, press releases, and blogs. Google News uses computer algorithms to search through 4,500 English-language information sources and then arranges them according to relevance. Google claims that this method allows news to be presented "without political viewpoint or ideology, enabling you to see how different organizations are reporting the same story."[34] In partnership with Reuters, Associated Press, and other news services, Yahoo News uses human editors and automation to select top stories. In 2005, it surpassed Google News in the number of unique visitors it received—24.5 million to Google's 7.1—but Google dominated in sheer number of searches.[35]

News aggregators provide both a challenge and an opportunity for older news outlets. They offer links and direct searchers to other news outlets, but also create greater competition for readers and advertising revenues. Older media make a great investment in the production of the original content used by news aggregators to boost their sites. But the climate may be changing. Some older news outlets, like the *Wall Street Journal* and the Associated Press, have begun charging for access. Therefore, the news aggregators may lose much of the free content on which they've relied. They may develop new business models, rely more on participatory journalism, or increasingly develop their own original content.

Culture: Newsrooms

The culture of journalism—its ways of life and work—is undergoing change, largely because of technological and economic convergence. Mainstream news organizations are under much greater pressure than they were in the past to make higher profits for their stockholders. Yet, they face declining or static audiences, which leads to fewer advertising revenues and less profit.[36] News staff have been laid off or face greater workloads as they may be expected to produce content across several platforms.

Financial imperatives combine with a twenty-four-hours-a-day, seven-days-a-week environment that many professional journalists feel has eroded the quality of the news. In his study of a major metro daily, Eric Klinenberg calls this a "news cyclone" which has "eliminated the temporal borders in the news day, creating an informational environment in which there is always breaking news to produce, consume, and—for reporters and their subjects—react against."[37] One of the consequences is that many news organizations, especially television networks, rely less on time-consuming, context-rich reporting, replacing these kinds of stories with quick blockbuster news, commercials, and self-promotions. The Project for Excellence in Journalism observes that "in cable and online, there is a tendency toward a jumbled, chaotic, partial quality in the reports, without much synthesis or even ordering of information."[38] Further, a "journalism of verification" has been replaced with a "journalism of assertion," in which reports are quickly made and verified later.[39]

In parallel with this trend is a declining public faith in journalistic credibility. Many leaders in the industry point to a crisis in trust, and are looking for ways to reaffirm journalism's role, including its values in the newsroom. Some argue that economic conditions must be improved for journalists without making business values more important than journalistic ones. The former Washington Bureau chief for Knight Ridder, Clark Hoyt, has argued that economic strength can help newsrooms resist demoralization in the face of change, increase their confidence, and give them the legal ability to stand up to government pressures.[40] Others argue that newsrooms need a shift in internal values to greater transparency. A professor at Northwestern University's Medill School of Journalism, Jon Ziomek, explains, "In journalism, transparent organizations open the processes by which facts, situations, events, and opinions are sorted, sifted, made sense of, and presented. They listen closely and responsively to their audiences and acknowledge that audience perspective in their work."[41] A common opinion is that news organizations must "adapt or die," as the *American Journalism Review's* managing editor,

Rachel Smolkin, put it.[42] However, just how news organizations will adapt is an evolving story.

Culture: Audiences

Audiences may distrust journalists, but journalists are also expressing an increasing distrust of audiences. After the 2004 election, when asked about their "confidence in the public's electoral judgments," only 31 percent of national journalists surveyed said they had "a great deal."[43] The Project for Excellence in Journalism hypothesizes several reasons for the lack of faith, including an increased market data on audiences, the public's favorable reception of shallow news, and the election outcome which is considered by liberal journalists to be a sign of their audience's lack of intelligence. The problem with such a pessimistic view is that it "becomes a self-fulfilling prophecy that leads journalists to produce a shallower product because they think the public cannot handle anything else."[44]

Another worry voiced about audiences is that the Internet is creating greater fragmentation, so that news consumers may seek out niches, like blogs, and use the filtering powers of search engines and RSS feeds to get carefully selected newsbites. Therefore, they will receive only the news and opinions that confirm their worldviews and never be confronted with unsettling information. CBS News president Andrew Heyward argues that young people are "not as engaged with public life as they are in their own peer group," and therefore are grazers rather than steady consumers of news. However, Heyward sees the responsibility as lying on the news media to find innovative ways to reach such audiences.

SUMMARY

■ The U.S. government is based on an assumption that information will be disseminated freely and that the people will be well informed.

■ The primary purpose of journalism is to inform, but it also often entertains and sometimes seeks to persuade.

■ The business of reporting developed as editors sought to achieve mass audiences.

■ The philosophy of the Enlightenment was used by American colonists to defend civil liberties.

■ Televised politics and the Internet have changed the nature of political campaigning.

■ Reporters have sought through the years to expose the corrupt or secretive dealings of business and of government. This activity has been called muckraking.

- Journalism has two traditions: one is the objective analysis of the facts at hand and the other is a narrative tradition, or storytelling.
- The role of the citizen Journalist is increasing in influence over the news.
- The financial pressure on newsrooms is creating difficult conditions for journalists.

NAVIGATING THE WEB Journalism

Columbia Journalism Review
cjr.org
The *Columbia Journalism Review,* published in conjunction with the Columbia School of Journalism, is a critique of modern media, but it offers excellent information for journalists about the business and about how to make ethical decisions. A similar publication, the *American Journalism Review,* can be accessed at www.wjr.org.

Poynter Institute
poynter.org
The Poynter Organization's site claims it has "[e]verything you need to be a better journalist." The Poynter Institute is a school dedicated to "teaching and inspiring journalists and media leaders. It promotes excellence and integrity in the practice of craft and in the practical leadership of successful businesses. It stands for a journalism that informs citizens and enlightens public discourse. It carries forward Nelson Poynter's belief in the value of independent journalism." Nelson Poynter is a former editor of the *St. Petersburg Times.*

Project for Excellence in Journalism
journalism.org
PEJ studies and evaluates the news media to aid journalists and citizens in understanding them.

QUESTIONS FOR REVIEW

1. What is the importance of the John Peter Zenger case?
2. What is the Bill of Rights?
3. What does the First Amendment protect?
4. What factors contributed to the development of the reporter?
5. What is the narrative tradition in journalism?

ISSUES TO THINK ABOUT

1. Try to imagine a society without any free dissemination of information. How would your life be different from the way it is today?
2. Should journalism be used to persuade and to entertain as well as to inform?
3. Explore the relationship of Enlightenment philosophy to the development of independent journalism in the United States.
4. How can news organizations effectively use citizen reporting?
5. Name several news values and critique them.
6. Discuss the occupation of journalist. What is attractive about it? What is not so attractive?
7. What is the role of a news organization on the Internet?

SUGGESTED READINGS

Downie, Leonard Jr., and Robert Kaiser, *The News about the News: American Journalism in Peril* (New York: Knopf, 2002).

Gans, Herbert. *Democracy and the News* (New York: Oxford University Press, 2003).

Gillmor, Dan, *We the Media: Grassroots Journalism by the People, for the People* (Sebastopol, CA: Farnham, 2004).

Glasser, Theodore L., and James L. Ettema, *Custodians of Conscience* (New York: Columbia University Press, 1998).

Mindich, David T., *Just the Facts: How "Objectivity" Came to Define American Journalism* (New York: New York University Press, 2000).

Public Relations

"Cruise Baby Suri in PR Nightmare" said the Fox News headline. The "nightmare" was that no one had seen a picture of eight-month-old Suri, born to Tom Cruise and Katie Holmes. Rumors were flying, with paparazzi attempting to get a shot of the elusive baby. "Does Baby Suri Really Exist?" asked Britain's *Daily Mail.*

To many Hollywood observers and celebrity gossips, Cruise's behavior surrounding his infant daughter further demonstrated his perceived strangeness, related to his promotion of Scientology and his attack on the mental health profession and Brooke Shield's use of psychiatric drugs. Cruise's Q Score, an annual poll of how many Americans like a given celebrity, plummeted from 30 percent to 19 percent. After *Mission Impossible III* did not do well at the box office, public relations professionals blamed bad handling for not keeping the actor "on a short leash."[1] Cruise had employed his sister, also a Scientologist, to be his publicist before replacing her with a professional known for his conservative approach and emphasis on celebrity privacy.

Because they offer their fans escapism and fantasy, celebrities are expected to maintain a carefully crafted image, even in their private lives. That image is created by a team, including an agent, a manager, a lawyer, a personal assistant, and a publicist. The team is responsible for transforming a person into a marketable commodity. Fans expect celebrities to do well at public relations, as when Angelina Jolie and Brad Pitt offered photographs of their baby, Shiloh, through *People*

Magazine while donating the proceeds to charity. Sometimes, the celebrity team has to engage in another form of public relations, crisis management, to restore its client's image. For example, Mel Gibson released a careful apology through his publicist after a disastrous drunken incident when he made anti-Semitic remarks.

Whether they promote a celebrity, a product, an organization, or even a nation, public relations attempt to influence public views, attitudes, and opinions. Edward L. Bernays, one of the public relations' instrumental pioneers, defined public relations as "the science of creating circumstances, mounting events that are calculated to stand out as genuine, staged and 'newsworthy.'" Both Bernays and journalist Walter Lippmann asserted the need for an elite group of opinion leaders who could control the masses by engineering their consent and manipulating their unconscious desires. Today, their ideas are still felt in the way public relations professionals attempt to exert influence on consumers and audiences behind the scenes.[2]

In 1988, the Public Relations Society of America established this definition of public relations: "Public relations help an organization and its publics adapt mutually to each other."

An examination of the terms in this definition help to clarify it. First, public relations usually involves *organizations,* though an individual celebrity may also hire publicists. Second, public relations differs from advertising because companies pay for advertising messages; they do not pay for media content that is generated by public relations activity. Advertising and public relations both fall under the heading of promotion, which is part of marketing, but PR is fundamentally different from advertising. Public relations practitioners hope that their materials will be used or will generate interest and news stories. Advertising practitioners simply buy time or space to advance the exact message they want to promote.

Publics—the people and organizations that the company deals with—constitute the audience for public relations practitioners. Consumers are a public for a department store because their purchases determine whether a store will make a profit. Television station owners consider the government to be one of their publics because the Federal Communications Commission licenses stations. Good public relations involves knowledge of publics and monitoring of their messages.

According to the definition, organizations and publics *adapt* to each other, suggesting that the public relations process is a two-way street, unlike Bernay's early idea that opinion leaders would persuade the unwitting masses.

Understanding public relations is essential to navigating through public life in the United States today. The pervasiveness of information generated through public relations efforts poses many issues such as the following:

- What is the role of public relations in a complex, highly technological, democratic society?

- What are the inevitable tensions for public relations practitioners whose commitment is to an organization but also to ethical standards of fairness and accuracy?

- What role do new technologies play in public relations?

- How does increased specialization affect public relations activities?

- What relationships do public relations professionals help establish between organizations and audiences?

publics

The various groups to whom PR professionals address messages. They may be internal or external to the organization.

Public Relations in Your Life

Do You Know It When You See It?

Sometimes it is difficult to decide what information comes from public relations sources and what constitutes news and entertainment. Think about some recent public events that you consider to be examples of PR and events you consider to be non–PR-generated news or entertainment. Considering these events, develop your own definition of public relations material.

PR-Generated Events	Non–PR-Generated News/Entertainment
Local radio station's sponsorship of a charity walkathon	Natural disaster, such as a flood

PUBLIC RELATIONS IN AMERICAN LIFE

Although communication between organizations and publics has occurred for thousands of years, public relations was perfected as an art and practice in the United States. In ancient Athens, orators in public forums provided information and persuaded people about public policy. Some historians describe Samuel Adams as the first American public relations practitioner. Adams was a radical patriot in Massachusetts who helped bring about the American Revolution. His goal was to whip up the fervor for rebellion and keep the public's ire sustained so that they would act, not just protest, against England. He used a variety of media, created an activist organization, employed symbols and slogans, created **pseudo-events** such as the Boston Tea Party, orchestrated conflict, and recognized the need for a sustained saturation campaign.[3] However, only in modern times have professional public relations people been paid to represent organizations through planned and sustained public relations activities.

Public relations history can be viewed from two perspectives. It can be understood as the evolution of professional public relations practice, and it can be recognized as a type of communication that evolved to serve specific social needs.

pseudo-event

An event created solely for the purposes of public relations to gain favorable notice for an organization.

Public Relations in Social Context

The *practice of public relations* developed from people's desire to hold political power and to profit from entertainment and business. As the United States grew and diversified during the early 1800s, Andrew Jackson sponsored a Kentucky editor named Amos Kendall, who supported Jackson's candidacy. Kendall wrote speeches and advised Jackson, while "Old Hickory" capitalized on his military image to

Key Concept

Practice of public relations Public relations—systematic, planned communication with an organization's publics—helps explain complex information and shape news agenda. It can also be used to mislead if practitioners do not adhere to ethical standards.

become president.[4] Although sponsored through government printing contracts rather than being paid directly, Kendall functioned as an early political PR consultant.

Jackson's use of PR to gain political office suggests a social condition in the United States that generated a need for public relations: the dispersion of power. Voters hold the power to choose from all available ideas. Strong monarchies and dictatorships can coerce; governments that hold less power rely on persuasion. Voters in a democracy have the power to influence their government, but they need information on which to base decisions. Ideally, the information is provided by knowledgeable, unbiased sources. However, when there is an information gap, it can be filled by those seeking office. Jackson, along with other government officials, used the power of persuasion to influence the voters (a significant public in U.S. society) to choose him. Political advertising, news, entertainment, and public relations efforts all crowd the marketplace of ideas.

Press Agents and Entertainment   *Early press agents* hawked their wares and worked doggedly with entertainment businesses to get publicity in newspapers. The first master of publicity was P. T. Barnum. In the late 1830s, he toured the eastern United States with an African American woman, Joice Heth, who claimed to be the 160-year-old nurse of George Washington. With a combination of advertising and **publicity** in newspapers, Barnum drew large crowds. When attendance slumped in Boston, he wrote a letter to a local newspaper claiming that Heth was an early form of robot run by springs. Attendance grew as people checked out the fraudulent story.[5] An autopsy of Heth after her death revealed that she was about half her announced age. Meanwhile, Barnum had been collecting about $1,500 a week from people who wanted a look at the pipe-smoking old woman.

When Barnum formed the Barnum and Bailey Circus with James A. Bailey, he hired his own press agent, Richard Hamilton. With the increased business responsibilities of running a company of 800 employees, Barnum could no longer afford to do what he did best—get people into the tent. The world's greatest press agent had to hire a press agent.

> **Key Concept**
>
> **Early press agents**   Press agentry, which was one of the earliest forms of public relations, involves publicizing an event or person or promoting a campaign. As press agents and those who hired them became more sophisticated about audience response to messages, publicity evolved into a process of communication.

publicity

Information disseminated to attract public interest.

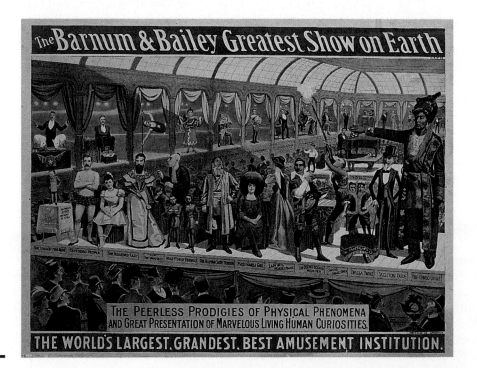

P. T. Barnum, who provoked curiosity for a variety of circus sideshows, was a genius at using publicity techniques to arouse expectations.

Press Agentry and Business In the mid-1800s, businesses began to experiment with similar press agentry techniques. However, in addition to publicity they also hired press agents to persuade government officials to serve their cause. During the 1850s, capitalizing on fears of a coming civil war, the Illinois Central Railroad organized a public relations campaign to get the government to construct a north–south railway that would bind the country together. This successful campaign for federal funds altered a historic pattern of local funding for railroad development. Other railroads used similar persuasion techniques. They argued that building railroads served the public, and Congress responded by giving forty grants to railroads between 1852 and 1857. Railroad companies continued to use lobbying and press relations throughout the nineteenth century, eventually influencing the Interstate Commerce Act of 1886 in their favor.[6]

Railroad executives were vulnerable public targets because they were viewed as land grabbers who had little regard for local communities. To create more positive public images, railroad officials became masters of early press relations. They offered editors appealing tours through various parts of the country in return for free advertising. At the turn of the century, most editors carried free railway passes in their wallets.

Emerging Professionalism During the last half of the 1800s, big business became a target of citizen anger as the public began to perceive it as a greedy octopus that grabbed power and money and worried little about the common person. Efforts to break up large steel, oil, and railroad monopolies increased as the twentieth century began. The muckrakers from *McClure's* magazine began to expose the excesses of wealthy industrialists such as J. P. Morgan, Cornelius Vanderbilt, and John D. Rockefeller. Recognizing that they needed a better public image, the captains of industry turned to public relations experts.

Ivy Ledbetter Lee emerged during this period as the model for public relations practitioners. Lee worked as a newspaper reporter for three years before becoming a PR counselor for a number of corporations. Lee advocated honest communication between his clients and their publics. John D. Rockefeller sought Lee's advice after two women and eleven children were killed during a strike at his Colorado coal mines in an incident known as the Ludlow Massacre. Lee replied that "the first and most important feature of any plan of publicity should be its absolute frankness; that there should be no devious ways employed."[7] Rockefeller hired Lee to tell his side of the labor war that had developed.

Not everyone believed that Lee lived up to his own words. Poet Carl Sandburg attacked Lee for his role in publicity following the Ludlow Massacre. In his 1919 book on the press, *The Brass Check,* Upton Sinclair gave Lee the nickname "Poison Ivy."[8] Nevertheless, Lee's admonition to avoid deceit remains the basis of the professional approach to public relations.

Public Relations and War During the early part of the twentieth century, much of the U.S. public did not believe that the country should take an active part in European affairs. To promote U.S. participation in World War I, President Woodrow Wilson set up the Committee for Public Information run by George Creel. Creel, a former newspaper editor, successfully ran a **propaganda** campaign that generated support for U.S. involvement and created hatred of Germans. The committee's efforts cost $4.5 million. It mailed 6,000 news releases that generated about 20,000 columns of newsprint each week. The committee developed cartoons, created posters, and issued war photographs to the schools. Part of the appeal was based on fear, and Germans were depicted as without morals. Many of those who worked for the Creel Committee took the techniques they learned with them and moved into the modern, postwar world of business and government public relations, in which they successfully blended *propaganda and public relations*. Edward Bernays, who worked on the Committee

Key Concept

Propaganda and public relations Some of the modern persuasive techniques of public relations were developed during World War I when the federal government conducted a propaganda campaign to encourage U.S. citizens to support an unpopular war. The connection between propaganda and public relations led to a negative perception which professional public relations practitioners had to overcome during the mid-twentieth century.

propaganda

Material disseminated by a group or cause to persuade another group of the validity of its own position.

Edward L. Bernays

Edward L. Bernays wrote the first book on public relations and taught the first public relations class at a major university. In 1989, *Life* magazine named him one of the most important Americans in the twentieth century.

The nephew of Sigmund Freud, Bernays sold the public on everything from presidents to Ivory soap. Clients whose images and products he promoted included singer Enrico Caruso, automobile manufacturer Henry Ford, inventor Thomas Edison, moviemaker Sam Goldwyn, and first lady Eleanor Roosevelt. Bernays worked for every president from Calvin Coolidge in 1925 to Dwight D. Eisenhower in the late 1950s. He is said to have turned down Adolf Hitler and Generalissimo Francisco Franco of Spain.

Bernays was born in Vienna, Austria, in 1891 and was brought to New York a year later. He received his bachelor's degree from Cornell University in 1912. During World War I, he worked for the War Department as a government propagandist, learning how to mold public opinion. He used this experience as a foundation when he opened his public relations business with Doris Fleishman in 1919.

Three years later, he married Fleishman. She kept her maiden name and was the first American woman to maintain it on her passport. Bernays and Fleishman ran their business together until she died in 1980.

In 1923, Bernays wrote *Crystallizing Public Opinion*, the first book on public relations. In this book, he moved from using mass communication to reach one large public to targeting specific audiences. He stressed that clients had different relations with different publics.

Bernays wrote fourteen books in all. In his 1965 autobiography, *Biography of an Idea*, he wrote that public relations had moved "from a one-way street of information and persuasion from client to public" to a two-way interaction between client and public. However, he was unsuccessful in his drive to have public relations practitioners licensed, an attempt to legitimize the field.

Bernays had about 350 clients, ranging from federal government departments to labor unions and from individuals to large corporations. He continued giving speeches until a few years before his death at age 103, on March 9, 1995, in his home in Cambridge, Massachusetts.

Sources: Harvey Smith, "The Original Persuader," *The Guardian* (March 24, 1995), the Guardian Features Page section, T21; "Edward Bernays," *The Boston Herald* (March 10, 1995), Obituary section, 61.

The Committee on Public Information helped develop a variety of public relations techniques during World War I. This Liberty Bond poster resembles many designed by the committee and those who supported its efforts.

for Public Information, wrote the first book about public relations in 1923. *Crystallizing Public Opinion* received mixed reviews, but it introduced hundreds of thousands of people to the activities of public relations.[9]

Bernays's career in public relations lasted more than five decades. He argued that public relations should be a profession in which social science principles are applied and consideration for the public takes precedence over profit:

> The standards of the public relations counsel are his own standards, and he will not accept a client whose standards do not come up to them. While he is not called upon to judge the merits of his case any more than a lawyer is called upon to judge his client's case, nevertheless he must judge the results which his work would accomplish from an ethical point of view.[10]

Public relations activities expanded during the 1930s, though most people in the United States were unaware of PR techniques until after World War II. The Office of War Information (OWI), created in June 1942, handled propaganda and absorbed the Office of Government Reports, the Office of the Coordinator of Information, the Office of Facts and Figures, and several smaller agencies. Elmer Davis, former *New York Times* staffer, directed the operation.

OWI's domestic and foreign operations in May 1945 at the peak of activity required the services of 9,600 persons, and the budget was $132,500,000 for the three years of operation.[11] Three experienced editors and publishers directed the domestic operation: Gardner Cowles Jr. of the *Des Moines Register and Tribune,* the *Minneapolis Star-Journal* and *Tribune,* and *Look* magazine; E. Palmer Hoyt, editor and publisher of the *Portland Oregonian;* and George W. Healy Jr., publisher of the *New Orleans Times-Picayune.* The government controlled the broadcasting facilities of five companies that had been disseminating shortwave programs from the United States, including CBS and NBC. News and other programs broadcast through these facilities to a variety of enemy and allied countries became known as the Voice of America, an operation still in existence. The Voice of America and related overseas activity constituted 85 percent of the total OWI budget.

Information and Persuasion

The *process of public relations* consists of PR activities as communication. Public relations specialists act as senders who encode messages and send them to receivers (the organization's publics). Because these messages are planned, they have purposes. The exact purpose may vary, but public relations messages usually aim either to inform or to persuade.

Informational messages make the receiver aware of some event or issue that the sending organization considers important. A public information director at a local community college sends course catalogs to residents of the community to inform them which classes are available. A sports information director mails pregame press releases to tell sportswriters about the importance of an upcoming basketball game. Publics cannot make effective decisions without information, so organizations must inform their publics.

Persuasion causes people to change their beliefs or to act in certain ways. The environmental lobbyist who talks with a senator over lunch tries to persuade the senator to vote for a bill that will protect an endangered species. The press release about a new department store aims to get a newspaper to publish an informational story about the grand opening.

Ultimately, whether PR practitioners use an informational or a persuasive model, they want to persuade their publics that the company's position is accurate, complete, and justified. However, effective public relations relies on accurate information. Consumers who do not trust a company's communication, or reporters who cannot trust a PR practitioner, will not be persuaded by communication from those organizations and people. Publics may be fooled a few times, but sustained PR efforts will falter without accurate information.

Public relations activities constitute a process. An organization and its publics are *interdependent.* Because of differences in exposure, attention, perception, and retention, people experience the same events in many different ways. Public relations communicates the organization's perspective on the events and, in doing so, tries to alter the results of consumers' selective processes. Hospital PR departments call patients after discharge to see how they feel about their stays. If the patients have a negative perception of the hospital, the specialists will talk with them or send them some printed material to change that perception. Perceptions of service, people, and products determine success.

Under some situations, such as special events, the process also will entertain. However, efforts to entertain primarily aim to attract an audience that can be informed or persuaded.

Internal Public Relations

Unlike **external PR,** which has been around in some form for almost 200 years, **internal PR** is relatively new. The study of communication in organizations progressed "from a footnote mention in pre–World War II days" to an entire area of study in the 1990s.[12] Before 1930, managers thought of employees as pieces of a big industrial machine. They did their work, got paid, and went home. However, in the process of studying the impact of lighting and environment on productivity, researchers at the Western Electric plants in Cicero, Illinois, discovered that relationships among employees were as important as technological working conditions. People who enjoyed their work

external PR

Messages directed at publics external to the organization.

internal PR

Communication within the various units and between individuals of the organization.

Dateline

Public Relations in Our Lives

1700s. Mercantile newspapers serve public relations goals.

1773. Boston Tea Party is early PR event.

Early 1800s. Amos Kendall helps elect Andrew Jackson president.

Mid-1800s. P. T. Barnum uses public relations techniques.

1850s. Railroad companies use public relations to influence Congress.

1900s. Ivy Ledbetter Lee improves John D. Rockefeller's image.

1917–1918. CPI handles PR during World War I.

1919. Upton Sinclair attacks PR practitioners in *The Brass Check*.

1923. Edward L. Bernays writes *Crystallizing Public Opinion*.

1924–1932. Hawthorne studies lead to human relations management.

1941–1945. OWI handles propaganda during World War II.

1948. Public Relations Society of America starts.

1400–1700	1800	1880	1900	1920	1930	1940

1620. Pilgrims land at Plymouth Rock.

1690. *Publik Occurrences* is published in Boston.

1741. First magazine is published in America.

1776–1783. American Revolution

1830s. The penny press becomes the first truly mass medium in the United States.

1861–1865. American Civil War

1892. Thomas Edison's lab develops the kinetoscope.

1914–1918. World War I

1915. *The Birth of a Nation* marks the start of the modern movie industry.

1920. KDKA in Pittsburgh gets the first commercial radio license.

1930s. The Great Depression

1939. TV is demonstrated at the New York World's Fair.

1939–1945. World War II

1949. First commercial electronic computer is produced.

Cultural Milestones

Key Concept

Human dimension In the late 1930s, some corporate managers began to realize that employees who were satisfied with their workplace performed better than those who disliked their jobs. Public relations then took on an internal dimension, and one goal was to inform employees so they would feel as though they were part of the overall company effort.

performed better. Managers began to think in terms of the **human dimension** and recognized that employee well-being and effective communication increased productivity.

In 1938, Chester Barnard, the former president of the New Jersey Bell Telephone Company, wrote in *Functions of the Executive* that three elements were essential to the existence of all organizations: a purpose, people willing to pursue that purpose, and communication to coordinate the pursuit.[13] As companies consolidated and increased in size, they also became more bureaucratic. Layers of management

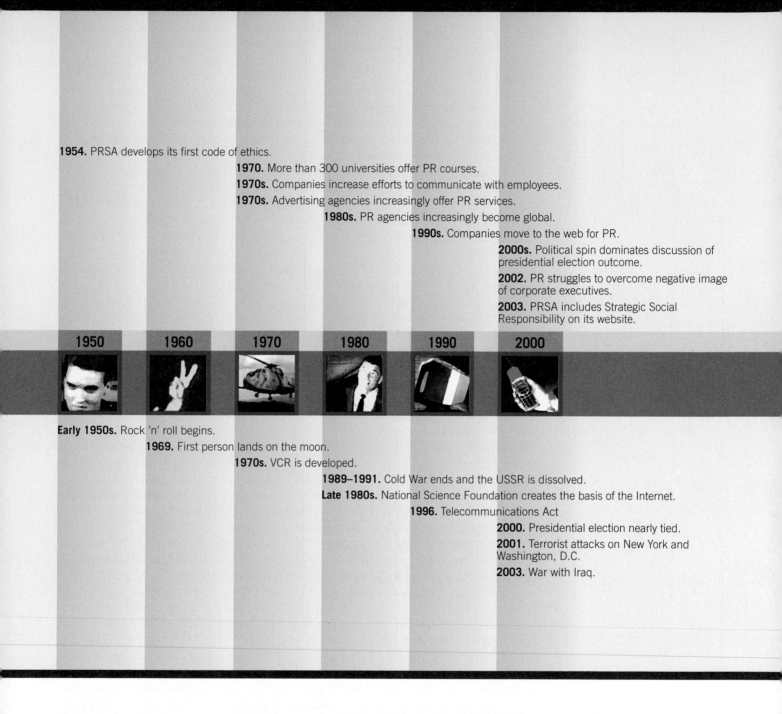

1954. PRSA develops its first code of ethics.

1970. More than 300 universities offer PR courses.

1970s. Companies increase efforts to communicate with employees.

1970s. Advertising agencies increasingly offer PR services.

1980s. PR agencies increasingly become global.

1990s. Companies move to the web for PR.

2000s. Political spin dominates discussion of presidential election outcome.

2002. PR struggles to overcome negative image of corporate executives.

2003. PRSA includes Strategic Social Responsibility on its website.

| 1950 | 1960 | 1970 | 1980 | 1990 | 2000 |

Early 1950s. Rock 'n' roll begins.

1969. First person lands on the moon.

1970s. VCR is developed.

1989–1991. Cold War ends and the USSR is dissolved.

Late 1980s. National Science Foundation creates the basis of the Internet.

1996. Telecommunications Act

2000. Presidential election nearly tied.

2001. Terrorist attacks on New York and Washington, D.C.

2003. War with Iraq.

often acted as blocks to communication, spurring the development of departments of internal communication during the last half of the twentieth century. Internal public relations then developed as a process of planned and sustained communication between the organizational leadership and its employees.

Internal relations was once a phenomenon of developed countries such as Japan and the United States. Now, in large global organizations which may have units in many parts of the world answering to a corporate center, internal public relations is important in linking employees together. Such efforts face many challenges, such as differences in time zones, government regulations, cultural expectations about confidentiality and privacy, and technological systems.[14]

SOCIAL AND CULTURAL IMPACT

Ethics and integrity within public relations practice are continuing issues. Journalists deride public relations as a profession not related to journalism and claim that PR people present only their employers' side of the story. However, public relations education is often included in journalism schools, and many journalists eventually become PR professionals. Since the time of Ivy Lee, PR practitioners have argued that honesty and accuracy must be the ethical foundation of the profession. Another ethical value of journalism—objectivity—does not apply to professional public relations. No one, journalist or ordinary citizen, expects public relations experts to present multiple views. The public relations view is one of persuasion within the marketplace of ideas. Often it is a powerful message generated by sophisticated communication techniques and supported by power and money.

Public relations practitioners organized after World War II to emphasize skill development and ethical applications. Growth in public relations education accompanied the quest for a more professional standing. In 1961 the American Public Relations Association, begun in 1944, merged with the Public Relations Society of America (PRSA), organized in 1948. PRSA is the most prestigious public relations professional group today.[15]

The degree of professionalism found in public relations is higher now than it was fifty years ago, but ethical problems remain. The heart of the professional approach to PR concerns openness between the organization and its publics. Advocates of professional PR, such as Bernays, argue that public relations practitioners should advise their clients to be honest with those affected by their business.

One of the classic cases in ethical public relations is that of Johnson & Johnson, a company that reacted with concern for the public after cyanide was discovered in some Extra-Strength Tylenol capsules in 1982. Seven people died in and around Chicago. Johnson & Johnson immediately stopped production and recalled all of its Tylenol capsules. The company contacted the media and federal government. Johnson & Johnson did not try to hide anything that had happened. Its first response involved protecting and warning the public. Instead of a knee-jerk reaction aimed at short-term results (keeping Tylenol on the shelves), Johnson & Johnson considered long-term goals and the importance of its credibility to continuing its business success. As a result, the company lived up to its business credo of public responsibility and regained its share of the market within a year. This strategy has been adopted by many companies, particularly those dealing with pharmaceuticals.[16]

In contrast to Johnson & Johnson, the Augusta National Golf Club, home of the Masters Tournament, created a public relations nightmare when the National Council of Women (NCW) asked in June 2002 that the club allow women to join. William Johnson, chairman of Augusta, replied that Augusta would not be forced into changing its rules. After Martha Burk, chairwoman of NCW, said that the group would ask companies to withdraw advertising from the 2003 Masters Tournament, Johnson declared that the tournament would go on without advertisers. During the controversy that followed, some of the 300 members of Augusta promised to work to admit women, and Tiger Woods said both sides are right.[17] In 2006, women were still not being admitted. Exxon, sponsor of the 2006 Masters Tournament, came under pressure from its shareholders to uphold the company's nondiscrimination policy and refuse to support the event. Several other companies, including SBC and IBM, had already refused to participate if the club discriminated against women and racial minorities.

DEMAND FOR PUBLIC RELATIONS

Public relations practitioners serve as a pipeline to move information from organizations to their publics. Demand for public relations activity can be viewed from both ends of the pipe: At one end, organizations demand services to get their information

McDonald's and Corporate Responsibility

The fast food restaurant, McDonald's, has long faced international criticism of its labor policies, unhealthy food, and environmental practices. In the late 1990s, the company sued two environmental activists for libel, taking the case to an English court. Though McDonald's won the widely publicized case in 1997, the judge wrote in his decision that the company endangered workers' health, used misleading advertising, and was cruel to animals.

Then, in 1999, a French farmer, José Bové, drove a tractor into a local McDonald's restaurant to protest genetically modified foods. Bové accused McDonald's of "malbouffe," bad food, further fueling the "slow food" movement, started in 1986 to protest the opening of a McDonald's in Rome. Especially in Europe, McDonald's became a symbol of globalization, industrialization, antienvironmentalism, and the eradication of local cultural traditions.

With the popularity of Eric Schlosser's book *Fast Food Nation* (2001) and Morgan Spurlock's film *Super Size Me* (2004), the company faced its severest difficulties with public opinion. A growing worldwide concern with obesity, especially in children, often focused on fast food restaurants, especially McDonald's. In its new public relations campaign to polish its image, the company began to feature health and wellness in its global "Balanced, Active Lifestyles Campaign," putting the burden on consumers to exercise and make wise choices. It also began revamping 5,000 of its over 30,000 restaurants, especially in Europe, to feature a more culturally integrated architecture, comfortable furniture, televisions, and Internet connections. In thirty European countries, the company began an "Open Doors" campaign, allowing customers to visit their kitchens. A McDonald's executive in Europe explained that this was part of a larger campaign of "trust-building activities."

On its webpage, McDonald's features corporate responsibility as number one on its list of key values. The company states, "At McDonald's, responsibility means striving to do what is right, being a good neighbor in the community, and integrating social

and environmental priorities into our restaurants and our relationships with suppliers and business partners."

Strategic social responsibility has become an important issue for public relations professionals. The Public Relations Society of American defines it as "a management model that encourages ethical values and practices for all sizes of businesses and nonprofits by creating a public relations platform to promote these practices to stakeholders." However, some business analysts question whether a company's mission to make profits for its shareholders can coexist with demands for social responsibility. For that reason, other critics wonder about the credibility of such efforts at companies like McDonald's.

Sources: Jeremy Grant, "McDonald's Responds to Customers' Beefs," *Financial Times,* September 24, 2005: 19; Public Relations Society of America, *Strategic Social Responsibility,* prsa.org; Center for Media and Democracy, Corporate Social Responsibility, sourcewatch.org/index.php?title=Corporate_Social_Responsibility; McDonald's, *McDonald's Corporate Responsibility,* mcdonalds.com.

---

out; at the other end, various publics demand information from the organizations. Newspapers use releases as the basis of news stories; government agencies use information in policy decisions; and consumers use information as a basis for voting and buying products.

Demand for Public Relations Services

The demand for public relations services depends on the types of publics that interact with the organization. In some cases, organizations depend on publics for revenue. Customers of JCPenney form a public for that company. In other cases, the organizations depend on a public for resources. General Motors communicates with its employees, who form a public that supplies labor. Consumers demand certain actions of JCPenney, and laborers demand fair treatment by General Motors. Communication is part of the process that ensures that consumers and laborers get what they need.

Most daily newspapers in the United States belong to the Newspaper Association of America (NAA). Through this membership, publishers constitute a public and express a demand for intelligent lobbying, that is, representing their interests to state and federal governments. The NAA tries to influence legislation that affects daily newspapers, such as laws that limit access to public meetings.

Public relations people deal with two types of publics: those inside their organization and those outside the organization. *Internal publics* include employees, managers, trustees, and stockholders. The inside publics have a much stronger commitment to the organization than do those outside. *External publics* include consumers and voters, government organizations, interest groups, business organizations, and media.

Demand for Public Relations Information

Just as organizations eagerly send out information about themselves, individuals and other groups seek information about those organizations. Press releases, electronic and print, and press conferences are prime ways in which journalists find out about the activities of organizations. Research indicates that small newspapers use press releases more often, sometimes without editing, than large newspapers. Up to 30 percent of the content in some small newspapers comes from press releases.

News media organizations' demand for information from organizations is much like automobile makers' demand for steel and plastic. Public relations information serves as a raw material for creating news content. Just as steel and plastic vary in quality, so does information. Inaccurate and misleading information, whether purposeful or accidental, does not adequately meet the general public's need for useful information.

SUPPLYING THE DEMAND FOR PUBLIC RELATIONS

Almost every organization has public relations needs. The manager of a small retail store can usually conduct all the public relations the store requires. However, large organizations require public relations specialists. At least four types of groups require public relations to fulfill their goals: political and government groups, interest groups, profit-seeking companies, and nonprofit organizations. All these organizations share common needs to inform publics about an event, product, or political position, and to persuade individual members of the publics to attend the event, use the product, or adopt the position.

Political and government groups inform citizens and advocate political candidates and positions. These groups include political parties, elected and appointed government officials, and candidates for public office. Information is supplied through videotapes, media interviews with politicians, press releases, newsletters, and advertisements. The Michigan Department of Natural Resources distributes information to residents about a variety of outdoor activities such as hunting, fishing, and gardening. Most of the newsletters sent by members of Congress during an election year try to influence the voters to reelect them. Table 11.1 describes different public relations functions used by a variety of organizations.

Interest groups attempt to influence politicians to achieve public policy decisions that favor the groups' interests. The National Rifle Association (NRA) is a powerful interest group that represents the interests of gun owners and manufacturers. For years the NRA has been able to limit legislation to control guns even though a majority of U.S. citizens support control of certain types of weapons.

Table 11.1	PR Functions (by Type of Organization)
Type of Organization	**PR Function**
Government and political organizations	Political PR Fund-raising Crisis management Event coordination
Interest groups	Political PR Fund-raising Lobbying Event coordination
For-profit organizations	Lobbying Crisis management Financial PR Event coordination
Nonprofit organizations	Fund-raising Event coordination Lobbying Crisis management

Almost every cause and profession imaginable has an organized interest group to advocate its political position. Offices for most interest groups are located in Washington, D.C., and state capitals, where they are close to the legislative processes.

Profit-seeking organizations use public relations to create and maintain favorable attitudes toward their goods and services. Consumers who do not trust a company or a particular product will be less likely to purchase it. PR practitioners in profit-seeking organizations use advocacy and information to maintain a positive image in the public's minds.

Nonprofit organizations depend heavily on public relations because much of their support comes from public donations. Organizations such as the Red Cross, the United Way, and the Salvation Army receive a large portion of their funds from individual donations. It is important for those fund-raising efforts that the public recognize the community work they do. In addition, people who use a nonprofit organization's services must be aware of the services it offers if they are going to use it.

The Public Relations Process

Often, public relations practitioners seem to do their jobs effortlessly. But PR works best when it is based on solid planning. Several models of the public relations process are available. In 1955, Edward L. Bernays listed the eight *components of public relations:*[18]

1. Define your objective.
2. Research your publics.
3. Modify your objectives to reach goals that research shows are attainable.
4. Decide on your strategy.
5. Set up your themes, symbols, and appeals.
6. Blueprint an effective organization to carry out the activity.
7. Chart your plan for both timing and tactics.
8. Carry out your tactics.

Key Concept

Components of public relations The public relations process starts with a goal, requires a plan, progresses through implementation, and then evaluates the plan for effectiveness. Successful public relations campaigns require careful planning and reliance on research.

Ongoing public relations efforts, including fundraising, ensure that agencies like the Red Cross can continue their work, such as aiding victims of the 2004 Indian Ocean tsunami.

The public relations process starts with an objective or goal. An automobile company might want to publicize its latest car. Its public relations objective would be getting as much mass media publicity as possible. Researching the publics would involve checking the media outlets that are most likely to carry information about a new auto model. These would include automotive magazines, the business and automotive sections of newspapers, and business-oriented television shows. Part of the research might include the probability that the media outlets would write stories about the new model.

A political party that seeks support for a candidate is in a similar situation. The party must identify the types of people who are likely to vote for that candidate and the particular issues that will convince them to vote for the person. Part of the research includes surveying the public about issues and reactions to a candidate's position. Without specific knowledge about these two topics, time and money will be wasted on people who will not be swayed or on issues that voters consider unimportant.

On the basis of the research, the automobile public relations practitioners would specify particular goals for publicity. For example, the PR department would aim for long articles in the *Wall Street Journal,* the *New York Times* business section, *Business Week,* and each of a dozen regional daily newspapers. With these goals set, the particular ways of approaching the various media outlets would be designed. These might include personal contact, press releases, video news releases, electronic press releases, and press conferences.

In the political example, public relations personnel and political consultants would examine the research, advise the candidate to modify his or her position on certain issues, and select appropriate media outlets and schedule public appearances so that the candidate could advance the message.

The fifth step involves creating the types of messages that will be used. For the automobile company, these messages would include special attributes of the car such as safety features, a sporty image, or mileage performance. A political candidate usually attempts to provide a cohesive and consistent message, which is often referred to as a campaign theme.

The sixth step requires specifying how people and financial resources will be used to carry out the campaign. Who will write what? Where and when will press conferences be held? Who will test drive the new car? Who will promote the candidate, raise funds, and plan public appearances? What is the budget for each type of activity?

As a seventh step, the practitioner plans detailed tactics. This includes the timing of various activities. For example, the car might be announced at a press conference, which would be followed by interviews with company officials and test drives by journalists. Tactics include national announcements and efforts to provide public relations at regional levels. The political candidate might tour a factory, meet with spouses, and give a speech on the factory steps.

Finally, the tactics are fulfilled. After the process begins, the results must be evaluated for the short term and the long term. An effective plan includes monitoring how the tactics are working as the plan is being executed. The practitioners monitor stories run in magazines, newspapers, and on television. Evaluation allows the PR practitioner to adjust the tactics as the plan unfolds. Finally, after the plan has been completed, the practitioner evaluates the overall success of the plan.

The unifying activity of all steps in the planning process is decision making. At each step, decisions must be made. Effective decisions are based on two important aspects of the process: specifying goals and conducting research. All PR activities should take place with a goal in mind; otherwise, the effort may be wasted. The goal may be to improve a car manufacturer's image or to increase the donations at a university, but without goals, efforts cannot be focused and cannot be evaluated. Research is the second critical activity because all planning must be based on knowledge.

The T-shirts on these children not only identify them as Head Start youngsters, but they also serve an identifying role for the importance of the program itself. Part of the public relations process requires maintaining a message presence before the various publics that an organization or program serves.

Conducting External Public Relations

External communication deals with publics outside the organization. Common activities include lobbying, political PR, financial PR, fund-raising, crisis management, and event coordination. This list is far from exhaustive, and even these activities vary with the publics addressed, the goals pursued, and the communication methods employed.

Lobbying   **Lobbying** is an effort to influence the legislative and administrative activities of government. Legislators need information when they are writing a law or considering whether to vote for it. They need to know who will be affected by the law, what will be the cost of administering it, and what effects, positive and negative, it is likely to have. A lobbyist provides the information that supports the organization's position. For example, oil companies have lobbied to open up the Arctic National Wildlife Refuge for drilling, hoping to obtain the 10 billion barrels of oil thought to be contained there. Their lobbyists argue that such drilling would reduce U.S. dependency on foreign oil. Opponents counter that it would destroy the environment without any great gain in energy reserves.

Political Public Relations   Political PR activities resemble lobbying efforts, but the voters form the public of interest. Political public relations tries to get a certain person elected or to influence public opinion about a political issue such as abortion or tax reform. During an election campaign, PR practitioners write news releases; set up print, radio, and television interviews; prepare campaign literature for voters; distribute yard signs and bumper stickers; answer questions from journalists; and plan advertising campaigns.

lobbying

Persuading legislators and other government officials to enact or support legislation favorable to one's cause.

Events Coordination   Public relations also includes coordinating events. These range from concert tours to political campaigns. A concert tour by the Dave Matthews Band requires public relations activity to help organize the tour, buy advertising, and communicate with various music media organizations. The PR practitioner creates and distributes media kits about the tour, coordinates media interviews for the artists, writes press releases, and makes sure reporters cover the tour stops.

Financial Public Relations   Financial public relations, sometimes called **investor relations,** are efforts by corporations to communicate with their investors, potential investors, and other interested parties, with the goal of maintaining the financial value of the company. The financial public relations practitioner communicates with three publics: investment analysts, financial journalists, and institutional investors.[19] Investment analysts advise the public about buying stocks and securities, and institutional investors represent investment organizations such as mutual funds that have large amounts of money to invest. Financial journalists from such publications as the *Wall Street Journal* provide information about businesses to a variety of audiences. Financial PR firms such as Financial Brokers Relations of Houston, Texas, usually provide a range of services. This includes finding financial support for projects such as expanding production plants and promoting the company's stock among mutual funds, retirement fund managers, and other institutional investors.

External public relations activities can be handled in-house by organizational employees, or they can be handled by consultants who are usually affiliated with a ***public relations agency.*** Each method has advantages and disadvantages. In some situations, a combination of in-house practitioners and consultants might work best. For example, media training might best be handled by a combination of internal media relations practitioners advising corporate officials on how to stick to a corporate theme, and consultants might provide on-camera training.

In-house practitioners are usually more familiar with the company's managers and operations than consultants. This gives them more credibility with media and allows for informal interaction with the press. This familiarity can make the practitioner a valuable member of the management team. In addition, an in-house public relations staff usually costs less than outside consultants unless activities are only periodic.

Despite the in-house advantages, it is not always the best approach in all situations. Some organizations do not need ongoing external public relations activities.

investor relations

Communication with those who invest in the company, that is, those who buy stock.

This Dave Matthews Band concert at Madison Square Garden required extensive public relations activity, from organizing the tour to informing music media organizations about the logistics.

For example, a small firm that sells manufacturing equipment to furniture companies deals with a small identifiable public and does not require extensive public relations, in such a case, an in-house staff would be an unnecessary expense.

PR consultants also may be used in specialized situations even if a company has an in-house public relations staff. If a cereal company plans to sell new public stock, a financial public relations firm might be hired. Most companies do not have in-house financial public relations personnel.

Public relations firms vary greatly in size. A few collect more than $250 million in fees annually; others have only a few employees. Small firms survive in a world of big companies because the heart of PR is mediated and interpersonal communication. From writing press releases to persuading a legislator to support a new bill, PR involves people with communication talent. Many of these people prefer to work for themselves rather than for larger companies.

Several of the larger firms work as subsidiaries of advertising agencies. Because public relations and advertising are both in the business of promotion, it often makes sense to have both types of services available in the same organization. A client can have both the public relations and ad campaigns planned and executed by the same organization. Table 11.2 shows the public relations fee income for the top ten independent firms. Of these firms, seven are associated with an advertising agency.

Fund-Raising Some public relations practitioners participate in fund-raising for nonprofit organizations. Public broadcasting stations exemplify this activity. Twice a year PBS stations interrupt their regular programming to ask viewers to donate money to pay for the station's operations. Many stations also hold auctions, soliciting donated goods and services from the community and then selling them to raise money. Philanthropic organizations, such as United Way, and universities and colleges also participate in fund-raising activities. Immediately on graduation, if not sooner, college

Table 11.2 — 2005 PR Fee Income for Top Ten Independent Firms

Firm	2005 Net Fees (Millions of Dollars)	Employees	% Fee Change from 2004
1. Edelman PR Worldwide	$261.9	1,848	+13.6
2. Ruder Finn	92.1	568	+2.7
3. Waggener Edstrom	84.9	594	+8.0
4. APCO Worldwide	73.3	405	+29.0
5. Text 100 Int'l	52.4	493	+16.0
6. Schwaetz Communications	22.1	156	−8.5
7. Zeno Group	19.9	113	+19.9
8. Dan Klotes Communications	19.5	131	+12.1
9. Qorvis Comms.	18.2	69	+19.1
10. Gibbs & Soell	17.2	105	+14.2

Source: O'Dwyer's Directory of Public Relations Firms, odwyerpr.com.

students receive solicitations for donations from their college's public relations department, which is usually called the development office.

Crisis Management

Public relations personnel develop long-range plans for managing issues so they can help companies avoid crises. Nevertheless, sometimes an unexpected catastrophe hits, and the public relations staff is called on for **crisis management.** Typical crises include product tampering, product recalls, serious accidents, and even some labor disputes. In addition to the potential financial damage done to a company by the crisis, the organization's image can be damaged if the crisis is not handled well.

The federal government's response to the Hurricane Katrina disaster was widely regarded as a failure because of belated action, bad communication, wasteful spending, and poor coordination. Disaster response turned into crisis management for the Federal Emergency Management Agency (FEMA), which had to defend itself as an organization. Receiving criticism for implying that the victims were to blame for their suffering, FEMA's director, Michael Brown, admitted to having underestimated the disaster. Brown resigned, and the government spent billions of dollars trying to fix the disgraced agency.

Crisis management requires **contingency plans** that anticipate possible crises. Such plans can't anticipate every scenario, and many public relations firms stress a corporation's social responsibility in avoiding such accidents in the first place. An unexpected crisis can be financially devastating to a business and even destroy it.

External Tools

Public relations uses a variety of tools; most either generate information or communicate information. Information-generating tools include research methods such as surveys, focus groups, and databases. Public relations specialists conduct *surveys* using telephone, mail, and personal interviews. In each situation, the respondent answers questions about topics of interest to the practitioner. The questions may concern a company's image, use of a product, or opinion about an issue. The answers to the questions are analyzed using computers, and the information facilitates planning and executing plans.

The second set of tools includes communication methods, both mediated and interpersonal, to inform and persuade people. A record company faxes news releases about a new album to music critics at newspapers and magazines. The releases provide information about the group, the album title, and the release date in order to get the critic to listen to the album and review it. A day or two after the release arrives, a practitioner will call to remind the music critic about the album. Both of these efforts are part of a larger plan to create publicity for the album. Interpersonal communication tools range from giving speeches to one-on-one discussions.

Spin Doctors and New Tools

Although spin doctors operate in the business world, the term is more often associated with those who work on political campaigns to "spin" a candidate's message. **Spin doctors** lobby journalists to influence coverage. The practice first gained attention during the 1988 presidential contest between George Bush and Michael Dukakis when the campaign managers contacted the press corps daily to put their candidate's spin on the coverage. Eventually, the spin doctors themselves became subjects of news stories.

Spin doctors provide information, but their real goal is to persuade journalists at least to look at an issue from their client's perspective. Spin doctors first master an understanding of the reporting and editing process and then use that understanding to appeal to journalistic routines and values to get reporters to pay attention to a particular candidate's point of view.[20]

Political spinning seemed to reach its peak after the disputed 2000 presidential election, when both parties tried to influence the courts' and the public's perceptions

contingency plan

Plan designed well in advance to accommodate situations in which the turn of events would be unpredictable; such plans help organizations cope with possible undesirable outcomes.

spin doctor

Public relations personnel, usually associated with political communication, who tries to get journalists and other publics to believe a particular interpretation of an event or information.

Media Convergence

Reaching the Blogosphere

Public relations is no longer simply a process of reading audiences through news professionals in print, television and radio. Since information and opinion are now widely shared through forums like websites, blogs, podcasts, and wikis, public relations professionals have adapted their strategies to take advantage of these new tools. Not all of their efforts have been successful, and some, especially stealth marketing campaigns using blogs, have become legendary failures in the blogosphere.

In 2004, Mazda created a fake blogger, twenty-three-year-old Kid Halloween, who listed music, cheeseburgers, and cars as interests in his user details. On his blog, Kid Halloween posted links to videos, which he claimed a friend had downloaded from public access television. These videos featured the Mazda M3 performing stunts and being driven on Halloween night. Bloggers recognized the Kid Halloween blog as fraudulent because of the videos' production values, among other hints. Many bloggers, including public relations professionals, reviled Mazda for the stunt, and the site was closed.

To launch its new Raging Cow milk drink in 2003, Dr. Pepper/7 Up hired the ad agency Richards Interactive, which created a mock blog, Angry Cow, supposedly written by a bovine. Since unlike Kid Halloween, the Angry Cow was obviously a fake without attempt to deceive, no one minded. However, Richards also enlisted six teenagers to blog about its drink, inviting them to company headquarters, giving them free samples, and asking them not to mention that they'd been enlisted by Dr. Pepper/7 Up. Other bloggers heard of the scheme, and angry at the deception, launched a boycott of the Raging Cow drink.

After these failures, public relations firms understood that the blogging world has unique characteristics. Based on the older form of the diary, a blog typically is supposed to be an honest record of an individual writer's thoughts, not a polished, top-down corporate marketing gimmick. Furthermore, many bloggers have thought of themselves as mavericks and whistle-blowers with a commitment to free speech. This can lead to a host of potential public relations problems for companies, including angry consumers blogging about bad products and disgruntled employees blogging about embarrassing company practices and trade secrets.

Despite the risks, many corporations are using blogs for promotion, including having their CEOs write for Internet audiences. Robert Scoble's "Corporate Weblog Manifesto" offers a widely used guide. His advice includes telling the truth, being open, promptly announcing both good and bad news, and using a human voice. Most public relations professionals now agree that honesty and transparency are essential to using blogs as a tool.

Sources: Rob Walker, "Blogging for Milk," *Slate,* April 14, 2003, slate.com/id/2081419; Ogilvy Public Relations Worldwide, *The Executive Blogger's Guide to Building a Nest of Blogs, Wikis & RSS,* Ogilvy Insight, ogilvypr.com/pdf/bloggers-guide.pdf.

---

of the election outcome. Democratic candidate Al Gore even appeared on television in an effort to influence the recount in Florida.

Problems Facing the Practitioner   Public relations practitioners deal with two primary problems: budget vulnerability and the need for respect. When the economy takes a downturn, many companies cut budgets to preserve profit levels. Because PR does not contribute directly to the production of goods and services and PR people do not run machines or wait on customers, communication departments often face the sharpest edge of the downsizing ax: Budgets are cut, and resources for outside consultants are reduced.

In addition, company managers do not always understand—or respect—the fact that practitioners have particular expertise in understanding the impact of communication. Managers assume that people in their organization who can write and speak well know as much about communication as the experts do. However, exercising the mechanical process of communicating is not the same as understanding how that communication will affect people.

Practitioners also encounter respect problems because their contributions are difficult to measure. Managers can determine how many people hours it takes to produce

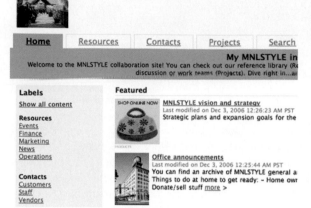

MNLSTYLE intranet

| Home | Resources | Contacts | Projects | Search |

My MNLSTYLE in
Welcome to the MNLSTYLE collaboration site! You can check out our reference library (Re
discussion or work teams (Projects). Dive right in...a

Labels
Show all content

Resources
Events
Finance
Marketing
News
Operations

Contacts
Customers
Staff
Vendors

Featured

SHOP ONLINE NOW **MNLSTYLE vision and strategy**
Last modified on Dec 3, 2006 12:26:23 AM PST
Strategic plans and expansion goals for the

Office announcements
Last modified on Dec 3, 2006 12:25:44 AM PST
You can find an archive of MNLSTYLE general a
Things to do at home to get ready: – Home owr
Donate/sell stuff more >

Many corporations have internal computer networks, called intranets, through which employees can share information, ideas, and resources. For example, fmyi (for my innovation) provides companies with a free and easy-to-use online workspace for internal communication (fmyi.com).

a car, but they cannot tell how many practitioner hours it took to get the public to think well of those cars.

The effect of a public relations campaign is difficult to measure, a problem that has been widely discussed in the profession. Mentions of a campaign in the media can be counted, but word of mouth is notoriously hard to assess. To demand bigger budgets, public relations firms are becoming more interested in developing measures to prove the worth of their campaigns. Sales figures and surveys of audience awareness and behavior are important components of evaluation. Some practitioners also see an advantage in surveying website visits, online chats, blogs, and other sources to provide more information.

Conducting Internal Public Relations

Internal public relations activities include all of the formal communications activities within an organization except for interpersonal communication in the organization's daily activities. Broadcasting a company news program to Ford plants around the United States is internal PR; an assembly line foreperson telling a welder to speed up is not.

As with external activities, internal activities are planned and sustained. They include company publications about social activities, communication about policies and goals, and training activities. Such communication becomes crucial if a company wants its employees to cooperate effectively and efficiently in achieving the organization's goals.

Both managers and employees of a company continually make decisions. The decisions affect the company's production and services and the lives of the people who work for the company. Employees deserve to know the truth about the company in which they work, and managers must know about their employees if they are to motivate them. Internal PR is a classic case of two-way communication, and much of PR success is determined by how much employees are "listened to" rather than "told to."

Key Concept

Directions of information exchange Good public relations and good business require more than one-way communication. Communication horizontally, or among publics, as well as from the top down and bottom up, is essential for harmonious production of products or services.

Who Communicates with Whom?   Internal communication involves four **directions of information exchange:** downward, upward, horizontal, and diagonal.[21] Figure 11.1 illustrates these four directions.

Downward communication (managers communicating with employees) is best exemplified by a president presenting a policy to employees. There are five main reasons for downward communication: (1) to explain the duties of a job and how to do them; (2) to provide a reason for doing a job and to explain how the job fits with other jobs; (3) to communicate an organization's policies, procedures, and practices; (4) to give employees feedback about their performance; and (5) to provide employees with a sense of the organization's missions and goals.[22] All of these are essential for employees to perform well. Upward communication (employees communicating with their supervisors) provides seven types of information: (1) feedback for managers about employees' attitudes; (2) suggestions for improving job procedures; (3) feedback about the effectiveness of downward communication; (4) the ability of employees to achieve company goals; (5) requests for assistance and supplies; (6) timely expressions of employee grievances; and (7) stimulation of employee involvement.[23] All effective communication requires feedback. Upward and downward communications feed each other; it is a mutual and symbiotic relationship. Without both, organizations cannot achieve their greatest potential.

Horizontal and diagonal communication, which involve communication between departments at different levels or between employees at similar levels, are just as crucial to an organization's performance as upward and downward communications.

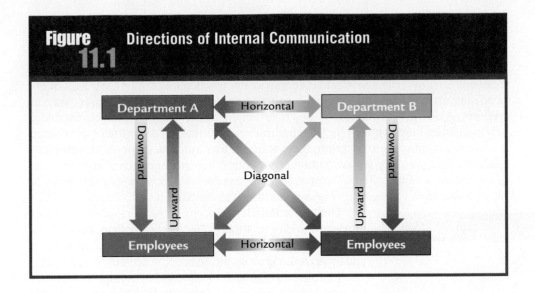

Figure 11.1 Directions of Internal Communication

A reporter may need to talk to the circulation director (diagonal communication), or directors of two different departments, such as editorial and circulation, may need to communicate (horizontal communication). These conversations usually involve direct communication among managers and employees without the intervention of a PR practitioner. Diagonal and horizontal communications typically involve small numbers of people, so interpersonal communication works best without someone intervening.

Methods of Internal Communication Company officials communicate with their employees through media and interpersonally. Many of the tools used are the same as those used in communicating to external publics. The more important the information is to the receiver, the more effective interpersonal communication will be. Information about layoffs and drastic changes in working conditions should be delivered face to face by the employees' supervisors. Under such conditions, the employees will have questions that need to be answered. E-mail notices or newsletters can be effective in explaining changes in policies and procedures.

The type of communication also depends on the number of people involved. Interpersonal communication with 10,000 people is not feasible, but a television broadcast would work. Many large companies with multiple plants have daily TV broadcasts with satellite distribution to keep employees up to date on corporate events and concerns.

The employees' media habits must be considered if communication is to work. Companies with large numbers of unskilled laborers will communicate more effectively through television and radio than through a newspaper. White-collar companies with highly educated staffs tend to use e-mail, newsletters, and memos to communicate.

The nature of the company itself is a factor. Some companies are scattered across the globe; others locate their branches close together or have a single location. Because of current technology, distance should not hamper good communication, but it will affect the method chosen.

Converging technologies have increased companies' ability to function world wide. Strategies may include electronic newsletters, instant messaging, mobile communications, and podcasts. Most large companies have private intranets that only employees can access; for example, IBM's intranet reaches 329,000 employees in 75 countries and has been recognized for its personalized news offerings, elaborate employee directory, blogging capabilities, and accessibility features for older users with memory and vision problems. IBM's intranet hosts around 2,800 employee blogs, mostly used for project management.[24]

Problems Facing Internal Public Relations Practitioners   Internal PR is usually conducted by practitioners who are hired by the organization and work for a supervisor or executive who controls information. The practitioner cannot release more information than is authorized. For public relations practitioners, trust between management and employees is essential in carrying out information tasks. Internal practitioners need support and honesty from management in order to communicate effectively. In addition, good internal public relations relies on credibility. One former PR person told of a manufacturing plant in which the internal communication department conducted a survey of employees to ascertain their attitudes toward management. The employees were told that they would remain anonymous, but managers used the returned questionnaires to identify troublemakers. The troublemakers were eventually fired. Additional efforts to measure employee attitudes at the plant had no success.

Key Concept

Code of ethics Ethical practice is most likely to exist within a society that values truth in communication and holds the people who have the most access to media to high ethical standards. Ethical practices are endorsed by professional public relations organizations, but practicing good ethics is ultimately the responsibility of the individual.

The Public Relations Society of America plays the most important role in promoting PR professionalism. PRSA has a **code of ethics,** a publication called *Public Relations Journal,* and an accrediting program. To become accredited, a PR practitioner must take an exam that tests knowledge of PR practices and ethics and communication law. Practitioners who pass the exam become accredited in public relations and can use the acronym APR after their names. Research indicates that accredited practitioners make an average of $102,031 a year, $16,759 more than unaccredited practitioners.[25] Accreditation is enforced through the code of ethics. Complaints can be filed against APR practitioners, and if they are found to have violated the PRSA Code of Ethics (see Figure 11.2), they can be stripped of their accreditation.

Figure 11.2   Public Relations Society of America Code of Ethics

CODE OF PROFESSIONAL STANDARDS
FOR THE PRACTICE OF PUBLIC RELATIONS

Declaration of Principles

Members of the Public Relations Society of America base their professional principles on the fundamental value and dignity of the individual, holding that the free exercise of human rights, especially freedom of speech, freedom of assembly and freedom of the press, is essential to the practice of public relations.

In serving the interests of clients and employers, we dedicate ourselves to the goals of better communication, understanding and cooperation among the diverse individuals, groups and institutions in society.

We pledge:

- To conduct ourselves professionally, with truth, accuracy, fairness and responsibility;

- To improve our individual competence and advance the knowledge and proficiency of the profession through continuing research and education;

- And to adhere to the articles of the Code of Professional Standards for the Practice of Public Relations as adopted by the governing Assembly of the Society.

Source: David A. Haberman and Harry A. Dolphin, *Public Relations: The Necessary Art* (Ames: Iowa State University Press, 1988), pp. 413–414. Reprinted by permission of the Public Relations Society of America.

Selling Nations

A nation's interests are often pursued not only through military and economic means, but through promotion of a national culture and image. This strategy has been called soft power, cultural diplomacy, public diplomacy, or, in a more negative view, propaganda. Nations may try to shape their international reputations to attract business investment, political support, tourist trade, or global events like the Olympics.

Some nations have government employees who are responsible for these public relations efforts. In the United States, the State Department's Under Secretary for Public Diplomacy and Public Affairs has the job of promoting U.S. values throughout the world. The State Department's cultural ambassadors, such as baseball player Bernie Williams and jazz musician Wynton Marsalis, also represent the United States abroad through arts and education programs. To "promote and sustain freedom and democracy," the United States sends radio and television broadcasts to many parts of the globe, including Cuba, through Radio Martí and TV Martí; the Middle East, through Alhurra television and Radio Sawa; and Europe, through the Voice of America and Radio Free Europe.

A nation may also hire a public relations firm to promote its interests. These efforts may include political lobbying, lining up media appearances for a visiting head of state, and cultivating supporters such as academics and business leaders. Because of growing anti-immigration feelings in the United States, Mexico hired a U.S. public relations firm, Allyn & Co., in 2006 to raise opposition against the extension of a border wall. Rob Allyn explained, "If people in the U.S. and Canada had an accurate view of the success of democracy, political stability, and economic prosperity in Mexico, it would improve their views on specific bilateral issues like immigration and border security." Since the September 11 attacks, Saudi Arabia has given over $20 million to public relations firms, like Qorvis Communications, to improve the country's image in the United States. However, the strategy has had little effect, with well over half of U.S. citizens believing that Saudi Arabia has a role in terrorist attacks.

Increasingly, governments are viewing their national image as a brand that distinguishes it from other national images and can be used to gain political and economic advantage. For example, South Korea has a "Dynamic Korea" campaign to attract tourists and investors by enhancing its image as a liberal democracy with a market economy. Many other countries have similar campaigns, such as "Malaysia, Truly Asia," "Amazing Thailand," "Costa Rica—No Artificial Ingredients," and "South Africa, Alive with Possibility." Such efforts can be traced back to England's "Cool Britannia" campaign in the 1990s, which attempted to shift the country's image from a quaint monarchy to a modern, high tech center of trade. Often, global sporting events provide opportunities for countries to polish their images. Before the 2006 World Cup, hosted by Germany, the German government started a "Land of Ideas" campaign to transmit its new image as "a hospitable, joyful, and modern nation."

Some marketing researchers argue that nations, unless they are very authoritarian, are far too complex and often inconsistent to be regarded as brands. Other critics, such as Naomi Klein, suggest that nation branding is nothing more than propaganda that disguises dissenting voices. Nevertheless, the nation branding movement is becoming well established, with many countries taking advantage of global communications to spread their carefully crafted images.

Sources: Mark Stevenson, "Mexico Promises to Block Border Wall Plan," Associated Press, December 20, 2005, breitbart.com/news/2005/12/20/D8EK9N0G6.html; Ajay Kumar, "Middle East: Getting a Facelift," *Harvard International Review* 27 (Fall 2005): 9–10; Andrew Purvis, "Germany's New Pitch," *Time International,* June 12, 2006: 43; *How the World Sees the World: The Anholt-GMI Nation Brands Index,* 2005, nationbrandindex.com; Naomi Klein, "The Spectacular Failure of Brand USA," nologo.org/features/02/03/11/158241.shtml.

The field continues to be redefined, with an emphasis on integrity of practice. When a *Public Relations Journal* article asked practitioners to comment about their role, eighty-four practitioners responded. Of these, 21 percent said that practitioners are advocates on behalf of clients, 7 percent said that practitioners are consensus builders who try to bring competing sides together to find solutions, and 57 percent said that practitioners must be both advocates and consensus builders. The remaining 15 percent said that practitioners should perform other functions, such as those of information broker, strategist, and educator.

However, the dichotomy between advocate and consensus builder misses the key issue that has always defined professionalism. The issue is not whether to advocate on behalf of clients but rather to determine the role of truth in public relations practice. The question is: Should practitioners purposely mislead any of their publics?

The professional practitioner, as defined by PRSA, would answer no to this question. The third article of the PRSA Code of Ethics says, "A member shall adhere to truth and accuracy and to generally accepted standards of good taste." However, most specialists are not members of the PRSA. The tobacco industry's efforts to persuade the public that smoking is not harmful is a classic case of questionable public relations.

TRENDS

In 2005, journalism and mass communications professor J. Sean McCleneghan sent an e-mail asking 231 public relations practitioners to rank nine issues facing the profession. In *The Practice of Public Relations,* Fraser P. Seitel had identified these as the key concerns for public relations firms in the twenty-first century. As a group, participants in McCleneghan's survey ranked them in the following order.

1. *Accountability:* Corporate morality, virtue, and ethics were ranked number one by PR professionals.
2. *Technology:* The changing world of communications technologies have led to great changes in the way public relations professionals target and reach their audiences.
3. *Corporate responsibility:* Corporations must maintain public trust by being responsible toward consumers and contributing to society.
4. Economic **globalization:** This issue has many dimensions, such as potential changes in the global economy, the effects of outsourcing jobs to other countries, the difficulties in communicating across cultures, and the impact of major events such as wars and disasters.
5. *Shifting of public opinion:* Because new technologies make communications fast and easy, opinions and perceptions can change rapidly.
6. *Global jealousies:* Economic disparities have created a situation leading to terrorism and anti-Western feeling in global publics.
7. *Aging of society:* Having the highest incomes, older audiences are concerned with health, quality of life, and the quality of consumer products.
8. *Leanness and meanness:* Public relations practitioners are more vulnerable to cost-cutting measures and have tighter budgets than in the past.
9. *Bigness is back:* The trend toward convergence of small firms into large corporations was ranked last among PR professionals.[26]

> **Key Concept**
>
> **Globalization** Globalization is a broad term that refers to changes brought by increased movement of people, financial capital, ideas, technologies, and media representations throughout the world. Communications technology has helped foster globalization.

Technology: New Ways to Contact Publics

Technology has transformed the public relations industry by allowing easier direct contact between professionals and their publics and by increasing the number of media outlets that carry information. Blogging has received great attention as a public relations tool, a way of carrying out the mission of the public relations professional to establish relationships with employees, clients, consumers, and other audiences. Satellite and radio media tours allow a PR spokesperson to meet with reporters in remote locations. Other new digital means of communications, such as podcasts, webcasts, and RSS feeds, have been touted as revolutionizing the industry. However, as of April 2006, many public relations professionals were still using more established means, such as print and video news releases, to communicate. A PR News/MediaLink survey of 459 practitioners found that 34 percent had used blogs and 10 percent had used podcasts. Few had used satellite and radio media tours. Webcasts were more popular, with 56 percent of respondents developing these for both external and internal communications.[27] Explanations for the lag include reluctance on the part of public relations professionals to devote attention to relatively untested, time-consuming methods.

Culture: Ethics Crisis

Accountability topped the list of issues facing the public relations industry in 2005, a year when ethics scandals beset its reputation. In January, a conservative commentator and public relations professional, Armstrong Williams, was revealed to have been paid $240,000 by the U.S. Department of Education, through its public relations firm Ketchum, to support the No Child Left Behind Act on his television show. Richard Edelman, president and CEO of one of the U.S.'s largest public relations firms, deemed the Armstrong incident "profoundly depressing" and called for the industry's "long term commitment to the best ethical behavior."[28] In December, the *Los Angeles Times* revealed that the U.S. Defense Department had hired a public relations firm, the Lincoln Group, to plant stories in Iraqi newspapers that put U.S. efforts in a positive light. Lincoln employees hid their connection to the military, sometimes pretending to be journalists, and offered payment to Iraqi news outlets to run their stories. Iraqi journalists and Muslim clerics were also on the payroll.[29] Citing these scandals that exposed a lack of disclosure and transparency, *PR News* named the "ethics miasma" as one of the profession's three main priorities, along with technology and measurement.[30]

Culture: Diversity in the Workforce

Researchers from the City College of New York and Howard University conducted a study in 2005 to assess diversity within the public relations profession. They invited 132 African-American, Latino, and Asian-American practitioners to respond. The study found that workplace conditions are less than desirable, with around half of the respondents reporting that they've been treated unfairly, have not been afforded the same opportunities as Caucasian Americans, and have experienced subtle discrimination. Sixty-three percent felt that the public relations industry is only "mildly committed" to improving diversity in the workforce, with little effort to recruit or retain minority employees. Further, minority employees are often given menial tasks and have suffered barriers to advancement. Despite talk in the field of reaching ethnic and minority audiences, the public relations profession is doing little to build and maintain a diverse workforce. The study recommends that public relations firms actively recruit minorities, provide diversity training for staff, and improve treatment of minority employees.[31]

SUMMARY

- Public relations concerns planned and sustained unpaid communication from organizations to publics.
- Practitioners communicate with internal and external publics.
- Any of an organization's many publics can influence whether that organization achieves its goals.
- The goals of public relations are to inform, persuade, and seek information from the organization's publics.
- Public relations did not become recognized by the general population until after World War II, although some corporations had used PR for almost one hundred years.
- External activities include lobbying, political PR, financial PR, fund-raising, crisis management, and events coordination.
- Public relations specialists can work in house for an organization or as a consultant for an organization.
- The public relations process includes setting goals, conducting research, creating a plan, and evaluating the success of the plan.
- The problems facing practitioners include low budgets and lack of respect from managers.
- Internal communication includes downward, upward, horizontal, and vertical communication.
- Ethnic and racial bias continues to plague the public relations field.
- A variety of technologies are available for PR communication, and the type that is used must be appropriate for the information needs and habits of the publics.
- A key concern for PR professionals is corporate responsibility, both for their own firms and for their clients.
- The growth of the international economic system has created global public relations, which in turn has created additional problems for practitioners.

NAVIGATING THE WEB Public Relations

The World Wide Web is an ideal public relations tool. In fact, many websites are promotional sites for organizations or corporations. In addition, various public relations firms maintain sites. Also included are trade publications that provide information about public relations.

PR Newswire
prnewswire.com
PR Newswire presents press releases and articles about industries in the United States and around the world. It organizes companies by industry and provides an overview of business and industry.

Public Relations Society of America
prsa.org
PRSA is a professional society that accredits PR practitioners. The site contains information about PRSA and its membership requirements, publications, and professional activities. This site also links to the PRSSA (Public Relations Student Society of America) site. The PRSSA promotes professional public relations on college campuses.

PR Watch
prwatch.org
The site is run by the Center for Media & Democracy, a nonprofit organization that criticizes the public relations industry for trying to manipulate the public. The site sells books and provides PR Watch online.

O'Dwyer's PR
odwyerpr.com
This is an excellent site for news and data about the industry. It offers O'Dwyer's PR Daily with news and pages aimed at public relations students.

QUESTIONS FOR REVIEW

1. Define public relations in your own words.
2. Describe public relations as an interactive process between an organization and its publics.
3. What contributions did Edward L. Bernays make to public relations?

4. What four groups require public relations in order to reach their goals?
5. What are the eight steps in the public relations process? Describe each briefly.

6. Why is accountability an issue for public relations personnel?

ISSUES TO THINK ABOUT

1. What is meant by the concept that public relations evolved to serve social needs?
2. What is the relationship between public relations and propaganda?
3. Why is it important for public relations professionals to be truthful?

4. Analyze the importance of directional communication in internal public relations.
5. What is the significance of nation branding? Can a nation be branded?

SUGGESTED READINGS

Anholt, Simon. *Brand New Justice: The Upside of Global Branding* (Oxford: Butterworth-Heinemann, 2005).

Cutlip, Scott M. *Public Relations History: From the Seventeenth to the Twentieth Century: The Antecedents* (Hillsdale, NJ: Lawrence Erlbaum Associates, 1995).

Flynn, Nancy. *Blog Rules: A Business Guide to Managing Policy, Public Relations, and Legal Issues* (New York: Amacom, 2006).

Ries, Al, and Laura Ries. *The Fall of Advertising and the Rise of PR* (New York: HarperBusiness, 2002).

Simmons, P. J., and Chantal de Jonge Ondraat, eds. *Managing Global Issues: Lesson Learned* (Washington, DC: Carnegie Endowment for International Peace, 2001).

12

Advertising

When word got out that Samuel L. Jackson was starring in a B-movie with the absurdly literal name, *Snakes on a Plane,* the Internet social world reacted with satirical fan fiction, spoof movie posters and trailers, music videos, and podcasts. Credited for helping start the buzz, screenwriter Josh Friedman suggested on his blog that "snakes on a plane" should become a philosophical answer to life's problems, like "whattya gonna do." The idea attracted a Georgetown law student, Brian Finkelstein, who started snakesonablog.com, where a growing number of fans shared their movie-related creations. Soon, the *Snakes on a Plane* buzz had spread to other sites, including dozens of videos on YouTube.

The free word-of-mouth publicity for *Snakes on a Plane,* fondly known as SoaP, seemed to be a dream for New Line Cinema, the studio that had produced the film. Finkelstein said of New Line's relationship with his promotional blog, "They are in no way in control of it. They don't pay me, for example, although I kind of wish they would."[1] The studio responded to the buzz by beefing up its own website and running a competition for the movie's theme song, receiving five hundred submissions. It altered the content of the film, adding a line for Samuel L. Jackson from a mock casting call video by impressionist D. C. Luigi and added other material that changed the movie's rating from PG to R. Advertisers watched to see if the mostly fan-generated hype would add up to box office success. They wondered if the movie would

KEY CONCEPTS

- Connection between Demand for News and Advertising
- Let the Buyer Beware Philosophy
- Advertising Agent
- Product Responsibility and Advertising
- Consumer Culture
- Advertising Affects Prices
- Social Cost of Advertising
- Four Effects of Advertising
- Consumer Behavior
- Types of Advertisements
- Targeted Advertising
- Online Advertising
- Viral Marketing
- Advertainment

launch a new way of advertising by tapping on-line social networks and allowing audiences to interact with content.

Beyond original expectations for the movie, *Snakes on a Plane* held the number one box office spot in its first weekend. However, its performance was generally seen as lackluster compared to summer blockbusters. Marketing experts looked for both positive and negative lessons, acknowledging that the viral spread of the SoaP phenomenon was all to the good, but that nobody knew yet how to fully exploit the Wild West of the Internet.

Because of the spread of communications systems, advertising increasingly permeates the social and cultural fabric not only of the United States but of the world. It clearly influences how we dress, eat, and even think, but advertising comes from biased sources. Some consumers see advertising as an effort to trick them into buying what they do not need. Some journalists see advertising as an unwanted influence on news coverage. Parents resist the brand-name appeals made to children and teenagers. Yet many consumers rely on advertising for information about products and to get a good deal. Each of these perspectives contains some truth.

Advertising is defined as a paid mediated presentation of information about services, products, or ideas with the specific goal of persuading consumers to act or think in a particular way. Advertising differs from news coverage and public relations activities because the advertising message is created, produced, and paid for by the advertiser, and the source of the information is clearly identified. Public relations practitioners must hope that a reporter will relay a message accurately; advertisers simply buy the message they want.

Advertising usually tries to sell products, such as soda, and services, such as health care. However, some ads try to promote ideas. All ads share the goal of trying to influence people in some way.

The effort to persuade is not a serious problem for consumers as long as they understand the purpose of advertisements. Many ads serve the basic media social function of coordinating economic activities. Advertising allows sellers to tell buyers what products and services are available at what prices and in what places. Without this exchange of information, consumers would waste time and money.

Advertising has been a controversial fact of American life. Because advertising has an economic and a social effect, the issues that it raises are complex:

- Advertising is most prominent in a free-market economy. As you read this chapter, try to analyze how and why advertising and the free market are related.

- Advertising uses social images and appeals to people's psychological and physical needs. Its content may sell a product through persuading people to adopt a specific lifestyle. Given this impact, think about how advertising is related to the marketplace of ideas.

- Some individuals think that certain types of advertising should be banned because well-produced messages have an enormous impact. After you read about the various types of influence advertising has on culture, try to decide whether advertising significantly changes our culture.

- Internet advertising is still in its infancy compared to more traditional forms of advertising. A major issue is how advertising will make use of the new electronic technologies in the long run. What are the implications for the ways people relate to advertising on the Internet?

- Brands have become important cultural symbols and some have spread globally. As you learn about brands, think about how they function in your own and other cultures.

Advertising in Your Life

Advertising as a Political and Social Message

Advertising is a controvepsial subject in the United States. Think about your own reactions to the ads you see, read, and hear. As you read this chapter, look for clues about the positive and negative aspects of advertising. Think about which forms of media you rely on for advertising and which forms of advertising you think are credible or effective.

Which Media Do You Most Rely on for Advertising? (Rank in Order of Importance to You)		Which Media Do You Most Trust? (Rank in Order of Trustworthiness)		Do You Think Advertising for Some Products Is More Credible than for Others? (Rank in Order of Credibility)		Which Types of Political Ads Are Most Effective? (Rank in Order of Effectiveness)		Which Types of Political Ads Contribute Most to Democracy? (Rank in Order of Contribution)	
Magazines	____	Magazines	____	Cosmetics	____	Issue-oriented	____	Issue-oriented	____
Newspapers	____	Newspapers	____	Household goods	____	Attack	____	Attack	____
Television	____	Television	____	Clothing	____	Personal	____	Personal	____
Radio	____	Radio	____	Cars	____	Informative	____	Informative	____
Direct mail	____	Direct mail	____	Appliances	____	Mood-creating	____	Mood-creating	____
Internet/online	____	Internet/online	____	Services	____	Other	____	Other	____

However, advertising has social costs. Some people argue that it raises the price of goods. Others fear that it alters cultural values; affects the attitudes of children and adults; and undermines the influence of family, religious institutions, and schools. Commercialization through advertising, they argue, directs society away from serious issues and raises the power of consumption to a new level.

For the service of connecting buyer and seller, U.S. media organizations receive large amounts of money. In 2005, media companies took in $271 billion in advertising. Ad spending has increased as companies market their products across media platforms and in every possible public space. Increasingly, inhabitants of consumer societies across the world live in ad-saturated environments, where brands have become symbols of pleasure, aspiration, status, and cosmopolitanism.

ADVERTISING IN AMERICAN LIFE

Advertising dates to the ancient Greek and Roman civilizations. In the cities, **criers** walked the street announcing commercial ventures, as well as providing information about religion, politics, and other public matters.[2] In a sense, these criers were verbal newspapers, with a mixture of news and advertising similar to that found today.

A more traditional definition of a medium would connect early advertising to printing. The earliest known printed advertisement was the **broadside,** or handbill, which was first produced in England in 1477, and the first known broadside was an advertisement for religious books. Although some disagreement exists, the first English newspaper advertisement has been dated from August 1622. A weekly publication of "Newes" carried an advertisement for two earlier copies of the newspaper.[3] Almost eighty years later, the first advertisement appeared in a U.S. newspaper, the *Boston News-Gazette.* The ad offered to sell advertising in the *News-Gazette.*

Key Concept

Connection between demand for news and advertising
Demand for news and for advertising created a demand for newspapers. Early newspaper ads were simple paragraphs of type promoting real estate, services, and goods for sale to retailers and consumers.

crier

In ancient Greece and Rome, a person who walked through the streets crying out news to the people. Preceded printed news.

broadside

Handbill, also called broadsheet, that was printed only on one side of the paper.

mercantile press

Early American newspapers that served businesses, shopkeepers, and tradespeople. These newspapers also contained political news.

The Mercantile Press and Advertising

As commerce grew in the American colonies, so did advertising in the **mercantile press.** The mercantile press was aimed at shopkeepers and other small business owners rather than at participants in political discussion. The first issue of the first U.S. daily newspaper, the *Pennsylvania Packet and Daily,* which began in 1784, contained 63 percent advertising. The next year a daily was started in New York with similar success in advertising. These cases suggest a *connection between demand for news and for advertising.* Demand for both promoted the creation of daily newspapers in the United States.[4]

Although most of today's newspaper ads are aimed at consumers, many of the mercantile press ads tried to sell goods to other businesspeople, often for use in their businesses. A shipping company would advertise a shipment of clothing so that retailers would buy it for resale. Early advertisements also promoted real estate, services, and goods for sale, just as newspapers do today. However, advertisements often read like announcements. For example, a small ad in the November 18, 1771, *Pennsylvania Packet and General Advertiser* read: "A few barrels of Carolina Pork to be sold by John Murgatroyd, in Water-street, near Tun-Alley."[5] By the 1820s, the

Advertising in the mercantile press often targeted other businesspeople. Today the tradition is carried forward at trade shows where businesses or companies try to attract product users through promotional favors.

mercantile newspapers had become important commercial bulletin boards with advertising and announcements for the business community.

Despite similarities in purpose, early advertisements looked nothing like the ads that are found in today's newspapers. Only a few crude illustrations were used, and printing technology limited the diversity of type. Ads were typically one column wide and rarely contained graphics.

The Development of Mass Advertising

Because of their focus on business and trade, the mercantile newspapers were poor advertising vehicles for consumer goods. Their small targeted audience kept their circulations low. In 1816 seven New York dailies sold only about 9,400 copies in a city of 125,000.[6] Average people could not afford these papers, nor did they like the content.

The penny press vitalized the consumer market and revolutionized **mass advertising.** By 1842, New York circulation had grown to 92,700 daily; two-thirds of these issues cost two cents or less.[7] Now merchants could reach large numbers of customers with one newspaper.

In addition to expanding the advertising market, the penny press changed the nature of advertising. Penny newspapers ran want ads similar to those found in English newspapers. They charged advertisers by a unit of space rather than the flat price charged by the mercantile press, and they separated advertising and news content.

Not everyone praised the penny press for its changes. The mercantile papers, which charged six cents for a copy, attacked various penny newspapers for printing patent medicine ads. These advertisements sold liquids and salves that at their best did no harm but at their worst could kill. These ads reflected the *let the buyer beware philosophy* of the newspapers. The criticism of penny newspapers was justified, but the mercantile press ignored the fact that some of its newspapers had been carrying patent medicine ads for decades.

After the Civil War, advertising increased rapidly. The Industrial Revolution contributed to an expanding middle class and encouraged an influx of immigrants, both of which increased the demand for goods and services. Businesses met the increasing demand for goods by advertising in the thousands of newspapers that were springing up around the country. Between the Civil War and 1900, printing and graphic technology facilitated visually appealing advertising. Ads with graphic illustrations became more common.

The post–Civil War period also saw the maturation of magazine advertising. An expanding national economy and a consumer thirst for the information and entertainment that were found in magazines created a national advertising market. A few magazines had reached large circulations before this period, but printing technology and localized economies had limited their advertising. Advertising became the mainstay of the big, high-quality monthlies. The November 1899 edition of Harper's magazine, for example, had 135 pages of advertising and 163 pages of editorial material, which reflected 45 percent advertising, only slightly lower than the percentage of advertising carried by many magazines today.[8]

Because of changes in the economy and mass media, *advertising agents* became more important in the late 1800s. They bought space in publications and resold it to advertisers. An agent could place an ad in a number of newspapers and magazines around the country for one price. This made advertising more efficient and simplified the process for the advertiser, who no longer had to buy ads separately for each newspaper and magazine.

Although several agents were in business before the Civil War, agents had no accurate listings of publications, circulation levels, and advertising rates. These problems

Key Concept

Let the buyer beware philosophy As newspapers grew in circulation, they advertised a wide variety of products about which the editor had no personal knowledge and, therefore, assigned the reader the responsibility of determining the truth of an ad and the worth of a product.

Key Concept

Advertising agent Agents facilitated more efficient advertising. They bought space in multiple newspapers and magazines and resold that space to advertisers for one price. As a result, companies could reach consumers in different geographic areas without having to buy ad space from large numbers of publications.

mass advertising

Advertising that aims to reach the largest number of people possible.

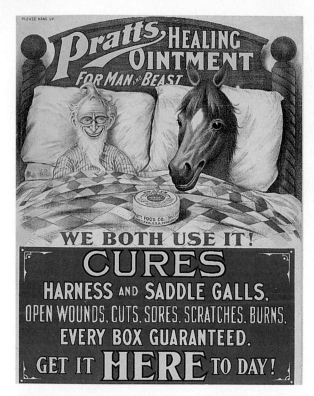

The graphics used in this patent medicine poster, circa 1880, were much more elaborate than the counterpart ads appearing in newspapers. In 1931, the Food and Drug Administration was created to address the patent medicine industry, requiring labeling of products.

were reduced by the George P. Rowell and N. W. Ayers & Sons agencies when they began publishing newspaper directories in 1869. The directories provided some information about where an ad might be placed to achieve a desired effect.

Even though the mercantile press had attacked the penny papers in the early part of the century for their reliance on patent medicine advertising, newspapers and magazines continued to carry ads for the popular medicines. Patent medicines did not cure people, but the high alcohol content in many of them often made people feel better, at least temporarily. Unfortunately, some patent medicines contained addictive drugs and deadly poisons.

The selling and advertising of patent medicines contributed to passage of the Pure Food and Drug Act in 1906, the establishment of the Federal Trade Commission (FTC) in 1914, and the establishment of the Food and Drug Administration (FDA) in 1931. These government initiatives represented efforts to connect **product responsibility and advertising.** Such regulations are based on the assumption that companies should be responsible for the impact of their products by truthfully labeling those products. The FTC and FDA had the power to limit false advertising of patent medicines, but the agencies continued to fight some of these companies into the 1940s.[9]

The Arrival of Broadcast Advertising

The creators of radio did not envision it as a mass medium, much less an advertising mass medium. It was supposed to be a form of wireless telephone. However, that idea did not last long.

Radio programming developed to sell radio sets, but as the cost of programming increased, more money was needed. In 1922, WEAF in New York sold five ten-minute advertising spots to Long Island real estate promoters. Radio advertising was born. Twenty years later, radio advertising was a $100 million business.[10]

Radio advertising prospered for several reasons. Radio was the first instantaneous national medium. Magazines circulated nationally, but they arrived in the mail and on newsstands days and weeks after they were printed. Radio was heard all across the country simultaneously. That's why General Motors spent $500,000 on radio advertising in 1928.[11] GM could announce the arrival of new car models to thousands of listeners at the same time.

Radio advertising also grew because the U.S. economy boomed through most of the 1920s. After World War I, industrial production and consumer buying expanded, and the middle class continued to grow. People had more discretionary income to spend on goods and services other than food and housing. Advertising helped them decide how to spend that money.

Broadcasting gave modern advertising agencies more choices to offer their clients. As agencies became full-service organizations, they bought advertising space, wrote copy, developed illustrations for ads, placed ads in newspapers and magazines, researched the wants and needs of the audience, and coordinated advertising in more than one publication. Now they could advise clients on where best to place their ads.

Until the early 1950s and the advent of television, radio was the prime broadcast advertising medium. But soon television eclipsed radio; consumers went wild for it, and advertisers capitalized on the fact that viewers could both see the product and hear the national message. In 1950, only 9 percent of U.S. homes had television sets; by 1960, 87 percent had television.[12] Advertisers could reach increasing numbers of people, and the ability to create positive images of a product on the new visual medium seemed limitless. The growth of television advertising contributed to the growth of a **consumer culture** in the United States, in which advertisements influenced not only economic decisions but popular culture as well.

By the 1970s, most of the current mass advertising options had developed, advertising expenditures were growing rapidly, and various forms of mass media were competing for advertising dollars. The amount of money spent on advertising grew from $2.1 billion in 1940 to $19.6 billion in 1970, a 933 percent increase. When adjusted for inflation, advertising increased by 337 percent during this thirty-year period.

A changing distribution of ad dollars among media also marked this period. Television enjoyed the great growth, moving from 3 percent of all advertising expenditures in 1940 to 18 percent thirty years later. The increasing proportion of ad dollars for television came at the expense of newspapers and radio. Magazines and direct mail also experienced a small decline as television boomed.

The growth of cable attracted advertisers during the 1980s. Cable, with its dozens of channels, provided segmented audiences for advertisers. Rather than advertising to mass audiences, advertisers could identify groups that watched specialized channels who might be more interested than the public at large in their products. Although cable offered more effective advertising than broadcast television could, it did not eliminate mass advertising. A 30-second commercial on the final summer episode of *Survivor* cost $1 million.

New media such as the Internet, mobile phones, and video on demand have created more competition and demands for new forms of advertising. Advertising revenues for the big online companies—Yahoo, Google, and AOL—rose to $11.9 billion in 2005, more than doubling from $5.1 billion in 2003. Total spending on the web was an estimated $16 billion in 2006, but still lagged far behind television and other advertising, which stood at $292 billion. However, online advertising revenues grew at the fastest rate as more consumers turned to digital media as their information and entertainment source.[13]

Advertising and the Price of Products

Economists disagree about how **advertising affects the prices** consumers pay for goods and services. Some argue that advertising increases prices because the money companies spend on advertisements is tacked onto the price of the goods. Campbell's tomato soup costs more than the store brand, they argue, to pay for Campbell's national advertising budget. Typically, nationally advertised products cost more than generic and regional brands.

Other economists argue that advertising reduces the cost of goods because it results in increased production. The more cans of Campbell's tomato soup produced, the less each can costs to make. The average cost of almost all goods will decrease as the number of units increases, up to the capacity of a production plant. Economists call the savings that result from producing large quantities **economies of scale.** The economies occur because a company has to invest a certain amount of money in a plant no matter how many units of the product are made. Producing the first 10,000 cans of tomato soup requires equipment to cook and can the soup. If a plant is already making 10,000 cans of tomato soup, producing another 1,000 will add only the cost of the ingredients, the cans, and some extra labor time.

Because advertising can increase the number of units people will buy, it decreases the average cost of making the product. The average cost per can of 11,000 cans of soup is less than the average cost per can of 10,000 cans. However, research is not conclusive on the impact of advertising on price. In some situations, the lower cost

economies of scale

As the number of units produced at a plant increases, the average cost per unit decreases. This comes about because the company has to invest large amounts of money just to produce the first unit.

Dateline

Advertising in Our Lives

1477. First handbill advertisement in England

1622. First English newspaper advertisement

1704. First newspaper advertisement in America

Late 1700s. Commercial notices grow as proportion of newspapers.

1830s. Penny press gets heavy advertising support.

1869. Rowell & Ayers publish newspaper directories for advertising.

Late 1800s. Printing technology allows visually appealing ads.

Late 1800s. Magazines provide a vehicle for mass national advertising.

Late 1800s. Advertising agencies grow in importance.

1906. First Pure Food and Drug Act is passed.

1914. Federal Trade Commission is created.

1922. First radio advertisement

1930s. Radio advertising booms as the audience grows.

1400–1700	1800	1860	1880	1900	1920	1930

1620. Pilgrims land at Plymouth Rock.

1690. *Publick Occurrences* is published in Boston.

1741. First magazine is published in America.

1776–1783. American Revolution

1830s. The penny press becomes the first truly mass medium in the United States.

1861–1865. American Civil War

1892. Thomas Edison's lab develops the kinetoscope.

1914–1918. World War I

1915. *The Birth of a Nation* marks the start of the modern movie industry.

1920. KDKA in Pittsburgh gets the first commercial radio license.

1930s. The Great Depression

1939. TV is demonstrated at the New York World's Fair.

1939–1945. World War II

Cultural Milestones

of increased production will be passed on to the consumers as price breaks. In other cases, the price of the product will be kept high, and the company will keep the difference as profit. Similarly, the advertising costs that companies pay may be added to the price of the product in some cases, but not in others. The impact of advertising on price varies based on a variety of factors, but a key element is competition. If consumers can buy the same quality of goods at a lower price, companies will probably not pass on the cost of advertising to consumers.

Interestingly enough, whether a similar good is perceived to be of equal quality to another sometimes depends on advertising. For example, advertising convinces some

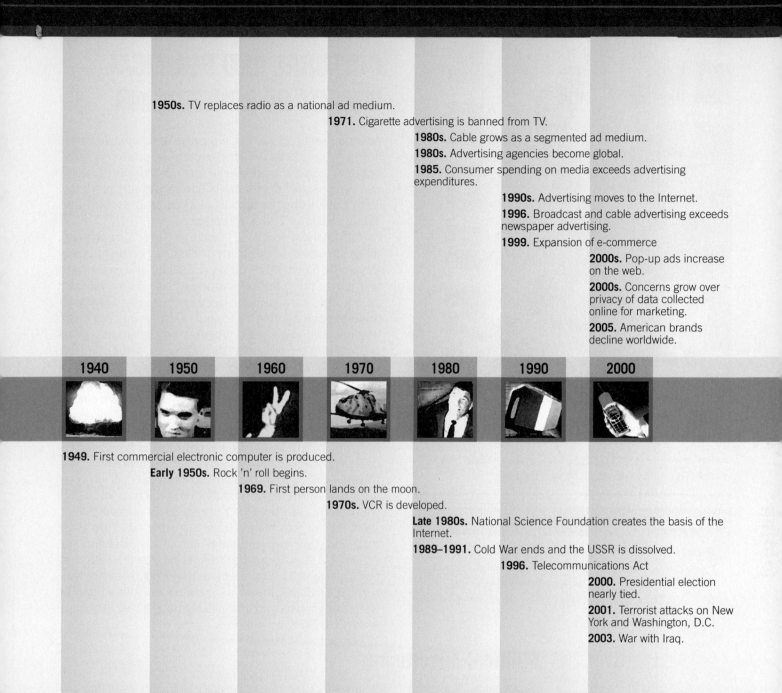

1950s. TV replaces radio as a national ad medium.

1971. Cigarette advertising is banned from TV.

1980s. Cable grows as a segmented ad medium.

1980s. Advertising agencies become global.

1985. Consumer spending on media exceeds advertising expenditures.

1990s. Advertising moves to the Internet.

1996. Broadcast and cable advertising exceeds newspaper advertising.

1999. Expansion of e-commerce

2000s. Pop-up ads increase on the web.

2000s. Concerns grow over privacy of data collected online for marketing.

2005. American brands decline worldwide.

| 1940 | 1950 | 1960 | 1970 | 1980 | 1990 | 2000 |

1949. First commercial electronic computer is produced.

Early 1950s. Rock 'n' roll begins.

1969. First person lands on the moon.

1970s. VCR is developed.

Late 1980s. National Science Foundation creates the basis of the Internet.

1989–1991. Cold War ends and the USSR is dissolved.

1996. Telecommunications Act

2000. Presidential election nearly tied.

2001. Terrorist attacks on New York and Washington, D.C.

2003. War with Iraq.

people that Campbell's tomato soup is better than the store brand. Much of television advertising aims to convince consumers that a product is better than other similar products. Nike spends millions of dollars to get people to believe that their athletic shoes are worth paying three times more for than some other athletic shoes. Burger King has long advertised its hamburgers as flame broiled rather than fried, implying that its burgers are better. This is called **differentiating the product,** that is, getting the consumer to believe one product is different in quality from other products.

Just how advertising affects price is a complicated process that varies from product to product. It depends on the level of demand, consumers' perceptions of quality,

differentiating the product

The process of trying to get the consumer to perceive one product as being different in nature and quality than other products.

In their advertising, corporations often promote lifestyles to enhance consumer identification with their brands.

the scale of production, and a variety of other business factors. Consumers can make better choices if they understand how these factors work.

CULTURAL AND POLITICAL IMPACT OF ADVERTISING

Advertising serves society in positive and negative ways. It brings buyers and sellers together in economic markets that supply the goods and services that people need and want. It also distributes economic resources for society. Advertising contributes to these processes by providing consumers with information.

On an individual level, advertising in some ways can make life easier. Without advertising, just getting the basics for living would be far more difficult and expensive. Imagine hunting for an apartment with no advertising except signs on apartment buildings. You would have to drive to each apartment to find out how much it cost. Without ads, you would not know which grocery store was offering the best specials each week. Price comparison would take enormous amounts of time.

However, the social contributions of advertising also have a **social cost.** The cost comes from negative effects that advertising can have on society. Some of these effects are direct, such as the manipulation of people's spending behavior; others are more indirect, such as the influence of advertising on news media and politics. Critics question the impact of advertising, especially in connection with television a medium on which children and young adults rely heavily. The concern is not only about short-term effects, but also about whether advertising actually changes expectations of normative behavior. For example, a short-term effect might be that teenage girls buy more lipstick. But a long-term effect of campaigns such as Levi's Skinnyjeans showing emaciated young people might be to persuade young people that they have to stay ultrathin, no matter what the cost to their health.

Political Advertising

Joe McGinnis published a book in 1969 called *The Selling of the President, 1968.* McGinnis claimed that Richard Nixon used television advertising techniques to win the presidency and that the 1968 election forever changed the nature of political advertising.[14] Since the 1968 election, advertising aimed at persuading, especially on television, has come to dominate elections at the state and national levels.

According to estimates, candidates for federal office spent more than $2.5 billion on advertising during the 2000 election campaign. This was a $500 million increase over the 1996 election.[15] Harold Ickes, an advisor to Hillary Rodham Clinton during her Senate race, said of the sum: "It even staggers me, and I'm pretty hard-core."

Critics of this trend are concerned about the content of ads and the influence that the candidates' need of advertising funds gives political donors. Political TV advertising often appeals to voters' emotions in an effort to persuade rather than inform. Images of crime and violence contribute little to the marketplace of ideas, but they do arouse concern among voters. Such ads attempt to identify a candidate's opponent with negative images and do not provide information for a rational political decision. Scholars and critics are concerned that such advertising emphasizes trivial problems and plays down the issues that are most urgent.[16] Even the heads of large advertising agencies question the usefulness of advertising in the political process.[17]

Critics also express concern about the influence that donors of advertising can have on political candidates. Campaign spending in 2000 resulted in national finance reform legislation that outlawed contributions to national political parties from wealthy individuals, labor unions, and corporations. Therefore, presidential candidates relied on grassroots fundraising through the Internet, mail, and telephone calls. They were aided by dozens of advocacy groups, called 527 committees. These groups, like MoveOn.org and Progress for America Voter Fund, raised over $400 million, but caused concern because of their negative campaigning and acceptance of substantial donations from wealthy individuals who could sway the election.[18]

Manipulation by Advertising

Even though advertising serves the legitimate function of bringing buyers and sellers together, not all advertising is designed simply to provide information. Many ads aim to persuade consumers to buy unneeded goods and services or to pay higher prices for particular brands.

Of particular concern in this area is advertising aimed at children. Children develop **rational thinking abilities** at about the age of twelve. Before that, children have trouble understanding the nature and purpose of advertising. Research indicates that children under the age of four cannot tell programs from commercials. Often the commercials, with quick camera cuts and lots of action, appeal even more to children than do the programs. The result is that parents hear their children say, "I want that" every time the children see a toy or cereal ad on television. Luckily for parents, advertisements have less influence over children as they grow older.

Political candidates and public officials increasingly use the web to communicate with voters. Here, Senator John McCain of Arizona provides his position on key issues facing the nation.

Advertising's Influence on Journalism

Because advertising provides all of the revenue for broadcast television news and 80 percent of the revenues for newspapers, media critics often raise the question of the advertiser's role in news content. The concern is justified. Advertisers increasingly succeed in influencing news coverage.

Because broadcast television networks face increased competition and loss of audience and advertising revenues, their news branches are under pressure to make their shows more entertaining. In 2005, Ted Koppel announced that he was leaving his serious television newsmagazine, *Nightline,* and moving from Disney-owned ABC to the Discovery Channel. ABC executives wanted Koppel to change the format of his show to attract younger viewers, with shorter segments on celebrity and entertainment news. When asked what he saw as the changes in television news, Koppel pointed to advertisers who were trying to capture an eighteen to forty-nine-year-old demographic: "People can't figure out why 24-hour cable news is about blondes reporting on missing blondes. It's because they're looking for that young-female

rational thinking abilities

The cognitive processing of information by considering options based on conscious comparison of influencing factors.

Children are especially susceptible to advertising of consumer goods like toys and food, since they have not yet developed rational thinking.

demographic."[19] However, because some cable networks like Discovery may obtain up to 50 percent of their revenues from cable operator fees, they are not as beholden to advertising. Instead, they try to enhance their brand so that they can be sold successfully as part of cable packages. Therefore, in his move to Discovery, Koppel and his team could maintain their commitment to serious journalism and add to the worth of the channel, even if their audience was composed of mature viewers with less appeal to advertisers.[20]

The concern for profit may also drive news organizations to provide favorable or avoid damaging coverage of the companies who advertise with them. Examples are many, ranging from companies' subtle influence on to outright purchase of the news. Companies can threaten to pull their advertising dollars if they are negatively portrayed. In 2005, both the oil company BP and the investment banker Morgan Stanley sent notices to publications in which they advertised, insisting that they be notified of any articles about their companies and given the option of pulling their ads in the case of negative coverage. Some journalists argued that such implicit threats would likely influence editorial decisions.[21]

Because of the economic power of advertising, issue advocacy groups sometimes try to influence or suppress media organizations by getting companies to withdraw their advertising. For example, in 2005, the conservative Christian American Family Association (AFA) threatened a boycott against the Ford Motor Company to persuade it to stop running commercials for luxury cars in gay-oriented magazines like *Out* and *The Advocate.* In AFA's view, Ford was supporting gay marriage and the "homosexual agenda" with this advertising, rather than remaining neutral in the "culture wars."[22] Ford initially agreed and withdrew its advertising, potentially alienating gays, a consumer group worth $610 billion. For *Out* and the *Advocate,* Ford's advertising made up only a small portion of their revenues so they were not much damaged. For them, the cultural issues were much more significant than the economic ones. Later, after meeting with gay and lesbian organizations, Ford reversed its decision, angering some of the company's dealers and investors who worried that the move might endanger profits.[23]

The relationships among audiences, news organizations, and advertisers can involve conflicts based on differing social goals and values. Wishing to attract advertisers, owners and their news divisions may also come into conflict between the need to make a profit and the responsibility to inform the public. Many journalists believe that the situation is worsening as news organizations face stiffer competition for audiences and greater managerial interference.

STRUCTURE OF ADVERTISING AND DEMAND

Advertising is a form of promotion. **Promotion** involves all the ways of gaining attention for a company, product, or service. In addition to advertising, these include public relations, packaging, personal selling, and gifts. Marketing experts divide the marketing process into four elements: product, price, place, and promotion. To market a product successfully, companies must start with a good product, price it correctly, place it well, and promote it. Advertising is interrelated with other aspects of marketing. Advertising cannot sell an inferior product for long, and advertising cannot convince most adults to buy overpriced, low-quality services and products.

The economics of advertising concerns the interaction of supply and demand in the advertising market and the connection between the advertising market and the consumer market. Advertisers buy ads in media because they want to reach the audience that is attracted by the information in the media. Some of the audience seeks the information in advertisements. Economists call serving two markets with the same production process a **joint product.**

To promote goods and services, a company enters the advertising market. Producers and sellers of goods and services pay media companies, which provide space and time in their media products. When a company spends more than $300,000 for thirty seconds on *Monday Night Football,* this exchange takes place in the advertising market.

There is also a connection between the advertising market and the consumer market. In the consumer market, people exchange their time and money for information. A person who watches *Monday Night Football* is part of the consumer market. This person is exchanging his or her attention for the entertainment of the game. The viewer would have no game to watch if advertising did not pay for it, and the advertiser would have no one to see the ads if the game was not provided.

The difference between the two markets is more clear cut with media that consumers buy. Readers buy newspapers for the information they contain, which comes in the form of news and advertising. Advertisers buy space and reader attention from the newspaper company. As a result, the newspaper simultaneously serves two different but interconnected markets with the same production process.

> ### Key Concept
>
> **Four effects of advertising** Advertising influences consumers four ways. It makes people aware of goods, gives them price information, provides quality information, and gets them to identify with people and activities.

Advertising's Effects on Consumers

Advertising influences consumers in four ways: (1) It makes people aware of a product or service; (2) it provides price information about a product or service; (3) it provides information about the quality of a product or service; and (4) it tries to persuade consumers to identify a product or service with a particular person or activity.[24]

The simplest effect is *awareness.* Consumers must know that a product or service exists before they can decide to buy it. In the 1980s, when General Motors planned to create a new car, the Saturn, it spent hundreds of millions of dollars to make the public aware of the car's existence. The advertisements began running before a single Saturn had been produced.

Price information plays an important part in advertising. From a business perspective, advertising that features special prices can attract customers to a store. Supermarkets run grocery prices in the local newspaper to bring customers into the store. The supermarket won't make much, if any, money on the advertised specials, but the customer will buy other products that are not on sale. From the customer's perspective, price advertisements save them time. A person who wants to buy a car will not waste time looking at models that are out of his or her price range.

promotion

The ways a company gains attention for its product or service, including advertising, public relations, packaging, and personal selling.

joint product

Term economists use when one production process serves two markets. For instance, the process of printing magazines serves readers in the consumer market and companies in the advertising market.

Product Placement

Two primary reasons exist for product placement in television shows, songs, movies, and books. Marketers make agreements with entertainment companies to feature their brands, and writers and directors feature brands because they have artistic worth, such as making a setting seem more real or providing a readily understood symbol.

Often, writers and artists provide free advertising for companies when they feature products. For example, in the movie *Cast Away*, the Tom Hanks character, Chuck Noland, befriends a Wilson volleyball because the screenwriter, while he was in the stages of invention, had come across such a ball stranded on a beach in Mexico. As media researchers Michael Maynard and Megan Scala point out, the ball evolves into a character, creating greater emotional involvement from the audience and potentially deepening an unconscious sales message. Wilson was on the screen for about eleven minutes, which would have been worth between $1.8 and $11.5 million of media exposure. Wonder Bread was featured in *Talladega Nights: The Ballad of Ricky Bobby* because Will Ferrell likes it, and as the *New York Times* put it, the brand has "an innocence about it, an almost sweet faith in scientific progress, that may be easy to snicker at but even easier to be nostalgic for." The approximately twelve minutes that the Wonder Bread logo appeared on the screen was free media exposure worth $4.3 million.

The economic success of product placement in mainstream rap music is said to have begun with this kind of free media exposure which then turned into a lucrative contract. According to legend, after recording a hit song called *My Adidas*, Run-D.M.C. was playing Madison Square Garden in 1986 when they stopped the music and asked everyone to take off their shoes and raise them in the air. Fans raised their thousands of shell-toed Adidas shoes, and the company executives who'd been secretly invited to the show by the group's manager, Russell Simmons, offered them a $1.5 million endorsement deal.

Since then, mainstream hip-hop artists have made deals for brand endorsements, though they more often mention products to evoke an identity, an urban scene and an aspirational lifestyle, providing symbols of luxury that most people can understand. The brand strategy agency, Agenda Inc., found over 1,000 brand mentions in the top one hundred and six Billboard songs of 2005. Mercedes was at the top of the list, with one hundred mentions, followed by Nike, Cadillac, Bentley, Rolls Royce, and Hennessy. The artist with the most mentions was 50 Cent, mostly for luxury cars.

Little is known about how much companies pay music artists for brand shoutouts, but Petey Pablo, in *Freek-a-leek*, revealed:

"Now I got to give a shoutout to Seagram gin, 'cus I drink it and they paying me for it." Since hip-hop artists have to preserve their aura of authenticity, they are not likely to mention any deal or product that would damage their credibility. Nevertheless, mainstream hip hop is a highly commercial enterprise, and companies such as Cadillac and Polaroid have actively courted artists with parties and music events to gain approval and mention. Hip-hop artists like Jay Z and 50 Cent have their own brands in partnership with companies like Reebok that they then promote in their tracks.

The relationship among advertisers, consumer products, and artists is a complicated one, since many believe that artists may be compromised if they are beholden to mentioning certain companies. Nevertheless, brands are embedded in the daily lives of people living in consumer cultures. Literary scholar James Twitchell describes brands as a kind of storytelling: "What marks the modern world is that certain brand fictions have been able to generate a deep and almost instantaneous bond between consumers." Both artists and corporations use that bond to create and maintain their own relationships with audiences.

Sources: James B. Twitchell, "An English Teacher Looks at Branding," *Journal of Consumer Research* 31 (2004): 488; Michael L. Maynard and Megan Scala, "Unpaid Advertising: A Case of Wilson the Volleyball in Cast Away," *Journal of Popular Culture* 39 (2006): 622–639; Rob Walker, "Free Ride," *New York Times Magazine,* September 17, 2006: 31.

Advertisers use a wide range of media to reach potential customers.

Quality advertising strives to influence the buyer's impression of how good a product or service is. Quality claims can be vague and unsupported, such as "the best burger in town." But quality claims can also have some authority behind them, such as the *Motor Trend* Car of the Year Award. Quality claims can influence the decision to buy, but they will not get consumers to buy a second time if the product turns out not to have the quality that was claimed.

Identity advertising attempts to get a customer to associate a product with a particular person or enjoyable activity. People in beer commercials always enjoy themselves. Only young, healthy people smoke cigarettes in magazine ads. If consumers associate products with pleasant activities and people, they will be more likely to buy them.

How effectively an advertisement achieves its purpose depends on several factors. Media type is among the most important. Price advertising seems to be most effective in print. Print is more permanent, and the listed prices can be cut out and kept. Prices that are broadcast over television and radio have to be remembered or written down, and both of these are inconvenient. Television works well with identity ads because of its visual nature. Influencing young people mentally to connect beer with fun at parties is much easier when the party is shown on a visual medium such as television.

A second important factor in advertising effectiveness concerns the habits and motivations of the consumer. Not all people can be reached effectively by the same medium. As a result, most advertising campaigns, especially for large companies, use several media; however, the central look and message of the brand remains the same. For example, the McDonald's arch is familiar around the world, on webpages, television and radio spots, print advertisements, cups and containers, t-shirts, hats, bags, mugs, and billboards. Advertising agencies help design plans that incorporate more than one medium to reach a variety of people with a variety of ads that all promote the same, recognizable brand identity.

The Influence of Advertising on Consumer Behavior

Marketing and psychology researchers call the study of how and why people buy products **consumer behavior.** This term encompasses many approaches, but most researchers are interested in people's **cognitive processes** and **affective responses** in their relationship to consumer goods. Their decisions to buy may be based on internal factors such as their individual goals, values, and feelings, and by external factors such as media messages and social networks with friends, family, and coworkers.[25] Marketers are interested in these internal and external factors so that they can better craft messages that will win consumers' purchasing power and brand loyalty. Consumer behavior studies can also be used to educate people about their buying habits and reactions to advertising messages.

Highly motivated consumers may go through rational, cognitive processes when choosing products. For example, a potential homebuyer may investigate neighborhoods, look through housing ads, hire an inspector, and compare prices before buying. Some companies try to tap into these rational processes, like marketing foods on the basis of their health benefits. However, many other affective factors may be at play, and decisions may be based on emotions, feelings, and moods. A product or a brand can appeal to a consumer because it evokes a memory or is associated with personal values and status. A consumer may also be stimulated to buy through feelings of sensual pleasure. For instance, Sony electronics stores have a deliberate special scent to lure women into an environment they might otherwise find intimidating.[26]

Consumer behavior also explores what social and cultural influences drive purchases. Placing movie and music advertisements in young teens' social networking spaces, media companies hope to tap the desire of teens to be popular and their susceptibility to peer pressure. When the Chicano population grew in the Midwest, so did imports of Mexican beers like Corona and Tecate because of brand loyalty associated with culture. Beauty companies like Avon successfully sell certain medicinal skin products to wealthy women in urban areas of China because these women come from a cultural tradition that values medicinal practices, lengthy beauty rituals, and an even skin tone.[27] Consumer products are associated with the histories, meanings, and values of cultural groups, which also shape individual cognitive and affective responses.

When researchers set out to understand consumers, they have traditionally relied on focus groups, consumer panels and surveys. However, in recent years, ethnographic study of consumer groups has become important. In an ethnographic study, marketers send in social scientists and camera operators to study how people use and react to brands in their ordinary settings and activities. The research team may observe people in their homes or travel around with them on their daily routines. Critics of the method charge that a serious ethnographic study takes training, time, and resources that are usually not fully expended by marketers.

In identifying customers for brands and products, advertising agencies classify them by demographics, geographics, and psychographics. *Demographics* concerns characteristics of people and households such as age, gender, income, marital status, and family size. *Geographics* concerns physical locations (state, region, or country) of potential buyers. *Psychographics* concerns the lifestyles and activities of people such as movie attendance, hobbies, and types of physical exercise.

cognitive process

In advertising, a consumer's rational process of product selection.

affective response

In advertising, a consumer's response to brands and products because of emotions, moods, and values.

SUPPLYING THE DEMAND FOR ADVERTISING

A business that wants to advertise its product or service faces an almost staggering number of advertising forms and advertising outlets. Businesses no longer can depend on just one form of advertising. Companies need to use a mix of media to reach all of their potential customers. This multimedia advertising approach explains why old advertising forms continue to survive as new forms develop.

Table 12.1 shows advertising revenue and proportion of revenues by medium for 2005. In 1988 about $118.4 billion was spent on advertising in the United States. In 2005 the figure was $262 billion.

Table 12.1 Advertising Revenues and Proportions, 2005

Print	Revenue (Billions of Dollars)	Percentage of Revenue	Electronic	Revenue (Billions of Dollars)	Percentage of Revenue
Daily newspaper	$49.4	18.1	Broadcast TV	44.3	16.3
Direct mail	55.2	20	Radio	19.6	7.2
Miscellaneous	35.7	13.1	Cable	23.6	8.7
Yellow Pages	14.2	5.2	Internet	7.7	2.9
Magazines	12.8	4.7	Total electronic	95.2	35.1
Total print	167.3	61.1			

Source: Newspaper Association of America; Universal McCann.

Advertising Support for Media

The growth of mass media during most of the twentieth century was interwoven with a simultaneous growth in advertising. As U.S. economic growth became more dependent on consumer spending, companies sought to reach increasingly larger audiences through their advertising. Media companies rightfully saw advertising as their biggest source of revenue. This gave advertisers more influence over media content than consumers had.

Advertising may take a variety of forms, including the sponsorship of events that enhance a company's brand identity.

Times have changed, however. In 1984 slightly more than 50 percent of all communication industry revenue came from advertising.[27] By 2004 advertising accounted for 23.4 percent of all communication revenue. Marketing schemes are expected to shift from traditional ad forms, such as thirty-second television commercials and print ads, to new media as advertisers woo young consumers. Increasingly important are product placements in movies, television shows, music, and video games, and sponsorships of entertainment events, like concerts and sporting events.[28]

Types of Advertisements Advertisements can be classified in a number of ways, but the two most common ways of classifying **types of advertisements** are geographic coverage and purpose. *Geographic coverage* is defined as the market in which the advertisements are placed and the advertised product is sold. The *purpose of the ad* reflects the type of influence the advertiser seeks to have over the customer.

Geographic Coverage. Depending on where their current and potential consumers live, companies advertise to local, national, and global communities. Local advertisements target a much smaller market such as a city or metropolitan area, while national advertisements are for products and services that are available throughout the country. As companies seek greater worldwide reach, global advertising becomes important. Multinational companies, such as Nike, Coke, and McDonald's must develop campaigns that reach local audiences from a variety of cultural backgrounds, but maintain a single brand identity.

Therefore, companies must develop various strategies for reaching local, national, and global audiences. A national restaurant chain might run commercials on a major television network while its local outlet runs print ads in the student newspaper. The local department store may benefit from Nike's national marketing, but also runs its own ads to tell customers when Nike shoes are on sale. Marketers may place regional ads in national media, as when cable companies set aside certain time slots for local commercials.

The Internet has both expanded and complicated these opportunities. A company wishing to advertise through Google's AdWords can choose to target ads locally or nationally. However the options and the keywords must be chosen carefully. Google can send ads to consumers it identifies as living in a specific area because of their network address (IP), but if they log in through AOL, they have an address that is nowhere near where they live. Therefore, a company may choose both options, setting up different keywords so that the national campaign includes local keywords and the local campaign includes more generic keywords.[29] On the websites of major multinational companies, like Coke and Avon, visitors may arrive at a generic company site from which they can choose using a menu that takes them to a country site in their own language and currency, and with more tailored messages.

Geographic coverage is important because some media serve local businesses better and some serve national and multinational businesses better. Newspapers excel as vehicles for local businesses, broadcast television had traditionally been strong for national advertising because of its national audience, cable television can reach niche audiences, and the Internet can be used to reach local, national and global audiences.

Geographic coverage also affects the price of advertising. The price that a business pays for an advertisement depends on the number of people who will be exposed to the ad. *Time* magazine

Multinational corporations work to make their brands easily recognizable to consumers worldwide.

The Ad Council offers public service announcements sponsored by non-profit and governmental organizations.

charges more for an ad than *Crain's Chicago Business* does. The first is a national publication; the other is a regional publication. A business that sells computers only in Chicago would be foolish to buy a national ad in *Time*. A regional ad in *Time* or an ad in *Crain's* would be more effective and efficient.

Advertisement's Purpose. Although most advertisements promote a product or service, not all do. Advertisements fall into three categories: business ads, public service ads, and political ads.

Business ads try to influence people's attitudes and behaviors toward the products and services a business sells, toward the business itself, or toward an idea that the business supports. Most of these ads try to persuade consumers to buy something, but sometimes a business tries to improve its image through advertising. This often occurs when a company has been involved in a highly publicized incident that might negatively affect its image, such as AOL's release of users' search data.

Public service ads promote behaviors and attitudes that are beneficial to society and its members. These ads may be either national or local and usually are the product of donated labor and media time or space. The **Advertising Council** produces the best-known public service ads. The council, which is supported by advertising agencies and the media, was formed during World War II to promote the war effort. It now runs about twenty-five campaigns a year. These campaigns must be in the public interest, timely, noncommercial, nonpartisan, nonsectarian, and nonpolitical.[30] The Ad

Advertising Council

Formed to promote the civilian efforts in World War II, the Advertising Council is supported by advertising agencies and media companies. It conducts advertising campaigns in the public interest.

Pepsi's global ad campaign includes recognizable stars, such as Jennifer Lopez, Beckham, and Beyonce.

PROFILE

Leo Burnett

As the founder of one of the top advertising firms in the world, Leo Burnett influenced what Americans and others around the world buy.

Burnett was born in a small town in Michigan in 1891 and lived to be seventy-nine. He claimed that his name was supposed to be George, but because of his father's tendency to abbreviate, coupled with bad handwriting, the "Geo" turned out to be "Leo"—and the name stuck.

Burnett's parents owned a small store in Michigan, and his first memory of advertising was seeing the store's name and slogan on the umbrella of its delivery cart. While he was growing up in Michigan, he claimed, "you could hear the corn growing on hot nights." By the time he reached Chicago and opened his advertising agency in 1935, he was forty-four years old.

In contrast to the stereotype of the gregarious advertising man, Burnett was shy. He was also short, slope-shouldered, and had a paunch. The front of his head was bald and freckled, and his lapels were often sprinkled with Marlboro cigarette ashes. His most prominent feature, however, was his lower lip, which became the focal point of his writers' and art directors' attention. The more displeased Burnett was with an idea, the farther out his lip would jut.

To Burnett, the most powerful ideas were nonverbal. Their true meanings were too deep for words, such as the large, playful Tony the Tiger and the strong Marlboro man atop his horse. A successful ad, he said, was one that made an audience respond not with "That is a great ad!" but with "That is a great product!"

For Burnett it was important to find the inherent drama of the product and present it. If no inherent drama could be found, it had to be created. Usually, the creation would be through *borrowed interest,* a concept that allows the drama to come from someone, such as the Lonely Maytag Repairman, or something, such as Morris the cat. Other successes for Burnett included animations such as the Keebler Elves, Charlie the Tuna, and the Jolly Green Giant.

In his sixties, Burnett had an enviable vitality that would not quit. David Ogilvy once said that he turned down Burnett's proposal to merge because Burnett was the only person he knew who worked harder than he did, and "[t]he thought of Leo ringing me in New York at 2 A.M. and asking me to meet him in Chicago for breakfast with some fresh campaign ideas was more than I could bear."

Burnett continued working hard into his seventies, and his loyalty to his clients was unwavering. When he grew faint from low blood sugar, someone ran for a candy bar. "Make sure it's a Nestlé," he cried hoarsely.

Sources: Michael L. Rothschild, *Advertising* (Lexington, MA: D.C. Heath, 1987), p. 217; Simon Broadbent, ed., *The Leo Burnett Book of Advertising* (London: Business Books, 1984), pp. ii and 1–8.

Council has consistently run campaigns against illegal drug use and in support of such organizations as the United Negro College Fund.

Political ads aim to persuade voters to elect a candidate to political office or to influence the public on legislative issues. These advertisements run at the local, state, and national levels. They incorporate most forms of media but use newspapers, radio, television, and direct mail most heavily. During a presidential election year, more than $1 billion is spent on political ads.

Mass versus Targeted Ads   As part of advertising planning, companies must decide how large an audience they want to reach. Not every product or service is designed for mass consumption, nor is it available in every geographic location. Advertising the performances of the Dallas Symphony Orchestra during an episode of Comedy Central's *South Park* would be inefficient and ineffective. Most viewers would be too far from Dallas to attend the symphony even if they wanted to, and the audience that watches *South Park* is probably not interested in attending symphony concerts.

Advertisements that target the largest audience possible constitute *mass advertising.* Advertisements that seek to reach a selected audience are classified as **targeted advertising.** Yellow pages serve as mass advertising because every household that has a telephone gets them. Direct mail

Key Concept

Targeted advertising Increasingly, advertisements are designed to appeal to a limited group of consumers who can be defined by demographics, geographics, and psychographics.

catalogs from retailers such as Lands' End are targeted advertising because they are mailed to people who are likely to buy clothing through the mail. The most appropriate type of advertising depends on the nature and price of the product or service.

Who Produces Advertisements?

The nature of jobs in advertising is diverse. Some involve creative writing and art; others consist of selling and buying advertising space and time. Most advertising personnel work either in an advertising agency or in the advertising department of a company. Others work within media advertising departments. Ad agencies try to connect advertising buyers with media organizations. Table 12.2 shows the amount of money billed by the top ten advertising agencies in the world. The advertising departments within companies may handle most of the same activities as an agency, or they may be small departments that rely heavily on agency services.

The most common services advertising agencies provide include creative production, media buying, research services, merchandising, and advertising planning.[31] *Creative production* includes all the steps in creating advertisements for various media. *Media buyers* place the advertisements in media outlets. *Research* involves determining the effectiveness of advertising. *Merchandise experts* oversee other forms of promotion besides advertising. *Advertising planning* incorporates all of these services.

There are two types of advertising agencies. *Full-service* advertising agencies offer a client all five services just mentioned. A *boutique* agency often specializes in creative services and restricts its activities to a few specialties. A large company, such as a soup manufacturer, would probably use a full-service agency to plan and produce multimedia advertising campaigns. The company's advertising manager would work closely with the agency. A small mail-order company might do most of its work in house and then contract the creation and production of a catalog to a boutique agency.

Table 12.2	Top Ten Advertising Agencies Worldwide (in millions of dollars)	
Agency	**U.S Gross**	**Worldwide Gross**
Omnicom (New York)	$5,743.9	$9,747.2
WPP Group (London)	$3751.6	$10,032.2
Interpublic Group of Cos. (New York)	$3,509.2	$6,274.3
Publicis Groupe (Paris)	$2,181.7	$5,107.2
Dentsu (Tokyo)	$48.4	$2,887.8
Havas (Suresnes, France)	$712.8	$1,808
Aegis Group (London)	$446.1	$1,577.6
Hakuhodo DY Holdings (Toyko)	0.0	$1,364
Asatsu-DK (Tokyo)	$2.7	$444.8
MDC Partners (Toronto/NY)	$328.1	$443.5

Source: Advertising Age, www.adage.com.

Global Brands

According to the consulting firm Interbrand, a global brand is defined as one that has a significant presence and earns a third of its profits from outside its home country. Even though the products represented in the brand may vary from country to country, the brand has a single, recognizable identity. As Interbrand puts it, "The brand's positioning, advertising strategy, personality, look and feel are, in most respects, the same but allow for regional customization. What remains consistent from market-to-market are the values communicated and delivered by the brand."

Interbrand/Business Week's top ten brands of 2006 were Coca-Cola, Microsoft, IBM, GE, Intel, Nokia, Toyota, Disney, McDonald's, and Mercedes. Of the top one hundred, 52 percent were U.S. companies, with Google, eBay, and Starbucks making the most gains. The popularity of global brands with teens worldwide generates a different list that reveals the influence of fashion, chocolate, and social networking: Sony, Nokia, Adidas, Nike, Colgate, Nestlé, Cadbury, Coca-Cola, M&Ms, and Kodak.

A global brand must be recognized in many places around the world, and therefore must have a simple name that is easy to remember and say. Companies with longer names shorten them as they go global. For example, General Electric is now known as GE. Company brands must also have a clear, simple, unique identity and a unified appeal that generates positive emotional responses in the consumer. For many people around the world, Disney is associated with safe, heart-warming family entertainment while Nike is connected with athletic performance. Hightech companies, like Intel, are valued more for their product performance. While research on how international audiences respond to global brands is scanty, some studies have found that Western brands are broadly associated with status, modernity, sexuality, and technology.

Most global companies recognize, however, that they must cater to local markets with potentially different responses to their products and advertising message. For example, McDonald's in England must address that population's deeper concerns with treatment of animals, while in India, it must be sure to explain its vegetarian offerings and kitchen practices so as not to offend people's religious beliefs. A study of McDonald's websites for countries around the world reveals many subtle variations in its menus and the way it addresses its diverse audiences. The beauty company Avon grew into a prominent global corporation because its brand identity included training local door-to-door salespeople— "Avon Ladies." This worked well in many places around the world, because these salespeople could speak their clients' languages and knew their lifestyles and interests.

A global brand can be a liability, especially if it is associated with political conflicts and economic disparities. Nike, McDonald's, Wal-Mart, and Disney have been targeted in many places because they represent the exploitation of workers, environmental destruction, and the spread of negative cultural values. In 2005, the marketing firm Energy/BBDO studied 3,222 teens in thirteen countries, concluding that they are becoming turned off by global brands, especially U.S. ones. Some marketing consultants speculated that teens may be reacting to the U.S. role in world affairs and feel more loyal to local brands in strengthening economies.

Sources: Interbrand/Businessweek, "Best Global Brands 2006," ourfishbowl.com/images/surveys/BGB06Report_072706.pdf; Valerie Seckler, "U.S. Brands Take a Tumble with Teens," *WWD*, January 25, 2006: 9; Energy/BBDO, "GenWorld: The New Generation of Global Youth," energybbdo.com/uploads/GenWorld%20Overview.pdf.

Full-service agencies have account teams that serve clients. The account teams provide the basic services previously mentioned. Typically, the account teams are headed by an account executive, who is the agency's contact with the client. The team also includes a media planner, who buys ad space and time; a research director; and creative people, who produce the ads. The creative process involves writing copy and creating illustrations. The copy director oversees the copywriters, and the art director supervises the artists and layout people.

The positions found in an agency team also can be found within the advertising departments of large companies. Larger companies such as department stores often have an in-house ad department because it cuts their expenses and gives them greater control over their advertising. These departments have media buyers and planners as well as creative staff.

TRENDS

Advertising in the twenty-first century faces changes generated by the same trends confronting all media. Technological change, globalization, and the greater participation of consumers in new media forms will continue to alter the advertising industry in the next decades. Technological change has created new advertising forms on the Internet, but businesses continue to experiment with what works best with consumers, especially those who have grown up in the digital age. Furthermore, as advertisers seek the attention of these consumers, they must address ethical questions related to extreme or surreptitious techniques.

Technology: Online Advertising

Always eager to reach customers, businesses began moving cautiously online during the early 1990s. The caution came from not knowing much about this new medium for reaching customers. However, by 2005, the amount of **online advertising** had grown to $7.7 billion, up from $4.33 billion in 2000. This increase has sparked the interest of many businesses in shaping online campaigns, using techniques appropriate to an environment where users are much more active in generating their own content and circulating messages. Online advertising forms have evolved considerably from banner ads and text-based e-mail.

One of the more important trends is **viral marketing,** which can mean any advertising message that spreads exponentially from consumer to consumer, often through e-mail. However, as major companies have adapted the technique, it has come to have a more specific meaning: the spread of short advertising videos or video games by Internet users. Marketers have observed the way that clips like the Numa Numa Dance, which featured a chubby computer user lip-syncing to a Romanian pop song, can catch the interest of Internet users who circulate them through their social networks, sometimes imitating them and hacking them into new forms along the way. However, that kind of interest is not easy to capture with a planned campaign, since one of the charms of such videos is their unexpectedness, spontaneity, and amateurishness. When Gary Brolsma, the original creator of the Numa Numa Dance, created a more polished followup video, many of his fans disapproved and accused him of selling out. Marketers face considerable challenges in trying to create a planned viral campaign, which must seem spontaneous or at least funny, sexy, or shocking enough to get potential customers involved in telling their friends.

Many major companies have tried viral marketing, with varying degrees of success. Marketing Sherpa, a business research firm, selected as its 2006 top viral advertisement a celebrity game for the Internet DVD seller, Peerflix, targeting twenty-five to fifty-four-year-old movie lovers. Game players, acting as paparazzi, scored points by taking virtual pictures of animated celebrities, like Michael Jackson. At the end of each set, players were given the opportunity to send a message about the game to a friend. Peerflix's ad agency, POD Design, "seeded" notices about the game on blogs and game directories, leading to almost two million visitors.

The cost of such campaigns can be relatively inexpensive, ranging from $50,000 to $100,000, compared to over $330,000 for a television spot.[32] Some of the most successful viral ads have been free, as when Fritz Grobe and Stephen Voltz created the video, Experiment No. 137, that showed them choreographing streams of Diet Coke fizzed with Mentos candy. However, as major businesses become more

Key Concept

Online advertising Advertising online continues to develop, and companies are experimenting with the effectiveness of different types of product services, advertising, and subscription fees. The evolution of how online material is paid for will determine, in large part, the tone and character of online content in the same way the commercial base of broadcast television has influenced the entertainment and news received through that medium.

Key Concept

Viral marketing Marketers in major companies have adapted this technique to generate word of mouth among consumers. It is usually used for online activities such as forwarding advertisements via e-mail and circulating video clips.

Media Convergence

Advertising in the Social Network

As of September 2006, Ricky Bobby, a fictional character from the movie *Talladega Nights,* had 110,803 friends on the popular social networking site, MySpace. John Tucker, from the movie *John Tucker Must Die,* had 145,906. The obviously plastic Burger King mascot had achieved 133,000 friends, though at least some of them may have been exploiting the King, who was giving away free downloads of the television shows *24, Pinks,* and *American Dad.*

The creation of fictional friends on MySpace was one of the latest advertising ploys to reach a desirable demographic, teenagers and young adults, and to generate the word-of-mouth publicity known as viral marketing within their social networking sites. The commercialization of many of these sites began to increase exponentially in 2005. Advertisers are attracted to them because they contain a potential consumer base that is both tech savvy and sociable, spreading publicity for free through their sometimes hundreds of online friends. Because teens, especially, may be influenced by peer pressure, tapping their social networking sites is a way of reaching them on the seemingly personal level of a friend. They are considered early adopters of new products and technologies and their loyalty to brands may last well into the future.

While many social networking sites are available, MySpace has proven the most successful. According to Nielsen/NetRatings, MySpace had over 49 million visitors in August 2006, ranking seventh of the most popular websites. It was also the fastest growing: Between June 2005 and June 2006 it experienced a 183 percent increase in audience. Originally started to help musicians promote their bands, MySpace is now owned by Rupert Murdoch's News Corp. It makes its money from advertising, mostly from Google which paid $900 million to put ads on the site, making for a total of $1,180 million. Spending on all other social networking sites in 2006 was expected to be about $100 million. Ads directed at these consumers range from banner ads, to fake personas like the Burger King, to promotional music and video contests.

Another model is evolving that sets up virtual worlds that double as online shopping malls. An early version is Cyworld, a South Korean site that boasts a third of the country's population as users, many of them in their twenties. In Cyworld, users pay to decorate their virtual characters and rooms with charms such as pets, furniture, and clothing, and businesses set up their own pages on the site to give away charms that carry advertising. Released in a BETA version in 2006, MTV's Virtual Laguna Beach will allow users to create a character, dress it, take it to virtual parties, and shop both for real and virtual consumer goods. Virtual Laguna Beach plans to eventually become a virtual mall as well as social hangout.

Some businesses are hesitant to get involved in social network advertising because they fear that such spaces attract sexual predators and don't want their businesses associated with these activities. Others feel uncomfortable with the personal, interactive aspects. On the other hand, some social networkers resent the intrusion of commercialization of their space and worry about privacy issues that may arise if businesses collect demographic and psychographic information from user data.

Sources: Kris Oser, "MySpace: Big Audiences, Big Risks," *Advertising Age,* February 20, 2006: 3, 25; Elizabeth Holmes, "On MySpace, Millions of Users Make 'Friends' with Ads," *Wall Street Journal,* August 7, 2006: B1; Debra Aho Williamson, "Advertising on Social Networks: The New Frontier?" eMarketer, September 8, 2006, emarketer.com.

interested in seeding their own viral ads, popular bloggers and other website owners are charging a hefty fee for mentioning them.

Despite the growing interest in them, viral campaigns are risky because businesses run the risk of losing control of their advertising. A case that has become legendary among advertisers is a 2006 Chevy campaign for its Tahoe SUV. Chevy invited visitors to its website to create their own thirty-second commercial for the Tahoe, adding text to stock footage. In terms of numbers, the campaign was a success, with 22,000 entries, attracting 5.5 million visitors.[33] However, environmental activists used the opportunity to make videos with captions like "Contributes to Glacier Melt World Wide" and "Responsible for Global Warming." Many of these were posted on YouTube. Questions arose over whether even bad publicity is good news for business, and how much control should be exercised over user-generated content. Another problem lies with the unintended association of a brand with violent or pornographic Internet content as it is spread from site to site.

Many of the issues facing advertising are similar to those faced by public relations practitioners and other media industries. Some questions that must be answered include:

■ How will the development of online advertising affect sales, consumers' attitudes toward companies and brands, and increased commercialization on the Internet?

■ To what extent should advertising be a form of entertainment?

■ Why have worldwide advertising and advertising agencies developed?

■ What are the implications of worldwide advertising for individuals and societies outside the United States?

■ How do global brands reach local audiences?

Culture: Advertainment

Viral ads are part of a wider trend, ***advertainment,*** which makes advertising look like entertainment, bordering very close to disguise. Marketers are looking for creative ways to make their advertisements more visible and interactive, so that consumers stay with them longer. Advertainment often goes beyond static product placements, lengthening the form of an ad to resemble a television show or a video game.

Television stations are especially interested in advertainments because consumers are increasingly discovering video on demand and DVRs, making it easier for them to filter out the traditional thirty-second commercial. Therefore, advertising spots have to be appealing enough to grab the viewer who is no longer sitting passively as advertisements flit past. Consumers are also watching television shows on their own schedules, making it harder for advertisers to isolate a target demographic who watches television during a certain time slot. Both broadcast and some cable networks are facing declining ad revenues. Some large companies are turning away from expensive television advertising to focus their efforts online. Therefore, the networks have turned to advertainments as a way of restoring and increasing revenues.

Advertainments expand the idea of product placement to make products part of dramatic scripts. For its launch, the CW network offered advertisers spots for mini-shows which followed a character through a series of episodes during commercial breaks. These mini-shows featured company brands. Some companies provide their video advertisements only on websites. An early instance of the technique was BMW's 2001 online film series, *The Hire,* with acclaimed directors such as John Woo and Ang Lee. They all starred Clive Owen driving various BMW models in action-adventures. Other companies followed suit. After cutting down its television advertising, American Express focused its marketing efforts online, offering a user-generated film competition and shorts from directors like M. Night Shyamalan.[34]

> ### Key Concept
>
> **Advertainment** A way to make advertising more visible is through the blend of advertising and entertainment. Usually, a marketer's goal is to make an advertisement seem like entertainment, but embed advertising messages, such as product placements.

Culture: Ethics and Responsibility in Advertising

Media critics and advertising watchdogs argue that one of the problems with advertainment is its surreptitiousness at a time when media organizations, like newspapers, are emphasizing greater transparency in what they do. For example, Procter & Gamble made a deal with the Perseus Books Group to include product placements for Cover Girl beauty products in a young adult novel, *Cathy's Book: If Found Call 650-266-8233.* A consumer organization, Commercial Alert, began a campaign to get magazine and newspaper editors not to review the book, arguing that it was nothing but an ad.[35] Commercial Alert argues that audiences have the right to be informed when they are watching or reading sales pitches. Surreptitious marketing is of special concern when aimed at children, who have less ability to discern media messages. In 2006, Nabiscoworld.com had an *advergame* on its website that involved the player catching Oreos in a glass of milk. Critics argue that such games manipulate children into unhealthy eating habits and should be regulated.[36]

New ad forms, like viral videos, have also pushed the boundaries of advertising ethics, especially when they disguise their purpose or incorporate extreme content to make their videos more likely to be spread. In England, a regulatory body set up by the advertising industry, the Advertising Standards Authority (ASA), included viral marketing in its ethics code after receiving many complaints about such ads. Of particular concern was a commercial for the game Moral Kombat: Shaolin Monks, which showed a businessman at a meeting decapitating and eating the heart of one of his colleagues. Arguing that online advertising should be held to the same standards as other forms, the ASA condemned the ad as indecent, potentially damaging to children, and an encouragement to violent and antisocial behavior. Critics of the move argued that the ASA's censorship of the ad only piqued interest in it, and that content on the Internet can't and shouldn't be regulated.

SUMMARY

- Advertising serves a basic economic function in the United States. It allows sellers and buyers of goods and services to find one another in the marketplace.
- Advertising sometimes aims at mass audiences and at other times concentrates on segmented audiences.
- Segmented audiences can be classified by demographics, psychographics, and geography.
- Advertisements can be classified by the geographic area they cover, the purpose of the ads, and the effect the ads have on consumers of media.
- Most advertising plans incorporate more than one type of medium.
- Cable, home video, and other new technologies compete for advertising that was supported in the past by traditional mass media.
- Not all of advertising's effects on society are positive. Some advertisers attempt to manipulate audiences to

buy certain products and services. This is especially problematic with very young television viewers.
- Advertisers sometimes influence the news coverage of media organizations with advertising boycotts and informal pressure that affect the contents of stories that are run.
- Political advertising can become problematic when it misleads or allows contributors to gain influence by donating money.
- Online advertising includes techniques different from traditional mass media.
- Online advertising attempts to target young audiences through viral marketing.
- The use of product placement is increasing.
- Global brands maintain brand identities within differing local market.

NAVIGATING THE WEB Advertising

More and more, advertising is seen on the World Wide Web. Many sites have advertising, but information about advertising is not plentiful. The following list presents a range of sites related to advertising.

Advertising Age
adage.com
Advertising Age is the dominant trade magazine for advertising. It contains a wide range of information about

media that carry advertising. Its website is the online version of the print magazine.

American Association of Advertising Agencies
aaaa.org
The AAAA site is maintained by a national trade organization for ad agencies. The association promotes integrity and ethics in advertising. The site contains information about the organization and its goals.

Interbrand
interbrand.com
This brand consulting agency tracks and rates global brands.

Scarborough Research
scarborough.com
This market research organization conducts research for media and advertisers. The site contains information about the services it offers.

QUESTIONS FOR REVIEW

1. What is the difference between advertising and entertainment?
2. What factors contributed to the development of mass advertising?
3. Why did some publications begin to refuse patent medicine advertising?
4. Why are advertisers concerned about geographic coverage?
5. What are the primary tasks of an advertising agency?
6. What is viral marketing?

ISSUES TO THINK ABOUT

1. What is the economic and social role of advertising in a free-market society?
2. How does cultural change affect advertising?
3. What impact did the arrival of the Internet have on advertising?
4. How does advertising have both a negative and a positive effect on journalism?
5. Does advertising coerce people into buying things they do not need?
6. What are the implications of heavy political advertising on the Internet?
7. How do global brands develop?

SUGGESTED READINGS

deMooij, Marieke K. *Consumer Behavior and Culture: Consequences for Global Marketing and Advertising.* (Thousand Oaks, CA: Sage, 2003).

Ewen, Stuart. *Captains of Consciousness: Advertising and the Social Roots of Consumer Culture* (New York: McGraw-Hill, 1976).

Gunter, Barrie, Caroline Oates, and Mark Blades. *Advertising to Children on TV: Content, Impact, and Regulation* (Mahwah, NJ: Lawrence Erlbaum, 2005).

Heath, Robert. *The Hidden Power of Advertising* (Oxfordshire, England: World Advertising Research Center, 2001).

Marchand, Roland. *Advertising the American Dream* (Berkeley: University of California Press, 1989).

Schudson, Michael. *Advertising: The Uneasy Persuasion* (New York: Basic Books, 1984).

Twitchell, James B. *Adcult USA: The Triumph of Advertising in American Culture* (New York: Columbia University Press, 1997).

Ethics

KEY CONCEPTS

- Ethical Decision Making
- Theoretical Approaches to Ethics
- Credibility as an Economic Incentive for Ethics
- Fundamental Ethical Standards
- Conflict of Interest
- Code of Ethics
- Moral Reasoning Process
- Sensationalism

In April 2004, twenty-nine U.S. newspapers and news websites emailed 13,642 readers asking them about a case of ethics. Did they feel that the news should carry a photograph of a few Iraqis cheering as the burned bodies of two American civilian workers were hung from a bridge in Fallujah? They also asked readers to consider whether it mattered if the bodies were of soldiers or civilians and were recognizable as human beings. The answer was divided: 58 percent of respondents approved of the photograph's publication, while 39 percent objected. Some readers felt that such images, no matter how gruesome, must be shown to reveal the truth about war and violence. Others felt that the photograph was inhumane and sensationalistic and might cause harm to the victims' families. A few readers refused to even look at it.[1]

News images during wartime have been powerful persuaders in the history of the United States, and journalists often face ethical questions in publishing them. Two photographs encouraged opposition to the Vietnam War: the execution of a Viet Cong police officer and a child fleeing from a napalm bombing. The U.S. police action in Somalia came under fire when a news photo showed anti-American protesters dragging the body of an American soldier through the streets.

More recently, over a thousand disturbing photographs from the Abu Ghraib prison showing brutalized, sexually degraded prisoners have challenged editors. They must decide whether to publish them, weighing news value against potential offense to audiences. When Islamic fundamentalists murdered Daniel Pearl in May 2002, they released a videotape of his beheading. The *Boston Phoenix* posted a link to an edited version of the tape, inciting a debate over whether the image had news value. Some argued that the video was gratuitous, while others felt the video had historical importance and that withholding it would be paternalistic. "There are awful things that happen in the world, and I don't believe people should be prevented from seeing them," Paul Lester, a professor at California State University, Fullerton, told the *American Journalism Review*. "Awful acts need to be shown, and we need to see as humans what other humans are capable of in this world. Visual images show this more powerfully than words can ever do."[2]

Ethical decision making is not easy to understand or to do. But because mass media permeate our society and are our primary sources of information, we need to address ethical issues. Some of those addressed in this chapter include the following:

- Why is adherence to ethical behavior an important consideration for media workers?

- How is ethical behavior related to political, social, and cultural issues?

- How do economic issues influence ethical behavior?

- What is the relationship of ethical behavior to the marketplace of ideas and to the nation?

Newsmakers must not only decide whether to publish such images, but how and where to place them. Pointing out the difference between the impact of text and visuals, journalist and ethicist Fred Brown explains, "The first photos from Abu Ghraib were properly on most front pages, but what about those charred corpses from Fallujah? Or stills from the beheading of Daniel Pearl? Both were relevant, but an ethical editor must consider whether it's really in everyone's best interest to play them large and in color on the front page."[3]

Newsmakers face dilemmas in making these kinds of decisions. Who is affected by publishing the image? Is it credible and authentic? Do less shocking alternatives exist that would work just as well? Is the photograph being shown just to gain audience? Should a news organization succumb to government pressure not to publish?

Welcome to the world of media ethics. In this world, political and economic pressures can affect the media content that consumers receive. *Ethics* is easily defined as standards of conduct and moral judgment. However, defining moral judgment requires judging the goodness or badness of human behavior and character. This is a difficult task both for those who supply news to reporters and for those who process news. When people question whether mass media employees have ethics, they are really asking whether these influential professionals have standards to guide their decisions and conduct and whether they adhere to those standards. News reporters and editors have long claimed that they adhere to standards of truth without obligation to any economic imperative, but research reveals that economics and politics often have dictated news content. Furthermore, although public relations personnel are often thought to be more loyal to the organization that employs them than to the truth, standards of professional conduct also are applied to decision making in public relations. Public relations professionals consider part of their job to be convincing upper management of the ethical position that a company should take regarding public service and information.

Ethics in Your Life

Whom Do You Trust?

Do you trust journalists to behave in ethical ways? What about public relations practitioners? If you had a discussion with your friends, what would they say? Do you think credibility is an important issue for information gatherers?

As you read this chapter, think about the various individuals who try to control the flow of information. To what extent does their credibility have an impact on your life?

Whom Do You Trust?	Who Is Most Likely to Adhere to Ethical Behavior?
Print journalists?	
Reporters and anchors for network television news?	
Reporters for special news programming, such as newsmagazines?	
Reporters and anchors for local news?	
Public relations practitioners who work for nonprofit companies?	
Public relations practitioners who work for profit-making companies?	
Citizen journalists on blogs?	
Sources for news: Politicians?	
Sources for news: People who hold high positions in the business world?	
Sources for news: Social and political activists?	

ETHICS IN AMERICAN LIFE

Media critics have long been concerned with ethical standards. That concern, reported as early as the eighteenth century, was part of a continuing dialogue about the role of a free press in a democratic society. If the media are to be protected—that is, if freedom of expression is to be paramount—then the public must be able to trust the media to adhere to well-understood standards. The political importance of ethical behavior is strongly connected to the concept of a free-flowing marketplace of ideas that is the foundation of a democratic society.

Key Concept

Ethical decision making Making ethical decisions has been a concern of journalists since at least the early twentieth century, when many reporters wanted to be among the emerging groups of professionals. However, attempts to determine exactly what standards of conduct and moral judgment constitute ethical behavior have resulted in a continuing debate rather than absolute standards.

History of Journalistic Standards

Ethical standards are intrinsically related to the political and cultural milieu in which the media operate. In colonial days, newspapers were highly partisan, and ***ethical decision making*** focused on whether editors should print points of view of competing parties rather than just the views of the party they supported. As newspaper editors adopted an **information model** during the middle of the nineteenth century, they

information model
Pattern of behavior for disseminating information as news; incorporates values such as objectivity over partisanship.

Sensational stories, such as those about murders and love triangles, have always been standard fare for newspapers. Critics have argued about whether the editor should decide what the reader needs to read or whether the reader can make intelligent individual choices. After World War II, the idea of a socially responsible press gained credence, and critics viewed it as the obligation of the press to report the news in the full context of political and social events.

remained partisan but also began to include stories about common people. This focus on individuals gave rise to new discussions about ethics. Critics denounced editors for trivializing the news, claiming that giving public notice to ordinary people was harmful to the public and "misled most people . . . into thinking them[selves] important."[4] After 1850, however, critics began to focus on the relationship between press and society, and they increasingly addressed press issues. They attacked editors for publishing trivial gossip and argued that publishing details of people's lives, such as accounts of weddings, invaded individuals' privacy.

With the rise of sensational journalism in the 1890s, critics began to focus on attributes of news. They argued that fact and opinion should be separated, that care "beyond the profit principle must be exercised in news selection," and that material that violated good taste and judgment should be avoided. Critics, of course, differed in their definitions of good taste. Some thought crime stories were not in good taste. Others thought editors should print only certain details about crime stories. Critics also noted that business and editorial operations should be separated. These discussions paved the way for the development of journalism education, ethics codes, and other means of monitoring journalistic conduct.[5]

In a study of journalistic standards, Marion Marzolf noted that by the end of the nineteenth century, commercial concerns were beginning to shape newspaper standards. Even though the newspaper was still seen as educational, with a moral obligation toward the public, profit goals were beginning to tip the press toward a "degrading vulgarity."[6] Marzolf's work reflects a concern that dominates criticism of the media today: the controversy between commercial gain and the traditional democratic values that a free press was thought to foster.

Development of Standards for Public Relations

By the end of World War I, extensive use of propaganda techniques during the war raised ethical issues for practitioners of public relations as well as for journalists. In 1923, Edward L. Bernays, who had developed campaigns for the War Department, published *Crystallizing Public Opinion,* which argued that the modern public demanded information and made up its own mind. However, because society was growing in complexity, Bernays said, someone was needed to bring specialized information to the public in an honest, ethical way. He and his colleague and wife, Doris Fleishman, coined the term "counsel on public relations" to describe the work of the public relations practitioner. In essence, Bernays argued that in the marketplace of ideas the job of the public relations counsel was to get a client the best possible hearing for a legitimate message.[7]

CLASSICAL ETHICS IN A MODERN SOCIETY

In their book *Media Ethics,* three prominent ethics scholars, Clifford G. Christians, Kim B. Rotzoll, and Mark Fackler, outline five **theoretical approaches** for understanding modern ethical decisions. Remember that these are philosophical principles that underlie discussions; they are not prescriptions for solutions, as you can see in the following examples.

1. *The Golden Mean.* Aristotle advocated the Golden Mean. He believed that moderation in life, as well as in eating habits, best serves the individual. Moderation as applied to ethics means operating somewhere between two extremes.
2. *The categorical imperative.* Eighteenth-century philosopher Immanuel Kant believed that ethical principles should be determined by analyzing what principles could be applied universally. This imperative is related to what some call **absolute ethics.** What is right for one is right for all, and what is right for one situation is right for all situations with similar circumstances.

    People who advocate absolutist positions believe that if lying, for example, is unethical, then all variations from the truth are wrong; it would be out of the question to utter a white lie or to lie to protect someone. If an editor decrees that names of suspects will not be published until they have been found guilty, then that rule covers all cases, with no exceptions.
3. *The principle of utility.* Nineteenth-century philosopher John Stuart Mill advocated that ethical decisions be made on the basis of what provides the greatest good for the greatest number of people. One could argue that public relations professionals who promote tobacco and media companies who reap profits from tobacco advertising are not operating according to the principle of utility. Medical science has found that tobacco is deleterious to a great number of people.
4. *The veil of ignorance.* John Rawls espouses a decidedly twentieth-century philosophical position, arguing that justice emerges when social differentiations are eliminated in the process of negotiation. Therefore, information is treated outside of the social context, and power, wealth, and other social factors do not enhance one position over another. This principle means that ABC reporters, for example, when covering Disney, would be able to disregard the power and wealth of the network's parent company.
5. *Judeo-Christian ethic.* The Golden Rule, "Do unto others as you would have them do unto you," applies here. Individuals who adhere to this religious ethic are encouraged to "love thy neighbor as thyself" and to treat all individuals with respect.[8]

POLITICAL AND ECONOMIC DEMAND FOR ETHICAL BEHAVIOR

The evolution of journalistic standards and concern about the ethics of reporting information from both journalistic and public relations standpoints clearly reveal that the public, press, educators, and critics demand ethical behavior. The standards are not always clear, and they change as cultural norms within society change. The nineteenth-century critics who thought that reporting on crime was distasteful would be laughed off the television screen, which thrives on realistic reenactments of police investigations.

However, there are also economic demands for ethical behavior because of the enormous impact of information dissemination in a free-market society. Economic demand involves several factors: (1) the **credibility** of the news organization and its ability to make a profit, (2) the economic concentration of media outlets, and (3) the impact on other industries affected by media coverage.

Credibility and Profit

When the public believes that those who work in the mass media act without thinking ethically, then media credibility is at stake. People listen to the radio, watch television, and read newspapers and magazines to find out what is going on in the world

absolute ethics

A code of ethics that allows no deviation from its rules.

credibility

A measurement of how well a journalist or media organization is trusted. If a high percentage of the public perceives a journalist as truthful, that person has credibility.

around them. If the local newspaper is known for routinely publishing inaccurate information, then people will stop buying the paper and turn to local television or radio for news.

If people question the credibility of one network news department, then they may turn to a more credible network for national news. For any of the news media to survive, *credibility is an economic incentive for ethics.*

An issue of credibility may arise, for example, when a public relations firm provides a free video news release (VNR) to a news broadcaster. Designed to look like a regular news story, the VNR may appear to be in the public interest, but also promotes a product. For example, a spot made for Masterfoods about providing a safe Halloween for kids also features shots of its candies: Snickers and M & Ms. In April 2006, the Center for Media and Democracy issued a controversial report showing that over a ten-month period, seventy-seven television stations used VNRs from public relations firms without mentioning their source. The firms worked for companies like General Motors, Intel, Pfizer and Capital One. The Center for Media and Democracy charged that the stations "actively disguised the sponsored content to make it appear to be their own reporting." Further, the VNRs were shown without any fact checking and sometimes without editing. Occasionally, anchors read directly from a script provided by the public relations firm, all without mentioning the source.[9] Critics of VNRs call them "fake news." Consumers, they say, should have truthful, unbiased news to make informed decisions about products. Public relations firms argue that VNRs are like the press releases often printed verbatim in newspapers. Further, VNRs aren't causing any great harm and can perform a valuable public service.

Public relations firms aren't the only providers of VNRs. In 2003, television stations received a VNR discussing the Medicare Prescription Drug Improvement and Modernization Act. The piece was aimed at seniors, advising them that the changes to Medicare were for their benefit. When the story broke that the U.S. government had funded the VNR, many critics questioned whether the government should be providing the news in a democracy. The U.S. Government Accountability Office (GAO) revealed that twenty agencies supplied VNRs to the media and accused the Bush administration of disseminating "propaganda." The administration replied that the GAO did not realize the difference between propaganda and "purely informational video news reports."[10]

There is no hard evidence yet that VNRs damage the credibility of news organizations that use them, but they raise questions about the independence of news reporting and audience trust in it. Some media analysts have said that television stations are more likely to use VNRs because of budget cuts, media consolidation, and the strain to produce twenty-four-hour-news.[11] The FCC has warned that it may provide rules that require disclosure when a VNR is aired.

Ethics and Media Concentration

With the increasing concentration of the ownership of media organizations, critics and the public have become more attuned to the possibilities and effects of unethical behavior. In 1996, Disney acquired two major media organizations: Cap Cities and ABC. Two years later, serious accusations arose about ABC's ability to cover the parent company. The case involved *20/20,* the ABC newsmagazine. After a top investigative reporter, Brian Ross, and his longtime producer, Rhonda Schwartz, spent months exposing unsavory practices at Disney theme parks, executives killed the story. "A draft story was submitted that did not work," ABC news spokeswoman Eileen Murphy said in a prepared statement. "This does not reflect badly on any reporter or producer involved."[12]

Impact on Other Industries

News stories affect not only readers but the subjects they cover. They can affect an industry's credibility or a company's profits; they can also affect the amount of government attention an industry gets. Such attention can result in a change in

Ethics, Media Frenzy, and True Crime

Nearly ten years after six-year-old JonBenet Ramsey was found dead in her family's basement, John Mark Karr was arrested in Thailand and confessed to the murder. In 1996, the case had been a sensational one, with seventy news organizations descending on the scene in Boulder, Colorado. The story made the covers of *People* and *Newsweek.* Over the next decade, the now-famous beauty pageant photos of JonBenet appeared in hundreds of media sources, like supermarket tabloids, webpages, magazines, and television shows. Two months before the arrest of Karr, the *New York Times* still found the case newsworthy, running a review of a documentary about it.

What made the JonBenet Ramsey case so fascinating to the press and its audiences? Al Tompkins, of the Poynter Institute, suggests the following factors for why some crime stories become sensational. The victim is famous, wealthy, or a child. Striking images or videos of the victim are available to the press. The crime happens in a major media market. The bad guy has not been found.

Media sensations can lead to questionable accusations and inaccurate reporting. In the Ramsey case, the press often seemed to accuse JonBenet's parents, John and Patsy Ramsey, to the point that, as British journalist Simon Hoggart said at the time, "they have been tried, condemned and to all purposes had their lives terminated by the media." For example, on his nightly news show, Geraldo Rivera, conducted a mock trial of the case that implied John's and Patsy's guilt. JonBenet's brother, Burke, was also tried and convicted in the media, even though the police had cleared him. Burke and his parents sued AOL-Time Warner for libel and defamation and were awarded $35 million.

When Karr was arrested in Thailand, some journalists were quick to rush to judgment. The *New York Daily News* ran the front-page headline: SOLVED! More responsible journalists urged caution. Bob Steele, who writes an ethics column for the Poynter Institute, cited the case of Richard Jewell, a security guard who had been falsely accused of the 1996 bombing of the Centennial

Olympic Park in Atlanta. Jewell had actually alerted the police and helped with rescue efforts. He sued *NBC,* the *Atlanta Journal-Constitution,* and the *New York Post* for libel. Evoking Jewell to discuss the latest media frenzy in the JonBenet Ramsey case, Steele argued that the press must be careful when covering sensational events like the arrest of Karr. Journalists must respect "innocent until proven guilty," avoid suggesting guilt, not let "competitive zeal cloud their judgment," and "respectfully challenge every statement made by law enforcement agencies and prosecutors." That advice turned out to be wise when police decided not to charge Karr for the JonBenet murder because his DNA did not match the DNA found at the crime scene.

Sources: Simon Hoggart, "Please Shut Up," *Spectator,* July 14, 2001: 43–44; Bob Steele, "An Arrest in the JonBenet Ramsey Case," *Everyday Ethics,* August 16, 2006, poynter.org; Al Tompkins, "Why Do Some Cases Like This One Get So Much Media Attention?" *Al's Morning Meeting,* August 18, 2006, poynter.org.

---

regulation, which may ultimately affect profit. Such coverage does have an impact that can improve or detract from a company's profitability.

A classic example is the story about Food Lion, Inc., that ABC ran on *Prime Time Live* during 1992. ABC accused the food chain based in North Carolina of selling out-of-date meat and substandard deli products. Within days, Food Lion stock dropped $1.5 billion in value and food sales declined. ABC producers had gotten jobs at Food Lion and hidden tiny cameras in wigs to shoot footage. Food Lion sued for fraud, deceptive trade practices, breach of loyalty, and trespassing.

Although ABC was found guilty on two counts, the fine was reduced to only one dollar for each count. The network maintained that its actions were ethical. ABC defended lying on the applications, the use of hidden cameras, and its selection of sources by saying that serving the public good—protecting the public from being exposed to bad food—outweighed other considerations. It may well have been a false argument because it is doubtful that bad food was ever the real issue. Even Diane Sawyer, the anchor, reported that no cases of illness from bad food purchased at a Food Lion store had been documented.

A more recent example shows how unquestioning news coverage of the latest miracle cures can help a company and hurt readers. Knowing that many Americans are interested in health news, the press often helps pharmaceutical companies promote their latest product. Health news is profitable. In 2004, ABC, NBC, CBS, Fox News, and CNN raked in $1.5 billion in advertising revenues from pharmaceutical companies, triple what they had received in 1999.[13] However, news organizations often carry stories about new drugs without rigorous investigation. The results can be dangerous for consumers. For example, the media helped promote Merck's VIOXX as a "super aspirin" for arthritis, migraines, and menstrual cramps. Reporters missed many warning signs from the FDA and the medical community about the dangers of VIOXX, and thousands of people may have died because of adverse side effects. In 2004, the FDA announced that all COX 2 drugs, such as VIOXX, may cause heart attacks.

One of the problems lies in the sources reporters use. Pharmaceutical companies may reward scientists who develop and test drugs, so their expert testimony about these products may constitute a conflict of interest.[14] Nevertheless, reporters often rely on the scientists for information. Pharmaceutical companies are unlikely to cooperate with reporters who ask the tough questions, but occasionally these watchdogs have done a great service in protecting the public interest. For example, stories by David Willman, of the *Los Angeles Times,* exposed the dangers of Rezulin, used to treat diabetes.

Basic Ethical Standards in U.S. Media

Key Concept

Fundamental ethical standards Although most individuals and groups agree on a few fundamental ethical standards, they often disagree about specifics and about whether fundamental standards are met. The commonly agreed-on standards are accuracy, fairness, balance, accurate representation, and truth.

Professional communicators recognize the value of fundamental standards of ethical behavior. In addition, media audiences have come to expect certain ***fundamental ethical standards.*** Among these are accuracy, fairness, balance, accurate representation, and truth. The Public Relations Society of America, for example, recognizes, in its code of professional standards, values such as truth, accuracy, fairness, responsibility to the public, and generally accepted standards of good taste.

Accuracy The bedrock of ethics is **accuracy.** For public relations professionals, reporters, and editors, being accused of inaccuracy is one of the worst charges that can be leveled. However, accuracy is not simply recording the facts, but selecting and weighing them for relevance and providing appropriate background and contact. Some inaccuracies can be damaging, such as the one revealed in this correction printed in the *Fulton County Expositor* in Wauseon, Ohio: "The *Fulton County Expositor* incorrectly reported in Tuesday's edition that recently deceased John T. Cline of Delta was a Nazi veteran of World War II. The obituary should have read he was a Navy war veteran."[15]

Some issues of accuracy are more complex because the news is more complex. For example, in September 2003, a team of researchers visited thirty homes in thirty-three neighborhoods in Iraq to compile a count of those who had been killed during the war. Led by Les Roberts, a researcher from Johns Hopkins University, the study concluded that the deaths numbered 100,000, a figure extrapolated from the survey. The count was much greater than any previous estimate.[16]

The prestigious British medical journal, the *Lancet,* published Roberts' findings just before the 2004 presidential election. The British foreign minister, Jack Straw, questioned whether the count was accurate because of the way the research had been conducted. Most epidemiologists, however, believed the team's methods to be

accuracy

The recording, selecting, and weighing of facts to provide a truthful account.

proper. Other critics questioned the researchers' decision to publish the report to co-incide with the election, creating skepticism about the their results and motivations. The report was not covered much in the U.S. mainstream media, with only a few newspapers mentioning it briefly in their back pages.[17] In the *New York Times,* Peter Steinfels responded, asking why the military wasn't keeping better track of Iraqi deaths.[18] Project Censored included the Roberts report in its 2005 list of top-ten stories that had been "overlooked, under-reported or self-censored."[19] The issues surrounding this case are complex because the research was published in the highly politicized environment of war.

Objectivity   To be truly unbiased is an admirable but unattainable goal. From birth on, society and familial upbringing subtly influence a person's view of the world. However, journalists who accept **objectivity** as a goal need to be aware of their biases and then report and produce as objective a story as possible.

Objectivity is more than simply being aware of personal biases. How objective should a journalist be? Perhaps some interpretation is necessary to present a complete story. For example, in the 1950s the media unwittingly helped Wisconsin Senator Joseph McCarthy to instill a fear of communism in U.S. society that caused serious harm to innocent people. Actors and others who had only attended a meeting of the Communist Party decades earlier were blacklisted and could not get jobs in their profession. McCarthy and his aides understood how the media operated, and they carefully timed speeches and press conferences close to deadlines, knowing that reporters would have to choose between checking facts and being scooped by another news organization. Often, reporters followed the dictates of objectivity, quoting McCarthy verbatim. However, some newspaper reporters questioned McCarthy's actions, and in his television program *See It Now,* Edward R. Murrow exposed the McCarthy witch-hunt.

Objectivity is not a fundamental ethical attribute of public relations and advertising personnel, whose goal is to persuade as well as to inform. But it has been a fundamental aspect of twentieth-century reporting, and it is one of the factors that distinguishes journalism from public relations and advertising.

Fairness and Balance   Fairness and balance often go hand in hand with accuracy and objectivity. Reporters attempt to investigate the many sides of a story. For example, abortion is a much-debated issue in many state legislatures. If the mass media quote and run video only of active demonstrators on the prochoice and prolife sides, the

objectivity
Reporting facts without bias or prejudice, including a deliberate attempt to avoid interpretation.

After the news media realized they had been duped by Senator Joseph McCarthy, they took steps to ensure that it could not happen again.

Reporters listen to spokespersons on a legal case involving the federal government's regulation of carbon dioxide and greenhouse gases.

complete story remains untold. Stories need to take into account the range of differing opinions. Often, complexity must be preserved for **journalistic balance** to be achieved.

The more complicated the news, the more difficult it is to provide balance. For example, reporting on global warming requires a sophisticated understanding of science, including the knowledge that science can be inconclusive and involve a range of outcomes. Global warming has generated significant debate and political conflict between scientists and politicians. Therefore, journalists try to explain the science while presenting what they see as two sides of the issue. Many climatologists feel that this attempt at balance in mainstream news coverage allows fringe ideas to undermine the accepted scientific view that global warming is occurring.[20]

Absence of Fakery One of the most blatant cases of **fakery** occurred in 1992 when NBC *Dateline* faked a truck explosion for a report about the dangers of crashes involving General Motors pickups. GM sued. NBC broadcast a retraction and NBC News President Michael Gartner resigned. The line between entertainment and news was badly blurred in the competition for viewers. Why did the network do it? "Because one side of the line is an Emmy. The other side, the abyss," said Jane Pauley, one of *Dateline*'s anchors.[21]

Many charges of fakery have involved photographs because they seem to represent reality, but can be easily manipulated. One of the best known cases was an altered photograph of O. J. Simpson that appeared on the cover of *Time* in 1994. The image generated charges of racism because it made Simpson appear darker. *National*

journalistic balance

Providing equal or nearly equal coverage of various points of view in a controversy.

fakery

Posing that which is false to be true.

In 2006, Reuters admitted that one of its photographs, showing the aftermath of an Israeli strike on Beirut, had been doctored to exaggerate the damage. Reuters apologized and ended its relationship with the freelance photographer who had provided the image.

Geographic admitted that in its July 2004 issue, a photograph of Tanzanian tribesmen carrying ivory tusks had been faked. When astute readers noticed that the tusks were marked with numbers, the photographer confessed that he had borrowed them from a wildlife agency and posed the Barabaigs with them. In 2006, Reuters ran doctored photographs of an Israeli strike on Lebanon, taken by a freelance photographer. The photographer had heightened the damage by digitally enhancing the black smoke plumes. Reuters admitted that the images were manipulated and ended its relationship with the freelancer. Such incidents can cause audiences to question the credibility of their news organizations.

Truth   Although journalists cannot always ensure that their stories are true, they can make an extra effort to be truthful and to avoid lying. In 2003, Jayson Blair was fired from the *New York Times* for plagiarizing and concocting his stories. It began over an article about a missing soldier in Iraq. Blair claimed to have interviewed the soldier's mother in San Antonio, but he had never made the trip. Rather he had stolen the story from a former intern at the *Times* who was working at the *San Antonio Express-News*. Eventually, the *Times* revealed that Blair had stolen or fabricated half of his stories. The Blair scandal had lasting repercussions, with the executive and managing editors eventually resigning because of criticisms that they had mismanaged the paper. The case was similar to Stephen Glass. A reporter for the *New Republic,* Glass had been fired in 1998 for fabricating many of his stories, including one about a teenage hacker.

It is possible to report material accurately and still not present the truth. Trying to attain truth requires accuracy, fairness, balance, and a variety of other aspects of reporting that combine to create a picture of the "whole truth."

Integrity of Sources   A journalist's story is only as good as its sources. In 1981, Janet Cooke, a twenty-six-year-old *Washington Post* reporter, won a Pulitzer Prize for a front-page article called "Jimmy's World." Jimmy was an eight-year-old heroin addict. Soon after receiving the award, Cooke confessed that she had concocted the story; Jimmy did not exist. She returned the prize and left the *Post.*[22]

Reporters who become too loyal to sources risk the possibility of being blinded and missing important cues to stories. The *Washington Post*'s revelations about the Watergate scandal initially came not from reporters covering the White House who had access to top-level sources, but from young metropolitan desk staffers Carl Bernstein and Bob Woodward, who connected one of the burglars who broke into the Democratic Party headquarters in the Watergate complex to the Central Intelligence Agency.

Avoiding Conflict of Interest   Outside business, social and personal activities, and contacts can subtly influence the ability of mass media professionals to conduct objective reporting. This is called **conflict of interest.** Examples include a technology journalist who receives free services from a technology company, a city council member writing about a housing bill, or the spouse of a political contender writing about a candidate's platform. The lack of objectivity these reporters experience originates in a conflict of interest—the conflict between trying to do one's job effectively and a belief system that adheres to the moral rightness of a cause or a desire to promote one's own interest.

> **Key Concept**
>
> **Conflict of interest**   Along with government officials and others in positions of responsibility, journalists are under pressure to avoid allowing personal activities or interests to interfere with their professional responsibilities. Journalists have an obligation to strive for unbiased coverage of an event or situation.

Stories of conflict of interest abound. For example, Suzy Wetlaufer, editor of the *Harvard Business Review,* had an affair with the married former chairman of General Electric Jack Welch after interviewing him for a story. Similarly, Andrea Mitchell, NBC's chief foreign affairs correspondent, and Federal Reserve Chairman Alan Greenspan dated for twelve years before their marriage in 1997. As Lori Robertson wrote in *American Journalism Review* about the topic, "Other ethicists and editors say that reporters romancing their sources is an issue they rarely face. But what many journalists do encounter is the larger grayer issue of personal relationships bumping up against coverage responsibilities. What if a reporter dates a former source, for instance?"[23]

SUPPLYING ETHICAL STANDARDS

Standards can be imposed through agreements among professionals to behave in certain ways and to punish certain behaviors. Ethical standards are upheld by educating professionals in moral reasoning processes that help individuals and organizations make decisions about how to handle specific situations.

Industry's Response

Media industries have tried to establish official positions that indicate their desire to increase credibility and avoid government regulation. Their responses have taken several forms, including establishing codes of ethics and ombudsman positions.

Codes of Ethics   Media organizations have established **codes of ethics** to standardize media behavior. Although critics argue that many of the codes are shallow, the code guidelines still serve as reminders that ethical standards are considered important for credibility, profitability, and the good of society.

The American Society of Newspaper Editors, in 1923, was the first national press association to draft an official code of ethics. Many news organizations did not adopt formal codes until the 1980s, when ethics became a hot topic for journalists. Instead of using ethics codes, some small news organizations have created firmly established verbal policies or guidelines set by precedent. Currently, the Society of Professional Journalists (SPJ), the Radio–Television News Directors Association (RTNDA), and the Public Relations Society of America (PRSA) are among prominent organizations that have formulated policies.[24] Figure 13.1 is the Society of Professional Journalists' Code of Ethics as revised in 1996.

In 1982, the television Code of Good Practice that the National Association of Broadcasters (NAB) had established was ruled unconstitutional by the Supreme Court. The industry code was seen as a violation of antitrust rules because the code required all broadcast bodies to be answerable to the same uniform policies.

National advertisers, public relations practitioners, filmmakers, TV program producers, and even **infomercial** producers have codes of ethics. These national policies serve primarily as voluntary guidelines for local member organizations. Some organizations simply follow the national or state code, or they modify the standard to fit their own news objectives and geographic areas. However, many media chains have lengthy written ethics policies that they expect their local affiliates to follow.

An organization's codes can be enforced in the same way as any other company policy. Adherence to the national codes is voluntary and cannot be enforced. Many professionals fear the adoption of mandatory codes, arguing that they would be used as the basis for lawsuits that would harm the media.

Ombudsmen   Another effort to enforce ethics originated at the *Louisville Courier-Journal and Times* in 1967, with the appointment of the first newspaper **ombudsman.** The primary function of the ombudsman is to represent the readers and to criticize the actions of the newspaper when the ombudsman believes it has done something wrong. An effective ombudsman will serve as the newspaper's conscience and help to ensure that readers and the community are served and that ethical standards are observed. The international Organization of News Ombudsmen maintains an active website, with information about the practice.

Critics' Response

By 1947, increased chain ownership of newspapers meant that fewer newspapers were independently owned. In the 1940s, the Hutchins Commission, which had been created by Henry Luce to analyze the impact of the modern press, addressed the issue

---

Key Concept

Code of ethics Many media organizations establish a code of ethics to standardize their employees' behavior in response to events and to safeguard themselves against increased government regulation. Guidelines remind employees that ethical standards are considered important to credibility, profit, and the good of society.

---

infomercial

A media message that offers consumer information.

ombudsman

A person within an organization who represents customers and investigates potentially unethical conduct of the organization and people within it.

Figure 13.1   Society of Professional Journalists: Code of Ethics

PREAMBLE

Members of the Society of Professional Journalists believe that public enlightenment is the forerunner of justice and the foundation of democracy. The duty of the journalist is to further those ends by seeking truth and providing a fair and comprehensive account of events and issues. Conscientious journalists from all media and specialties strive to serve the public with thoroughness and honesty. Professional integrity is the cornerstone of a journalist's credibility. Members of the Society share a dedication to ethical behavior and adopt this code to declare the Society's principles and standards of practice.

SEEK TRUTH AND REPORT IT

Journalists should be honest, fair and courageous in gathering, reporting and interpreting information.

JOURNALISTS SHOULD:

- Test the accuracy of information from all sources and exercise care to avoid inadvertent error. Deliberate distortion is never permissible.
- Diligently seek out subjects of news stories to give them the opportunity to respond to allegations of wrongdoing.
- Identify sources whenever feasible. The public is entitled to as much information as possible on sources' reliability.
- Always question sources' motives before promising anonymity. Clarify conditions attached to any promise made in exchange for information. Keep promises.
- Make certain that headlines, news teases and promotional material, photos, video, audio, graphics, sound bites and quotations do not misrepresent. They should not oversimplify or highlight incidents out of context.
- Never distort the content of news photos or video. Image enhancement for technical clarity is always permissible. Label montages and photo illustrations.
- Avoid misleading re-enactments or staged news events. If reenactment is necessary to tell a story, label it.
- Avoid undercover or other surreptitious methods of gathering information except when traditional open methods will not yield information vital to the public. Use of such methods should be explained as part of the story.
- Never plagiarize.
- Tell the story of the diversity and magnitude of the human experience boldly, even when it is unpopular to do so.
- Examine their own cultural values and avoid imposing those values on others.
- Avoid stereotyping by race, gender, age, religion, ethnicity, geography, sexual orientation, disability, physical appearance or social status.
- Support the open exchange of views, even views they find repugnant.
- Give voice to the voiceless; official and unofficial sources of information can be equally valid.
- Distinguish between advocacy and news reporting. Analysis and commentary should be labeled and not misrepresent fact or context.
- Distinguish news from advertising and shun hybrids that blur the lines between the two.

- Recognize a special obligation to ensure that the public's business is conducted in the open and that government records are open to inspection.

MINIMIZE HARM

Ethical journalists treat sources, subjects and colleagues as human beings deserving of respect.

JOURNALISTS SHOULD:

- Show compassion for those who may be affected adversely by news coverage. Use special sensitivity when dealing with children and inexperienced sources or subjects.
- Be sensitive when seeking or using interviews or photographs of those affected by tragedy or grief.
- Recognize that gathering and reporting information may cause harm or discomfort. Pursuit of the news is not a license for arrogance.
- Recognize that private people have a greater right to control information about themselves than do public officials and others who seek power, influence or attention. Only an overriding public need can justify intrusion into anyone's privacy.
- Show good taste. Avoid pandering to lurid curiosity.
- Be cautious about identifying juvenile suspects or victims of sex crimes.
- Be judicious about naming criminal suspects before the formal filing of charges.
- Balance a criminal suspect's fair trial rights with the public's right to be informed.

ACT INDEPENDENTLY

Journalists should be free of obligation to any interest other than the public's right to know.

JOURNALISTS SHOULD:

- Avoid conflicts of interest, real or perceived.
- Remain free of associations and activities that may compromise integrity or damage credibility.
- Refuse gifts, favors, fees, free travel and special treatment, and shun secondary employment, political involvement, public office and service in community organizations if they compromise journalistic integrity.
- Disclose unavoidable conflicts.
- Be vigilant and courageous about holding those with power accountable.
- Deny favored treatment to advertisers and special interests and resist their pressure to influence news coverage.
- Be wary of sources offering information for favors or money, avoid bidding for news.

BE ACCOUNTABLE

Journalists are accountable to their readers, listeners, viewers and each other.

JOURNALISTS SHOULD:

- Clarify and explain news coverage and invite dialogue with the public over journalistic conduct.
- Encourage the public to voice grievances against the news media.
- Admit mistakes and correct them promptly.
- Expose unethical practices of journalists and the news media.
- Abide by the same high standards to which they hold others.

Source: Sigma Delta Chi's first Code of Ethics was borrowed from the American Society of Newspaper Editors in 1926. In 1973, Sigma Delta Chi wrote its own code, which was revised in 1984 and 1987. The present version of the Society of Professional Journalists' Code of Ethics was adopted in September 1996. Reprinted by permission.

of chain-owned media. The commission feared that such media would not freely criticize themselves and recommended the establishment of news councils to counter this trend. In subsequent years, journalism reviews developed as another way of monitoring the press and its behaviors. Today, newspapers print news and editorial comment on press behavior.

News Councils   The Hutchins Commission recommended the establishment of **news councils,** which would hear complaints against news media, investigate each complaint, pass judgment on the complaint, and publicize the judgment.

During the 1950s and 1960s, several European countries, including Germany, England, and Sweden, established press councils. In 1972, a consortium of foundations started the Council on Press Responsibility and Press Freedom in the United States. It later became the National News Council, and its role was to investigate public complaints about national news organizations. Newspaper owners reacted to the News Council with the same vehemence they had shown the Hutchins Commission. The vast majority of newspapers did not support the News Council and criticized the very idea of an independent watchdog for news organizations. In 1984, the National News Council closed because of lack of money and support from the news media.

In 2006, two remaining state news councils in Minnesota and Washington began a grant program to encourage the formation of such councils to encourage fair coverage and promote credibility in the media.

Journalism Reviews   Only a small percentage of newspapers have ombudsmen, and news media have failed to support news councils, but another forum for criticizing media behavior exists: the journalism review. These publications report and analyze examples of ethical and unethical journalism. Three national reviews provide extensive criticism of the media: *Quill, American Journalism Review,* and *Columbia Journalism Review. Quill* is published by the Society of Professional Journalists; *American Journalism Review* is published by the University of Maryland College of Journalism, and *Columbia Journalism Review* is published by Columbia University.

Moral Reasoning Processes for Ethical Decisions

Codes of ethics are good for outlining standard practices and procedures, but they cannot take every situation into account. Media practitioners must go through a ***moral reasoning process*** to help them make decisions. Instead of simply saying that the decision "felt like the thing to do," professionals need to be able to articulate and justify why a decision was made. Journalists must be accountable.

Several ethical decision-making procedures and models have been developed to help professionals make ethical decisions. We will discuss four of them: (1) an ethical framework advanced by philosopher Sissela Bok; (2) a decision-making process designed by Roy Peter Clark of the Poynter Institute; (3) a values-oriented-series-of-questions approach advocated by media ethics expert H. Eugene Goodwin; and (4) the Potter Box. Not every model or every item within each model will be equally pertinent to every situation; however, decision makers should discuss each item.

Bok's ethical framework is based on three questions designed to help all types of professionals make ethical decisions. Each question is discussed in great detail in her book *Lying: Moral Choice in Public and Private Life:*[25]

1. How do you feel about the action? (Look inside yourself and have a talk with your conscience.)
2. Is there any other way to achieve the same goal that will not raise ethical issues? (Talk to others to find out what they would do. Or think about what a trusted friend or ancient philosopher would suggest.)

> **Key Concept**
>
> **Moral reasoning process**   Media ethicists have developed various moral reasoning processes that communication professionals can use to help them make ethical decisions from a principled basis rather than by reacting intuitively.

news council

A committee that reviews potentially unethical activities of news organizations.

3. How will my actions affect others? (Think about what readers, viewers, sources, and those affected by the story might feel or say.)

The moral reasoning model advanced by Roy Peter Clark of the Poynter Institute for Media Studies suggests that all journalists carefully examine their consciences before making deadline decisions. He offers five questions that should be answered before a story is published or broadcast:[26]

1. Is the story, photo, or graphic complete and accurate to the best of my knowledge?
2. Am I missing an important point of view?
3. How would I feel if this story or photo were about me?
4. What good will publication do?
5. What does my reader or viewer need to know?

Goodwin discusses his values-oriented approach in his book *Groping for Ethics in Journalism,* which he wrote after "becoming bothered by some of the things journalists and news media proprietors do. They do not always seem to have a strong sense of morality, of what is right and wrong." He recorded seven useful questions for successful teaching in journalism ethics and for working journalists:[27]

1. What do we usually do in cases like this? (Consider whether a policy for this situation has been established. Is it a good policy or does it need to be modified?)
2. Who will be hurt and who will be helped? (Recognize that most stories will hurt someone or some group. Weigh that hurt against benefits to the community. "Realizing who is apt to be hurt and whether the benefits can justify that hurt can help us make an intelligent decision.")
3. Are there better alternatives? (Think about all alternatives before making a decision. Harmful results often can be softened or eliminated by going a different route.)
4. Can I look at myself in the mirror again? (You must think about how you feel personally. Can you live with yourself afterward? James D. Squires, formerly of the *Chicago Tribune,* advised media people not to "do anything that your momma would be ashamed of.")
5. Can I justify this to other people and the public? (If you know that you will have to explain your decisions, in an editor's column or television newscast, for example, you are often more careful with your decisions.)
6. What principles or values can I apply? (Some established principles, such as truth, justice, or fairness, take priority over others.)
7. Is this decision appropriate for the kind of journalism I believe in; does it coincide with how people should treat one another? (Your judgments should correspond with the way you believe that media ought to act and how "people in a civilized society ought to behave.")

The Potter Box, constructed by Harvard philosopher and theologian Ralph Potter, is a sequence of four steps designed to help people reason their way to an ethical decision:[28]

1. Find out what happened.
2. Analyze the values.
3. Identify loyalties.
4. Look at the principles involved.

Sometimes the initial reaction to a set of circumstances is not the final judgment one reaches after progressing through facts, values, principles, and loyalties. The Potter Box is depicted in Figure 13.2.[29]

Stephen Ward, director of Journalism Ethics for the Global Citizen, has offered further considerations for covering global issues. Journalists should:

1. Act as global agents, informed by values of tolerance and diversity.
2. Serve the citizens of the world, avoiding factionalism and loyalty only to one's own community.
3. Promote nonparochial understandings that go beyond ethnocentrism and patriotism to provide broad, impartial coverage from a diversity of sources.[30]

Figure 13.2 Modified Potter Box

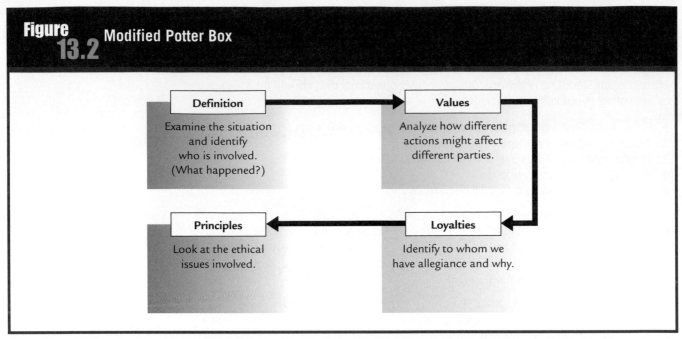

Source: The original version is described in Ralph B. Potter, "The Structure of Certain American Christian Responses to the Nuclear Dilemma, 1958–1963" (Ph.D. dissertation, Harvard University, 1965).

ETHICAL SITUATIONS AND DILEMMAS

Some situations are variations on common dilemmas. Because these dilemmas recur often, personnel in many news organizations have developed consistent ways of dealing with them.

Business and Media Content

Most media outlets are businesses, and many depend heavily, if not entirely, on advertising revenue, which often creates ethical dilemmas for people who create media content. Businesses can affect content in a variety of ways, but the most effective impact is created through advertising. Advertisers can withhold advertising in what is called an advertising boycott, or they may seek favorable treatment by buying advertising.

Businesses, religious groups, and civic activists have used advertising boycotts to try to persuade publishers to change their editorial stance. In January 1998, Harry Ashmore died. Ashmore was a civil rights writer who won a Pulitzer Prize for his editorials on desegregating Little Rock's Central High School. Ashmore's fame may have died before he did, but his experience is central to journalism in the United States. Ashmore edited the now-defunct *Arkansas Gazette* in 1957 when Arkansas Governor Orval E. Faubus ordered the National Guard to stop nine black students from entering Little Rock Central High School. Eisenhower sent in federal troops to counteract Faubus's action. Ashmore urged Little Rock's citizens to accept a desegregation plan, a plea that resulted in death threats, an advertising boycott, and a decline in circulation. In 1959, Ashmore left Little Rock.[31]

Just how advertising and business pressure affects content depends on the ethics of the individual journalists and media managers. Some managers give in to pressure more quickly than others, and some do not give in at all. Allowing advertisers to influence news and information has at least two dangers—one for consumers and one for the media companies. If consumers know that the information they receive represents a business's bias, they can take this into consideration when using that information. If they don't know, as may happen when media are influenced by advertisers, then they can be influenced to act in ways that may not be in their interest.

Decades ago, Heywood Campbell Broun gave journalists a motto to remember as they work in the marketplace of ideas: "For the truth, there is no deadline."

Broun, a prominent newspaper columnist during the 1920s and 1930s, showed perpetual concern for the underdog. Today, the Heywood Broun Award is given to select journalists who have helped right a wrong or correct an injustice.

Broun began writing for newspapers in 1908 and did not stop until his death in 1939. He wrote novels, political tracts, and pieces about sports and drama. He invented the newspaper column in which writers expressed opinions that could differ from those of the owners. His six columns a week rooted out injustices, and they were read by thousands of people who felt that he was their friend.

Broun was educated at Harvard University. From 1912 to 1920, he was a drama critic and then literary editor for the *New York Tribune.* He and his wife, Ruth Hale, whom he married in 1917, also spent time in Europe, he as a war correspondent and she as editor of a Paris-based edition of the *Chicago Tribune.*

In 1921, he began a daily column, "It Seems to Me," for the *New York World,* but in 1928 he was fired from the *World* because of his support for Italian anarchists Nicola Sacco and Bartolomeo Vanzetti, who were convicted of murder on

Heywood C. Broun

slight evidence but in an atmosphere of fear of anarchists.

Ruth Hale was the United States' first female movie critic, a reporter for the *New York Times,* and a drama critic for *Vogue.* This professionally successful couple led a somewhat tortured private life and after seventeen years of marriage were divorced, although they maintained what their son called a "special intimacy." Ruth Hale battled the State Department for the right to carry a passport bearing her name rather than her husband's, and she founded the Lucy Stone League, a group of women who championed the right to retain their birth names.

Broun ran for Congress as a Socialist in 1930. A few years later he became the founding president of the American Newspaper Guild. When he died in 1939, more than ten thousand people, some of them readers, attended his funeral. In 1941, two years after his death, the guild established the Heywood Broun Award for outstanding journalistic achievement that reflects "the spirit of Heywood Broun."

Sources: William Hunter, "In Bed with Broun, Star of the Liveliest Sheets," *The Herald* [Glasgow], March 14, 1995: 14; Mary Anne Ramer, "A PR Practitioner's Memo to Journalists," *Editor & Publisher,* October 10, 1992: 64; Joseph McLellan, "His Mother, His Father, Himself; Whose Little Boy Are You? *A Memoir of the Broun Family* by Heywood Hale Broun," *The Washington Post,* August 8, 1983, Book World: C8.

Freebies and Junkets

Until the 1980s, at least some people who worked in mass media took for granted that their low pay would be supplemented by **perks** such as gifts, free meals, and trips—freebies and junkets. These blatant handouts were among the first practices to be attacked as unethical. During the early 1900s, editors began to reject free railroad passes in return for advertising. But freebies persisted well into the 1990s, with sports reporters continuing to accept free rides to accompany teams on trips and movie reviewers accepting free movie passes. Most of these practices have now ceased, not only among journalists, but among public relations practitioners as well. One element of a respectful relationship between journalists and public relations professionals has been an acknowledgment that public relations is most effective when it is based on accurate and convincing information and that journalists can best act with integrity when they are not indebted to specific organizations or people. If journalists are accepting free trips, movie passes, or other perks, they are less likely to report a story with full objectivity.

Anonymous Attribution

The use of anonymous sources has long been problematic with journalists. Journalist Richard Blow said of them:

> They [anonymous sources] can say what they want without having to take responsibility if their information isn't accurate. Another problem is that for the subject of anonymous criticism, it's almost impossible to respond; knowing the source of an attack is often crucial to rebutting it.[32]

perk

Short for *perquisite,* or payment for something in addition to salary.

Bloggers' Ethics

In the Internet world of blogging, ethical issues abound. A central question is whether bloggers who offer serious news should be held to the same standards as other journalists. Furthermore, newspapers have gotten into the business of blogging, prompting discussion of the roles and responsibilities of journalist bloggers.

These cases illustrate the challenges:

- Several conservative bloggers who had supported Wal-Mart received press releases from Wal-Mart's public relations firm, Edelman, offering them tips, information, and invitations to tour the company's headquarters. Some bloggers simply copied the press releases into their blogs, without attribution, igniting questions about bloggers' independence and ethics, especially concerning plagiarism.
- The *Los Angeles Times* closed down Pulitzer Prize–winning journalist Michael Hiltzik's blog after it found that Hiltzik used pseudonyms to post to his own and other blogs. The paper said that its ethics policy "requires editors and reporters to identify themselves when dealing with the public."

- A student at the University of Oklahoma killed himself by setting off a bomb outside the stadium where 85,000 people were watching the game. Rumors quickly spread among bloggers that the students was a suicide bomber who had intended to blow up the stadium. Local television stations repeated their speculations. The FBI found no connection to terrorism, and some journalists condemned the bloggers for spreading stories without fact-checking.

While many bloggers reject the idea of a formal code of ethics, especially from an external authority, others argue that bloggers have a responsibility to standards like fairness, accuracy, honesty, accountability, and transparency. Several websites offer codes of ethics for bloggers, including CyberJournalist.net and Microcontentnews.com.

Sources: Steve Yahn and Jake Whitney, "Defending Blogs," *Editor & Publisher,* August 2006: 20–25; Michael Barbaro, "Wal-Mart Enlists Bloggers in Its Public Relations Campaign," *New York Times,* March 7, 2006: C1; Cathy Young, "Smears in Cyberspace," *Reason* 37 (2006): 19–20.

A survey of 419 newspaper editors by the Associated Press Managing Editors (APME) in 2005 found that one in four newspapers do not allow their reporters to use anonymous sources. Most other newspapers have strict guidelines so that reporters must have a very compelling case for including an unnamed source.[33] A recent controversy involved a *New York Times* reporter, Judith Miller. Miller refused to reveal the name of a source—the Vice President's chief of staff—who leaked the identity of a CIA agent. Miller was imprisoned for eighty-five days, provoking debate over whether laws should protect journalists from divulging their sources. Released from jail in September 2005, Miller announced her retirement from the *New York Times* two months later.

Journalists admit to abuses, but argue that some stories could not be reported without protection of anonymity. Marshall Loeb, a columnist for *CBS Market Watch* and former editor of *Columbia Journalism Review,* said, "In reporting, there is a tension between using named sources and anonymous sources. But I've spent most of my life covering business, and you can't get a story about corporate abuse without granting your source anonymity."

Checkbook Journalism

News organizations, both broadcast and print, sometimes pay sources for story ideas and information. In the past, such **checkbook journalism** occurred mostly in entertainment, but with the lines blurring between news and entertainment, journalistic standards quickly can take a backseat. ABC paid the $25,000 bill for Monica Lewinsky's lawyer so he would persuade special prosecutor Kenneth Starr's office to let Lewinsky be interviewed by Barbara Walters in March 1999.[34] ABC also paid a friend of one of the Columbine killers $16,000 for videotapes and photographs of the killer. The material aired on *Good Morning America* in 1999, a week after the friend, Nathan

checkbook journalism

Paying subjects or witnesses for information or interviews.

Dykeman, appeared for an interview. ABC has a policy against paying for interviews but will pay for newsworthy images. An ABC spokesperson said the network did not know the visual material existed when Dykeman was first interviewed.[35] Similarly, Michael Jackson was not directly paid for an interview on CBS' *60 Minutes,* but the network promised him $1 million for an entertainment special, raising questions about CBS' ethics.[36]

Most incidents of paying for news content reflect the need to attract audience in order to sell advertisements. This emphasis on profit, wrote Stuart Loory of the *Kansas City Star,* puts "hard news into the same category as major-league sports as a profit center and throws the whole purpose of news presentation—information for consumers versus profit for disseminators—into question."[37]

Privacy versus People's Need to Know

Many media professionals believe that there are times when the public's right to know takes precedence over the **right of privacy** of an individual. When does information change from news to voyeurism? Is it necessary to watch a woman cry on television about the death of her spouse? Is it important to write that the man who rescued a drowning child was also gay? When should journalists report that a political candidate has been unfaithful to a spouse? Although some reporters believe that personal life has nothing to do with business or politics, others think that personal actions illuminate character. A candidate who breaks a solemn vow to someone as important as his or her spouse might also break promises to constituents. The question here is whether the account serves a public interest. What constitutes "the public's right to know" is an ethical question that media workers and the public share.

Public figures are not given as much consideration as private citizens. Public figures such as politicians or movie stars deliberately place themselves in the limelight and know that their lives and movements will be constantly scrutinized by the press. However, the relationship between celebrities and the press is not always harmonious. When Brad Pitt and Angelina Jolie went to Namibia to have their baby, the Namibian government cooperated in providing security and creating a "paparazzi-free" environment for them. A no-fly zone was set up, and some journalists had their cameras confiscated and were even deported because they lacked approval from Pitt and Jolie.[38]

While celebrities must expect intrusiveness, private citizens have indirectly attracted publicity. Since they haven't courted the limelight, they have more right to privacy. Therefore, ethical journalists look at whether someone is a private citizen or a public figure when considering whether to include potentially harmful images or information about that person.

Sensationalism, Decency, and Good Taste

Some material, especially visual information, will always be more offensive to some viewers than others. **Sensationalism**—the use of material merely to shock, startle, or violate a person's sense of decency—may attract attention, but it is not newsworthy.

Stanley Forman, a photojournalist for the Boston *Herald-American,* took several photos of a young woman and little girl standing on a fire escape about to be rescued from a burning building. Suddenly, the fire escape collapsed, and Forman took dramatic pictures of the two falling. Although the woman died, newspapers all over the world published the photos, and Forman was awarded a Pulitzer Prize. But, as mass media educator Fred Fedler noted, readers "accused the newspapers of sensationalism: of poor taste, insensitivity, an invasion of the victims' privacy, and a tasteless display of human tragedy to sell newspapers."[39]

The realism of images can create controversy, as it did with video and photographic images from 9/11.[40] Many people, including some of the family members of

right of privacy

An ethical and legal area of decision making. The right to be protected from unwaranted intrusion by the government, media, or other institutions or individuals.

Court cases involving celebrities, such as Michael Jackson, can create a media frenzy and descend into sensationalism.

those who died in the attacks, objected to the use of graphic images on the anniversary of the terrorist attacks. In particular, people did not want to see scenes of people jumping or falling from the World Trade Towers or the towers collapsing. Defenders of using the images argued that people need to know about the horrors of terrorism if the United States is to maintain its resolve to fight it.

However, some journalists and media analysts have pointed out that terrorists exploit the news media's attraction to sensationalism. Mark Bowden, national correspondent for the *Atlantic Monthly*, explains: "What disturbs me is the way terrorists use sensationalism to vastly amplify their message. They know that horror and drama capture the media's attention, so they manufacture them."[41]

Sensationalism can distort serious thought and debate about crucial issues. For example, researchers at the Institute for Public Policy Research, a progressive think tank in London, studied 600 news articles, 40 television and radio news reports and advertisements, and 30 press advertisements on global warming. They found that many were alarmist, presenting global warming as "awesome, terrible, and immense and beyond human control." The authors concluded that this kind of sensational coverage, which they called "climate porn," might cause detachment and despair that leads to inaction in reducing carbon emissions.[42]

Reporting on crime investigations and disasters can lead to sensational reporting that may harm people. During the Hurricane Katrina disaster, some reporters presented a portrait of violence and mayhem. Rumors were perpetuated in the news, such as the exaggerated claim that ten thousand people were dead, that rape and murder were rampant, and that bodies were piled up in the Convention Center's freezer. Such stories overlooked the real plight and humanity of the victims. Many were ignored, such as Hispanic and Asian residents of New Orleans and people outside of the city. However, a move to avoid sensationalism raised questions when FEMA asked reporters not to photograph the bodies of the victims. Communications professors Karen Slattery and Erik Ugland write, "Properly covered, elements or images that are normally associated with sensationalism but are central to the story can stimulate debate and lead to better social and political practices."[43] A big question is what does or does not constitute sensationalism, especially in covering crimes and disasters.

Concern about sensational media coverage and images remains an international concern. It has been an ongoing concern in Great Britain for decades because their tabloid newspapers continue the types of coverage popularized by Hearst and Pulitzer during the "yellow journalism" period. Codes of ethics from such countries as Macedonia, Pakistan, Peru, Portugal, Tanzania, Bangladesh, and Thailand have strictures against sensational reporting.[44]

Direct Quotations

Quote marks signify the exact words of a source. However, research shows that media professionals do not agree on the practice of quoting bad grammar, cursing, ramblings, and accents.[45] Nor do they agree on when a quote should be edited. For example, cursing might be edited out of a quote from a student but left untouched in one from a ball player or politician (or the other way around, depending on the subject). If a quotation has to be changed, it should be paraphrased, using indirect or partial quotations. Journalists almost universally denounce making up quotes, even if they are based on notes and represent a partial reconstruction of what the person might have said.

Correction of Errors

Media sometimes publish or broadcast inaccurate information, yet often the public is never notified of the inaccuracy. When was the last time a network news anchor admitted a mistake was made the previous night? While covering the September 11 attacks, the networks produced live reports and inevitably broadcast a variety of mistakes while trying to be first with the news. Most of these mistakes were never identified or addressed. Instead, more accurate news was broadcast in a followup story.

Newspapers are usually better than magazines, television, and radio about rectifying errors. However, readers rarely know where to look for corrections because notifications are not a standard practice. When a correction is made, it is usually published on an inside page, not in a prominent position. Some newspapers, such as the *Chicago Tribune,* either place corrections at the same location as the original story or put the corrections in the same location every day.

Fiction and Fact

When real-life events provide the basis for entertainment, audiences are often confronted with a mix of fact and fiction. Docudramas and creative reenactments mix documentary techniques and dramatic action: they make great viewing. But they often blur the lines between fact and fiction in such a compelling way that viewers may remember the visual representation as history even if it distorts historical realities.

Most historians are not worried so much by small factual errors as they are by broad misinterpretations of history, especially the glamorization of figures like Alexander the Great, Benedict Arnold, and Pontius Pilate. They also are concerned by events taken out of context, so that audiences never know what social and political currents helped create them. Military historian Lawrence Suid has compiled a five-page list of errors in the movie *Pearl Harbor,* but his greatest concern is that "audiences will come away from the film with no real understanding of what happened and why."[46] The filmmaker's interpretation becomes murkier when little evidence exists as to what really happened, as in Paul Greengrass's *United 93* and Steven Spielberg's *Munich,* which recreate terrorist attacks.

A distorted history can have consequences, especially if it affects the traditions and beliefs of a people. *The Patriot,* directed by Roland Emmerich and starring Mel Gibson,

The Catholic Church has criticized the international bestseller, *The Da Vinci Code*, for historical inaccuracies in its portrayal of Biblical figures, such as Mary Magdalene.

The Danish Cartoons

Twelve cartoons in a provincial Danish newspaper on September 30, 2005 caused an ethical crisis for many editors worldwide. The newspaper, *Jyllands-Posten,* had commissioned cartoons of the Prophet Muhammad to test the limits of freedom of expression. Many, though not all, Muslims feel that representations of Muhammad constitute blasphemy, and consider the publication of the cartoons an insult. In January 2005, after some Danish Muslims had taken news of the cartoons to the Middle East, mass demonstrations erupted throughout the Arab and Muslim world. Some turned violent, leading to a number of deaths and the burning of Danish embassies.

Several major newspapers and magazines in Europe, including Germany's *Die Welt,* Italy's *La Stampa,* and Spain's *El Periódico de Catalunya,* published the offending cartoons, upholding freedom of speech as the reason. For some editors, the decision had repercussions. They were either fired, as was *France-Soir's* editor in chief, or forced to apologize, as did *Rzeczpospolita's* editor in chief in Poland.

In the United States, a State Department spokesperson spoke in defense of religious tolerance and called for press responsibility. Most major newspapers in the country, as well as in Britain, decided not to print the cartoons; however, two editors of the campus newspaper, the *Daily Illini,* were suspended for doing so.

Attempts at parodying the cartoon controversy also ran into trouble. The American Family Association launched a campaign of protest against an alternative newspaper, the *Insurgent,* at the University of Oregon that printed cartoons of a sexualized Jesus. The University president, David Frohnmayer, upheld the paper's right to free speech, provoking Bill O'Reilly, on his national television show, to demand that Frohnmayer be fired. Similarly, against strong protest, the University of Toronto's president supported the decision by its student newspaper to publish a cartoon representing Jesus and Muhammad kissing.

South Park's creators, Matt Stone and Trey Parker, faced censorship when they tried to parody the Danish cartoons, and Comedy Central executives would not allow them to caricature Muhammad. Stone and Parker retaliated by including satires of the censorship in two episodes, pointing out that Comedy Central had allowed parodies of Jesus, but not of Muhammad.

The main debate over the Danish cartoons was between the need for cultural sensitivity and the value of free speech in a networked world where images can spread rapidly. Hundreds of publications commented on the events, even if they decided not to publish the cartoons. Cochairman of the Society of Professional Journalists Ethics Committee, Fred Brown, gives guidelines for how journalists might cover such a story ethically. He advises journalists to do the reporting, assembling the facts, describing the situation, and posing the ethical dilemma. They should try to account for all differences of opinion and pose every possible question that might be relevant. Then, they must take into account all the people who might be affected. They should establish the principles for their decision: "Is it freedom of expression? Or is it unnecessary provocation? Is there an acceptable middle ground between showing the blunt truth and minimizing the harm of insult?" What's important, Brown says, is that such decisions be guided by serious discussions and solid reasons.

Sources: Svenning Dalgaard, "The Right to Offend: The Causes and Consequences of the 'Danish Cartoon Affair,'" *RUSI Journal,* April 2006: 28–33; Duncan Currie, "The Cartoon Wars Are Over," *Weekly Standard,* May 1, 2006: 14–15; "Success Stories," *Newsletter on Intellectual Freedom,* July 2006: 211–212; Fred Brown, "Share Your Ethical Cases So Everyone Can Learn," *Quill,* August 2006: 40.

outraged the British press because of its portrayal of atrocities during the American Revolution. In one scene, British soldiers burn down a church containing screaming women and children, a wild inaccuracy. Similarly, Tony Blair publicly objected to the film *U-571* that showed Americans recovering the Enigma code-breaking machine instead of the British. The screenwriter admitted that he had purposely changed history to appeal to an American audience.[47] Many Catholics were angered by the account of Jesus' life as presented in Dan Brown's book, *The Da Vinci Code,* which was made into a film. The Conference of Catholic Bishops set up a webpage (jesusdecoded.com/truthbetold8 .php) with a checklist of the movie's errors.

Screenwriters and directors argue that in filmmaking, drama is more important than history. However, the question remains as to how much alteration is permissible, whether the audience should be notified of deliberate distortions, and whether makers of docudramas need to be responsible to the legacies of others.

TRENDS

Technology: Protecting Privacy Online

One of the greatest concerns about digital technologies is that they increase the potential for surveillance and violations of privacy. Ethically, media professionals must protect sensitive information, such as personal information about audiences, that may be kept in their databases. In 2006, AOL's release of 658,000 users' search histories led to severe criticism. Many electronic privacy advocates complained that the company had not asked users' permission before making very sensitive data available to the public. AOL retracted the data and apologized for its ill-considered actions.

Protection of confidential information has become a big issue for journalists facing possible surveillance of their e-mail and phone records by the National Security Agency and the Department of Justice. Under the USA Patriot Act, the FBI can request such information from phone companies, which must keep these requests secret. In May 2006, two ABC reporters discovered that the FBI had looked at their phone records searching for sources as part of a leak investigation.[48] Advocates for freedom of the press argue that these measures stand in the way of the press' watchdog role, while government officials defend surveillance as necessary to the war on terrorism.

Chat on the Internet has also led to questions related to journalism and privacy. Surreptitiously lurking on the Internet generally violates the ethical standard to "avoid undercover or other surreptitious methods of gathering information when traditional open methods will not yield information vital to the public."[49] In Spokane, Washington, the editor of the *Spokesman-Review* decided to send a forensic computer expert into a chatroom disguised as an eighteen-year-old gay man. His object was to verify reports that the city's mayor, Jim West, was using his position to gain sexual favors. When the newspaper published its report, including all documents related to the case, on its website, West was recalled from office. Some journalists questioned the *Spokesman-Review's* methods, but the paper won a 2006 Payne Award for Ethics in Journalism for its "careful consideration of ethical issues and transparency in explaining its decision-making process, both in the paper and on its website."[50]

Culture: Objectivity in Journalism

Trends in ethics depend on changes in economic structures of media institutions, including increased competition and targeting of niche audiences. As media companies compete for readers, viewers, and listeners in a fast-paced environment, organizations are tempted to emphasize sensational content and lower their ethical standards. Some journalists see unsubstantiated opinion and emotional storytelling, often featuring disease and murder, as negative trends at the expense of serious news. Others point to the role of commercialism and pressures from profit-driven management as influences on a downward trend. The Society of Professional Journalists made this point when they awarded their 2006 Ethics in Journalism Award to nine former employees of the *Santa Barbara News-Press.* They had quit their jobs because the publisher had allegedly interfered with editorial content to protect her friends, most notably the actor Rob Lowe, who was involved in a controversy over building a mansion in the area.

Taking advantage of the interactive capabilities of digital technologies, an increasingly participatory audience has challenged the power of media institutions, including their gatekeeping role. This challenge has led to a host of unresolved ethical issues, such as to what extent citizen journalists and other media producers, outside of institutions, are beholden to traditional ethical standards. News organizations, especially, defend their social importance by pointing out their reportorial skills, including objectivity and accuracy. But the media landscape has changed dramatically to allow a greater diversity of voices, more ways to gather and disseminate information, and new ways to

During times of economic and technological change and political crisis, pressures on media organizations and journalists can increase. Media must provide information that is profitable but doesn't compromise their ethics or the security of the country. As competition for attention increases, ethical standards can become even shakier. This leads to a range of complex questions that can test individual and organizational ethics:

- How can a news organization provide truthful, balanced, and fair coverage of a community with shrinking newsroom budgets?
- Should citizen journalists be expected to uphold the same standards?
- Will the need to attract audience in TV news outweigh the desire to maintain ethics in an increasingly fragmented industry?
- When is it acceptable to conduct a surreptitious news investigation?

- Should freedom of speech outweigh cultural sensitivity, and if so, when?
- How can self-criticism within news media help police unethical behavior?

Equally difficult will be covering a war on terrorism and maintaining balanced reporting and ethical behavior.

- In wartime, should news media continue to provide balanced and fair reporting of all sides?
- Should news media fight for individuals' rights as government aims to increase security and curtail the flow of information?
- How can the public and news media differentiate between issues of national security and efforts by government to hide its mistakes?
- To what extent should the news media cooperate with government demands that they reveal their sources?

generate multimedia content.[51] Since the late 1990s, media organizations, such as the Society of Professional Journalists and the Poynter Institute, have tried to develop or adapt codes of ethics to accommodate these changes, while upholding the principles of fairness, balance, and accuracy.

SUMMARY

- Media ethics are important because citizens rely heavily on media to make informed decisions in a democratic framework and because media credibility is necessary to attract and keep an audience.
- Ethical behavior has political and economic implications.
- In the nineteenth century, editors were criticized for trivializing the news when they printed material about the details of people's lives.
- Standards for ethical behavior vary within and across cultures.
- The increasing volume and complexity of information in the early twentieth century led to the development of professional public relations practitioners whose task was to get a client the best possible hearing for a legitimate message.
- If media organizations do not regulate themselves (with standards of good taste and decency), then government is more likely to impose regulations.

- Five classical positions for understanding modern ethical dilemmas include the principles of (1) the Golden Mean, (2) the categorical imperative, (3) utility, (4) the veil of ignorance, and (5) the Judeo-Christian ethic.
- Accuracy, fairness, balance, and accurate representation are fundamental ethical standards accepted by most professional communicators. Objectivity is a basic value of most journalists.
- Some media organizations joined together to support the National News Council, but it lacked support throughout the industry; other organizations have hired ombudsmen to act as internal critics.
- Industry ethics codes are used as guidelines for media professionals. Adherence is voluntary. Many local media operations have devised their own codes, enforcing adherence in the same way that other company policies are enforced.

- Although many media organizations follow a code of ethics, such codes are not enough. Individuals need to develop a process of moral reasoning and understand ethical issues at all levels to articulate and justify the reasons behind their decisions and actions.

- The rise of citizen journalists and new media have posed new questions concerning ethics.
- Business and government attempt to shape the news for their own interests.

NAVIGATING THE WEB Ethics

Ethics-related websites provide information about ethics in the United States and in the world. These sites may include journalistic codes of ethics, reports from think tanks, and journalism magazine articles that discuss ethical issues.

AJR NewsLink
ajr.org
AJR NewsLink is the online version of the *American Journalism Review*. Maintained by the University of Maryland College of Journalism, this site provides articles and links about journalism performance.

Fairness and Accuracy in Reporting (FAIR)
fair.org
FAIR is a liberal media watch group that criticizes media for their biased coverage of minorities, women, and labor. FAIR's site provides reports and a variety of links.

The Media Institute
mediainstitute.org
As a conservative think tank that criticizes media, lobbies Congress about media policy, and supports deregulating media, The Media Institute's site provides articles and reports.

Poynter Online
poynter.org
The Poynter Institute for Media Studies is a nonpartisan, nonprofit organization that studies media ethics, management, and graphics. It conducts seminars on a variety of these topics.

Society of Professional Journalists
spj.org
SPJ was founded by Sigma Delta Chi in 1909 to promote ethical behavior and freedom of the press.

QUESTIONS FOR REVIEW

1. Why did social responsibility replace the libertarian philosophy as the basis for the U.S. press system?
2. Under what conditions can profit affect news credibility?
3. Why is accuracy a basic element of most communication ethics?
4. What types of impact can business and government have on media content?

ISSUES TO THINK ABOUT

1. How might questionable ethics, such as doctored photographs, affect the way people think about news? What could news departments do about this?
2. How might media organizations be forced to behave ethically? What drawbacks would this method create?
3. What can companies and organizations do if they think the news media are not being fair and balanced in their coverage?
4. How do personal ethics affect professional ethics?
5. Do you use a moral reasoning process in making decisions? How would you describe that process?
6. How would you go about writing a code of ethics for a news organization in the digital age? Who would you consult about what should be in the code?
7. How are ethical and legal problems similar? How are they different?

SUGGESTED READINGS

Christians, Clifford G., et al. *Media Ethics: Cases and Moral Reasoning,* 6th ed. (New York: Longman, 2002).

Jaksa, James A., and Michael S. Pritchard. *Communication Ethics: Methods of Analysis* (Belmont, CA: Wadsworth, 1988).

Jacquette, Dale. *Journalistic Ethics: Moral Responsibility in the Media* (New York: Prentice Hall, 2006).

Lynch, Dianne, ed. *Stand! Virtual Ethics: Debating Media Values in a Digital Age* (Boulder, CO: Coursewise Publishing, 1999).

Meyer, Philip. *The Vanishing Newspaper: Saving Journalism in the Information Age* (Columbia, MO: University of Missouri Press, 2004).

Regulation

During the MTV-produced 2004 Super Bowl halftime show, while singing *Rock Your Body,* Justin Timberlake reached over and ripped off part of Janet Jackson's leather bustier. For a second, Jackson's breast, with a metal star ornament, was exposed to 90 million television viewers, many of whom didn't quite catch it. The scene was replayed a record number of times on TiVos, and "Janet Jackson" became the most used search term on the Internet.

The singers, CBS, and MTV all apologized for the incident, which Timberlake called a "wardrobe malfunction." Timberlake and Jackson claimed that only Jackson's red lace bra was supposed to have been exposed. Officials at the FCC, which received over 500,000 complaints about the incident, were skeptical. Though CBS continues to disavow any prior knowledge of a plan to expose Jackson's breast, the FCC slapped the network with a $550,000 fine.

The breast-baring incident focused much public attention on broadcast indecency, which the FCC defines as "language or material that, in context, depicts or describes, in terms patently offensive as measured by contemporary community standards for the broadcast medium, sexual or excretory organs or activities." The debate over indecency and federal regulation is nothing new, stemming back to the Radio Act of 1927. But since the 1980s, indecency has become a central concern of the U.S. Congress and the FCC.

KEY CONCEPTS

- Regulatory Concept
- 1996 Telecommunications Act
- Freedom of Expression
- Balancing Theory
- Competition Benefits Consumers
- Direct Telecommunications Regulation
- Fairness Doctrine
- Business Regulation
- Content Regulation
- Controlling Obscenity and Indecency
- Chilling Effect
- Control of Media Content during War
- Libel and Slander
- Voluntary Rating System

Arguing for self-regulation, broadcasters say that they have little guidance from the FCC in determining what is indecent or profane and that the rules are unconstitutionally vague, unevenly applied, and obsolete. Family values groups, like the Parents' Television Council, continue to urge the FCC to uphold stricter rules against indecency and Congress to broaden FCC oversight to include all media platforms such as cell phones. Cultural critics point to the sexism directed at women's breasts, a "danger zone, a territory that authority must control and restrict." A student e-mailed a basic question to the Media Guy, Simon Dumenco, of *Advertising Age:* "Does the FCC or anyone in particular actually gain anything by placing all these restrictions on what we watch?"[1]

The issue of who loses and who gains freedom is at the heart of regulation. Whenever people interact, conflicts arise. Ethics and social norms provide standards for behavior, but they have no formal power of enforcement. Some entity must balance the rights of individuals against those of society. Ultimately, governments determine which behaviors will be punished as illegal and the form of punishment that will be applied. Therefore, regulation—the process of enforcing rules that mediate societal conflicts—occurs in all societies.

Because of the media's potential for changing society and harming individuals, media content and the behavior of people who work in the media are regulated throughout the world. A person in the United States cannot legally start broadcasting without permission from the federal government. A Chinese journalist can be sentenced to jail for criticizing the government. The degree of speech and press freedoms varies from country to country, but in no country is it absolute.

The issues surrounding regulation are always complex because they involve the rights of society versus the rights of individuals and they must cope with changing technologies and changing economic factors. Some of the issues addressed in this chapter include the following:

- As new technologies develop and channels of information proliferate, what justifications will be used to regulate new technologies? Will these be legitimate bases for regulation, or will they merely serve political or economic purposes?

- As electronic delivery of information increases throughout the world, how will governments regulate this activity, which freely crosses national boundaries?

- How does regulation achieve a balance between the right of free expression and societal concerns about media depictions of violence and sexual activity?

- Are journalists' right to access compatible with individuals' rights to privacy and freedom from libel?

- Who receives First Amendment protection in the United States and who does not?

- How will the need to control information during war affect individual rights of expression?

REGULATION IN AMERICAN LIFE

Although few people dispute a government's right to regulate, nearly everyone disagrees about what the regulation should cover. The founders of the United States, fearing that government officials would exercise arbitrary power, created the Bill of Rights to protect citizens from government encroachment on private affairs and to promote the concept that government is by consent of its citizens.

Regulation in Your Life

Freedom and Restraint

As you read this chapter, think about how free speech has been restrained at different times in society. Can you think of some examples that might enrich a discussion of how free speech is important to your life as a student? As you think about your own examples of restrictions on freedom of speech, would you say they fit into the five categories listed below? Or do they fit into other categories?

Why Governments Regulate	Examples of Restrictions
Economic reasons	
Product or company has negative impact on society as a whole	
Product or company has negative impact on individuals that outweighs benefits to society	
Preservation of security during war	
Preservation of government's power	
Other	

Reasons for Regulation

In the United States, the *regulatory concept* is widely accepted. Federal, state, and local governments use regulatory power for five reasons.

1. *Government regulates when people or organizations interfere with the workings of the economic market system.* The United States has a **market economy** based on two assumptions: that competition works best for society and that unfair business practices must not be allowed to reduce competition. Competition has been favored because it is believed to force companies to respond to the demands of the public and keep prices low. Theoretically, the company that produces the best product at the lowest price will continue in business.

Even though competition does not always provide immediate benefits to media consumers, the federal government assumes that in most situations competition is better than monopoly. Such was the assumption when the courts broke the AT&T monopoly in 1984. AT&T, the giant telephone monopoly, was stifling competition for long-distance services and making monopoly profits through high prices. The largest company in the world at the time, AT&T was forced to split its local telephone services among seven independent regional operating systems called Baby Bells. It continued to provide long-distance service, competing against providers such as MCI and Sprint, and could enter into unregulated enterprises.

Key Concept

Regulatory concept Regulation is designed to maintain a balance between the needs and rights of the society as a whole and the needs and rights of individuals. Therefore, government legitimately may regulate mass media to ensure that their behavior does not have an impact on society that outweighs their contributions to society.

market economy

An economy in which the interaction of supply and demand determines the prices of goods and services and the levels of production. In a nonmarket economy, government determines prices and production.

AT&T split its companies into AT&T, AT&T Wireless and AT&T Broadband. As a result of the **1996 Telecommunications Act**, Comcast acquired AT&T Broadband, forming the largest cable company. In the climate of deregulation and consolidation, one of the Baby Bells, Southwestern Bell, became SBC. It acquired AT&T and another Baby Bell, BellSouth, in 2005, renamed itself AT&T, and continued with plans to expand its empire into WiFi, digital subscriber lines (DSL), and satellite TV. Thus, AT&T seemed to be gathering itself back together.

Key Concept

1996 Telecommunications Act This landmark legislation represented the first major revamping of federal telecommunications legislation since the Federal Communications Act was passed in 1934. An attempt to increase competition through deregulation, the act included provisions that applied to radio, broadcast and cable television, the Internet, and telecommunications equipment manufacturing.

2. *Government regulates when the use of a product or an industry or company's behavior has a negative impact on society as a whole.* The ongoing struggle between the tobacco industry and the government illustrates this point. By the early 1950s, the U.S. medical community was convinced that cigarettes posed serious health hazards for the public. The tobacco industry responded with a public relations and advertising effort that clouded the issue and sought to minimize health problems related to smoking.[2] In 1964 the U.S. Surgeon General pronounced publicly that cigarettes cause cancer. Seven years later, Congress passed legislation prohibiting radio and television from carrying cigarette advertising. The federal and state governments have taken several regulatory steps to control smoking, including banning and controlling smoking in public places.

The ability of tobacco companies to influence policy declined in 1997 when the cigarette manufacturer Liggett Group released about 175 boxes of internal documents to state prosecutors as part of a lawsuit settlement. Liggett admitted that company executives knew cigarettes were habit forming and caused cancer, something tobacco companies had denied for decades.

Despite the settlement of a class action lawsuit by forty states against the tobacco industry and calls from lawmakers that cigarettes be regulated, smoking continues to threaten the lives of millions of Americans. The fact that cigarettes have not been banned entirely illustrates the influence of powerful and wealthy industries over government regulation.

3. *Government regulates when a product or behavior has a negative impact on individuals that outweighs its contribution to society as a whole.* Laws concerning privacy, libel, and slander are examples of this form of regulation. In 1942, *Time* published a story about Dorothy Barber, a woman who ate constantly but still lost weight, calling her a "starving glutton." She sued, and the courts ruled for Mrs. Barber, arguing that the hospital was one place you should be able to go for privacy. Her disease, rather unusual at the time, is now more widely known as anorexia nervosa.

A journalist cannot enter a person's house carrying hidden cameras and microphones. When a *Life* magazine journalist and a photographer did this for an article called "Crackdown in Quackery," *Life* was sued for invasion of privacy and lost. The courts ruled that the journalist's entry into A. A. Dietemann's home was an illegal intrusion of privacy even though he was practicing a questionable form of medicine in his home.[3]

4. *Government regulates the flow of information during times of war.* Unrestricted publication and broadcasting could endanger the lives of U.S. troops and could affect the outcome of battles and wars. **Censorship** during war is not mentioned in the Constitution, but courts have supported the government's right to censor ever since the Civil War.

The exact relationship between the press and government during war remains unsettled. Because the Vietnam conflict was never declared a war, formal censorship was never invoked. Since that time, the federal government tried to regulate the media in war by creating **press pools** and by limiting access.

The relationship between the press and the government in wartime became even more complicated when the war was expanded to a worldwide battle against terrorist threats. The Patriot Act of 2001 gave the U.S. Justice Department broadened

censorship

Restriction of access to information; deletion of information from a story; or refusal to let a correspondent mail, broadcast, or otherwise transmit a story.

press pool

A small group of reporters selected to gather information and pass it on to the larger group of press people. Used when the number of reporters gathering in one spot is problematic.

Some countries strictly regulate advertising of potentially harmful products, such as cigarettes, while others are more tolerant.

powers of search and seizure, affecting both individual rights and journalists' access to information. In 2006, revelations that the National Security Agency (NSA) had eavesdropped on citizens' phone records and e-mail without a warrant led to an outcry against the government's abuses of power during wartime. Seventeen lawsuits were brought against U.S. telephone companies, including AT&T and Verizon, claiming that they had released phone records to the NSA.

5. *Government seeks to preserve its own security and power.* Government officials sometimes try to regulate information for illegitimate reasons, to avoid political embarrassment, or to hide illegal activities. Most citizens and journalists would argue that using government laws to avoid embarrassment is an improper use of political power. Two important events came about primarily because citizens, journalists, and the U.S. courts agreed that government officials' use of laws to avoid embarrassment is a misuse of political power: the overturn of the Alien and Sedition Acts and the resignation of President Nixon. The Alien and Sedition Acts, passed in 1798 by a Federalist-controlled Congress, allowed the government to imprison and fine its critics. Representative Matthew Lyon was imprisoned for four months and fined $1,000 for suggesting that President John Adams's administration had "an unbounded thirst for ridiculous pomp, foolish adulation, and selfish avarice."[4] Congress overturned these acts after only two years. Two historic clashes in the early 1970s between the press and President Nixon illustrate cover-up efforts by a U.S. president. The first was the battle between the press and the government over the Pentagon Papers, which are historical documents chronicling the Vietnam conflict. The second was the Watergate affair. Both involved an attempt by government to withhold information because it would be personally (or governmentally) embarrassing.

In the Pentagon Papers case, major newspapers published government documents that they believed had been misclassified, and they were vindicated by the Supreme Court. The government's ability to hide information legally had not been destroyed, but it had been significantly damaged. The term *Watergate* applies to a wide range of illegal and unethical behavior by the Nixon White House during his re-election campaign in 1972. These activities included disruption of Democratic campaign activities, burglary, wiretapping, and taking illegal campaign contributions. Nixon and his advisers got even further into trouble when they tried to cover up their activities as the Senate held hearings. Nixon resigned in 1974 when it became obvious that he would have to endure impeachment proceedings if he remained president.

The initial story of a break-in at Democratic headquarters located in the Watergate office complex led to a series of investigations by *Washington Post* reporters Bob Woodward and Carl Bernstein. These reporters won the Pulitzer Prize for their stories, which revealed the corruption and illegal activity within the Nixon administration.

Lobbying

The government may use its regulatory power because of lobbying. Lobbying is the business of persuading government entities, such as federal and state representatives, to support a public or private interest. Major corporations hire professional lobbyists to represent their interests in approving, modifying, or removing legislation that affects them.

For example, in 2003, the FCC reconsidered its rules limiting media ownership, allowing a media company to own a daily newspaper, eight radio stations, and three TV stations in a single market. Big media corporations were in favor of a relaxation of these rules, and as early as 1998 had begun an extensive lobbying campaign. Between 1998 and 2003, the broadcast industry's spending on lobbyists rose 74 percent. In 2000, the major television networks—ABC, CBS, NBC, CNN, and Fox—invested $27 million, and in 2003, Clear Channel invested $2.28 million to persuade Congress to allow further media consolidation. The industry also wooed FCC commissioners by sponsoring trips to destinations like Las Vegas.[5] The FCC revised its rules, but a grassroots movement spurred 2 million public comments opposing the changes. Federal courts struck down the new rules in 2004. In 2006, the FCC began to revisit the issue of media ownership.

Lobbying by advocacy groups can also affect government regulation. The conservative organization, Parents' Television Council, pressured the FCC to increase the number of fines it gave for broadcast indecency and raise the cap on these fines from $32,500 to $325,000.[6]

Regulation of Media and the First Amendment

Not all media are equal when government attempts to regulate *freedom of expression.* Print media initially gained their freedom through the First Amendment to the Constitution because the founders believed that a self-governing populace needed a free flow of information. The press enjoys a higher level of protection than broadcast and cable media. The limited number of channels available to broadcast and cable technology and public fear of broadcasting's power to influence elections and social values have created an atmosphere in which regulation has been thought necessary and beneficial.

First Amendment press guarantees are not unique. For example, Japan's constitution guarantees freedom of the press and speech. Great Britain also protects its press, although their protection is more limited than in the United States. One difference is that in the United States the balance of power among the executive, legislative, and judicial branches prohibits one branch of government from creating regulation without review. Each branch of government provides a check on the others that limits, but does not prevent, political abuse.

L. Brent Bozell III and his organization, the Parent's Family Council, argue for stricter government regulations against broadcast indecency.

Teach Your Children Well: Schools and the First Amendment

A democracy such as the United States exists on the free flow of information and ideas. The First Amendment rests on this foundation, and the preservation of this delicate and crucial relationship depends on citizens understanding it. If the United States must depend on its schools to teach this heritage, its democracy may well be in serious trouble. Since 1988, high school students have had little or no First Amendment protections, and efforts to reduce First Amendment protection for college students continue in U.S. courts.

Until the Supreme Court's *Hazelwood School District v. Kuhlmeier* decision, high school students could exercise free expression unless it would disrupt school or affect others' rights. The 1988 *Hazelwood* ruling presented school administrators with almost unlimited power to censor high school journalists. Officials use the ruling to control information that might simply be embarrassing. *Hazelwood* did not extend the ruling to student journalists at colleges and universities.

Certainly, many principals and superintendents do not exercise their power to censor, but the fact that they *can* censor content tells their students something about the role of the First Amendment in a democracy.

In general, courts have upheld that at colleges and universities student editors control the content of their newspapers, though they may be required to submit them to a faculty advisor for comment. Once they are established as a campus forum, student newspapers are protected against censorship from university administrators.

However, the case of *Hosty vs. Carter* sent an ominous message. The controversy began in fall 2002 when the *Innovator,* a student newspaper at Governors State University, published articles that university administrators found offensive, including one on their decision not renew the contract of the paper's faculty advisor. The University president and the Dean of the College of Arts and Sciences accused the *Innovator* of "irresponsible and defamatory journalism." Another university official insisted that the paper's printer send issues to her for review before they went to press. The student journalists refused to submit to the review, and took the case to court. In June 2005, a judge ruled that "*Hazelwood*'s framework applies to subsidized student newspapers as well as elementary and secondary schools." The students attempted to have their case heard by the Supreme Court, but on February 21, 2006, the court refused.

Arguments in support of controlling student expression contend that student mistakes could hurt others and that controversy

can disrupt schools. Critics reply that these are certainly possibilities, but these possibilities can be reduced by teaching students about press responsibility, and that sometimes these mistakes are the price for having freedom.

If U.S. high school and college students are denied protection of expression by the First Amendment, how can they develop an appreciation for the main pillar of democracy in the United States? How can young people support what they cannot experience? Is the danger of harm from exercising First Amendment rights greater than the negative effects of denying those rights to young people? These are the issues that regulation must address.

In August 2006, in reaction to the *Hosty* decisions, the California state senate approved a bill called the Hosty Bill that would prohibit college and university administrators from censoring student publications like newspapers and yearbooks. Signed by governor Arnold Schwarzenegger, the bill made California the first state to protect such publications. Journalism professors and free speech advocates applauded the decision.

Sources: Ken Paulson, "Too Free?" *American Journalism Review,* September 2002, ajr.org; Jill Rosen, "High School Confidential," *American Journalism Review,* June 2002, ajr.org; "*Hosty v. Carter* Information Page," Student Press Law Center, splc.org. "Two Houston Area Schools Censor Stories about Gay Students," Student Press Law Center, May 24, 2002, splc.org.

Dateline

Regulation in Our Lives

1790. First copyright law is passed.

1791. Bill of Rights (first ten Constitutional Amendments) is ratified.

1798. Alien and Sedition Acts are passed.

1861–1865. Press is censored during Civil War.

1890. Sherman Antitrust Act is passed.

1906. Pure Food and Drug Act is passed.

1914. Federal Trade Commission is established.

1914. Clayton Antitrust Act is passed.

1917. Espionage Act is passed (World War I prior restraint).

1918. Sedition Act is passed (World War I prior restraint).

1927. Radio Act of 1927 is passed.

1931. *Near v. Minnesota* (prior restraint) is decided.

1934. Federal Communications Act is passed (FCC established).

1937. National Labor Relations Act is applied to newspapers.

1400–1700	1800	1860	1880	1900	1920	1930

1620. Pilgrims land at Plymouth Rock.

1690. *Publick Occurrences* is published in Boston.

1741. First magazine is published in America.

1776–1783. American Revolution

1830s. The penny press becomes the first truly mass medium in the United States.

1861–1865. American Civil War

1892. Thomas Edison's lab develops the kinetoscope.

1914–1918. World War I

1915. *The Birth of a Nation* marks the start of the modern movie industry.

1920. KDKA in Pittsburgh gets the first commercial radio license.

1930s. The Great Depression

1939. TV is demonstrated at the New York World's Fair.

1939–1945. World War II

Cultural Milestones

The almost mythical stature the First Amendment has gained over the years hides the controversy that originally surrounded it and the other nine amendments in the Bill of Rights. During the 1787 Constitutional Convention, the Federalists argued against the inclusion of a bill of rights. They said that it was unnecessary because any powers not specifically given the central government would be left to the states. The Anti-Federalists, who were suspicious of a strong central government, said that the absence of specific protections for individuals' rights would allow the federal government to supersede such rights granted at the state level.

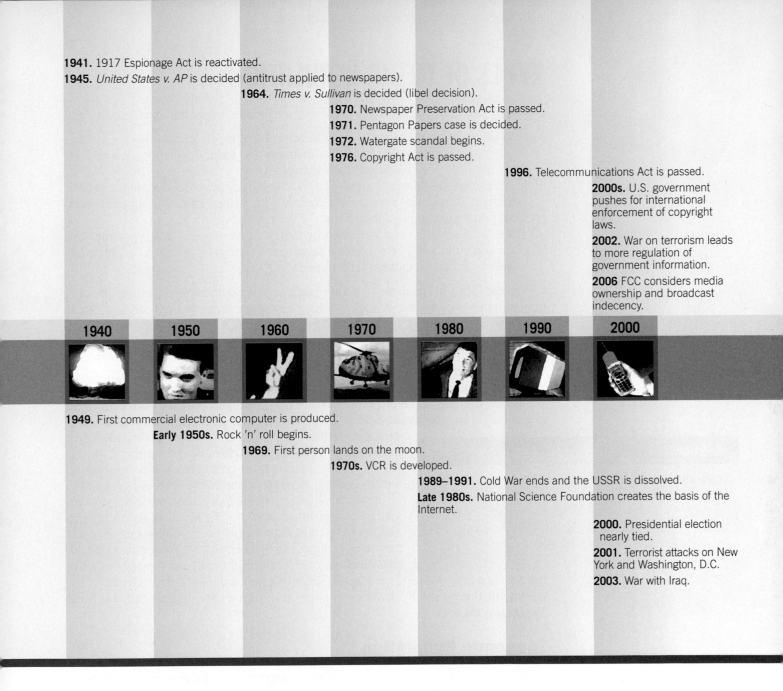

1941. 1917 Espionage Act is reactivated.

1945. *United States v. AP* is decided (antitrust applied to newspapers).

1964. *Times v. Sullivan* is decided (libel decision).

1970. Newspaper Preservation Act is passed.

1971. Pentagon Papers case is decided.

1972. Watergate scandal begins.

1976. Copyright Act is passed.

1996. Telecommunications Act is passed.

2000s. U.S. government pushes for international enforcement of copyright laws.

2002. War on terrorism leads to more regulation of government information.

2006 FCC considers media ownership and broadcast indecency.

| 1940 | 1950 | 1960 | 1970 | 1980 | 1990 | 2000 |

1949. First commercial electronic computer is produced.

Early 1950s. Rock 'n' roll begins.

1969. First person lands on the moon.

1970s. VCR is developed.

1989–1991. Cold War ends and the USSR is dissolved.

Late 1980s. National Science Foundation creates the basis of the Internet.

2000. Presidential election nearly tied.

2001. Terrorist attacks on New York and Washington, D.C.

2003. War with Iraq.

Some states were reluctant to ratify the Constitution without a bill of rights. To secure ratification, the Federalists agreed that such a bill would be added as amendments. This compromise allowed ratification of the Constitution by the original thirteen states. The Bill of Rights was drafted by the first U.S. Congress and ratified by the states in 1791.

For almost two hundred years, scholars have debated the exact reason for writing the First Amendment. However, one component is clear. The founders intended to preserve a marketplace of ideas, particularly in the realm of politics. Many who helped write the Constitution believed that distasteful and unpopular content must be protected so that democracy did not become mob rule. Today, as then, the press is an essential contributor to public debate. A valid fear is that censorship of unpopular content can become a precedent for censoring a wide variety of material. The slow erosion of protection could result in a tyranny of majority opinion that would damage the vitality of the entire democratic system.

TYPES OF MEDIA REGULATION

Governments in the United States exercise three types of regulation over mass media:

1. Governments regulate the economic behavior of media companies in the consumer and advertising markets. For example, the federal government limits the number of television stations a company can own in a city.
2. Governments regulate certain internal business activities of media companies. For example, a media company must comply with federal laws that prohibit racial and gender discrimination in hiring.
3. Despite the existence of the First Amendment, governments regulate some content and information. For example, a company cannot broadcast a deceptive advertisement that might harm consumers.

These forms of regulation can take place at several levels of government. Local governments pass ordinances about where newspapers can put news racks. States pass libel laws. The federal government has created the Federal Communications Commission (FCC), which regulates telecommunications, and the Federal Trade Commission (FTC), which regulates advertisements. The higher the level, the more power the government has to affect content.

Media regulation evolved through a series of legislative actions and court interpretations that are sometimes inconsistent and confusing. A valid libel defense in one state may not be a valid defense in another. One court decision may set a precedent that conflicts with another. The inconsistencies reflect the nature of a democratic style of government and the difficulties of interpreting laws on the basis of a constitution written in 1789. Table 14.1 outlines the sources of regulatory laws, which range from the federal Constitution to laws created by judicial interpretation. The ability of media organizations to monopolize a market through more efficient technology did not exist when the Constitution was ratified. Nevertheless, one common thread runs throughout all of the ad hoc public policy: Regulation attempts to balance the information needs of society with the rights of media companies and individual citizens. This is called **balancing theory.**

> **Key Concept**
>
> **Balancing theory** The Supreme Court, as well as the Congress, adheres to a balancing theory, which expresses the need for balance between individual rights and the rights of society as a whole. This balance is essential to a democratic government.

Economic Regulation

Media economics concerns the way media companies produce and sell products in the information and advertising markets. Two types of regulation affect these markets most often: antitrust laws and direct regulation by government agencies such as the FCC and FTC.

Antitrust Law   Antitrust laws are intended to promote competition in markets and to prevent or break up monopolies. They outlaw several practices aimed at closing down a company's competitors, including selling a product for less than it costs to make and joining with another company to drive others out of business.

The Sherman Act, passed in 1890, and the Clayton Act, passed in 1914, are the core of antitrust law. Congress passed them in part as a reaction to the "robber barons" of

Table 14.1 — Sources of Laws

These are listed in order of power. For example, the U.S. Constitution takes precedence over federal statutory laws. Federal statutory laws can be challenged as being unconstitutional.

- *Federal Constitution:* laws established by articles and amendments to the U.S. Constitution.

- *Federal Statutory:* laws passed by the federal legislative body, the U.S. Senate and House of Representatives.

- *Federal Administrative:* laws established by federal administrative bodies that were set up by statute, such as the FCC and FTC.

- *State Constitution:* laws established by the various state constitutions.

- *State Statutory:* laws passed by various state legislatures.

- *State Administrative:* laws established by various state administrative bodies that were set up by statute.

- *State Common Law:* laws created by judicial interpretation; few apply to communication law.

Source: Todd F. Simon, Professor and Director, A. Q. Miller School of Journalism and Mass Communication, Kansas State University.

---

the late nineteenth century. Industrialists J. P. Morgan, Cornelius Vanderbilt, and John D. Rockefeller, among others, used unfair business practices to monopolize markets. As monopolists, they were able to increase prices and profit considerably more than they would have if competition had existed.

The underlying assumption of antitrust laws is that ***competition benefits consumers.*** Experience shows that competition can reduce prices and allow consumers to influence products through their purchasing choices. This holds for news media competition at a local level. Competition among newspapers and among television news departments lowers subscription prices (for newspapers), increases news department budgets, increases amounts of information, and causes journalists to work harder to get news quickly and accurately. These advantages have a cost. Competition also can result in an emphasis on sensationalism and in unethical behavior to get stories.[7]

The impact of competition in the advertising market is more straightforward. Theoretically, competition keeps advertising prices low and improves service from the media companies. However, competition can increase advertisers' influence over editorial content. For example, because of the high degree of competition in the field, magazines are far more likely to allow advertisers to influence content than other media might be. If a company does not like what a magazine has written about its product, the company can ask for a change in that content and threaten to take its advertising elsewhere. Research shows that publications with extensive alcohol advertising also contain favorable editorial content toward drinking.[8] In another study, five large-circulation women's magazines with high amounts of cigarette advertising between 1983 and 1987 carried no feature-length articles about the hazards of smoking.[9]

> **Key Concept**
>
> **Competition benefits consumers** Government regulation of economic affairs of media companies is based on the assumption that competition is good because it provides a better product to consumers for less cost. Therefore, government regulates media through antitrust laws to ensure competition.

Media Convergence

Dividing the Airwaves

As the mediascape changes with the rise of wireless technologies, the way that the airwaves are allocated has become an important public issue. Not everyone agrees on the future of the airwaves, which newspaper columnist William Safire called "the most valuable natural resource of the information age."

Historically, the airwaves have belonged to the public and broadcasters have been given free licenses for parts of the radio spectrum. In the 1990s, many new wireless devices, such as mobile phones, created a much greater demand for the airwaves, and the federal government began auctioning frequencies to phone companies. Therefore, while radio and television providers do not have to pay for their use of the airwaves, phone companies do. In 2006, the FCC auctioned off another 1,122 licenses for a portion of the spectrum dedicated to Advanced Wireless Services (AWS-1), which may enable companies to offer bundles of services, including high-speed Internet, cellular phone, and video. Another set of licenses is set to be auctioned in 2009. With the switch from analog to digital television, more portions of the spectrum, called white space, have become available.

The argument lies in whether the airwaves should be open access, owned by licensees, or something in the middle. One group consists of public interest and consumer advocates, technology experts, and corporate interests who favor an *open-access*, or *commons* approach, in which the airwaves are a public resource that can be freely used by anyone. The need for regulation will eventually be outdated because new technologies will create unlimited spectrum capacity. In this vision, for example,

high-speed Internet would be completely free because computer users would route wireless signals through each other's computers instead of using cable modems.

A second group consists mostly of corporate interests and free market economists who favor a *property-rights* approach, privatizing the airwaves. Companies would own portions of the spectrum like real estate, and use it for whatever they like. This policy would maintain economic and political stability and foster more sound innovation.

A third group argues for a middle way, allowing corporations to lease parts of the spectrum while converting as much as possible for public use. The New America Foundation has argued that the white space freed up by digital technology should be open for unlicensed use. In this way, citizens in rural and poverty-stricken areas could be equipped with Internet access, and networks could be easily created to foster social and economic growth in local communities.

In 2006, it seemed unlikely that the FCC would undergo a major revision of its policies, but with the advent of new technologies and increased convergence, the issue of the airwaves will continue.

Sources: Neil Carlson, "The Airwaves Explained," *Ford Foundation Report,* Summer 2003, fordfound.org; Pierre de Vries, *Populating the Vacant Channels,* New America Foundation, August 2006, newamerica.net.

Direct Telecommunications Regulation   During the early stages of broadcasting, government gave three justifications for **direct telecommunications regulation:** (1) The airwaves are a limited commodity, (2) the airwaves belong to the public, and (3) broadcasters should be responsive to the community and work in its best interest. The first justification reflected the confusion that arose as the number of radio stations grew during the 1920s. Often, two stations would broadcast on the same radio frequency, which meant that one or both could not be heard clearly. Because the stations did not cooperate, Congress decided to regulate signals. The second justification concerns the physics of broadcasting. Radio and television use electromagnetic waves that move through the air. Because the government controls the air, the signal belongs to the public. The third justification reflects the assumption that giving a broadcasting company a license to use the public airwaves means that the company owes the public various kinds of services in return.

Key Concept

Direct telecommunications regulation Since the early stages of broadcasting, government regulated broadcast in more direct ways than it did print media. Supporters of government regulation argued that the airwaves, which are limited in quantity, belong to the people, not to the broadcasters, and that station owners should be responsive to the community and work in its best interest. This is often referred to as the trusteeship model or the scarcity doctrine.

A series of congressional acts in 1912, 1927, and 1934 reflected a compromise between the desire to safeguard the public interest and efforts by broadcasters to preserve a commercially oriented broadcasting system.

The Radio Act of 1912 was the first effort to regulate wireless communication. The Radio Act covered regulations for maritime radio behavior and required that the federal government give radio licenses on request. However, the 1912 act did not provide criteria for rejecting licenses, and as the radio industry developed commercially, stations broadcast over the same frequencies, creating chaos in the air.

In 1927, Congress recognized that radio would be more than wireless communication and passed the second radio act, which created a five-member Federal Radio Commission that could assign radio licenses and require records of programming and technical operations. Congress created the FCC with the Federal Communications Act of 1934. The FCC had the power to regulate both wireless and wired communications, which at the time included radio and telephone. Most of the procedures developed under the Radio Act of 1927 continued under the FCC. The act provided for FCC control of broadcast licenses and ownership rules, as well as for regulation of some types of content. The 1934 act was amended and extended in a variety of ways as new technology developed, but federal communication regulations did not receive a major overhaul until 1996.

During the 1960s, citizens began to take an active interest in television content and in access to these channels of information. In this activist period, regulation increased. For example, in the case *Office of Communication, United Church of Christ v. FCC,* citizens gained *standing,* or the ability to take part in a license hearing. In this case, citizens challenged the renewal of a license to a Jackson, Mississippi, television station because of what they believed to be racist policies. During the 1970s, guarantees of equal time to candidates for federal offices had been expanded to include equal access to stations and equality in desirability of air time. For example, a station cannot sell prime time to one candidate and only early Sunday morning time to another.

Deregulation In the 1980s, technology allowed fifty or more radio stations and a dozen or more television stations in large markets to broadcast without any signal overlap. This improvement in technology, combined with the rapid rise in cable television, caused critics to question whether scarcity of channels was an issue. The political climate also changed. The Republican administrations of Presidents Ronald Reagan and George Bush had a more conservative approach toward federal government policy than previous administrations had had. The FCC reduced its regulation of broadcasting in ways that reflected the Reagan and Bush administrations' aim to limit government activities in economic markets.

The broadcast industry changed drastically as a result of deregulation. Companies no longer have to carry public affairs programs; a station's license does not have to be renewed as often as before; a company can own multiple radio and television stations in the same city; and stations no longer have to observe the ***fairness doctrine,*** a collection of rules that required stations to air opposing viewpoints concerning controversial issues. However, Congress retained the *equal time rule,* which affects political elections.

> ### Key Concept
>
> **Fairness doctrine** The collection of FCC rules that was first passed in the 1940s required broadcast stations to air competing views on controversial issues, although earlier regulations had prohibited such debate. The FCC no longer enforces the rules, and some critics claim that the result has been a watering down of public debate.

The law that governs direct telecommunication underwent its first complete revision in sixty-two years with the 1996 Telecommunications Act. The package of regulations that govern the **telecommunications industry** ended several years of congressional debate and altered the relationships among the various types of media.

The act removed barriers that prohibited cable and telephone companies from competing against each other. Now telephone and cable companies can provide entertainment, information, and telephone service. In addition, the Telecommunications Act allows local Bell telephone companies to provide long-distance service if the local companies are competitive for telephone service and the FCC decides that

telecommunications industry

Organizations that are involved in electronic media such as broadcast television, cable, radio, and telephone, or the transmission of information over wires and with satellites.

such entry serves the community's interests. Price regulation for cable ended in March 1999.

Ownership regulation changed as well. The number of radio and television stations a company can own nationally is no longer regulated. However, a single company's television stations cannot reach more than 35 percent of all households in the country. Radio stations have no household limit. In radio, a company can own multiple stations in a market, but the number varies with market size. In markets with forty-five commercial stations, a company can own up to eight stations but no more than five of a particular type (AM or FM). In the smallest markets, those with fourteen or fewer stations, a company can own five stations but no more than three of a particular type. Three years after the Telecommunications Act, the FCC ruled that one company could own two television stations and six radio stations in a market with twenty or more unaffiliated newspapers, radio stations, and television stations.

Proponents of the 1996 Telecommunications Act claimed it would promote competition that would lower prices and increase diversity of content. Opponents said it would result in media concentration that would reduce competition and increase prices.

Despite the massive deregulation of the telecommunications industry, large media companies continue to press for more changes in the ownership rules. Efforts by radio and television corporations to change ownership rules in their favor in 2003 did not succeed. In 2006, the FCC began to revisit the issue, inviting public comment. The new proposed rules would allow cross-ownership, such as two television stations or a daily newspaper and television station in the same market. Broadcasters could also own more than one national TV network. The rapid changes in media, especially digital convergence and broadband access, have challenged regulators negotiating between the commercial marketplace and the public interest, including the protection and encouragement of democratic discourse.[10]

The 1996 Telecommunications Act did not entirely deregulate the cable industry. In 1992, Congress passed the Cable Consumer Protection and Competition Act, which required cable systems to carry the signals of local television stations. Cable operators argued that the law violated their free speech rights because they could not open these channels to other cable networks, such as C-SPAN and Comedy Central. If the law did not exist, channels used for smaller local stations would likely be used for cable channels and possibly for pay-per-view programming. In 1997, the Supreme Court upheld the law five to four and required cable systems to continue carrying local station signals.

Business Regulation

Although economic regulations govern the interaction among competitors, the concerns of **business regulation** are less abstract. Business regulations affect the way an organization treats its employees and the impact that it might have on society. Media companies are concerned primarily with labor laws, discrimination laws, and other laws that affect media business practices.

Labor Laws   Treatment of employees makes up a large portion of business regulation. Until the early years of the twentieth century, laborers usually worked six days a week for ten to twelve hours a day. Even children under the age of twelve worked under these conditions. However, in the 1930s the National Labor Relations Act (NLRA) and the Fair Labor Standards Act (FLSA) were passed as part of President Franklin Roosevelt's New Deal package. The NLRA outlawed antilabor activities by employers such as refusing to bargain collectively with employees and firing individuals because they participate in labor unions or publish criticism of an employer. The FLSA established the minimum wage and set limits on the number of hours a person could be required to work.

> **Key Concept**
>
> **Business regulation** Mass media outlets are usually owned by large corporations. As big businesses, media owners are required to adhere to labor laws, environmental regulations, and such standards as postal law. In many cases, media owners have protested having to abide by these laws, arguing that the laws infringe on their First Amendment rights.

Many media companies fought against the application of labor laws to their activities. Although they argued that the First Amendment guarantee of freedom of the press should protect them from having to adhere to laws that affected other businesses, media business owners generally were more concerned with the effect on their profits than on their freedom. The NLRA was applied to newspapers in 1937 after the Associated Press attempted to fire Morris Watson for trying to form a union. The AP argued, to no avail, that the NLRA abridged freedom of the press. The NLRA was ruled applicable to broadcast stations the same year. The Watson case was part of the American Newspaper Guild's efforts to unionize reporters; the guild, begun in 1933, continues today with contracts at more than one hundred newspapers.

Discrimination Laws Congress passed a series of laws between 1964 and 1992 that concern discrimination against employees who are members of various groups. The most important law in this area is the Civil Rights Act of 1964. Title VII of this act makes illegal any employment discrimination based on "race, color, religion, sex or national origin." The Americans with Disabilities Act (ADA), passed in 1990, prohibits most employers from discriminating against people on the basis of a disability.

As part of its broadcast licensing, the FCC prohibits discrimination based on race, color, religion, and national origin and requires reporting from licensees about their recruitment, hiring, and employment practices. However, as documented elsewhere in this text, media companies have not performed well in hiring women and minorities or allowing them to advance in their organizations. Issues concerning women, minorities, disabled and other marginalized groups not only involve hiring, but related aspects of access and representation.

Content and Information Regulation

Direct **content regulation** emerged from government efforts to balance the free flow of information and ideas against the negative effects of media products. Part of the news media's role, as H. L. Mencken said, is "to comfort the afflicted and afflict the comfortable." Content regulation tries to reduce *unjustified, unnecessary,* and *unreasonable* harm to people from media content. Such regulation can occur before or after distribution. Some types of speech, such as political speech, are more protected than others, such as commercial speech. Figure 14.1 outlines the levels of protected speech.

Regulating Content Before Distribution Regulation of media content before it is distributed is used to control content in times of war and for economic reasons. Such regulation falls into three areas: prior restraint, controlling government documents, and copyright law. The first two concern access to information about governments and their activities, and the third concerns protection of content created by individuals and organizations.

Prior Restraint. Through prior restraint, a government body prevents the public from getting certain types of information. In some cases, the government body reviews content before publication and censors it. In other cases it mandates that some types of content cannot be distributed.

The classic legal case involving prior restraint on newspapers is *Near v. The State of Minnesota.*[11] In this 1931 case, the State of Minnesota tried to stop the publication of the *Saturday Press,* a smear sheet that viciously attacked Jews and Catholics. In one story, the *Press* charged that gangsters controlled Minneapolis while law enforcement officers turned the other way. The publishers, Howard Guilford and J. M. Near, were charged under a Minnesota statute that prohibited anyone from publishing a "malicious, scandalous and defamatory newspaper, magazine or other periodical." The U.S. Supreme Court overturned the conviction of Guilford and Near and let them continue to publish. Although the Supreme Court allowed the *Saturday Press* to continue

Figure 14.1   Levels of Protected Communication

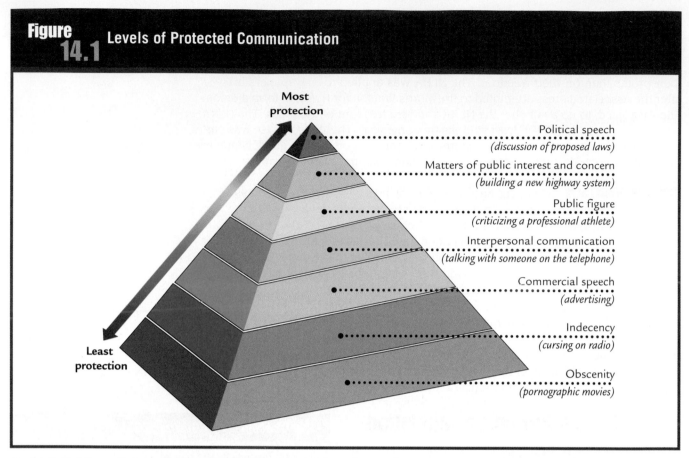

Source: Todd F. Simon, Professor and Director, A. Q. Miller School of Journalism and Mass Communication, Kansas State University.

publication and, in effect, struck down the Minnesota "press as public nuisance" law, the court also recognized that these press freedoms are not absolute. It said that prior restraint can be exercised under conditions of national security, situations involving obscenity, and when the public order is threatened through violence. Prior restraint was often exercised during the mid-twentieth century when local and state censorship committees ruled on whether a film could be shown or whether it should be banned because of violence, sexual content, or unacceptable moral prescriptions.

Obscenity and Indecency.   Prior restraint often has been exercised when ***controlling obscenity and indecency.*** Such restraint was employed—sometimes illegally—by postmasters who took it on themselves to censor the mail they handled. In 1873, Congress adopted the Hicklin Rule, which defined obscenity as anything with a tendency to corrupt people whose minds might be open to immoral influences. Critics later argued that the rule treated all citizens as though they were children. During the 1950s, the Supreme Court adopted a new definition, which eased the standards by which something was deemed obscene. The Roth-Memoirs Rule, named for two Supreme Court cases, declared that material deemed obscene for children was not necessarily obscene for all. The rule also required that the entire work, not just a portion, be considered in judging whether material was obscene. In 1973, with the case of *Miller v. California,* the court devised a three-part rule for determining obscenity:

> **Key Concept**
>
> **Controlling obscenity and indecency**   Whether to protect obscene speech and how to define it have been enduring issues for the public, Congress, and the Supreme Court. The evolution of new technologies such as color photo printing and new media such as the Internet create issues that generate further discussions about the problems surrounding obscenity and indecency.

1. An average person, applying contemporary local community standards, finds that the work, taken as a whole, appeals to prurient interest.
2. The work depicts in a patently offensive way sexual conduct specifically defined by applicable state law.
3. The work in question lacks serious literary, artistic, political, or scientific value.

Because the rules are community based, what is deemed obscene in Shreveport, Louisiana, may be determined by community standards in New York City to be purely artistic.

In 1978, the Supreme Court's ruling in *FCC v. Pacifica Foundation* added the term "indecency" to the mix. From this decision, the FCC defines indecency as "language or material that, in context, depicts or describes, in terms patently offensive as measured by contemporary community standards for the broadcast medium, sexual or excretory organs or activities." Broadcasters are forbidden from broadcasting obscene programming at any time, and indecent programming during the hours of 6 A.M. to 10 P.M. In March 2006, the FCC imposed the strictest fine in U.S. history: $3.6 million against CBS for airing an episode of *Without a Trace* that allegedly included a teen sex orgy. In June 2006, President George W. Bush signed the Broadcast Decency Enforcement Act that raised indecency fines from $32,500 to $325,000 per incident.

Some critics argue that vague legal definitions of obscenity and indecency lead to a **chilling effect** on free speech. They point to the aftermath of the Janet Jackson breast-baring incident when sixty NBC affiliates decided not to air an uncut version of *Saving Private Ryan,* which contained strong language. The medical drama *E.R.* aired only after a scene that briefly revealed an elderly patient's breast was removed, and MTV decided to show Britney Spears' video *Toxic* only between 10 P.M. and 6 A.M.[12]

In 2005, the U.S. Congress decided to expand its discussions of content regulation to cable and satellite TV. A survey by SRBI Research and *Time* magazine found that over half of respondents did not approve of further content regulation of satellite radio and cable television, while 51 percent felt that the FCC should more strictly control sexual language on traditional broadcast radio.[13] The Internet and cell phones, as well as parental control devices like the V-chip, are also technologies that concern the FCC as it considers content regulation.

Censorship during War. Despite concerns about prior restraint, most journalists have accepted some censorship during times of war. The **control of media content during war** dates to the Civil War, when President Lincoln shut down the *New York Journal of Commerce* for publishing a forged presidential proclamation announcing the draft of 400,000 men. But Lincoln was generally tolerant of the press and remanded an order by General A. E. Burnside to close the *Chicago Times,* arguing that such action would be more detrimental than criticism of the war effort.

Congress formalized war censorship of the press during World War I when it passed the Espionage Act in 1917 and the Sedition Act in 1918. These acts prohibited publishing "disloyal" information and bringing the U.S. government into "contempt, scorn or disrepute." The enforcement of these laws was the responsibility of the Postmaster General, who could prevent offending publications from being mailed. At least forty-four publications lost second-class mailing privileges as a result of the Espionage Act.[14]

During World War II, the 1917 Espionage Act was reactivated, and President Franklin Roosevelt declared a limited national emergency, which allowed him to control broadcasting. Hoping to avoid more stringent regulation, the National Association

Key Concept

Chilling effect Advocates of absolute free expression argue that most regulations have a chilling effect on the media; the regulations may prevent reporters from going after tough stories because they fear being sued. If lawsuits become too oppressive, they affect how information is disseminated and debated in the marketplace of ideas.

Key Concept

Control of media content during war Techniques for controlling media content during wartime include censorship and restriction of access. The overriding question is whether the distribution of material will harm the war effort or endanger national security, or whether censorship will restrict information the public has a legitimate right to know so as to make political decisions.

Global Impact

The Internet: What's in a Domain Name?

To varying degrees, over one billion people all around the world use the Internet. Mostly, they are concerned with access, cost, privacy, and safety rather than who manages and regulates the vast global network. Yet one key global technology issue is the management of the domain name system (DNS), which may radically change the shape of the Internet.

Currently, a nonprofit organization, the Internet Corporation for Assigned Names and Numbers (ICANN), has oversight over DNS, as well as allocating Internet protocol (IP) addresses around the world. The organization was established by the U.S. Department of Commerce in 1998, and is subject to U.S. veto. In 2006, ICANN became the subject of much criticism for representing U.S. interests instead of global ones appropriate to a worldwide technological system.

In 2005, a British businessman, Stuart Lawley, began negotiations with ICANN to establish a top-level domain name, .xxx, for pornography sites. Other top-level domain names include .edu, .gov, and .org. Lawley hoped to make it rich by providing .xxx domain names, though he marketed the idea by suggesting that they could be used in child safety filters. However, conservative family groups, like the Family Research Council, opposed the idea, arguing that it would increase and legitimate online pornography. Jan LaRue, a lawyer with Concerned Women for America, argued, "Anybody who thinks [the .xxx domain] would help parents protect kids from porn on the Internet has crashed in the cranium." Conservative family groups were responsible for more than 6,000 letters sent to the Department of Commerce, which persuaded ICANN to vote down adding .xxx.

The decision had global implications because many members of the world Internet community, including the European Union, felt that the U.S. had exercised unilateral power under the political influence of conservatives. They argued that such decisions are purely technical matters and that the Internet is a global resource beyond a single country's political control. The debate publicized concerns expressed at the United Nation's 2005 World Summit on the Information Society in Tunisia, in which many countries, especially China, Iran, Saudi Arabia, and members of the European Union, argued for the complete transformation of ICANN into an international body.

Shortly after the .xxx fracas, China announced that it was developing its own top-level domain names, .com, and .net, in Chinese script. A government-approved major Chinese newspaper reported: "It means Internet users don't have to surf the web via the servers under the management of ICANN, of the U.S." Other countries, like Japan, Korea, Greece, India, and Israel, were already using domain names with non-Roman characters, but had not altered top-level domain names; .com and .net were supposed to be under the control of ICANN. China's announcement generated fears that the Internet could become fragmented into separate networks, with confusion and duplication in domain names like the popular MySpace.

When the Department of Commerce held a hearing on ICANN in June 2006, it received over seven hundred comments from people in many countries, including Canada, Morocco, Nigeria, Sweden, and Tobago. Many of them said, "No single government should have a pre-eminent role in Internet governance." The U.S. government has historically argued that its role in ICANN's operations has helped maintain Internet stability and prevents countries like China and Saudi Arabia from imposing censorship. However, critics like Milton Mueller of the Internet Governance Project counter that "no national government is exempt from politics, and no national government can be expected to resist the imprecations of domestic politics on its supervision of the Internet."

The United States government has stated that it will eventually relinquish its control over the domain name system. The Center for Democracy and Technology maintains that the alternative might turn out to be worse, leading to more government involvement. Whatever the case, who manages the Internet not only has implications for technology, but for global economics and politics.

Sources: Christopher Rhoads, "Red-Light District," *Wall Street Journal,* May 10, 2006: A1; Mark Gibbs, "ICANN," *Network World,* May 22, 2006: 92; Nikki Swartz, "China Launches Chinese Language Domains," *Information Management Journal* 40 (May/June 2006): 11; Internet Governance Project, "Review of the Documents Released under the Freedom of Information Act in the .xxx Case," May 19, 2006, internet governance.org/pdf/xxx-foia.pdf, accessed on August 14, 2006; Anne Broache, "U.S. Voices Openness to Private Net Control," CNET News, July 27, 2006, news.rom.com, accessed August 13, 2006.

of Broadcasters asked its commentators not to editorialize. Because of widespread fear and public support of the war, the media cooperated in most censorship during that war. The Office of Censorship, created in 1941, administered a voluntary code of censorship and controlled communications coming into and leaving the country.

Because the United States never declared war on North Vietnam, wartime censorship was never imposed during that conflict. The media were free to report the war as they saw it, though military personnel often gave inaccurate information in news briefings. Although research indicates that public protest of the war coincided with official concern about the conduct of the war—and that negative media coverage followed, but did not precede, the official concern—many military officials believed that the media had helped to lose the war in Vietnam. Government efforts to prevent publication of the Pentagon Papers under the guise of national security created further mistrust between journalists and government.

After Vietnam, the military tried to improve its management of the media by controlling access rather than by engaging in official censorship. This strategy was used in 1983 in Grenada and in 1989 in Panama. It also proved fairly successful during the initial stages of the Gulf War in 1991. However, some daring journalists were able to bypass military controls and pursue their own stories. Peter Arnett challenged U.S. control by remaining in Baghdad and reporting from the enemy capital, despite censorship by the Iraqis.

In 2003, Arnett again remained in Baghdad during the early stages of the war in Iraq, but after granting an interview to Iraqi State Television during the first two weeks of the war in which he stated that the U.S. war plan had "failed," he was fired by NBC and *National Geographic*. Many journalists believed that Arnett had "cozied up" to the Iraqi War Ministry to try to get an interview with Saddam Hussein. In doing so, he crossed the line from accurate reporting to airing his personal opinion as fact.

During the 2003 conflict, reporters were embedded with troops and gave real-time coverage to military actions. Government officials hoped such reporting would show how the United States strived to provide humanitarian aid and avoid civilian casualties.

In 2006, revelations that the federal government had wiretapped millions of Americans' phone calls and e-mails without a warrant led to discussions of illegal search and seizure as enshrined in the Fourth Amendment. The question is whether the President has the Constitutional right to evoke executive privilege, including wiretapping of citizens, in times of war.

Controlling Government Documents.   Prior restraint and censorship are not the only ways in which government controls information. It can also control access to material that affects the decision-making process. Many federal agencies exist just to provide information to Congress and the administrative branch. At the federal level, the president controls information because of the doctrine of **executive privilege,** which dates to the time of George Washington and James Madison. This doctrine states that the president may withhold information when disclosure might injure the public.

During the 1960s, press associations and other citizens' groups lobbied extensively for open meetings and records acts, often called **sunshine laws.** As a result, all fifty states have some form of open records laws. However, just how information is released varies. Some states, such as Florida and New York, allow more access to computerized data than do others. The denial of access to databases reflects a desire to protect individual privacy. However, as more records are stored electronically, states will have to make such databases available as part of open records acts.

In an effort to make government information more available to the public, Congress passed the Freedom of Information Act (FOIA) in 1967. The act specified that a federal agency can withhold information in only nine areas: national security, agency interpersonal activities, statutory exemptions, trade secrets, some intra-agency and interagency memos, issues involving personal privacy, police investigations, protection of government-regulated financial institutions, and information about oil and gas wells.

A difficulty with the FOIA is that agencies have extensive leeway in following the act. Bureaucracies can make information access easier or harder to obtain, depending on what the particular administrator wants to do. For example, the person seeking information is expected to pay reasonable fees for searching and copying. What is reasonable can vary from department to department and across time. The 1986 FOIA Reform Act tried to define the issues of national security and law enforcement exemptions, but it also gave departments more power to make some information less accessible.

executive privilege

The president's right to withhold information if disclosure might harm the executive branch's functions and decision-making processes.

sunshine laws

Laws requiring that meetings of federal or state administrative agencies be open to the public.

Concern over how forthcoming the federal government would be increased in 2002 with the revelation that U.S. Attorney General John Ashcroft wrote a memo to government agencies on October 12, 2001, encouraging them to be more restrictive with FOIA requests for information.[15]

In February 2006, the National Security Archive reported that the CIA and other federal agencies had reclassified 55,000 records, making them unavailable to the public. Many historians, journalists, and archivists were concerned about the trend toward greater secrecy.

Controlling News Events.　At times, reporters need information that cannot be found in documents. During breaking news stories, journalists want access to the people and locations involved in the news. Other important news events include governmental meetings at which ordinances and laws are decided. Because historically many government bodies have sought to close meetings, all states and the federal government have enacted open meetings laws known as *sunshine laws.* These laws require official government meetings to be open to the public, and thus the press, except under specific conditions.

The federal Government-in-Sunshine Act that took effect in 1977 applies to about fifty agencies, departments, and other groups. Their meetings can be closed if circumstances meet one of ten exemptions. State laws vary. Typical exemptions include meetings to discuss personnel matters, lawsuits, and land acquisition. Discussions about personnel could involve private material, considerations of lawsuits might involve confidential client–attorney information, and deliberating over land acquisitions could result in the premature release of information that could affect the price of land.

In breaking news situations, such as the Montreal school shooting in September 2006, journalists want total access. However, law enforcement officials can legally exclude journalists from crime scenes during and after the crime. Nevertheless, police sometimes restrict journalists when it is not necessary to do so, causing speculation that law enforcement personnel are simply trying to control information.

Copyright Regulation.　Copyright law stems from a power granted by the Constitution to Congress. The first copyright law was passed in 1790. The original purpose of the law was to grant property rights to authors in order to promote knowledge in the arts and sciences for the public good. Initially, copyright law extended protection

Public officials and corporate leaders often try to control the news, especially in a damaging crisis. After Hewlett Packard executives, such as Mark Hurd, were accused of electronically spying on journalists and their own board members, they said little to explain their actions.

to the author for fourteen years, but since that time, the protection has expanded. In 1998, the Sonny Bono Copyright Term Extension Act was passed, protecting works for the duration of the author's life plus seventy years, and ninety-five years for a work of corporate authorship. Critics deemed the law the "Mickey Mouse Protection Act" because the Disney Corporation had strongly lobbied for its passage.

Copyright law applies to newspapers, magazines, books, video, film, photographs, computer programs, speeches, websites, and even professors' lecture notes. By providing the creator with control over the created material, the government hopes to encourage as much participation in the consumer market and marketplace of ideas as possible. People who make their living as writers, journalists, artists, and scholars cannot do so without legal control of the material they create.

Although the law has protected creators of information, it has not been proved perfect in its promotion of an active marketplace of ideas. For example, **fair use** is a problematic issue. Teachers, reporters, book reviewers, and researchers exercise fair use when they excerpt material for scholarly use or comment and criticism. Fair use also allows parody and comedic use of a work. However, it is often difficult to determine just exactly what constitutes fair use. Therefore, in lawsuits that involve fair use, the courts look at (1) the purpose of the use, (2) the nature of the work being used, (3) the amount used in relation to the size of the full work, and (4) the impact of use on the market for the content.

New technologies have raised further challenges to copyright law. In 1998, the U.S. Congress passed the Digital Millennium Copyright Act containing provisions that protect software from piracy and obligate service providers to remove offending material when notified of copyright infringement. The Church of Scientology International used the bill to force service providers to remove documents posted by its critics and Google to block links to anti-Scientology websites through its search engine.

The development of peer-to-peer (P2P) file sharing has posed challenges to copyright protection. By 2002, a survey found more than 17 percent of adults who used the Internet had downloaded music from P2P file sharing services like Napster.[16] Napster was forced to discontinue its service by court order, but new services have arrived that allow music and video sharing and are much more difficult to control. In 2005, the Supreme Court ruled on a landmark case, *MGM Studios v. Grokster,* holding that P2P file sharing companies could be sued. The music and movie industries had already begun suing individual file sharers, resulting in thousands of lawsuits. However, these efforts seem to have had little effect either on company profits or file sharing.[17]

> ### Key Concept
>
> **Libel and slander** Libel, the written defamation of a private individual, and slander, spoken defamation, have always been considered beyond the bounds of free expression. A more complicated issue is the libel of a public figure. In 1964, the Supreme Court ruled in *New York Times v. Sullivan* that a reporter had to show disregard for the truth or falsify a report to be convicted of libeling a public official.

Regulating Content after Distribution Regulating content before the fact usually involves some conflict between the news media and the government. The government wants to keep something secret. Regulating content after distribution, such as through libel and privacy law, usually involves an individual or nongovernmental organization and the media. Regulating after publication or broadcast can take two forms. First, the media organization must pay the person or organization damages for the negative impact. These are *compensatory damages.* Second, the media organization might also be punished for its actions in an effort to discourage such actions in the future. These are *punitive damages.*

Libel and Slander. *Libel and slander* are probably the best-known types of regulation after distribution. Libel occurs when a person is defamed falsely in written form. Slander is spoken **defamation.** However, it is generally accepted that when a person is defamed through a broadcast, the defamation constitutes libel, not slander. Because broadcasting is not **limited speech,** as is person-to-person speech, it is considered to have the same impact as libel.[18] When libel or slander occurs, a person's reputation and character are damaged in some way. Comedian and actress Carol Burnett sued the *National Enquirer* in 1981 for running a story saying that she

fair use

Use of a small portion of a copyrighted work by scholars, teachers, or reporters to further enlighten the public.

defamation

To misconstrue facts or misrepresent a person in such a way as to lower the individual in the estimation of others.

limited speech

Speech that is not widely disseminated.

Few people who spend their time immersed in media legislation have enough glamour to be portrayed as characters on television's *West Wing* or have *Wired Magazine* call them "the Elvis of cyberlaw." However, Lawrence Lessig has gained that kind of popularity for his vision of the Internet as a creative space where ideas are exchanged without restrictive copyright law.

Lawrence Lessig

Rather than a marketplace of ideas, the Internet is and should remain a creative commons. Lessig has argued against what he sees as an "extremist conception of intellectual property" applied to cases like Napster, the once popular peer-to-peer music file-sharing system. Lessig holds up the band Wilco's decision to make its fourth album available free on the Internet after Warner refused to release it. *Yankee Hotel Foxtrot* became an enormously popular album and catapulted Wilco to fame.

Born in South Dakota in 1961, Lessig spent his early years in Williamsport, Pennsylvania, where his father owned a steel factory. As a high school student, he was active in the Republican Party. He entered the University of Pennsylvania in 1980, earning degrees in business management and economics, and went on to study philosophy at Cambridge University, where his politics began to shift. When he returned to the United States, he studied law at the University of Chicago and Yale, specializing in constitutional law. After teaching at Harvard, he became professor of law at Stanford University, where he directs the Center for Internet and Society.

In 1999, Lessig challenged the Sonny Bono Copyright Term Extension Act. The chief plaintiff in the case was Eric Eldred. Eldred had been about to publish some Robert Frost poems in his online library of works in the public domain. Then the Bono Act was passed along with the 1998 No Electronic Theft Act, preventing him from doing so. The Supreme Court heard the case, *Eldred vs. Ashcroft,* in 2002. Lessig filed briefs that included a statement by the economist Milton Friedman and a Hollywood studio interested in film preservation. The opposing argument marshaled representatives from the estate of Theodor Geisel (Dr. Seuss), whose representatives worried that his works would be used "to glorify drugs or to create pornography." In the end, Lessig lost the case, but it helped cement his reputation as the leading thinker on intellectual property in the digital age.

Lessig's works include *Code: and Other Laws of Cyberspace* (2000), *The Future of Ideas: The Fate of the Commons in a Connected World* (2001), and *Free Culture: How Big Media Uses Technology and the Law to Lock Down Culture and Control Creativity* (2004). *Free Culture* is published under a creative commons license, an alternative copyright system offered by Lessig's nonprofit corporation, Creative Commons. The license allows anyone to distribute, copy, or reuse/remix the book for noncommercial purposes, and it has helped spark an international student movement to promote the free, creative exchange of information, including music, and oppose regulations on the distribution of content.

Sources: Steven Levy, "Lawrence Lessig's Supreme Showdown," *Wired,* October 2002, wired.com/wired/archive/10.10/lessig_pr.html; Lawrence Lessig, "How I Lost the Big One," *Legal Affairs,* March/April 2004, legalaffairs.org/issues/March-April-2004/story_lessig_marapr04 .msp; Lawrence Lessig, "Why Wilco is the Future of Music," *Wired,* February 2005, wired.com/wired/archive/13.02/view.html?pg=5.

was drunk at a restaurant. She won. In 2006, a seller on eBay obtained a court order ordering the site to remove comments from a buyer he said had defamed him. A small claims court agreed, but eBay resisted removing the offending remarks. Internet companies are usually held to be protected from liability for users' posted comments.

Libel cases often are perceived as the results of profit-hungry media organizations trying to build circulation or ratings by lying about someone. In reality, libel can result from mistakes, poor reporting skills, and arrogance when a news organization is asked to correct a mistake. The suits that get attention are not the average cases, and often the results of trials are changed by higher courts.

The difference between the initial jury awards and the eventual resolution during the appeal process reflects the complexity of libel laws. Just damaging a person's reputation is not enough to justify a judgment against a journalist. Several defenses can either absolve the journalist or reduce the impact of a judgment against the journalist.

Truth is a defense for libel. Reporting that someone is a convicted murderer constitutes defamation, but if that person was indeed convicted of murder, the report is not libelous. Even during the period of the Alien and Sedition Acts, truth was considered a defense for libel.

Qualified privilege is a second defense for libel. Privilege developed to make happenings in government proceedings available to citizens. Under qualified privilege, a journalist is protected while reporting statements from a public meeting as long as the report is accurate. However, the definition of what privileged information is varies from state to state. Usually, remarks made in a trial are privileged, but informal remarks made by a police officer during an investigation are not.

Fair comment and criticism defenses allow a journalist to express opinion in the most offensive ways without committing libel. The statement must be presented as opinion and not fact. This allows a no-holds-barred criticism of anything from political ideas to artistic performances. Perhaps the most famous case of fair comment and criticism was the review of the Cherry Sisters' vaudeville act at the turn of the twentieth century. The sisters sued when this critique ran in the *Des Moines Leader*:[19]

> Billy Hamilton, of the *Odebolt Chronicle,* gives the Cherry Sisters the following graphic write-up on their late appearance in his town: "Effie is an old jade of 50 summers, Jessie a frisky filly of 40, and Addie, the flower of the family, a capering monstrosity of 35. Their long skinny arms, equipped with talons at the extremities, swung mechanically, and anon waved frantically at the suffering audience. The mouths of their rancid features opened like caverns, and sounds like the wailing of damned souls issued therefrom. They pranced around the stage with a motion that suggested a cross between the danse du ventre and fox trot—strange creatures with painted faces and hideous mien. Effie is spavined, Addie is stringhalt, and Jessie, the only one who showed her stockings, has legs with calves as classic in their outline as the curves of a broom handle."[20]

This review is cruel, but according to the Iowa Supreme Court, it is not libelous. The review is fair comment and criticism.

Absence of actual malice, perhaps the strongest libel defense for journalists other than truth, reflects the legal status of the subject being covered. People who find themselves in the public eye have less libel protection than a private person does, and they must prove actual malice on the part of a reporter to win a libel suit. There are two types of public persons: public officials and public figures. A *public official* is someone who holds a position in government that affects public policy. A *public figure* is someone who places herself or himself before the public through the media or someone who is swept involuntarily into public controversy. Published comments about the second type of public figure can be protected only if they concern the controversy.

In 1964, a Supreme Court decision in the *New York Times v. Sullivan* case assured reporters that as long as they followed careful reporting procedures, random errors would not result in large libel judgments. The Supreme Court ruled that public officials—elected officials and individuals appointed to high offices—had to carry a heavier burden than did private individuals in libel judgments. The case arose from a *New York Times* advertisement titled "Heed Their Rising Voices," which appeared in March 1960, shortly after whites used violence at Alabama State College in Montgomery against black demonstrators who were protesting the segregation of public facilities. Alabama Police Commissioner L. B. Sullivan filed suit against the *Times,* which was considered a northern liberal newspaper, charging that he was libeled by the ad's general references to the police. The advertisement did contain errors. For example, it claimed that the students had sung "My Country, 'Tis of Thee," when in fact they had sung "The Star-Spangled Banner." Although the errors were minor, the implications of the suit were not. State libel laws were being used by southern states to attempt to control news coverage of civil rights demonstrations. The *Times* alone was facing eleven other libel suits in Alabama courts. When the case reached the Supreme Court on appeal, Justice William Brennan wrote that something far more crucial than an individual seeking to protect a reputation was at stake: the right to be able to discuss and to criticize government and government officials. The Supreme Court enacted the *rule of actual malice,* requiring that public officials had to prove that statements were made with actual malice, or "knowledge that information is false or with reckless disregard of whether it was false or not." Brennan argued that the case had to be considered "against the background of a profound national commitment to the principle that debate on public issues should be uninhibited, robust, and wide-open."

Celebrities have fewer privacy protections than ordinary citizens, and are often followed by paparazzi.

Since 1964 and the *Sullivan* ruling, the court has extended the actual malice rule to public figures. Michael Jordan and Madonna are public figures because they have voluntarily placed themselves before the public through the media. Because they have sought public attention, they must tolerate the comments and criticism that come with it. A private person can demonstrate libel merely by showing that a journalist was negligent in carrying out his or her work or that a journalist showed a lack of care in collecting information and writing stories.

The difference between private and public people represents the concern Justice William Brennan voiced in the *Sullivan* case for a free and open marketplace of ideas. The need of a democratic society to explore as many ideas as possible, even despised ones, has led the courts to allow error on the side of open discussion. For this reason, people who are in the public spotlight are open for more criticism than those who are not. A sloppy journalist has some protection with public figures, though a malicious one does not.

A new type of libel law emerged during the 1990s. Thirteen states passed "veggie libel laws," which make it illegal to issue false statements that defame farming industries. Cattle rangers in Texas sued Oprah Winfrey in 1998 because she said on her television show that she would stop eating hamburgers. Following her show, beef prices dropped. She won the suit, but critics of the law are afraid other defendants will not have the $1 million she spent to defend herself. The U.S. Court of Appeals for the Fifth Circuit upheld the decision in 2000, and an effort to repeal the Texas veggie law failed in 1999.

Privacy.   Privacy laws are similar to libel laws because they also involve protection of individuals from media abuse. Privacy laws address the right of a person to be left alone. People are entitled to keep parts of their lives away from public scrutiny. Although privacy is not written into the Constitution, it is derived from the Constitution's protection from unreasonable search and seizure and from self-incrimination. This area of law has become much more active as the number and type of national media outlets, both print and broadcast, have increased during the past thirty years.

Invasion of privacy can take several forms. Physically invading a person's solitude is classified as *intrusion*. A radio journalist cannot hide a microphone or camera in someone's room to collect information. Putting someone in a commercial without getting permission—*commercial appropriation*—also is an invasion of privacy.

Disclosing embarrassing facts can invade privacy through the release of information a person would consider awkward. A television program cannot broadcast details of a private person's sexual behavior without permission. A person cannot be portrayed in a *false light* by media. Journalists cannot imply something about someone that is not true. For example, a camera crew cannot record video of people on the street and use the tape while talking about sexually transmitted diseases. However, victims who claim they have been portrayed in a false light must prove actual malice. The Hill family, who had been held hostage in their home for nineteen hours during a weekend in 1952, sued Time, Inc., for invasion of privacy when *Life* reported on a Broadway play that depicted the Hills as having heroically resisted brutish conduct by the invaders. In reality, the Hills' captors had treated them courteously. On appeal, the Supreme Court ruled that even private individuals must prove actual malice if they are involved in a newsworthy issue.

As with libel, laws regarding invasion of privacy are not equally applicable to all people. People who are part of newsworthy events can lose their right to privacy, but courts differ in their interpretations of newsworthiness. Although the purpose of these laws is to protect people who are forced into embarrassing situations, sometimes media cover such situations as newsworthy events. In 1929, for example, Mrs. Lillian Jones sued the *Louisville Herald-Post* for quoting her as saying she "would have killed" the people who stabbed her husband to death on a Louisville street. Mrs. Jones lost her case when the newspaper claimed it had simply covered a newsworthy event.

In 1999, the Supreme Court ruled unanimously in *Wilson v. Layne* that reporters and camera crews entering a home during a "ride-along" violated the homeowners' rights. If law enforcement officers allow this entry, they can be subjected to civil law suits.

Regulating Advertising Content. Advertising falls under the heading of commercial speech, which is information aimed at promoting a commercial transaction. Until 1976, commercial speech was outside the protection of the First Amendment. That year, however, the Supreme Court ruled in the case of *Virginia State Board of Pharmacy v. Virginia Citizens Consumer Council*[21] that commercial speech that serves consumers with accurate and useful information deserves First Amendment protection. The Court did state that some forms of commercial speech should be subject to regulation.

The primary justification for advertising regulation is the protection of consumers from false claims that would mislead them. This justification dates to the late 1700s, when newspapers and other print media carried advertisements for patent medicines. Patent medicines were salves, ointments, and liquid concoctions that claimed to cure a wide range of illnesses and ailments. The following example ran in the *Pennsylvania Gazette* in 1777 for "Dr. RYAN'S incomparable WORM destroying SUGAR PLUMS, Necessary to be kept in all FAMILIES:"[22]

> The plum is a great diuretic, cleaning the veins of slime; it expels wind, and is a sovereign medicine in the cholic and griping of the guts. It allays and carries off vapours which occasion many disorders of the head. It opens all obstructions in the stomach, lungs, liver, veins, and bladder; causes a good appetite, and helps digestion.

The effects of patent medicines never lived up to the advertising claims, and in some cases the contents of the patent medicine could kill. The *New York Evening Post* temporarily stopped taking patent medicine ads in 1805 after a young girl died from using a patent medicine.[23]

Concerns about patent medicine advertising and other forms of consumer abuse led to the passage of the Pure Food and Drug Act in 1906 and the creation of the Federal Trade Commission (FTC) in 1914. The Pure Food and Drug Act gave the federal government regulatory powers over foods and medicines, and the FTC gave the government the power to control false advertising. Until 1934 the FTC was concerned with consumer protection only in the context of antitrust actions. That year the Supreme Court extended the FTC's authority to cover non–anti-trust cases, and in 1938, Congress made unfair and deceptive acts and practices in commerce illegal by passing the Wheeler–Lea Act.[24] In addition to enforcement specified by the act, the FTC also enforces several other consumer protection laws.

Unfair advertisements and practices are ones that cause substantial injury without offsetting benefits to consumers and businesses. The FTC uses its power to regulate businesses that mistreat consumers, although unfairness can also apply to advertising. For example, Orkin Exterminating Company was forced to cancel a rate increase for treating houses against termites. The company had signed a contract with homeowners at a lower price.

For the FTC to decide that an advertisement is deceptive, the ad must be misleading *and* it must cause the reasonable consumer to act in a way that results in real injury to the consumer. The FTC does not pursue cases that involve obviously inflated claims, such as "The Greatest Soda Ever Invented," because only an "unreasonable" person would believe such a claim. Real injury occurs when something is purchased; if the claim will not lead to a consumer's purchase, it is not likely to be regulated by the FTC.

If the FTC finds an advertisement deceptive, it can take a variety of actions. A consent agreement, for example, allows the company to stop the advertisement without admitting guilt. The FTC can also get a cease-and-desist order, which prohibits the practice in the future. It can even require corrective advertising, which attempts to correct false impressions created by past ads. For example, in 1975 the Warner–Lambert Company, which produces Listerine mouthwash, was required to include in Listerine ads a statement that the mouthwash does not prevent colds and sore throats. The corrective ads continued until $10 million was spent on Listerine ads. The FCC has continued to prosecute cases against misleading advertising, especially in weight loss ads.

The FCC also regulates advertising aimed at children. The Children's Television Act of 1991 established standards for broadcasters who must provide three hours a week of children's TV programs but limit commercial time to 10.5 minutes per hour or less on weekends and 12 minutes per hour on weekdays. In 2005, the FCC added new rules, including limitations on mentioning websites unless they were substantially related to the TV program, weren't primarily for commercial purposes, and didn't provide a link to commercial content.

The Telecommunications Act and Content Regulation. The 1990s saw heated debates in Congress and elsewhere about regulation of television content. The decade began with the passage of the Children's Television Act, followed five years later by the passage of the Telecommunications Act of 1996.

Although most of the 1996 act concerns business activities, controversial portions cover content regulation. The act prohibits the transmission by means of computer of pornographic material to minors, requires television manufacturers to include a microchip (called a **V-chip**) in each set that allows electronic blocking of programs on the basis of a ratings system, increases fines from $10,000 to $100,000 for television and radio obscenity, and requires cable to scramble programs for subscribers who think the programs are unfit for children. After the act was passed, hundreds of websites changed their background screens to black and issued protest statements about the new regulations. At issue in the Internet-related cases is whether online communications will enjoy the broad protection given print media or the more narrow rights traditionally given broadcasting.

The regulation against indecent material on the Internet faced court challenges immediately after the act went into effect. The lawsuits involve arguments about the impact of the regulations on First Amendment rights. In June 1997, the Supreme Court ruled that the Computer Decency Act was unconstitutional. Justice John Paul Stevens wrote the majority opinion for the Supreme Court, noting that the Computer Decency Act cast a "shadow over free speech" and "threatens to torch a large segment of the Internet community." Stevens argued that an attempt to protect children from harmful materials "does not justify an unnecessarily broad suppression of speech addressed to adults."

In March 1996, the top executives in the television industry met with President Clinton and agreed to pursue a *voluntary rating system* similar to the one used by

Many parents and educators have turned to technology to block potentially harmful content from reaching their children.

the motion picture industry. The system identifies six types of content with icons in the upper left corner of the TV screen during the first fifteen seconds of the program. The levels are age based and start with TV-Y for programs suitable for all children and end with TV-M, which is content not suitable for children under age seventeen. The ratings system allows the V-chip to filter out programs that parents deem unsuitable.

The Threat of Regulation

Regulations do not have to be enforced to change media content. The very threat of filing action under one of the regulatory laws affects what media organizations do. In some cases, this benefits people. The knowledge that they could be sued for intrusion keeps most media organizations from sending a reporter to a person's house with a hidden camera to record what happens. Not all such threats are beneficial, however. The threat of a costly libel suit can have a chilling effect on the work of journalists because the journalists will avoid covering a story or will change their writing because they fear a lawsuit.

Litigation can be expensive even if the newspaper wins the case. In addition, time spent on the case is time away from gathering news. People who appear in the news understand this and often file nuisance suits. Although the plaintiffs know that they will probably not win, they also know that the newspaper or other organization will have to spend money to defend itself. The plaintiff also may hope that the editors will be more reluctant to publish controversial articles in the future.

Measuring the impact of the chilling effect is difficult; it requires measuring what did not happen. Fear of adverse reactions leads to self-censorship. The process occurs in people's minds, often out of habit, and goes against the principles of open discussion of ideas and information in the marketplace of ideas.

Media organizations are not the only groups that can be chilled by lawsuits. Libel suits can be filed against anyone. Lawsuits called Strategic Lawsuits against Public Participation (SLAPPs) have been used against activist groups to discourage their activism. A public person who has been attacked can file such suits to discourage critics. Columnist Molly Ivins listed a number of SLAPP suits in one of her columns. These included suits against a Las Vegas doctor for saying a city hospital violated a state law, against members of a Baltimore community group for questioning the property-buying practices of a real estate developer, and against a West Virginia environmental activist for criticizing a coal mining company.[25] Such suits do not even need a chance of winning to be effective. The cost of litigation is often enough to keep the critics quiet.[26] Because the obvious purpose is the stifling of open discussion of matters that interest the public, SLAPP suits are being fought with countersuits. Many states have laws against such lawsuits.[27]

GAINING ACCESS TO JOURNALISTS' INFORMATION

Most media laws deal with either content or business operations. Another area of law that concerns media and focuses specifically on newsgathering is called **evidentiary privilege.** Although this privilege is not universally granted to journalists, when it is, journalists who have promised a source anonymity do not have to identify that source in court. Such protection for confidentiality has long existed for lawyers and doctors; it has become an issue for journalists in the second half of the twentieth century.

Privilege involves three types of litigation: (1) the court seeking the identity of an anonymous source, (2) the court demanding materials such as notes and videotapes, and (3) the court asking journalists who witnessed an event to testify. When a court seeks information, it issues a subpoena that orders the journalists to provide information or testify in court. The journalist and news organization can ask the court to quash, or dismiss, the subpoena.

The U.S. Supreme Court has not accepted the concept of journalists' privilege based on the First Amendment. But as of 1996, twenty-nine states had *shield laws* protecting journalists from being forced to disclose information. Another seventeen states and the District of Columbia have recognized privilege under common law or state constitutions.

Government officials argue that journalists should have no more privilege than ordinary citizens because such privilege can hamper police and prosecutors' investigations. Journalists respond that the absence of such privilege would prevent sources from revealing information to them. They argue that privilege allows them to question people who are afraid to talk with police or other government officials. Many sources, such as government employees and crime witnesses, face retaliation if their identity is made public. As a result, a valuable source of information might be eliminated, and the public good might be harmed.

The protection of bloggers under shield law became an issue in 2005 when Apple Computer charged that two bloggers had disclosed trade secrets involving a WiFi interface the company had developed for its GarageBand music program. A circuit court ruled that the bloggers had to reveal their sources, but the decision was overturned on appeal when the judge delivered his decision that an online journalist deserved the same protection as any other.

TRENDS

The extent and nature of regulation reflect changes in society. As the economy, culture, and politics of a country evolve, so does the regulation, or lack of regulation. Recent rapid changes in U.S. society have led to a variety of regulatory trends.

Technology: Copyright Regulation

Convergence of content prompted by the digitization of media has enhanced the ability to steal copyrighted material. Naturally, holders of copyright want to see the laws enforced in order to protect both their profits and their intellectual property. However, enforcement has become increasingly difficult for two reasons. First, not all countries adhere to copyright laws and such countries often become homes for digital **piracy.** Second, individual Internet users download and share digitized music and video, bypassing the distributors and the cost of purchasing music.

evidentiary privilege

Rule of law allowing journalists to withhold the identification of confidential sources.

piracy

Using material without securing appropriate copyright authorization.

The ease of pirating is forcing large corporations that control copyright to confront large corporations that control Internet distribution. The outcome of this battle has yet to be determined. Some critics are concerned that the outcome will dry up the free exchange of information. Copyright law has always tried to protect intellectual property but at the same time promote public discourse. In some cases, the development of profit-driven corporations has diminished the concern about public discourse, despite its importance to democracy.

In 2005, eyes were on the search engine company Google for new rulings on copyright law. The company had developed the Google Book Search project to scan millions of books into an online database. Some of these books are being scanned as part of an agreement with publishers, the copyright holders, and so do not provoke any copyright issues. But when Google announced that it had partnered with five major research libraries to scan their books, the Authors Guild and several authors brought suit against the company for copyright infringement. They were followed by five major book publishers who also sued. Google has made it clear that it will only show highlights of books under copyright, not the entire texts, and that publishers can opt out of the project by providing a list. One of the issues, however, is whether the scanning process itself is a copyright violation. Other companies have begun to partner with libraries, such as Microsoft with the British Library. Legal decisions on these activities will affect how users can access content on the web.

Technology: Net Neutrality

Net neutrality is a complicated economic, political, and technical issue which has several interpretations, depending on what stake the interpreter has in the outcome. Under net neutrality, Internet service providers (ISPs) allow a free flow of data, treating all bits equally. In essence, a change from net neutrality would allow ISPs to give some users preference over others, usually based on how much they pay. Some argue that this will stifle competition and give ISPs too much power that they might use to censor some users and sites. As the U.S. Congress considers new telecommunications regulations, major Internet users, like cable companies, have lobbied to overturn net neutrality because they need greater bandwidth.

Culture: Access to Information

For the past twenty years, governments have become increasingly active in trying to withhold information from journalists and other citizens. Since the September 11 attacks, control has been placed on more government documents. The Bush administration has withheld many documents for security reasons and encouraged government agencies to slow down the process by which people can request to see documents. The White House has told its agencies not to disclose any records that refer to "weapons of mass destruction" or are related to national security.

In the summer of 2002, Governor James McGreevey of New Jersey used national security as an excuse to try to seal five hundred categories of state documents. After public protest, journalists discovered that much of the information did not pertain to national security. A memo from Attorney General John Ashcroft encouraging federal department officials to be less cooperative with FOIA requests has led to withholding information. A person who works for the federal government told a journalist, "There was a dramatic, clearly visible change throughout these agencies after Bush came in. Sometimes the Clinton people would be reluctant, but they would go ahead and obey the law. These guys have a meeting and try to figure ways to have FOIA requests delayed."[28] Similar events are happening in local government all over the United States.

The long-term trend toward withholding information explains the skepticism toward the Patriot Act of 2001. Few would argue that the U.S. government does not need the power to fight the continuing war on terrorism. However, the Patriot Act increased the power of the federal government to withhold and limit access to information, and the current government has shown a willingness to use this power. At a time when the public needs to trust its government, there are reasons not to.

Discussing Trends

Although the First Amendment allows far more freedom of speech and press in the United States than that found in almost all other countries in the world, U.S. citizens still face constraints. The constraints can come from the marketplace or from government regulation, but the two are connected. As regulation declines, economic concentration often increases. Because of changes in technology, economics, and politics, the United States faces the possibility of changes that could shape media for decades to come. As the changes occur, consumers must confront a variety of questions about regulation:

■ How much access should journalists and citizens have to government information?

■ How has the war on terrorism affected what should and should not be available?

■ How much copyright enforcement should the government pursue?

■ Some surveys show that a majority of young people think it's acceptable to download music free online. What is the justification for this?

■ To what extent should information be freely available on the Net?

■ Does copyright protection encourage or discourage creativity?

SUMMARY

■ Regulation exists to mediate conflicts between the rights of two individuals or between a government or corporation and an individual.

■ The Bill of Rights was created to limit government control of private affairs and to preserve individual liberties.

■ Government imposes regulations (1) when people or organizations interfere with the workings of the economic market system, (2) when the use of a product or an industry or company's behavior has a negative impact on society as a whole, (3) when a product or behavior has a negative impact on individuals that outweighs its contribution to society as a whole, (4) during times of war, and (5) to preserve its own security and power.

■ The First Amendment was designed to protect robust intellectual exchange within a democratic society.

■ Governments regulate (1) the economic behavior of media companies in the consumer and advertising markets, (2) certain internal business activities of media companies, and (3) some content and information.

■ Media regulation evolved not only from federal and state legislation, but from court decisions.

■ Economic regulations include antitrust laws and direct regulation by government agencies such as the FCC and FTC.

■ Direct telecommunication regulation covers broader areas than print because in the early years government sought to avoid chaos in the airwaves, to allocate scarce resources (airwaves), and to force licensees to act in the public interest.

■ Media companies are also subject to regulations that affect most businesses, such as labor laws.

■ Content can be regulated before or after distribution. Regulation before distribution includes prior restraint, controlling government documents, and copyright law. Prior restraint includes laws relating to obscenity and government regulation of the press during wartime. Regulation after distribution includes libel laws and privacy laws.

■ Open meetings laws, such as the federal Government-in-Sunshine Act, increase access of the public and journalists to the decisions of government bodies.

■ *New York Times v. Sullivan* was a landmark decision because it assured reporters that random errors in covering the conduct of a public official would not result in huge libel judgments against them. The Supreme Court decision further ruled that government entities could not use libel suits as a way of silencing the press.

■ Advertising is subject to all regulations affecting regular content and to additional controls that are intended to protect the consumer from misleading and dangerous claims.

■ Although the Telecommunications Act of 1996 primarily affected business practices, it also initiated new content regulation.

■ Often, the threat of regulation can have a chilling effect that not only curbs the excesses of media, but also sometimes curbs their desire to address controversial issues.

- State shield laws protect journalists from being forced to reveal information to courts and government agencies.

NAVIGATING THE WEB Regulation

Most websites that cover media regulations are maintained by either universities or governments. They provide access to material about regulation and law, including full texts of some legal documents.

Communication Media Center at New York Law School
nyls.edu/pages/107.asp
This law school site contains background about cases, statutes, and scholarly papers related to media law and regulation.

Creative Commons
creativecommons.org
Lawrence Lessig's nonprofit organization provides information on creative commons licensing.

Libel Defense Resource Center, Inc.
medialaw.org
This site is a New York nonprofit clearinghouse for information about libel law in the United States.

Student Press Law Center
splc.org
This nonprofit center aims to promote freedom of the press in high schools and colleges. The site contains a variety of information, including reports and news articles about events relating to student press issues.

Telecommunications Act of 1996
fcc.gov
This FCC site contains the full text of the 1996 Telecommunications Act, as well as material about the proceedings and various FCC activities after its passage.

QUESTIONS FOR REVIEW

1. What are the five reasons government regulates media in the United States?
2. Why are broadcast media regulated to a greater degree than print media?
3. What are the three types of regulation of mass media in the United States?
4. What are the justifications for direct regulation of the telecommunications industry?
5. How do courts determine if media content is obscene?
6. What are the defenses against a libel suit?
7. What are the major types of regulation before publication?
8. What are the major types of regulation after publication?

ISSUES TO THINK ABOUT

1. Traditionally, broadcast media have been subject to more regulation than print media. In the computer age, broadcast and print blend. How would you apply traditional laws, such as those protecting copyright and restrictions against pornography, in the online world?
2. To what extent is the public adequately protected from invasion of privacy? How would you reconcile the right to privacy with the public's right to know?
3. How should indecency be defined and treated?
4. To what extent do you think the threat of regulation restricts reporters' desire to present full information about public behavior?

SUGGESTED READINGS

Clayton, Richard, and Hugh Tomlison. *Privacy and Freedom of Expression* (New York: Oxford University Press, 2002).

Litman, Jessica. *Digital Copyright: Protecting Intellectual Property on the Internet* (New York: Prometheus, 2000).

McChesney, Robert W. *Rich Media, Poor Democracy: Communication Politics in Dubious Times* (Urbana: University of Illinois Press, 1999).

Middleton, Kent, Robert Trager, and Bill Chamberlin. *The Law of Public Communication*, 5th ed. (New York: Longman, 2000).

Overbeck, Wayne, and Bradford J. Hill. *Major Principles of Media Law* (Belmont, CA: Wadsworth, 2002).

Soley, Lawrence. *Censorship Inc.: The Corporate Threat to Free Speech in the United States* (New York: Monthly Review Press, 2002).

Mass Communication Research
From Content to Effects

Voters who went to bed early on the 2004 election night may have thought John Kerry had won instead of George W. Bush. Throughout the day, television networks received information from a consortium of news organizations, the National Election Pool, that predicted a Kerry victory based on early exit polls. Although these polls were supposed to be kept under wraps, they were quickly leaked on the Internet, where many voters were eagerly keeping track of the election on websites like Electoral-Vote.com and political blogs like the Drudge Report. The Kerry campaign planned an acceptance speech and the stock market plunged. When the final vote was tallied and George W. Bush was declared the winner, some voters reacted with dismay, charging election fraud.[1]

Many political scientists and long-time professional pollsters agree that the 2004 election demonstrated a changing landscape for the use of polls. The rising importance of the Internet as a provider of political information has resulted in a proliferation of polls and has changed the way people access and respond to them, sometimes with strong public criticism of pollsters. Further, the Internet and automated phone technologies have provided new ways of conducting surveys, leading to questions about methodology. At the same time, the cell phone and call screening have made it more difficult to reach a broad, representative sample of voters. Therefore, changes in culture and technology

KEY CONCEPTS

- Mass Communication Research
- Basic and Practical Mass Communication Research
- Critical/Cultural Research Approach
- Qualitative Research
- Quantitative Research
- Media Theory
- Magic Bullet Theory
- Limited Effects Model
- Moderate Effects Research
- Cultivation Research
- Agenda-Setting Research
- Dependency Theory
- Uses and Gratifications Research
- Transmission Model
- News Net
- Ideology Influences Media Content
- Media and Culture

have led to many questions about the polls and their influence on news organizations that often rely on them.

Research for elections is just one type of research used by media. Research affects every aspect of every medium in ways most people do not realize. It helps determine the topics covered in newspapers and magazines, the endings of movies, and the content of advertisements. Its influence extends beyond media to all aspects of society. Research affects what automobiles look like, who runs for public office, and the taste of hamburgers sold in fast-food restaurants. Research influenced Congress to require the V-Chip in television sets and to outlaw various chemicals from use in the environment. Research affects society and people because it helps us predict and explain human behavior, both of which are crucial in making decisions about the future.

Research is conducted by university scholars who build theories to explain the impact of media on individuals and society. Media companies and media consulting firms also conduct research. They use the results to design content, to sell content to individuals, and to track who uses what media and when.

This chapter helps explain how research contributes to the understanding of mass communication on both a practical and a theoretical level. The issues addressed include the following:

- How do media directly and indirectly affect individuals and groups?
- What forces shape media technology and content?
- How do media affect individuals' knowledge of public issues and events?
- How do people use media?
- How do political and economic structures shape media culture?
- How do media organizations use research?
- What is the relationship between research and government policy?

DEFINING MASS COMMUNICATION RESEARCH

Key Concept

Mass communication research Mass communication researchers have developed a systematic study of media technology and content, the forces that shape their creation, how and why people use media, and the impact of media institutions on individuals and society.

Key Concept

Basic and practical mass communication research Mass communication research involves both practical and basic research. Practical research aims to help media organizations increase their audiences. Basic research aims to create a more theoretical understanding of human communication using mass media.

Mass communication research involves the systematic study of media technology and content, the forces that shape their creation, how and why people use media, and the impact of media institutions on individuals and society. The reasons for conducting mass communication research vary with the researcher and the organization funding the research. **Basic mass communication research** is pursued primarily by academic researchers who want to develop theory that explains the relationship between people and media. For instance, one issue of interest in basic research is determining how violent programming affects children. Media organizations conduct **practical research** in an effort to understand what content and services their audiences want and need; the goal is to predict consumer behavior in order for media organizations to increase their audiences. The movie industry conducts research to determine the popularity of particular actors. Often the same research topic can be examined by basic and practical researchers. Determining

Research in Your Life

What Do You Think? What Do You Know?

Often people think they know how mass media affect them. They make comments such as, "I never buy a product because it's advertised on television." Or, "I already know who I'm going to vote for. I don't care how candidates advertise themselves on television." Use the following questions to decide what you think the media's effects are on you. Then,

as you read this chapter, consider whether the research you read about makes you change your mind about these effects. What you thought about media's effects on yourself may be correct—or you may discover that the media have a more powerful effect on you than you thought.

Possible Effect	Yes	No
Do advertising and public relations affect the brand of product that I buy?		
Does media coverage of a political candidate affect what I think of him or her?		
Does media coverage of issues cause me to think more about certain issues than others?		
Do I act in ways similar to those I admire on television and in movies?		

how advertising affects voting can be considered basic research when it is done by political scientists or practical research when it is done by campaign consultants.

Approaches to Mass Communication Research

Mass communication research begins with a *paradigm,* which is a set of assumptions about the nature of human behavior. A variety of paradigms are available for scholars to use.[2] Each is based on previous scholarship. However, two paradigms dominate mass communication research. One uses a social science approach, and the other uses a critical approach. Of course, each of these can be broken down into many subdivisions.

The **social science approach** emphasizes the use of theory building and empirical measurement to learn about human behavior. The basic unit that is studied is the individual or small social group. The origins of this approach lie in an effort to adapt scientific methods to the study of human behavior. The social science approach involves studies such as experiments and surveys. For example, researchers at the University of Oklahoma exposed 181 students to photographs from the war in Iraq and, using scientific assessment, determined what kinds of emotions and attitudes the images evoked. The researchers were concerned with the question of whether such images "may undermine attitudes in support of war," and concluded, in part, that women are more "casualty sensitive."[3]

The *critical/cultural approach* seeks an understanding of the relationship between mass communication systems and cultural, social, and political life, often including issues of race, ethnicity, and gender. It often has an interpretive component,

Key Concept

Critical/cultural research approach The critical/cultural research approach studies the connection between media and society along with the impact of those connections on culture.

social science approach

Research approach that emphasizes theory building and quantitative methods for testing theory.

so that the researcher is actively engaged in interacting with and creating meaning from the texts, artifacts, and people being studied. Many different kinds of analysis fall under the critical/cultural approach, and researchers may define themselves as qualitative analysts or as *critical* or *cultural theorists*. They may use ethnography, analysis of language and images, and historical context, and may incorporate quantitative research to bolster qualitative arguments. For example, Lisa Flores, Dreama Moon, and Thomas Nakayama studied the racial language used in the political debate over California's "Racial Privacy Initiative" in order to understand its defeat.[4]

Each approach is limited by its paradigm. No single method of inquiry is sufficiently comprehensive to explain all cultural activity and human behavior adequately. In the late twentieth century, despite significant differences in point of view, scholars began to try to combine the two approaches into better media and communications theories.

Types of Research Methods

A number of research approaches have developed as a result of both basic and practical research. They are classified as qualitative or quantitative. The National Science Foundation, a government body that funds many researchers, defines *qualitative research* as a detailed focus on a small number of cases "with the goal of finding out 'how' things happen" and to "make the facts understandable."[5] It does not report its findings in numbers. *Quantitative research* involves the use of statistical analysis with units of content or observations about individual behaviors or attitudes. The responses and content are assigned numbers. Both approaches have advantages and disadvantages and can be used for both practical and basic research.

In the world of academic research, both qualitative and quantitative research are used to understand human behavior. However, businesses and policymakers depend increasingly on quantitative methods. Statistics can analyze the responses from large numbers of people, and the quantitative approach includes a system for selecting a representative sample of individuals from a large group of people. Most of this chapter concentrates on the social science approach and quantitative methods rather than on qualitative research, which reflects the dominance of the social science approach in applied research rather than an ordering of importance. Qualitative research methods serve a significant role in the quest to understand the relationship between humans and their media. Qualitative and quantitative supplement and complement each other in this quest.

participant observation

Research where researchers observe research subjects in everyday behavior.

textual analysis

Research where researchers interpret texts to find the social meanings underlying them.

in-depth interviewing

Research where subjects are selected for study and several detailed interviews are conducted at different times.

Qualitative Research Qualitative research works well when researchers want to understand behavior in great depth through case studies and to recognize potentially multiple points of view. In media research, many kinds of cases may be chosen, such as language, texts, images, events, identities, and group and organizational behaviors. The approach is sometimes, but not always, associated with critical studies. Examples of qualitative methods include participant observation, textual analysis, and in-depth interviewing. In **participant observation,** the researcher observes the subjects of the research in their everyday behavior. In **textual analysis,** a researcher examines a writing or other cultural product, such as a painting or music video, to unpack its meanings. The researcher may consider the author's intention, the way audiences read the text, or the relationships between texts that reveal cultural assumptions. **In-depth interviewing** involves selecting subjects for study and conducting several detailed interviews at different times.

One qualitative method often used by practical researchers is the focus group, in which a researcher assembles people at a given location with a facilitator. The people in the group may have a wide range of backgrounds, in an attempt to

Media researchers listen to focus groups, comprised of consumers, to judge whether and how to market their products, from carbonated beverages to blockbuster Hollywood films.

replicate the individuals found in a community, or they may be individuals with similar characteristics, such as men more than fifty years old. The facilitator asks questions of the group and follows up answers with additional questions. Such an approach allows a researcher to collect in-depth information. Facilitators also may seek responses from participants who view videos or read magazine or newspaper articles. Focus groups can be used to test political ads, evaluate newspaper design changes, and test campaign strategies.

The main limitation of focus groups is that they are not large enough to accurately represent large social groups. When researchers mistakenly assume that focus group conclusions can be generalized, the goals of the research may not be achieved. For example, a group of suburban daily newspapers in the southwest that had covered only local news decided to shift to a combination of local and wire service coverage. The change resulted from a decision based on a series of focus groups. However, as local content declined, subscriptions did too. A survey using a random sample of readers of the local papers, which could have been generalized to the whole population, probably would have prevented the change. A year after adding wire service content, the dailies went back to all local coverage.

Quantitative Research Quantitative research involves turning observations into numbers in order to use statistical analysis. It helps researchers make general statements about large groups, such as all the voters in a state or all individuals who usually vote Republican. People who participate in quantitative studies are selected through random methods that then allow researchers to make generalizations from the data. However, although quantitative research allows for generalizations, it does not allow researchers to gain an in-depth understanding of individual behaviors and attitudes. If two voters support a particular candidate, their responses will seem equal in a computer, but that does not mean they both support the candidate to the same degree. This explains the great variation in support a candidate receives in political polls early in an election. Some voters who express support early in a campaign may change their minds. Those who changed their minds probably did not support the candidate to the same degree as those who did not change their minds, but in the earlier survey they were grouped together.

There are three primary methods in quantitative media research: experiments, surveys, and content analysis. **Experiments** involve the application and manipulation of a treatment given to groups. For instance, an experiment to test whether information graphics affect newspaper readers' interest in the front page of a paper

experiment

A quantitative research method that involves the application and manipulation of a treatment given to groups of people, and then tests the result.

might involve giving one group of readers a front page with information graphics and another group a front page with photographs. Then the members of the two groups would be asked to rate their interest in the front pages. Their responses would be compared to see which group found which front page more interesting. With experiments, researchers can control the nature of the treatment and the surroundings of the research, which helps establish **causation.** However, because most experiments occur in artificial settings, their results may not represent everyday behavior.

Survey research involves randomly selecting a small group of people, called a sample, from a larger group, called a population, and asking them questions. The

people in the sample can be interviewed in person, over the telephone, through e-mail, or with a printed questionnaire through the regular mail. If the sample is randomly selected, surveys should result in accurate predictions of behaviors, such as voting, in the population. Nielsen ratings, for example, use a sample of households to infer what is being watched on television in all U.S. households. In addition, survey data can be used to break down such characteristics by demographic groups. For instance, Nielsen reports the TV viewing habits of men and women in various age groups.

When surveys are used in politics, they are called polls. Polls can represent accurate measures of how a group of people feels about issues, but it is difficult to phrase questions so that respondents understand them in similar ways. In addition, it cannot be assumed that responses about future behavior are accurate. How likely a respondent is to follow through with a stated intention can vary greatly. One of the best skills a pollster can have is the ability to phrase questions carefully to produce accurate and informative results.

Quantitative content analysis provides a systematic way of categorizing media content and using statistics to analyze patterns in the content. Content analysis uses a **protocol** to instruct coders how to assign numbers to diverse content. Coders can classify sentences, paragraphs, stories, photographs, characters in a movie, and actions in a video game. Before the numbers assigned to the content can be analyzed statistically, the reliability of the protocol must be established. A protocol is considered reliable when several coders use it to categorize the same content and agree on how the content should be categorized.

Just as with surveys, when researchers select samples of content randomly, they can draw conclusions about the larger population of content. If they are selected randomly, only fourteen editions of a daily newspaper are needed to describe accurately the content that appears in the paper for the year. Content analysis can describe a characteristic of content, such as the number of violent acts during an hour of television, and allow the characteristics to be compared and contrasted across media and organizations. Content analysis can answer questions such as: Is there a disproportionate number of African Americans and Latinos represented as criminals on reality cop shows? Do newspaper companies with high profit margins publish lower quality news content than newspapers with low profit margins?

If a researcher is not careful, a protocol can result in coders counting events and losing context. For example, a coder could count the same number of violent acts in Shakespeare's *Macbeth* as in a network television program, but the context and meaning of the two would be very different.

The Role of Theory in Research

Media theory involves generalizing about the relationships between people and media and society and media. Theory goes beyond research findings that apply to limited groups of people to abstractions that apply to large numbers of people. A study of how news media coverage affected the issues that concerned voters in the 2000 presidential election would be a research project. The theory would be a set of statements explaining how news media coverage affects the issues that concern voters in

causation

The process by which one or more factors result in the occurrence of an event, behavior, or attitude. A variety of factors cause human behavior. For example, genetics, parental behavior, peer associations, media consumption, and other factors combine to create certain behaviors in children.

survey research

A quantitative research method that involves randomly selecting a small group of people, called a sample, from a larger group, called a population, and asking them questions from a questionnaire.

quantitative content analysis

A quantitative research method that provides a systematic way of categorizing media content and using statistics to analyze patterns in the content.

protocol

Content analysis that contains instructions that researchers use to assign units of content to categories that in turn receive numbers. The instructions contain detailed steps every coder must follow.

all presidential elections. As with research, theory falls into social science and critical approaches.

Social science theory has adapted the scientific method used in the natural sciences. A social science theory is a set of related statements about people's behavior that (1) categorizes phenomena, (2) predicts the future, (3) explains past events, (4) gives a sense of understanding of why the behaviors occur, and (5) provides the potential for influencing future behavior.[6]

Building social science theory begins with empirical research, which is the systematic collection and analysis of data. From these data, researchers draw generalizations about social behavior and form theories. Creating a theory from research is only part of the process. The theory must be tested with further research and modified when necessary. Social science theories are based on **hypotheses,** which are statements of relationships between people and things. For example, the statement "the more violent television a child watches, the more aggressive acts the child will exhibit toward his or her playmates" is a hypothesis connecting violence on television with play behavior of children. Research tests these hypotheses. If the research results support the hypothesis, the theory that generated the hypothesis becomes stronger and more useful in explaining behavior. If the research does not support the theory, the theory must be modified to make it more consistent with reality, or it may be discarded entirely. Figure 15.1 shows that the relationship between social science theory and research is dynamic and that new hypotheses constantly lead to more research and theory modification.

Over time, most social science theory gets modified for several reasons:

1. Behavior changes as societies and humans evolve.
2. The ability to measure social behavior improves, facilitating better tests.
3. The accumulation of research further facilitates better theory.

The critical approach also develops theoretical frameworks, but the researcher engages in interpretation based on informed, subjective knowledge and experience. For example, ethnographic description may be used to describe and document the language, behaviors, emotions, and attitudes of a given social group, and the researcher may speak personally of her experience of the encounter to emphasize that her own beliefs and values necessarily affect her interpretation. Because of its historical development, critical theory is often concerned with issues of mass media's relationship to social, economic, and political power.

hypothesis

A theoretical statement of a relationship between a causing agent and a resulting action, behavior, or attitude.

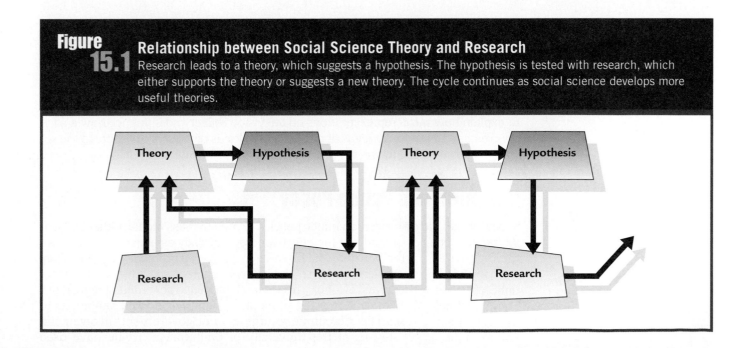

Figure 15.1

Relationship between Social Science Theory and Research

Research leads to a theory, which suggests a hypothesis. The hypothesis is tested with research, which either supports the theory or suggests a new theory. The cycle continues as social science develops more useful theories.

Internationally known communications researcher Wilbur Schramm wrote more than one hundred journal articles and books, including *Mass Communication,* which was one of the world's most widely used textbooks on communication.

Schramm graduated Phi Beta Kappa from Marietta College in his hometown, Marietta, Ohio, in 1928. He obtained a master's degree from Harvard University in 1930 and a doctorate from the University of Iowa in 1932.

Schramm worked his way through school. He worked as a waiter, was a reporter and editor at the *Marietta Daily Herald* and the *Boston Herald,* wrote for the Associated Press, and played semipro baseball with a farm club of the Pittsburgh Pirates for five dollars a game. Later he played flute with the Boston Pops symphony before a Harvard professor told him he had to choose between playing the flute and his studies at Harvard.

From 1934 to 1947, Schramm taught at the University of Iowa, starting as a part-time teacher of honors English and eventually becoming an associate professor and the first director of the nationally known Writers Workshop. When World War II broke out, he took a two-year leave to become director of the Office of Facts and Figures for the U.S. Office of War Information. One of his jobs was writing speeches for Roosevelt's "fireside chats."

Schramm returned to the University of Iowa in 1943 as a communications scholar and the director of the Iowa Journalism

Wilbur Schramm

School. Five years later the department was granting the first doctorates of mass communication in the country. In 1947, Schramm transferred to the University of Illinois to start the Institute of Communications Research. By the time he left in 1955, he had also been a research professor, director of the University Press, and dean of the division of communications. At Stanford he was the founder and director of the Institute for Communication Research, a research professor, a fellow at the Center for Advanced Study in the Behavioral Sciences, and the Janet M. Peck professor of communication.

Schramm retired in 1973, only to join the East West Center in Honolulu as director of its Communication Institute and then its Distinguished Center Researcher. He also taught for two years at the Chinese University of Hong Kong as the Aw Boon Au professor in the Department of Communication. He conducted extensive research in many parts of the world, including Asia, Africa, El Salvador, Samoa, India, and Israel.

Schramm's last book, *The History of Communication,* was published a few days before he died at home in Honolulu on December 27, 1987, at eighty years of age.

Sources: "Stanford; Obit/Wilbur Schramm, Internationally Known Communications Researcher," *Business Wire,* January 12, 1988; "Wilbur Schramm Wrote Many Works on Communications," *The New York Times,* January 1, 1988, sec. 1, p. 64; Max MacElwain, "Meet Wilbur Schramm," *Saturday Evening Post* 257 (April 1985): 49.

The importance of developing theory can be illustrated by considering how racial and ethnic groups are represented on television. Using a content analysis, a social scientist might develop a formal theory that would categorize ways these groups are represented according to stereotypes, and explain why the repetition of these stereotypes is harmful because they become psychologically internalized. Based on reviewing a television series and interpreting what she sees, a critical theorist may set out to explain how racial representations on television reflect and influence how a society creates and reinforces ideas about race. Both kinds of theory contribute to the social good by pointing to ways to reduce racism.

Research and Public Policy

Research can have an effect on public policies related to mass media, either by instigating new policies or studying the effectiveness of already established ones. Since the 1970s, a strong tradition in media research has involved protecting children from the harmful effects of violent, obscene, and indecent content and advertisements for unhealthy food, tobacco, and alcohol. This research has led to government regulations and guidelines on children's exposure to media content considered dangerous to them, and some researchers continue to urge greater government involvement. For example, psychologists at the University of California at Irvine have used

Cultural Impact

Researching Race and Television

What is the role of the mass media in a multiethnic society? To what extent do the mass media educate society about racism or reinforce racist assumptions? What impact do representations of ethnic and minority groups have on viewers? Do media companies suffer from institutional racism in their hiring practices and creation of media content? These are some of the questions posed by researchers who study the relationships between mass media and racial and ethnic groups.

Since the 1980s, a substantial body of research has grown on the representation of African Americans in the news and other television programs. Researchers have particularly focused on the question of whether African Americans are overrepresented as having a tendency toward violence and crime. In the 1990s, several content analyses found that in local news stories, African Americans were more often portrayed as suspects in mug shots, shown as handcuffed and being attacked by the police, and more likely to have damaging information presented about them before trial, potentially leading to jury bias. Further, they were rarely portrayed as officers. Whites, on the other hand, were more often portrayed as victims and in the role of officers. In 2003, researchers found that on network news, more whites are portrayed in all roles, while African Americans, when they are portrayed, more often appear as perpetrators. They concluded that because network news is targeted at a national white audience, it both blames African Americans and overrepresents whites to attract the interest of white viewers.

Communications researchers have also examined crime dramas like *Law & Order* and *NYPD Blue* and reality crime shows like *Cops* and *America's Most Wanted,* finding many of the same distortions. For example, a content analysis of *Law & Order* revealed that African Americans were five times more likely to be shown as perpetrators than victims, and were more often portrayed in handcuffs. Paying special attention to the narrative voiceover, a rhetorical analysis of *Cops* and *World's Wildest Police Videos* argued that the shows portrayed the police as always right, no matter how aggressive, and the criminals, mostly people of color, as unpredictable, irrational, and crazy. Furthermore, the police were frequently shown stopping African-American and Latino males on a pretext which then led to an arrest for a more significant crime such as grand larceny. These scenes justified police hunches that were based in racial profiling.

Racial bias also affects television sports reporting. A study of sports commentary for the men's NCAA Division I-A intercollegiate football and basketball games found that announcers emphasized African-American players' physicality and "natural" ability, while portraying whites as using brains and hard work. African Americans were frequently subjected to negative comments about their lives, character and intelligence, while white players received no such criticism. The researchers concluded that "through their negative descriptions, the announcers portray African American athletes as being at odds with society."

A growing body of cognitive psychology and communications research shows that repetition of these associations in media content reaffirms and exacerbates racial stereotyping. Even subtle negativity and bias may subconsciously affect television viewers, especially heavy television viewers who are more likely to have a distorted view of their fellow citizens and of their society. Many social scientists argue that the exaggerated association of people of color with crime has implications for the criminal justice system, such as citizens' greater support of the death penalty, longer and harsher prison sentences, and racial profiling. They also point out the need for continuing research in efforts to enhance the media's role in creating a more just society.

Sources: Travis L. Dixon, Cristina L. Azocar, and Michael Casas, "The Portrayal of Race and Crime on Television Network News," *Journal of Broadcasting & Electronic Media* 47 (2003): 498–523; Sarah Eschholz, Matthew Mallard, and Stacey Flynn, "Images of Prime-Time Justice: A Content Analysis of 'NYPD Blue' and 'Law & Order,'" *Journal of Criminal Justice and Popular Culture* 10.3 (2004): 161–180; Theodore O. Prosise and Ann Johnson, "Law Enforcement and Crime on *Cops* and *World's Wildest Police Videos:* Anecdotal Form and the Justification of Racial Profiling," *Western Journal of Communication* 68.1 (2004): 72–91; James A. Rada and K. Tim Wulfemeyer, "Color Coded: Racial Descriptors in Television Coverage of Intercollegiate Sports," *Journal of Broadcasting & Electronic Media* 49.1 (2005): 65–85.

neurological studies of adolescent brain development to argue that teens are more vulnerable to advertisement of addictive substances. They suggest that the federal government consider more comprehensive regulation to control advertising content and teens' exposure to it.[7]

Government agencies like the FCC and the FTC also conduct research to guide their decisions in policy making. Since 2000, for example, the FTC has conducted a series of research projects to support its policy of persuading the movie, music, and video game industries to exercise greater control over teens' access to violent content. The agency conducts an undercover operation, sending 13–16-year-olds into shops to purchase products with adult ratings. It then uses the findings to pressure entertainment industries to adhere to guidelines and marketing codes related to ratings systems.

Research and Media Organizations

Media managers use research to understand what their audiences want, to decide what they should charge their advertisers, and to develop news and information. Determining what a media audience wants allows companies to produce media content that people will be likely to use and buy. Motion picture studios, for example, hire research firms to survey audiences before beginning production on a film. During production, three to five previews are shown to several hundred likely viewers who answer a questionnaire about aspects of the film, like the ending. Focus groups of about twenty persons are also used to discuss the film in greater detail. Even trailers, commercials, and other promotional materials are test-screened to hone marketing campaigns. From the data collected, movies may be tweaked or even undergo major changes, such as the addition and deletion of scenes and alternative endings. DVDs often contain the original scenes that retain the director's vision. Sometimes, directors will refuse test screenings, and studios may forgo test screenings for fear that premature reactions might damage the movie's release. For example, Sony's *The Da Vinci Code* and Fox's X-Men series were not prescreened.[8]

Television news departments also use research by gathering viewers and showing them videotapes of various anchors. The researchers collect and assess reactions and suggest which anchor should be hired. Not everyone believes such research is appropriate. Changing movies to meet audience demand takes away the creative control of directors and tends to produce mediocre movies. Allowing viewers to pick anchors or TV reporters based on videos emphasizes image, often at the price of journalistic ability.

Research also helps determine what advertisers will pay for space or time. The need for an independent organization to measure audience size arose during the 1800s, when newspapers and magazines inflated their circulation numbers in order to draw advertisers away from other publications. The companies that bought advertisements rebelled against this practice and threatened not to buy advertising unless they could get independent confirmation of circulation. Today, the Audit Bureau of Circulations (ABC) conducts research to measure circulation for almost all U.S. daily newspapers and for some weekly newspapers. Nielsen Media Research estimates how many people watch particular television programs. These estimates become the basis for what stations and networks charge for advertising time or space. As use of the Web increases, companies demand accurate estimates of how many people visit sites before they will buy advertising on a particular site.

Research contributes to news coverage as well as business at media organizations. National and regional news organizations often contract for surveys to determine who is leading an election and what issues affect the race. These research results are used to develop election stories. Critics of polls argue that their use for determining who is winning treats the election like a horse race rather than a debate about important public policy issues. Polls might even influence voters and the election outcome.

MASS COMMUNICATION RESEARCH IN AMERICAN LIFE

Mass communication research started two decades into the twentieth century. During the 1920s and 1930s, researchers concluded that mass media had powerful effects on individual behavior. From the 1940s through the 1960s, researchers took the opposite tack and argued that the effects of mass media on people were limited. During this time, researchers also began to explore the factors that influence media content and the social impact of media technologies. After the 1970s, research into content influences grew enormously. Effects and uses research indicate that the impact of mass media on people and society is neither as powerful as once was thought nor as limited as researchers later claimed, but that the impact of content depends on many factors. Critical/cultural studies scholars have pursued a variety of topics during recent years, with an emphasis on the commercialization of culture and the role of media in maintaining power structures.

Effects Model

Mass media effects research studies the influence of media content on audiences and how powerful that influence might be. Media effects have been characterized as powerful, moderate, or weak, depending on the number of people who exhibit the effects. Over time, however, a more nuanced approach has developed in effects research that recognizes that people are not all alike when it comes to media impact. On the whole, research indicates that media do not have either powerful or weak effects; they have *contingent* effects. Media's impact is dependent on many factors. Some involve the content, some reflect the situation surrounding media use, and some involve the social and cultural backgrounds of media consumers.

History of Effects Research

Media effects research began during World War I. Over the years the research methods became more sophisticated, but controversy still remains about the impact of media on individuals.

Powerful Effects   Early research into the impact of mass communication developed from World War I propaganda. Governments, including that of the United States, supported mass communication efforts to mobilize their citizens in support of the war and to discourage the populations in enemy countries. Although some political and social groups in the United States opposed its entry into the war, the U.S. propaganda arm, the Committee on Public Information, flooded the country with leaflets, programs, and other materials that were designed to reduce media and citizen opposition to the war. Reflecting on these activities, Harold Lasswell published *Propaganda Techniques in the World War* in 1927.[9] The conclusions of Lasswell and others that media propaganda had been successful in generating support for the war led to the concept of universal, powerful media effects, which is known as the ***magic bullet theory.*** Scholars argued that the media worked like a bullet in their powerful persuasive impact on audiences.

Support for the *powerful effects theory* grew after the war, with a series of studies between 1929 and 1932 that examined the impact of movies on children. In response to concern about the influence of movie sex and violence, the Payne Fund financed studies of adolescents that concluded that media—in the form of movies—did indeed have powerful effects.[10] For example, W. S. Dysinger and Christian A. Ruckmick used

Posters distributed during World War I, such as this one encouraging people to grow vegetables to support the war effort, were considered to be highly effective propaganda pieces. This belief led to a supposition that mass media effects were exceedingly powerful and resulted in the "magic bullet theory" of media effects.

Key Concept

Magic bullet theory Propaganda efforts during World War I suggested that media were all-powerful. Propagandists believed that you could simply hit individuals with information, as though it were a bullet, and it would have powerful and immediate effects.

Mass Communication Research in Our Lives

1880. Marx introduces survey techniques in a study of French workers.

1927. Lasswell publishes *Propaganda Techniques in the World War.*

1920s. Frankfurt School emerges.

1929–1932. Payne studies examine movies' impact on children.

1930s–1940s. Professional pollsters develop survey techniques.

1942–1945. Hovland studies attitude change for the U.S. Army.

1948. Lazarsfeld, Berelson, and Gaudet publish *The People's Choice.*

1400–1700	1800	1900	1920	1930	1940

1620. Pilgrims land at Plymouth Rock.

1690. *Publick Occurrences* is published in Boston.

1741. First magazine is published in America.

1776–1783. American Revolution

1830s. The penny press becomes the first truly mass medium in the United States.

1861–1865. American Civil War

1892. Thomas Edison's lab develops the kinetoscope.

1914–1918. World War I

1915. *The Birth of a Nation* marks the start of the modern movie industry.

1920. KDKA in Pittsburgh gets the first commercial radio license.

1930s. The Great Depression

1939. TV is demonstrated at the New York World's Fair.

1939–1945. World War II

1949. First commercial electronic computer is produced.

Cultural Milestones

experiments in the early 1930s to study the emotional response of children to movies. They charted physiological responses, such as breathing, while the children watched the films and found that the children showed greater emotional arousal to films than did adults. They concluded that adults treated film as fantasy, but children did not.[11]

Scholars who developed the powerful effects approach conducted research at a time when social science methods were evolving. Often such research failed to control for influences that could have caused the effects the researchers found. Furthermore, the studies began with the simplistic assumptions that genetics determined all people's behavior and that all people are motivated in similar ways. Today, we know better.

1950. White publishes the first gatekeeping study.

1954. Berelson, Lazarsfeld, and McPhee publish *Voting*.

1955. Breed publishes "Social Control in the Newsroom."

1959. Katz suggests the uses and gratification line of research.

1970. Tichenor, Donohue, and Olien publish knowledge gap research.

1971. Surgeon General issues a report on TV violence's impact.

1970s. Carey revives community orientation of U.S. cultural studies.

1972. McCombs and Shaw begin agenda-setting research.

1973. Noelle-Neumann hypothesizes the spiral of silence.

1970s. Gerbner and colleagues develop cultivation theory.

1976. Ball-Rokeach and DeFleur publish dependency theory.

1982. National Institutes of Health issue a report on television violence.

Late 1980s. Media economics research increases.

1991. Shoemaker and Reese publish *Mediating the Message*.

2000. On the basis of exit polls, TV networks mistakenly announce Al Gore wins Florida popular vote.

1950	1960	1970	1980	1990	2000

Early 1950s. Rock 'n' roll begins.

1969. First person lands on the moon.

1970s. VCR is developed.

1989–1991. Cold War ends and the USSR is dissolved.

Late 1980s. National Science Foundation creates the basis of the Internet.

1996. Telecommunications Act

2000. Presidential election nearly tied.

2001. Terrorist attacks on New York and Washington, D.C.

2003. War with Iraq.

Limited Effects　At the beginning of World War II, the U.S. government again used communication to develop support for the war effort. Carl Hovland and his colleagues used more sophisticated social science methods and found evidence for a ***limited effects model***. Although films and other forms of communication did motivate troops, their effects were specific and limited.[12] These results surprised communication scholars because they contradicted the powerful effects research of the previous two decades.

Key Concept

Limited effects model　The media have limited effects on individuals—interpersonal impact is more important in influencing attitude and creating change. This approach recognizes that individuals interact with one another as well as respond to the media messages they receive.

Media scholars are concerned about the effects of television on individuals, particularly children. Studies of violence and of heavy television watching indicate that media effects can be negative as well as positive. The critical question is whether media contribute to the development of a good society. Such a statement involves many assumptions and unanswered questions.

However, the conclusion that mass media had limited effects on people found increasing support during the 1940s, particularly in studies of voting behavior. Researchers studied the voters in Erie County, Ohio, during the 1940 presidential election[13] and the voters in Elmira, New York, during the 1948 election.[14] They found that mass media converted only a small percentage of voters. Interpersonal communication played a greater role in influencing voting behavior than did media.

Moderate Effects   During the early 1970s, government and university interest in media research grew. Researchers shifted direction and began to label effects as "moderate," rather than "limited."[15] *Moderate effects research* found that media content had a greater impact on people's behavior than limited effects studies suggested, but the impact was not as great as was found by the powerful effects researchers.

An important contribution to moderate effects research was the 1972 Report to the Surgeon General on TV Violence and Children. It concluded that a connection exists between TV violence and some children's antisocial behavior. Controversy followed the release of the forty research projects that were part of the report. The television industry argued that the research had not shown a causal relationship. Some researchers argued that the report's conclusions were weaker than the research warranted.

The Surgeon General's report was followed four years later by another study of violent content by George Gerbner and his associates at the University of Pennsylvania. They found that heavy television viewing influences people to adopt values, roles, and worldviews that are based on the content they watch. If television programs are violent, heavy viewers believe that the real world is violent and frightening.

This research introduced *cultivation research,* which concerns the effect of television viewing on how people perceive the world. It states that heavy television viewers are more likely than light viewers to think that the world is actually like what is presented on television.

A steady viewing diet of *The Shield, Cops,* and other graphically violent shows could easily create the impression of a scary, violent world. Just as important as what is watched is how much viewing takes place. Time spent watching television reduces exposure to reality. Without experience to counteract television, the TV world becomes reality. Dozens of studies have found a variety of limited cultivation effects in addition to violence. These include depression, changed political attitudes, sexism, and stereotyping.

Most scholars do not doubt that television affects people's perceptions of reality. However, just how much impact it has, and on how many people, remains an issue. Cultivation research has found a consistent but weak relationship between television viewing and some people's view of the world.

Key Concept

Moderate effects research   Research after the 1970s found that media content had a greater impact on people's behavior than limited effects studies suggested, but the impact was not as great as was found by the powerful effects researchers. Therefore, the impact was labeled moderate.

Key Concept

Cultivation research   Cultivation research looks at the effect that television viewing has on how people perceive the world. The theory states that heavy television viewers are more likely than light viewers to think that the world is as it is presented on television. Heavy viewers perceive the world as being more violent than it is.

Effects and Contingencies

contingent factors

Effects that are caused by contingent, or indirect, variables rather than by the direct impact of media content.

In its early history, the effects model depended on a simple causal relationship between media content and audiences, and implied top-down, unidirectional effects. However, as researchers refined the model, they realized the importance of **contingent factors,** like the personal interests, motivations, settings, and cultural and educational backgrounds of viewers. Part of this more recent research still assumes a mostly passive audience, but takes into consideration these other factors. Other research emphasizes the active participation of audiences in seeking out and interacting with media content.

Political Effects of Mass Media Much research into the political effects of mass media has been concerned with the power that politicians may wield through image advertising, spin doctors, and manipulation of the news. The drafters of the Bill of Rights granted freedom of expression because they believed that public debate would guard against the imposition of arbitrary power by a repressive government and would create an informed populace that would be capable of governing itself. Therefore, the relationship between politics and mass media continues to be an important one for mass communications researchers in the United States and other democracies.

Agenda-setting research contends that the media influence the importance individuals place on public issues. The agenda-setting process involves placing an issue and ranking it by importance on the public agenda. The original agenda-setting research by McCombs and Shaw questioned one hundred undecided voters in Chapel Hill, North Carolina, during the 1968 presidential election.[16] The researchers analyzed the media content that the voters used and ranked the importance of issues on the basis of the amount of time and space the issue received. The voters then ranked the importance of the same issues. The ranking of coverage in the media and the ranking of issues by the voters came close to being an exact match. The conclusion from the study was that media can affect politics by influencing what the public considers important.

> ### Key Concept
>
> **Agenda-setting research** Media research seeks to understand the relationship between readers' determination of important issues and politicians, and the press treatment of them. The research focuses not on how media cover an issue, but on how they set an agenda for the issues they cover.

Audience characteristics affect individual agendas. How important an issue is to individuals, or its *salience,* affects the placement of an issue on the public agenda. For example, if unemployment is higher in the automobile industry than in other industries, unemployment will be a more salient issue to employees in the automobile industry. Salience interacts with media coverage. In Detroit, where the automobile industry is a major employer, unemployment has salience for many individuals. That salience reinforces the media's agenda-setting role. If media do not cover salient issues, their agenda-setting role is reduced.

Related to salience is the idea of obtrusiveness. An issue is *obtrusive* if an individual can experience something about it directly. An issue that is beyond direct personal experience is *unobtrusive.* If the price of a pound of hamburger goes up every week, most U.S. consumers have firsthand experience of inflation. Other issues, such as drought in Africa, are unobtrusive for most people in the United States because they have not experienced it directly. Media have more power when people do not have direct experience; this is why media play such a big role in international policy.

Research in agenda setting shows that mass media influence the public issues people discuss, and that, in turn, affects political behaviors. However, the importance of media in setting the agenda varies from person to person and from issue to issue. The goal of scholars in this area is to better explain contingencies and to explore the relationship among media, government officials, and the public in setting the public policy agenda.[17]

Shortly after the original agenda-setting study, Elisabeth Noelle-Neumann published a theory called "the spiral of silence."[18] This theory concerns the impact of mass media on public opinion. It states that three characteristics of mass media produce powerful effects on people: (1) *cumulation,* or the increasing effect of media across time; (2) *ubiquity,* or the experiencing of media messages almost all of the time; and (3) *consonance,* or the presentation of a consistent unified picture of the political world.

According to the spiral of silence, the unified, constant, and consistent picture of the world that the mass media present shapes people's perceptions of dominant political ideas. The majority of people do not share the ideas expressed by the media, the spiral of science theory argues, but media consumers think they do because of the power of media coverage. People in the majority assume they are in the minority, an assumption that makes them less likely to speak out about the issues. Over time, as the "silent majority" remains quiet, ideas that are held by a minority of people come to dominate the political discussion.

A study of the spiral of silence in Austin, Texas, found that a person's perception of public opinion did influence outspokenness.[19] However, the person's perception was only one of several factors that had an influence. Gender, age, education, income, and political opinion also affected whether people would express their political opinions. The impact of this spiral of silence on people will likely decline as the fragmentation of audiences through convergence and interactivity reduces the consonance found in mass media.

Dependency Theory   In the mid-1970s, Sandra Ball-Rokeach and Melvin DeFleur tied together a variety of effects research with ***dependency theory.***[20] Their theory explains why the impact of media varies from person to person and from situation to situation. It states that the system of media organizations controls information that people depend on to live. At the same time, people and groups in a society control scarce resources, such as information and money, that media companies need to survive. This mutual dependency between media and individuals contributes to the effects that each group has on the other.

The community newspaper illustrates this mutual dependency. Readers depend on the newspaper to help them know what has happened and what will happen in a community. People read the newspaper to learn about the decisions of the city council, the results of the high school football game, who is getting married, who died, and when local events will take place. The newspaper journalists in turn depend on the local citizens to tell them what is happening in the community. The newspaper company depends on the community to support the newspaper with advertising and subscriptions.

In addition to dependency between media organizations and individuals, dependency theory also states that social systems are interdependent. The political system depends on media to help inform the electorate, and the media system depends on the political system to define its freedoms and to maintain a stable economic environment. The mutual dependency among social systems, groups, and individuals means that all these types of units affect one another.

Dependency theory suggests that media influences individuals in six ways:

1. *Self-understanding:* People depend on media to learn about themselves and to grow as individuals.
2. *Social understanding:* People depend on media to learn about the world and their community.
3. *Action orientation:* People depend on media to decide what to buy and how to act.
4. *Interaction orientation:* People depend on media to decide how to behave toward other people.
5. *Solitary play:* People depend on media to divert and entertain them when they are alone.
6. *Social play:* People depend on media to entertain them when they are with friends and family.

The importance of media in these six activities varies from person to person, across time, and from activity to activity. An introverted person may use media more for solitary play; an extrovert may use media to interact with others. People create their own mix of media information, and some people depend more on one type of media than on another.

The overall impact of media on a person depends on availability of nonmediated information, the individual's goals and interests, and the individual's background. The stereotypical "couch potato," for instance, depends greatly on television for play and social orientation. The couch potato's images of society and how people act reflect what he or she sees on television. However, if that couch potato gets tired of watching reruns on cable and joins in church activities, his or her ideas about how other people behave will also be shaped by the church members. Media content alone does not shape people's images of their surroundings.

Uses and Gratifications Research *Uses and gratifications research* tries to identify why and how people use various media and what types of rewards they get from media content. Effects research examines what media *do to people;* uses and gratifications research examines what people *do with* media.

Early uses and gratifications research classified the reasons people decide to view, read, or listen to media. Research since the 1970s has consistently found four classifications for media uses: (1) surveillance of the environment, (2) social interaction, (3) entertainment, and (4) understanding and developing personal identity.[21] A more recent classification added the concept of using information for decision making.[22]

Using media for surveillance involves a person attending to events that may be important to him or her. Checking the baseball scores and reading about the stock market performance every day are forms of surveillance. Using media for social interaction occurs when people discuss what they watched on television or heard on radio or become part of fan groups. For instance, *Survivor* fans sharing thoughts on the Internet create group identity and understanding.

Entertainment is a way people use media to escape their problems or even everyday activities. Watching *The Lord of the Rings* trilogy allows viewers to lose themselves in the movie and forget reality for a while. In developing and understanding personal identity, people use media to analyze and come to terms with emotions, thoughts, and attitudes. For example, everyone has favorite songs that express how they feel about another person or life itself. Decision making with media information occurs when a person consults the Internet, newspapers, or magazines to help solve a specific problem—buying a car, for example.

Uses and gratifications research has developed fairly consistent categories for the way people use media. However, this area of research has not produced an accepted theory that connects people's motivations with the use classifications. There is no doubt that people often use mass media for entertainment, but questions as to why people select media over other forms of entertainment have yet to be adequately explained. Equally important are questions about why individuals select specific media to meet their needs. For instance, why do young people around the world use popular music in their social interactions?

> **Key Concept**
>
> **Uses and gratifications research** Research that tries to identify why and how people use various media and what types of rewards they receive from media content is known as uses and gratifications research. Five categories seem to classify most people's media uses: surveillance, decision making, social/cultural interaction, diversion, and personal identity.

> **Key Concept**
>
> **Transmission model** Using information theory, the Shannon–Weaver transmission model views communication as a technical process involving a source, an encoder, a message, a decoder, and a receiver.

Transmission Theory

A long-lasting influence on media theory has been Claude Shannon's and Warren Weaver's more general *transmission model,* which views communication as an information process. Shannon and Weaver were engineers at Bell Telephone in the 1940s, and were interested in understanding how information is transmitted through communications technologies. In Shannon and Weaver's **model** (see Figure 15.2), the sender translates an idea into symbols, such as words, drawings, or gestures. The symbols create a message that is communicated across a **channel,** or system, that physically transfers the message from the sender to another person or group of people. A telephone, a television set, and the human voice are all channels. The person or people who get the message are receivers. The receiver translates the message from the channel into a mental image. One can assess the accuracy of the process by asking whether the mental image of the receiver corresponds to the idea of the sender. This process can be applied to all human communication.

model

A diagram or picture that attempts to represent how something works. In communication, models are used to try to explain what happens in the creation, sending, and receiving of a message.

channel

A way of transmitting a message from a person or group of people to a person or group of people, e.g., a telephone line or newspaper.

Figure 15.2
The Communication Process (modified Shannon–Weaver model)

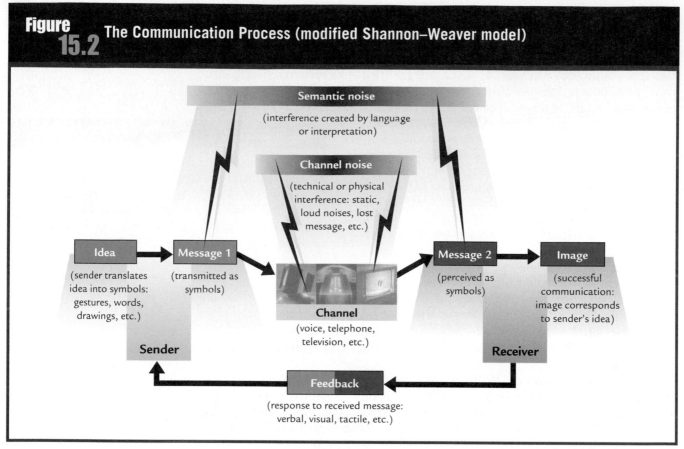

Semantic noise
(interference created by language or interpretation)

Channel noise
(technical or physical interference: static, loud noises, lost message, etc.)

Idea
(sender translates idea into symbols: gestures, words, drawings, etc.)

Message 1
(transmitted as symbols)

Channel
(voice, telephone, television, etc.)

Message 2
(perceived as symbols)

Image
(successful communication: image corresponds to sender's idea)

Sender

Receiver

Feedback
(response to received message: verbal, visual, tactile, etc.)

Source: Claude Shannon and Warren Weaver, *The Mathematical Theory of Communication* (Urbana: University of Illinois Press, 1949), p. 98.

However, the process of sending and receiving a message is not as simple as it may seem. **Channel noise** (technical or physical interference) or **semantic noise** (the interference created by language or interpretation) can disrupt or distort the message. Sometimes channel noise can be solved rather simply by increasing the capacity or the quality of the technology. Historically, technological improvements have solved many problems of channel noise, such as radio static.

Semantic noise, however, is less easily reduced or ended because it involves underlying meaning. For example, when a word has more than one meaning, readers or listeners may be confused. Careful crafting of the message by the sender reduces semantic noise.

Another element in the model, **feedback,** also helps reduce semantic noise. Feedback usually starts from the receiver in response to a message, but a series of messages may generate many feedback messages. Feedback can take many forms: verbal, visual, and tactile.

Media theorists have argued that even as the transmission model has been refined, it still oversimplifies the communications process as a one-way flow, and does not adequately take into account the interpretations, meanings, and sensory impressions generated by audiences or the contexts in which messages are exchanged. Furthermore, the interactive and multitasking abilities made possible by new media are difficult to accommodate in the transmission model.

Content Studies

During the 1940s, people also began to study the forces that shape mass media content. Critics had always assumed that mass media content reflected the rational decisions of the people who created the content. If a story on government corruption

channel noise

Interference in a communication channel, e.g., static on a radio.

semantic noise

An interference with communication because of misunderstandings about the meaning of words or symbols.

feedback

Signals sent in response to a message. These may be verbal or nonverbal.

Figure 15.3 The Process of Creating Media Content

The creation of media content begins with observations and interviews with sources. The creator generates content that is edited by managers. The creation process is influenced by routines and social interaction within the media organization. In addition, economic, political, and social forces outside the organization help shape the process. Ultimately, the content is used by media consumers, and it affects them in a variety of ways.

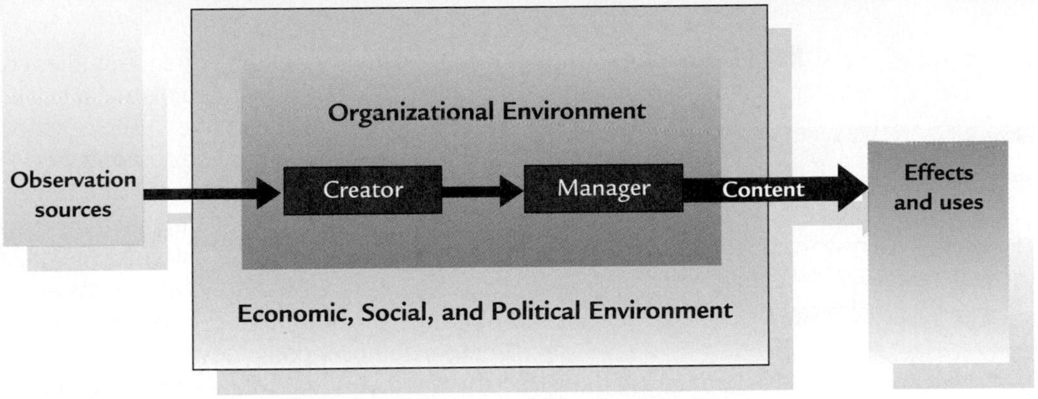

Observation sources → Organizational Environment [Creator → Manager] → Content → Effects and uses

Economic, Social, and Political Environment

appeared in a newspaper, it ran only because the editors wanted to achieve some specific goal, such as the punishment of crooked politicians. This approach seemed to explain media creation, but it failed to acknowledge that media workers face pressure as they create content. The pressure comes from advertisers, readers, sources of news, and even other journalists. Figure 15.3 indicates the complexity of creating media content and emphasizes that both external and internal forces are at work.

Gatekeeping   The earliest content influence research involved gatekeeping studies. David Manning White in 1950 studied the decisions of a wire service editor as he selected material to put in the newspaper.[23] White asked the editor to explain why he excluded and included particular articles. The editor ran stories according to personal biases, his perceptions of what readers wanted, and the editorial policies of the newspaper. The editor was acting as a **gatekeeper** of information.

Since that time, numerous studies have found that a variety of factors influence the gatekeeper's decisions. For example, how often a particular type of article appears in the wire or other news services influences the gatekeepers' decisions more than do their shared news values.[24] If 25 percent of Associated Press stories are about other countries, about 25 percent of the newspaper's stories will be about other countries. Television gatekeepers are influenced by their biases, the visual impact of stories, and how attractive the stories will be to viewers.[25] One evening a house fire will get thirty seconds on the local TV news, and the next evening another house fire will get a one-minute story. The two stories are similar, but the station shot video of the second fire.

Social Influences   Soon after the first gatekeeping study, researchers began studying the role of news organizations as social influences on news selection. Researcher Warren Breed interviewed 120 newspaper journalists during the early 1950s to determine how editors enforce newsroom policy.[26] He found that a **socialization process** taught reporters news policy without the editors having to explicitly tell them. Journalists learn what the paper's editors will accept as news from what was and was not printed in the newspaper, the way their stories were edited, and their knowledge of the editors' interests.

Reporting   Another area of exploration involves the relationship between reporters and sources. In 1961, Walter Gieber and Walter Johnson published a study of reporters

gatekeeper

A person who controls the flow of information into and through the mass media.

socialization process

Process by which reporters learn patterns of behavior by observing others and by learning to recognize the systems of rewards and punishments in a newsroom.

covering their local city hall and found that reporters often shared the values of their sources. The beat reporters and government officials depended on each other to do their jobs. Their informal relationships resulted in collaboration and cooperation in gathering and writing news.[27] Fairness and balance can become difficult when sources become more like friends than sources.

These early studies of gatekeepers and socialization showed that journalists were not autonomous individuals exercising their freedom of expression. Rather, journalists face a complex series of interactions with people who influence their actions in ways journalists do not even recognize.

News Gathering   During the 1970s, many content influence studies concentrated on newsgathering. In 1978, sociologist Gaye Tuchman published a book that created a whole new research language.[28] She described the routines that are used to gather news as a **news net.** The net catches some types of events, which become news, and it allows others to pass through. Events that are prescheduled, such as city council meetings, or nonscheduled, such as earthquakes, may qualify as news. Problems and issues that are not connected to public events, such as unequal pay for women, do not become news.

> ### Key Concept
>
> **News net** The typical routines that a reporter uses to gather news are known as a news net. Because reporters often go to the same places repeatedly, the traditional news net sometimes omits certain types of news.

Tuchman's criticism of the media grew out of her feminism and the failure of news organizations to adequately cover the women's and civil rights movements of the 1960s and 1970s. It took some time, but many newspapers eventually discovered what she found: Using topical beats improves news coverage. Today, reporters cover the environment and civil rights beats as well as the city hall and school beats.

INFLUENCES ON CONTENT

Just as a variety of factors determine the uses and effects of media, several types of influences shape media content. The influences can be classified as individual, organizational, economic, and ideological factors. *Individual influences* include the psychological makeup of the people creating the content. *Organizational influences* involve the work routines, social interaction, and ownership goals found in media organizations and in the organizations covered by media. *Economic influences* involve the demand for media content and competition for media consumers. *Ideological influences* include the shared values and beliefs that are found in a social system. These factors can work singly or together to influence media content.

Individual Factors

As was mentioned earlier, gatekeeping research examines the role of individual biases on the selection of news. As with all decisions, a journalist's perceptions affect the decisions to include one source instead of another, to emphasize a particular idea, and to pick a particular quotation. During the past twenty years, scholars have examined the impact of individual characteristics such as political beliefs, social identity, basic values, and professional ethics on content creation.

For example, when researchers at Southern Illinois University studied 159 journalists' perceptions of embedded reporting in Iraq, they included questions about the journalists' personal attitudes toward the war. They found that over half of the respondents perceived their attitudes toward the war as having "little or no influence on reporting the conflict." However, 7.4 percent stated that their attitudes had "much" or "very much" influence. Researchers often weigh the importance of individual factors against other factors, such as organizational influences, to deem which is most important.[29]

Organizational Factors

Organizational factors take two forms. The first includes the socialization processes and work routines that are found within media organizations. The other involves the interaction between journalists and people from outside the organization, such as choice of sources. The study of organizational factors dates from the beginning of research on content influences. Warren Breed's 1955 study of socialization in news organizations continues to be applicable today. Breed argued that media organizations enforce policy more through social interaction than through formal policy.[30]

Changes in newsrooms have altered the social world in which journalists make content decisions. Recent research on the influence of socialization has found that a large number of minority employees in a news organization leads to greater minority hiring and more favorable editorial comment on affirmative action. The news staff begins to share the value of cultural diversity, and this affects newspaper content.[31] Another change in newsrooms is convergence, potentially causing changes in work routines and role perceptions. Researchers have asked whether online journalists are working under different organizational influences that make speed of delivering content more important than investigation.[32] Further, they may explore whether content remains the same for the newspaper and its webpage, or is tailored for each medium, based on new organizational routines.[33]

Market Factors

Market factors include forces outside the organization, such as government regulations, economic competition, and consumer demand. Government regulations establish acceptable types of market behavior. Governments regulate some media more than others; television is the most regulated, followed by cable and radio, and finally, the Internet.

An example of how regulations affect content can be found in the history of cable and direct broadcast satellite (DBS) transmission. As the FCC has removed regulatory barriers from the expansion of cable and DBS, the number and diversity of programming

The press secretary for George W. Bush, Robert Anthony Snow, is responsible for representing the President's point of view to the press, thereby shaping news coverage.

choices for viewers have boomed. The average amount of money spent to create network prime-time programs has increased as well. One can argue about whether the changes benefit viewers, but not that regulation changes affect content.

Competition can have an impact on content depending on the type of competition and the intensity. Competition between newspapers can affect the amount of money that is available to the newsrooms and the amount of space that is available to readers. This is called the *financial commitment model*.[34] As competition increases, newspaper managers spend more money to make their newspaper different from the competition's paper. This differentiation tries to attract readers from the competition, but the news product must also remain similar enough to its competition to be considered a substitute.

Ideology

How *ideology influences media content* has been studied more by critical/cultural theorists than by social scientists. Social scientists tend to concentrate on microlevel

factors, such as individual, organizational, and market factors, rather than broad cultural beliefs. Ideology is a complex term which has been debated since Karl Marx argued that the dominant class in capitalist societies secured its power by convincing members that oppression and exploitation were natural, a form of "common sense." Though ideology has often come to mean the collection of values, beliefs, and meanings that a group of people shares, the term refers to underlying power structures: who has power and why. Most critics who use the term ideology no longer view it as a ruling class exercising its power over the masses. Rather, ideology is a competition for control over social reality, and that competition often favors those with money and other resources who can then persuade others to share their worldview.

Media theorists are interested in ideology because the mass media represent and shape social relationships, helping determine who has power and conveying "common sense" through images and texts. These theorists may explore how media institutions sustain dominant values like nationalism, consumerism, technological progress, and traditional social roles. For example, scholars have argued that rap music perpetuates an ideology of hatred of women because of casual, demeaning references to violence against women and treatment of them as manipulators and sex objects. Such portrayals "ultimately support, justify, instill, and perpetuate ideas, values, beliefs, and stereotypes that debase women."[35] These attitudes are not unique to rap, the argument goes, but are embedded in a broader society which still upholds the power of men over women, making it seem acceptable and natural. Theorists may also examine the ways groups interact with persuasive ideological messages, sometimes adapting or resisting them.

CRITICAL/CULTURAL MEDIA STUDIES

Critical/cultural media studies takes many forms, but is primarily concerned with the way people make meaning from media technologies and cultural texts. The phrase *cultural text* refers to any human-made thing that people in a culture find meaningful. It can apply not only to printed pages, but to other forms, such as films, soap operas, song lyrics, artworks, fashions, political speeches, bodies, places, and events. Attention is often paid to *cultural practices:* how people incorporate media forms into their everyday lives and communities. Historically, critical/cultural theorists often have had a skeptical view of mass media, arguing that media institutions have too much destructive influence in their conveying of dominant values and their emphasis on their own power and profit. However, other theorists emphasize that encounters between audiences and texts produce multiple meanings that can't be so easily summed up.

Early Critical/Cultural Media Studies Research in the United States

Three strains of critical studies were developed during the late nineteenth and twentieth centuries that would influence media studies.

In Chicago, Charles Cooley, Robert Park, and John Dewey explored the positive possibilities of modern communication. They saw communication as the foundation for developing a sense of community in an industrialized world. A second group of communication scholars came to the United States from Frankfurt, Germany. Theodor Adorno, Herbert Marcuse, and Max Horkheimer, theorists associated with the Frankfurt Institute for Social Research, fled Hitler's fascist regime in 1933 and established themselves in New York. The Frankfurt School's thought was more pessimistic than that of the Chicago School. Frankfurt theorists did not believe that modern media had the potential to improve society. Their theoretical approach was based on the economics of media organizations, and so they considered the specifics of professional practice to be irrelevant.

Finally, in the 1960s, scholars at the Centre for Contemporary Cultural Studies at the University of Birmingham, England, tied the insights of the Frankfurt School to other studies of language and meaning. The Birmingham School emphasized the importance of audiences in interpreting media texts.

Chicago School The work of Charles Horton Cooley, John Dewey, and Robert E. Park ushered in a new way of thinking about modern media. Theorizing from philosophical and sociological traditions, these **pluralist** social reformers believed that modern media could make possible a truly democratic community. Together, writes Daniel Czitrom in *Media and the American Mind*, they "construed modern communication essentially as an agent for restoring a broad moral and political consensus to America, a consensus they believed to have been threatened by the wrenching disruptions of the nineteenth century: industrialization, urbanization, and immigration."

Cooley tried to understand the interplay between modern media and social groups, such as the family, friends, play group, and peer group. He laid the foundation for later empirical research into how media effects are moderated and changed by interaction with other individuals and groups. Dewey and Park addressed the form and content of journalism, occasionally lamenting that it too often lined the pockets of the businessperson, but also speculating about a newspaper that would carry no advertising and would appeal to the higher intellect. Unlike the Frankfurt theorists, these communication scholars of the **Progressive generation** had great hopes about the effect of media on modern society. Dewey wrote in 1915, in *Democracy and Education,* "There is more than a verbal tie between the words *common, community,* and *communication.* Men live in a community in virtue of the things they have in common; and communication is the way in which they come to possess things in common."

As the Progressive era gave way to the Great Depression of the 1930s, the emphasis on empirical research and social science approaches gained ascendancy. The daring hopes of the Progressives for a new form of community were dashed as the economy plummeted. Scholars turned tn empirical methods to document media effects, and empiricism and social science approaches dominated in media studies, just as they dominated in other emerging fields such as political science.

Frankfurt School The Frankfurt School's theories developed out of traditional Marxist thought. Principles of Marxist thought include a belief that the economic basis of a society determines its social structure as a whole as well as the psychology of the people within it. Historical change was thought to have been a result of conflict between owners of property and workers, and class struggle is inevitable within a capitalist society. Marxist theorists believe that only revolution, not reform, can accomplish change; therefore, although labor unions might be useful training grounds for radicals, they only temporarily relieve the conditions of workers. Because reform creates only temporary relief, conditions will worsen until the workers' misery drives them to

pluralist

One who espouses coexistence and cooperation among different elements of a power structure.

progressive generation

Group of individuals in the early 1900s who championed political and social reform.

revolution. The government in capitalist societies is perceived to be the coercive instrument of property owners.

The young Marxist intellectual radicals who made up the Frankfurt School were disappointed that the 1917 Russian revolution had not spread throughout Europe. The dark years of fascism in Europe affected them deeply, and they were concerned that the postwar Western world appeared to be politically stable. Such stability, in their minds, meant an end of a conscious recognition of the need for radical change from within the working class. They saw the workers as suppressed by the culture industries—by the mass media. They viewed the Western press as being organized through rules and institutions.[36] The Frankfurt School theorists believed that within a capitalist society art could not be a revolutionary force. They argued that the media made art part of the established order, and although it might have made certain forms of high culture more accessible to the middle class, it did so at the expense of robbing high culture of its critical substance. Art thus became intertwined with official function. Herbert Marcuse, a founder of the Frankfurt Institute of Social Research, argued that language constantly imposed images, which worked against conceptual thinking. As a group, the Frankfurt School rejected the idea that theory could affect practice, and they retreated from allowing their research to lead them into a dialogue about modern media. Although there are now many strains within the cultural studies traditions, both in the United States and abroad, the traditions of the Frankfurt School had an enormous impact on the development of U.S. cultural theory.

Birmingham School In the late nineteenth century, the Swiss linguist Ferdinand de Saussure and American philosopher Charles Peirce introduced the field of semiotics, which would have as much influence as Marxism on the development of media studies. Semiotics is the study of signs. Signs are anything that stands for something else, just as a photograph of a tree stands for trees, a flag stands for national identity, and a road sign stands for stop. Signs can only be understood in their similarity and difference to other signs, and become part of systems of signs that have meaning when someone interprets them. For example, a later philosopher, Roland Barthes, studied how fashion magazines have a system of texts and images that present an idea of Fashion.

In the 1960s, scholars at the Centre for Contemporary Cultural Studies at the University of Birmingham, England, brought semiotics together with Marxist theory to create a new field of media studies. British theorists like Raymond Williams and Stuart Hall argued that audiences create meaning by decoding the cultural codes implicit in media texts. Audiences have freedom in the meanings they generate from a media text, but the text guides them toward preferred ideological interpretations, such as those promoting consumerist values and proper gender roles. Although it has been questioned and refined by later scholars, the encoding/decoding model is still highly influential in critical/cultural media studies.

Critical/Cultural Media Studies Today

While social science approaches continue to dominate mass media research, critical/cultural studies have gained in importance with the establishment of scholarly publications and university programs and courses. Raising new questions, their emphasis on culture, text, and interpretation is an important contribution to a holistic understanding of people and media.

Media and Culture Addressing questions about the relationship between **media and culture,** James Carey, writing from the mid-1970s onward, revived the community orientation of U.S. cultural studies. Carey argued that the transmission model did not adequately represent communication; instead, communication should be viewed as a process through which a shared culture is created, modified, and transformed. Communication is not an extension of messages in space, but the maintenance of society across time.

Media Convergence

Researching Video Games

Convergent media has challenged researchers and theorists to come up with new models and ideas, and to adapt old ones. Electronic video games are an interesting case, because even though video games have been around since Ralph H. Bauer invented Pong in the late 1960s, they have only recently gained broad attention, both by quantitative and qualitative analysts.

As the video game industry has begun rivaling other media industries, advertisers have had a greater interest in marketing through games, either by product placement, developing gaming advertainments, or including commercials before and after game play. Therefore, advertisers want measurements of who plays video games, when and how they play, what other media content interests them, and whether they buy products based on ads. In October 2006, Nielsen introduced GamePlay Metrics to meet this demand by recording information about games played through television sets. This required a change to Nielsen's People Meter technology to include an audio device that identifies the video game being played.

Other researchers have been interested in the effects of violent content on video game players, especially children and young adults. Their studies extend earlier work on television violence, and have an impact on public policy regarding the rating and censorship of video games. Psychologist Craig Anderson points to two reasons why video games have required new research: young players' increasing exposure to ultraviolent content, and their interactive participation in violent scripts that potentially make video games more dangerous than violent movies and television. Research may take the form of surveys, observation of player behaviors, and measurement of physiological factors like brain activity and heart rate. Because of the changed demographics of game players, more research has been done on the effects of violent content on female players and their relationship to male and female characters.

Qualitative research on video games has also expanded, as critics have examined the artistic, social, and cultural dimensions of play. Some theorists examine the relationship of video game content to other media forms, focusing on games as cultural texts.

For example, Jay David Bolter and Richard Grusin have argued that digital multimedia forms like video games adapt their content from older storytelling forms, such as print fiction and movies. Narrative theorists may look at how traditional devices such as plot, character, and point of view are developed in electronic games, or how their content may reflect social and political ideologies. The notion of storytelling is also important in discussions of how content is delivered across media platforms, from movies to video games, and from books to video games.

However, other theorists called "ludologists"—derived from the Latin for "play"—are more interested in the way users interact with the technology and game design and the pleasure they take in play. Editor of *Game Studies,* Espen Aarseth, has argued that games "can't be read as texts or listened to as music, they must be played. Playing is integral, not coincidental like the appreciative reader and listener." Therefore, video games are fundamentally different than other media forms, and elements like a user's interface with technology, skill, creativity, and social adeptness must be taken into account. Aarseth has suggested three interrelated areas of game research: game play, such as psychological and social factors; game rules, such as design parameters; and game world, such as artistic qualities.

With the appearance of scholarly books and journals, academic institutes, and university courses devoted to game studies, they have become a recognized field of inquiry devoted to a new media form.

Sources: Craig A. Anderson, "Violent Video Games: Myths, Facts and Unanswered Questions," *Psychological Science Agenda,* American Psychological Association (October 5, 2003), apa.org/science/psa/sb-anderson.html; Espen Aarseth, "Computer Game Studies, Year One," *Game Studies* 1.1 (2001), gamestudies.org/0101; Jay David Bolter, *Writing Space: Computers, Hypertext, and the Remediation of Print* (Mahwah, NJ: Lawrence Erlbaum, 2001); Special Issue on Games, *Popular Communication* 4 (2006); Espen Aarseth, "Playing Research: Methodological Approaches to Game Analysis," Melbourne DAC (2003), hypertext.rmit.edu.au/dac/papers.

Carey further argued that communication was not the imparting of information or influence but the creation and transmission of shared beliefs.

Communication, writes Carey, "is a symbolic process whereby reality is produced, maintained, repaired, and transformed."[37] Carey helped introduce a North American cultural media studies that shifted the focus away from ideology and content, focusing instead on how individuals interact with media forms and technologies within everyday situations.[38]

Carey's work contributed to the study of media ecology, which grew out of Marshall McLuhan's claim that "the medium is the message." Neil Postman writes that media

Media Research and Global Flows

In a world transformed by the mass migration of peoples, the spread of communication technologies, and the flow of media forms across borders, the comparative study of media is a complex undertaking. A central question for media researchers and theorists is how people in different cultures respond to different media forms, and how their understanding of the global and the local interact. For example, when a Chinese youth buys a Nike shoe, what cultural and psychological forces influence that decision? What knowledge, feelings, and values embodied in the Nike shoe and its related advertising make sense to this consumer, and why? If the Chinese youth has migrated to the United States, are different influences at work involving cultural assimilation?

Figuring out the needs and desires of the global youth market is important to multinational corporations and other investors who need to know how to design marketing campaigns. Thus, some researchers and marketing consultants carry out studies to assess foreign consumers' response to brands and products. For example, a study conducted through focus group interviews with students in Kazakhstan found that many of them wanted to own a Mercedes-Benz, wear Armani, and furnish their dwellings with IKEA. Since Kazakhstan is a transitional economy, lifting trade barriers and encouraging foreign investment, the researchers suggested that their results might represent the "special credibility and authority" of Western brands in such economies. Western brands are associated with affluence, success, and modernity for young people with a desire to participate in a new global consumer culture associated with a global youth identity.

Other scholars are interested not in the marketing potential, but in the cultural impact of media forms. They examine the ways people come into contact with a media product, accept some foreign influences, reject or adapt others to suit their own cultural desires and expectations, and possibly even forget its association with the originating country. For example, a quiz show like *Who Wants to Be a Millionaire* is broadcast around the world using a similar format, but the exact content may be different to make sense to local audiences. In India, a question like "Who painted the Mona Lisa?" is worth many more points because of the audience's lack of familiarity with Western culture. In countries with similar language and background, such as the United States and the United Kingdom, the versions of *Who Wants to Be a Millionaire* are more alike. In countries like Singapore, where Christian holidays are celebrated and the government urges citizens to imitate Western behaviors, the version is also similar to the original British version. Such examinations explore the complicated relationship of the local and the global in understanding media flows.

Sources: Jung-Wan Lee and Simon Tai, "Young Consumers' Perceptions of Multinational Firms and Their Acculturation Channels Towards Western Products in Transition Economies," *International Journal of Emerging Markets* 1 (2006): 212–224; Amir Hetsroni, "Rule Britannia! Britannia Rules the Waves: A Cross-Cultural Study of Five English-Speaking Versions of a British Quiz Show Format," *Communications* 30 (2005): 129–153.

---

ecology "tries to find out what roles media force us to play, how media structure what we are seeing, why media make us feel and act as we do."[39] Related to media ecology is *medium theory,* which focuses on the characteristics of media rather than the content that they convey. For example, theorists in medium theory and media ecology ask in what ways new media are changing users' perceptions of time and space.

Critical Discourse Analysis   In critical discourse analysis, media theorists examine texts to see how society is represented through language. They may look at political rhetoric, advertising copy, or letters to the editor, or conduct interviews to obtain a sample of the way people talk about a subject. In general, critical discourse analysts are interested in examining how social power is created and circulated through discourse. For example, to examine how a leader rallies a country to war, an analyst might study President George W. Bush's speech on Iraq for religious imagery, vision of national identity, and use of the word "terrorist."

Media Representations of Race, Class, and Gender   Because the media reproduce, encourage and challenge social constructions of race, class, and gender, many media theorists are concerned with the representation of identity. Using a variety of analytical tools, such as discourse analysis, the economics of media production, and social theory, these scholars look critically at media forms such as soap operas, horror films, advertising, rap music, celebrity images, and sports broadcasts. In general, their aim is to promote critical thinking about race, class, and gender in and through media, and to encourage change and activism in creating a more just and equitable society.

TRENDS

While much media research still relies on traditional models such as surveys and focus groups, new technologies have created opportunity for new methods, approaches, and theories. As study of new media has grown, researchers from many disciplines have joined to create new fields, such as social informatics, which looks at the use of information and communications technologies in specific environments, and game studies, which brings together computer scientists, graphic designers, philosophers, cognitive scientists, and cultural theorists. New technologies have provided opportunities for measuring media use. Two trends—brain scanning and frame analysis—try to get at underlying motivations and responses of media producers and consumers.

Technology: Brain Imaging

Functional magnetic resonance imaging (fMRI) is a noninvasive technology that measures neural activity in specific areas of the brain. Researchers claim that they can give stimuli to a test subject wearing a sensor net, and measure brain activity related to feelings such as identification, fear, sexual pleasure, indecision, and empathy. In media research, fMRI has been used to measure consumer behavior and reactions to violent content. A key assumption is that people have hidden responses and motivations beyond what they say, and that can't be understood through traditional methods, such as interviews and surveys.

In consumer research, the technology has been used to assess test subjects' response to advertising, including commercials, brands, and spokespersons. For example, working with a marketing firm, neuroscientists at UCLA tested five subjects during the 2006 Super Bowl, finding that an "I'm Going to Disney World" ad stimulated responses related to identification, empathy, and reward gratification.[40] In another experiment, test subjects were asked to judge brands using a list of 450 adjectives that usually apply to personality, such as "pleasant" and "cheerful." The researchers

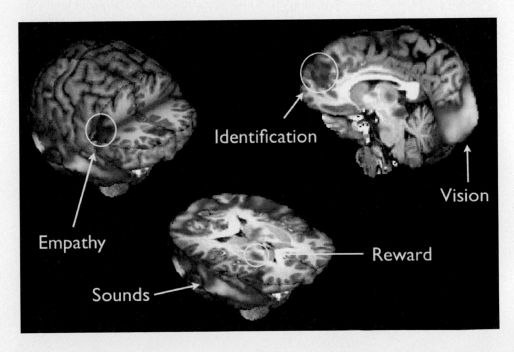

A research team led by Marco Iacoboni at the University of California, Los Angeles, has used brain scans to gauge viewers' emotional responses to a series of 2006 Super Bowl advertisements.

Changes in technology, laws, and aims of researchers are affecting the nature of communication research. The power that such research can have on society also seems to be growing. Underlying these trends is the importance of research in making decisions—an importance often lost on most U.S. citizens because research seems alien to them. This importance suggests that more people should understand the trends that are occurring and be ready to discuss these trends by answering questions such as:

■ Why is developing mass communication theory important? What are the advantages of integrating communication research into theories? Can scholars create a theory that will integrate the factors that affect media content with the effects of content on people?

■ What role does research play in shaping government and laws? Should this be the case? Are there ways

other than research for government officials to know what the public supports? Is knowing public opinion important? Why?

■ How will technology affect the ability of researchers to understand the use and impact of media?

■ What role does research play in shaping public policy? Are there ways other than research for government officials to know what the public supports? Is knowing public opinion important? Why?

■ How will technology affect the ability of researchers to understand the use and impact of media? What are the ethical implications of new research technologies?

■ What new questions do digital media technologies and contents pose for researchers? What traditional research approaches are still relevant and why?

---

concluded that people don't respond to brands and persons in the same way, since different areas of the brain are employed.[41]

fMRI has also been used in the longstanding debate over the effects of media violence on children. Communications researchers have observed that adolescent test subjects playing *Tactical Ops: Assault on Terror* show higher cortical activity related to aggression. Similarly, a study of the effects of violent television on children found increased brain behavior related to aggression and memory that may influence social behavior.[42]

These experiments require an effective interdisciplinary team, careful design, great skill, and expensive technology to construct. The technology is still relatively new, and is extremely limited in the extent to which it can "mind read" and predict what a person is actually thinking. Critics charge that human behavior is far more complex than a scan implies, because it involves social behaviors, practices, and choices within real-life environments.

Culture: Framing and Second-Level Agenda Setting

Frame analysis stems from the work of sociologists Gregory Bateson and Erving Goffman in the 1970s. Bateson and Goffman argued that people make sense of reality through unconscious frames, selecting some details and placing others in the background. A frame answers the question, "What is going on here?" The selection process takes place primarily because of a person's social background and influence. In the 1990s, frame analysis proliferated in a number of fields, such as law and psychology, taking a variety of forms.

In media research, frame analysis has increasingly been used to examine the way journalists construct news stories through conscious and unconscious selection processes. Because it also builds on earlier agenda-setting research, this research is often referred to as "second-level agenda setting." First-level agenda setting research focuses on *what* issues are covered; second-level agenda setting research focuses on *how* issues are represented and defined. Three approaches apply: studying journalists' thought processes and resulting news coverage; examining how politicians and other newsmakers compete to have their frames represented; and looking at how the perceptions, attitudes, and feelings of audiences might change in exposure to journalistic frames.[43]

Much of the focus in this research is on language and image as a way of understanding frames and framing. Researchers examine the visual and verbal content of news stories, press releases, and news blogs, and survey public attitudes through phone surveys. For example, because of the high impact of visual images, researchers may study images and video of political candidates along with newscasters' positive, negative, or neutral comments about them. Then, a survey may be conducted to assess whether viewers' emotional responses to the candidates correlate with the news content. For example, television exposure to 2000 campaign images in which Al Gore smiled and looked directly at the camera led viewers to feel "hopeful and proud."[44] Thus, a news organization's selection of images to include in its coverage has an effect on public opinion.

SUMMARY

- Mass communication research plays an important role in public policy media literacy, and solving practical problems for media organizations.
- Basic mass communication research takes two approaches. The social science approach examines the behavior of individuals and groups associated with mass communication, and the critical/cultural approach emphasizes the connections between media and culture.
- Communication research is classified as qualitative and quantitative, which represent a variety of methods. Each of these methods has strengths and weaknesses.
- Early social science communication research concentrated on media effects.
- Critical studies developed from three major schools: the Frankfurt School, the Chicago School, and the Birmingham School.
- Supporters of the Chicago School took a more positive approach toward the impact of communication in society than did scholars in the Frankfurt School.
- World War I propaganda led researchers to believe that media had an all-powerful (magic bullet) effect.
- By 1940, researchers began to shift their thinking to a limited effects model, which suggests that interpersonal influences were as great as media influences.

- An active area of political effects research is agenda setting, which deals with the impact of media on the political issues that are discussed by the public and addressed by government.
- Media uses and gratifications research is an offshoot of effects studies. Uses and gratifications research explores why and how people select media content.
- Dependency theory holds great promise for individual effects research. It identifies the dependency relationships among people, media, and social systems, and explains how these influence people and groups.
- Media uses research is an offshoot of effects studies. Uses research explores why and how people select media content.
- Research about factors that determine media content concentrates on several types of influences. Important among these are individual, organizational, economic, and ideological influences.
- Critical/cultural studies research involves the study of power and ideology. It can take the form of historical analysis, textual analysis, technology and society studies, as well as other investigations into media and culture.
- Political polls are survey research tools that under some conditions can have a strong impact on public policy.

NAVIGATING THE WEB Mass Communication Research

Communication, Cultural and Media Studies
cultsock.ndirect.co.uk/MUHome/cshtml/index.html
This site, developed by Mick Underwood, offers a searchable database of key media terms, along with definitions and discussions.

Nielsen Media Research
nielsenmedia.com
Nielsen Media provides audience measurement for television, advertising, and portable media.

Popular Culture: Resources for Critical Analysis
wsu.edu/~amerstu/pop
Created by T. V. Reed, a professor at Washington State University, this page provides a guide to resources for studying cultural texts, such as television, film, comic books, fashion, sports, and digital media.

QUESTIONS FOR REVIEW

1. What are the differences between quantitative and qualitative research methods?
2. How does the cultural studies approach to the study of mass media differ from the social science approach?
3. What is social science theory? What is it used for?
4. What is the difference between effects and uses research?
5. What is agenda setting?
6. What is frame analysis?

ISSUES TO THINK ABOUT

1. What are the possible effects of the gatekeeping process on news content?
2. Pick a current topic in the news and discuss the implications of the agenda-setting concept on how this issue became news.
3. Discuss dependency theory and its connection to media effects.
4. Explain the different theoretical perspectives in social science research and cultural studies approaches. What separate contribution does each approach make to understanding mass communication?
5. Discuss some possible organizational influences on content.
6. Discuss some possible individual influences on content.

SUGGESTED READINGS

DeFleur, M. L., and Sandra Ball-Rokeach. *Theories of Mass Communication,* 2nd ed. (New York: David McKay, 1982).

Downing, John D. H., et al. *The Sage Handbook of Media Studies* (Thousand Oaks, CA: Sage, 2004).

McQuail, Dennis. *McQuail's Mass Communication Theory: An Introduction,* 5th ed. (Thousand Oaks, CA: Sage, 2005).

Severin, Warner J., and James W. Tankard. *Communication Theories: Origins, Methods and Uses in the Mass Media,* 5th ed. (Boston: Addison-Wesley, 2002).

Williams, Kevin. *Understanding Media Theory* (London: Arnold, 2003).

Endnotes

Chapter 1

1. Deborah Potter, "Bearing Witness," *American Journalism Review,* Oct./Nov. 2005: 88.
2. Qtd. in Lisa de Moraes, "Kanye West's Torrent of Criticism," *Washington Post,* September 3, 2005: C01.
3. Yahoo, Inc. and Carat North America, Press Release, July 24, 2003, docs.yahoo.com/docs/pr/release1107.html, accessed on August 19, 2006.
4. David Manning White, "The 'Gatekeeper': A Case Study in the Selection of News," *Journalism Quarterly* 27 (1950): 383–390.
5. S. H. Steinberg, *Five Hundred Years of Printing* (New York: Criterion Books, 1959), pp. 21–22.
6. For a detailed discussion of the impact of the printing revolution on Western society, see Elizabeth L. Eisenstein, *The Printing Revolution in Early Modern Europe* (Cambridge, England: Cambridge University Press, 1983). See also David Hall, "The World of Print and Collective Mentality," in John Higham and Paul K. Conkin, eds., *New Directions in American Intellectual History* (Baltimore: Johns Hopkins University Press, 1980), pp. 166–180. Eisenstein and Hall demonstrate the impact of technological change on society.
7. Richard Schwarzlose, *The Nation's Newsbrokers: The Formative Years from Pretelegraph to 1865,* vol. 1 (Evanston, IL: Northwestern University Press, 1989). Schwarzlose's volumes are the first complete history of the wire services.
8. Christopher Sterling and John Kittross, *Stay Tuned,* 2nd ed. (Belmont, CA: Wadsworth, 1990), pp. 52–55. This is a complete history of broadcast media.
9. "Internet: The Undiscovered Country," *PC Magazine* (March 15, 1994): 116–118.
10. "Media Wars," *Media Studies Journal* 6:2 (Spring 1992): Preface.
11. Mark A. Thalhimer, "A National Information Service Background Paper," Freedom Forum Media Studies Center, December 1991.
12. William B. Blankenburg and Gary W. Ozanich, "The Effects of Public Ownership on the Financial Performance of Newspaper Corporations," *Journalism Quarterly* 70 (1993): 68–75.
13. Harold Lasswell, "The Structure and Function of Communication in Society," in Lyman Byron, ed., *The Communication of Ideas* (New York: Institute for Religious and Social Studies, 1948), pp. 37–51; Charles R. Wright, *Mass Communication: A Sociological Perspective,* 3rd ed. (New York: Random House, 1959), pp. 4–6. Together these scholars listed four functions of mass communication for society. Two of these, surveillance and entertainment, take place at the individual level and are considered individual uses here. Self-understanding as a use is taken from dependency theory. See Melvin DeFleur and Sandra Ball-Rokeach, *Theories of Mass Communication,* 5th ed. (New York: Longman, 1989), pp. 305–310.

Chapter 2

1. Jonathan Franzen, "Jonathan Franzen Uncorrected," Powell's Books, October 4, 2001, powells.com/authors/franzen.html, accessed May 16, 2006.
2. National Endowment for the Arts, *Reading at Risk: A Survey of Literary Reading in America* (Washington, D.C.: NEA, 2004), pp. ix–x.
3. Elizabeth L. Eisenstein, *The Printing Revolution in Early Modern Europe* (Cambridge, England: Cambridge University Press, 1983); David Hall, "The World of Print and Collective Mentality," in *New Directions in American Intellectual History,* John Higham and Paul K. Conkin, eds. (Baltimore: Johns Hopkins University Press, 1980); Jeffery A. Smith, *Printers and Press Freedom: The Ideology of Early American Journalism* (New York: Oxford University Press, 1988).
4. Moira Davison Reynolds, *Uncle Tom's Cabin and Mid-Nineteenth Century United States: Pen and Conscience* (Jefferson, NC: McFarland & Company, 1985); and Thomas F. Gossett, *Uncle Tom's Cabin and American Culture* (Dallas, TX: Southern Methodist University Press, 1985).
5. J. Preston Dickson, *Young Frederick Douglass: The Maryland Years* (Baltimore: Johns Hopkins University Press, 1980); William Andrews, "An Introduction to the Slave Narrative," North American Slave Narratives Online Collection, University Library, University of North Carolina at Chapel Hill, December 1, 2005, docsouth.unc.edu/neh/intro.html, accessed on May 17, 2006.

6. Lewis A. Coser, Charles Kadushin, and Walter W. Powell, *Books: The Culture and Commerce of Publishing* (New York: Basic Books, 1982). This comprehensive volume thoroughly explores the relationship between economics and culture in book publishing.

7. Christine Bold, "Popular Forms I," in *Columbia History of the American Novel,* Emory Elliott, ed. (New York: Columbia University Press, 1991), p. 298. The *Columbia History* is particularly useful for studying genres historically and for understanding content in the context of history.

8. Association of American Publishers, "Book Publishing Industry Net Sales Totalled $25.1 Billion in 2005," press release, March 6, 2006.

9. Bowker, "U.S. Book Production Plummets 18K in 2005," press release, May 9, 2006, bowker.com/press/bowker/2006_0509_bowker.htm, accessed on May 17, 2006.

10. "Potter Leads the Pack," *Publishers Weekly,* March 27, 2006: 27.

11. Association of American Publishers, "Book Publishing Industry."

12. National Endowment for the Arts, *Reading at Risk,* p. ix.

13. Jacqueline Blais and Anthony DeBarros, "Reading the Trends," *USA Today,* January 19, 2006: D6.

14. Association of American Publishers, "Book Publishing Industry."

15. Qtd. In Steven Waldman, "Belief Watch," *Newsweek,* May 22, 2006, 10.
Jim Milliot, "Top Five Pubs Take Half of Sales," *Publishers Weekly,* April 25, 2005, 5.

16. National Endowment for the Arts, *Reading at Risk,* p. 9.

17. John F. Baker, "Reinventing the Book Business," *Publishers Weekly,* March 14, 1994: 36.

18. Don R. LeDuc, *Law of Mass Communications,* 7th ed. (Westbury, NY: Foundation Press, 1992), p. 695; see also John F. Baker, "Reinventing the Book Business."

19. "Largest Trade Publishers," *Publishers Weekly,* April 25, 2005, 5.

20. "Paramount's Last Chapter—Not Quite," *U.S. News & World Report,* February 28, 1994; "Business Notes," *Maclean's,* February 28, 1994: 40; Mark Landler and Gail DeGeorge, "Sumner at the Summit," *Business Week,* February 28, 1994: 32; John Greenwald, "The Deal That Forced Diller to Fold," *Time,* February 28, 1994: 50; Don Jeffrey, "Industry Awaits Fallout of Paramount Deal; Victors in Takeover Battle Now Must Pay Down Debt," *Billboard,* February 26, 1994: 6.

21. "Titanic Tidings," July 12, 2002, www.publishersweekly.com/articles/19980914_70408.asp.

22. Caitlin Kelly, "The Oprah Effect," *Broadcasting & Cable,* January 24, 2005: 58.

23. Ashwin Ahmad, "Hurry Potter: 1 lakh copies sold in India," Knight Ridder *Tribune Business News,* July 18, 2005, 1; Viva Sarah Press, " 'Harry' in Hebrew in Time for Hannuka," *Jerusalem Post,* November 22, 2005: 24.

24. International Movie Database, Inc., "All-Time Non-USA Box Office," 2006, imdb.com/boxoffice/alltimegross?region=non-us, accessed on May 19, 2006.

25. John F. Baker, "Reinventing the Book Business," *Publishers Weekly,* March 14, 1994: 36

26. *Hoover's Company Records,* May 15, 2006, 16513, 14665, 42887.

27. "The Book Marketplace II," in *Reading in America: Literature and Social History,* Cathy Davidson, ed. (Baltimore: Johns Hopkins University Press, 1989), pp. 687–688.

28. weeklywire.com/disk$ebony/tw/www/ww/09–29–97/knox_feat.html, September 29, 1997.

29. E. A. Vander Veer, "The Revolution That Wasn't," *The Writer,* January 2002: 18.

30. "Sexual Intelligence," *Publishers Weekly,* August 28, 2005: 47.

31. Paula Berinstein, "Using Statistics," *Searcher,* May 2005: 52.

32. National Endowment for the Arts, *Reading at Risk,* 24.

33. Lawrence Hardy, "Forgetting How to Read, or Just Relocating It?" *Education Digest,* Feb. 2005, 33–41.

34. Jim Milliot, "It's All About Content," *Publishers Weekly,* June 24, 1996: 28–30.

Chapter 3

1. Devin Leonard, "What Price Knight Ridder?" *Fortune,* March 6, 2006: 63.

2. Qtd. in Rachel Smolkin, "Adapt or Die," *American Journalism Review,* April/May 2006, ajr.org/Article.asp?id=4111, accessed May 29, 2006.

3. Thomas C. Leonard, *The Power of the Press* (Oxford, England: Oxford University Press, 1986), p. 4.

4. U.S. Senate (May 1832), *Postage on Newspapers,* Report 147, 22, 1, cited in Richard Kielbowicz, "Modernization, Communication Policy, and the Geopolitics of News, 1820–1860," in *Media Voices: An Historical Perspective,* Jean Folkerts, ed. (New York: Macmillan, 1992), p. 130.

5. Richard Kielbowicz, *News in the Mail: The Press, Post Office and Public Information, 1700–1860* (Westport, CT: Greenwood Press, 1989).

6. *New York Sun,* September 3, 1833: 1.

7. Gerald Baldasty, *The Commercialization of News in the Nineteenth Century* (Madison: University of Wisconsin Press, 1992).

8. Project for Excellence in Journalism, *The State of the News Media 2006,* Annual Report, stateofthenewsmedia.com/2006, accessed May 31, 2006.

9. Stephen Lacy, "Understanding and Serving Newspaper Readers: The Problem of Fuzzy Market Structure," *Newspaper Research Journal* 14:2 (Spring 1993): 55–67.

10. Project for Excellence in Journalism, *State of the News Media 2006.*

11. Project for Excellence in Journalism, *State of the News Media 2006;* Newspaper Association of America, "NAA Releases ABC FAS-FAX Analysis," November 7, 2005, naa.org, accessed May 31, 2006.

12. Adam Clymer, speech, George Washington University Graduate School of Political Management class, "Politics and the Media," 1994.

13. Project for Excellence in Journalism, *State of the News Media 2006.*

14. Hamilton Nolan, "Fate of the *Voice* Could Impact All Alt-Media," *PR Week,* May 1, 2006: 12.

15. William Blankenburg and Gary W. Ozanich, "The Effects of Public Ownership on the Financial Performance of Newspaper Corporations," *Journalism Quarterly* 70 (Spring 1993): 68–75; and Stephen Lacy, Mary Alice Shaver, and Charles St. Cyr, "The Effects of Public Ownership and Newspaper Competition on the Financial Performance of Newspaper Corporations: A Replication and Extension," *Journalism & Mass Communication Quarterly* 73 (Summer 1996): 332–341.

16. Stephen Lacy and Todd F. Simon, *The Economics and Regulation of United States Newspapers* (Norwood, NJ: Ablex, 1993).

17. Lori Robertson, "The Chronicle Chronicles," *AJR,* October/November 2005, ajr.org/Article.asp?id=3965, accessed June 1, 2006.

18. Joseph Hallinan, "Local Story," *Wall Street Journal,* February 8, 2006: A1.
19. Joe Nicholson, "News Industry Anguish over Crumbling Credibility," *Editor & Publisher,* July 18, 1998: 8.
20. Pew Research Center, "Online Newspapers Modestly Boost Newspaper Readership," people-press.org/reports, accessed July 30, 2006.
21. New California Media, "Ethnic Media in America: The Giant Hidden in Plain Sight," Survey, June 7, 2005, ncmonline.com/polls, accessed June 1, 2006.
22. "Black Publishers Believe FCC Ruling Threatens Minority Press," *Knight Ridder Tribune Business News,* June 14, 2003: 1.
23. Latino Print Network, *The State of Hispanic Print 2005,* Annual Report, latinoprintnetwork.com/research.html, accessed June 1, 2006.
24. New California Media, "Ethnic Media in America."
25. "Black Publishers," 1.
26. Carolyn Foreman, *Oklahoma Imprints, 1835–1907: Printing before Statehood* (Norman: University of Oklahoma Press, 1936), cited in Sharon Murphy, "Neglected Pioneers: 19th Century Native American Newspapers," *Journalism History* 4:3 (Autumn 1977): 79.
27. Richard LaCourse, "A Native Press Primer," *Columbia Journalism Review* (November/December 1998): 51.
28. New California Media, "Ethnic Media in America."
29. Chris Hamby, "Native American Press Freedom," *Native American Times,* August 19, 2005: 4.
30. Carlos E. Cortes, "The Mexican-American Press," in *The Ethnic Press in the United States: A Historical Analysis and Handbook,* Sally M. Miller, ed. (Westport, CT: Greenwood Press, 1987), pp. 247–260.
31. Allied Media Corporation, www.allied-media.com/Publications/hispanic-publications.htm, accessed on December 25, 2002.
32. New California Media, "Ethnic Media in America."
33. Pat Twair and Samir Twair, "AAPG Forum Launched Program to Acquaint Candidates with Concerns of the Minority Press," *Washington Report on Middle East Affairs,* September 30, 2000: 65.
34. Takeya Mizuno, "Federal Government Uses of the Japanese-Language Press from Pearl Harbor to Mass Incarceration," *Journalism and Mass Communication Quarterly* 82 (Spring 2005): 149–150.
35. Debbi Gardiner, "Asian American Print Media," *Asian Week,* May 4, 2000, asianweek.com/2000_05_04/biz_apiprintmedia.html, accessed June 3, 2006.
36. "Darts and Laurels," *Columbia Journalism Review* (March/April 1998): 15.
37. Randal A. Beam, "What It Means to Be a Market-Oriented Newspaper," *Newspaper Research Journal* 19:3 (Summer 1998): 2–20.
38. John T. Russial, "Topic-Team Performance: A Content Study," *Newspaper Research Journal* 18:1–2 (Winter/Spring 1997): 126–144.
39. Leo Bogart, *Press and Public,* 2nd ed. (Hillsdale, NJ: Lawrence Erlbaum Associates, 1989), p. 196.
40. Bogart, *Press and Public,* p. 322.
41. Project for Excellence in Journalism, *State of the News Media 2006.*
42. Michael Gawenda, "U.S. Times Changing for U.S. Papers," *AsiaMedia,* October 24, 2005, asiamedia.ucla.edu/article.asp?parentid=32132, accessed June 3, 2006.
43. Matt Villano, "Teenage Wasteland?" *Editor & Publisher Interactive,* May 27, 1999, www.mediainfo.com.
44. Readership Institute, "Reinventing the Newspaper for Young Adults," April 2005, readership.org/experience/startrib_overview.pdf, accessed on June 3, 2006.
45. "Newsroom Diversity Still an Uphill Battle," *Black Issues in Higher Education,* June 30, 2005: 13.
46. "News and Views," *Journal of Blacks in Higher Education* 44 (Summer 2004): 59.
47. Native American Journalists Association, "ASNE Survey Shows Slight Growth of Native Americans," May 1, 2006, naja.com/news/releases/060501_asne/, accessed June 2, 2006.
48. "Minorities in the Newsroom," *ASNE Bulletin* (September 1993): 26–29.

Chapter 4

1. "The Wedding Report," 2005, theweddingreport.com, accessed June 8, 2006.
2. Richard Kielbowicz, *News in the Mail: The Press, Post Office, and Public Information, 1700–1860s* (New York: Greenwood Press, 1989), pp. 130–132.
3. Theodore Peterson, *Magazines in the Twentieth Century* (Urbana: University of Illinois Press, 1972), p. 60.
4. Peterson, *Magazines in the Twentieth Century,* p. 60.
5. *National Directory of Magazines,* 2006, American Society of Magazine Editors, *Editorial Trends and Magazine Handbook,* magazine.org/editorial/editorial_trends_and_magazine_handbook, accessed June 5, 2006.
6. Project for Excellence in Journalism, *State of the News Media 2006.*
7. John Wolfe, "Women's and Lifestyle Mags Top New Launches," *Media Daily News,* January 23, 2006, publications.mediapost.com/index.cfm?fuseaction=Articles.san&s=38802&Nid=17897&p=15617, accessed June 7, 2006.
8. American Business Media, "Business Publications Continue Strong Ad Revenue Growth," press release, January 23, 2006, americanbusinessmedia.com/abm/Press_Releases.asp?SnID=304622704, accessed June 7, 2006.
9. Lorraine Calvacca, "Shared Approach: Similarities between Association and Commercial Publications," *Folio,* March 15, 1994: 5.
10. Magazine Publishers of America, "2005 ABC Digital Circulation," magazine.org/digital/14328.cfm, accessed June 7, 2006.
11. min Online, "New Media Boxscores," 2006, minonline.com/top10_boxscore.htm, accessed June 7, 2006.
12. Katharine Q. Seelye, "As Magazine Readers Increasingly Turn to the Web, So Does Condé Nast," *New York Times,* April 3, 2006: C1.
13. Samir Husni, "How Magazines Are Born," *Folio* (October 1, 1991): 54–55.
14. Bruce Sheiman, "From Start-up Idea to Magazine," *Folio,* January 15, 1994: 118.
15. Some examples of combination financing are from Gloria Steinem, "Sex, Lies & Advertising," *Ms.,* July/August 1990: 18–28; Michael Hoyt, "When the Walls Come Tumbling Down," *Columbia Journalism Review* (March/April 1990): 35–41.
16. Deirdre Carmody, *New York Times,* as it appeared in "Lear's Lived and Died on a Whim," *Houston Chronicle,* March 15, 1994: 1.

17. Magazine Publishers Association, magazine.org/index.html and magazine.org/mpa/content/map.handbook/advertising/fcb_media_research.html.

18. Project for Excellence in Journalism, *State of the News Media 2006.*

19. Reed Phillips, "What We Learned from the Recession: Or Should Have," *Folio,* February 1, 1993: 61.

20. Liz Borod, "Finally, a Little More in the Paycheck," *Folio,* May 2004: 18.

21. "Production Salary Survey 2002: The Producers," *Folio,* August 2002: 31–37.

22. "Editorial Salary Survey," *Folio,* December 2005: 44.

23. Nat Ives, "Why *Time* Will Now Hit Your Mailbox on Friday," *Advertising Age,* August 21, 2006: 3–4.

24. Bert Langford, "Six Ways Technology is Changing Publishing," *Folio,* July 2005: 46–51.

25. Annenberg Public Policy Center, "Women Fail to Crack the Glass Ceiling in Communication Companies," press release, August 27, 2002, http://www.annenbergpublicpolicycenter.org/02_reports_releases/report_2002.htm, accessed November 30, 2006.

26. Derek T. Dingle, "Essence of the Deal," *Black Enterprise,* March 2005: 69.

Chapter 5

1. Spike Lee, Interview by George Avgerakis, *Digital Cinema,* www.bvr.com/images/library/1026312946.pdf, accessed on August 28, 2006; "Spielberg at the Revolution," Interview, *Time,* March 14, 2006, www.time.com/time/arts/article/0,8599,1173367.00.html, accessed August 28, 2006.

2. Louis Giannetti and Scott Eyman, *Flashback: A Brief History of Film* (Englewood Cliffs, NJ: Prentice-Hall, 1986), p. 15.

3. From an original transcript in the collection of Gordon Hendricks, New York, cited in *The American Film Industry,* rev. ed., Tino Balio, ed. (Madison: The University of Wisconsin Press, 1985), p. 45.

4. Russell Merritt, "Nickelodeon Theatres, 1905–1914: Building an Audience for the Movies," in Balio, *The American Film Industry,* p. 86.

5. Robert Anderson, "The Motion Picture Patents Company: A Reevaluation," in Balio, *The American Film Industry,* p. 134.

6. Douglas Gomery, "The Coming of Sound: Technological Change in the American Film Industry," in Balio, *The American Film Industry,* p. 230.

7. Giannetti and Eyman, *Flashback,* p. 372.

8. Clayton R. Koppes and Gregory D. Black, *Hollywood Goes to War: How Politics, Profits and Propaganda Shaped World War II Movies* (New York: Free Press, 1987).

9. Koppes and Black, "Blacks, Loyalty, and Motion Picture Propaganda in World War II," *Journal of American History* (September, 1986): 394.

10. DeWayne Wickham, "Bassett Criticism Has Its Merits," *USA Today,* July 8, 2002, www.usatoday.com.

11. Jacquelyn Kilpatrick, *Celluloid Indians: Native American on Film* (Lincoln: University of Nebraska Press, 1999), pp. xv–xviii.

12. Joann Faung Jean Lee, *Asian American Actors: Oral Histories from Stage, Screen, and Television* (Jefferson, NC: McFarland & Sons, 2000).

13. Daniel J. Leab, *From Sambo to Superspade: The Black Experience in Motion Pictures* (Boston: Houghton Mifflin, 1975), pp. 70–72.

14. Leab, *From Sambo to Superspade,* pp. 173–174.

15. Gary D. Keller, *Hispanics and United States Films: An Overview and Handbook* (Tempe, AZ: Bilingual Press, 1994), pp. 195–196.

16. Mark A. Reid, *Redefining Black Film* (Berkeley: University of California Press, 1993).

17. Gomery, "Hollywood's Business," p. 98.

18. Bruce Owen and Steve Wildman, *Video Economics* (Cambridge, MA: Harvard University Press, 1992).

19. "Hollywood Suffers Fall," *Knight Ridder Tribune Business News,* March 11, 2006: 1.

20. Motion Picture Association, *MPA Snapshot Report,* March 2005, mpas.org/us%20theatrical%20snapshot.pdf.

21. J. D. Reed, "Plugging Away in Hollywood," *Time,* January 2, 1989: 103, as cited in *International Journal of Advertising* (January, 1993): 1–3.

22. Reed, "Plugging Away in Hollywood" D.C. McGill, "Questions Raised on 'Product Placements,'" *New York Times* (April 13, 1989): D18; J. Schlosberg, "Film Flam Men," *Inside Media,* June 13, 1990: 34.

23. Josh Grossberg, "Minority Reports Product Placement," E! Online news, June 21, 2002, www.eonline.com/news/Items/Pf/0,1527,10138,00.html.

24. Gomery, "Hollywood's Business," 107.

25. John Latchem, "Theatrical Beats Home Viewing, MPA Study Says," *Home Media Retailing,* March 19, 2006: 6.

26. Sklar, *Film: An International History of the Medium,* pp. 508–517.

27. Rana Foroohar, "Hurray for Globowood," *Newsweek,* May 27, 2002: 51.

28. Michael Goldman, "Exclusive: The Lucas POV," *Millimeter,* March 2004: 19.

29. Paul Taylor, "Coming Soon," *Financial Times,* May 31, 2006: 12.

30. Roger O'Crockett, "Hauling in the Hollywood Hackers," *Business Week,* May 15, 2006: 80.

31. Edward J. Epstein, "Hollywood, the Remake," *Wall Street Journal,* December 29, 2005: A10.

32. Ibid.

33. Sharon Waxman, "Hollywood Losing Biggest Fans to Digital World," *New York Times,* October 9, 2005, ngt.com.

34. "Studios See the Light," *Video Business,* February 13, 2006: 1.

Chapter 6

1. Bill McConnell, "Rapper Sues FCC," *Broadcasting & Cable,* Febuary, 4, 2002, broadcastingcable.com; FCC, Memorandum Opinion and Order, In the Matter of the KBOO Foundation, February 20, 2003.

2. Bill McConnell, "New Rules for Risqué Business," *Broadcasting & Cable,* March 4, 2002, broadcastingcable.com.

3. *Broadcasting & Cable Yearbook* (New Providence, NJ: Bowker Publications, 2001), p. D639, and more than 12,000 people work in commercial radio news; Vernon Stone, "News Operations at U.S. Radio Stations," August 3, 2002, missouri.edu/~jourvs/graops.html.

4. Thomas W. Hoffer, "Nathan B. Stubblefield and His Wireless Telephone," *Journal of Broadcasting* 15 (Summer 1971): 317–329.

5. Elliot N. Sivowitch, "A Technological Survey of Broadcasting's Prehistory, 1876–1920," *Journal of Broadcasting* 15 (Winter 1970–1971): 1–20.

6. George H. Gibson, *Public Broadcasting: The Role of the Federal Government, 1912–76* (New York: Praeger, 1977), pp. 2–3.

7. Federal Communication Commission, "Early History of Network Broadcasting (1923–1926) and the National

Broadcasting Company," *Report on Chain Broadcasting* (Commission Order No. 37, Docket 5060, May 1941), pp. 5–20.

8. Lawrence W. Lichty and Malachi C. Topping, "Audiences," in *American Broadcasting: A Source Book on the History of Radio and Television,* Lawrence W. Lichty and Malachi C. Topping, eds. (New York: Hastings House, 1975), pp. 445–457.

9. John W. Spalding, "1928: Radio Becomes a Mass Advertising Medium," *Journal of Broadcasting* 8 (Winter 1963–1964): 31–44.

10. Gibson, *Public Broadcasting,* p. 21.

11. David H. Hosley, *As Good as Any: Foreign Correspondence on American Radio, 1930–1940* (Westport, CT: Greenwood Press, 1984), pp. 8–9. See also Jean Folkerts and Dwight Teeter, *Voices of a Nation,* 2nd ed. (New York: Macmillan, 1994), pp. 382–385.

12. Edwin Emery and Michael Emery, *The Press and America,* 4th ed. (Englewood Cliffs, NJ: Prentice Hall, 1978), p. 400.

13. Arbitron, "Radio Today: How American Listens to Radio," 2006, arbitron.com/downloads/radiotoday06.pdf, accessed June 13, 2006.

14. Bill McConnell, "Radio Giants Want More Turf," *Broadcasting & Cable,* March 8, 2002, broadcastingcable.com.

15. Newspaper Association of America, 2004 Horizon Watching Initiative: Radio, June 30, 2004, naa.org/horizon/mt/radio .ppt#614, accessed June 14, 2006; Arbitron, *Audience Composition Report,* 2006, wargod.arbitron.com/scripts/ ndb/audience2.asp, accessed June 14, 2006.

16. Arbitron, "Radio Today."

17. Project for Excellence in Journalism, *State of the News Media 2006.*

18. Glen T. Cameron, Glen J. Nowak, and Dean M. Krugman, "The Competitive Position of Newspapers in the Local Retail Market," *Newspaper Research Journal* 14 (Summer–Fall 1993): 70–81.

19. Bruce Girard, "Introduction," in *A Passion for Radio,* Bruce Girard, ed. (Montreal: Black Rose Books, 1992), p. 6.

20. Bruce Porter, "Has Success Spoiled NPR?," *Columbia Journalism Review* (September–October 1990): 26–32.

21. NPR, *Annual Reports, Audited Financial Statements, and Form 990s,* 2006, npr.org/about/privatesupport.html, accessed June 14, 2006.

22. Sarah McBride, "Mixed Messages," *Wall Street Journal,* March 17, 2006: A1.

23. Project for Excellence in Journalism, *State of the News Media 2006.*

24. Ibid.

25. Steve Emmons, "Just What Do Talk Shows Listen For?" *Los Angeles Times,* Orange County edition, May 10, 1995: E1.

26. Ibid.

27. Peter Laufer, *Inside Talk Radio: America's Voice or Just Hot Air?* (Secaucus, NJ: Carol Publishing Group, 1995).

28. Donald R. Browne, *International Broadcasting: The Limits of a Limitless Medium* (New York: Praeger, 1982), p. 48.

29. George Wedell and Philip Crookes, *Radio 2000* (Manchester, England: The European Institute for the Media, 1991), p. 52.

30. *Financial Times,* June 9, 2006: 10.

31. Richard Robinson, "Still Making Waves," *Americas,* July 1994: 44–50.

32. *Australian Commercial Radio—A Study of Listener Attitudes* (Sydney: Federation of Australian Radio Broadcasters, 1979).

33. Katy Bachman, "Radio," *Mediaweek,* January 2, 2006: 15.

34. Antony Bruno, "Web Radio Starts to Cast a Wide Net," *Billboard,* April 29, 2006: 14.

35. Arbitron. *Internet and Multimedia 2006,* arbitron.com/ downloads/im2006study.pdf, accessed June 15, 2006.

36. Ibid.

37. Ibid.

38. "U.S. Senator Arlen Specter Holds a Hearing on Parity, Platforms, and Protection," *Political Transcript Wire,* April 28, 2006. Proquest.

39. Abbey Klaasen, "Reggaeton Spices Up Radio," *Advertising Age,* January 30, 2006: S4.

40. New America Media, "Ethnic Media in America."

41. L. A. Lorek, "Hispanic Radio is Boosting Clear Channel," *Knight Ridder Tribune Business News,* September 11, 2005: 1.

42. Victor Manuel Ramos, "Radio Tunes in Cultural Uproar," *Knight Ridder Tribune Business News,* February 4, 2005: 1.

43. New America Media; Arbitron, *Black Radio Today 2006,* arbitron.com/downloads/Black_Radio_Today_06.pdf, accessed June 15, 2006.

44. Quoted in Kenneth Meeks, "Back Talk," *Black Enterprise,* November 2005: 188.

45. Bob Papper, *Running in Place,* Radio-Television News Directors Association & Foundation, 2005, rtnda.org/communicator/ pdfs/072005-26-32.pdf, accessed June 15, 2006.

46. *Broadcasting & Cable,* January 14, 2002, broadcastingcable.com.

47. "Indecency Debate," *Cablefax Daily,* May 22, 2006: 1.

Chapter 7

1. John Colapinto, "The Most Trusted Name in News," *Rolling Stone,* October 28, 2004, ProQuest.

2. Lauren Feldman, "The News About Comedy: Young Audiences, *The Daily Show,* and Evolving Notions of Journalism," delivered at the International Communication Association Annual Meeting, New York (2005) all academic.com, accessed August 10, 2006.

3. Lynn Spigel, *Make Room for TV* (Chicago: University of Chicago Press, 1992).

4. For a discussion of the early debate over technical standards, see Christopher H. Sterling and John M. Kittross, *Stay Tuned: A Concise History of American Broadcasting,* 2nd ed. (Belmont, CA: Wadsworth, 1990), pp. 526–527.

5. Sterling and Kittross, *Stay Tuned,* pp. 265, 267.

6. *Broadcasting-Telecasting,* December 21, 1953: 29, cited in James Scofield O'Rourke IV, "The Development of Color Television: A Study in the Freemarket Process," *Journalism History* 9:3–4 (1982): 78–85, 106.

7. For a thorough discussion of legal issues from 1945 to 1952, see Chapter 7, "Era of Great Change," in Sterling and Kittross, *Stay Tuned.*

8. James L. Baughman, *The Republic of Mass Culture: Journalism, Filmmaking, and Broadcasting in America since 1941* (Baltimore: Johns Hopkins University Press, 1992), p. 54.

9. Sterling and Kittross, *Stay Tuned,* p. 278.

10. Melvin Patrick Ely, *The Adventures of Amos 'n' Andy* (New York: Free Press, 1991), pp. 1–10. The quote is cited in Ely from a resolution in Herbert L. Wright, letter to NAACP Youth Councils, College Chapters and State Youth Conferences, July 19, 1951, in National Association for the Advancement of Colored People Papers, II, A, 479, Manuscript Division, Library of Congress.

11. Stephen Fox, *The Mirror Makers* (New York: Random House, 1984), p. 212.

12. Walter Karp, "The Quiz-Show Scandal," *American Heritage,* May–June 1989: 77–88.

13. Fox, *The Mirror Makers,* p. 215.

14. Stuart Taylor Jr., "Witch-Hunt or Whitewash?" *The American Lawyer* (April 1995): 60.

15. "Fox and Murdoch Win a Big One," *U.S. News & World Report,* May 15, 1995: 17+.

16. "Congressional Testimony Reveals Market Statistics," *Broadcast Engineering,* June 8, 2005, broadcastengineering .com/newsletters/hd_tech/20050608/Congress-market-stats-20050608/index.html, accessed August 7, 2006.

17. Sydney W. Head and Christopher Sterling, *Broadcasting in America: A Survey of Electronic Media,* 2nd ed. (Boston: Houghton Mifflin, 1996), pp. 82–85.

18. ComScore Networks, press release, August 15, 2006, comscore.com/press/release.asp?press=982, accessed August 17, 2006.

19. Adam L. Penenberg, "The Death of Television," *Slate,* October 17, 2005, slate.com/id/2128201, accessed August 17, 2006.

20. Stephanie McKinnon, "Looking Ahead for PBS," *Lansing State Journal,* January 19, 1995: B1, B5.

21. Richard Campbell, "TV News in the Corporate Era," *Television News* 35 (2005): 10–20.

22. Terry Eastland, "The Shrinking News Audience," *Wilson Quarterly* 29 (2005): 47.

23. Susan Whiting, "What Now for Audience Measurement Techniques?" *Television Quarterly* 36 (2006): 9–13.

24. James G. Webster, "Beneath the Veneer of Fragmentation: Television Audience Polarization in a Multichannel World," *Journal of Communication* 55 (2005): 366–382.

25. Lynn Spigel, "Entertainment Wars: Television Culture After 9/11," *American Quarterly* 56 (2004): 235–270.

26. Rebecca Pirito, "New Markets for Cable TV," *American Demographics* (June 1995): 40.

27. IBM Institute for Business Value, "The End of Television As We Know It," 2006, ibm.com/services/us/imc/pdf/ge510-6248-end-of-tv-full.pdf, accessed August 10, 2006.

28. *Marketing Week,* March 2 2006: 34.

29. Nielsen Media Research, press release, October 6, 2005.

30. "FAQ-Research and Product Questions," Nielsen Media, October 26, 2002, www.nielsenmedia.com.

31. Russ Lemmon, "WTVG Beats WTOL for Key Audience in 3 of 5 Newscasts," *Toledo Blade,* June 16, 2006, toledoblade.com, accessed January 6, 2007.

32. Jens Manuel Krogstad, "Network Fall Lineup Lacking Minority Leads," *Knight Ridder Tribune Business News,* (August 3, 2006): 1.

33. Snapshot International LTD., *US Satellite TV Broadcasting 2006,* April 2006, Proquest.

34. Stuart Elliott, "Advertising," *The New York Times,* October 2, 2002: C9.

35. Ted Kulfan, "Marlboro Is Ordered to Butt Out," *The Detroit News,* June 7, 1995: 1B.

36. Center on Alcohol Marketing and Youth, "Children, Youth Saw Over 30% More Alcohol Ads on Television in 2004 than in 2001," camy.org/factsheets/index.php?FactsheetID=25, accessed August 17, 2006.

37. LInnea Anderson, CNN, *Hoover's,* 2006, Proquest.

38. Linnea Anderson, Al Jazeera, *Hoover's* 2006, Proquest.

39. Fauzi Najjar, "The Arabs, Islam and Globalization," *Middle East Policy* 12 (Fall 2005): 91–107.

40. John Lansing, "Time to Embrace the Promise of Broadband," *Television Week,* December 12, 2005: 10.

41. Quoted in Ira Teinowitz, *Advertising Age,* July 24, 2006: 1.

Chapter 8

1. David Kusek, "The New Artist Model," *The Future of Music* (June 26, 2006), futureofmusicbook.com/2006/06/, accessed November 2, 2006.

2. David Ewen, *Panorama of American Popular Music* (Englewood Cliffs, NJ: Prentice Hall, 1957), p. 58.

3. Ewen, *Panorama of American Popular Music,* p. 145.

4. John Rublowsky, *Popular Music* (New York: Basic Books, 1967), pp. 63–80.

5. Hitchcock, *Music in the United States,* p. 141.

6. Ronald L. Davis, *A History of Music in American Life: The Gilded Years, 1865–1920,* Vol. 2 (Huntington, NY: Robert Krieger, 1980), p. 63.

7. Hitchcock, *Music in the United States,* p. 276.

8. Hitchcock, *Music in the United States,* pp. 276–277.

9. Steven Feld, "A Sweet Lullaby for World Music," *Public Culture* 12.1 (2000): 145–171.

10. Eric Berman, "The Godfathers of Rap," *Rolling Stone,* December 23, 1993: 137–142, 180.

11. Hitchcock, *Music in the United States,* pp. 286–291.

12. John Lannert, "U.S. Latin Market Slows a Bit after Explosive Growth," *Billboard,* September 4, 1999, via Nexis-Lexis.

13. Diana Saenger, "Reggaetón—Red Hot in the Latino Music World," *Hispanic Outlook in Higher Education,* July 31, 2006: 30–32.

14. Recording Industry Association of America, *2005 Consumer Profile,* riaa.com/news/marketingdata/pdf/2005consumerprofile.pdf, accessed November 1, 2006.

15. John von Rhein, "It's Not Over, Beethoven," *Chicago Tribune,* January 10, 1997, sec. 7: p. 1–13.

16. Allan Kozinn, "Check the Numbers: Rumors of Classical Music's Demise Are Dead Wrong," *New York Times* May 28, 2006, newyorktimes.com, accessed November 2, 2006.

17. Andrew Edgecliffe-Johnson, "CD as We Know It 'Dead', Says EMI Chief," *Financial Times,* October 28, 2006: 16.

18. IFPI, *Digital Music Report,* 2006, ifpi.org/content/library/digital-music-report-2006.pdf, accessed October 30, 2006.

19. Recording Industry Association of America, 2005 *Year-End Statistics,* riaa.com/news/newsletter/pdf/2005yrEndStats .pdf, accessed October 30, 2006.

20. National Association of Music Merchants, *Music USA 2005,* namm.org/press-room/music-usa, accessed October 20, 2006.

21. Paul Betts, "Court Edict Puts Record Industry in a Spin," *Financial Times,* July 14, 2006: 22.

22. Ibid.

23. Jennifer C. Lena, "Social Context and the Musical Content of Rap Music, 1979–1995," *Social Forces* 85 (2006): 479–492.

24. Mary Madden, *Artists, Musicians, and the Internet,* Pew Internet & American Life Project, December 5, 2004, pewinternet.org, accessed November 1, 2006.

25. Geoffrey P. Hull, *The Recording Industry* (New York: Routledge, 2004): p. 261.

26. Electronic Frontier Foundation, *RIAA v. the People: Two Years Later,* eff.org/IP/P2P/RIAAatTWO_FINAL.pdf, accessed November 9, 2006.

27. Hull, *The Recording Industry,* 62.

28. Recording Industry Association of America, *2004 Consumer Profile*, riaa.com/news/marketingdata/pdf/2004consumerProfile.pdf, accessed October 30, 2006.

29. Russell Sanjek, *From Print to Plastic: Publishing and Promoting America's Popular Music (1900–1980)* (New York: Brooklyn College of the City of New York, 1983), p. 54.

30. Keith Negus, *Producing Pop: Culture and Conflict in the Popular Music Industry* (London: Edward Arnold, 1992), p. 13.

31. "Rock and Roll Forever," *Newsweek*, July 5, 1994: 48.

32. Kerry Segrave, *Payola in the Music Business: A History from 1880–1991* (Jefferson, NC: McFarland, 1994), pp. 92–93.

33. Fredric Dannen, *Hit Men: Power Brokers and Fast Money inside the Music Business* (New York: Times Books, 1990).

34. Joshua Chaffin, "Music Videos Become Hits All Over Again," *Financial Times*, October 11, 2006: 24.

35. Norbert J. Michel, "The Impact of Digital File Sharing on the Music Industry: An Empirical Analysis," *Topics in Economic Analysis and Policy* 6 (2006), Article 18.

36. Alain Levy, "Digital Music and How the Consumer Became King," LBS London Media Summit, IFPI, October 2006, ifpi.com/content/section_views/view024.html, accessed November 10, 2006.

37. Leila Abboud, "Ringing in the Change at France Telecom," *Wall Street Journal*, May 4, 2006: B4.

38. Patrick Burkart and Tom McCourt, *Digital Music Wars: Ownership and Control of the Celestial Jukebox* (Oxford: Rowman & Littlefield, 2006).

39. J. Scott Orr, "Code Makers Battle Breakers Over Digital Protections," Newhouse News Service, 2006, newhousenews.com/archive/orr110806.html, accessed November 10, 2006.

40. Sasha Frere-Jones, "1+1+1=1," *New Yorker*, January 3, 2005, newyorker.com/critics/content/articles/050110crmu_music, accessed October 30, 2006.

41. *Free the Grey Album*, greytuesday.org.

42. Lawrence Lessig, Interview with Richard Koman, "Remixing Culture: An Interview with Lawrence Lessig," O'Reilly, oreillynet.com/pub/a/policy/2005/02/24/lessig.html, accessed November 2, 2006.

Chapter 9

1. Sid Yadav, "Facebook—The Complete Biography," *Mashable!*, August 25, 2006, mashable.com/2006/08/25/facebook-profile/; John Cassidy, "Me Media," *New Yorker*, May 25, 2006: 50.

2. Danah Boyd and Henry Jenkins, Interview with Sarah Wright, *Henry Jenkins*, May 30, 2006, web.mit.edu/cms/People/henry3/myspaceissues.htm.

3. Quoted in Shayne Bowman and Chris Willis, "We Media," *The Media Center*, July 2003, hypergene.net/wemedia/download/we_media.pdf, accessed October 30, 2006.

4. Ibid.

5. Vannevar Bush, "As We May Think," *Atlantic Monthly*, July 1945, America Online, accessed in July 2000.

6. Larry Press, "Before the Altair: The History of Personal Computing," *Communications of the ACM* (September 1993): 27+, Lexis-Nexis.

7. Press, "Before the Altair." See also D. C. Engelbart and W. K. English, "A Research Center for Augmenting Human Intellect," *Proceedings of the 1968 Fall Joint Computer Conference* (Washington, DC: Thompson Book Co.), pp. 395–410.

8. Eugene Marlow, "The Electrovisual Manager: Media and American Corporate Management," *Business Horizons*, March 1994: 61+, via Lexis-Nexis; see also a website describing Atanasoff's contributions at www.lib.iastate.edu/arch/jva.html.

9. Cited in Denise W. Gurer, "Pioneering Women in Computer Science," *Communications of the Association for Computing Machinery* (January 1995): 58.

10. Gurer, "Pioneering Women," p. 50.

11. Michael Swaine, "The Programmer Paradigm," *Dr. Dobbs' Journal of Software Tools*, p. 109+, Lexis-Nexis.

12. For a full discussion of the network, see "What Is the Internet?" in Ed Krol, *The Whole Internet User's Guide and Catalog* (Sebastopol, CA: O'Reilly & Associates, 1992).

13. Mary Madden, "Internet Penetration and Impact," press release, Pew/Internet April 2006, pewinternet.org/pdfs/PIP_Internet_Impact.pdf, accessed October 4, 2006.

14. John Horrigan and Lee Rainie, "The Internet's Growing Role in Life's Major Moments," Pew Internet & American Life Project, April 19, 2006, pewinternet.org/pdfs/PIP_Major%20Moments_2006.pdf, accessed October 5, 2006.

15. Mary Madden, "Internet Penetration and Impact," Pew Internet & American Life Project, April 2006, pewinternet.org/pdfs/PIP_Internet_Impact.pdf, accessed October 5, 2006.

16. Michelle Kessler, "Dot-com Bust Isn't Over for Workers," *USA Today*, March 12, 2004, usatoday.com/money/industries/technology/2004-04-12-tech-recovery_x.htm, accessed October 20, 2006.

17. Tracy Gordon Fox, "Park Provides Internet Access: Is First in State to Go Wireless," *Knight Ridder Tribune Business News*, September 18, 2006: 1.

18. Snapdata International Ltd., "U.S. PCs 2006," *Snapshots Series*, May 2006, Proquest.

19. Software Division, Software & Information Industry Association, *Packaged Software Industry Revenue and Growth*, siia.net/software/pubs/growth_software06.pdf, accessed October 18, 2006.

20. Michael Barbaro and Tom Zeller, Jr., "A Face Is Exposed for AOL Searcher No. 4417749," *New York Times*, August 9, 2006: A1.

21. Privacy, Electronic Freedom Foundation, eff.org/Privacy/, accessed October 18, 2006; Rich Haglund, "What Happens to the Fourth Amendment When the USA Patriot Act Enters Wireless Hot Spots," *Journal of Internet Law* 9 (July 2005): 12–22.

22. Nikki Swartz, "U.S. Demands Google Web Data," *Information Management Journal* (May/June 2006): 18–19.

23. Mary Madden and Susannah Fox, "Finding Answers Online in Sickness and Health," Pew Internet & American Life Project, May 2, 2006, pewinternet.org/pdfs/PIP_Health_Decisions_2006.pdf, accessed October 22, 2006.

24. John B. Horrigan, "Politics Online," Pew Internet & American Life (August 2006), pewinternet.org/pdfs/PIP_Politics%20Aug06_Memo.pdf, accessed October 22, 2006.

25. Kavan Peterson, "Integrity of Electronic Voting Questioned," Stateline.org, May 3, 2004; Eric Kelderman, "Ballot Blunders Abound as Election Nears," Stateline.org (October 20, 2006), accessed October 22, 2006.

26. Joan Johnson, "Increased Internet Shopping Leads to Online Sales Clerks to Assist the Customers," *Colorado Springs Business Journal,* October 6, 2006, Proquest.

27. Mary Madden, "Internet Penetration and Impact," Pew Internet & American Life, April 2006, pewinternet.org/pdfs/PIP_Internet_Impact.pdf, accessed October 22, 2006; Danielle Long, "Four in Five Shoppers Feel 'Web Rage,'" *Revolution,* September 2006: 27.

28. Susannah Fox and Jean Beier, "Online Banking 2006: Surfing to the Bank," Pew Internet & American Life, June 14, 2006, pewinternet.org/pdfs/PIP_Online_Banking_2006.pdf, accessed October 22, 2006.

29. U.S. Department of Labor, "Tellers," August 4, 2006, bls.gov/oco/ocos126.htm, accessed October 22, 2006.

30. Thomas Friedman, *The Lexus and the Olive Tree* (New York: Farrar, Straus, Giroux, 2000).

31. Paul Hitlin and Lee Rainie, "Teens, Technology, and School," Pew Internet & American Life, August 2005, pewinternet.org/pdfs/PIP_Internet_and_schools_05.pdf.; National Center for Education Statistics, *Digest of Education Statistics: 2005,* June 2006, nces.ed.gov/programs/digest/d05, accessed October 23, 2006.

32. Kathleen Debevec, Mei-Yau Shih, and Vishal Kashyap, "Learning Strategies in a Technology Integrated Classroom," *Journal of Research on Technology in Education* 38 (2006): 293–307; David Noble, *Digital Diploma Mills: The Automation of Higher Education* (New York: Monthly Review Press, 2001); Edward Tufte, "PowerPoint Is Evil," *Wired,* September 2003, wired.com/wired/archive/11.09/ppt2.html.

33. Point Topic, USA Broadband Overview, September 11, 2006, point-topic.com/content/operatorsource/profiles, accessed October 4, 2006; Vince Chook, *World Broadband Statistics, Q2, 2006,* Point Topic, September 2006, point-topic.com, accessed September 13, 2006.

34. John B. Horrigan, *Home Broadband Adoption is Going Mainstream and That Means User-Generated Content is Coming from All Kinds of Internet Users,* Pew/Internet, May 28, 2006, pewinternet.org/pdfs/PIP_Broadband_trends2006.pdf, accessed October 4, 2006.

35. Tim O'Reilly, "What Is Web 2.0?" O'Reilly Media, September 30, 2005, oreillynet.com/pub/a/oreilly/tim/news/2005/09/30/what-is-web-20.html?page=1, accessed October 5, 2006.

36. Leida Chen and Ravi Nath, "Nomadic Culture: Cultural Support for Working Anytime, Anywhere," *Information Systems Management* 22.4 (2005): 57.

37. Wade-Hahn Chan, "Inside OPM's New Telework Guidelines," *Federal Computer Week,* August 21, 2006: 42–43.

38. Susannah Fox, Janna Quitney Anderson, Lee Rainie, *The Future of the Internet,* Pew Internet & American Life, June 9, 2005; Janna Quitney Anderson and Lee Rainie, *The Future of the Internet II,* Pew Internet & American Life, September 24, 2006, pewinternet.org, accessed October 22, 2006.

39. Tony Salvador and John Sherry, "The Anna Karenina Principle: What It Takes to Own a PC," Intel, 2006, intel.com/research/exploratory/papr/anna_karenina_principle.htm, accessed October 20, 2006.

Chapter 10

1. George W. Bush, press conference, December 19, 2005, whitehouse.gov/news/releases/2005/12/20051219-2.html, accessed December 7, 2006.

2. See Jeffery A. Smith, *Printers and Press Freedom* (New York: Oxford University Press, 1990), pp. 42–53.

3. *1791–1991: The Bill of Rights and Beyond* (Washington, DC: Library of Congress, 1991), p. 18.

4. Stephen Botein, "'Meer Mechanics' and an Open Press: The Business and Political Strategies of Colonial American Printers," *Perspectives in American History* 9 (1975): 140–150.

5. Paul Finkelman, "The Zenger Case: Prototype of a Political Trial," in *American Political Trials,* Michael R. Belknap, ed. (Westport, CT: Greenwood Press, 1981); David Paul Nord, "The Authority of Truth: Religion and the John Peter Zenger Case," *Journalism Quarterly* 62 (Summer 1985): 227–235; James Alexander, *A Brief Narrative of the Case and Trial of John Peter Zenger,* 2nd ed. (Cambridge: Harvard University Press, 1971), p. 13. A narrative relates the text of the trial.

6. For a description for the times, see William E. Ames, *A History of the National Intelligencer* (Chapel Hill: University of North Carolina Press, 1972). The *National Intelligencer* was the prime political newspaper in early Washington, D.C. See also Richard B. Kielbowicz, "The Press, Post Office, and Flow of News in the Early Republic," *Journal of the Early Republic* (Fall 1983): 269–280. Kielbowicz connects the flow of news to congressional debates over postal policy.

7. Jeffery A. Smith, *Franklin and Bache: Envisioning the Enlightened Republic* (New York: Oxford University Press, 1990), pp. 147–148. Jeffery Smith, also the author of *Printers and Press Freedom,* explains the intellectual dimensions of the press in the early republic.

8. Jerilyn McIntyre, "Repositioning a Landmark: The Hutchins Commission and Freedom of the Press," *Critical Studies in Mass Communication* 4 (June 1987): 141; Commission on Freedom of the Press, *A Free and Responsible Press* (Chicago: University of Chicago Press, 1947), p. vi. See also Margaret Blanchard, "The Hutchins Commission, the Press and the Responsibility Concept," *Journalism Monographs* 49 (May 1977): 1–59, and D. L. Smith, *Zechariah Chafee, Jr.: Defender of Liberty and Law* (Cambridge: Harvard University Press, 1986).

9. Quotation is from McIntyre, "Repositioning a Landmark," p. 143.

10. McIntyre, "Repositioning a Landmark," p. 150.

11. John H. Colburn, "What Makes a Good Newspaper?" *Saturday Review,* June 9, 1952: 50, 52, cited in Ernest C. Hynds, *American Newspapers in the 1980s* (New York: Hastings House, 1980), p. 29.

12. Bruce A. Williams and Michael X. Delli Carpini, "Monica and Bill All the Time and Everywhere: The Collapse of Gatekeeping and Agenda Setting in the New Media Environment," *American Behavioral Scientist* 47 (2004): 1208–1231.

13. Project for Excellence in Journalism, *State of the News Media 2004,* stateofthenewsmedia.org/2004, accessed August 31, 2006.

14. David Mindich, *Just the Facts: How 'Objectivity' Came to Define American Journalism* (New York: New York University Press, 1998).

15. Michael Robertson, *Stephen Crane, Journalism, and the Making of Modern American Literature* (New York: Columbia University Press, 1997).

16. Stephen Lacy and Hugh Martin, "Profits Up, Circulation Down for Thomson Papers in 80s," *Newspaper Research Journal* 19.3 (1998): 63–76.

17. Alan Blanchard and Stephen Lacy, "The Impact of Public Ownership, Profits, Competition on Newsroom Employees

and Starting Salaries in Mid-Sized Daily Newspapers," paper delivered to the Association for Education in Journalism and Mass Communication, Miami, Florida, August 2002.

18. "Knight Ridder Honored for Stories on Veterans' Issues," *Knight Ridder Tribune Business News,* January 11, 2006: 1.

19. Alicia C. Shepard, "The Gospel of Public Journalism," *American Journalism Review,* September 1994: 29–30.

20. Shepard, 34.

21. Leonard Witt, "Do We Need a Name Change?" *Civic Journalism Group News* (Winter 2004): 3.

22. General Assembly of the United Nations, Universal Declaration of Human Rights, adopted December 10, 1948, www.un.org/Overview/rights.html, accessed August 31, 2006.

23. Reporters Without Borders, "Worldwide Press Freedom Index 2005," rsf.org/, accessed September 12, 2006.

24. Stephen J. A. Ward, "Global Journalism Ethics," *Journalism Ethics for the Global Citizen,* 2005, journalismethics.ca/ global_journalism_ethics, accessed September 8, 2006.

25. Pew Research Center for the People and the Press, "Online Papers Modestly Boost Newspaper Readership," July 30, 2006, people-press.org/reports, accessed September 2, 2006.

26. Pew Research Center for the People and the Press, "Public's News Habit Little Changed by September 11," June 9, 2002, people-press.org/reports, accessed September 2, 2006.

27. Pew Internet & American Life Project, "Bloggers: A Portrait of the Internet's New Storytellers," July 19, 2006, www .pewinternet.org, accessed September 1, 2006.

28. J. D. Lasica, "What Is Participatory Journalism?" *Online Journalism Review,* August 7, 2003, ojr.org/ojr/workplace/ 1060217106.php, accessed September 1, 2006.

29. Dan Gillmor, *We the Media: Grassroots Journalism by the People, for the People* (Sebastopol, CA: O'Reilly, 2004).

30. Jay Rosen, "Bloggers vs. Journalists Is Over," PressThink, January 15, 2005, journalism.nyu.edu/pubzone/weblogs/ pressthink/2005/01, accessed September 1, 2006.

31. Nicholas Lemann, "Amateur Hour; The Wayward Press," *New Yorker,* August 7, 2006, Proquest.

32. John Burke, "Citizen Journalism vs. Professional Journalism," Editors Weblog, April 28, 2006, www.editorsweblog.org/ analysis//2006/04, accessed September 1, 2006.

33. J. Patrick Coolican, "Unregulated Blogs Promote Wild Political Rumors," *Scripps Howard News Service,* August 9, 2006, Lexis-Nexis.

34. About Google News, news.google.com/intl/en_us/ about_google_news.html, accessed September 2, 2006.

35. Greg Jarboe, "Beyond Beta: Google News Graduates," SearchEngine Watch, January 25, 2006, searchenginewatch.com/showPage.html?page=3579746, accessed September 3, 2006.

36. Project for Excellence in Journalism, *State of the News Media 2004;* Project for Excellence in Journalism, "Network TV Audience Trends," March 13, 2006, journalism.org/ node/1178, accessed August 20, 2006.

37. Eric Klinenberg, "Convergence: News Production in a Digital Age," *Annals,* AAPSS 597 (January 2005), 54.

38. Project for Excellence in Journalism, *State of the News Media 2004.*

39. Project for Excellence in Journalism, *State of the News Media 2006.*

40. Clark Hoyt, "Future of News Is Secure," Poynter Institute, June 21, 2006, poynter.org/content/content_view.asp? id=102161, accessed September 20, 2006.

41. Jon Ziomek, *Journalism, Transparency and the Public Trust* (Washington, D.C., Aspen Institute, 2005), p. 4.

42. Rachel Smolkin, "Adapt or Die," *American Journalism Review,* June/July 2006, ajr.org/Article.asp?id=4111, accessed September 20, 2006.

43. Pew Research Center for People & the Press, "Bottom-Line Pressures Now Hurting Coverage, Say Journalists," May 23, 2004, people-press.org/reports, accessed September 20, 2006.

44. Project for Excellence in Journalism, *State of the News Media 2006.*

Chapter 11

1. "Cruise's Rebound Will Be Tough, But Not Impossible," *PR Week,* May 15, 2006: 8.

2. Edward L. Bernays, *Crystallizing Public Opinion* (New York: Boni and Liveright, 1923), p. 215.

3. Scott Cutlip, "Public Relations and the American Revolution," *Public Relations Review* 2 (Winter 1976): 11–24.

4. David A. Haberman and Harry A. Dolphin, *Public Relations: The Necessary Art* (Ames: Iowa State University Press, 1988), pp. 14–15.

5. Neil Harris, *Humbug: The Art of P. T. Barnum* (Boston: Little, Brown, 1973), pp. 21–25.

6. Marvin N. Olasky, "The Development of Corporate Public Relations," *Journalism Monographs* 102 (April 1987): 2–15.

7. Ray Eldon Hiebert, *Courtier to the Crowd: The Story of Ivy Lee and the Development of Public Relations* (Ames: Iowa State University Press), pp. 99–100.

8. Hiebert, *Courtier to the Crowd,* pp. 298–299.

9. Edward L. Bernays, *Biography of an Idea: Memoirs of Public Relations Counsel Edward L. Bernays* (New York: Simon & Schuster, 1965), pp. 291–292.

10. Edward L. Bernays, *Crystallizing Public Opinion* (New York: Boni and Liveright, 1923), p. 215.

11. Elmer Davis, "Report to the President," in Ronald T. Farrar, ed., *Journalism Monographs* 7 (August 1968): 39.

12. William V. Ruch, *Corporate Communications: A Comparison of Japanese and American Practices* (Westport, CT: Quorum Books, 1984), p. 107.

13. Chester Barnard, *Functions of the Executive* (Cambridge: Harvard University Press, 1938).

14. Sabine Jaccaud and Bill Quirke, "Structuring Global Communication to Improve Efficiency," *Strategic Communication Management* 10 (August/September 2006): 18–21.

15. Haberman and Dolphin, *Public Relations,* pp. 19–20.

16. Lee W. Baker, *The Credibility Factor: Putting Ethics to Work in Public Relations* (Homewood, IL: Business One Irwin, 1993), pp. 54–59.

17. Clifton Brown, "Woods Says Each Side Must Bend on Augusta," *The New York Times,* October 17, 2002, nytimes.com.

18. Edward Bernays, "The Theory and Practice of Public Relations: A Resume," in *The Engineering of Consent,* Edward Bernays, ed. (Norman: University of Oklahoma Press, 1955), pp. 9–10.

19. Wragg, *The Public Relations Handbook,* pp. 87–89.

20. Randy Sumpter and James W. Tankard Jr., "The Spin Doctor: An Alternative Model for Public Relations," *Public Relation Review* 20.1 (1994): 19–27.

21. Gibson and Hodgetts, *Organizational Communication,* pp. 212–230.

22. Daniel Katz and Robert Kahn, *The Social Psychology of Organizations* (New York: John Wiley & Sons, 1966), p. 239.

23. Gibson and Hodgetts, *Organizational Communication*, pp. 219–220.

24. "IBM's Intranet One of the World's Top Ten," *Yahoo Finance*, January 26, 2006, biz.yahoo.com/iw/060126/0107490.html, accessed August 27, 2006; Phil Borremans, "Blogging at IBM," IAOC Blog, March 4, 2005, iaocblog.com/blog/_archives/2005/3/4/396555.html, accessed August 27, 2006.

25. Universal Accreditation Board, "Accreditation Linked to Higher Salaries," PRSA, June 22, 2005, praccreditation.org/news/prweek.asp, accessed August 27, 2006.

26. J. Sean McCleneghan, "PR Practitioners and 'Issues' in the Early Millennium," *Public Relations Quarterly* 50 (Summer 2005): 17–23.

27. "Exclusive PR News," *PR News*, April 17, 2006, ProQuest.

28. Richard Edelman, "Pay to Play PR is Not On," Edelman, January 7, 2004, edelman.com/speak_up/blog/archives/2005/01/pay_to_play_pr.html, accessed August 27, 2006.

29. "Controversy Builds Over Planted Stories in Iraqi Press," *Editor and Publisher*, December 1, 2005, editorandpublisher.com/eandp/news/article_display.jsp?vnu_content_id=1001613273, accessed August 27, 2006; David S. Cloud and Jeff Gerth, "Iraqi Clerics Found on Pentagon Payroll," *International Herald Tribune*, January 2, 2006, iht.com/articles/2006/01/01/news/cleric.php, accessed August 27, 2006.

30. "PR Professionals Cite Blog Mania, Ethics Miasma as Top Trends," *PR News*, December 21, 2005, ProQuest.

31. Rochelle L. Ford and Lynn Appelbaum, *Multicultural Public Relations Practitioner Study*, CUNY, www.ccny.cuny.edu/prsurvey/, accessed August 27, 2006.

Chapter 12

1. Josh Friedman, "Snakes on a M____ing Plane," I Find Your Lack of Faith Disturbing, August 17, 2005, hucksblog.blogspot.com/2005/08/snakes-on-motherfucking-plane.html, accessed September 5, 2006, C. Spencer Beggs, "Why Will 'Snakes on a Plane' Be a Hit?" Fox News, August 18, 2006, foxnews.com/story/0,2933,209101,00.html, accessed September 5, 2006; Brian Finkelstein, quoted on CNN, "'Can 'Snakes on a Plane' Live Up to the Hype?" August 16, 2006, YouTube.com, accessed September 5, 2006.

2. Philippe Schuwer, *History of Advertising* (London: Leisure Arts, 1966), pp. 9–10.

3. Blanche Elliot, *A History of English Advertising* (London: Business Publications, 1962), pp. 20–21.

4. Frank Presbrey, *The History and Development of Advertising* (Garden City, NY: Doubleday, Doran, 1929), p. 161.

5. Ibid.: 160.

6. Ibid.: 180–181.

7. Ibid.: 201.

8. James Wood Playsted, *The Story of Advertising* (New York: Ronald Press, 1958), p. 200.

9. G. Allen Foster, *Advertising: Ancient Market Place to Television* (New York: Criterion Books, 1967), pp. 120–121.

10. Foster, *Advertising: Ancient Market Place to Television*, pp. 156–157.

11. Presbrey, *The History and Development of Advertising*, p. 579.

12. Lawrence W. Lichty and Malachi C. Topping, *American Broadcasting: A Source Book on the History of Radio and Television* (New York: Hastings House, 1975), p. 522.

13. Aline van Duyn, "Internet Advertising Stymied by Lack of Experienced Staff," *Financial Times*, August 30, 2006: 15.

14. Joe McGinnis, *The Selling of the President, 1968* (New York: Trident Press, 1969).

15. Alan C. Miller and T. Christen Miller, "Election Was Decisive in Arena of Spending," December 8, 2000, latimes.com.

16. Ralph L. Lowenstein and John C. Merrill, *Macromedia: Mission, Message and Morality* (New York: Longman, 1990), p. 80.

17. Michael L. Rothschild, *Advertising: From Fundamentals to Strategies* (Lexington, MA: D.C. Heath, 1987), p. 755.

18. "United States: '527 Committees' Play Key Campaign Role," *Oxford Analytica*, 2005, ProQuest.

19. Mark Laswell, " 'Nightline': Exit Interviews," *Broadcasting & Cable*, November 14, 2005: 16.

20. Project for Excellence in Journalism, *State of the News Media 2006*.

21. Matthew Creamer, "Ad-Pull Edicts Elicit Nary a Whimper of Protest," *Advertising Age*, May 30, 2005: 3–4.

22. American Family Association, Action Alert, BoycottFord.com, boycottford.com/, accessed August 31, 2006.

23. Stephanie D. Smith, "Ford Ads Just 1% of Gay Mags' Revenue," *Adweek*, December 12, 2005: 8.

24. Stephen Lacy and Todd F. Simon, *The Economics and Regulation of United States Newspapers* (Norwood, NJ: Ablex, 1993), pp. 41–42.

25. "Consumer Behavior," *Encyclopedia of Business and Finance* Allison McClintic Marion, ed., Thomson Gale, 2001, eNotes.com 2006, business.enotes.com/business-finance-encyclopedia/consumer-behavior, accessed September 20, 2006.

26. Mindy Fetterman and Jayne O'Donnell, "Just Browsing the Mall?" *USA Today*, September 1, 2006: B1.

27. Joseph T. Hallinan, "Imported Beers Win Converts in the Heartland," *Wall Street Journal*, July 25, 2006: B1; Liz Grubow, "Chinese Culture and Its Effect on Skin Care Trends in China," *Global Cosmetic Industry* (August 2006), pp. 26–27.

28. Veronis Suhler Stevenson, "Highlights," *Communications Industry Forecast*, 2005, vss.com/pubs/pubs_cif_highlights.html, accessed December 11, 2006.

29. Richard Ball, "Google AdWords: Local Advertising," Search Engine Guide, June 21, 2006, www.searchengineguide.com/ball/007816.html, accessed September 20, 2006.

30. Rothschild, *Advertising: From Fundamentals to Strategies*, p. 729.

31. David W. Nylen, *Advertising: Planning, Implementation & Control* (Cincinnati, OH: Southwestern Publishing), pp. 72–74.

32. Suzanne Vranica, "Leadership," *Wall Street Journal*, July 10, 2006: R4.

33. Carlos Grande, "Online Marketers Urged to Go Viral," *Financial Times*, June 23, 2006: 26.

34. Daren Fonda, "Prime-Time Peddling," *Time*, May 30, 2005: 50.

35. Jack Neff, "Disclosure Deabate Hits Novel Ideas," *Advertising Age*, June 19, 2006: 4.

36. Seth Grossman, "Grand Theft Oreo: The Constitutionality of Advergame Regulation," *Yale Law Journal* 115 (2005): 227–237.

Chapter 13

1. Phil H. Shook, "Readers Repond to Fallujah Photos," *Ethics*, Poynter Online, April 13, 2004, poynter.org/content/content_view.asp?id=63968, accessed August 20, 2006.

2. Doug Brown, "How Much Is Too Much?" *American Journalism Review,* July/August 2002, ajr.org.

3. Quoted in Robert Buckman, "Daily Dilemma," *Quill,* April 2006: 35.

4. Hazel Dicken-Garcia, *Journalistic Standards in Nineteenth-Century America* (Madison: University of Wisconsin Press, 1989), p. 229.

5. See Jean Folkerts's review of Hazel Dicken-Garcia, *Journalistic Standards in Nineteenth-Century America* (Madison: University of Wisconsin Press, 1989) in *Journalism Quarterly* (Autumn 1990). Dicken-Garcia's book outlines the development of ethics within the context of the press as a social institution.

6. Marion Marzolf, *Civilizing Voices: American Press Criticism, 1880–1950* (New York: Longman, 1991), pp. 16–17.

7. Marzolf, *Civilizing Voices,* p. 106.

8. Clifford G. Christians, Kim B. Rotzoll, and Mark Fackler, *Media Ethics,* 2nd ed. (New York: Longman, 1987), pp. 9–17.

9. Diana Farsetta and Daniel Price, "Fake TV News: Widespread and Undisclosed," *Center for Media and Democracy,* April 6, 2006, prwatch.org/fakenews/execsummary, accessed August 13, 2006.

10. Ron Chepesiuk, "Fake News or Valuable Resource? The Controversy Surrounding the VNR," *Quill,* Jan./Feb. 2006: 10

11. Ibid.

12. Carol Guensburg, "When the Story Is About the Owner," *American Journalism Review* (December 1998), http://www.ajr.org, accessed in January 2003.

13. Trudy Lieberman, "Bitter Pill," *Columbia Journalism Review* (July/August 2005): 51.

14. Ibid.: 49.

15. "Take 2," *American Journalism Review* (January–February 1996): 15.

16. Les Roberts et al., "Mortality Before and After the 2003 Invasion of Iraq," *Lancet* 364 (2004): 1857–1864.

17. Lila Guterman, "Lost Count," *The Chronicle of Higher Education,* February 4, 2005: A10.

18. Peter Steinfels, "In the Brutality of War, the Innocents Have Become Lost in the Crossfire," *New York Times,* November 20, 2004: B6.

19. "About Us," Project Censored, projectcensored.org, accessed August 15, 2006.

20. Chris Mooney, "Blinded by Science," *Columbia Journalism Review,* 2004, cjr.org/issues/2004/6/mooney-science.asp, accessed August 11, 2006.

21. Jane Pauley, "Defending Dateline," *Quill* (November–December 1994): 63–69.

22. James Warren, "Paths of Janet Cooke and Marion Barry Cross," *Chicago Tribune,* July 4, 1996: 2.

23. Lori Robertson, "Romancing the Source," *American Journalism Review* (May 2002): 44.

24. Updated versions of these and other industry codes can be found in Conrad C. Fink, *Media Ethics* (Boston: Allyn and Bacon, 1995), or on request from the organizations themselves. Many organizations also publish their codes of ethics on their web sites.

25. Sissela Bok, *Lying: Moral Choice in Public and Private Life* (New York: Random House, 1989), pp. 111–112.

26. Jay Black and Deni Elliott, "Justification Models for Journalists Facing Ethical Dilemmas." Unpublished materials presented at a teaching ethics seminar by Jay Black, Philip Patterson, and Lee Wilkins, Association for Education in Journalism and Mass Communication annual meeting, Kansas City, MO, 1993.

27. Eugene Goodwin, *Groping for Ethics in Journalism,* 2nd ed. (Ames: Iowa State University Press, 1987), pp. 24–25. For additional suggestions on what an ethical journalist should do in various situations, refer to the last sections in each chapter in Gene Goodwin and Ron F. Smith, *Groping for Ethics in Journalism,* 3rd ed. (Ames: Iowa State University Press, 1994).

28. Clifford G. Christians, Mark Fackler, and Kim B. Rotzoll, *Media Ethics: Cases and Moral Reasoning,* 4th ed. (White Plains, NY: Longman, 1995), pp. 3–10.

29. The Potter Box has been adapted and edited many times since Ralph Potter presented it in his 1965 dissertation. This version appears in Black and Elliott, "Justification Models for Journalists Facing Ethical Dilemmas."

30. Stephen J. A. Ward, "Global Journalism Ethics," Journalism Ethics for the Global Citizen, 2005. journalismethics.ca/global_journalism_ethics/index.htm.

31. Myrna Oliver, "Harry Ashmore: Arkansas Editor Fought Segregation," *Los Angeles Times,* January 22, 1998: A20.

32. Richard Blow, "Gagging on 'Deep Throat,' " *TomPaine .common sense,* June 19, 2002, www.tompaine.com.

33. David Crary, "Survey Shows Many Newspapers Never Permit Use of Anonymous Sources," APME, apme.com/news/2005/060805anonymous.shtml, accessed August 25, 2006.

34. From Paul Farhi, *Philadelphia Inquirer,* August 10, 2002, posted online under "Media/1999: ABC Paid Lawyer for Lewinsky Interview," at Signs of the Times, george.loper.org/trends/2000/aug/93.html.

35. "ABC Just Can't Justify Paying Interviewee," *Chicago Headliner Club: Chicago Journalist,* August 1999, www.headlinerclub.org/journalist/1999/0899eth.html.

36. Sharon Waxman, "Michael Jackson's $1 Million Interview Deal," *New York Times,* December 31, 2003: E1.

37. Stuart H. Loory, "Pursuit of Profit Hampers Journalistic Standards," *Kansas City Star,* May 8, 1999: B6.

38. Brendan O'Neill, "Africa's New Royals," *New Statesman,* June 19, 2006: 18.

39. Fred Fedler, *Reporting for the Print Media,* 5th ed. (Fort Worth, TX: Harcourt Brace Jovanovich, 1993), p. 477.

40. Jennifer Harper, "Sensationalism Calls as 9/11 Anniversary Approaches," *Washington Times,* August 30, 2002, washtimes.com.

41. Mark Bowden, "News Judgment and Jihad," *Atlantic Monthly,* December 2004: 41.

42. Gill Ereaut and Nat Segnit, *Warm Words,* Institute for Public Policy, August 2006, ippr.org.uk/publicationsandreports, accessed August 25, 2006.

43. "Karen Slattery and Erik Ugland, "The Truth and Nothing But the Truth," *Digital Journalist,* September 2005, digitaljournalist.org/issue0509/ethics.html, accessed August 25, 2006; "Journalist Groups Protest FEMA Ban on Photos of Dead," *Editor & Publisher,* September 7, 2005, mediainfo.com/eandp/news/article_display.jsp?vnu_content_id=1001055768, accessed August 25, 2005.

44. *Codes of Ethics,* International Journalists' Network, ijnet.org/Director.aspx?P=Ethics, accessed August 25, 2006.

45. Lucinda D. Davenport, "News Quotes: Verbatim?" Paper presented to the annual meeting of the Association for Education in Journalism and Mass Communication, Portland, OR, 1988.

46. Lawrence Suid, review of *Pearl Harbor, Journal of American History* 88 (December 2001).

47. "Ayer Admits Distorting U-571 History," *PR Inside,* August 18, 2006, pr-inside.com/ayer-admits-distorting-u-571-history-r15624.htm, accessed August 25, 2006.

48. Brian Ross and Richard Esposito, "FBI Acknowledges: Journalists' Phone Records are Fair Game," *Blotter,* May 16, 2006, blogs.abcnews.com/theblotter/2006/05/fbi_acknowledge.html, accessed August 25, 2006.

49. Society of Professional Journalists, *Code of Ethics,* 1996, www.spj.org/ethicscode.asp, accessed August 25, 2006.

50. Payne Awards, 2006, payneawards.uoregon.edu/, accessed August 25, 2006.

51. Kendyl Salcito, "Online Journalism Ethics: New Media Trends," *Journalism Ethics for the Global Citizen,* 2005, journalismethics.ca/online_journalism_ethics/new_media_trends.htm, accessed August 25, 2006.

Chapter 14

1. "Is It Legal?," *Newsletter on Intellectual Freedom,* July 2006: 213; Jeffrey D. Mason, " 'Affront or Alarm': Performance, the Law and the 'Female Breast' from Janet Jackson to *Crazy Girls,*" *New Theatre Quarterly* 21 (May 2005): 179; Simon Dumenco, "The FCC Thinks You Look Totally Hot in a Diaper," *Advertising Age,* June 5, 2006: 45.

2. Karen Miller, "Smoking Up a Storm: Public Relations and Advertising in the Construction of the Cigarette Problem, 1953–1954," *Journalism Monographs* 136 (December 1992).

3. Harold L. Nelson and Dwight L. Teeter Jr., *Law of Mass Communications: Freedom and Control of Print and Broadcast Media,* 4th ed. (Mineola, NY: Foundation Press, 1982), pp. 189–190.

4. Harold L. Nelson and Dwight L. Teeter Jr., *Law of Mass Communications: Freedom and Control of Print and Broadcast Media,* 2nd ed. (Mineola, NY: Foundation Press, 1973), pp. 26–27.

5. Alexander Lynch, "The Media Lobby," *AlterNet,* March 11, 2005, alternet.org/mediaculture/21477, accessed August 13, 2006.

6. Doug Halonen, "Indecency Warrior's Campaign Peaking," *TelevisionWeek,* May 15, 2006: 1.

7. Bruce M. Owen, *Economics and Freedom of Expression* (Cambridge, MA: Ballinger, 1975); Stephen Lacy and Todd F. Simon, *The Economics and Regulation of United States Newspapers* (Norwood, NJ: Ablex, 1993).

8. James W. Tankard Jr. and Kate Pierce, "Alcohol Advertising and Magazine Editorial Content," *Journalism Quarterly* 59 (Summer 1982): 302–305.

9. Lauren Kessler, "Women's Magazines' Coverage of Smoking Related Health Hazards," *Journalism Quarterly* 66 (Summer 1989): 316–322, 445.

10. Mark Cooper, *Media Ownership and Democracy in the Digital Information Age,* cyberlaw.stanford.edu/blogs/cooper/archives/mediabooke.pdf, accessed August 14, 2006.

11. *Near v. Minnesota,* 283 U.S. 697, 51 S.CT. 625, 75 L. ED. 1357 (1931).

12. Julie Hilden, "How the Janet Jackson 'Nipplegate' Scandal Illustrated the Dangers of Chilling Free Speech," February 17, 2004, writ.news.findlaw.com/hilden/20040217.html, accessed August 15, 2006.

13. Project for Excellence in Journalism, *State of the News Media 2006.*

14. Jean Folkerts and Dwight L. Teeter Jr., *Voices of a Nation: A History of Media in the United States,* 4th ed. (Boston: Allyn and Bacon, 2002), p. 319.

15. Ruth Rosen, "The Day Ashcroft Censored Freedom of Information," *San Francisco Chronicle,* January 7, 2002, Common Dreams News Center, commondream.org.

16. David Lieberman, "Piracy or Fair Use?" *Lansing State Journal,* April 23, 2002: 6C, 7C.

17. Electronic Freedom Foundation, "MPAA vs. the People," eff.org/IP/P2P/MPAA_v_ThePeople/, accessed August 15, 2006.

18. Donald M. Gillmor, Jerome A. Barron, Todd F. Simon, and Herbert A. Terry, *Mass Communication Law: Cases and Comment,* 5th ed. (St. Paul, MN: West Publishing, 1990), p. 172.

19. Gillmor et al., *Mass Communication Law,* p. 173.

20. *Cherry v. Des Moines Leader,* 86 N. W. 323 (Iowa 1910).

21. *Virginia State Board of Pharmacy v. Virginia Citizens Consumer Council, Inc.,* 425 U.S. 748, 96 S. CT. 1817, 48 L. ED.2D. 346 (1976).

22. Nelson and Teeter, *Law of Mass Communications,* 2nd ed., p. 517.

23. Alfred McClung Lee, *The Daily Newspaper in America* (New York: Macmillan, 1937), pp. 314–316.

24. Gillmor et al., *Mass Communication Law,* pp. 525–526.

25. Molly Ivins, "Curbing Free Speech," NewsMax.com, January 18, 2000, newsmax.com.

26. Kent R. Middleton and Bill F. Chamberlin, *The Law of Public Communication,* 3rd. ed. (New York: Longman, 1994), p. 128.

27. Donald M. Gillmor, Jerome A. Barron, Todd F. Simon and Herbert A. Terry, *Fundamentals of Mass Communication Law* (Minneapolis/St. Paul, MN: West Publishing, 1996), p. 121.

28. Charles Layton, "The Information Squeeze," *American Journalism Review,* September 2002, ajr.org.

Chapter 15

1. Michael Traugott, Benjamin Highton, and Henry E. Brady, *A Review of Recent Controversies Concerning the 2004 Presidential Election Exit Polls,* National Research Commission on Elections and Voting, March 10, 2005, elections.ssrc.org/research/ExitPollReport031005.pdf, accessed October 19, 2006.

2. Robert K. Avery and David Eason, *Critical Perspectives on Media and Society* (New York: Guilford Press, 1991), pp. 3–6.

3. Michael Pfau, "The Effects of Print News Photographs of the Casualties of War," *Journalism & Mass Communication Quarterly* 83.1 (2006): 150–168.

4. Lisa A. Flores, Dreama G. Moon, and Thomas K. Nakayama, "Dynamic Rhetorics of Race: California's Racial Privacy Initiative and the Shifting Grounds of Racial Politics," *Communication & Critical/Cultural Studies* 3.3 (2006): 181–201.

5. Charles C. Ragin, Joane Nagel, and Patricia White, *Workshop on Scientific Foundations of Qualitative Research,* National Science Foundation, 2004, www.nsf.gov/pubs/2004/nsf04219/nsf04219.pdf, accessed October 11, 2006.

6. Earl Babbie, *The Practice of Social Research,* 6th ed. (Belmont, CA: Wadsworth, 1992), pp. 27–48; and Paul Davidson Reynolds, *A Primer in Theory Construction* (Indianapolis, IN: ITT Bobbs-Merrill Educational Publishing, 1971), pp. 3–11.

7. Cornelia Pechmann, et al., "Impulsive and Self-Conscious: Adolescents' Vulnerability to Advertising and Promotion," *Journal of Public Policy & Marketing* 24.2 (2005): 202–221.

8. Stephen Galloway, "Test Screenings," *Hollywood Reporter,* July 25, 2006, hollywoodreporter.com/thr/film/feature_

display.jsp?vnu_content_id=1002878620, accessed October 19, 2006.

9. Harold D. Lasswell, *Propaganda Techniques the World War* (New York: Peter Smith, 1927).

10. Shearon A. Lowery and Melvin L. DeFleur, *Milestones in Mass Communication Research: Media Effects,* 5th ed. (New York: Longman, 1989), pp. 31–54.

11. W. S. Dysinger and Christian A. Ruckmick, *The Emotional Responses of Children to the Motion Picture Situation* (New York: Macmillan, 1933).

12. Carl I. Hovland, Arthur A. Lumsdaine, and Fred D. Sheffield, *Experiments on Mass Communication* (Princeton, NJ: Princeton University Press, 1949).

13. Paul F. Lazarsfeld, Bernard Berelson, and Hazel Gaudet, *The People's Choice* (New York: Columbia University Press, 1948).

14. Bernard Berelson, Paul F. Lazarsfeld, and William McPhee, *Voting: A Study of Opinion Formation in a Presidential Campaign* (Chicago: University of Chicago Press, 1954).

15. Werner J. Severin and James W. Tankard Jr., *Communication Theories: Origins, Methods, and Uses in the Mass Media,* 3rd ed. (New York: Longman, 1992), p. 260.

16. Maxwell E. McCombs and Donald L. Shaw, "The Agenda Setting Function of Mass Media," *Public Opinion Quarterly* 36 (1972): 176–187.

17. Wayne Wanta, *The Public and the National Agenda: How People Learn about Important Issues* (Mahwah, NJ: Lawrence Erlbaum Associates, 1997).

18. Elisabeth Noelle-Neumann, "Return to the Concept of Powerful Mass Media," in *Studies of Broadcasting: An International Annual of Broadcasting Science,* H. Eguchi and K. Sata, eds. (Tokyo: Nippon Hoso Kyokai, 1973), pp. 67–112.

19. Dominic L. Lasorsa, "Political Outspokenness: Factors Working against the Spiral of Silence," *Journalism Quarterly* 68 (Spring/Summer 1991): 131–140.

20. Sandra J. Ball-Rokeach and Melvin L. DeFleur, "A Dependency Model of Mass Media Effects," *Communication Research* 3 (1976): 3–21.

21. Dennis McQuail, J. G. Blumler, and J. R. Brown, "The Television Audience: A Revised Perspective," in *Sociology of Mass Communications,* D. McQuail, ed. (Harmondsworth, England: Penguin, 1972).

22. Stephen Lacy and Todd F. Simon, *The Economics and Regulation of United States Newspapers* (Norwood, NJ: Ablex, 1993), p. 28.

23. David Manning White, "The 'Gatekeeper': A Study in the Selection of News," *Journalism Quarterly* 27 (Winter 1950): 383–390.

24. D. Charles Whitney and Lee B. Becker, "'Keeping the Gates' for Gatekeepers: The Effects of Wire News," *Journalism Quarterly* 59 (Spring 1982): 60–65.

25. Dan Berkowitz, "Refining the Gatekeeping Metaphor for Local Television News," *Journal of Broadcasting & Electronic Media* 34 (1990): 55–68; and John H. McManus, *Market-Driven Journalism: Let the Citizen Beware?* (Thousand Oaks, CA: Sage, 1994).

26. Warren Breed, "Social Control in the Newsroom: A Functional Analysis," *Social Forces* 33 (May 1955): 326–335.

27. Walter Gieber and Walter Johnson, "The City Hall 'Beat': A Study of Reporter and Source Roles," *Journalism Quarterly* 38 (Summer 1961): 289–297.

28. Gaye Tuchman, *Making News: A Study in the Construction of Reality* (New York: Free Press, 1978).

29. Shahira Fahmy and Thomas J. Johnson, "'How We Performed': Embedded Journalists' Attitudes and Perceptions Towards Covering the Iraq War," *Journalism and Mass Communication Quarterly* 82 (2005): 301–317.

30. Gieber and Johnson, "The City Hall Beat."

31. John D. Richardson and Karen M. Lancendorfer, "Framing Affirmative Action: The Influence of Race on Newspaper Editorial Responses to the University of Michigan Cases," *Press/Politics* 9 (Fall 2004): 74–94; Frederick Fico, Eric Freedman, and Brad Love, "Partisan and Structural Balance in Newspaper Coverage of U.S. Senate Races in 2004 with Female Nominees," *Journalism and Mass Communication Quarterly* 83 (2006): 46–47.

32. William P. Cassidy, "Variations on a Theme: The Professional Role Conceptions of Print and Online Newspaper Journalists," *Journalism and Mass Communication Quarterly* 82 (2005): 264–280.

33. Larry Daily, Lori Demo, and Mary Spillman, "Most TV/Newspaper Partners at Cross Promotion Stage," *Newspaper Research Journal* 26 (2005): 47.

34. Barry R. Litman and Janet Bridges, "An Economic Analysis of Daily Newspaper Performance," *Newspaper Research Journal* 9 (Spring 1986): 9–26.

35. Terri M. Adams and Douglas B. Fuller, "The Words Have Changed, But the Ideology Remains the Same: Misogynistic Lyrics in Rap Music," *Journal of Black Studies* 36 (2006): 940.

36. James Curran, Michael Gurevitch, and Janet Woollacott, "The Study of the Media: Theoretical Approaches," in *Culture, Society and the Media,* Michael Gurevitch, Tony Bennett, James Curran, and Janet Woollacott, eds. (London: Methuen, 1982), pp. 11–29.

37. James Carey, *Communication as Culture: Essays on Media and Society* (Boston: Unwin-Hyman, 1989), Chap. 1.

38. Donna Flayhan, "Hidden Dimensions of Hall in Media Ecology," *Proceedings of the Media Ecology Association* 3, 2002, media-ecology.org/publications/proceedings/v3/, accessed October 22, 2006.

39. *What is Media Ecology?* Media Ecology Association, 2006, media-ecology.org/mecology/, accessed October 22, 2006.

40. Marco Iacoboni, "Who Really Won the Super Bowl?" *Edge,* 2006, edge.org/3rd_culture/iacoboni06/iacoboni06_index.html, accessed October 30, 2006.

41. René Weber, Ute Ritterfeld, Klaus Mathiak, "Does Playing Violent Video Games Induce Aggression? Empirical Evidence of a Functional Magnetic Resonance Imaging Study," *Media Psychology* 8 (2006): 39–60; Carolyn Yoon, et al., "A Functional Magnetic Resonance Imaging Study of Neural Dissociations Between Brand and Person Judgments," *Journal of Consumer Research* 33 (2006): 31–40.

42. John P. Murray, et al., "Children's Brain Activations While Viewing Televised Violence Revealed by fMRI," *Media Psychology* 8 (2006): 25–27.

43. Editorial, Special Issue on Media Frames, *Gazette: The International Journal for Communication Studies* 67 (2005): 378–380.

44. Renita Coleman and Stephen Banning, "Network TV News' Affective Framing of the Presidential Candidates: Evidence for a Second-Level Agenda-Setting Effect Through Visual Framing," *Journalism & Mass Communication* 83 (2006): 320.

Glossary

35 millimeter: Photographic film that has a frame for exposure 35 millimeters in length. It is used for both still and moving pictures.

3-D: Film technique designed to create a sense of depth. Viewers wore special glasses for viewing.

8-track tape: A plastic cartridge that holds a continuous recording tape. Invented primarily for automobile play during the 1960s, its eight tracks allowed high-quality stereo reproduction in an easy-to-handle cartridge.

A and B pictures: A films are usually high-budget films that studios expect to be box-office hits. B films are low-budget films designed to make money.

absolute ethics: A code of ethics that allows no deviation from its rules.

accuracy: The recording, selecting, and weighing of facts to provide a truthful account.

Advertising Council: Formed to promote the civilian efforts in World War II, the Advertising Council is supported by advertising agencies and media companies. It conducts advertising campaigns in the public interest.

affective response: In advertising, a consumer's response to brands and products because of emotions, moods, and values.

Alien and Sedition Acts: Federalist laws passed in 1798 to restrict freedom of information. They were used to quell political dissent.

AM: Amplitude modulation attaches sound to a carrier wave by varying the intensity, or amplitude, of the carrier wave.

analog: Transforms one form of energy into another to transport content, as when a telephone converts sound vibrations into electrical vibrations.

anthology: A favorite television format of the 1950s that consisted of stage plays produced for TV.

areas of dominant influence (ADI): Areas defined by the ratings company Arbitron for purposes of reporting listener data.

art theater: Outlet for films designed for their artistic quality rather than for their blockbuster audience appeal that usually are produced by independent companies rather than by the big studios.

association magazines: Magazines published by various associations to publicize their activities and communicate with their members.

audience fragmentation: The division of audiences into small groups consuming more specialized offerings of diverse media outlets.

audion: A three-electrode vacuum tube amplifier, which was the basis of the electronic revolution that permitted the development of radio.

auteur: A director with a highly personal cinematic style who maintains creative control over his or her film.

beat: A beat is a regularly covered topic of news such as police and science. Reporters contact sources on a beat regularly to check for events that might be newsworthy. Desks have one or more beats connected with them.

blacklist: A list of individuals compiled with the express purpose of forcing them out of their jobs. Blacklisting was used during the 1950s to label certain individuals as Communists and to force them out of the information and entertainment industries.

Blaxploitation films: A film genre that arose in the 1970s featuring black actors, urban scenes, and funk and soul music.

blind booking: Marketing strategy common in the 1930s and 1940s that required theaters to book movies before they were produced.

block booking: The practice of forcing a theater to book movies as a package, rather than individually. Declared illegal in the 1940s.

437

bop: Jazz that developed during the 1940s as a reaction to big band swing music. Usually performed by small groups with fast tempos and conflicting rhythms. Also called be-bop.

breakout boxes: Shorter pieces of information, often direct quotes, that are connected to the larger story being covered. They are used to emphasize specific points and for design relief.

broadband: Fiber-optic cable with the capacity to carry large amounts of information.

broadside: Handbill, also called broadsheet, that was printed only on one side of the paper.

cable modem: Device used to connect computers to the Internet and other online services that operate through cable, rather than telephone, lines.

capital intensive: A production process that requires a large investment of money.

causation: The process by which one or more factors result in the occurrence of an event, behavior, or attitude. A variety of factors cause human behavior. For example, genetics, parental behavior, peer associations, media consumption, and other factors combine to create certain behaviors in children.

censorship: Restriction of access to information; deletion of information from a story; or refusal to let a correspondent mail, broadcast, or otherwise transmit a story.

channel: A way of transmitting a message from a person or group of people to a person or group of people, e.g., a telephone line or newspaper.

channel noise: Interference in a communication channel, e.g., static on a radio.

chapbooks: Cheaply printed paperback books produced during the 1700s.

checkbook journalism: Paying subjects or witnesses for information or interviews.

cinerama: Trade name for process that produces widescreen images.

circulation: The number of copies sold by a newspaper during its production cycle (week or day).

coaxial cable: Cable that contains two conductors: a solid central core surrounded by a tubelike hollow one. Air or solid insulation separates the two. Electromagnetic energy, such as television transmission signals, travels between the two conductors.

cognitive process: In advertising, a consumer's rational process of product selection.

computer language: An intermediate programming language designed for programmers' convenience that is converted into machine language.

conglomerate: Large company formed by consolidating two or more small companies.

contingency plan: Plan designed well in advance to accommodate situations in which the turn of events would be unpredictable; such plans help organizations cope with possible undesirable outcomes.

contingent factors: Effects that are caused by contingent, or indirect, variables rather than by the direct impact of media content.

controlled circulation: Technique of sending magazines free to individuals within an industry to increase identification with an organization.

copyright: A law that protects authors, playwrights, composers, and others who construct original works and keeps others from reproducing their work without permission.

credibility: A measurement of how well a journalist or media organization is trusted. If a high percentage of the public perceives a journalist as truthful, that person has credibility.

crier: In ancient Greece and Rome, a person who walked through the streets crying out news to the people. Preceded printed news.

crossover artist: A top-selling musical artist in more than one music segment. Country and rhythm and blues often cross over with Top 40 music.

cultural appropriation: Capitalizing on musical forms that belong to disempowered social groups.

cumulative weekly audience: The total number of people who listen to radio during a given week in a given market.

customer-relationship management: A system that allows consumers to customize musical offerings.

Dark Ages of journalism: Period when the republic was formed and reporters and editors were highly partisan in their efforts to build a new political system.

database: Software for recording statistics. Data can be sorted into categories and reports printed in various forms. Used by businesses that need to sort customers by zip code, for example.

defamation: To misconstrue facts or misrepresent a person in such a way as to lower the individual in the estimation of others.

demographics: Characteristics of an audience for mass media based on age, gender, ethnic background, education, and income.

design: Visual elements, including headlines, photographs, and graphics, organized to make the newspaper interesting and easy to read.

desk: A newspaper department with an editor in charge. Most newspapers, for example, have a city desk and a sports desk.

desktop publishing: Writing, illustrating, and designing publications with a personal computer.

differentiating the product: The process of trying to get the consumer to perceive one product as being different in nature and quality than other products.

digital: Transforms information into binary form, as when computers convert sound vibrations to 1s and 0s.

Digital Millennium Copyright Act: Act that protects service providers from liability for copy-right infringement.

dime magazine: Magazine that cost ten cents and appealed to a broad class of readers. These magazines were less expensive than the quality monthlies that preceded them.

dime novel: Cheap, paperback fiction produced in the midnineteenth century.

distributor: Company that helps get magazines from the printer to the wholesalers.

distributors: The people of the movie industry who arrange to engage movies in theaters, then on television.

documentary: Film or video investigation. Based on the term documents—such accounts document the details of a historical or current event. Often used as a term that implies investigative reporting.

dot.com bubble: A period of inflated expansion of new Internet business in the late 1990s.

downlink: Transmitting an electronic signal from a satellite to a ground facility.

DSL: Telephone lines that foster extremely fast connection to the Internet and other online services.

economies of scale: As the number of units produced at a plant increases, the average cost per unit decreases. This comes about because the company has to invest large amounts of money just to produce the first unit.

editing: The technique of joining pieces of film or of digitally manipulating images in a creative process.

electrotyping: A metal plate used in letterpress printing by coating a lead or plastic mold of the page to be printed.

evidentiary privilege: Rule of law allowing journalists to withhold the identification of confidential sources.

executive privilege: The president's right to withhold information if disclosure might harm the executive branch's functions and decision-making processes.

experiment: A quantitative research method that involves the application and manipulation of a treatment given to groups of people, and then tests the result.

external PR: Messages directed at publics external to the organization.

fair use: Use of a small portion of a copyrighted work by scholars, teachers, or reporters to further enlighten the public.

fakery: Posing that which is false to be true.

fast film: Generic term for the film that photographers use to stop fast action. Does not need long exposure to light to capture the photographic image.

feature story: Story that emphasizes activities of people instead of "hard news events" such as crime and disasters.

feedback: Signals sent in response to a message. These may be verbal or nonverbal.

fellow travelers: During the period of intense fear of Communism in the 1950s, people in the broadcast and entertainment industry who were unfairly accused of sympathizing with the beliefs of the Communist Party.

fiction factory: Late nineteenth-century publishing of formulaic books, in which publishers dictated story lines.

film genre: A kind or style of movie.

FM: Frequency modulation attaches sound to a carrier wave varying the frequency of the carrier wave.

focus groups: Groups of individuals representing different interests who are assembled to discuss a topic. A form of research used to get in-depth information, but not information that is representative of an entire audience.

folksonomy: A method for users to label the content they create with identifying words and phrases.

full-power television station: A station that reaches a large percentage of households in its market and that must broadcast a schedule of programs.

gatekeeper: A person who controls the flow of information into and through the mass media.

genre: A type of literary or cinematic work, classified by elements such as similar plots, characters, and themes.

graphical user interface (GUI): Arrangement on the screen that imitates a desktop.

high fidelity: Reproduction of sound with minimal distortion.

high-definition television (HDTV): Digital transmission that produces the highest level of TV reproduction quality.

historical epic: Film genre focusing on heroic myths, legends, and historical incidents and requiring an expensive, large-scale production.

hoax: An act or story intended to deceive; a tall tale; a practical joke or serious fraud.

Horatio Alger story: Story that began as a real account of how Horatio Alger worked his way up the social and economic ladder, but soon developed into a term to represent the glorification of individualism in American life.

household penetration: The number of households subscribing to a newspaper compared to the number of potential households in an area.

Hutchins Commission: Commission established in the 1940s to review press conduct. The commission argued that the press should provide intelligence that would enable the public to understand the issues of the day.

hybrid: A new form created from the combination of two or more different elements.

hypertext: A group of texts, sounds, graphics, and video connected by links rather than arranged linearly. Also called hypermedia.

hypothesis: A theoretical statement of a relationship between a causing agent and a resulting action, behavior, or attitude.

in-depth interviewing: Research where subjects are selected for study and several detailed interviews are conducted at different times.

infomercial: A media message that offers consumer information.

information model: Pattern of behavior for disseminating information as news; incorporates values such as objectivity over partisanship.

infotainment: A blend of information and entertainment. Critics believe such treatments masquerade as journalism and deceive the public.

interactive: Systems that involve two-way communication. The information receivers act as senders and vice versa.

internal PR: Communication within the various units and between individuals of the organization.

investor relations: Communication with those who invest in the company, that is, those who buy stock.

joint product: Term economists use when one production process serves two markets. For instance, the process of printing magazines serves readers in the consumer market and companies in the advertising market.

journalistic balance: Providing equal or nearly equal coverage of various points of view in a controversy.

jump music: Small band music that merged swing and electric blues during the late 1940s. Jump developed into rhythm and blues music.

kilobyte: A measure of memory size equal to 1,024 bytes.

kinetoscope: A boxlike mechanism used to view short films during the late 1800s. The viewer looked into an opening and watched film move past a lightbulb.

limited speech: Speech that is not widely disseminated.

lobbying: Persuading legislators and other government officials to enact or support legislation favorable to one's cause.

market: A geographic area in which businesses and consumers exchange goods and services for money. *Major markets* include a metropolitan area and have many media choices; *outstate markets* are removed from metropolitan areas but are not rural and include some diversity in media choice; *isolated markets* include rural areas with limited media choices.

market economy: An economy in which the interaction of supply and demand determines the prices of goods and services and the levels of production. In a nonmarket economy, government determines prices and production.

market niche: Portion of the audience a particular magazine gains as subscribers or buyers.

market segments: The target audience. The group of individuals a magazine selects to target for its readership.

mashup: A remix of two or more recordings that creates a new one.

mass advertising: Advertising that aims to reach the largest number of people possible.

mass media: A form of communication (radio, newspapers, television, etc.) used to reach a large number of people.

media kit: A collection of information about a particular event or person, such as a recording release. The kit can include text, photographs, audiotapes, and even computer discs and CD-ROMs.

media mix: Consumers' use of a variety of media, such as newspapers, television, and the World Wide Web.

melodrama: Film genre characterized by exaggerated emotions, stereotypical characters and overblown storylines having to do with fate.

mercantile press: Early American newspapers that served businesses, shopkeepers, and tradespeople. These newspapers also contained political news.

microcomputer: A small computer using a microprocessor as its central processor.

mid-list: Titles that sell less than the "frontlist" bestsellers or are on the "backlist" of older titles.

minstrel: An entertainer, with blackened face, performing songs and music of African-American origin.

model: A diagram or picture that attempts to represent how something works. In communication, models are used to try to explain what happens in the creation, sending, and receiving of a message.

modulator: Device that processes the carrier wave so that its amplitude or frequency varies. Amplitude modulation (AM) is constant in frequency and varies the intensity, or amplitude, of the carrier wave. Frequency modulation (FM) is constant in amplitude and varies the frequency of the carrier wave.

muckraking: Using the journalism of exposure. The term was given to the press by Theodore Roosevelt, who claimed the press "raked the muck" but refused to regard the "celestial crown." Often used as a term for reporting on business.

narrowcasting: Transmission of data, like a television program, to a specific demographic of viewers, listeners, or subscribers.

network: Computers that are connected by communications lines. The computers may be connected within a restricted geographic area, such as a laboratory in a mass communication program. This network is a local area network (LAN). The Internet networks millions of computers worldwide through telephone and fiber-optic lines.

new journalism: Journalism that expresses the social context. Used at different times in the history of journalism, in the 1890s, it defined sensationalism. In the 1960s, the term was used to describe experimentation in reporting strategies and writing styles.

news council: A committee that reviews potentially unethical activities of news organizations.

newsmagazine: Fifteen- to twenty-minute news segments put together to form an hourlong electronic magazine such as 60 Minutes or Dateline. Such programs combine soft features with hard-hitting investigative reporting.

niche publisher: Small publishing house that serves very narrowly defined markets.

nickelodeon: Small storefront functioning as a theater; popular about 1910. These preceded the grand movie palaces.

objectivity: Reporting facts without bias or prejudice, including a deliberate attempt to avoid interpretation.

oligopoly: A business situation in which a few dominant companies control enough of the business that each one's actions will have a significant impact on the actions of the others.

ombudsman: A person within an organization who represents customers and investigates potentially unethical conduct of the organization and people within it.

on-air personalities: A personality listeners identify with and tune in to regularly on the radio. Whether the radio host reads the news or announces music, the on-air personality gives a station a singular identity.

open source code: Programming code that is freely available to anyone to use and manipulate.

open video system: A system that rents entire channels or time on channels to unaffiliated programmers without discrimination.

operating system: A program that tells the computer how to behave. DOS and Windows, produced by Microsoft, dominate the world market for operating systems. The Macintosh operating system is second, used by about one-tenth as many machines as the Microsoft systems.

option: A contractual agreement between an author and a producer, giving the producer temporary rights to a story.

package deals: A series of media tie-ins.

Panavision: System of lenses used in filming that enabled a film shot in one wide-screen version (Cinemascope, for example) to be shown in theaters without the lenses for that type of projection.

participant observation: Research where researchers observe research subjects in everyday behavior.

pass-along rate: The total number of readers who read a magazine regularly, including those who read copies that were given, or passed along, to them by other readers.

patent medicines: Packaged drugs that can be obtained without a prescription. Before the Food and Drug Administration was created, these drugs often contained large amounts of alcohol and sometimes opium.

perk: Short for perquisite, or payment for something in addition to salary.

phonorecord: Mechanical sound recording that falls under copyright protection.

piracy: Using material without securing appropriate copyright authorization.

pluralist: One who espouses coexistence and cooperation among different elements of a power structure.

popular government: Government that is controlled by the citizenry rather than an elite cadre of officials.

postmodern film: Using various techniques such as a collision of styles and a suspension of historical time, a postmodern film emphasizes artificiality and creates emotional detachment in its audience.

precedent: A legal decision that sets a standard for how subsequent cases are decided.

press pool: A small group of reporters selected to gather information and pass it on to the larger group of press people. Used when the number of reporters gathering in one spot is problematic.

press release: An announcement of some event, such as a recording release, sent to various news media outlets.

prior restraint: Restricting publication before the fact rather than banning material or punishing an individual after the material is already printed.

professional communicator: Person who selects information from sources and processes them for delivery to an audience.

profit margin: The difference between revenue and expenses.

progressive generation: Group of individuals in the early 1900s who championed political and social reform.

promotion: The ways a company gains attention for its product or service, including advertising, public relations, packaging, and personal selling.

propaganda: Material disseminated by a group or cause to persuade another group of the validity of its own position.

protocol: Content analysis that contains instructions that researchers use to assign units of content to categories that in turn receive numbers. The instructions contain detailed steps every coder must follow.

pseudo-event: An event created solely for the purposes of public relations to gain favorable notice for an organization.

public domain: The status of publications that are not under copyright. No one has exclusive rights to them, and the public owns them.

public investment: The buying of stock in a company by the general public.

publicity: Information disseminated to attract public interest.

publics: The various groups to whom PR professionals address messages. They may be internal or external to the organization.

pundit: An expert on a particular topic; a person consulted because of his or her knowledge.

quantitative content analysis: A quantitative research method that provides a systematic way of categorizing media content and using statistics to analyze patterns in the content.

quiz show: Show on which contestants answer questions that show their knowledge of selected material.

radio frequency: An electromagnetic wave frequency used in radio transmission.

rational thinking abilities: The cognitive processing of information by considering options based on conscious comparison of influencing factors.

remix culture: A global movement to promote the creation of new forms remixed from former creative recordings and other products.

right of privacy: An ethical and legal area of decision making. The right to be protected from unwaranted intrusion by the government, media, or other institutions or individuals.

RSS: A data file that notifies users of updates to webpage contents.

sampling: The electronic borrowing and incorporation of sounds and rhythms from prior recordings.

seditious libel: Criticism of the government. In colonial times, such criticism was considered libelous even if it was true.

semantic noise: An interference with communication because of misunderstandings about the meaning of words or symbols.

serialized book: A book printed in parts in a magazine or newspaper over a certain period of time.

social responsibility theory: As applied to freedom of the press, a philosophy that states that with freedom comes responsibility to the social good.

social science approach: Research approach that emphasizes theory building and quantitative methods for testing theory.

socialization process: Reporters learn patterns of behavior by observing others and by learning to recognize the systems of rewards and punishments in a newsroom.

softpower: The use of media persuasion, rather than violence, to promote a nation's interests.

Software-as-a-Service: Software programs accessed over the Internet. SaaS providers make money either through usage fees or advertising.

sound bite: A short quotation used on radio or television to express an idea.

specialized publisher: Publishing house that produces a particular type of book, such as religious or children's books.

spin doctor: Public relations personnel, usually associated with political communication, who tries to get journalists and other publics to believe a particular interpretation of an event or information.

spot news: News based on one-time events such as accidents or crimes.

spreadsheet: Software that allows for organization and tabulation of financial data; commonly used in planning budgets.

stereotyping: The use of a paper mat to make cylindrical molds for printing.

stringer: A reporter, often at a location remote from the newspaper, who sells occasional pieces at "space rates," or by the column inch.

studio film rental: Movie produced by studios to rent to distributors and/or theaters.

sunshine laws: Laws requiring that meetings of federal or state administrative agencies be open to the public.

superstation: A station that reaches hundreds of markets throughout the country by means of satellite distribution of a signal to cable systems.

survey research: A quantitative research method that involves randomly selecting a small group of people, called a sample, from a larger group, called a population, and asking them questions from a questionnaire.

swing: Big band music played with a jazz rhythm that was popular during the 1930s and early 1940s. Swing enjoyed a revival during the 1990s.

syncopated beat: The regular metrical accent that shifts temporarily to stress a beat that is normally weak. Syncopation is important in African and African-American musical traditions and is considered the root of most modern popular music.

syndicated material: Programs made available for sale directly to stations or cable channels rather than distributed by networks to affiliates. Examples are *Xena: Warrior Princess* and *The Oprah Winfrey Show*. Discontinued network shows that have had long successful runs, such as Cheers, are also candidates for syndication.

syndicated programming: Nationally produced programming that is supplied to stations through telephone lines and by satellite.

targeted advertising: Trying to sell a product or service to a particular group of people.

telecommunications industry: Organizations that are involved in electronic media such as broadcast television, cable, radio, and telephone, or the transmission of information over wires and with satellites.

telenovela: A soap opera with a finite number of episodes.

television network: A system of linked communication technologies that transmits video, audio, and text to many stations. Network-affiliated stations rebroadcast programs and advertising to viewers in a geographic area, and may also provide locally produced content.

textbook: Book used for elementary school, middle school, high school, or college classroom work.

textual analysis: Research where researchers interpret texts to find the social meanings underlying them.

tie-in: The connection made when a magazine runs a story about a product advertised in the magazine.

trade book: Mass marketed books sold at bookstores or through book clubs. Excludes textbooks.

trade press: Periodicals that target a specific industry. *Broadcasting & Cable* magazine, for example, targets the broadcast and cable industry and is an example of a trade magazine.

traffic: Department that controls movement of programming through the day, logs what goes on the air, and supplies information for billing advertisers.

transistor: A small electronic device containing a semiconductor. A key component of an integrated circuit that paved the way for portability.

uplink: Transmitting an electronic signal to a satellite for storage or further distribution.

user-friendly: Software that is designed for use by individuals who are not familiar with complex computer languages.

V-Chip: An electronic device in a television set that blocks certain television programs.

venture funding: Funding of an enterprise with cash from several investors who are interested in innovative enterprises that carry both risk and the potential for large profits.

vertical integration: A system in which a single corporation controls production (including obtaining the raw materials), distribution, and exhibition of movies. Declared illegal in the 1940s.

wave band: An electromagnetic wave within the range of radio frequencies.

wholesaler: Company that delivers magazines from a warehouse to dealers, such as bookstores.

wire service: Organization that collects and distributes news and information to media outlets. Referred to as "wire" because before computer transmission, these services relied on use of the telegraph wires.

WYSIWYG: Text on a computer screen that corresponds exactly to the printout: What you see is what you get.

zoning: Printing an edition of a newspaper for a specific geographic area (or zone) that has content aimed at that area, usually in a specific section of the paper.

Index

Photo Credits

Chapter 1: pp. xxxii, 3, © Susan Poag/Newhouse News Service/ Landov; p. 4, © Win McNamee/Getty Images; p. 5 top, © AP Images/The Daily Times/Dave Watson; p. 5 bottom, p. 7 top, © North Wind Picture Archives; p. 7 bottom, © The Granger Collection, New York; p. 9, © Scott Peterson/Getty Images; p. 18, © Hal Stoelzle/ Denver RMN/Corbis Sygma; p. 20, © AP Images. Chapter 2: pp. 24, 27, © AP Images/Stuart Ramson; p. 28, © The Granger Collection, New York; p. 32, © AP Images/J. Pat Carter; p. 33, © The Granger Collection, New York; p. 35, © Keith D. Bedford/ Getty Images; p. 37, © AP Images/Damian Dovarganes; p. 38, © AP Images/Xinhua/Zhang Ming; p. 40, © Will Faller; p. 41, © AP Images/Tim Boyd; p 44, © Stephen Hird/Reuters/Landov. Chapter 3: pp. 48, 51, © AP Images/Jeff Chiu; p. 52 top, © Bettmann/CORBIS; p. 52 bottom, © The Granger Collection, New York; p. 53, Library of Congress; p. 62, Courtesy of the Daily Herald; p. 64, © John P. Filo/CBS Photo Archive/Getty Images; p. 66, © AP Images/Tony Dejak; p. 67, © AP Images/Nick Ut; p. 70, © AP Images/Bebeto Matthews; p. 73, © E. W. Scripps Archive/ Archives & Special Collections/Ohio University Libraries. Chapter 4: pp. 76, 79, © Michael Newman/PhotoEdit; p. 80, © The Granger Collection, New York; p. 82, © Bettmann/CORBIS; p. 83 top, © Edward Clark/Time Life Pictures/Getty Images; p. 83 bottom, Library of Congress; p. 87, Courtesy of Essence Communications, Inc.; p. 88, © Slate.com and Washingtonpost. Newsweek Interactive. All rights reserved; p. 91, Courtesy of Grrrlzines; p. 95, © Andy Uzzle/Corbis Sygma. Chapter 5: pp. 100, 103, © Lions Gate/Courtesy Everett Collection; p. 104, © Bettmann/CORBIS; p. 105, © Wark Producing Company/The Kobal Collection; p. 107, © JSP/Shooting Star; p. 110, © Svensk Filmindustri/Photofest; p. 114, © APA/Getty Images; p. 115, © Warner Independent Pictures/Courtesy Everett Collection; p. 116, Courtesy Everett Collection; p. 118, © Paramount/Courtesy Everett Collection; p. 119 top, © Focus Features/Courtesy Everett Collection; p. 119 bottom, © Universal/Courtesy Everett Collection; p. 121, © Miramax/ Courtesy Everett Collection; p. 124, © Eros International/Courtesy Everett Collection. Chapter 6: pp. 130, 133, © Prashant Nadkar/ Reuters/Landov; p. 134, p. 135 top, © Bettmann/CORBIS; p. 135 bottom, © The Granger Collection, New York; p. 144, © Ethan Miller/Getty Images; p. 145, © Ray Tamarra/Getty Images; p. 148, © AP Images/Richard Drew; p. 149, © David McNew/Getty Images; p. 152, © AP Images/Manish Swarup. Chapter 7: pp. 158, 161, © Peter Kramer/Getty Images; p. 162, Library of Congress; p. 165, © The Kobal Collection; p. 168, © NBC Television/Getty Images; p. 169, Ron P. Jaffe/© UPN/Courtesy Everett Collection; p. 173, © AP Images/CSPAN; p. 175, TM and Copyright © 20th Century Fox Film Corp. All rights reserved. Courtesy Everett Collection; p. 176, © NBC/Photofest; p. 182, © Bill Inoshita/CBS/ Landov; p. 183 top, Katherine Bomboy/© ABC/Courtesy Everett Collection; p. 183 bottom, Robert Voets/© CBS/Courtesy Everett Collection; p. 186, © AP Images/Natacha Pisarenko. Chapter 8: pp. 192, 195, © AP Images/Sang Tan; p. 196, p. 200, © Frank Driggs Collection/Getty Images; p. 202, © Bill Levy/Shooting Star;

p. 203, © Megan Garvin/Retna Ltd.; p. 205, © AP Images/Oded Balilty; p. 206, © Photofest; p. 207, © Gary Hershorn/Reuters/ Landov; p. 210, © Bill Freeman/PhotoEdit; p. 211, © Steve Double/ Retna Ltd.; p. 214, © Brian Smith; p. 217, © AP Images/Chitose Suzuki. Chapter 9: pp. 222, 225, © Rachel Watson/Getty Images; p. 227, © Bettmann/CORBIS; p. 229, © Maiman/Corbis Sygma; p. 234, © FAHD SHADEED/AFP/Getty Images; p. 235, © Chris Smith/PhotoEdit; p. 236, © Yonathan Weitzman/Reuters/Landov; p. 242, © Ed Bock/CORBIS; p. 243, © Stanley Walker/Syracuse Newspapers/The Image Works; p. 246, © Nick North/CORBIS. Chapter 10: pp. 250, 253, © Brooks Kraft/CORBIS; p. 254, © Bettmann/CORBIS; p. 257, © Jason Forman; p. 261 top, © Bettmann/ CORBIS; p. 261 bottom, Street Arabs at Night, Photograph, Circa 1890, The Jacob Riis Collection, #123, © Museum of the City of New York; p. 263, © Bettmann/CORBIS; p. 265, © Chris Graythen/Getty Images; p. 269 left, © Chris Graythen/Getty Images; p. 269 right, © AP Images/Dave Martin; p. 270, © PAUL J. RICHARDS/AFP/Getty Images; p. 272, © AP Images. Chapter 11: pp. 278, 281, © AP Images/Reed Saxon; p. 282, © The Granger Collection, New York; p. 284 top, © AP Images/Sean Kardon; p. 284 bottom, © The Granger Collection, New York; p. 289, © AP Images/Lauren Burke; p. 292, © JIMIN LAI/AFP/ Getty Images; p. 293, © AP Images/The Daily Sentinel/Andrew D. Brosig; p. 294, © Getty Images; p. 298, Courtesy of fmyi (www .fmyi.com). Chapter 12: pp. 306, 309, © New Line/The Kobal Collection/Dittiger, James; p. 310, © Brian Smith; p. 312, © The Granger Collection, New York; p. 316, © Bill Aron/PhotoEdit; p. 317, Courtesy of John McCain; p. 318, © AP Images/Sang Tan; p. 320, © Sony Pictures/Courtesy Everett Collection; p. 321, © Mike Stone/Reuters/Landov; p. 323, © Colin Young-Wolff/ PhotoEdit; p. 324, © Claro Cortes IV/Reuters/CORBIS; p. 325 top, Courtesy of the Environmental Protection Agency and the Ad Council; p. 325 bottom, Photo by Getty Images for Pepsi; p. 326, Courtesy of the Leo Burnett Company. Chapter 13: pp. 334, 337, © Chris Hondros/Getty Images; p. 338, © Bettmann/ CORBIS; p. 341, © AP Images/Apichart Weerawong; p. 343, © Bettmann/CORBIS; p. 344 top, © Matthew Cavanaugh/epa/ CORBIS; p. 344 bottom, © AP Images/Reuters/Adnan Hajj; p. 351, © Bettmann/CORBIS; p. 354, © AP Images/Michael A. Mariant; p. 355, © Columbia/Courtesy Everett Collection. Chapter 14: pp. 360, 363, © AP Images/Elise Amendola; p. 365, © JOHN MACDOUGALL/AFP/Getty Images; p. 366, © David Scull/ Bloomberg News/Landov; p. 367, Photo by Brian Baer/Sacramento Bee/ZUMA Press. © Copyright 2006 by Sacramento Bee; p. 380, © AP Images/Benjamin Sklar; p. 382, © AP Images/ Canadian Press/Paul Chiasson; p. 384, © AP Images/STR; p. 387, © David Young-Wolff/PhotoEdit. Chapter 15: pp. 392, 395, © MANDEL NGAN/AFP/Getty Images; p. 397, © Spencer Grant/ PhotoEdit; p. 400, Courtesy of the East West Center; p. 401, Courtesy Everett Collection; p. 403, © The Granger Collection, New York; p. 406, © John Coletti/Index Stock Imagery; p. 413, © Jim Young/Reuters/Landov; p. 419, Courtesy of Dr. Marco Iacoboni.